CRITICAL AND EXEGETICAL

COMMENTARY

ON

THE NEW TESTAMENT.

BY

HEINRICH AUGUST WILHELM MEYER, Th.D.,

OBERCONSISTORIALRATH, HANNOVER.

From the German, with the Sanction of the Author.

THE TRANSLATION REVISED AND EDITED BY

WILLIAM P. DICKSON, D.D.,

AND

FREDERICK CROMBIE, D.D.

PART IX.

THE EPISTLES TO THE PHILIPPIANS AND COLOSSIANS.

EDINBURGH:

T. & T. CLARK, 38 GEORGE STREET.

MDCCCLXXXIII.

PRINTED BY MORRISON AND GIBB,

FOR

T. & T. CLARK, EDINBURGH.

LONDON, ... HAMILTON, ADAMS, AND CO.

DUBLIN, ... GEORGE HERBERT.

NEW YORK, ... SCRIBNER AND WELFORD.

CRITICAL AND EXEGETICAL

HANDBOOK

TO

THE EPISTLES

TO THE

PHILIPPIANS AND COLOSSIANS.

BY

HEINRICH AUGUST WILHELM MEYER, Th.D.,

OBERCONSISTORIALRATH, HANNOVER.

TRANSLATED FROM THE FOURTH EDITION OF THE GERMAN BY

REV. JOHN C. MOORE, B.A.

THE TRANSLATION REVISED AND EDITED BY

WILLIAM P. DICKSON, D.D.,

PROFESSOR OF DIVINITY IN THE UNIVERSITY OF GLASGOW.

EDINBURGH:

T. & T. CLARK, 38 GEORGE STREET.

MDCCCLXXXIII.

PREFATORY NOTE.

THE Commentary on the Epistle to the Philippians was translated from the third edition of the German by the late Mr. G. H. Venables; but, as it became necessary to incorporate the numerous alterations and additions made by Dr. Meyer for the fourth edition, the work of revising and completing the version of Mr. Venables has been entrusted to the Rev. John C. Moore, who has also executed independently the greater portion of the translation, from the fourth German edition, of the Commentary on the Epistle to the Colossians. I have myself translated a small portion of the latter, and, as in previous volumes, have revised the whole with some care, and carried it through the press.

It is stated by Dr. Meyer's son, in the Preface to the new edition of this volume, that his father had, before his fatal illness, despatched the one half of the manuscript of his revision to the printers, and that the other half was found labelled "ready for the press." The book, therefore, although issued subsequently to the author's death, is entirely his own work. I have reserved the biographical sketch of Dr. Meyer given by his son for the first volume of the series. The Commentary on the Epistle to Philemon, which in the German accompanies those now issued, will also appear subsequently.

It is scarcely necessary to say that the explanations given in preceding volumes as to the principles on which this translation is issued, and the caveat inserted regarding the views or opinions occasionally expressed by Dr. Meyer, are equally applicable to the present.

W. P. D.

GLASGOW COLLEGE,
October 1875.

EXEGETICAL LITERATURE OF THE EPISTLES

TO THE

PHILIPPIANS AND COLOSSIANS.

[FOR commentaries or collections of notes embracing the whole New Testament, see Preface to the Commentary on the Gospel of St. Matthew; for those which deal with the Pauline, or Apostolic, Epistles generally, see Preface to the Commentary on the Epistle to the Romans. The following list includes only those which concern the Epistle to the Philippians or the Epistle to the Colossians, or in which one of these Epistles holds the first place on the title-page. Works mainly of a popular or practical character have, with a few exceptions, been excluded, since, however valuable they may be on their own account, they have but little affinity with the strictly exegetical character of the present work. Monographs on chapters or sections are generally noticed by Meyer *in loc.* The editions quoted are usually the earliest; *al.* appended denotes that the book has been more or less frequently reprinted; † marks the date of the author's death.]

AIRAY (Henry), † 1616, Provost of Queen's College, Oxford : Lectures upon the whole Epistle to the Philippians . . .   4°, Lond. 1618, *al.*

AM ENDE (Johann Gottfried), † 1821, Superintendent at Neustadt on the Orla : Pauli Epistola ad Philippenses Graece . . . nova versione Latina et annotatione perpetua illustrata.   8°, Viteb. 1798, *al.*

BÄHR (Carl Christian Wilhelm Felix), Ministerialrath, Baden : Commentar über den Brief Pauli an die Colosser, mit stäter Berücksichtigung der ältern und neuern Ausleger.   8°, Basel, 1833.

BAUMGARTEN (Sigmund Jakob).   See GALATIANS.

BAUMGARTEN-CRUSIUS (Ludwig Friedrich Otto), † 1843, Prof. Theol. at Jena : Commentar über den Brief Pauli an die Epheser und Kolosser . . . 8°, Jena, 1845.—Commentar über die Briefe an die Philipper und Thessalonicher . . .   8°, Jena, 1848.

BAYNE (Paul), † 1617, Min. at Cambridge: A Commentarie upon the I. and II. chapters of Saint Paul to the Colossians . . .

4°, Lond. 1634, *al.*

BEELEN (Jean-Théodore), R. C. Prof. Or. Lang. at Louvain: Commentarius in Epistolam S. Pauli ad Philippenses.   8°, Lovanii, 1852.

BLEEK (Friedrich), † 1859, Prof. Theol. at Berlin: Vorlesungen über die Briefe an die Kolosser, den Philemon und die Epheser . . .

8°, Berl. 1865.

BÖHMER (Wilhelm), Prof. Theol. at Breslau: Theologische Auslegung des paulinischen Sendschreibens an die Colosser.   8°, Breslau, 1835.

BRAUNE (Karl), Superintendent at Altenburg in Saxony: Die Briefe S^{ti}. Pauli an die Epheser, Kolosser, Philipper. Theologisch-homiletisch bearbeitet. [In Lange's Bibelwerk.]   8°, Bielefeld, 1867. [Translated from the German, with additions (Philippians), by Horatio B. Hackett, D.D., and (Colossians) by M. B. Riddle, D.D.]

8°, New York and Edin. 1870.

BREITHAUPT (Joachim Justus), † 1732, Prof. Theol. at Halle: Animadversiones exegeticae et dogmatico-practicae in Epistolam ad Philippenses.

4°, Halae, 1703

BRENZ [or BRENTIUS] (Johann), † 1570, Provost at Stuttgart: Explicatio Epistolae ad Philippenses.   8°, Francof. 1548.

BYFIELD (Nicholas), † 1622, Vicar of Isleworth: An Exposition upon the Epistle to the Colossians . . .   4°, 1617, *al.*

CALIXTUS (Georg). See ROMANS.

CARTWRIGHT (Thomas), † 1603, Prof. Theol. at Cambridge: Commentary on the Epistle to the Colossians.   4°, Lond. 1612.

DAILLE (Jean), † 1670, Pastor at Paris: Exposition sur la divine Épître de l'apôtre S. Paul aux Filippiens.   8°, Genev. 1659.

DALMER (Karl Eduard Franz): Auslegung des Briefes Pauli an die Colosser.

8°, Gotha, 1858.

DAVENANT (John), † 1641, Bishop of Salisbury: Expositio Epistolae Pauli ad Colossenses, 2°, Cantab. 1627, *al.* [Translated, with notes, by Josiah Allport. 2 vols.   8°, Lond. 1831.]

DAVIES (JOHN LLEWELYN), Rector of Christ Church, Marylebone: The Epistles of St. Paul to the Ephesians, the Colossians, and Philemon, with introduction and notes, and an essay on the traces of foreign elements in the theology of these Epistles.

8°, Lond. 1867.

EADIE (John), D.D., Prof. Bibl. Lit. to the United Presbyterian Church: A Commentary on the Greek Text of the Epistle of Paul to the Philippians.   8°, Edin. 1859. A Commentary on the Greek Text of the Epistle to the Colossians.

8°, Lond. and Glasg. 1856.

ELLICOTT (Charles John), D.D., Bishop of Gloucester and Bristol: A Critical and Grammatical Commentary on St. Paul's Epistles to the Philippians, Colossians, and Philemon, with a revised translation.
8°, Lond. 1857, *al.*

ELTON (Edward), Minister at Bermondsey : An Exposition of the Epistle to the Colossians . . . 4°, Lond. 1615, *al.*

FERGUSON (James), † 1667, Min. at Kilwinning : A Briefe Exposition of the Epistles of Paul to the Philippians and Colossians.
8°, Edin. 1656, *al.*

FLATT (Johann Friedrich), † 1821, Prof. Theol. at Tübingen : Vorlesungen über die Briefe Pauli an die Philipper, Kolosser, Thessalonicher, und den Philemon, herausgegeben von Chr. F. Kling.
8°, Tübing. 1829.

HEINRICHS (Johann Heinrich), Superintendent at Burgdorf: Testamentum Novum Graece perpetuo annotatione illustravit J. P. Koppe. Vol. vii. p. 2. Complectens Pauli Epistolas ad Philippenses et Colossenses. Continuavit J. H. Heinrichs. 8°, Götting. 1803, ed. II., 1826.

HENGEL (Wessel Albert van), Prof. Theol. at Leyden : Commentarius perpetuus in Epistolam Pauli ad Philippenses. 8°, Lugd. Bat. 1839.

HOELEMANN (Hermann Gustav), Teacher in Gymnasium at Zwickau : Commentarius in Epistolam divi Pauli ad Philippenses. [THEILE : Comment. in N. T., vol. xxii.] 8°, Lips. 1839.

HOFMANN (Johann Christian Konrad von), Prof. Theol. at Erlangen : Die Heilige Schrift des N. T. zusammenhängend untersucht. IV. 2. Die Briefe Pauli an die Kolosser und Philemon. IV. 3. Der Brief Pauli an die Philipper. 8°, Nördlingen, 1870–2.

HUTHER (Johann Eduard), Pastor at Wittenförden, Schwerin : Commentar über den Brief Pauli an die Colosser. 8°, Hamb. 1841.

JATHO (Georg Friedrich), Director of Gymnasium at Hildesheim : Pauli Brief an die Philipper. 8°, Hildesheim, 1857.

JUNKER (Friedrich) : Historisch-kritischer und philologischer Commentar über den Brief Pauli an die Colosser . . . 8°, Mannheim, 1828.

KÄHLER (C. R.) : Auslegung der Epistel an die Philipper.
8°, Kiel, 1855

KRAUSE (Friedrich August Wilhelm), † 1827, Tutor at Vienna : Die Briefe an die Philipper und Thessalonischer übersetzt und mit Anmerkungen begleitet. 8°, Frankf. 1790.

KRAUSE (Johann Friedrich), † 1820, Superintendent at Weimar : Observationes critico-exegeticae in Pauli Epistolae ad Philippenses c. i. et ii.
4°, Regimont. [1810].

LIGHTFOOT (Joseph Barber), D.D., Hulsean Professor of Divinity at Cambridge: St. Paul's Epistle to the Philippians. A revised text, with introductions, notes, and dissertations.

8°, Lond. and Camb. 1868, *al.*

St. Paul's Epistles to the Colossians and Philemon. A revised text, with introductions, notes, and dissertations.   8°, Lond. 1875.

MATTHIAS (Konrad Stephan), Prof. Theol. at Greifswald: Erklärung des Briefes Pauli an die Philipper.   8°, Greifswald, 1835.

MAYERHOFF (Ernst Theodor): Der Brief an die Kolosser mit vornehmlicher Berücksichtigung der Pastoralbriefe kritisch geprüft.

8°, Berl. 1838.

MELANCHTHON (Philipp), † 1560, Reformer: Enarratio Epistolae Pauli ad Colossenses.   8°, Viteb. 1559, *al.*

MICHAELIS (Johann David). See GALATIANS.

MÜLLER (Cornelius): Commentatio de locis quibusdam Epistolae ad Philippenses.   4°, Hamburgi, 1844.

MUSCULUS [or MEUSSLIN] (Wolfgang), † 1563, Prof. Theol. at Berne: In Epistolas ad Philippenses, Colossenses, Thessalonicenses ambas et primam ad Timotheum commentarii.   2°, Basil. 1565, *al.*

NEANDER (Johann August Wilhelm), † 1850, Prof. Theol. at Berlin: Der Brief Pauli an die Philipper praktisch erläutert . . .

8°, Berl. 1849.

PEIRCE (James), † 1726, Minister at Exeter: A Paraphrase and Notes on the Epistles of St. Paul to the Colossians, Philippians, and Hebrews, after the manner of Mr. Locke . . .   4°, Lond. 1727, *al.*

RETTIG (Heinrich Christian Michael), † 1836, Prof. Theol. at Zürich: Quaestiones Philippenses.   8°, Giessen. 1831.

RHEINWALD (Georg Friedrich Heinrich), † 1849, Prof. Theol. at Bonn: Commentar über den Brief Pauli an die Philipper.

8°, Berl. 1827.

RILLIET (Albert), Prof. Theol. at Geneva: Commentaire sur l'épître de l'apôtre Paul aux Philippiens . . .   8°, Génève, 1841.

ROELL (Herman Alexander), † 1718, Prof. Theol. at Utrecht: Brevis Epistolae Pauli ad Colossenses exegesis.   4°, Traject. 1731.

SCHENKEL (Daniel), Prof. Theol. at Heidelberg: Die Briefe an die Epheser, Philipper, Kolosser. Theologisch - homiletisch bearbeitet. [In Lange's Bibelwerk.]   8°, Bielefeld, 1862.

SCHINZ (Wilhelm Heinrich): Die christliche Gemeinde zu Philippi.

8°, Zürich, 1833.

SCHMID (Sebastian). See ROMANS.

SCHOTANUS (Meinardus H.), † 1644, Prof. Theol. at Utrecht: Analysis et Commentaria in Epistolam Pauli ad Philippenses.

4°, Franek. 1637.

STEIGER (Wilhelm), † 1836, Prof. Theol. at Geneva: Der Brief Pauli an die Colosser; Uebersetzung, Erklärung, einleitende und epikritische Abhandlungen.   8°, Erlangen, 1835.

STORR (Gottlob Christian), † 1805, Prof. Theol. at Tübingen: Dissertatio exegetica in Epistolam ad Philippenses. . . . Dissertatio exegetica in Epistolae ad Colossenses partem priorem [et posteriorem] . . .

4°, Tübing. [1783–87].

Expositions of the Epistles of Paul to the Philippians and Colossians by John Calvin and D. Gottlob Christian Storr.   Translated from the original by Robert Johnston.   [Biblical Cabinet.]   12°, Edin. 1842.

SUICERUS [SCHWEITZER] (Johann Heinrich), Prof. of Greek in Heidelberg: In Epistolam ad Colossenses commentarius critico-exegeticus.

4°, Tiguri, 1699.

TIL (Salomon van).   See ROMANS.

VELASQUEZ (Juan Antonio), S. J.: In Epistolam Pauli ad Philippenses commentaria et adnotationes.   2°, Lugd. et Paris. 1628–33.

VICTORINUS (C. Marius), about A.D. 360, teacher of rhetoric at Rome: In Epistolam ad Philippenses liber unicus.   [In Mai's *Scrip. Vet. Nov. Coll.* iii. 1.]

WEISS (Bernhard), Prof. Theol. at Kiel: Der Philipperbrief ausgelegt, und die Geschichte seiner Auslegung kritisch dargestellt.

8°, Berl. 1859.

WIESINGER (J. C. August), Pastor at Untermagerbein, near Nördlingen: Die Briefe des Apostel Paulus an die Philipper, an Titus, Timotheus und Philemon erklärt.   [In Olshausen's Commentar.]   8°, Königsb. 1850.   [Translated by the Rev. John Fulton, A.M.

8°, Edin. 1851.]

ZACHARIAE (Gotthilf Traugott).   See GALATIANS.

THE

EPISTLE TO THE PHILIPPIANS.

—◆—

INTRODUCTION.

§ 1. THE PHILIPPIAN COMMUNITY.[1]

THE fortified city of *Philippi*[2] was situated in Macedonia, on the borders of Thrace ; in earlier times, as a Thasian colony, it was called, from its site abounding in springs, Κρηνίδες (Diodor. S. xvi. 3. 8 ; Strabo, vii. p. 490), but it changed this name for that of its enlarger and fortifier, *Philip*, the son of Amyntas. It was rich in gold mines (Herod. vi. 46 ; Appian. *Bell. civ.* iv. 15 ; Strabo, vii. p. 511) ; and the victory over Brutus and Cassius made it a landmark in the history of the world. Through this overthrow of Roman freedom it acquired a high rank as a Roman colony with the *Jus Italicum* (see on Acts xvi. 11) ; but it obtained another and higher historical interest, attended by a greater gain for the Roman Empire, through the fact that it was the first city in Europe in which Paul, under the divine direction in a nocturnal vision (see on Acts xvi.

---

[1] See generally, Mynster, *Einleit. in d. Br. an d. Philipper*, in his *Kl. theol. Schriften*, p. 169 ff. ; Hoog, *de coetus Christ. Philipp. conditione*, etc., Lugd. Bat. 1825 ; Rettig, *Quaest. Philipp.*, Giess. 1831 ; Schinz, *d. christl. Gem. z. Phil.*, Zürich, 1833 ; J. B. Lightfoot, *St. Paul's Ep. to the Philippians*, Lond. 1868, p. 46 ff.

[2] Now the village of *Felibah*. On the site and the ruins, see Cousinéry, *Voyage dans la Macéd.*, Paris, 1831, II. ch. x. p. 1 ff. ; Perrot in the *Revue archéolog.* 1860, II. pp. 44 ff., 67 ff.

9 f.), and amid ill-treatment and persecution (Acts xvi. 16 ff. ;
1 Thess. ii. 2), planted Christianity. Thus did the city vindi-
cate its original name, in a higher sense, for the entire West.
This event took place in the year 53, during the second
missionary journey of the apostle, who also, in his third
journey, laboured among the Macedonian churches (Acts xx.
1 f.), and especially in Philippi (Acts xx. 6). With what
rich success he there established Christianity is best shown
by our epistle itself, which exhibits a more cordial, affectionate,
and undisturbed relation between the church and the apostle,
and bears a more unalloyed testimony to the distinction of the
church (comp. especially iv. 1), than we find in any other
apostolic letter. This peculiar mutual affection also explains
the fact that Paul, contrary to his usual custom, accepted aid
on more than one occasion from the Philippians (iv. 10 ff. ;
2 Cor. xi. 9); from which, however, on account of this very
love, we are not entitled to infer that they were specially
wealthy. The Jews were so few in number that they had
only a προσευχή (see on Acts xvi. 13), and the Christian
church was one consisting mostly of those who had been
Gentiles. The view which discovers a Judaizing faction
(iii. 2) in it (Storr, Flatt, Bertholdt, Eichhorn, Rheinwald,
Guericke, and others), seems all the more unwarrantable, when
we consider how deeply the apostle was concerned to ward off
from his beloved Philippians the *danger*, at that time everywhere so imminent, of the intrusion of Judaistic disturbance,
and how susceptible the Philippians themselves were to such
a danger, owing to a certain spiritual conceit[1] which had
already impaired their unanimity (i. 12–ii. 16, iv. 2). Comp.
i. 28. See, against the view of heretical partisanship, Schinz,
p. 48 ff. ; Rilliet, *Commentaire*, Geneva, 1841, p. 352 ff. ;
Weiss, Introduction to his *Ausleg.*, Berl. 1859 ; compare,
however, Huther in the *Mecklenb. theolog. Zeitschrift*, 1862,
p. 623 ff.

---

[1] Credner, § 158 f., represents the conceit of the Philippians as apparent also
in "the servile courting of the rank of a πρώτη πόλις." But the statement in
Acts xvi. 12, which, besides, is purely historical, gives no warrant for the charge
of any arbitrary assumption of rank.

§ 2. PLACE AND TIME OF COMPOSITION, OCCASION, AND CONTENTS.

It is justly the universal tradition (Chrysostom; Euthalius, in Zacagni, *Coll. vet. mon.* pp. 547, 642, 648; *Synopsis* of Athanasius, Syrian Church, the subscriptions), and the almost unanimous view of modern writers, that the epistle was written in *Rome*. We are pointed to Rome by the οἰκία Καίσαρος (iv. 22), and by the crisis between life and death in which Paul was placed,—a crisis which presupposes his appeal to the emperor as the ultimate legal resort (i. 20 ff., ii. 17),—as well as by the entire conformity of his position and work (i. 12 ff.) to what we find recorded in Acts xxviii. 16 ff. The epistle must, moreover, have been written during the *later* period of the Roman captivity; for the passages, i. 12 ff., ii. 26 ff., betoken that a somewhat lengthened course of imprisonment had elapsed, and the apostle was already abandoned by all his more intimate companions (ii. 20), except Timothy (i. 1). A more precise specification, such as Hofmann in particular gives (that the apostle had then been transferred from his hired dwelling to the prison-house), is not deducible either from i. 12 ff., or from the mention of the Praetorium and the imperial house. We must reject the isolated attempts to transfer its composition to Corinth (Acts xviii. 12; Oeder, *Progr.*, Onold. 1731) or to Caesarea (Acts xxiii. 23–xxvi. 32; Paulus, *Progr.*, Jen. 1799; and Böttger, *Beitr.* I. p. 47 ff.; favoured also by Rilliet, and Thiersch, *Kirche im apost. Zeitalt.* p. 212). Concerning and against these views, see particularly Hoelemann, *Commentar*, 1839, p. iii. ff.; Neander, *Gesch. d. Pflanzung*, etc., p. 498 f.

We are to assume, therefore, as the date of composition, not indeed the full *expiration* of the διετία ὅλη of Acts xxviii. 30 (Hofmann), but the latter *portion* of that period,—in the year 63 possibly, or the beginning of 64.[1] See on Acts, *Introd.* § 4. ✗ The *occasion* of the epistle was the fact that the Philippians had sent Epaphroditus with *pecuniary aid* to Paul, who, on

---

[1] Marcion properly assigned to our epistle the *last* place, in point of time, among his ten Pauline epistles.

the return of the former after his recovery from " a sickness
nigh unto death," made him the bearer of the letter (ii. 25–28).
In the utterances of the epistle, however, there is nothing to
suggest any *special change* in the situation of the apostle as
having afforded a motive for this gift on the part of the
church; and it is an uncertain reading between the lines to
assume, with Hofmann, not merely that the apostle was transferred to the prison-house, but that with that transference
the process had reached the stage of its judicial discussion,
in which the Philippians believed that they could not but
discern a change to the worse for Paul, whom they regarded
as suffering privations in prison.   Those traces, also, which
Hofmann has discovered of a *letter of the church* brought to
Paul by Epaphroditus along with the contribution, and expressing not only the concern of the Philippians for the apostle,
but also their need of instruction regarding the assaults to
which their Christianity was exposed, and regarding various
other matters of theirs that required to be settled and arranged,
are so far from being warranted by the exegesis of the passages
in question, that there is neither direct occasion nor any other
sufficient reason for going beyond the oral communications of
Epaphroditus in order to account for the apostle's acquaintance
with the circumstances of the Philippians.   And just as the
aid tendered by the careful *love of the church* had furnished
the occasion for this letter to them, so also does its entire
tenor breathe forth the heartfelt and touching *love*, which the
captive apostle cherished *towards his Philippians*.   Not one
of his epistles is so rich as this in hearty effusions of affection
and in tender references; and not one of them is so characteristically *epistolary*, without any rigid arrangement, almost
without dogmatic discussion, as also without quotations from the
Old Testament or dialectic chains of reasoning.   Not one is so
eminently an epistle *of the feelings,* an outburst of the moment,
springing from the deepest inward need of loving fellowship
amidst outward abandonment and tribulation; a model, withal,
of the union of tender love, and at times an almost elegiac
impress of courageous resignation in the prospect of death,
with high apostolic dignity and unbroken holy joy, hope, and

victory over the world. "Summa epistolae: *Gaudeo, gaudete,*" Bengel; comp. Grotius: "laetior alacriorque et blandior ceteris."

After the apostolic salutation (i. 1 f.), Paul, with heart-winning fervour, expresses thanks, intercession, and confidence as regards his readers (i. 3–11), and then enlarges on his present position, with his hope of a speedy return (i. 12–26); after which he exhorts them to unanimity and humility, and generally to the Christian life (i. 27–ii. 18). He promises to send Timothy to them soon, yet trusts that he himself shall also soon come to them (ii. 19–24); in the meantime he sends away to them Epaphroditus, their messenger, who is delicately and touchingly commended to them (ii. 25–30). On the point, apparently, of passing on to a conclusion (iii. 1) he proceeds to deal with his Jewish opponents, with whom he compares himself at some length, thereby inciting his readers to be like-minded with him, to keep in view the future salvation, and so to maintain their Christian standing (iii. 2–iv. 1). After a special exhortation to, and commendation of, two women (iv. 2, 3), the apostle subjoins the concluding words of encouragement (iv. 4–9), to which he had already set himself in iii. 1, adds yet another grateful effusion of his heart on account of the aid given to him (iv. 10–20), and ends with a salutation and a blessing (iv. 21–23).

§ 3. GENUINENESS AND UNITY.

The *genuineness* of this epistle is established *externally* by the continuous testimonies of the ancient church from Polycarp, iii. 11, onwards; see Marcion in Epiph. *Haer.* 42; Canon Murat.; Tertull. *c. Marc.* v. 19, *de praescr.* 36; literal use made of it, as early as the epistle from Vienne and Lyons, in Eus. v. 2; direct quotations from it in Iren. iv. 18. 4, v. 13. 3; Cypr. *Test.* iii. 39; Clem. *Paed.* i. 107; Tert. *de resurr.* 23, 47,—in the presence of which testimonies it is unnecessary to adduce uncertain allusions from apostolic Fathers and Apologists. *Internally* it bears the seal of genuineness in the thoroughly Pauline character of its contents, of its spirit, of its emotions, of its delicate turns and references, of its whole diction and form, and in the comparative absence, moreover, of doctrinal definition properly so called, as well as in the prominence throughout of the features characteristic of its origin as a cordial and fresh occasional letter.   Nevertheless, Baur, after repeated threats (see *die sogen. Pastoralbr.* pp. 79, 86, and *Tüb. Zeitschr.* 1836, 3, p. 196), has directed his bold attacks against this epistle also (see his *Paulus der Ap. Jesu Christi*, 1845, p. 458 ff., and second ed. II. p. 50 ff.; also in the *theol. Jahrb.* 1849, p. 501 ff., 1852, p. 133 ff.[1]); and Schwegler, *nachapostol. Zeitalt.* II. p. 133 ff., has adopted the same views.   See, against these attacks, now hardly worth the trouble of refutation, besides the Commentaries and Introductions, Lünemann, *Pauli ad Phil. epist. contra Baurum defend.*, Gött. 1847; Brückner, *Ep. ad Phil. Paulo auctori vindicata contra Baur.*, Lips. 1848; Ernesti in the *Stud. u. Krit.* 1848, p. 858 ff., 1851, p. 595 ff.; Grimm in the *Lit. Bl.* of the *Allg. K.Z.* 1850, No. 149 ff., 1851, No. 6 ff.; Hilgenfeld in his *Zeitschr.* 1871, p. 309 ff.   According to the opinion of Baur, the epistle moves in the circle of *Gnostic* ideas and expressions, to which it attaches itself; but the only passage adduced as a proof is ii. 5 ff., and this entirely under mistaken explanations or arbitrary references of the several elements of that passage. Comp. the commentary on this passage, and the remark after ii. 11.   The further charges—that the epistle labours under feeble repetitions (copies of passages in other epistles, as iii. 4 ff. from 2 Cor. x. 18, *et al.*), under a want of connection, and poverty of ideas (in proof of which stress is laid on iii. 1, as the author's own confession)—rest entirely on uncritical presupposition, and on a mistaken judgment as to the *distinctive epistolary peculiarity* of the letter, and as to the special *tone of feeling* on the part of the apostle in his present position generally and towards his Philippians.   Lastly, we must reckon as wholly fanciful the doubt thrown upon what is said at i. 12, for which a combination of this passage with iv. 22 is alleged to furnish ground, and to which the mention of Clement, iv. 3,

---

[1] Compare also Plank in the same, 1847, p. 481 f. ; Köstlin in the same, 1850, p. 263 ff.

who is taken to be Clement of Rome, and is supposed to weave
the bond of unity round Paul and Peter, must supply the key;
while the supposed anachronism in the mention of the bishops
and deacons in i. 1, the Euodia and Syntyche in iv. 2, and the
σύζυγος γνήσιος in iv. 3, are likewise wrongly adduced against
the Pauline authorship. Indeed, even the historical occasion
of the epistle—the aid sent to Paul—is made to appear as a
fictitious incident at variance with 1 Cor. ix. 15. The special arguments of Baur are set aside by an impartial interpretation of the passages to which they refer, and the same may
be said with regard to the latest attacks of Hitzig (*zur Kritik
d. paulin. Briefe*, 1870) and of Hinsch (in Hilgenfeld's *Zeitschrift*, 1873, p. 59 ff.) on the genuineness. The latter,
though independent in his movement, stands on the ground
occupied by Baur; the former has no ground whatever.
Against Hinsch, see Hilgenfeld in his *Zeitschr.* 1873, p. 178 ff.

Heinrichs, with whom Paulus in the main concurred, *Heidelb.
Jahrb.* 1817, 7, has sought to do away with the *unity* of the
epistle by the assumption that there were originally *two* epistles,
—one *exoteric*, addressed to the whole church, consisting of
i. 1–iii. 1, χαίρετε ἐν κυρίῳ, and the salutations, iv. 21–23; the
other *esoteric*, to the apostle's more intimate friends, which contained from iii. 1, τὰ αὐτὰ γράφειν, down to iv. 20.[1] But this
idea is nothing but a consequence of misconceiving the free
epistolary movement, which, especially in a letter like this called
forth by a special occasion, and addressed to a community so
dear to him, might naturally be most unfettered (see on iii. 1);
and in this case, the distinction of exoteric and esoteric
elements is a mistake, which is no less unhistorical than contrary to all psychological probability.

From iii. 1 we must, moreover, assume that, prior to our
epistle, Paul had addressed another letter to the Philippians,
which is not now extant; and this is confirmed by Polycarp
(*Phil.* 3). See on iii. 1, remark.

[1] Without any grounds whatever, Weisse (see his *Beiträge z. Krit. d. paulin.
Briefe*, edited by Sulze, 1867) has found himself forced, in accordance with his
criticism based on style, to regard the portion from chap. iii. onwards as the
fragment of a second Epistle to the Philippians.

Παύλου ἐπιστολὴ πρὸς Φιλιππησίους.[1]

A B D E F G ℵ have merely *πρὸς Φιλιππησίους.*

CHAPTER I.

Ver. 1. Ἰησοῦ Χριστοῦ] Lachm. and Tisch. read Χριστοῦ Ἰησοῦ. The same in vv. 6 and 8. This is to be preferred on account of the strong attestation of B D E ℵ (the latter, however, only in vv. 1 and 8), which is reinforced in ver. 8 by A ; it was readily supplanted by the more usual Ἰ. Χ. — Ver. 7. Elz. has merely τῇ ἀπολογ. *without* ἐν. Lachm. has ἐν, which Griesb., Matth., Scholz, and Tisch. adopt, in brackets. It is found in B D** E K L P ℵ, min. Syr. Copt. Arr. Vulg. It. and some Fathers. Looking at this indecisive attestation, and seeing that ἐν might more readily be supplementarily or mechanically added than omitted, it should be deleted. — Ver. 8. ἐστίν] after μου is defended by Griesb., bracketed by Lachm., omitted by Tisch., following B F G ℵ*, min. Vulg. It. Aeth. Chrys. An addition made from a reminiscence of Rom. i. 9. — Ver. 9. περισσεύῃ] B D E have περισσεύσῃ. So Lachm., who has placed περισσεύῃ in the margin, and Tisch. 7. With the considerable testimony which exists in favour of the *Recepta,* restored also by Tisch. 8, it should be retained, as περισσεύσῃ might very easily originate in the similarity of sound in the following final syllables : ἐπιγνώΣΕΙ, πάσΗΙ, and αἰσθήΣΕΙ. The *Recepta* is also supported by the readings περισσεύει and περισσεύοι. — Ver. 11. Elz. has καρπῶν . . . τῶν, against decisive testimony. An emendation. — Ver. 14. Lach. and Tisch. 8 have τοῦ Θεοῦ after λόγον, although, according to testimony of some weight (such as A B ℵ, Clem.), only an explanatory addition, which some Codd. give in a different position, while others change it into τοῦ κυρίου. — Vv. 16, 17. Elz. reverses their position : οἱ μὲν ἐξ ἐριθείας . . . μου· οἱ δὲ ἐξ ἀγάπης . . . κεῖμαι, against decisive testimony. A transposition intended to produce uniformity with ver. 10. — Instead of ἐγείρειν (Griesb., Lachm., Tisch.) Elz. has ἐπιφέρειν, which is defended by Matth. and Scholz, and vindicated by Reiche. But

---

[1] The Philippians are also called Φιλιππήσιοι by Steph. Byz., Φιλιππηνοί by Polyb. (according to Steph. Byz.), Φιλιππεῖς in the Corp. Inscript.

ἐγείρ. is decisively attested by the preponderance of uncials (including ℵ) and vss.; ἐπιφέρειν, instead of which Theophyl. ms. has προσφέρειν, is an ancient gloss. — Ver. 18. πλήν] B has ὅτι; A F G P ℵ, min. some vss. and Fathers: πλὴν ὅτι. So Lachm. and Tisch. 8. But the reference of the πλήν not being understood, it was explained by the ὅτι written on the margin, which has in some cases (B) *supplanted* the πλήν, and in others passed into the text *along with* it. — Ver 21. Χριστός] χρηστόν was so isolated and weak in attestation (Ar. pol.), that it should not have been recommended by Griesb., following earlier authority. — Ver. 23. Elz. has γάρ instead of δέ, against decisive testimony. The γάρ after πολλῷ is neither critically nor exegetically to be rejected. See Reiche, *Comm. crit.* — Ver. 24. ἐν τῇ σαρκί] ἐν is wanting in A C P ℵ, min. Clem. Or. Petr. alex. Cyr. Chrysost. Wrongly condemned by Griesb. and Tisch. 8; for ἐν might easily be absorbed by the final syllable of ἐπιμένειν, especially as it is frequently used elsewhere with the simple dative. — Ver. 25. συμπαραμενῶ] Lachm. and Tisch. 8 read παραμενῶ, which Griesb. also approved of, following A B C D* F G ℵ, min. A neglect of the doubly compound verb, attested certainly more weakly, but yet by D*** E K L P, Chrys. al. and many min., which took place all the more readily, because the word does not occur elsewhere in the N. T., and even its meaning might be offensive. — Ver. 27. Instead of ἀκούσω, Lach. and Tisch. 8 read ἀκούω, but without a preponderance of testimony in its favour. — Ver. 28. ἐστὶν αὐτοῖς] Elz. has αὐτοῖς μὲν ἐστίν, against decisive testimony. — ὑμῖν] A B C** ℵ, min. vss. Aug. read ὑμῶν. So Lachm. and Tisch. Rightly; the dative is a mechanical alteration in accordance with the preceding αὐτοῖς and the following ὑμῖν. — Ver. 30. Elz. has ἴδετε. But εἴδετε is attested by A C D* E* ℵ, min. and Fathers, and was supplanted by ἴδετε through Itacism.

CONTENTS.—After the greeting to his readers (vv. 1, 2), Paul assures them of his gratitude towards God on account of their condition as Christians (vv. 3–5), while as regards the future also he has confidence, in accordance with his heartfelt love towards them, as to the continued work of God in their case (vv. 6–8). His prayer is, that their love may increase yet more and more on behalf of Christian perfection to the glory of God (vv. 9–11). He then declares how his present position redounds to the furtherance of the gospel, to which even the preaching of those who are actuated by impure motives contributes

(vv. 12–18), because Christ in fact is preached, which must tend to his—the apostle's—salvation, since now nothing else but the glorification of Christ in his case will be the result, whether he remains alive in the body or not (vv. 19–21). Which of the two he should prefer, he knows not; since, however, the former is more needful for the sake of his readers, he is convinced that it will be the case for their furtherance and joy (vv. 22–26). Only their conduct should be in conformity with the gospel, in order that he, if he should come again to them, or should be absent, might learn their Christian unity and fearlessness (vv. 27–30).

Vv. 1, 2. Καὶ Τιμόθ.] not as *amanuensis*, although he may have been so (comp. 1 Cor. xvi. 21; 2 Thess. iii. 17; Col. iv. 18; and see on Gal. vi. 11), for from Rom. xvi. 22 we must assume that the amanuensis *as such* is not included in the superscription; nor yet merely as taking part in the *greeting* (Estius, Weiss), for ver. 1 is the *address* of the epistle, and as such names *those from whom it emanates;* but as subordinate *joint-writer of the letter* (comp. on 1 Cor. i. 1; 2 Cor. i. 1; Col. i. 1; Philem. 1), who, as a distinguished helper of the apostle, and well known to the readers, adopts the teachings, exhortations, etc. of the letter, which the apostle had previously discussed with him, as his own. At the same time, the apostle himself remains so completely the proper and principal writer of the epistle, that so early as ver. 3 he begins to speak solely in his own person, and in ii. 19 speaks of Timothy, who was to be sent to them, as a third person. Nevertheless this joint mention of Timothy must have been as accordant with the personal relation existing between the latter and the readers (Acts xvi. 10 ff., xix. 22), as it was serviceable in preparing the way for the intended sending of Timothy (ii. 19), and generally edifying and encouraging as a testimony of the intimate fellowship between the apostle and his subordinate fellow-labourer.[1] — δοῦλοι X. 'I] The fact that

[1] In general, when Paul names others besides himself in the address, the ground for it must be sought for in the relation in which those named—who were then present with Paul—stood to the churches concerned, and not in any wish on his part to give by that means to the epistles an *official and public cha·*

Paul does not expressly assert his *apostolic* dignity by the side of Timothy (as in 2 Cor. i. 1, Col. i. 1), may be explained by the intimate and cordial relation in which he stood to the Philippians; for in regard to them he saw no external cause, and felt no internal need, for making this assertion; and we may assume the same thing in Philem. 1. The non-mention of his apostolic dignity in the First and Second Epistles to the Thessalonians is, considering the early date at which they were composed, to be similarly explained (see Lünemann on 1 Thess. i. 1). In their joint designation as δοῦλοι ᾽Ι. Χ. (see on Rom. i. 1),—a designation resulting from the deep consciousness of the specific vocation of their lives (1 Cor. iv. 1),—both the *apostleship* of *Paul* and the official position of *Timothy* (comp. Rom. xvi. 21 : Τιμόθ. ὁ συνεργός μου; Col. iv. 12) are included. Compare σύνδουλος, Col. i. 7, iv. 7. — τοῖς ἁγίοις ἐν Χ. ᾽Ι.] see on Rom i. 7, and on ἡγιασμένος ἐν Χ. ᾽Ι., 1 Cor. i. 2.— σὺν ἐπισκ. κ. διακόν.] *along with overseers and deacons*. Paul writes to *all*[1] the Christians at Philippi (comp. Rom. i. 7), bishops and deacons being expressly *included* (σύν,

racter (Huther *on Col.* p. 45, with whom Corn. Müller agrees, *Commentat. de loc. quibusd. ep. ad Phil.*, Hamb. 1843, p. 5) ; for in that case the Epistles to the Romans and Ephesians would least of all bear the apostle's name *alone*. To him, too, with his personal consciousness of his high apostolic standing (Gal. i. 1), the need of any confirmation or corroboration *by others* must have been an idea utterly foreign. Lastly, this very Epistle to the Philippians bears less of the *official* and more of the *familiar* character than any of the others. —The fact, moreover, that in almost *all* the epistles, in the superscription of which Paul does not name himself alone, *Timothy* is mentioned with him (*Silvanus* being named with the latter in 1 and 2 Thessalonians), is a proof that Timothy was the apostle's *most intimate* companion, and was *highly esteemed* among the churches. In 1 Corinthians only, Sosthenes, and not Timothy, is mentioned along with Paul in the address.

[1] For *all* had, in fact, by their common readiness in offering given occasion to the apostolic letter. Thus the decorum of reply naturally gave rise to the insertion of the otherwise superfluous πᾶσι, without its implying any special design of not putting to shame those who possibly had not contributed (van Hengel). And when Paul still further in this Epistle makes mention repeatedly and earnestly of *all* his readers (i. 4, 7 f., 25, ii. 17, 26, iv. 25), the simple and natural explanation is to be sought in the feeling of *special all-embracing love*, by which he was attached to this well-constituted church not divided by any factions. Hence there is no ground for seeking further explanation, as *e.g.* de Wette does, by suggesting erroneously that "Paul wished to manifest his *impartiality* with regard to the dissension in the church."

comp. Acts xiv. 5).   As *official designations,* the words did not
require the article (Kühner, *ad. Xen. Anab.* iii. 5. 7 : στρατη-
γοὶ δὲ καὶ λοχαγοί), although particular persons are meant (in
opposition to Hofmann), who are regarded, however, just as
office-bearers.   The reason why the latter are specially mentioned in the salutation, in a way not found in any other epistle,
must be sought in the special occasion of the letter, as the
aid which had been conveyed to Paul could not have been
collected without the guidance, and co-operation otherwise, of
these office-bearers.[1]   They might even have transmitted to
him the money by means of *an accompanying letter* in the
name of the church (Ewald; compare Hofmann); there is,
however, no trace elsewhere of this.   Arbitrary suggestions are
made by Cornelius a Lapide and Grotius : that he thus
arranged the salutation *with reference to Epaphroditus,* who
was one of the ἐπίσκοποι; by Matthias : that the ἐπίσκοποι
and διάκονοι had *specially distinguished* themselves among the
Philippians by their zeal and energy; by Rilliet and Corn.
Müller : that the intention was to describe the church as a
regularly constituted one, or as an undivided whole (Rheinwald),
a collective body organized into unity (Hofmann) (which,
in fact, other churches to whom Paul wrote were also); or
that, with the view of preventing disunion, Paul wished to
suggest to them the recognition of the office as an antidote to
self-exaltation (Wiesinger).   Other expositors have given yet
other explanations.—The writing of the words as one : συν-
επισκόποις (B** D*** K, Chrysost. Theophyl. min.) is to be rejected, because σὺν would be without appropriate reference, and
the epistle is addressed to the whole community.   See already
Theodore of Mopsuestia.—As to the *bishops,* called from their
official duty ἐπίσκοποι (Acts xx. 28 ; 1 Tim. iii. 2 ; Tit. i. 7),
or figuratively ποιμένες (Eph. iv. 11), and after the Jewish-
theocratic analogy πρεσβύτεροι, see on Acts xx. 28, Eph.
iv. 11.   And how much the *plural* is at variance with the

---

[1] There is therefore the less ground for Baur bringing forward the mention
of bishops and deacons in this passage to help the proof of a post-apostolic composition of the epistle, as is also done by Hinsch in the passage specified. See,
against this, Hilgenfeld in his *Zeitschr.* 1873, p. 178 f.

Catholic doctrine of the episcopate, see in Calovius. The
absence also of any mention of *presbyters*[1] strikingly shows
that the latter were still at that time identical with the
bishops. Comp. particularly Acts xx. 17, 28 ; and see
Ritschl, *altkath. Kirche*, p. 400 ff. ; also J. B. Lightfoot, p.
93 ff., and Jul. Müller, *dogmat. Abh.* p. 581. Mistaken view in
Döllinger's *Christenthum u. Kirche*, p. 308, ed. 2, who makes
out of σύζυγε γνήσιε the bishop κατ᾽ ἐξοχήν. As to the
διακονία, the care of the poor, sick, and strangers, comp. on
Rom. xii. 7, xvi. 1 ; 1 Cor. xii. 28. We may add that the
placing of the officials *after the church generally*, which is not
logically requisite, and the mere subjoining of them by σὺν,
are characteristic of the relation between the two, which
had not yet undergone hierarchical dislocation. Comp. Acts
xv. 4 ; Heb. xiii. 24. Cornelius a Lapide, following Thomas
Aquinas, sagely observes, that " the shepherd who rules *goes
behind the flock !*" — χάρις ὑμῖν κ.τ.λ.] See on Rom. i. 7.

Ver. 3 f. Comp. Rom. i. 9 ; 1 Cor. i. 4 ; Eph. i. 16 ; 1
Thess. i. 2 ; Philem. 4 ; Col. i. 3. — ἐπὶ πάσῃ τῇ μνείᾳ ὑμ.]
not: in *every* recollection, but, as the article requires : in my
whole recollection of you, so that the sense is not : *as often as*
I remember you (so usually, following Chrysostom and Luther),
but : my remembrance of you *in its entire tenor and compass* is
mingled with thankfulness towards God. On ἐπί with the
dative, comp. ii. 17. Maldonatus, Homberg, Peirce, Michaelis,
Bretschneider, Hofmann, are mistaken in making ὑμῶν genitive of the *subject* (and ἐπί as stating the ground, 1 Cor. i. 4) :
" *that ye are constantly mindful of me,*" or " *on account of your
collective remembrance*" (Hofmann), which is supposed to imply
and include the *aid* transmitted to him as a single μνεία. *That
for which* Paul thanks God—and it is here, as in the openings
of the other epistles, something of a far higher and more
general nature—does not follow until ver. 5. — μνείᾳ] is to
be rendered in the usual sense of *remembrance* (comp. 1 Thess.

---

[1] In the Epistle of Polycarp to the Philippians, πρεσβύτεροι and διάκονοι are
spoken of as existing in Philippi, but no ἐπίσκοπος. See especially chap. v. 6.
Therefore even at this later period bishops and presbyters were identical in
Philippi.

iii. 6 ; 2 Tim. i. 3), and not, as by van Hengel, in that of *mention*, which it only obtains in the passages—certainly otherwise corresponding—Rom. i. 9, Eph. i. 16, 1 Thess. i. 2, Philem. 4, by the addition of ποιεῖσθαι. In this case it is the μνείαν ἔχειν (1 Thess. iii. 6 ; 2 Tim. i. 3 ; Plat. *Legg.* vii. p. 798 A), and not the μν. ποιεῖσθαι, that is thought of. —— πάντοτε] cannot belong to εὐχαριστῶ in such a way that the following ἐν πάσῃ δεήσει κ.τ.λ. should be separated from it and joined to the participial clause, as Hofmann[1] desires. It is true that πάντοτε down to ὑμῶν is closely linked with what precedes ; but the connection is of such a character that πάντοτε already finds the befitting limitation through ἐπὶ πάσῃ τ. μνείᾳ ὑμῶν, and now by πάντοτε κ.τ.λ. can be announced, *when* the εὐχαριστῶ τ. Θ. μ. ἐπὶ π. τ. μν. ὑμ. takes place, namely, "*at all times, in every request which I make for you all,* thanksgiving towards my God is joined with my entire remembrance of you." Negatively expressed, the sense up to this point therefore is : "*I never* (πάντοτε) *make my intercessory prayer for you all, without always* (πάντοτε, as in Rom. i. 10, Col. i. 4) *in it associating thanks towards my God with my entire remembrance of you.*" This does not render the πάντων inappropriate, as Hofmann objects, the fact being that the apostle constantly bears *all* his Philippians upon his heart, and cannot help praying for them *all ;* he *feels* this, and *ex-presses* it. If we should, with Castalio, Beza, and many others, including Weiss, connect as follows : "*whilst I at all times in all my praying for you all make the prayer with joy,*" the expression ἐν πάσῃ δεήσει τὴν δέησιν ποιούμενος, as thus linked together, would be only a burdensome tautology. Instead of μετὰ χαρ. τ. δ. ποιούμ., Paul would have simply and naturally written the mere χαίρων. This applies also to the view of Huther, who (in the *Mecklenb. Zeitschr.* 1863, p. 400) substantially agrees with Weiss. Hoelemann incorrectly

---

[1] According to whom Paul is supposed to say that "*he thanks his God for their collective remembrance at all times, in each of his intercessory prayers making the request for them all with joy.*" Thus, however, the apostle would in fact have expressed himself in a manner *extravagant* even to falsehood, because implying an impossibility.

connects ὑπὲρ παντ. ὑμ. with εὐχαριστῶ (Rom. i. 8; Eph. i. 16; 1 Thess. i. 2; 2 Thess. i. 3). Against this it may be urged, that the otherwise too general ἐν πάσῃ δεήσει μου needs[1] an addition more precisely defining it; and the words μετὰ χαρ. τὴν δέησ. ποιούμ. which follow, show that the thought is still occupied with the *prayer*, and *has it* as yet *in prospect* to express the object of the *thanks*. Lastly, the article in τὴν δέησιν points back to a *more precisely defined* δέησις, the specification of which is contained in this very ὑπ. π. ὑμ. Comp. Col. i. 3. — As to the distinction between δέησις and προσευχή (ver. 9, iv. 6), see on Eph. vi. 18.—On the emphatic sequence of πάσῃ, πάντοτε, πάσῃ, πάντων, comp. Lobeck, *Paral.* p. 56. Paul does not aim at such accumulations, but the fulness of his heart suggests them to him; comp. 2 Cor. ix. 8. — μετὰ χαρᾶς κ.τ.λ.] His heart urges him, while mentioning his prayer for them all, to add: " when I make *with joy* the (mentioned) prayer (τὴν δ.),"—a feature which is met with in the opening of *this* epistle *only*. Ver. 4 is not to be placed in a parenthesis (as by Luther), nor yet from μετὰ χαρ. onwards, for ποιούμ. is connected with εὐχαριστῶ (in opposition to Heinrichs), as containing the characteristic definition of mode for δέησις ὑπ. πάντ. ὑμ.

Ver. 5 f. Ἐπὶ τῇ κοινων. ὑμ. εἰς τὸ εὐαγγ.] is to be taken together with εὐχαριστῶ, ver. 3 (1 Cor. i. 4), and not with μετὰ χαρ. κ.τ.λ. (Calvin, Grotius, van Hengel, de Wette, Ewald, Weiss, Hofmann); for in that case, with the right explanation of ἐπὶ πάσῃ τ. μν. ὑμ., the specification of the ground for thanks would be entirely wanting, or would at all events result only indirectly, namely, as object of the *joy*. *On account of your fellowship in respect of the gospel;* by this Paul means the common brotherly coherence (Acts ii. 42) which united the Philippians together for the gospel (as the aim to which the κοινωνία has reference), that is, for its furtherance and efficiency. The great cause of the gospel was the end at which, in their mutual coherence, they aimed; and this, therefore, gave to their

---

[1] This applies also in opposition to Ewald, who attaches ὑπὲρ πάντων ὑμῶν, and to Hofmann, who at the same time joins ἐν πάσῃ δεήσει, *to the participial clause.* The participial clause only begins with the emphatically prefixed μετὰ χαρᾶς.

fellowship with one another its specific character of a holy destination. The correctness of this interpretation is confirmed by the context in ver. 9, where that which is here expressed by ἡ κοινωνία ὑμῶν is characterized, under the category of the *disposition* on which this κοινωνία is based, as ἡ ἀγάπη ὑμῶν. As this view is in full harmony with both words and sense, and is not dependent on anything to be supplied, it excludes divergent interpretations. We must therefore reject not only the explanation which refers κοινωνία to the *aid* sent to Paul (Zeger, Cornelius a Lapide, Estius, Wetstein, Michaelis, Bisping, and others), so that it is to be taken actively as *communication* (see Fritzsche, *ad Rom.* III. p. 81, 287), although it is never so used in the N. T. (comp. on Rom. xv. 26 ; Gal. vi. 6 ; Philem. 6), but also the view of Theodoret, Luther, Beza, Calvin, Grotius, Heinrichs, and others : "*quod evangelii participes facti estis*," as if it ran τοῦ εὐαγγελίου (Theodoret: κοινωνίαν δὲ τοῦ εὐαγγελίου τὴν πίστιν ἐκάλεσε). Chrysostom and Theophylact, who are followed by most of the recent interpreters (including Schinz, Weiss, Schenkel, Huther, Ellicott, J. B. Lightfoot, Hofmann), understand the fellowship of the Philippians *with the apostle*, that is, ὅτι κοινωνοί μου γίνεσθε κ. συμμερισταὶ τῶν ἐπὶ τῷ εὐαγγ. πόνων, Theophylact ; consequently, their *co-operation with him* in spreading the gospel, in which case also a reference to the aid rendered is included. In this case, since the text says nothing about a "*service*" devoted to the gospel (Hofmann), an addition like μετ᾽ ἐμοῦ (1 John i. 3, *et al.*), or some other more precise definition, like that in ver. 7, would be an essential element— not arising (as in Gal. ii. 9) out of the context—which therefore must have been *expressed*, as indeed Paul must have *said* so, had he wished to be understood as referring to fellowship *with all who had the cause of the gospel at heart* (Wiesinger). The *absolute* "your fellowship," if no arbitrary supplement is allowable, can only mean *the mutual fellowship* of *the members of the church themselves*.—The *article* is not repeated after ὑμῶν, because κοινωνία εἰς τὸ εὐαγγ. is conceived as forming a single notion (comp. on κοινωνεῖν εἰς, iv. 15 ; Plato, *Rep.* p. 453 A). — ἀπὸ πρώτης ἡμ. ἄχρι τοῦ νῦν] is *usually* connected with τῇ κοινωνίᾳ κ.τ.λ.   This connection is the *true one*, for the *constancy* of the κοινωνία, that has been attested hitherto, is the very thing which not only supplies the motive for the apostle's thankfulness, but forms also the ground of his just confidence for the future.   The connective article (τῇ before ἀπό) is not requisite, as ἐπὶ τῇ κοινωνίᾳ ὑμῶν was construed as ἐπὶ τῷ κοινωνεῖν ὑμᾶς (Winer, p. 128 [E. T. 171]).   It cannot be connected with τ. δέησιν ποιούμ. (Weiss), unless ἐπὶ τ. κοινων. κ.τ.λ. is also made to belong hereto.   If joined with πεποιθώς (Rilliet, following Lachmann, ed. min.), it would convey an emphatically prefixed definition of the apostle's confidence, whereas the whole context concerns the previous *conduct of the readers,* which by the connection with πεποιθ. would be but indirectly indicated.   If connected with εὐχαριστῶ (Beza, Wolf, Bengel), the words—seeing that the expression πάντοτε ἐν πάσῃ δεήσει has already been used, and then in ἐπὶ τῇ κοινωνίᾳ κ.τ.λ. a transition has already been made to the object of the thanks — would contain a definition awkwardly postponed.—The *first* day is that in which he first preached the gospel to them, which was followed by immediate and decided results, Acts xvi. 13 ff.   Comp. Col. i. 6.— πεποιθώς] *confidence* by which Paul knows his εὐχαριστεῖν, vv. 3–5, to be *accompanied*.   Without due ground, Hofmann confuses the matter by making a new prolonged paragraph begin with πεποιθώς.[1] — αὐτὸ τοῦτο] if taken according to the common usage as the accusative of the *object* (comp. ver. 25), would not point to what follows, as if it were τοῦτο merely (Weiss), but would mean, being confident of *this very thing,* which is being spoken of (ii. 18; Gal. ii. 10; 2 Cor. ii. 3).   But nothing has been yet said of the contents of the confidence, which are to follow.   It is therefore to be taken

[1] He makes ver. 6, namely, constitute a *protasis,* whose apodosis is again divided into the protasis καθώς ἐστιν δίκαιον ἐμοί and the apodosis corresponding thereto. But this *apodosis of the apodosis* begins with διὰ τὸ ἔχειν με, ver. 7, and yet is only continued after the words μάρτυς γ. ὁ Θεός, ὡς ἐπιποθῶ ὑμᾶς, which are a *parenthesis,* in vv. 8, 9.   Such a dialectically involved and complicated, long-winded period would be most of all out of place in *this* epistle ; and what reader would have been able, without Hofmann's guidance, to detect it and adjust its several parts ?

as *ob id ipsum*,[1] *for this very reason* (2 Pet. i. 5 ; Plato, *Symp.*
p. 204 A, and Stallb. *ad loc. ; Prot.* p. 310 E ; Xen. *Anab.* i.
9. 21, and Kühner *in loc.*, also his *Gramm.* II. 1, p. 267 ; see
also Winer, p. 135 [E. T. 178], and comp. on Gal. ii. 10),
namely, because your κοινωνία εἰς τὸ εὐαγγ., from the first day
until now, is that which alone can warrant and justify my
confidence for the future, ὅτι ὁ ἐναρξάμενος κ.τ.λ. — ὁ ἐναρξάμενος κ.τ.λ.] *God.* Comp. ii. 13. That which He has begun
He will complete, namely, by the further operations of His
grace. The idea of resistance to this grace, as a human possibility, is not thereby excluded ; but Paul has not to fear this
on the part of his Philippian converts, as he formerly had in
the case of the Galatians, Gal. i. 6, iii. 3. — ἐν ὑμῖν] That Paul
did not intend to say *among you* (as Hoelemann holds), but
in you, in animis vestris (comp. ii. 13 ; 1 Cor. xii. 6), is shown
by ὑπὲρ πάντων ὑμῶν following, by which the language
ὁ ἐναρξ. ἐν ὑμιν κ.τ.λ. expresses a *confidence* felt in respect
to all *individuals.* — ἔργον ἀγαθόν] without article, hence :
an excellent work, by which is meant, in conformity with
the context, the κοινωνία ὑμ. εἰς τὸ εὐαγγ. — ἄχρις ἡμέρας
'Ι. Χ.] corresponding to the ἀπὸ πρώτης ἡμέρ. ἄχρι τοῦ νῦν,
ver. 5, presupposes the *nearness* of the παρουσία (in opposition to Wiesinger, Hofmann, and others), as everywhere in
the N. T., and especially in Paul's writings (Weiss, *bibl. Theol.*
p. 297, ed. 2). Comp. ver. 10, iii. 20. The device by
which the older expositors (see even Pelagius) gratuitously introduce qualifying statements, " Perseverat autem in illum usque
diem, quicunque perseverat *usque ad mortem suam* " (Estius),
whereby is meant not " *continuitas usque ad illum diem,*" but
" *terminus et complementum perfectionis, quod habituri isto die
erimus* " (Calovius), is just as un-Pauline as Calvin's makeshift,
" that the dead are still *in profectu,* because they have not yet
reached the goal," and as Matthies' philosophical perverting of
it into the *continual* and *eternal* Parousia.

Ver. 7. Subjective justification of the confidence expressed
in ver. 6. How should he otherwise than cherish it, and
that on the ground of his objective experience (αὐτὸ τοῦτο),

---

[1] Hofmann also adopts this explanation of αὐτὸ τοῦτο.

since it was to him, through his love to his readers, a *duty*
and *obligation !* *Not* to cherish it would be *wrong.* " Caritas
enim omnia sperat," Pelagius.—As to καθώς, which, in the
conception of the *corresponding* relation, states the *ground*,
comp. on iii. 17 ; 1 Cor. i. 6 ; Eph. i. 4 ; Matt. vi. 11.
—On δίκαιον, comp. Acts iv. 19 ; Eph. vi. 1 ; Phil. iv. 8 ;
Col. iv. 1 ; 2 Pet. i. 12.   A classical author would have
written : δίκαιον ἐμὲ τοῦτο φρονεῖν (Herod. i. 39 ; Dem. 198.
8 ; Plat. *Symp.* p. 214 C), or : δίκαιός εἰμι τοῦτο φρ. (Herod.
i. 32 ; Dem. 1469. 18, and frequently ; Thuc. i. 40. 3). —
τοῦτο φρονεῖν] *to have this feeling*, this practical bent of mind
in favour of you, by which is meant *the confidence* expressed
in ver. 6, and not *his striving in prayer for the perfecting of
his readers' salvation* (ver. 4), which the sense of the word
φρονεῖν does not admit of (in opposition to Weiss), as it is
not equivalent to ζητεῖν (comp. on Col. iii. 2).   See besides,
Huther, *l.c.* p. 405 f.—On ὑπέρ, comp. iv. 10 ; 2 Macc. xiv. 8 ;
Eur. *Archel. fr.* xxv. 2 f. ; Plut. *Phil. c. Flam.* 3 ; on τοῦτο φρ.,
Gal. v. 10, οὐδὲν ἄλλο φρ.   The special reference of the sense
of φρονεῖν : *to be mindful about something*, must have been suggested by the context, as in iv. 10 ; but is here insisted on by
Hofmann, and that in connection with the error, that with
καθώς the protasis of an apodosis is introduced.   The φρονεῖν
is here perfectly general, *cogitare ac sentire*, but is characterized
by τοῦτο as a εὖ φρονεῖν, which Paul feels himself bound to
cherish in the interest of the salvation of all his readers (ὑπὲρ
πάντων ὑμῶν). — διὰ τὸ ἔχειν με ἐν τῇ καρδίᾳ ὑμᾶς] An expression of *heartfelt love* (comp. 2 Cor. vii. 3) *on the part of
the apostle towards his readers*, not on the part of his *readers*
towards *him* (Oeder, Michaelis, Storr, Rosenmüller, am Ende,
Flatt), thus making ὑμᾶς the subject ; although the sing.
καρδίᾳ (comp. Eph. iv. 18, v. 19, vi. 5 ; Rom. i. 21 ; 2 Cor.
iii. 15, and elsewhere) is not against this view, the position of
the words is opposed to it, as is also the context, see ver. 8.
The readers are present to the apostle in his loving heart. —
ἔν τε τοῖς δεσμοῖς κ.τ.λ.] so that, accordingly, this state of
suffering, and the great task which is incumbent on me in it,
cannot dislodge you from my heart.   See already Chrysostom

and Pelagius.   These words, ἔν τε τοῖς δεσμοῖς κ.τ.λ., set
forth the *faithful* and *abiding* love, which even his heavy
misfortunes cannot change into concern for himself alone.
They contain, however, the two points, co-ordinated by τέ . . .
καί (*as well . . . as also*): (1) The *position* of the apostle, and
(2) his *employment* in this position.   The latter, which, through
the non-repetition of the article before βεβ., is taken as a whole
(Buttmann, *neut. Gr.* p. 294 [E. T. 342]), is both *antithetical*,
the *defence* of the gospel, and also *thetical*, the *confirmation* of it,
that is, the corroboration of its truth by proof, testimony, etc.,
its *verification ;* comp. Heb. vi. 16 ; Rom. xv. 8 ; Mark xvi.
20 ; Thucyd. i. 140. 6, iv. 87. 1 ; Plat. *Polit.* p. 309 C ;
Wisd. v. 18.   For an instance of this kind of βεβαίωσις
during the earliest period of the apostle's captivity at Rome,
see Acts xxviii. 23.   Hofmann, taking a groundless objection
to our explanation from the use of τέ . . . καί (see, however,
Baeumlein, *Partik.* p. 225), refuses to connect the τέ with the
following καί; he prefers to connect with the one ἔχειν, namely
with the ἔχειν ἐν τῇ καρδίᾳ, another, namely an ἔχειν συγκοινωνούς.   This is an artificial conjunction of very different
references of the ἔχειν, yielding the illogical formalism : I have
you (1) *in my heart,* and (2) *for my companions,* etc.   The
latter would indeed be only a more precise qualitative definition of the former.   The question, moreover, whether in τῇ
ἀπολ. κ. βεβ. τοῦ εὐαγγ. Paul intended to speak of his *judicial*
examination (Heinrichs, van Hengel), or of his *extra-judicial*
action and ministry during his captivity, cannot be answered
without arbitrariness, except by allowing that *both* were meant.
For the words do not justify us in excluding the judicial
defence (Wieseler, *Chronol. d. apostol. Zeitalt.* p. 430), since the
ἀπολογία might be addressed not merely to Jews and Judaists,
but also to Gentile judges.—τοῦ εὐαγγ.] belongs to τῇ ἀπολ. κ.
βεβαιώσει, and *not* to βεβ. only ; the latter view would make
τῇ ἀπολ. denote the *personal* vindication (Chrysostom, Estius,
and others), but is decisively opposed by the non-repetition
—closely coupling the two words—of the article before βεβ.
But to interpret ἀπολογία and βεβαίωσις as *synonymous* (Rheinwald), or to assume an ἐν διὰ δυοῖν for ἀπολογίᾳ εἰς βεβαίωσιν

(Heinrichs), is logically incorrect, and without warrant in the connection. It is also contrary to the context (on account of τῇ ἀπολογίᾳ) to understand the βεβαίωσις τ. εὐαγγ. as the *actual* confirmation afforded by the apostle's *sufferings* (Chrysostom, Theodoret, Erasmus, and others). — συγκοινωνούς μου κ.τ.λ.] characterizes the ὑμᾶς, and supplies a motive for the ἔχειν με ἐν τῇ καρδίᾳ ὑμᾶς κ.τ.λ. : *since you*, etc. This love to you, unalterable even in my affliction, is based on the real *sympathy*, which results from *all of you being joint-partakers* with me in the grace. The emphasis is laid, primarily on συγκ. and then on πάντας, which is correlative with the previous πάντων. The idea of the *grace which the apostle had received* (τῆς χάριτος) is defined solely from the connection, and that indeed by the two points immediately preceding, ἔν τε τοῖς δεσμοῖς μου and τῇ ἀπολ. κ. βεβ. τοῦ εὐαγγ., namely, as God's gift of grace enabling them to *suffer* for the gospel (comp. ver. 29 f.; see also Acts v. 41; 1 Pet. ii. 19), and therewith to *defend* and *confirm* instead of falling away from and denying it. "Magnus in hac re honos, magna praemia" (Grotius). Paul knew that the experience of this grace—for the setting forth of which the context itself amply suffices, without the need of any retrospective ταύτης (as is Hofmann's objection)— had been vouchsafed not only to himself, but also to all his Philippian converts, who like him had had to suffer for Christ (ver. 29 f.); and thus, in his bonds, and whilst vindicating and confirming the gospel, conscious of the holy similarity in this respect between his and their experience, sympathetically and lovingly he bore them, as his *fellow-sharers* of this grace, in his heart. He knew that, whilst he was suffering, and defending and confirming the gospel, he had all his readers as συμπάσχοντες, συναπολογούμενοι, συμβεβαιοῦντες τὸ εὐαγγέλιον, and that in virtue of the above-named grace of God, as a manifestation of which he had recognised his bonds, and his activity for the gospel in these bonds. Others interpret it much too generally and vaguely, looking at the tender and *special* references of the context, as the "gratiosa *evangelii* donatio" (Hoelemann, comp. Wolf, Heinrichs, de Wette, and others). Likewise without any

more immediate reference to the context, and inappropriate, is
its explanation of the *apostolic office* (Rom. i. 5, *et al.*), the
Philippians being said to be active promoters of this through
their faith (see Theodore of Mopsuestia); along with which
a reference is introduced to the *assistance* rendered (Storr,
am Ende, Rosenmüller, Flatt, Hofmann; comp. also Weiss)—
which assistance has come to be regarded as a κοινωνία εἰς τὸ
εὐαγγέλιον (but see on ver. 5), as Hofmann expresses it.
Those who feel dissatisfied that Paul does not mention at the
very beginning of the epistle the assistance rendered to him,
prescribe a certain line for the apostle; which, however, he does
not follow, but gives expression first of all to his love for the
Philippians in subjects of a higher and more general interest,
and puts off his expression of thanks, properly so called, to
the end of the epistle.   Lastly, the translation *gaudii* (Vulgate,
Itala, Ambrosiaster, Pelagius, Primasius, Sedulius) is derived
from another reading (χαρᾶς).—The σύν in συγκοινωνούς refers
to μου, *my joint-partakers* (iv. 14) *of the grace*, thus combining συγκ. with a double genitive of the person and the
thing, of the subject and the object (Kühner, II. 1, p. 288;
Winer, p. 180 [E. T. 239]), and placing it first with emphasis;
for this *joint fellowship* is the *point* of the love in question.
—As to the repetition of ὑμᾶς, see Matthiae, p. 1031, and on
Col. ii. 13; comp. Soph. *O. C.* 1278, and Reisig *in loc.*

REMARK.—Whether ἔν τε τοῖς δεσμοῖς . . . εὐαγγ. should be connected with the preceding διὰ τὸ ἔχειν με ἐν τῇ καρδίᾳ ὑμᾶς (Chrysostom, Erasmus, Castalio, Luther, and many; also Huther),
or with συγκ. κ.τ.λ. which follows (Beza, Calvin, Calovius, Cornelius a Lapide, Storr, Flatt, Lachmann, van Hengel, Tischendorf,
Wiesinger, Ewald, Weiss, Hofmann, and others), cannot be
determined. Still the former, as of a less periodic character,
is more in harmony with the fervent tone of feeling. Besides,
the repetition of ὑμᾶς betrays a break in the flow of thought
after τ. εὐαγγ.

Ver. 8. A solemn confirmation of the preceding assurance,
that he had his readers in his heart, etc. Comp., on the
connection, Rom. i. 9.   Theophylact, moreover, strikingly
observes: οὐχ ὡς ἀπιστούμενος μάρτυρα καλεῖ τὸν Θεόν, ἀλλὰ
τὴν πολλὴν διάθεσιν οὐκ ἔχων παραστῆσαι διὰ λόγου. — ὡς

ἐπιποθῶ κ.τ.λ.] *how much I long after you all*, etc., which
would not be the case if I did not bear you in my heart
(γάρ), as announced more precisely in ver. 7.   On ἐπιποθῶ,
comp. Rom. i. 11; Phil. ii. 26; 1 Thess. iii. 6; 2 Tim. i. 4.
The *compound* denotes the *direction* (Plat. *Legg.* ix. p. 855 F;
Herod. v. 93; Diod. Sic. xvii. 101; Ecclus. xxv. 20), not the
strength of the ποθεῖν (comp. on 2 Cor. v. 2), which is conveyed
by ὡς; comp. Rom. i. 9; 1 Thess. ii. 10. — ἐν σπλάγχνοις
Χριστοῦ Ἰησοῦ] is not, with Hofmann,[1] to be connected with
what follows (see on ver. 9); it is an expression of the
heartiness and truth of his longing, uttered in the strongest
possible terms.   ἐν, on account of the sensuous expression
which follows (σπλάγχνα, like רַחֲמִים, as seat of the affections,
especially of heartfelt love, ii. 1; Col. iii. 12; Philem. 7,
12, 20; also in classical authors), is to be taken *locally*:
in the heart of Jesus Christ; that is, so that this longing of
mine is not my own individual emotion, but *a longing which
I feel in virtue of the dwelling and working of Christ in me.*
Paul speaks thus from the consciousness that his inmost life
is not that of his human personality, of himself, but that
Christ, through the medium of the Holy Spirit, is the personal
principle and agent of his thoughts, desires, and feelings.
Comp. on Gal. ii. 20.   Filled with the feeling of this holy
fellowship of life, which threw his own individuality into the
background, he could, seeing that his whole spiritual ζωή was
thus the life of Christ in him, represent the circumstances
of his ἐπιποθεῖν, as if the *viscera Christi* were moved in him,
as if Christ's heart throbbed in him for his Philippians.   Bengel
aptly says: "In Paulo non Paulus vivit sed Jesus Christus;
quare Paulus non in Pauli, sed Jesu Christi movetur vis-
ceribus."   Comp. Theodoret: οὐκ ἀνθρώπινον τὸ φίλτρον,
πνευματικόν.   Not doing justice to the Pauline consciousness
of the *unio mystica* which gives rise to this expression, some
have rendered ἐν in an *instrumental* sense, as in Luke i. 78
(Hofmann); others have taken it of the *norma*: "according

[1] According to Hofmann, namely, ἐν σπλ. Χ. Ἰ. asserts with reference to the
following καὶ τοῦτο προσεύχ. that Christ's heart towards those who are His produces such prayer in the apostle, and manifests itself therein.

to the pattern of Christ's love to His people " (Rosenmüller,
Rilliet) ; and some have found the sense of the *norma* in the
genitival relation : " in animo penitus affecto ut animus fuit
Christi " (van Hengel).   So also Wetstein, Heinrichs, and
earlier expositors ; whilst Storr refers ἐν σπλ. 'I. X. even
to the readers (*sc.* ὄντας).   For many other interpretations,
see Hoelemann and Weiss.   The merely approximate statement of the sense, given by Grotius and others : " amore non
illo communi, sed *vere Christiano*," is in substance correct, but
fails to give its full development to the consciousness of the
Χριστὸς ἐν ἡμῖν (Gal. ii. 20, iv. 19 ; Rom. viii. 10 ; 2 Cor.
xiii. 5 ; Eph. iii. 17) ; notwithstanding which Hofmann regards
the identification of Paul's own heart with the heart of Christ
as simply *impossible ;* thus, however, applying to the mysti-
cism of deep pious feeling, and the living immediate plastic
form in which it finds expression, a criterion alien to its
character, and drawing around it a literal boundary which
it cannot bear.

Ver. 9. After having stated and discussed, in vv. 3–8,
the reason why he *thanks* God with respect to his readers,
Paul now, till the end of ver. 11, sets forth what it is that he
asks in prayer for them.   " Redit ad precationem, quam obiter
tantum uno verbo attigerat (namely, ver. 4) ; exponit igitur
summam eorum, quae illis petebat a Deo" (Calvin).—καί] the
simple *and*, introducing the new part of,[1] and thus continuing,
the discourse : *And this* (which follows) *is what I pray*,—so
that the *object* is placed first in the progress of the discourse ;
hence it is καὶ τοῦτο προσεύχομαι, and not κ. προσεύχ. τοῦτο.
Hofmann's explanation of the καί in the sense of *also*, and his
attaching ἐν σπλ. X. 'I. to ver. 9, are the necessary result of

---

[1] The word προσεύχομαι, which now occurs, points to a *new* topic, the thanksgiving and its grounds having been previously spoken of.   Therefore κ. τ.
προσεύχ. is not to be attached, with Rilliet and Ewald, to the preceding verse :
and (how I) *pray this*.   Two different things would thus be joined.   The
former portion is *concluded* by the fervent and solemn ver. 8.   Jatho also
(*Br. an d. Phil.*, Hildesh. 1857, p. 8) connects it with ὡς, namely thus : *and
how I pray for this*, namely, to come to you, *in order* that I may edify you.
But to extract for τοῦτο, out of ἐπιποθῶ ὑμᾶς, the notion : "my presence with
you," is much too harsh and arbitrary ; for Paul's words are not even ἐπιποθῶ
ἰδεῖν ὑμᾶς, as in Rom. i. 11.

his perverse metamorphosis of the simple discourse, running on from πεποιθώς in ver. 6, into a lengthened protasis and apodosis,—a construction in which the apodosis of the apodosis is supposed to begin with ἐν σπλ. Χ. Ἰ.; comp. on ver. 6.— ἵνα] introduces the contents of the prayer conceived of under the form of its *design* (Col. i. 9 ; 1 Thess. i. 11 ; Matt. xxiv. 20), and thus explains the preparatory τοῦτο.   Comp. on John vi. 29.   "*This* I pray, *that your love should more and more*," etc. — ἡ ἀγάπη ὑμῶν], not love *to Paul* (van Hengel, follow-ing Chrysostom, Theophylact, Grotius, Bengel, and others),—a reference which, especially in connection with ἔτι μᾶλλον κ. μᾶλλον, would be all the more unsuitable on account of the apostle having just received a practical proof of the love of the Philippians.   It would also be entirely inappropriate to the context which follows (ἐν ἐπιγνώσει κ.τ.λ.).   Nor is it their love *generally*, without specification of an object for it, as a proof of faith (Hofmann) ; but it is, in accordance with the context, the brotherly love of the Philippians *one to another*, the common disposition and feeling at the bottom of that κοινωνία εἰς τὸ εὐαγγ., for which Paul has given thanks in ver. 5.[1]   This previous *thanksgiving* of his was based on the confidence, ὅτι ὁ ἐναρξάμενος κ.τ.λ., ver. 6, and *the contents of his prayer* now is in full harmony with that confidence.   The connection is misapprehended by Calovius and Rheinwald, who explain it as love *to God and Christ ;* also by Matthies (comp. Rilliet), who takes it as love to everything, *that is truly Christian ;* comp. Wiesinger : love to the Lord, and to all that belongs to and serves Him ; Weiss : zeal of love for the cause of the gospel,—an interpretation which fails to define the necessary personal object of the ἀγάπη, and to do justice to the idea of co-operative fellowship which is implied in the κοινωνία in ver. 5. — ἔτι μᾶλλον] quite our: *still more.*   Comp. Homer, *Od.* i. 322, xviii. 22 ; Herod. i. 94 ; Pind. *Pyth.* x. 88, *Olymp.* i. 175 ; Plat. *Euthyd.* p. 283 C ; Xen. *Anab.* vi. 6.

---

[1] The idea that "your love' means the *readers themselves* (Bullinger), or that this passage gave rise to the mode of addressing the hearers that has obtained since the Fathers (very frequently, *e. g.* in Augustine) in the language of the church (Bengel), is purely fanciful.

35 ; Diog. L. ix. 10. 2. See instances of μᾶλλον καὶ μᾶλλον in Kypke, II. p. 307. With the reading περισσεύῃ note the sense of *progressive development*. — ἐν ἐπιγνώσει κ. πάσῃ αἰσ-θήσει] constitutes that *in which*—*i.e. respecting which*—the love of his readers is to become more and more abundant. Comp. Rom. xv. 13 ; 2 Cor. iii. 9 (*Elz.*), viii. 7 ; Col. ii. 7 ; Ecclus. xix. 20 (24). Others take the ἐν as instrumental: *through* (Heinrichs, Flatt, Schinz, and others) ; or as local : *in, i.e. in association with* (Oecumenius, Calvin, Rheinwald, Hoelemann, and others),—περισσ. being supposed to stand *absolutely* (*may be abundant*). But the sequel, which refers to the ἐπίγνωσις and αἴσθησις, and not to the love, shows that Paul had in view not the growth in *love*, but the increase in ἐπί-γνωσις and αἴσθησις, which the love of the Philippians was more and more to attain. The less the love is deficient in knowledge and αἴσθησις, it is the more deeply felt, more moral, effective, and lasting. If ἐπίγνωσις is the penetrating (see on 1 Cor. xiii. 12 ; Eph. i. 17) *cognition* of divine truth, both theoretical and practical, the true knowledge of salvation,[1] which is the source, motive power, and regulator of love (1 John iv. 7 ff.) ; αἴσθησις (only occurring here in the New Testament), which denotes *perception* or *feeling* operating either through the bodily senses[2] (Xen. *Mem.* i. 4. 5, *Anab.* iv. 6. 13, and Krüger *in loc. ;* Plat. *Theaet.* p. 156 B), which are also called αἰσθήσεις (Plat. *Theaet.* p. 156 B), or spiritually [2] (Plat. *Tim.* p. 43 C ; Dem. 411. 19, 1417. 5), must be, according to the context which follows, *the perception which takes place with the ethical senses,*—an activity of moral perception which apprehends and makes conscious of good and evil as such (comp. Heb. v. 14). The opposite of this is the dulness and inaction of the inward sense of ethical feeling (Rom. xi. 8 ; Matt. xiii. 15, *et al.*), the stagnation of the αἰσθητήρια τῆς καρδίας (Jer. iv. 19), whereby a moral unsusceptibility, in-

---

[1] Not a mere knowledge of the *divine will* (Rheinwald), which leads to the right objects, aims, means, and proofs of love (Weiss ; comp. Hofmann). This, as in Col. i. 9, would have been *expressed* by Paul. Neither can ἐπιγν. be limited to the knowledge of *men* (Chrysostom, Erasmus, and others).

[2] "Nam etiam spiritualiter datur visus, auditus, olfactus, gustus, tactus, i. e. sensus investigativi et fruitivi" (Bengel).

capacity of judgment, and indifference are brought about.
Comp. LXX. Prov. i. 7; Ex. xxviii. 5; Ecclus. xx. 17, Rec.
(αἴσθησις ὀρθή); 4 Macc. ii. 21.   Paul desires for his readers
every (πάσῃ) αἴσθησις, because their inner sense is in no given
relation to remain without the corresponding moral activity
of feeling, which may be very diversified according to the
circumstances which form its ethical conditions.   The relation
between ἐπίγνωσις and αἴσθησις is that of spontaneity to
receptivity, and the former is the ἡγεμονικόν for the efficacy
of the latter.   In the contrast, however, mistaking and misapprehending are not correlative to the former, and deception
to the latter (Hofmann); both contrast with both.

Vv. 10, 11. Εἰς τὸ δοκιμάζειν κ.τ.λ.] states the *aim* of the
περισσ. ἐν ἐπιγν. κ. π. αἴσθ., and in ἵνα ἦτε εἰλικρ. κ.τ.λ. we
have the *ultimate design*.   δοκιμάζειν τὰ διαφέροντα is to
be understood, as in Rom. ii. 18 : *in order to approve that
which is* (morally) *excellent.*   So the Vulgate, Chrysostom,
Theodore of Mopsuestia, Theophylact, Erasmus, Castalio,
Grotius, Calovius, Estius, Bengel, Michaelis, Flatt, Rheinwald,
Rilliet, Ewald, and others.   See on διαφέρειν, *praestantiorem
esse* (Dem. 1466. 22; Polyb. iii. 87. 1; Matt. x. 31), and
τὰ διαφέροντα, *praestantiora* (Xen. *Hier.* i. 3; Dio Cass. xliv.
25), Sturz, *Lex. Xen.* I. p. 711 f.   Comp. διαφερόντως, *eximie*
(Plat. *Prot.* p. 349 D, and frequently).   For δοκιμάζ., comp.
Rom. xiv. 22, *et al.*   Others understand it as *a testing of
things which are morally different* (Theodoret, Beza, Grotius,
Wolf, and others; also Matthies, Hoelemann, van Hengel, de
Wette, Corn. Müller, Wiesinger, Weiss, Huther).   In point
of usage, this is equally correct; see on δοκιμάζ., in both
senses, 1 Thess. ii. 4.   But in our view the sense which yields
a *definition of the aim* of the words περισσ. ἐν ἐπιγν. κ. π. αἴσθ.,
as well as *the antecedent of the* εἰλικρίνεια *which follows*,
seems more consistent with the context.   The *testing* of good
and evil is not the aim, but the expression and function, of
the ἐπίγνωσις and αἴσθησις.   Looking at the stage of Christian
life which must be assumed from vv. 5 and 7 (different in
Rom. xii. 2), the former, as an aim, does not go far enough;
and the εἰλικρίνεια is the result not of that testing, but of *the*

approbation of the good. Hofmann's view is therefore unsuitable, that it means the proving *of that which is otherwise;* otherwise, namely, than that towards which the Christian's love is directed. This would amount merely to the thought of testing *what is unworthy of being loved* (= τὰ ἕτερα)—a thought quite out of keeping with the *telic* mode of expression. — εἰλικρινεῖς], *pure, sincere* = καθαρός ; Plat. *Phil.* p. 52 D. Comp., on its *ethical* use, Plat. *Phaedr.* p. 66 A, and Stallbaum *in loc.*, 81 C ; 2 Pet. iii. 1 ; 1 Cor. v. 8 ; 2 Cor. i. 12, ii. 17 ; Wisd. vii. 25, and Grimm *in loc.* — ἀπρόσκοποι] practical proof of the εἰλικρίνεια in reference to intercourse with others (2 Cor. vi. 3): *giving no offence;* 1 Cor. x. 32 ; Ignat. *Trall. interpol.* 7 ; Suicer, *Thes. s.v.* As Paul decidedly uses this word in an *active* sense in 1 Cor. *l.c.* (comp. Ecclus. xxxv. 21), this meaning is here also to be preferred to the in itself admissible *intransitive,*—viz. *not offending* (Acts xxiv. 16 ; comp. John xi. 9),—in opposition to Ambrosiaster, Beza, Calvin, Hoelemann, de Wette, Weiss, Huther, Hofmann, and others. — εἰς ἡμέρ. X.], *to,* i.e. *for,* the day of Christ, when ye are to *appear* pure and blameless before the judgment-seat. Comp. ii. 16 ; Eph. iv. 30 ; Col. i. 22 ; 2 Pet. ii. 9, iii. 7 ; 2 Tim. i. 12 ; also Jude 24 f. These passages show that the expression is not equivalent to the ἄχρις ἡμέρας X. in ver. 6 (Luther, Erasmus, and others), but places what is said in relation to the decision, unveiling, and the like of the day of the Parousia, which is, however, here also looked upon as near. — Ver. 11. πεπλ. καρπὸν δικ.] modal definition of the εἰλικριν. κ. ἀπρόσκ., and that from the *positive* side of these attributes, which are manifested and tested in this fruitfulness—*i.e.* in this rich fulness of Christian virtue in their possessors. καρπὸς δικαιοσ. is the fruit *which is the product of righteousness,* which proceeds from a righteous moral state. Comp. καρπ. τοῦ πνεύματος, Gal. v. 22 ; κ. τοῦ φωτός, Eph. v. 9 ; κ. δικαιοσύνης, Jas. iii. 18, Heb. xii. 11, Rom. vi. 21 f., Prov. xi. 30. In *no* instance is the genitive with καρπός that of *apposition* (Hofmann). The δικαιοσύνη here meant, however, is not *justitia fidei* (*justificatio*), as many, even Rilliet and Hoelemann, would make it, but, in conformity with ver. 10, a righteous *moral* condition, which is the moral *consequence*, because the necessary *vital expression*, of the righteousness of faith, in which man now καρπcφορεῖ τῷ Θεῷ ἐν καινότητι πνεύματος, Rom. vii. 5 f.; comp. vi. 2, viii. 2; Col. i. 10. We must observe that the emphasis is laid not on δικαιοσύνης, but on καρπόν,—which therefore obtains more precise definition afterwards,—so that δικαιοσύνης conveys no new idea, but only represents the idea, *already conveyed* in ver. 10, of the right moral condition. Comp. on δικαιοσύνη, Eph. v. 9; Rom. vi. 13, 18, 20, xiv. 17, *et al.* —On the *accusative of the remote object*, comp. Ps. cv. 40, cxlvii. 14; Ecclus. xvii. 6; Col. i. 9 (not 2 Thess. i. 11); Winer, p. 215 [E. T. 287]. A classical author would have used the genitive (*Elz.*) or the dative.— τὸν διὰ 'I. X.] *sc.* ὄντα, the more exact specific definition of this fruit, the peculiar *sacred essence and dignity* of which are made apparent, seeing that it is produced, not through observance of the law, or generally by human power, but *through Christ*, who brings it about by virtue of the efficacy of the Holy Spirit (Gal. ii. 20, iii. 22; Eph. iv. 7 f., 17; John xv. 14, *et al.*).— εἰς δόξαν κ.τ.λ.] belongs to πεπληρ. κ.τ.λ., not specially to τὸν διὰ 'I. X. *How far* this fruitfulness tends to the honour of God (comp. John xv. 8), see Eph. i. 6–14. God's δόξα is His *majesty in itself*; ἔπαινος is the *praise* of that majesty. Comp. Eph. i. 6, 12, 14. This ἔπαινος is *based on matter of fact* (its opposite is ἀτιμάζειν τ. Θεόν, Rom. ii. 23), in so far as in the Christian moral perfection of believers God's work of salvation in them, and consequently His glory, by means of which it is effected, are manifested. Comp. 1 Cor. vi. 20. The whole work of redemption is the manifestation of the divine δόξα. See John xii. 27 f. The glory of God is, however, the ultimate aim and constant refrain of all Christian perfection, ii. 11; 1 Cor. x. 31; Eph. iii. 31; 1 Pet. iv. 11; Rom. xi. 36.

Ver. 12. See, on vv. 12–26, Huther in the *Mecklenb. Zeitschr.* 1864, p. 558 ff.—Paul now proceeds by the δέ of continuation to depict *his own position* down to ver. 26. See the summary of contents.—The element of transition in the train of thought is that of the *notification* which Paul now

desires to bring before them; γινώσκειν is therefore placed
first: but ye are to know. It is otherwise in 2 Tim. iii. 1,
also 1 Cor. xi. 3, Col. ii. 1. — τὰ κατ᾽ ἐμέ] *my circumstances,*
my position, as in Eph. vi. 21 ; Col. iv. 7 ; Tob. x. 9 ; 2 Macc.
iii. 40, *et al. ;* Xen. *Cyr.* vii. 1. 16 ; Ael. *V. H.* ii. 20. — μᾶλλον]
not *to the hindrance,* but much *the contrary.* See Winer, p. 228
[E. T. 304]. He points in this to the *apprehension* assumed
to exist, and certainly confirmed to him by Epaphroditus as
existing, on the part of his readers, which, before going further,
he wishes to relieve. There is no trace even here of a *letter*
received from them with the contribution (Hofmann; comp.
Wiesinger) ; comp. on ver. 1. Hoelemann : " magis, *quam antea
contigerat ;*" but this meaning must have been intimated by a
νῦν or ἤδη. — προκοπήν] *progress, i.e.* success. Comp. ver. 25 ;
1 Tim. iv. 15. As to the later Greek character of this word,
see Lobeck, *ad Phryn.* p. 85. In consequence of the apostle's
fate, the gospel had excited more attention, and the courage
of its preachers had increased ; see ver. 13 f. As to whether
a *change* had taken place *in his condition,* which the readers
regarded as a change for the worse, as Hofmann requires us to
assume, we have no specific hint whatever. The situation of
the apostle generally, and in itself, abundantly justified their
concern, especially since it had already lasted so long. — ἐλή-
λυθεν] *evenit, i.e. has redounded.* Comp. Acts xix. 27 ; Wisd.
xv. 5 ; Herod. i. 120 ; Soph. *Aj.* 1117 (1138) ; Plat. *Gorg.*
p. 487 B. So the matter *stands ;* note the *perfect.*

Ver. 13. Ὥστε κ.τ.λ.] *so that my bonds became manifest in
Christ,* etc. This ὥστε introduces the actual *result* of that
προκοπή, and consequently a more precise *statement of its
nature.*[1] Ἐν Χριστῷ does not belong to τοὺς δεσμούς μου,
alongside of which it does not stand ; but φανεροὺς ἐν Χριστ.
is to be taken together, and the emphasis is laid on φανερούς,
so that the δεσμοί did not remain κρυπτοί or ἀπόκρυφοι ἐν
Χριστῷ, as would have been the case, if their relation to Christ

---

[1] "Rem, qualis sit, addita rei consequentis significatione definit," Ellendt,
Lex. Soph. II. p. 1012. Hofmann's view, that it stands in the sense of εἰς τοῦτο
ὥστε, also amounts to this. But Hoelemann is in error in making it assert the
greatness of the προκοπή. Not the greatness, but the *salutary effect,* is indicated.

had continued unknown, and if people had been compelled to
look upon the apostle as nothing but an ordinary prisoner
detained for examination.   This ignorance, however, did not
exist ; on the contrary, his bonds became *known in Christ,* in so
far, namely, that *in their causal relation to Christ*—in this their
specific peculiarity—was found information and elucidation with
respect to his condition of bondage, and thus the specialty of
the case of the prisoner, became notorious.   If Paul had been
only known generally as δέσμιος, his bonds would have been
οὐκ ἐμφανεῖς ἐν Χριστῷ ; but now that, as δέσμιος ἐν κυρίῳ
or τοῦ κυρίου (Eph. iv. 1, iii. 1 ; Philem. 9), as πάσχων ὡς
Χριστιανός (1 Pet. iv. 16), he had become the object of public
notice, the φανέρωσις of his state of bondage, as *resting* ἐν
Χριστῷ, was thereby brought about,—a φανερὸν γίνεσθαι, consequently, which had its distinctive *characteristic quality* in the
ἐν Χριστῷ.   It is arbitrary to supply ὄντας with ἐν Χριστῷ
(Hofmann).   Ewald takes it as : *"shining* in Christ," *i.e.* much
sought after and *honoured* as Christian.   Comp. also Calvin, and
Wieseler, *Chronol. d. apost. Zeitalt.* p. 457.   But, according to
New Testament usage, φανερός does not convey so much as this ;
in classical usage (Thuc. i. 17. 2, iv. 11. 3 ; Xen. *Cyr.* vii. 5. 58,
Anab. vii. 7. 22 and Krüger *in loc.*) it may mean *conspicuous,
eminent.* — ἐν ὅλῳ τῷ πραιτωρίῳ] πραιτώριον is not the *imperial palace* in Rome (Chrysostom, Theodoret, Oecumenius,
Theophylact, Erasmus, Luther, Beza, Calvin, Estius, Cornelius
a Lapide, Grotius, Bengel, and many others, also Mynster,
Rheinwald, and Schneckenburger in the *Deutsch. Zeitschr.*
1855, p. 300), which is denoted in iv. 22 by ἡ Καίσαρος
οἰκία, but was never called *praetorium.*[1]   It could not well,
indeed, be so called, as τὸ πραιτώριον is the standing appellation
for the palaces of the chief governors of *provinces* (Matt. xxvii.
27 ; John xviii. 28, xix. 9 ; Acts xxiii. 35) ; hence it might
and must have been explained as the Procurator's palace in

---

[1] *Act. Thom.* § 3, 17, 18, 19, in Tischendorf, *Act. apocr.* pp. 192, 204 f.,
cannot be cited in favour of this designation (in opposition to Rheinwald) ; the
πραιτώρια βασιλικά there spoken of (§ 3) are *royal castles,* so designated after the
analogy of the residences of the Roman *provincial rulers.*   Comp. Sueton. *Aug.*
72 ; *Tib.* 39, *et al. ;* Juvenal, x. 161.

Caesarea, if our epistle had been written there (see especially Böttger, *Beitr.* I. p. 51 f.). But it is the Roman *castrum praetorianorum*, the *barracks of the imperial body-guard* (Camerarius, Perizonius, Clericus, Elsner, Michaelis, Storr, Heinrichs, Flatt, Matthies, Hoelemann, van Hengel, de Wette, Rilliet, Wiesinger, Ewald, Weiss, J. B. Lightfoot, and others), whose chief was the *praefectus praetorio*, the στρατοπέδων ἔπαρχος, to whom Paul was given in charge on his arrival in Rome (Acts xxviii. 16). It was built by Sejanus, and was situated not far from the Porta Viminalis, on the eastern side of the city.[1] See Suet. *Tib.* 37 ; Tac. *Ann.* iv. 2 ; Pitiscus, *Thesaur. antiq.* III. 174 ; and especially Perizonius, *de orig., signif. et usu vocc. praetoris et praetorii*, Franeq. 1687, as also his *Disquisitio de praetorio ac vero sensu verborum Phil.* i. 13, Franeq. 1690 ; also Hoelemann, p. 45, and J. B. Lightfoot, p. 97 ff. τὸ πραιτώριον does not mean the *troop of praetorian cohorts* (Hofmann), which would make it equivalent to οἱ πραιτωριανοί (Herodian, viii. 8. 14).[2]—The *becoming* known *in the whole praetorium* is explained by the fact, that a praetorian was always present with Paul as his guard (Acts xxviii. 16), and Paul, even in his captivity, continued his preaching without hindrance (Acts xxviii. 30 f.). — καὶ τοῖς λοιποῖς πᾶσι] not in the sense of locality, dependent on ἐν (Chrysostom, Theodoret, Calvin), but : *and to all the others,* besides the praetorians. It is a popular and inexact way of putting the fact of its becoming still more widely known among the (non-Christian) Romans, and therefore it must be left without any more specific definition. This extensive pro-

---

[1] Doubtless there was a praetorian guard stationed in the imperial palace itself, on the Mons Palatinus, as in the time of Augustus (Dio. Cass. liii. 16). See Wieseler, *Chronol. d. apost. Zeitalt.* p. 404, who understands the station of this palace-guard to be here referred to. But it cannot be proved that after the times of Tiberius, in whose reign the *castra praetoriana* were built in front of the Viminal gate (only three cohorts having previously been stationed in the city, and that *sine castris*, Suetonius, *Octav.* 49), anything else than these *castra* is to be understood by the wonted term *praetorium*, στρατόπεδον, when mentioned without any further definition (as Joseph. *Antt.* xviii. 6. 7 : πρὸ τοῦ βασιλείου).

[2] Not even in such passages as Tacitus, *Hist.* ii. 24, iv. 46 ; Suetonius, *Ner.* 7 ; Plin. *H. N.* xxv. 2, 6, *et al.*, where the prepositional expression (*in* praetorium, *ex* praetorio) is always *local.*

clamation of the matter took place in part directly through
Paul himself, since any one might visit him, and in part
indirectly, through the praetorians, officers of justice, disciples, and friends of the apostle, and the like.[1]   Van
Hengel, moreover, understands it incorrectly, as if οἱ λοιποί
were specially " homines *exteri*," " *Gentiles*,"—a limitation
which could only be suggested by the context, and therefore
cannot be established by the use of the word in Eph. ii. 3,
iv. 17 ; 1 Thess. iv. 13.   Equally arbitrary is the limitation of
Hofmann : that it refers to those, *who already knew about him.*

   Ver. 14. τοὺς πλείονας] the *majority*, 1 Cor. x. 5, xv. 6, *et
al.*   It is not to be more precisely specified or limited. — ἐν
κυρίῳ] belongs not to ἀδελφῶν (Luther, Castalio, Grotius,
Cornelius a Lapide, Heinrichs, van Hengel, de Wette, Ewald,
Weiss, and others)—in which case it would not indeed have
needed a connecting article (Col. i. 2, iv. 7), yet would have
been entirely superfluous—but to πεποιθότας, along with which,
however, it is not to be rendered : *relying upon the Lord with
respect to my bonds* (Rheinwald, Flatt, Rilliet, comp. Schneckenburger, p. 301).   It means rather : *in the Lord trusting my
bonds*, so that ἐν κυρίῳ is the specific modal definition of
πεποιθ. τοῖς δ. μ., *which trust is based and depends on Christ.*
Comp. ii. 24 ; Gal. v. 10 ; Rom. xiv. 14 ; 2 Thess. iii. 4.   On
the dative, comp. 2 Cor. x. 7 ; Philem. 21, and the ordinary
usage in the classics ; in the New Testament mostly with ἐπί
or ἐν.   Ἐν κυρίῳ is placed *first* as the correlative of the ἐν
Χριστ., ver. 13.   As the apostle's bonds had become generally

---

[1] This suffices fully to explain the situation set forth in ver. 13.   The words
therefore afford no ground for the historical combination which Hofmann here
makes : that during the two years, Acts xxviii. 30, the apostle's case was held
in abeyance ; and that only now had it been brought up for *judicial discussion*,
whereby first it had become manifest that his captivity was caused, not by his
having committed any crime against the state, but by his having preached Christ,
which might not be challenged (?) on the state's account.   As if what is expressly
reported in Acts xxviii. 31 were not sufficient to have made the matter known, and
as if that διετία ἐν ἰδίῳ μισθώματι precluded the judicial preparation of the case
(ver. 7)!   As if the increased courage of the πλείονες, ver. 14, were intelligible
only on the above assumption !   As if, finally, it were admissible to understand,
with Hofmann, among these πλείονες all those who *" even now before the conclusion of the trial were inspired with such courage by it"* !

known as *in Christ*, so also *in Christ* (who will not abandon
the work of His prisoner that had thus become so manifest)
may be found the just ground of the confidence which encourages the brethren, Paul's fellow-Christians in Rome, ἀφόβως
τ. λ. λαλεῖν. They trust *the bonds* of the apostle, inasmuch as
these bonds exhibit to them not only an encouraging example
of patience (Grotius), but also (comp. iii. 8; Col. i. 24 f.;
2 Tim. ii. 8 f.; Matt. v. 11 f., and many other passages) a
practical guarantee, highly honourable to Christ and His gospel,
of the complete truth and justice, power and glory of the word,[1]
for the sake of which Paul is in bonds; thereby, instead of
losing their courage, they are only made all the bolder in virtue
of the elevating influence of moral sympathy with this situation
of the apostle in bonds. Weiss explains as if the passage ran
τῇ φανερώσει τῶν δεσμῶν μου (which would tend to the recommendation of the gospel); while Hofmann thinks that, to guard
themselves *against the danger of being criminally prosecuted on
account of their preaching*, they relied on the apostle's imprisonment, in so far as the latter had *now* shown itself, in the
judicial process that had at length been commenced, to be *solely
on account of Christ*, and not *for anything culpable*. The
essential elements, forsooth, are thus introduced in consequence
of the way in which Hofmann has construed for himself the
situation (see on ver. 13). — περισσοτ.] *i.e.* in a higher degree
than they had formerly ventured upon, before I lay here in
bonds. Their ἀφοβία in preaching had *increased*. This, however, is explained by Hofmann, in accordance with the above
hypothesis, by the fact that the *political guiltlessness* of preaching Christ had now been established,—thus referring, in fact,
the increase of their fearless boldness to a sense of *legal security*.
But the reason of the increased ἀφοβία lay *deeper*, in the sphere
of the *moral* idea, which manifested itself in the apostle's
bonds, and in accordance with which they trusted those bonds
in the Lord, seeing them borne for *the Lord's* sake. They
animated the brethren *to boldness through that holy confidence,
rooted in Christ*, with which they imbued them.—τὸν λόγον

---

[1] Oecumenius well says: εἰ γὰρ μὴ θεῖον ἦν, φησὶ, τὸ κήρυγμα, οὐκ ἂν ὁ Παῦλος
ἠνείχετο ὑπὲρ αὐτοῦ διδόσθαι. Comp. ver. 16.

λαλεῖν] *i.e.* to let the gospel become known, to preach, Acts
xi. 19, and frequently.   On ἀφόβως, comp. Acts iv. 31.

Ver. 15. This is *not* indeed the case *with all*, that they
ἐν κυρίῳ πεποιθότες τοῖς δεσμ. μου περισσοτ. τολμ. κ.τ.λ.   No,
some in Rome preach with an improper feeling and design;
but some also with a good intention. (Both parties are described in further detail in vv. 16, 17.)   In either case—Christ
is preached, wherein I rejoice and will rejoice (ver. 18). —
τινὲς μὲν καὶ διὰ φθόνον κ. ἔριν] These do not form a part of
those described in ver. 14 (Ambrosiaster, Erasmus, Calvin, and
others, also Weiss, Hofmann, and Hinsch), for these latter are
characterized by ἐν κυρίῳ πεποιθ. τοῖς δεσμ. μου quite otherwise,
and indeed in a way which excludes the idea of envy and contention (comp. also Huther, *l.c.*), and appear as the *majority* to
which these τινές stand in contrast as *exceptions ;* but they are
the *anti-Pauline* party, Judaizing preachers, who must have
pursued their practices in Rome, as in Asia and Greece, and
exercised an immoral, hostile opposition to the apostle and
his gospel.[1] We have no details on the subject, but from
Rom. xiv. we see that there was a fruitful field on which
this tendency might find a footing and extend its influence
in Rome.   The idea that it refers to certain members of the
Pauline school, who nevertheless hated the apostle *personally*
(Wiesinger, comp. Flatt), or were envious of his high reputation, and impugned his mode of action (Weiss), is at variance
with the previous ἐν κυρίῳ, assumes a state of things which is
in itself improbable, and is not required by the utterance of
ver. 18 (see the remark after ver. 18).   See also Schneckenburger, p. 301 f. — καί] indicates that, whilst the majority were
actuated by a good disposition (ver. 14), an *evil motive also*
existed in several,—expresses, therefore, the *accession of something else* in *other* subjects, but certainly not the accession of a
subordinate co-operating motive in a portion of the *same* persons

---

[1] For the *person* to whom individually their φθόνος and ἔρις (as likewise the
subsequent εὐδοκία) had reference was self-evident to the readers, and Paul, moreover, announces it to them in ver. 16 f.   Without due reason Hinsch finds in this
the mark of a *later period*, when the guarding of the apostle's *personal* position
alone was concerned.   See against this, Hilgenfeld in his *Zeitschr.* 1873, p. 180 f.

designated in ver. 14 (Hofmann). — διὰ φθόνον κ. ἔριν] *on account of envy and strife,* that is, for the sake of satisfying the strivings of their jealousy in respect to my influence, and of their contentious disposition towards me. Comp. ver. 17. On διὰ φθόνον, comp. Matt. xxvii. 18 ; Mark xv. 10 ; Plat. *Rep.* p. 586 D : φθόνῳ διὰ φιλοτιμίαν. — Τινὲς δὲ καί] *But some also ; there also are not wanting such as,* etc. Observe that the δὲ καί joins itself with τινές, whereas in μὲν καί previously the καί is attached to the following διὰ φθόνον. The τινές here are they who in ver. 14 were described as πλείονες, but are now brought forward as, in contrast to the τινὲς μέν, the *other portion* of the preachers, without any renewed reference to their preponderance in numbers, which had been already intimated.[1] — δι᾽ εὐδοκίαν] *on account of goodwill,* that is, because they entertain a feeling of goodwill towards me. This interpretation is demanded by the context, both in the antithesis διὰ φθόνον κ. ἔριν, and also in ver. 16 : ἐξ ἀγάπης. As to the linguistic use of εὐδοκία in this sense (ii. 13), see Fritzsche, *ad Rom.* II. p. 372. Comp. on Rom. x. 1. Others take it, contrary to the context, as : " ex benevolentia, *qua desiderant hominum salutem*" (Estius, comp. already Pelagius) ; or, "*quod ipsi id probarent,*" from conviction (Grotius, Heinrichs, and others), from taking delight *in the matter* generally (Huther), or in the cause of *the apostle* (de Wette), or in his *preaching* (Weiss).

[1] Van Hengel has not taken this into account, when he assumes that in τινὲς δὲ καί Paul had in view only *a portion* of those designated in ver. 14. It is an objection to this idea, that what is said subsequently in ver. 16 of the τινὲς δὲ καί completely harmonizes with *that,* whereby the πλείονες *generally,* and not merely a portion of them, were characterized in ver. 14 (ἐν κυρ. πεπ. τ. δεσμ.). This applies also in opposition to Hofmann, according to whom the *two* τινές, ver. 15 f., belong to the πλείονες of ver. 14, whom they divide into two classes. Hofmann's objection to our view, viz. that the apostle does not say that the one party preach *solely* out of envy and strife, and the other *solely* out of goodwill, is irrelevant. He could not, indeed, have desired to say this, and does not say it ; but he could describe in general, as he has done, the *ethical antitheses* which characterized the two parties. Moreover, ἔρις means everywhere in the N. T., and especially here in its conjunction with φθόνος (comp. Rom. i. 29 ; 1 Tim. vi. 4), not *rivalry*—the weaker sense assigned to it here, without a shadow of justification from the context, by Hofmann ("they wish to outdo him")—but *strife, contention.* Just as little is ἐριθεία to be reduced to the general notion of *egotism,* as is done by Hofmann ; see on ver. 17.

Vv. 16, 17. We have here a more detailed description of both parties in respect to the motives which actuated them in relation to the δεσμοί of the apostle. — οἱ μέν . . . οἱ δέ] corresponds to the two parties of ver. 15, but—and that indeed without any particular purpose—in an *inverted* order (see the critical remarks), as in 2 Cor. ii. 16, and frequently in classical authors (Thuc. i. 68. 4.; Xen. *Anab.* i. 10. 4). In ver. 18 the order adopted in ver. 15 is again reverted to. — οἱ ἐξ ἀγάπης] sc. ὄντες, a *genetic* description of the *ethical condition* of these people : *those who are of love,* i.e. *of loving nature and action;* comp. Rom. ii. 8 ; Gal. iii. 7 ; John xviii. 37, *et al.* We must supply what immediately precedes : τὸν Χριστὸν κηρύσσουσιν, of which εἰδότες κ.τ.λ. then contains the particular *moving cause* (Rom. v. 3, 6, 9 ; Gal. ii. 16 ; Eph. vi. 8 f., *et al.*). We might also take οἱ μέν (and then οἱ δέ) absolutely : *the one,* and then bring up immediately, for ἐξ ἀγάπης, the subsequent τ. Χριστὸν καταγγέλλουσιν (so Hofmann and others). But this would be less appropriate, because the progress of the discourse does not turn on the saying that the one preach out of love, and the other out of contention (for this has been said in substance previously), but on the internal determining motives which are expressed by εἰδότες κ.τ.λ. and οἰόμενοι κ.τ.λ. ; besides, οὐχ ἀγνῶς would then follow as merely a weak and disturbing auxiliary clause to ἐξ ἐριθείας. — ὅτι εἰς ἀπολ. τοῦ εὐαγγ. κεῖμαι] *that I am destined,* am *ordained* of God *for* (nothing else than) *the defence of the gospel*—a destination which they on their parts, in consequence of their love to me, feel themselves impelled to subserve. They labour sympathetically hand in hand with me. — κεῖμαι] as in Luke ii. 34 ; 1 Thess. iii. 3 ; comp. Plat. *Legg.* x. p. 909 ; Thuc. iii. 45, 2, 47, 2 ; Ecclus. xxxviii. 29, and other passages in which "κεῖσθαι tanquam passivum verbi ποιεῖσθαι vel τιθέναι videtur," Ellendt, *Lex. Soph.* I. p. 943. Others render : *I lie in prison* (Luther, Piscator, Estius, Wolf, am Ende, Huther, and others) ; but the idea *of lying under* fetters, which κεῖμαι would thus convey (comp. Eur. *Phoen.* 1633; Aesch. *Ag.* 1492), does not harmonize with the *position* of the apostle any more than the reference of its meaning thereby introduced : they

know that I am *hindered in my preaching*, and therefore they
" *supplent hoc meum impedimentum sua praedicatione*," Estius.
See, on the contrary, Acts xxviii. 30, 31; Phil. i. 7. Van
Hengel also imports (comp. Weiss) : " me ad causam rei Chris-
tianae, ubi urgeat necessitas, coram judice defendendam hic *in
miseria jacere*." Comp. Hom. *Od.* i. 46 ; Soph. *Aj.* 316 (323) ;
Pflugk, *ad Eur. Hec.* 496. — οἱ δὲ ἐξ ἐριθ.] *sc.* ὄντες, the *factious*,
the *cabal-makers*. See on Rom. ii. 8 ; 2 Cor. xii. 20; Gal.
v. 20. So also Ignatius, *ad Philadelph.* 8. It corresponds
with the φθόνον κ. ἔριν, ver. 15. — τὸν Χ. καταγγ. οὐχ ἁγνῶς]
belong together. καταγγ. is, in substance, the same as κηρύσ-
σειν, but more precisely defining it as the *announcement* of the
Messiah (Acts xvii. 3, 23 ; Col. i. 28, *et al.*). The words τ.
Χριστὸν καταγγέλλουσιν might have been left out, following
the analogy of ver. 16, but are inserted to bring out the *tragic
contrast* which is implied in preaching Christ, and yet doing
so οὐχ ἁγνῶς, *non caste*, not *in purity of feeling and purpose.*
καθαρῶς is synonymous (Hom. *H. in Apoll.* 121), also with a
mental reference (Hesiod. ἔργα, 339). Comp. Plat. *Legg.* viii.
p. 840 D; 2 Cor. vii. 11, xi. 2 ; Phil. iv. 8, *et al. ;* 2 Cor.
vi. 6. — οἰόμενοι κ.τ.λ.] *thinking to stir up affliction for my
bonds*, to make my captivity full of sorrow. This they *intend*
to do, and that is the immoral moving spring of their unworthy
conduct; but (observe the distinction between οἰόμενοι and
εἰδότες in ver. 16) Paul hints by this purposely-chosen word
(which is nowhere else used by him), that what they imagine
fails to happen. On οἶμαι with the *present* infinitive, see
Pflugk, *ad Eur. Hec.* 283. The future infinitive would not
convey that what is meant is *even now* occurring. See generally Stallbaum, *ad Plat. Crit.* p. 52 C ; comp. *Phaed.* p. 116 E.
How far they thought that they could effect that injurious
result by their preaching, follows from ver. 15 and from ἐξ
ἐριθείας; in so far, namely, that they doubtless, rendered the
more unscrupulous through the captivity of the apostle, sought
by their preaching to prejudice his authority, and to stir up
controversial and partisan interests of a Judaistic character
against him, and thus thought thoroughly to embitter the
prisoner's lot by exciting opponents to vex and wrong him.

This was the *cabal* in the background of their *dishonest* preaching. That by the spread of the gospel they desired to provoke the hostility of the heathen, especially of Nero, against Paul, and thus to render his captivity more severe, is a groundless conjecture imported (Erasmus, Cornelius a Lapide, Grotius, and others; comp. already Chrysostom, Oecumenius, Theophylact, Pelagius). — On ἐγείρειν (see the critical remarks) comp. ἐγ. ὠδῖνας, Plat. *Theaet.* p. 149 C, and similar passages.

Ver. 18. On τί γάρ, *scil.* ἐστι, comp. on Rom. iii. 3, where, however, γάρ is not, as here, *conclusive* (see on 1 Cor. xi. 22[1]); comp. also Klotz, *ad Devar.* p. 245. It is rendered necessary by the πλήν that the mark of interrogation should not be placed (as it usually is) after τί γάρ, but the question goes on to καταγγέλλεται (comp. Hofmann); and it is to be observed that through πλήν the τί γάρ receives the sense of τί γὰρ ἄλλο (see Heindorf, *ad Plat. Soph.* p. 232 C). Hence: *what else takes place therefore* (in such a state of the case) *except that*, etc., *i.e. what else than that by every sort* of preaching, *whether it is done in pretence or in truth, Christ is proclaimed? and therein*, that it is always *Christ* whom they preach, *I rejoice*, etc. How magnanimous is this liberality of judgment as to the existing circumstances in their reference to Christ! By προφάσει and ἀληθείᾳ is indicated the characteristic difference in the two kinds of preachers, vv. 15–17, and thus παντὶ τρόπῳ receives the more precise definition of its respective parts. As regards the first class, the preaching of Christ was not a matter of sincerity and truth—wherein they, in accordance with their sentiments, were really concerned about Christ, and He was the real αἰτία of their working (see on the contrast between αἰτία and πρόφασις, Polyb. iii. 6. 6 ff.)—but a matter of *pretence*, under the cloak of which they entertained in their hearts envy, strife, and cabal, as the real objects of their endeavours. For instances of the antithesis between πρόφασις and ἀλή-

---

[1] According to Weiss, γάρ is intended *to establish* the οἰόμενοι κ.τ.λ., so far as the latter is only an *empty imagination*. But this is an unnecessary seeking after a very obscure reference. The τι γάρ draws, as it were, the result from vv. 15–17. Hence also we cannot, with Huther, adopt as the sense: "*Is it then so, as they think?*"

θεια or τἀληθές, see Raphel, *Polyb.;* Loesner and Wetstein. To take πρόφασις as *opportunity, occasion* (Herod. i. 29, 30, iv. 145, vi. 94; Dem. xx. 26; Antiph. v. 21; Herodian, i. 8. 16, v. 2. 14),—as, following the Vulgate, Luther, Estius, Grotius (" nam *occasione* illi Judaei, dum nocere Paulo student, multos pertrahebant ad evang."), and others understand it,—is opposed to the context in vv. 15–17, in which the *want of honest disposition* is set forth as the characteristic mark of these persons. On πλήν in the sense of ἤ, comp. Kühner, II. 2, p. 842. — ἐν τούτῳ] the neuter: *therein,* in accordance with the conception of that *in which* the feeling *has its basis.* Comp. Col. i. 24; Plat. *Rep.* x. p. 603 C; Soph. *Tr.* 1118; Kühner, II. 1, p. 403. In the Χριστὸς καταγγέλλεται lies the apostle's joy.—ἀλλὰ καὶ χαρήσομαι] surpassing the simple χαίρω by a *plus,* and therefore added in a corrective antithetical form (*imo etiam*); comp. on 1 Cor. iii. 2; 2 Cor. xi. 1. To begin a new sentence with ἀλλά (Lachmann, Tischendorf), and to sever χαρήσομαι from its connection with ἐν τούτῳ (Hofmann, who makes the apostle only assert generally *that he will continue to rejoice also in the future*), interrupts, without sufficient reason, the flow of the animated discourse, and is also opposed by the proper reference of οἶδα γάρ in ver. 19. This applies also in opposition to Hinsch, p. 64 f.

REMARK.—Of course this rejoicing does not refer to the impure intention of the preachers, but to the objective result. See, already, Augustine, *c. Faust.* xxii. 48; *c. Ep. Parm.* ii. 11. Nor does παντὶ τρόπῳ apply to the doctrinal *purport* of the preaching (Gal. i. 8), but to its *ethical* nature and method, to disposition and purpose. See Chrysostom and those who follow him. Nevertheless the apostle's judgment may excite surprise by its mildness (comp. iii. 2), since these opponents must have taught what in substance was anti-Pauline. But we must consider, first, the *tone of lofty resignation* in general which prevails in this passage, and which might be fitted to raise him more than elsewhere above antagonisms; secondly, that in this case the danger did not affect, as it did in Asia and Greece, in Galatia and Corinth, his *personal sphere of apostolical ministry;* thirdly, that *Rome* was the very place in which the preaching of Christ

might appear to him *in itself* of such preponderating importance as to induce him in the meantime, while his own ministry
was impeded and in fact threatened with an imminent end,
to allow—in generous tolerance, the lofty *philosophical* spirit of
which Chrysostom has admired—of even un-Pauline admixtures
of doctrine, in reliance on the discriminating power of the
truth ; lastly, that a comparison of iii. 2 permits the assumption,
as regards the teachers referred to in the present passage, of a
less important grade of anti-Pauline doctrine,[1] and especially of
a tenor of teaching which did not fundamentally overthrow
that of Paul. Comp. also on iii. 2. All the less, therefore, can
the stamp of mildness and forbearance which our passage bears
be used, as Baur and Hitzig [2] employ it, as a weapon of attack
against the genuineness of the epistle. Comp. the appropriate
remarks of Hilgenfeld in his *Zeitschr.* 1871, p. 314 ff. ; in opposition to Hinsch, see on ver. 15. Calvin, moreover, well says :
" Quamquam autem gaudebat Paulus evangelii incrementis,
nunquam tamen, si fuisset in ejus manu, tales ordinasset
ministros."

Ver. 19. Reason assigned not only for the ἀλλὰ καὶ χαρήσομαι, but for the entire conjoint assertion : ἐν τούτῳ χαίρω,
ἀλλὰ κ. χαρ. For both, for his present joy and for his future
joy, the apostle finds the subjective ground in the certainty
now to be expressed. — τοῦτο] the same thing that was conveyed by ἐν τούτῳ in ver. 18, *this fact of Christ's being
preached,* from whatever different motives it may be done,—
not: *my present,* τὰ κατ᾽ ἐμέ (Hofmann). — εἰς σωτηρίαν] is,
in conformity with the context, not to be explained of the
deliverance from captivity (Chrysostom, Theophylact, Musculus,
Heinrichs), or of the *preservation of the apostle's life* (Oecumenius), or of the *triumph over his enemies* (Michaelis), or of
the salvation *multorum hominum* (Grotius) ; nor is it to be
more precisely defined as the *eternal Messianic redemption* (van
Hengel, Weiss ; comp. Matthies and Hoelemann), or as *spiritual*
salvation (Rheinwald, de Wette). On the contrary, the expression : " it will turn out *to my salvation*" (comp. Job xiii. 16),
will be *salutary* for me, is, without anticipating the sequel,

---

[1] Comp. Lechler, *apost. Zeitalt.* p. 388.

[2] Who thinks that he recognises here an indistinct shadow of Tacitus, *Agric.*
41 : " *Optimus quisque amore et fide, pessimi malignitate et livore.*"

to be left *without any more precise modal definition;* for Paul
himself only announces, as the discourse proceeds (ver. 20),
how far he expects salutary results for himself to arise out of
the state of things in question. Bengel aptly remarks : " non
modo *non in pressuram,*" ver. 17. On ἀποβήσεται, *will turn
out, issue,* comp. Luke xxi. 13 ; Job xiii. 16 ; 2 Macc. ix. 24;
Plat. *Lys.* p. 206 A; *de virt.* p. 379 C; *Rep.* p. 425 C; Dem.
1412. 10.—*Through the entreaty of his Philippians,* Paul knows,
it will be salutary for him (comp. 2 Cor. i. 11 ; Rom. xv.
31 ; 2 Thess. iii. 12 ; Philem. 22), and *through supply of the
Spirit of Christ,* that is, through the Spirit of Christ supplying him with help, strength, courage, light, etc. (comp. on
ἐπιχορηγ., Eph. iv. 16). The words διὰ τῆς ὑμῶν δεήσεως
. . . Χριστοῦ, embrace, therefore, *two* elements whick work together and bring about the ἀποβήσ. εἰς σωτηρ., one of these
on the part of *the readers themselves* (hence ὑμῶν is placed
first), the other on the part of the *Holy Spirit.* After καί,
διά is to be again understood ; the article, however, is not
repeated before ἐπιχορ., not because the entreaty and the
ἐπιχορηγία are to be taken together as one category, which
in this passage would be illogical,[1] but because Paul *conceived*
the second member of the clause *without the article: supply*
(not *the* supply) of the Spirit. τοῦ πνεύματος is the genitive
of the subject; as genitive of the *object* (Wiesinger, in accordance with Gal. iii. 5) the expression would be inappropriate,
since Paul already *has* the Spirit (1 Cor. vii. 40), and does
not merely expect it to be supplied, though in his present
position he does expect the *help,* comfort, etc., *which the Spirit
supplies.* Comp. Theodoret: τοῦ θείου μοι πνεύματος χορη-
γοῦντος τὴν χάριν. Respecting the πνεῦμα Χριστοῦ, see on
Rom. viii. 9 ; Gal. iv. 6 ; 2 Cor. iii. 17. Paul *here* designates
the Holy Spirit thus, because *Jesus Christ* forms, in the
inmost consciousness of the apostle, the main interest and aim
of his entire discourse, ver. 18 ff.

---

[1] Bengel well says: "precationem *in coelum ascendentem;* exhibitionem *de
coelo venientem.*" If, however, ἐπιχορηγίας is still to be included in dependence
on τῆς ὑμῶν (so Buttmann, *neut. Gr.* p. 87 [E. T. p. 100]), the *readers* would at all
events appear as those communicating, which would yield an incongruous idea.

Ver. 20. It will prove salutary for me *in conformity with my earnest expectation* (see, regarding ἀποκαραδοκία, on Rom. viii. 19) *and my hope*, that I, etc. (object of the earnest expectation and hope). Others take ὅτι as *argumentative* (Vatablus, Estius, Matthies) ; but by this interpretation the κατὰ τ. ἀποκ. κ. ἐλπ. μ. seems, after the οἶδα already expressed, to be an addition for which there is no motive, and the flow of the discourse is interrupted. No, when Paul says with ὅτι κ.τ.λ. *what it is that* he earnestly expects and hopes (comp. Rom. viii. 20 f.), he thereby supplies the precise definition of the former merely general expression εἰς σωτηρίαν.—This is neither *clumsy* nor *unsuited* to the meaning of ἀποκαραδ., as Hofmann thinks, who goes back with ὅτι to the far distant οἶδα, and finds it *convenient* to co-ordinate it with the first ὅτι. Paul would have made this alleged conjunction convenient and at the same time intelligible, only in the event of his having written καὶ ὅτι. — ἐν οὐδενὶ αἰσχυνθήσομαι] that *I shall in no point* (2 Cor. vi. 3, vii. 9 ; Jas. i. 4), in no respect, *be put to shame;* that is, in no respect will a result ensue tending to my shame, — a result which would expose me to the reproach of having failed to accomplish my destiny (comp. the sequel). Comp. on αἰσχύνεσθαι, 2 Cor. x. 8, 1 John ii. 28, and the passages of the LXX. in Schleusner, I. p. 98 f.; also Xen. *Cyr.* vi. 4. 6 ; Plut. *Mor.* p. 1118 E. Matthies understands it differently : " in nothing shall *I show myself shamefaced and fearful ;*" comp. van Hengel : " pudore confusus *ab officio deflectam.*" But the context, in which Paul desires to explain more in detail (comp. ver. 21) the words μοι ἀποβήσεται εἰς σωτηρίαν, ver. 19, will not harmonize with any other than the above-named purely passive interpretation ; not even with the sense that Paul would not " *stand* disgraced " (Weiss, comp. Huther), that is, be found unfaithful to his office, or deficient in the discharge of its duties to the glorifying of Christ. The connection requires a description, not of Paul's *behaviour,* but of the *fate* in which the τοῦτο of ver. 19 would issue for him. Hoelemann takes ἐν οὐδενί as *masculine,* of the *preachers* described in ver. 15 ff., who in their ministry, though actuated by such various motives, " ita esse versaturos, ut inde non oriatur, de quo erubescat et doleat quum ipse, tum etiam in re sua quasi Christus." This inter-pretation is opposed both by the context, which from ver. 18 onwards brings forward *no persons* at all ; and also by the sense itself, because Paul, thus understood, would be made to express a *confidence* in the labours of those teachers which, as regards the malicious portion of them (ver. 17, comp. ver. 15), would not be befitting. The αἰσχύνεσθαι of the apostle was indeed the very object which they had in view ; but, he means to say, οὐκ αἰσχύνομαι, τουτέστιν οὐ περιέσονται, Chrysostom.—ἀλλ᾽ ἐν πάσῃ παρρησίᾳ κ.τ.λ.] the contrast to ἐν οὐδενὶ αἰσχυνθή-σομαι ; for the apostle can receive no greater honour and triumph (the opposite to the αἰσχύνεσθαι) than to be made the instrument of glorifying Christ (iii. 7 f.): *but with all freeness, as always, so also now, Christ will be magnified in my body.*—ἐν πάσῃ παρρησ.] ἐν πάσῃ corresponds to the previous ἐν οὐδενί, so that *every kind* of freeness, which is no way re-strained or limited (comp Acts iv. 29, xxviii. 31; 2 Cor. iii. 12), is meant, which amounts *substantially* to the idea, " une *pleine* liberté " (Rilliet and older expositors) ; comp. Wunder, *ad Soph. Phil.* 141 f. The *subject* of the freeness is *Paul himself*, inas-much as it was in his *body* that the fearless glorifying of Christ was to be manifested (see below) ; but he expresses himself in the *passive* (μεγαλυνθήσεται) and not in the *active*, because, in the feeling of his being the organ of divine working, the μοι ἀποβήσεται εἰς σωτηρίαν (ver. 19) governs his conceptions and determines his expression. Hofmann's view, that ἐν π. παρρησ. means " in full *publicity*," as an unmistakeable fact before the eyes of all, is linguistically erroneous. See, in opposition to it, on Col. ii. 15. — ὡς πάντοτε καὶ νῦν] so that the present circumstances, however inimical they are in part towards me (vv. 15-18), will therefore bring about no other result than this most happy one for me, which has always taken place.—ἐν τῷ σώματί μου] instead of saying : ἐν ἐμοί, he says : *in my body*, because the decision was now close at hand, whether his body should remain alive or be put to death. But whichever of these possible alternatives should come to pass, he earnestly expected and hoped that the glory of Christ would be thereby secured (εἴτε διὰ ζωῆς εἴτε διὰ θανάτου), in so far, namely, as *through his remaining in the body* his apostolic labours would be continued to the glory of Christ, and *by the slaying of his body* there would take place, not the mere closing of his witness for Christ, as Hofmann, in opposition to the text (vv. 21–23), refines away this point, but his union with Christ. Thus, therefore, he will not be put to shame even by his death; but, on the contrary, Christ will be freely glorified by it, namely, *practically glorified, inasmuch as Paul, conscious of the great gain which he shall acquire through death* (ver. 21), *will with unwavering joyfulness*—with the frank joyful courage of the martyr who is being perfected—*die to the glorifying of Christ.* Comp. John xxi. 19. In any case, accordingly, the result must ensue, that *in his body*, just as it has always hitherto been the living personal instrument of Christ's glory, now also the free glorification of Christ shall be made manifest, whether this result be secured *through its being preserved alive or being slain;* "nam et corpus *loquitur* et corpus *moritur*," Grotius. Hoelemann erroneously refers ἐν πάσῃ παρρ. to the bold preaching of the various *teachers* described in vv. 15–18; from which now, as always, the glory of Christ shall result; and that indeed, through the influence which such a fearless working would have on the fate of the apostle, in his *body*, whether Christ grant to him a longer course of life or death, in either of which cases the Lord will manifest Himself to him as *augustissimum auxiliatorem.* But against this view it may be urged, that ἐν οὐδενί does not refer to the teachers (see above); that παρρησίᾳ is the contrast to αἰσχυνθήσομαι, so that the subject of the latter must be also the subject of the former; and lastly, that Paul would thus be made to say that the fearless working of others had *always* shown forth Christ's honour *in his body*,—an expression which, as regards the last point, might be suited to the *present* position of the apostle, but not to the ὡς πάντοτε. Rilliet takes μεγαλυνθήσεται not in the sense of *praising* (Luke i. 46; Acts v. 13, x. 46, xix. 17; Thuc. viii. 81; Xen. *Hell.* vii. 1. 13), but in the material signification of *grandir* (Matt. xxiii. 5; Luke i. 58; 2 Cor. x. 15), making it apply to the *mental indwelling of Christ*

(Gal. ii. 20 ; Rom. viii. 10 ; Gal. iv. 19) ; so that Paul is made
to hope that Christ may *grow* ever more and more in him,
that is, may more and more reveal Himself as the principle
of his life, and that this growth will be perfected whether he
himself live or die. But ἐν πάσῃ παρρησίᾳ would be an
inappropriate definition of this idea ; and ἐν τῷ σώματί μου
would also be *inappropriate*, as if Christ would have, even by
the apostle's *death*, to grow in his body ; lastly, neither the
foregoing nor the subsequent context points to the peculiar
mystical idea of a *growth of Christ in the human body ;* while
the similar idea in Gal. iv. 19 is there very peculiarly and
clearly suggested by the *context.*

Ver. 21. Justification not of the joy, ver. 18 (Weiss), which
has already been justified in ver. 19 f., but of the εἴτε διὰ ζωῆς
εἴτε διὰ θανάτου just expressed : *For to me the living is Christ,*
that is, if I remain alive, my prolonged life will be nothing
but a life of which the whole essential element and real
tenor is Christ (" quicquid vivo, vita naturali, Christum vivo,"
Bengel), as the One to whom the whole destination and
activity of my life bear reference (comp. on Gal. ii. 20) ; *and
the dying[1] is gain,* inasmuch as by death I attain to Christ ;
see ver. 23. *Whichever,* therefore, of the two may come to
pass, will tend to the free glorification of Christ ; *the former,*
inasmuch as I continue to labour freely for Christ's glory ;
the latter, inasmuch as in the certainty of that gain I shall
suffer death with joyful courage. Comp. Corn. Müller, who,
however, assumes that in the second clause Paul had the
thought : *" et si mihi moriendum est, moriar Christo, ita etiam
morte mea Christus celebratur,"* but that in the emotion of
the discourse he has not expressed this, allowing himself to
be carried away by the conception of the *gain* involved in
the matter. This assumption is altogether superfluous ; for,
to the consciousness of the Christian reader, the reference of

---

[1] Not *the being dead* (Huther, Schenkel). On the combination of the Inf.
pres. (continuing) and *aor.* (momentary), comp. Xen. *Mem.* iv. 4. 4 : προείλετο
μᾶλλον τοῖς νόμοις ἐμμένων ἀποθανεῖν ἢ παρανομῶν ζῆν, Eur. *Or.* 308 : σὺν σοὶ κατθα-
νεῖν αἱρήσομαι καὶ ζῆν, Epictet. *Enchir.* 12 ; 2 Cor. vii. 3. See generally Mätzn.
ad Antiph. p. 153 f. ; Kühner, II. 1, p. 159. The *being dead* would have been
expressed, as in Herod. i. 31, by τιθνάναι.

the κέρδος to Christ must of itself have been clear and certain. But the idea of κέρδος, which connects itself in the apostle's mind with the thought of death, prevents us from assuming that he meant to say that *it was a matter of no moment* to him personally whether he lived or died (Wiesinger); for on account of the κέρδος in death, his own personal wish must have given the preference to the dying (see ver. 23). Others (Calvin, Beza, Musculus, Er. Schmid, Raphel, Knatchbull, *et al.*) have, moreover, by the non-mention of Christ in the second clause, been led to the still more erroneous assumption, in opposition both to the words and linguistic usage, that in both clauses Christ is the subject and κέρδος the predicate, and that the infinitives with the article are to be explained by πρός or κατά, so that *Christ " tam in vita quam in morte lucrum esse praedicatur."*   Lastly, in opposition to the context, Rheinwald and Rilliet take τὸ ζῆν as meaning life *in the higher, spiritual* sense, and καί as : *and consequently,* which latter interpretation does not harmonize with the preceding alternative εἴτε . . εἴτε.   This explanation is refuted by the very τὸ ζῆν ἐν σαρκί which follows in ver. 22, since ἐν σαρκί contains not an antithesis to the absolute τὸ ζῆν, but on the contrary a more precise definition of it.   Although the διὰ θανάτου and τὸ ἀποθανεῖν contrasted with the ζῆν, as also ver. 20 generally, afford decisive evidence against the view that takes τὸ ζῆν in the *higher ethical* sense, that view has still been adopted by Hofmann, who, notwithstanding the correlation and parallelism of τὸ ζῆν and τὸ ἀποθανεῖν, oddly supposes that, while τὸ ἀποθανεῖν is the subject in the second clause, τὸ ζῆν is yet *predicate* in the first.   Like τὸ ἀποθανεῖν, τὸ ζῆν must be *subject* also. — ἐμοί] is emphatically placed first : *to me,* as regards my own person, though it may be different with others.   Comp. the emphatic ἡμῶν, iii. 20. — For profane parallels to the idea, though of course not to the Christian import, of τὸ ἀποθανεῖν κέρδος,[1] see Wetstein. Comp. Aelian. *V. H.* iv. 7 ; Soph. *Ant.* 464 f. ; Eur. *Med.* 145.

Ver. 22. *Δέ*] *carrying onward* the discourse to the *compari-*

[1] Compare also Spiess, *Logos Spermaticos*, 1871, p. 330 f.

son between the two cases as regards their desirability. Weiss understands δέ as *antithetic,* namely to τὸ ἀποθανεῖν κέρδος, and Hofmann as in contrast also to the ἐμοὶ τὸ ζῆν Χριστός, but both proceed on an erroneous view of what follows ; as does also Huther.—According to the τὸ ἀποθανεῖν κέρδος just expressed, the ἀποθανεῖν was put as the case *more desirable* for Paul personally ; but because the ζῆν, in which indeed Christ is his one and all, conditioned the continuance of his *official labours,* he expresses this now in the hypothetical protasis and, as consequence thereof, in the apodosis, that *thus he is in doubt respecting a choice between the two.*—The *structure* of the sentence is accordingly this, that the apodosis sets in with καὶ τί αἱρήσομαι, and nothing is to be supplied : *" But if the remaining in my bodily life, and just this, avails for my work, I refrain from a making known what I should choose."* We have to remark in detail : (1) that εἰ does not render problematical that which was said of the ζῆν ἐν σαρκί, but in accordance with the well-known and, especially in Paul's writings, frequent (Rom. v. 17, vi. 15, and often) syllogistic usage (Herbst and Kühner, *ad Xen. Mem.* i. 5. 1), posits the undoubted certainty (Wilke, *Rhetor.* p. 258), which would take place in the event of a continuance of life ; (2) that Paul was the more naturally led to add here the specially defining ἐν σαρκί to τὸ ζῆν (comp. Gal. ii. 20 ; 2 Cor. x. 3), because, in the previously mentioned κέρδος, the idea of life apart from the body (comp. 2 Cor. v. 8) must have been floating in his mind ; (3) that τοῦτο again sums up with the emphasis of emotion (comp. Rom. vii. 10) the τὸ ζῆν ἐν σαρκί which had just been said, and calls attention to it (Bernhardy, p. 283 ; Kühner, II. 1, p. 568 f. ; Fritzsche, *ad Matth.* p. 219), for it was the remaining in life, *just this,* this and nothing else (in contrast to the ἀποθανεῖν), which was necessarily to the apostle καρπὸς ἔργου ; (4) that καρπός is correlative to the preceding κέρδος, and embodies the idea *emolumentum* (Rom. i. 13, vi. 21, *et al.* ; Wisd. iii. 13), which is more precisely defined by ἔργου : *work-fruit, gain of work,* i.e. *advantage which accrues to my apostolical work ;* comp. on the idea, Rom. i. 13 ; (5) that καί, at the commencement of the apodosis, is the subjoining *also,* showing that if the one thing takes place, the other *also* sets in; see Hartung, *Partikell.* I. p. 130 f.; Baeumlein, *Partik.* p. 146; Nägelsbach, *z. Ilias,* p. 164, ed. 3; comp. on 2 Cor. ii. 2; (6) that τί stands in the place of the more accurate πότερον (Xen. *Cyrop.* i. 3. 17; Stallbaum, *ad Phileb.* p. 168; Jacobs, *ad Del. epigr.* p. 219; Winer, p. 159 [E. T. 211]), and that the *future* αἱρήσομαι (what I *should* prefer) is quite in order (see Eur. *Hel.* 631, and Pflugk *in loc.;* and Winer, p. 280 [E. T. 374]), while also the sense of the *middle,* to choose *for himself,* to prefer *for himself,* is not to be overlooked; comp. 2 Thess. ii. 13; Xen. *Mem.* iv. 2. 29: οἱ δὲ μὴ εἰδότες ὅ τι ποιοῦσι, κακῶς δὲ αἱρούμενοι, Soph. *Ant.* 551: σὺ μὲν γὰρ εἵλου ζῆν; (7) that οὐ γνωρίζω is not to be taken, as it usually has been, according to the common Greek usage with the Vulgate, in the sense of *ignoro,* but, following the invariable usage of the N. T. (comp. also 3 Macc. ii. 6; 3 Esr. vi. 12; Aesch. *Prom.* 487; Athen. xii. p. 539 B; Diod. Sic. i. 6), as: *I do not make it known, I do not explain myself on the point,* give no information upon it.[1]   Comp. van Hengel, Ewald, Huther, Schenkel, also Bengel, who, however, without any ground, adds *mihi.*   Paul refrains from making and declaring such a choice, because (see ver. 23 f.) his desire is so situated between the two alternatives, that it *clashes* with that which he is compelled to regard as the better.—The conformity to words and context, and the simplicity, which characterize the whole of this explanation (so, in substance, also Chrysostom, Theodoret, Oecumenius, Theophylact, Erasmus, Luther, Calvin, and many others, including Heinrichs, Rheinwald, van Hengel, de Wette, Wiesinger, Ewald, Ellicott, Hilgenfeld),—in which, however, καρπ. ἔργου is not to be taken as *operae pretium* (Calvin, Grotius, and others), nor καί as superfluous (Casaubon, Heinrichs, and others), nor οὐ γνωρίζω as equivalent to οὐκ οἶδα (see above), —exclude decisively all other interpretations, in which τοῦτο

---

[1] Not as if Paul intended to say that *"he kept it to himself,"* a sense which Hofmann wrongly ascribes to this declaration. He intends to say rather that he *refrains from a decision regarding* what he should choose. The dilemma in which he found himself (comp. ver. 23) caused him *to waive the giving of such a decision,* in order not to *anticipate* in any way the divine purpose *by his own choice.*

and the καί of the apodosis have been the special stumbling-
blocks. Among these other explanations are (*a*) that of
Pelagius, Estius, Bengel, Matthies, and others (comp. Lachmann, who places a stop after ἔργου), that ἐστί is to be understood with ἐν σαρκί, that the apodosis begins with τοῦτο, and
that καὶ τί αἱρ. κ.τ.λ. is a proposition by itself : "*if the living
in the flesh is appointed to me, then this has no other aim for me
than by continuous labour to bring forth fruit,*" etc. (Huther, *l.c.*
p. 581 f.). But how arbitrarily is the simple ἐστί, thus supplied, interpreted (*mihi constitutum est*) ! The words τοῦτό μοι
καρπὸς ἔργου, taken as an apodosis, are—immediately after the
statement ἐμοὶ γὰρ τὸ ζῆν Χριστός, in which the idea of καρπὸς ἔργου is substantially conveyed already—adapted less for
a new emphatic inference than for a supposition that has been
established ; and the discourse loses both in flow and force.
Nevertheless Hofmann has in substance followed this explanation.[1] (*b*) Beza's view, that εἰ is to be taken as *whether :* "*an
vero vivere in carne mihi operae pretium sit, et quid eligam ignoro.*"
This is linguistically incorrect (καρπὸς ἔργου), awkward (εἰ . . .
καὶ τί), and in the first member of the sentence un-Pauline
(vv. 24–26). (*c*) The assumption of an *aposiopesis* after ἔργου :
if life, etc., is to me καρπὸς ἔργου, "*non repugno, non aegre fero*"
(so Corn. Müller), or, "*je ne dois pas désirer la mort*" (Rilliet).
See Winer, p. 557 f. [E. T. 751] ; Meineke, *Menand.* p. 238.
This is quite arbitrary, and finds no support in the emotional
character of the passage, which is in fact very calm. (*d*) Hoelemann's explanation—which supplies καρπός from the sequel
after ζῆν, takes τοῦτο, which applies to the ἀποθανεῖν, as the
beginning of the apodosis, and understands καρπὸς ἔργου as
an *actual* fruit : "*but if life is a fruit in the flesh (an earthly
fruit), this (death) is also a fruit of (in) fact (a substantial,
real fruit)*"—is involved, artificial, and contrary to the genius

---

[1] *If it be life in the flesh,* namely, which I have to expect instead of dying (?),
then this, namely the life in the flesh, *is to me produce of labour,* in so far as by
living I produce fruit, *and thus then* (καί) *it is to me unknown,* etc. This interpretation of Hofmann's also is liable to the objection that, if Paul intended to
say that he produced fruit by his life, logically he must have predicated of his
ζῆν ἐν σαρκί, not that it was to him καρπὸς ἔργου, but rather that it was ἔργον καρ-
ποῦ, a work (a working) which produces fruit.

of the language (καρπ. ἔργου !).   (e) The explanation of Weiss
is that, after ἐν σαρκί, κέρδος is to be again supplied as a predicate, so that τοῦτο, which is made to apply to the entire
protasis, begins the apodosis : " but if life is a gain, that is a
fruit of his labour, because the successes of his apostolic
ministry can alone make his life worth having to him" (ver.
24).   This supplying of κέρδος, which was predicated of the
antithesis of the ζῆν, is as arbitrary as it is intolerably
forced ; and, indeed, according to ver. 21, not κέρδος merely
would have to be supplied, but ἐμοὶ κέρδος ; and, since κέρδος
is not to be taken from ἀποθανεῖν, of which it is predicate, we
should have to expect an *also* before τὸ ζῆν, so that Paul
would have written : εἰ δὲ (or ἀλλ᾿ εἰ) καὶ τὸ ζῆν ἐν σαρκὶ
ἐμοὶ κέρδος κ.τ.λ.

Ver. 23. Respecting the τί αἱρήσομαι οὐ γνωρίζω, Paul expresses himself more fully in vv. 23, 24, proceeding with the
explicative δέ ; for δέ is not *antithetical* (Hofmann : " on the
contrary"), but, in fact, the reading γάρ is a correct gloss,
since the *situation* now follows, which *necessitates* that relin-
quishment of a choice.   *But I am held in a strait* (comp.
Luke xii. 50 ; Acts xviii. 5 ; 2 Cor. v. 14 ; Wisd. xvii. 11 ;
Dem. 396. 22, 1484. 23 ; Plat. *Legg.* vii. p. 791 E, *Theaet.*
p. 165 B ; Heind. *ad Plat. Soph.* 46) *of the two points*, namely
the ἀποθανεῖν and the ζῆν,[1] of which he has just said, τί αἱρ.
οὐ γνωρ.   These δύο are not conceived in an *instrumental*
sense, which is expressed with συνέχ., by the *dative* (Matt.
iv. 24 ; Luke viii. 37 ; Acts xviii. 5 ; Plat. *Soph.* p. 250
D ; Eur. *Heracl.* 634), but as that from which the συνεχέσθαι
proceeds and originates (Bernhardy, p. 227 f. ; Schoem. *ad Is.*
p. 348 ; Mätzner, *ad Antiph.* p. 167). — τὴν ἐπιθυμ. ἔχων
κ.τ.λ.] *since my longing is* to die.   The *article* denotes, not
" votum *jam commemoratum*" (Hoelemann), for Paul has not

---

[1] It is therefore more in harmony with the context to refer ἐκ τῶν δύο to *what*
precedes than to *what follows* (Luther, Rheinwald, Corn. Müller, and others).
Note that the *emphasis* is laid on συνέχομαι, which is the *new climactic* point in
the continuation of the discourse.   The word συνέχ. itself is rightly rendered by
the *Vulgate : coarctor.*   The mere *teneor* (Weiss and earlier expositors) is not
sufficient according to the context.   Paul feels himself *in a dilemma* between two
opposite alternatives.

indeed as yet expressed an ἐπιθυμεῖν, but doubtless the desire, *which Paul has.* He says that his *desire* tends towards dying, etc.,[1] but that life is *more necessary ;* and therefore he knows that not that for which he longs, but that which is the more necessary, will come to pass, and that he will remain alive (ver. 25). Augustine aptly observes : " Non patienter moritur, sed patienter vivit et delectabiliter moritur." — ἀναλῦσαι] comp. 2 Tim. iv. 6 ; Isa. xxxviii. 12. Dying is conceived as a *breaking up* (a figure taken from the camp) for the departure, namely, from this temporal life to Christ (comp. ὑπάγειν, Matt. xxvi. 24 ; ἐκδημεῖν, 2 Cor. v. 8 f. ; and similar passages) ; hence the καὶ σὺν Χριστῷ εἶναι immediately added.[2] — πολλῷ γ. μᾶλλ. κρεῖσσον] *by much in a higher degree better ;* a cumulative expression in the strength and vividness of feeling. As to μᾶλλον with the comparative, see on Mark vii. 36 ; 2 Cor. vii. 13 ; and Kühner, II. 2, p. 24 f., and *ad Xen. Mem.* iii. 13. 5 ; Bornemann, *ad Cyrop.* p. 137, Goth. If here interpreted as *potius* (ver. 12), it would glance at the preference usually given to *life ;* but nothing in the context leads to this. The predicate κρεῖσσον (a much *better, i.e. happier* lot) refers to *the apostle himself ;* comp. below, δι' ὑμᾶς. Eur. *Hec.* 214 : θανεῖν μου ξυντυχία κρείσσων ἐκύρησεν.

Ver. 24. Ἐπιμένειν involves the idea : to remain *still* (still further), *to stay on,* comp. Rom. vi. 1. — ἐν τῇ σαρκί] *in my flesh.* Not quite equivalent to the idea involved in ἐν σαρκί without the article (ver. 22). The reading without the ἐν (see the critical remarks) would yield an *ethical* sense here unsuitable (Rom. vi. 1, xi. 22 ; Col. i. 23).—ἀναγκαιότ.] namely, than the for me far happier alternative of the ἀναλῦσαι κ. σ. Χ. εἶναι. The necessity *for that* is only a subjective want

---

[1] It is thus explained why Paul did not write τοῦ ἀναλῦσαι (as Origen reads). εἰς is not dependent on τὴν ἐπιθ. (ἐπιθ. is never so construed ; comp. Corn. Müller) ; but τὴν ἐπιθ. is absolute, and εἰς τὸ ἀναλ. expresses the direction of τὴν ἐπιθ. ἔχων : *having my longing towards dying.* Comp. Thuc. vi. 15. 2.

[2] Bengel : "*Decedere* sanctis nunquam non optabile fuit, sed *cum Christo esse* ex novo testamento est." This Christian longing, therefore, has in view anything rather than a "having emerged from the limitation of personality" (Schleiermacher).—The translation *dissolvi* (Vulgate, Hilary) is to be referred to another reading (ἀναλυθῆναι).

felt by the pious mind. But the objective necessity of the
other alternative has precedence as the greater ; it is more
precisely defined by δι’ ὑμᾶς, regarded from the standpoint of
love. " Vitae suae adjici nihil desiderat sua causa, sed eorum,
quibus utilis est." Seneca, *ep.* 98 ; comp. *ep.* 104. — δι’ ὑμᾶς]
applies to *the Philippians,* who would naturally understand,
however, that Paul did not intend to refer this point of
necessity to them *exclusively.* It is the *individualizing* mode
of expression adopted by special love.

Vv. 25, 26. Τοῦτο πεποιθ.] τοῦτο does not belong to οἶδα,
but to πεποιθ., and refers to the case of necessity just expressed ; having which is the object of his confidence, Paul
knows that, etc., so that ὅτι is dependent on οἶδα alone,—
in opposition to Theophylact, Erasmus, Calovius, Heinrichs,
Flatt, and others, under whose view the οἶδα would lack the
specification of a reason, which is given in this very τοῦτο
πεποιθ., as it was practically necessary. On the accusative of the
object with πεποιθ., comp. Bernhardy, p. 106 ; Kühner, II. 1,
p. 267 ; also Wunder, *ad Soph. O. T.* 259 f. Observe that
we may say : πεποίθησιν πέποιθα, 2 Kings xviii. 19. Comp.
on ii. 18. — μενῶ] *I shall remain ;* contrast to the ἀναλῦσαι,
which was before expressed by ἐπιμένειν ἐν τ. σαρκί. Comp.
John xii. 34, xxi. 22 f. ; 1 Cor. xv. 6. The loving emotion
of the apostle (ver. 8) leads him to add to the absolute μενῶ :
καὶ συμπαραμενῶ πᾶσιν ὑμῖν, *and I shall continue together
with all of you ;* I shall with you all be preserved in temporal
life. From vv. 6 and 10 there can be no doubt as to the *terminus ad quem* which Paul had in view ; and the πᾶσιν (comp.
1 Cor. xv. 51 ; Rom. xiii. 11) shows how *near* he conceived
that goal to be (iv. 5). Notwithstanding, Hofmann terms this
view, which is both verbally and textually consistent, quixotic,
and invents instead one which makes Paul mean by μενῶ the
remaining *alive without his co-operation,* and by παραμενῶ,
which should (according to Hofmann) be read (see the critical
remarks), *his remaining willingly,* and which assumes that
the apostle did not conceive the καὶ παραμενῶ πᾶσιν ὑμῖν as
dependent on ὅτι, but conveys in these words a *promise* to
remain with those, *" from whom he could withdraw himself."*

What a rationalistic, artificial distinction of ideas and separation of things that belong together ! and what a singular promise from the apostle's lips to a church so dear to him : that
he *will not withdraw himself*, but will *remain faithful* to them
(Schneider and Krüger, *ad Xen. Anab.* ii. 6. 2) ! If παραμενῶ
is the true reading, Paul says quite simply : *I know that I
shall remain* (shall not be deprived of life), *and continue with
you all*, *i.e.* and that I shall be preserved to you all; comp.
Heb. vii. 23 ; Ecclus. xii. 15 ; Hom. *Il.* xii. 402 ; Plat. *Menex.*
p. 235 B ; Lucian. *Nigr.* 30 ; Herodian. vi. 2. 19.—παραμενῶ,
to continue there, just like μενῶ in the sense of *in vita manere*,
Herod. i. 30.   Hence συμπαραμένειν (Thuc. vi. 89. 3 ; Men.
in Stob., lxix. 4, 5), to continue there with, *to remain alive
along with*.   Thus LXX. Ps. lxxii. 5 ; Basil, I. p. 49 ; Gregory
of Nazianzus, I. p. 74 (joined with συνδιαιωνίζειν). — εἰς τὴν
ὑμῶν . . . πίστ.] ὑμῶν, as the personal subject of the προκοπή
and χαρὰ τῆς πίστεως, is placed first, with the emphasis of
loving interest ; the latter genitive, however, which is the real
genitive of the subject, belongs to both words, προκοπὴν κ.
χαράν.   Hence : *for your faith—furtherance and joy.* Both
points are to be advanced by the renewed labours of the apostle
among them (ver. 26).   The blending of them together by an
ἐν διὰ δυοῖν (Heinrichs, Flatt) is erroneous.   Weiss, however,
is also in error in urging that τῆς πίστ. cannot belong to
προκοπήν also, because it would be in that case the genitive of
the *object ;* the faith also is to be an increasing and progressive
thing, 2 Cor. x. 15. — Ver. 26. ἵνα τὸ καύχημα κ.τ.λ.] the
special and concrete aim of the general proposition εἰς τὴν ὑμῶν
προκ. κ. χ. τ. πίστ., which is consequently represented as the
ultimate aim of the μενῶ καὶ συμπαραμ. πᾶσ. ὑμ. Comp.
ver. 10.   The καύχημα, because ὑμῶν is placed along with it
(comp. 1 Cor. v. 6, ix. 15 ; 2 Cor. ii. 14, ix. 3), is that of the
readers and *not* of the *apostle* (Chrysostom : μειζόνως ἔχω
καυχᾶσθαι ὑμῶν ἐπιδόντων, Ewald : *my pride in you* at the
last day) ; nor is it equivalent to καύχησις, *gloriatio* (Flatt and
many others), but it denotes, as it invariably does,[1] *materies*

---

[1] This applies also against Huther, *l.c.* p. 585, who, in support of the
signification *gloriatio*, appeals to Pind. *Isth.* v. 65 : καύχημα κατάβρεχε σιγᾷ. But

gloriandi (Rom. iv. 2 ; 1 Cor. v. 6, ix. 15 f. ; 2 Cor. i. 14,
v. 12 ; Gal. vi. 4). Hence : *that the matter in which you have to
glory, i.e.* the bliss as Christians in which you rejoice (compare
previously the χαρὰ τῆς πίστεως), *may increase abundantly*
(comp. previously the προκοπὴ τῆς πίστεως). The ἐν Χριστῷ
Ἰησοῦ that is added expresses the *sphere in which* the περισσεύειν is to take place, and characterizes the latter, therefore,
as something which only develops itself in Christ as the
element, in which both the joyful consciousness and the
ethical activity of life subsist. If the περισσεύειν took place
otherwise, it would be an egotistical, foreign, generally abnormal and aberrant thing ; as was the case, for example,
with some of the Corinthians and with Judaistic Christians,
whose καυχᾶσθαι was based and grew upon works of the law.
The normal περισσεύειν of the καύχημα of the Philippians,
however, namely, its περισσεύειν ἐν Χριστῷ Ἰησοῦ, shall take
place—and this is specially added as the concrete position of
the matter—ἐν ἐμοὶ διὰ τῆς ἐμῆς παρουσίας π. πρὸς ὑμᾶς,
that is, *it shall have in me by my coming again to you its procuring cause ;* inasmuch as through this return in itself, and
in virtue of my renewed ministry among you, I shall be the
occasion, impulse, and furtherance of that rich increase in your
καύχημα, and thus the περισσεύειν *will rest in me.* Consequently the ἐν in ἐν Χ. Ἰ., and the ἐν in ἐν ἐμοί, are *differently*
conceived ; the former is the *specific, essential definition* of
περισσεύῃ, the latter the *statement of the personal procuring
ground* for the περισσ. ἐν Ἰ. Χ., which the apostle has in
view in reference to the καύχημα of his readers,—a statement
of the ground, which is not surprising for the service of an
instrument of Christ (Hofmann), and which quite accords
with the concrete *species facti* here contemplated, the personal
return and the apostolic position and ministry. The interpretation of Hofmann is thus all the more erroneous, viz. that
the increase of their glorying is given to the readers in the
person of the apostle, *in so far as the having him again among*

---

in this passage also καύχημα means that *in which one glories,* as the Scholiast
has appropriately explained it : εἰ καὶ τηλικαῦτα εἰσὶ τῶν Αἰγινητῶν τὰ κατορθώ-
ματα, βρέχει καὶ ἐπικάλυπτι τῇ σιωπῇ.

them would be a matter of Christian joy and pride to them.
Thus would the apostle make himself in fact the object and
contents of the καυχᾶσθαι, which would neither be consistent
with the logical relation of the ἵνα to the preceding εἰς τ. ὑμ.
προκοπὴν κ.τ.λ., nor with Paul's own deep humility (1 Cor.
iii. 21, xv. 9 ; Eph. iii. 8), which he satisfies also in 2 Cor. i.
14 by the *mutual nature* of the καύχημα between himself and
his friends, and in view of the *day of Christ.* By many (see
Calvin, Heinrichs, Rheinwald, Rilliet, and others) ἐν Χ. Ἰ.,
and by some even ἐν ἐμοί (Storr, Flatt, Huther), are referred,
contrary to the position of the words, to τὸ καύχημα ὑμῶν,
with various arbitrary definitions of the sense, *e.g.* Flatt : " so
that ye shall have still more reason, in reference to me, to
glorify Jesus Christ (who hath given me again to you) ;"
Rheinwald : "If I shall be delivered by the power of Christ,
ye will find abundant cause for praising the Lord, who has
done such great things for me." — πάλιν] is connected, as an
adjectival definition, with παρουσ. See on 2 Cor. xi. 23 ;
Gal. i. 13 ; 1 Cor. viii. 7.

REMARK.—From vv. 20–26 we are not to conclude that
Paul at that time was in doubt whether he should live to see
the Parousia (Usteri, *Lehrbegr.* p. 355, and others). For in ver.
20 *he only supposes the case of* his death, and that indeed, in
ver. 21, as the case which would be *profitable* for himself, and
for which, therefore, he protests in ver. 23 *that he longs.* But
on account of the need for his life being prolonged (ver. 24), he
knows (ver. 25) that that case will *not* come to pass. This
οἶδα (ver. 25) is not to be weakened into a *probabiliter sperare*
or the like (Beza, Calvin, Estius, and many others, also Heinrichs, Rheinwald ; comp. Matthies, van Hengel, Rilliet), with
which Grotius, from connecting οἶδα πεποιθ., even brings out
the sense, "*scio me haec sperare,* i.e. *malle* ;" whilst others fall
back upon the *argumentum a silentio,* viz. that Paul says
nothing here of any *revelation* (see Estius, Matthies, and
others), but only expresses *an inference* in itself liable to error
(Weiss). No, although he has supposed the *possibility* (comp.
ii. 17) of his being put to death, he nevertheless *knew* that
he should remain alive ; and it must withal be confessed
that the *result* did *not correspond* to this definite οἶδα, which
Bengel even goes so far as to refer to a *dictamen pro-*

pheticum. By no means, however, is an *imaginary situation*[1]
to be suspected here (Baur), and just as little can a *second*
imprisonment at Rome be founded on this passage (Chrysostom,
Oecumenius, Theodoret, Bullinger, Piscator, Calovius, Estius,
Bengel, and many others, also Wiesinger); as to the relation of
this passage to Acts xx. 25, see on Acts.—We have further to
notice that Paul, according to ver. 23, assumes that, in case he
should be put to death, he would go *not into Hades*, but *into
heaven to Christ*,—a conviction of the bliss attending martyrdom which is found in 2 Cor. v. 8 and in the history of Stephen,
Acts vii. 59, and therefore does not occur for the first time in
the Apocalypse (vi. 9 ff., vii. 9 ff.).[2] Wetstein's idea is a mere
empty evasion, that by ἀναλῦσαι is doubtless meant the dying,
but by σὺν Χ. εἶναι only the time following the resurrection
(comp. also Weitzel, *Stud. u. Krit.* 1836, p. 954 ff.); as also is
that of Grotius, that σὺν Χ. εἶναι means : " *in Christi custodia esse*,"
and " *nihil hinc de loco definiri potest*." It is also altogether at
variance with the context (see vv. 20, 21), if, with Kaeuffer, we
interpret ἀναλῦσαι as the change that takes place at the Parousia
(" ut quasi eximeretur carne "). Comp. on the contrary, Polycarp : *ad Phil.* 9, ὅτι εἰς τὸν ὀφειλόμενον αὐτοῖς τόπον εἰσὶ παρὰ τῷ

---

[1] Hinsch even assigns, *l.c.* p. 71, to the passage with its vivid emotion the
character of a *historico-critical reflection*. He represents the author of the
epistle as having in view the various opinions current in his age regarding the
close of the apostle's life, in other words, the question, whether his captivity
at that time ended in his being put to death, or in his being set at liberty and
beginning a new course of labour. The author adduces the *grounds* of both
views, *putting them in the mouth of the apostle*, and in ver. 24 decides in favour
of the second ; the original, of which the present passage is an imitation, is to
be found (as Baur also thinks) in 2 Cor. v. 8, Rom. xiv. 8. See Hilgenfeld,
in opposition to Baur and Hinsch.

[2] All we can gather from Rom. viii. 10 f. is merely that the life of believers
remains unaffected by the death of the body ; as at John xi. 25 f. They remain in fellowship with Christ ; but as to the mode and place of this fellowship,
of which they might indeed be partakers even in *Hades* (Paradise, Luke xvi.
22 ff., xxiii. 43 ; Phil. ii. 10), as little is said in that passage as in viii. 38, xiv. 8.
But in the passage we are considering, the words σὺν Χριστῷ εἶναι point to an
actual being with the Lord in heaven (comp. 1 Thess. iv. 14, 17 ; Acts vii. 59 ;
2 Cor. *l.c.*), and do not therefore apply to the state in Hades (in opposition to
Güder, *Erschein. Chr. unt. d. Todten*, p. 111, and others) ; see also 2 Cor. v. 8.
This union with Christ, however, is not the δόξα as the ultimate goal of hope ;
see iii. 20 f. ; Col. iii. 3. To the latter belongs also the *bodily* transfiguration,
which can only take place at the Parousia, 1 Cor. xv. 23. This applies also in
opposition to Gerlach, *d. letzt. Dinge*, p. 79 ff., whose distinction between
corporeality and materiality [*Leiblichkeit und Körperlichkeit*] is not in harmony
with the New Testament, which distinguishes rather between σῶμα and σάρξ.

κυρίῳ, ᾧ καὶ συνέπαθον, Clem. Rom. 1 *Cor.* 5, of *Peter* : μαρτυρήσας ἐπορεύθη εἰς τὸν ὀφειλόμενον τόπον τῆς δόξης, and of *Paul* : εἰς τὸν ἅγιον τόπον ἐπορεύθη, Martyr. Ignat. 26. It is an *intermediate state*, not yet the fully perfected glory, but *in heaven*, where Christ is (iii. 20 f.). Georgii, in Zeller's *theolog. Jahrb.* 1845, I. p. 22, following Usteri, *Lehrbegr.* p. 368, erroneously discovers in our passage a *modification* of the New Testament view, developed only when the hope of a *speedy* Parousia fell into the background. Comp. Neander and Baumgarten Crusius (whose view amounts to an inconsistency of the conceptions). Opposed to these views, even apart from 2 Cor. v. 8 and Acts vii. 59, is the fact that the *speedy* Parousia appears still to be very distinctly expected in this epistle. See particularly iii. 20 f. But we find nothing said in the New Testament as to an *intermediate body* between death and resurrection. See remark on 2 Cor. v. 3. There is a vague fanciful idea in Delitzsch, *Psychol.* p. 443 f., who in p. 419 ff., however, forcibly shows the incorrectness of the doctrine of the *sleep of the soul.*

Ver. 27. To these accounts regarding his own present position Paul now subjoins certain exhortations to right conduct for his readers. — μόνον] without connecting particle, as in Gal. ii. 10, v. 13. With the above assurance, namely, that he shall continue alive, etc., he, in order that the object of this preserving of his life (ver. 25) may be accomplished in them, needs *only* to summon them *to be* in a way *worthy* of the gospel *members of the Christian community* (πολιτεύεσθε) ; nothing *further* is needed. Hofmann, in consequence of his finding previously a *promise,* finds here, equally erroneously, *the only counter-demand made for it.* — τοῦ Χριστοῦ] *of Christ.* See on Mark i. 1. — πολιτεύεσθε] comp. on Acts xxiii. 1. See also 2 Macc. vi. 1, xi. 25 ; 3 Macc. iii. 4 ; Joseph. *Antt.* iii. 5. 8, Vit. 2 ; Wetstein *ad loc.,* and Suicer, *Thes.* II. p. 709 ff. The word, which is not used elsewhere by Paul in the epistles to express the conduct of life, is here *purposely chosen,* because he has in view the moral life, internal and external, *of the Christian commonwealth,* corresponding to the purport of the gospel (πολιτεύεσθαι, *to be citizen of a state, to live as citizen*). See the sequel. It is also selected in Acts xxiii. 1, where the idea of the *official* relation of service is involved (πολιτεύεσθαι, to administer *an office in the state*). Comp. 2 Macc. vi. 1, xi. 25 ;

3 Macc. iii. 4. In the absence of such references as these, Paul says περιπατεῖν (Eph. iv. 1; Col. i. 10, with ἀξίως). Comp. however, Clement, *Cor.* i. 3: πολιτεύεσθαι κατὰ τὸ καθῆκον τῷ Χριστῷ, and ch. 54: πολιτευόμενος τὴν ἀμεταμέλητον πολιτείαν τοῦ Θεοῦ, ch. 21: ἀξίως αὐτοῦ πολιτευόμενοι. — εἴτε ἐλθὼν κ.τ.λ.] a parenthetic definition as far as ἀπών, so that ἀκούσω then depends on ἵνα : *in order that I —whether it be when I have come and seen you, or during my absence from you—may hear,* etc. The two cases εἴτε . . . εἴτε do not refer to the liberation *and non-liberation* of the apostle; but they *assume the certainty of the liberation* (ver. 25 f.), after which Paul desired to continue his apostolic journeys and to come again to the Philippians; and indeed trusted that he should come (ii. 24), but yet, according to the circumstances, might be led elsewhere and be far away from them (εἴτε ἀπών). In either event it is his earnest desire and wish that he may *come to learn* the affairs of the church in their excellence as described by ὅτι στήκετε κ.τ.λ. It cannot surprise us to find the notion of *learning* expressed by the common form of the *zeugma*,[1] corresponding to the εἴτε ἀπών; and from the ἀκούσω accordingly employed there naturally suggests itself a word of kindred import to correspond with εἴτε ἐλθὼν κ.τ.λ., such as γνῶ. The rash opinion, repeated even by Hofmann, that ἀκούσω *only* refers to the second case, does the apostle the injustice of making his discourse *"hiulca"* (Calvin), and even *grammatically faulty* (Hofmann), it being supposed that he intended to write either: " ut sive veniens *videam* vos, sive absens audiam," or: " sive quum venero et videro vos, sive absens audiam de statu vestro, *intelligam utroque modo*," etc. Calvin allows a choice between these two interpretations; the latter is approved of by de Wette and Weiss (comp. Rilliet and J. B. Lightfoot). Hofmann also accuses the apostle of the confusion of having written εἴτε

---

[1] It is a mistake (notwithstanding Winer, p. 578 [E. T. 777]) to suppose that in a zeugma the directly appropriate verb must be joined to the *first* member. It can also be joined with the *second*, as here. Comp. Xen. *Anab.* vii. 8. 12, and Kühner *in loc. ;* Plat. *Rep.* p. 589 C, and Stallbaum *in loc. ;* Hom. *Il.* iii. 327, and Faesi *in loc. ;* generally Nägelsbach, *z. Ilias,* p. 179, ed. 3 ; Bremi, *ad Lys.* p. 43 ff. ; Kühner, II. 2, p. 1075 f.

ἀπὼν¹ ἀκούσω τὰ περὶ ὑμῶν (which words are to be taken together), as if he had previously put εἴτε ἐλθὼν ὄψομαι ὑμᾶς; but of having *left it to the reader mentally to supply* the verbs that should have depended on ἵνα, and of which *two*¹ would have been needed! The passage employed for comparison, Rom. iv. 16, with its close, concise, and clear dialectic, is utterly a stranger to such awkwardness. Hoelemann finally interprets the passage in a perfectly arbitrary way, as if Paul had written : ἵνα, εἴτε ἐλθὼν κ. ἰδὼν ὑμᾶς, εἴτε ἀπὼν καὶ ἀκούσας τὰ περὶ ὑμῶν, στήκητε κ.τ.λ., thus making the participles *absolute* nominatives. — τὰ περὶ ὑμῶν] the object of ἀκούσω, so that ὅτι στήκετε κ.τ.λ., *that*, namely, *ye stand*, etc., is a more precise *definition* arising out of the loving confidence of the apostle, analogous to the familiar attraction οἶδά σε τίς εἶ, and the like; Winer, p. 581 [E. T. 781]. It has been awkwardly explained as *absolute :* " *quod attinet ad* res vestras" (Heinrichs, Rheinwald, Matthies, and others), while van Hengel not more skilfully, taking εἴτε ἀπὼν ἀκούσω τ. π. ὑμ. together, afterwards supplies ἀκούσω again. Grotius, Estius, and am Ende take τά even for ταῦτα, and Hoelemann makes Paul express himself here also by an *anakoluthon* (comp. above on εἴτε ἐλθὼν κ.τ.λ.), so that either ὅτι should have been omitted and στήκητε written, or τά should not have been inserted. — ἐν ἑνὶ πνεύματι] is to be joined with στήκετε, alongside of which it stands, although Hofmann, without any reason, takes it absolutely (2 Thess. ii. 15). It is the common element, *in which* they are to *stand, i.e.* to remain stedfast (Rom. v. 2 ; 1 Cor. xv. 1, xvi. 13) ; πνεύματι, however, refers not to the *Holy Spirit* (Erasmus, Beza, and others, also Heinrichs, Rheinwald, Matthies, van Hengel, Weiss), but, as the context shows by μιᾷ ψυχῇ, to the *human* spirit ; comp. 1 Thess. v. 23. The perfect *accord* of their minds in conviction, volition, and feeling, presents the appearance of *one* spirit which the various persons have in common. De Wette well says : " the practical

---

¹ But why *two ?* He would only have needed to insert μαθῶ or γνῶ before ὅτι. This would have suited both halves of the alternative discourse, in the confused form in which Hofmann makes it run ; and there would be no necessity whatever for *two* verbs.

community of spirit." Comp. Acts iv. 32.   It is, as a matter of
course, plain to the Christian consciousness that this unity of
the human spirit is *brought about* by the *Holy Spirit* (see on
Eph. iv. 3 f., 23), but ἑνὶ πνεύμ. *does not say* so.   Moreover
the *emphasis* is on this ἐν ἑνὶ πν., and therefore μιᾷ ψ. is
subsequently placed first.—The *special mode*, which this standing fast in one spirit desired by the apostle is to assume, is
contained in the sequel down to ἀντικειμ. — μιᾷ ψυχῇ συναθλ.
κ.τ.λ.] The ψυχή, as distinguished from the πνεῦμα, is the
principle of the individual personal life, which receives its
impressions on the one hand from the πνεῦμα as the principle
of the higher divine ζωή, and on the other hand from the
outer world, and is the seat of the activity of feeling and
emotion, the *sympathetic unity* of which in the church is here
described (comp. on Luke i. 46 f.).   Comp. ἰσόψυχος, ii. 20 ;
σύμψυχοι, ii. 2 ; Herodian. viii. 5. 15 : μιᾷ τε γνώμῃ καὶ
ψυχῇ, Rom. xv. 6, ὁμοθυμαδόν, 4 Macc. xiv. 20, ὁμόψυχος,
1 Pet. iii. 8, ὁμόφρων.   But μιᾷ ψ. does not also belong to
στήκετε (Chrysostom, Theophylact, Luther, Er. Schmid, and
others), for συναθλ. requires a modal definition in harmony
with the context. — συναθλοῦντες] in keeping with στήκετε,
according to the conception of a *contest* (comp. ver. 30), under
which the activity of Christian *faithfulness* is presented in
relation to all hostile powers.   Comp. Col. ii. 1 ; 1 Thess. ii. 2 ;
1 Tim. vi. 12 ; 2 Tim. iv. 7, *et al.;* also Soph. *O. C.* 564 ; Eur.
Suppl. 317 ; Aesch. *Prom.* 95.   The compound, *striving together*
(comp. iv. 3, and συναγωνίζεσθαι, Rom. xv. 30), is not to be
overlooked, as if συναθλ., with the dative of the thing expressed merely the *entering* or *stepping into the lists* for it
(Hofmann).   It does not refer, however, to *the fellowship of
the Philippians* themselves ("quasi facto agmine contra hostes
evang.," Grotius ; comp. Hoelemann, Rilliet, de Wette, Wiesinger, Weiss, and others, following Chrysostom, Theodoret,
Theophylact, Oecumenius).   Paul looks upon *himself* as a
combatant (ver. 30, comp. ver. 7), and the Philippians as
striving *with* him, and affording him *assistance* (Diod. iii. 4)
as his σύναθλοι in defending the faith (objectively viewed),
protecting it and rendering it victorious.   That they were to

do this *with one accord*, is stated emphatically by μιᾷ ψυχῇ, but is not conveyed by συναθλ. in itself. If, however, *Paul* is the combatant, the passage cannot be understood in the sense : " *adjuvantes decertantem* adversus impios evangelii *fidem*," Erasmus, *Paraphr.* ; comp. Castalio, Michaelis, Mynster, Flatt, Lightfoot,—even apart from the fact that *such a personification* of πίστις is unprecedented, and must have been suggested by the text, as in the case of τῇ ἀληθείᾳ, 1 Cor. xiii. 6.—τῇ πίστει is the dative *commodi* (comp. Jude 3), not *instrumenti* (Beza, Calvin, Grotius, Calovius, Loesner, Rheinwald, and others), which μιᾷ ψυχῇ was. As to the genitive of the object with πίστις, see on Rom. iii. 22.

Ver. 28. On πτύρεσθαι, *to become frightened* (of horses, Diod. ii. 19, xvii. 34 ; Plut. *Fab.* 3 ; *Marc.* 6), *to be thrown into consternation* (Diod. xvii. 37 f. ; Plat. *Ax.* p. 370 A ; Plut. *Mor.* p. 800 C), see Kypke, II. p. 312. In Gen. xli. 8 Aquila has καταπτύρεσθαι. — ἐν μηδενί] *in no point, nulla ratione*, ver. 20 ; 2 Cor. vi. 3, vii. 9 ; Jas. i. 4. — The ἀντικείμενοι (comp. 1 Cor. xvi. 9) are the *non-Christian opponents of the gospel* among Jews and Gentiles, and *not* the *Judaizers* and their adherents (Flatt), or the malevolent *false teachers* (Matthies). This follows from ver. 30, since the whole position and ministry of the apostle was a conflict with *such* adversaries, comp. ver. 7. — ἥτις ἐστὶν αὐτοῖς κ.τ.λ.] *which is indeed*, etc., refers to the preceding μὴ πτύρεσθαι ὑπὸ τῶν ἀντικειμ., to which Paul desires to *encourage* them. This *undauntedness* in the συναλθεῖν, and not the latter itself (Hofmann), is now the leading idea, with which what has further to be said connects itself ; hence ἥτις is not to be taken as referring to the *sufferings*, as it is by Ewald (comp. 2 Thess. i. 5), who subsequently, although without critical proof, would read ἀπωλείας ὑμῶν, ὑμῖν δέ. — αὐτοῖς] τοῖς ἀντικειμένοις is to be taken simply as dative *of reference : which is to them an indication of perdition*. Ὅταν γὰρ ἴδωσιν, ὅτι μυρία τεχναζόμενοι οὐδὲ πτῦραι ὑμᾶς δύνανται, οὐ δεῖγμα τοῦτο σαφὲς ἕξουσιν, ὅτι τὰ μὲν αὐτῶν ἀπολοῦνται, τὰ δὲ ὑμέτερα ἰσχυρὰ καὶ ἀνάλωτα καὶ αὐτόθεν ἔχοντα τὴν σωτηρίαν ; Theophylact. The ἥτις involving a *reason* is just as in Eph. iii. 13.

See on that passage. This would be still more emphatically expressed by ἥτις γε (Klotz, *ad Devar.* p. 305). But the fact that the ἀντικείμενοι *do not recognise* in the undauntedness of those persecuted a proof (not : *causa,* as in the *Vulgate ;* but comp. Rom. iii. 25 f. ; 2 Cor. viii. 24 ; Plat. *Ep.* vii. p. 341 E ; *Legg.* xii. p. 966 C) of their own perdition, and on the other hand of the salvation of the persecuted (ὑμῶν δὲ σωτηρίας), does not alter the state of the case in itself, that the μὴ πτύρεσθαι *is in reality* objectively such an ἔνδειξις to them. It is, indeed, the σημεῖον of the righteous divine cause, and of its necessary final victory. *Perdition* and *salvation :* both without more precise definition ; but the reader *knew* what reference to assign to each, viz. the *Messianic* perdition and salvation. Comp. on the matter, 2 Thess. i. 5 ff. ; Rom. viii. 17 ; 2 Tim. ii. 12 ; Luke xii. 32, *et al.* — καὶ τοῦτο ἀπὸ Θεοῦ] *and that* (see on Rom. xiii. 11) *of God,* thus certain, therefore, and infallible. It adds force to the encouragement conveyed by ὑμῶν δὲ σωτηρίας ; for the context shows by the ὑμῖν which is emphatically placed first in ver. 29,—without making the reading ὑμῖν necessary, however, in ver. 28 (Hofmann) ; see the critical remarks,—that τοῦτο refers only to this second and main part of ἥτις κ.τ.λ. (Calvin, Piscator, Calovius, Flatt, and others, also Ewald and Hofmann), and not to both halves of ἥτις (Beza, Grotius, and many others, also Wiesinger, Weiss, and Ellicott). Entirely foreign to the connection is any purpose of *humiliation* (Hoelemann and older expositors, following the Greek Fathers). Nor are the words to be attached to *what follows* (ὅτι, *that*) (Clemens Alex., Chrysostom, Theodoret, Erasmus, and others, and recently Rilliet) ; in which case the (preparative) τοῦτο would receive an uncalled-for importance, and yet ἀπὸ Θεοῦ would be obviously intelligible through ἐχαρίσθη.

Ver. 29. Ὅτι is argumentative. " Καὶ τοῦτο ἀπὸ Θεοῦ," I say, "*since indeed to you* it was *granted,*" etc. This grant distinguishing *you* is the practical proof, that the just expressed ἀπὸ Θεοῦ is indubitably right, and that consequently the ἔνδειξις of your final salvation which is afforded to the adversaries in your undauntedness is a *divine* ἔνδειξις, *a token given by God.*[1] Hofmann's view, that ὅτι specifies the reason why God imparts to them what has been before stated, is based upon the erroneous reading ὑμῖν in ver. 28 ; and is itself erroneous, because ὅτι would introduce merely the self-evident thought that they had *not sought out* their suffering *wilfully*, but had had it given to them *by God*, and because, for the purpose of marking the alleged contrast to the wilfulness, not ὑμῖν, but ἀπὸ Θεοῦ again would have been emphatically prefixed, and consequently Paul must have written : ὅτι ἀπὸ Θεοῦ ὑμῖν ἐχαρίσθη κ.τ.λ. Hofmann curiously explains the emphasized ὑμῖν, as if Paul meant to say that with respect to their sufferings *the case stood exactly as with his own.* In that case he must at least have written, in prospect of ver. 30, καὶ ὑμῖν, *to you also.* — ὑμῖν] emphatically put first, corresponding to the previous ὑμῶν δὲ σωτηρίας. — ἐχαρίσθη] *donatum est ;* by whom, is self-evident. 1 Cor. ii. 12. — τὸ ὑπὲρ Χριστοῦ] as if the πάσχειν was immediately to follow. The apostle does not leave this unwritten purposely, in order to bring into prominence in the first place the idea of ὑπέρ, as Hofmann artificially explains. But here his full heart interposes, after τ. ὑπὲρ Χριστοῦ, and before he writes πάσχειν, the fresh thought οὐ μόνον τὸ εἰς αὐτ. πιστεύειν, so that ἀλλὰ καὶ must now be also added ; and, on account of the different prepositional relation (εἰς) introduced, the τὸ ὑπὲρ Χριστοῦ already expressed is again taken up by τὸ ὑπὲρ αὐτοῦ. Thus οὐ μόνον . . . ὑπὲρ αὐτοῦ appears as a parenthesis of more special definition, after which the πάσχειν, which had been prepared for by τὸ ὑπὲρ Χριστοῦ, but is only now introduced, is to be dwelt upon with emphasis : " *to you the gift of grace is granted, in behalf of Christ*—not only to believe on Him, but also for Him—*to suffer.*" Plat. *Legg.* x. p. 802 C : εἰ δὲ φανήσεται ψυχὴ πρῶτον, οὐ πῦρ οὐδὲ ἀὴρ, ψυχὴ δὲ ἐν πρώτοις γεγενημένη. See also Dissen, *ad Dem. de cor.* p. 431 ; Fritzsche, *ad Matth.* p. 501. It is an awkward construction, to take τὸ ὑπὲρ Χ. absolutely and (notwithstanding the subsequent ὑπὲρ αὐτοῦ) in the sense : *as to what concerns Christ* (Beza,

---

[1] At the same time it is to be observed here also (comp. on ver. 28) that this divine pointing to the final salvation of believers was *in fact* before the adversaries, and that their non-recognition of it altered nothing in this *objective* relation.

Camerarius, Calovius, and others, including Matthies and Rilliet). For the conception of *suffering* for Christ as a high divine *distinction*, see already Acts v. 41; comp. Matt. v. 11 f. Comp. on ver. 7.

Ver. 30. *So that ye have the same conflict*, etc., serves to characterize the ὑμῖν ἐχαρ. τὸ ὑπὲρ X. πάσχειν just asserted; and Paul's intention in thus speaking, is to bring home to them the *high dignity and distinction* of suffering for Christ, which is involved in the consciousness of fellowship in conflict with the apostle. It is impossible, in accordance with the true explanation of what goes before (see on ver. 29), to find in τὸν αὐτόν, that they have themselves sought their conflict of suffering as little as the apostle had sought his, but, on the contrary, have received it as a gift of grace from God (Hofmann). The participle might have been put by Paul in the *nominative* (instead of the dative), because ὑμεῖς was floating before his mind as the *logical* subject of the preceding clause. Comp. on Eph. iii. 18, iv. 2; 2 Cor. i. 7; Col. ii. 2, iii. 16; Phil. iii. 19; Kühner, II. 2, p. 661 f. There is therefore neither a logical nor a grammatical reason, with Bengel, Michaelis, Lachmann, Ewald (comp. also Buttmann, *Neut. Gr.* p. 256 [E. T. 299]), to treat ἥτις . . . πάσχειν as a parenthesis,—a construction which would be only an injurious interruption to the flow of the discourse. — τὸν αὐτόν] namely, in respect of the *object;* it is the conflict *for Christ* (ver. 29) *and His gospel* (ver. 7). — οἷον εἴδετε κ.τ.λ.] *as ye have seen it in my person* (viz. whilst I was still with you in Philippi; see scenes of this conflict in Acts xvi. 16 ff.; comp. 1 Thess. ii. 2), *and now* (from my epistle which is read out to you) *ye hear in my person.* Paul, in his epistle, *speaks* to the Philippians as if they were listening to him in person; thus *they hear in him* his conflict, which is made known to them in the statements of the apostle. This explanation is all the less unfitting, as Hofmann terms it (comparing the ἐν ἡμῖν in 1 Cor. iv. 6), since Paul must necessarily have assumed that the statements in the epistle regarding his sufferings would not fail to receive more detailed description in Philippi on the part of Epaphroditus. The rendering *de me* for the second ἐν ἐμοί, adopted by Peschito, Vulgate, Erasmus, Beza, Calvin, Grotius, and others, including Flatt, is erroneous.

CHAPTER II.

VER. 1. Instead of εἴ τι παραμ., D* L, min. have: εἴ τις παραμ. Approved by Griesb., adopted by Matth. It is nothing but a mechanical repetition of the preceding εἴ τις. The same judgment must be passed on the reading: εἴ τις σπλάγχνα, although *this* τις (instead of which the *Recepta* τινα is to be restored) has the greatly preponderant attestation of A B C D E F G K L P ℵ, min. Bas. Chrys. (?) Damasc. Oec. Theoph., and is adopted by Griesb. Matth. Scholz, Lachm. and Tisch. Τινα (as early as Clem. Al. *Strom.* iv. p. 604, Pott.; also Theodoret) is, notwithstanding its small amount of cursive attestation, we do not say absolutely necessary,[1] but requisite for such an understanding of the entire verse as naturally offers itself to the reader; see the exegetical remarks. — Ver. 3. ἤ] Lachm. and Tisch. read, and Griesb. also recommended: μηδὲ κατά, following A B C ℵ, min. vss. and Fathers. An attempt at interpretation, as are also the readings ἢ κατά, καὶ κατά, μηδὲν κατά. — Ver. 4. Elz. Scholz, have ἕκαστος in both places, which is defended also by Reiche. But ἕκαστοι, which is confirmed by preponderating testimony even before σκοποῦντες (in opposition to Hofmann), was supplanted by the singular, as only the latter occurs elsewhere in the N. T. — Elz. has σκοπεῖτε instead of σκοποῦντες, against decisive testimony. — Ver. 5. τοῦτο γάρ] A B C* ℵ*, min. vss. Fathers, Lachm. and Tisch. 8 have τοῦτο only. But what led to the omission of γάρ was, that, φρονεῖτε being subsequently read, the preceding ἕκαστοι was looked upon as the beginning of the new sentence (A C ℵ). Moreover, the commencement of a lesson at τοῦτο favoured the omission. — φρονείσθω] The reading φρονεῖτε appears to have decisive attestation from the uncials, of which only C*** K L P favour the *Recepta* φρονείσθω. But it is incredible, if the well-known and very common imperative form φρονεῖτε was the original reading, that it should have been exchanged for the otherwise

---

[1] Reiche, *Comment. crit.* p. 213, would read τι instead of τινα; but the former is found only in min., and is scarcely susceptible of a forced explanation ("*si qua est vobis*," or "*si quid valet*").—The old Latin versions, with their *si qua* or *si quid*, leave us uncertain as to their reading. But the Vulg. Lachm. has: *si quis*.

unusual passive form φρονείσθω, merely for the reason that it was sought to gain a passive form to be supplied with the following words ὁ καὶ ἐν X. Ἰ. (where the supplying of ἦν would have been sufficient). And as the very ancient testimony of most Greek authorities since Origen, also of the Goth. Copt. Arm. and nearly all min., is in favour of φρονείσθω, we must retain it as the original, which has been made to give way to the more current φρονεῖτε. The latter, however, is adopted by Tisch. 8, following Lachmann. — Ver. 9. Elz. Scholz, Tisch. 7 have ὄνομα alone instead of τὸ ὄνομα, in opposition to A B C א, 17, and several Fathers. The article has been suppressed by the preceding syllable. — Instead of ἐξομολογήσηται the future ἐξομολογήσεται is decisively attested. — Ver. 13. The article before Θεός (Elz. Scholz) is condemned by preponderating testimony. — Ver. 15. γένησθε] A D* E* F G, Vulg. It. Cypr. have ἦτε. So also Lachm. But the testimony is not decisive, and there is the more reason for defending the *Recepta*, because γένησθε might be more readily glossed by ἦτε than the converse, both in itself, and also here on account of the following ἐν οἷς φαίνεσθε κ.τ.λ. — ἀμώμητα] Lachm. Tisch. 8 have ἄμωμα, following A B C א, min. Clem. Cyr. But the latter is the *prevailing* form in the N. T., and readily crept in (comp. *var.* 2 Pet. iii. 14). — ἐν μέσῳ] A B C D* F G א, min. Clem. have μέσον. Approved by Griesb., and adopted by Lachm. and Tisch. Rightly; the *Recepta* is explanatory. — Ver. 19. κυρίῳ] Lachmann reads Χριστῷ, upon too weak authority. — Ver. 21. Elz.: τὰ τοῦ Χριστοῦ Ἰησοῦ. But τὰ Ἰησοῦ X. (Tisch.: τὰ Χριστοῦ Ἰησοῦ) has the preponderance of evidence in its favour. — Ver. 26. After ὑμᾶς, A C D E א*, min. vss. and some later Fathers have ἰδεῖν, which Lachm. places in brackets. To be adopted; because, after i. 8, its omission would be very probable, and there is no reason why it should have got in as a gloss here and not at i. 8. — Ver. 27. Elz.: ἐπὶ λύπῃ, against decisive testimony in favour of ἐπὶ λύπην. — Ver. 30. τὸ ἔργον τοῦ Χριστοῦ] Tisch. 7 reads τὸ ἔργον merely; following, indeed, only C, but correctly, for the bare τὸ ἔργον appeared to need some defining addition, which was given to it by τοῦ Χριστοῦ or Χριστοῦ (Tisch. 8), or even by κυρίου (A א). — παραβουλ.] The form παραβολ. has preponderant attestation, and is to be preferred. See the exegetical remarks.

Ver. 1. Οὖν] infers from i. 30 what is, under these circumstances, the most urgent duty of the readers. If they are engaged in the same conflict as Paul, it is all the more im-

peratively required of them by the relation of cordial affection, which must bind them to the apostle in this fellowship
that they should fulfil his joy, etc. Consequently, although,
connecting what he is about to say with what goes immediately before (in opposition to Hofmann), he certainly, after
the digression contained from ἥτις in ver. 28 onwards, leads
them back to the exhortation to *unanimity* already given in
ver. 27, to which is then subjoined in ver. 3 f. the summons to mutual *humility.* — εἴ τις κ.τ.λ.] *four* stimulative
elements, the existence of which, assumed by εἰ (comp on Col.
iii. 1), could not but forcibly bring home to the readers the
fulfilment of the apostle's joy, ver. 2.[1] With each ἐστί simply
is to be supplied (comp. iv. 8): *If there be any encouragement* *Encouragement*
in Christ, if any comfort of love, etc. It must be noticed that
these elements fall into *two parallel sections,* in each of which
the first element refers to the *objective* principle of the Christian
life (ἐν Χριστῷ and πνεύματος), and the second to the *subjective*
principle, to the specific *disposition* of the Christian (ἀγάπης
and σπλάγχνα καὶ οἰκτιρμοί). Thus the inducements to
action, involved in these four elements, are, in equal measure,
at once objectively *binding* and inwardly *affecting* (πῶς
σφοδρῶς, πῶς μετὰ συμπαθείας πολλῆς! Chrysostom). —
παρακλ. ἐν Χ.] ἐν Χ. defines the παρακλ. as *specifically Chris-*
tian, having its essence and activity in Christ; so that it
issues from living fellowship with Him, being rooted in it, and
sustained and determined by it. Thus it is *in Christ,* that
brother *exhorteth* brother. παράκλησις means *exhortation*
(1 Cor. xiv. 3; Rom. xii. 8; Acts iv. 36, ix. 31, xiii. 15,
xv. 31), *i.e.* persuasive and edifying address; the more special
interpretation *consolatio,* admissible in itself, anticipates the
correct rendering of the παραμύθιον which follows (in opposition to Vulgate, Chrysostom, Theodoret, Oecumenius, Erasmus,
Beza, Calvin, Estius, Grotius, Heinrichs, and many others;
and recently Hoelemann and Ewald). — εἴ τι παραμ. ἀγάπ.]

---

[1] Hitzig, z. *Krit. Paul. Briefe,* p. 18, very erroneously opines that there is
here a *made* excitement, an emphasis in which not so much is felt as is put
into the words; and the four times repeated *if* is to cover the defect,—in connection with which an utterly alien parallel is adduced from Tacit. *Agric.* 46.

παραμύθιον (see generally Schaefer *ad Bos.* p. 492; Lobeck *ad Phryn.* p. 517; Jacobs *ad Ach. Tat.* p. 708) corresponds to the fourth clause (σπλάγχνα κ. οἰκτ.), and for this reason, as well as because it must be different from the preceding element,[1] cannot be taken generally with Calovius, Flatt, Matthies, de Wette, Hoelemann, van Hengel, Ewald, Weiss, J. B. Lightfoot, and Hofmann as *address, exhortation* (Plat. *Legg.* vi. p. 773 E, xi. p. 880 A), but definitely as _comfort_ (Thuc. v. 103; Theocr. xxiii. 7; Anth. Pal. vii. 195, 1; Wisd. iii. 18; Esth. viii. 15; comp. παραμυθία, Plat. *Axioch.* p. 375 A; Luc. *Nigr.* 7; Ps. lxv. 12; Wisd. xix. 12; 1 Cor. xiv. 3). 'Αγάπης is the genitive of *the subject:* a consolation, *which love gives,* which flows from the brotherly love of Christians. In order to make out an allusion to the *Trinity* in the three first points, dogmatic expositors like Calovius, and also Wolf, have understood ἀγάπης of the love *of God* (to us). — εἴ τις κοινων. πν.] *if any fellowship of the Spirit* (*i.e.* participation in the Spirit) exists; comp. on 2 Cor. xiii. 13. This is to be explained of the *Holy* Spirit, not of the *animorum* conjunctio (Michaelis, Rosenmüller, am Ende, Baumgarten-Crusius, de Wette, Hoelemann, Wiesinger, Hofmann, and others; Usteri and Rilliet mix up the two), which is inconsistent with the relation of this third clause to the first (ἐν Χριστῷ), and also with the sequel, in which (ver. 2) Paul *encourages* them to *fellowship of mind,* and cannot therefore *place* it in ver. 1 as a *motive.* — εἴ τινα σπλ. κ. οἰκτ.] *if there be any heart and compassion.* The former used, as in i. 8, as the seat of cordial loving affections generally; the latter, specially as *misericordia* (see on Rom. ix. 15), which has its seat and life in the heart. See also on Col. iii. 12; comp. Luke i. 28; Tittmann, *Synon.* p. 68 f.—It must further be remarked, with regard to *all four points,* that the context, by virtue of the exhortation based upon them πληρώσατέ μου τὴν χαράν in ver. 2, certainly presupposes their existence in the Philippians, but that the

---

[1] Hofmann erroneously makes the quite arbitrary distinction that παρακλ. refers to the *will,* and παραμ. to the *feelings.* The will, feelings, and intellect are called into exercise by both. Comp., especially on παραμύθ., Stallbaum, *ad Plat. Rep.* p. 476 E; *Phaed.* p. 70 B; *Euthyd.* p. 272 B; Thuc. viii. 86, 1.

general expression (*if there is*) forms a *more moving* appeal, and is not to be limited by the addition of *in you* (Luther, Calvin, and others). Hence the idea is: "*If there is exhortation in Christ*, wherewith one brother animates and incites another to a right tone and attitude; *if there is comfort of love*, whereby one refresheth the other; *if there is fellowship in the Spirit*, which inspires right feelings, and confers the consecration of power; *if there is a heart and compassion*, issuing in sympathy with, and compassion for, the afflicted,—manifest all these towards me, in that *ye make full my joy* (μου τὴν χαράν)." Then, namely, I experience practically from you that Christian-brotherly *exhortation*,[1] and share in your *comfort of love*, and so ye put to proof, in my case, the *fellowship in the Spirit* and the *cordial sympathy*, which makes me not distressed, but glad in my painful position.—There is much that is mistaken in the views of those who defend the reading τις before σπλ. (see van Hengel and Reiche), which cannot be got rid of by the assumption of a *constructio ad synesin* (in opposition to Buttmann, *Neut. Gr.* p. 71 [E. T. 81]). Hofmann is driven by this reading, which he maintains, to the strange misinterpretation of the whole verse as if it *contained only protases and apodoses*, to be thus divided: εἴ τις οὖν παράκλησις, ἐν Χριστῷ· εἴ τι παραμύθιον, ἀγάπης· εἴ τις κοινωνία πνεύματος, εἴ τις, σπλάγχνα κ. οἰκτιρμοί; this last εἴ τις being a *repetition* of the *previous one* with an *emphasizing* of the εἰ. Accordingly the verse is supposed to mean: "If exhortation, let it be exhortation in Christ; if consolation, let it be a consolation of love; if fellowship of the Spirit, if any, let it be cordiality and compassion." A new sentence would then begin with πληρώσατε.[2] Artifices such as this can only serve to recommend the reading εἴ τινα.

---

[1] In the *application* of the general εἴ τις παράκλησις ἐν Χ., the *subjects* of this παράκλησις must, following the rule of the other elements, be the *Philippians*; Paul (Wiesinger, comp. Ewald) cannot be conceived as the παρακαλῶν.

[2] From this interpretation of the whole passage he should have been deterred by the forlorn position which is assigned to the εἴ τις before σπλάγχνα as the stone of stumbling, as well as by the purposelessness and even inappropriateness of an oddly emphasized *problematical* sense of this εἴ τις. — If it be thought that the reading εἴ τις σπλ. must be admitted, I would simply suggest the following

Ver. 2. The joy which Paul already feels in respect to the Philippians (i. 4), they are *to make full* to him, like a measure (comp. John iii. 29, xv. 11, xvii. 13; 1 John i. 4; 2 John 12; 2 Cor. x. 6). For the circumstances of the case, comp. i. 9. The μου represents, as it very often does in the N. T. (*e.g.* iv. 14; Col. iv. 18; Philem. 20), and in Greek authors, the dative of interest. — ἵνα] *The mode in which* they are to make his joy full is conceived in *telic* form, as that which is *to be striven for* in the action of making full; and in this aim of the πληροῦν the regulative standard for this activity was to consist. Paul might quite as fitly have put the τὸ αὐτὸ φρονεῖν in the imperative, and the πληροῦν τὴν χαράν in the telic form; but the immediate relation *to himself*, in which he had conceived the whole exhortation, induced him to place the πληροῦν τ. χ. in the foreground. — τὸ αὐτὸ φρονῆτε] denotes generally *harmony*, and that, indeed, more closely defined by the sequel here as *identity of sentiment*. See Tittmann, *Synon.* p. 67; Fritzsche, *ad Rom.* III. p. 87 f.; comp. Herod. i. 60, ix. 54, and the passages in Wetstein. The opposite: ἀμφὶς φρ., Hom. *Il.* xiii. 345; ἄλλη φρ., *hymn. Ap.* 469; διχοφρονεῖν, Plut. *Mor.* p. 763 E; διχόμητις, Nonn. *ev. Joh.* xx. 29; and similar forms. Hoelemann interprets τὸ αὐτό as *illud ipsum*, that, namely, which was said in ver. 1, the παράκλησις ἐν X. down to οἰκτιρμοί. This is at variance with the context (see

by way of necessary explanation of the passage :—1st, Let the verse be regarded as consisting of a series of *four protases*, on which the apodosis then follows in ver. 2; 2d, Let ἐν Χριστῷ, ἀγάπης, πνεύματος and σπλάγχνα κ. οἰκτιρμοί be taken uniformly as *predicative* specifications; 3d, Let κοινωνία be again understood with the last εἴ τις. Paul would accordingly say : " *If any exhortation is exhortation in Christ, if any comfort is comfort of love, if any fellowship is fellowship of the Spirit, if any* (fellowship) *is cordiality and compassion* (that is, full of cordiality and compassion) *fulfil ye,*" etc. The apostle would thus give to the element of the κοινωνία, besides the *objective* definition of its nature (πνεύματος, referring to the *Holy* Spirit), also a *subjective* one (σπλ. κ. οἰκτιρμ.), and mark the latter specially by the repetition of εἴ τις *sc.* κοινωνία, as well as designate it the more forcibly by the *nominative* expression (σπλάγχνα κ. οἰκτ., not another genitive), inasmuch as the latter would set forth the *ethical nature* of such a κοινωνία (comp. such passages as Rom. vii. 7, viii. 10, xiv. 17) in the form of a direct predicate. The εἰ, moreover, would remain uniformly the *syllogistic* εἰ in all the four clauses, and not, as in Hofmann's view, suddenly change into the problematic sense in the fourth clause.

the following τ. αὐτ. ἀγάπ. and ἕν φρον.), and contrary to the
wonted use of the expression elsewhere (Rom. xii. 16, xv. 5;
2 Cor. xiii. 11; Phil. iv. 2). — τὴν αὐτὴν ἀγ. ἔχ., σύμψ. τὸ
ἐν φρον.] Two more precise definitions of that like-minded-
ness, so far as it is *identity of* (mutual) *love*, and *agreement of
feeling and active impulse*, sympathy (σύμψυχοι, only found
here in the N. T.; but see Polemo, ii. 54, and comp. on i. 27,
also on ἰσόψυχον, ver. 20). This *accumulation* of definitions
indicates *earnestness;* Paul cannot sever himself from the
thought, of which his heart is so full. Comp. Chrysostom:
βαβαὶ, ποσάκις τὸ αὐτὸ λέγει ἀπὸ διαθέσεως πολλῆς! He
also well remarks on τ. αὐτ. ἀγάπ. ἔχ.: τουτέστι ὁμοίως φιλεῖν
καὶ φιλεῖσθαι. The following τὸ ἐν φρονοῦντες is to be closely
connected with σύμψ., so that σύμψυχοι has the emphasis
and adds the *more precise definition* of the previously mentioned unity of mind: *with harmony of soul cherishing the one
sentiment.* There are therefore only *two,* and not *three,* special
explanations of the τὸ αὐτὸ φρονῆτε; and ἕν *with the article*
points back to the previous τὸ αὐτό, which is now represented
by τὸ ἕν without any essential difference in sense. Expositors, not attending to this close connection of σύμψ. with τὸ
ἐν φρον. (which Wiesinger, Weiss, Ellicott, and Schenkel have
acknowledged), have either made the apostle say the very same
thing twice over (Oecumenius: διπλασιάζει τὸ ὁμοφρονεῖν), or
have drawn entirely arbitrary distinctions between τὸ αὐτό and
τὸ ἐν φρον.—*e.g.* Bengel, who makes the former refer to the
same *objects* of the sentiment, and the latter to the same *sentiment itself;* Tittmann, *l.c.,* that the former is *idem sentire, velle
et quaerere,* and the latter *in uno expetendo consentire;* Beza and
others, that the former means the agreement of *will,* the latter
the agreement in *doctrine;* while others put it inversely; Hofmann thinks that ἕν with the article means the one thing, *on
which a Christian must inwardly be bent* (comp. Luke x. 42).
It means, on the contrary, the one thing which has just been
designated by τὸ αὐτὸ φρονῆτε (as in iv. 2; Rom. xii. 16;
and other passages); the context affords no other reference for
the article. — It is usual, even in classical authors, for the
participle of a verb to stand by the side of the verb itself, in

such a way that one of the two conveys a more precise
specification. See Stallb. *ad Plat. Hipp. m.* p. 292 A; Bornemann, *ad Cyrop.* viii. 4. 9; Lobeck, *Paral.* p. 532 f.

Ver. 3 f. Μηδὲν κατὰ ἐριθ. ἢ κενοδοξ.] *sc.* φρονοῦντες (not
ποιοῦντες, Erasmus, Luther, Beza, Camerarius, Storr, am Ende,
Rheinwald, Flatt, van Hengel, and others); so that, accordingly, what was *excluded* by the previous requirement τὸ αὐτὸ
φρονῆτε . . . φρονοῦντες, is here described.   To take, as in Gal.
v. 13, μηδὲν . . . κενοδοξίαν as a prohibition *by itself*, without
dependence on φρονοῦντες (see on Gal. *l.c.*), as J. B. Lightfoot
does, is inappropriate, because the following participial antithesis discloses the dependence of the μηδὲν κ.τ.λ. on the
previous participle; hence also Hofmann's view, that there is an
intentional leaving the verb *open*, cannot be admitted.   Hoelemann combines it with ἡγούμ., and takes μηδὲν as *neutiquam*;
but incorrectly, for ἡγούμ. κ.τ.λ. affirms the esteeming others
better *than oneself*, which, therefore, cannot take place in a
factious (κατὰ ἐρίθειαν, see on i. 17) or in a vainglorious (ἢ κενοδοξίαν) way.   The κατὰ denotes that *which is regulative* of the
state of mind, and consequently its *character*, and is exchanged
in the antithetic parallel for the *dative of the instrument: by
means of humility*, the latter being by the article set down as a
generic idea (by means of the virtue of humility).   The mutual
brotherly humility (Eph. iv. 2; Col. iii. 12; Acts xx. 19) is
the *determining principle*, by which, for example, Caius is
moved to regard Lucius as standing higher, in a moral point
of view, than himself, and, on the other hand, Lucius to pro-
nounce Caius to be of a higher moral rank than himself (*i.e.*
ἀλλήλους . . . ἑαυτῶν). Hoelemann erroneously refers τῇ ταπεινο-
οφρ. to ὑπερέχ., so that it "*excellentiae* designet *praesidium*,"
—a view which the very *position* of the words should have
warned him not to adopt. — κενοδοξία] *ostentation*, only here
in the N. T.   Comp. Wisd. xiv. 14; Polyb. iii. 81. 9; Lucian,
D. Mort. x. 8, xx. 4; and see on Gal. v. 26. — Ver. 4. μὴ τὰ
ἑαυτῶν ἕκαστοι σκοπ.] The humble mind just indicated cannot
exist together with *selfishness*, which has its own interests in
view.   See instances of σκοπεῖν τὰ τινος, to be mindful of
any one's interests, in Herod. i. 8; Plat. *Phaedr.* p. 232 D;

Thuc. vi. 12. 2 ; Eur. *Supp.* 302. Comp. Lucian, *Prom.* 14 :
τἀμαυτοῦ μόνα σκοπῶ. The opposite of τὰ ἑαυτῶν σκ. may be
seen in 2 Macc. iv. 5 : τὸ δὲ συμφέρον κοινῇ . . . σκοπῶν.
Comp. ζητεῖν τὰ ἑαυτοῦ, 1 Cor. x. 24, 33, xiii. 5 ; Phil. ii. 21,
where ζητεῖν presents no essential difference in sense. Others
consider that the having regard to *gifts and merits* is intended
(Calvin, Hammond, Raphel, Keil, *Commentat.* 1803, in his
Opusc. p. 172 ff., Hoelemann, Corn. Müller), which, after the
comprehensive τῇ ταπεινοφρ. κ.τ.λ., would yield a very insipid
limitation, and one not justified by the context. — ἕκαστοι] It
is usually, and in other passages of the N. T. invariably, the
singular that is used in this distributive apposition ; the plural,
however, is not unfrequently found in classical authors. Hom.
Od. ix. 164 ; Thuc. i. 7. 1 ; Xen. *Hell.* ii. 4, 38 ; Herodian,
iii. 13, 14. — ἀλλὰ καὶ κ.τ.λ.] *a weaker* contrast than we
should have expected from the absolute negation in the first
clause ;[1] a softening modification of the idea. *In strict consistency* the καί must have been omitted (1 Cor. x. 24).
Comp. Soph. *Aj.* 1292 (1313) : ὅρα μὴ τοὐμὸν ἀλλὰ καὶ τὸ
σόν ; and see Fritzsche, *ad Marc.* p. 788 ; Winer, p. 463 f.
[E. T. 624]. The second ἕκαστοι might have been dispensed
with ; it is, however, an *earnest* repetition. — *The influences
disturbing unity* in Philippi, disclosed in vv. 2–4, are not,
according to these exhortations, of a *doctrinal* kind, nor do
they refer to the *strength and weakness* of the knowledge and
conviction of individuals, as was the case in Rome (Rom. xiv.)
and Corinth (1 Cor. viii. and x.)—in opposition to Rheinwald
and Schinz ;—but they were based upon the *jealousy of moral
self-estimation,* in which Christian perfection was respectively
ascribed and denied to one another (comp. ver. 12, iii. 12 ff.).
Although this necessarily implies a certain difference of opinion
as to the ethical *theory,* the epistle shows no trace either of
any actual *division into factions,* or of *ascetic* jealousy (which

---

[1] In which, in fact, it is not merely the *limitation* (Hofmann) to one's own that
is forbidden, as if μόνον stood along with it. What Hofmann at the same time
deduces from the reading ἕκαστος (before σκοποῦντες), which he follows, as distinguished from the subsequent ἕκαστοι (with a here wholly irrelevant comparison of Plat. *Apol.* p. 39 A), is sophistical, and falls, moreover, with the reading
itself.

de Wette assumes as co-operating).   But the exhortations to unity are too frequent (i. 27, ii. 2 f., iii. 15, iv. 2 f.) and too urgent to justify us in questioning generally the existence (Weiss) of those disturbances of harmony, or in regarding them as mere *ill humour* and *isolation* disturbing the cordial fellowship of life (Hofmann).   Comp. Huther, in the *Mecklenb. Zeitschr.* 1862, p. 640 ff.

Ver. 5. Enforcement of the precept contained in ver. 3 f. by *the example of Jesus* (comp. Rom. xv. 3 ; 1 Pet. ii. 21 ; Clem. *Cor.* I. 16), who, full of humility, *kept not His own interest in view*, but in self-renunciation and self-humiliation sacrificed it, even to the endurance of the death of the cross, and was therefore exalted by God to the highest glory ;[1] this extends to ver. 12.   See on this passage Kesler in *Thes. nov. ex mus. Has. et Iken.* II. p. 947 f. ; Schultens, *Dissertatt. philol.* I. p. 443 ff. ; Keil, two *Commentat.* 1803 (*Opusc.* p. 172 ff.) ; Martini, in Gabler's *Journ. f. auserl. theol. Lit.* IV. p. 34 ff. ; von Ammon, *Magaz. f. Pred.* II. 1, p. 7 ff. ; Kraussold in the *Annal. d. gesammt. Theol.* 1835, II. p. 273 ff. ; Stein in the *Stud. u. Krit.* 1837, p. 165 ff. ; Philippi, *d. thätige Gehors. Chr.* Berl. 1841, p. 1 ff. ; Tholuck, *Disp. Christol. de l. Phil.* ii. 6–9, Halle 1848 ; Ernesti in the *Stud. u. Krit.* 1848, p. 858 ff., and 1851, p. 595 ff. ; Baur in the *theol. Jahrb.* 1849, p. 502 ff., and 1852, p. 133 ff., and in his *Paulus*, II. p. 51 ff. ed. 2 ; Liebner, *Christol.* p. 325 ff. ; Raebiger, *Christol. Paulin.* p. 76 ff. ; Lechler, *Apost. u. nachapost. Zeitalt.* p. 58 ff. ; Schneckenburger in the *Deutsch. Zeitschr.* 1855, p. 333 ff. ; Wetzel in the *Monatschr. f. d. Luth. Kirche Preuss.* 1857 ; Kähler in the *Stud. u. Krit.* 1857, p. 99 ff. ; Beyschlag in the *Stud. u. Krit.* 1860, p. 431 ff., and his *Christol. d. N. T.* 1866, p. 233 ff. ; Rich. Schmidt, *Paul. Christol.* 1870, p. 163 ff. ; J. B. Lightfoot's Excursus, p. 125 ff. ; Pfleiderer in Hilgenfeld's *Zeitschr.*

---

[1] Christ's example, therefore, in this passage is one of *self-denial*, and not of *obedience to God* (Ernesti), in which, in truth, the self-denial only manifested itself along with other things.   It is, however, shown by the very addition of *καί*, that Paul really intended to adduce the *example* of Christ (in opposition to Hofmann's view) ; comp. Rom. xv. 3.   Christ's *example* is the moral, ideal, historically realized.   Comp. Wuttke, *Sittenl.* II. § 224 ; Schmid, *Sittenl.* p. 355 ff. ; and as early as Chrysostom.

1871, p. 519 ff.; Grimm in the same *Zeitschr.* 1873, p. 33 ff.
Among the more recent dogmatic writers, Thomasius, II. p.
148 ff.; Philippi, IV. 1, p. 469 ff.; Kahnis, I. p. 458 ff.
— φρονείσθω ἐν ὑμ.] *sentiatur in animis vestris.* The parallelism
with the ἐν which follows prohibits our interpreting it *intra
vestrum caetum* (Hoelemann, comp. Matthies). The *passive*
mode of expression is unusual elsewhere, though logically
unassailable. Hofmann, rejecting the passive reading, as also
the passive supplement afterwards, has sadly misunderstood
the entire passage.[1] — ὃ καὶ ἐν X. 'I.] *sc.* ἐφρονήθη. On ἐν,
comp. the Homeric ἐνὶ φρεσί, ἐνὶ θυμῷ, which often occurs
with φρονεῖν, *Od.* xiv. 82, vi. 313; *Il.* xxiv. 173. καί is not
cum maxime, but the simple *also* of the comparison (in opposition to van Hengel), namely, of the pattern of Christ.

Ver. 6. The classical passage which now follows is like an
Epos in calm majestic objectivity; nor does it lack an epic
minuteness of detail. — ὅς] epexegetical; subject of what
follows; consequently Christ Jesus, but in *the pre-human state,*
in which He, the Son of God, and therefore according to the
Johannine expression as the λόγος ἄσαρκος, was with God.[2]

---

[1] Reading φρονεῖτε, and subsequently explaining the ἐν Χριστῷ Ἰησοῦ as a frequent
expression with Paul for the ethical Christian quality (like ἐν κυρίῳ in iv. 2),
Hofmann makes the apostle say that the readers are to *have their mind so directed
within them, that it shall not be lacking in this definite quality which makes it
Christian.* Thus there would be evolved, when expressed in simple words,
merely the thought: "Have in you *the* mind which is also the Christian
one." As if the grand outburst, which immediately follows, would be in harmony
with such a general idea! This outburst has its very ground in the lofty
example of the Lord. And what, according to Hofmann's view, is the purpose of
the significant καί? It would be entirely *without correlation* in the text; for in ἐν
ὑμῖν the ἐν would have to be taken as *local,* and in the ἐν Χριστῷ, according to that
misinterpretation, it would have to be taken in the sense of *ethical fellowship,*
and thus relations *not at all analogous* would be marked.

[2] That Christ in His Trinitarian pre-existence was already the eternal *Principle and Prototype of humanity* (as is urged by Beyschlag), is self-evident; for
otherwise He would have been one essentially different from Him who in the
fulness of time appeared in the flesh. But this does not entitle us to refer the
pre-existence to His *whole divine-human person,* and to speak of an *eternal
humanity,*—paradoxes which cannot exegetically be justified by our passage and
other expressions such as 1 Cor. xv. 47; Rom. v. 12 ff., viii. 29; Col. i. 15.
The Logos pre-existed as the *divine* principle and *divine* prototype of humanity;
Θεὸς ἦν ὁ λόγος, and this, apart from the form of expression, is also the teaching

The *human* state is first introduced by the words ἑαυτὸν ἐκένωσε in ver. 7. So Chrysostom and his successors, Beza, Zanchius, Vatablus, Castalio, Estius, Clarius, Calixtus, Semler, Storr, Keil, Usteri, Kraussold, Hoelemann, Rilliet, Corn. Müller, and most expositors, including Lünemann, Tholuck, Liebner, Wiesinger, Ernesti, Thomasius, Raebiger, Ewald, Weiss, Kahnis, Beyschlag (1860), Schmid, *Bibl. Theol.* II. p. 306, Messner, *Lehre d. Ap.* 233 f., Lechler, Gess, *Person Chr.* p. 80 f., Rich. Schmidt, *l.c.*, J. B. Lightfoot, Grimm; comp. also Hofmann and Düsterdieck, *Apolog. Beitr.* III. p. 65 ff. It has been objected (see especially de Wette and Philippi, also Beyschlag, 1866, and Dorner in *Jahrb. f. D. Th.* 1856, p. 394 f.), that the name *Christ Jesus* is opposed to this view; also, that in vv. 8–11 it is the exaltation of the *earthly* Christ that is spoken of (and not the return of the Logos to the divine δόξα); and that the *earthly* Christ only could be held up as a *pattern*. But Χριστὸς Ἰησοῦς, as subject, is all the more justly used (comp. 2 Cor. viii. 9; 1 Cor. viii. 6; Col. i. 14 ff.; 1 Cor. x. 4), since the subject not of the pre-human glory *alone*, but at the same time also of the human abasement[1] and of the subsequent exaltation, was to be named. Paul joins on to ὅς the *whole summary* of the history of our Lord, including His pre-human state (comp. 2 Cor. viii. 9 : ἐπτώχευσε πλούσιος ὤν); therefore vv. 8–11 cannot by themselves regulate our view as regards the definition of the subject; and the force of the *example*, which certainly *comes first to light* in the historical Christ, has at once historically and ethically its deepest root in, and derives its highest, because divine (comp. Matt. v. 48; Eph. v. 1), obligation from, just what is said in ver. 6 of His state *before* His human appearance. Moreover, as the context introduces the incarnation only at ver. 7, and introduces it as that by which the subject divested Himself of His divine appearance, and as the earthly Jesus never was in the form of

---

of Paul. Only *in time* could He enter upon the *human existence;* the notion of *eternal* humanity would refute itself.

[1] Hence Philippi's objection, that φρονεῖν is elsewhere applied to *man* only, and not to *God*, is devoid of significance. Unfounded is also Beyschlag's objection (1866) drawn from the word σχήματι; see below.

God (comp. Gess, p. 295), it is incorrect, because at variance
with the text and illogical, though in harmony with Lutheran
orthodoxy and its antagonism to the Kenosis of the Logos,[1]
to regard the *incarnate historical* Christ, the λόγος ἔνσαρκος, as
the subject meant by ὅς (Novatian, *de Trin.* 17, Ambrosiaster,
Pelagius, Erasmus, Luther, Calvin, Cameron, Piscator, Hunnius,
Grotius, Calovius, Clericus, Bengel, Zachariae, Kesler, and
others, including Heinrichs, Baumgarten-Crusius, van Hengel,
de Wette, Schneckenburger, Philippi, Beyschlag (1866), Dorner, and others; see the historical details in Tholuck, p. 2 ff.,
and J. B. Lightfoot). Liebner aptly observes that our passage
is "*the Pauline* ὁ λόγος σὰρξ ἐγένετο ;" comp. on Col. i. 15. —
ἐν μορφῇ Θεοῦ ὑπάρχων] not to be resolved, as usually, into
"*although*, etc.," which could only be done in accordance with
the context, if the ἁρπαγμὸν ἡγεῖσθαι κ.τ.λ. could be presupposed as something proper or natural to the being in the
form of God; nor does it indicate the *possibility* of His divest-
ing Himself of His divine appearance (Hofmann), which was
self-evident; but it simply *narrates* the former divinely glorious
position which He afterwards gave up: *when He found Himself
in the form of God,* by which is characterized Christ's pre-
human form of existence. Then He was forsooth, and that
objectively, not merely in God's self-consciousness—as the not
yet incarnate Son (Rom. i. 3, 4, viii. 3; Gal. iv. 4), according
to John as λόγος—with God, in the fellowship of the glory
of God (comp. John xvii. 5). It is this divine glory, in which
He found Himself as ἴσα Θεῷ ὤν and also εἰκὼν Θεοῦ—as such
also the instrument and aim of the creation of the world, Col.
i. 15 f.—and into which, by means of His exaltation, He again
returned; so that this divine δόξα, as the possessor of which
before the incarnation He had, without a body and invisible to

---

[1] According to which Christ had the full divine majesty "statim in sua con-
ceptione, etiam in utero matris" (*Form. Conc.* p. 767). But He had it in His
state of humiliation *secreto,* and only manifested it occasionally, *quoties ipsi
visum fuerit.* In opposition to this, Liebner rightly observes, p. 334 : "This is
altogether inadequate to express the powerful N. T. feeling of the depth and
greatness of our Lord's humiliation. This feeling unmistakeably extends to the
unique personal essence of the God-man, and in conformity with this, to the
very heart of the act of incarnation itself."

the eye of man (comp. Philo, *de Somn.* I. p. 655), the form of God, is now by means of His glorified body and His divine-human perfection visibly possessed by Him, that He may *appear* at the παρουσία, not again without it, but in and with it (iii. 20 f.). Comp. 2 Cor. iv. 4; Col. i. 15, iii. 4. Μορφή, therefore, which is an appropriate concrete expression for the divine δόξα (comp. Justin, *Apol.* I. 9), as the glory visible at the throne of God, and not a "fanciful expression" (Ernesti), is neither equivalent to φύσις or οὐσία (Chrysostom, Theodoret, Oecumenius, Theophylact, Augustine, Chemnitz, and many others; comp. also Rheinwald and Corn. Müller); nor to *status* (Calovius, Storr, and others); nor is it the godlike *capacity* for *possible equality with God* (Beyschlag), an interpretation which ought to have been precluded both by the literal notion of the word μορφή, and by the contrast of μορφὴ δούλου in ver. 7. But the μορφὴ Θεοῦ presupposes[1] the divine φύσις as ὁμόστολος μορφῆς (Aesch. *Suppl.* 496), and *more precisely* defines the divine status, namely, as *form of being,* corresponding to the essence, consequently to the homoousia, and *exhibiting* the condition, so that μορφὴ Θεοῦ finds its exhaustive explanation in Heb. i. 3 : ἀπαύγασμα τῆς δόξης κ. χαρακτὴρ τῆς ὑποστάσεως τοῦ Θεοῦ, this, however, being here conceived as predicated of the *pre-existent* Christ. In Plat. *Rep.* ii. p. 381 C, μορφή is also to be taken strictly in its literal signification, and not less so in Eur. *Bacch.* 54; Ael. *H. A.* iii. 24; Jos. *c. Ap.* ii. 16, 22. Comp. also Eur. *Bacch.* 4: μορφὴν ἀμείψας ἐκ Θεοῦ βροτησίαν, Xen. *Cyr.* i. 2. 2: φύσιν μὲν δὴ τῆς ψυχῆς κ. τῆς μορφῆς. What is here called μορφὴ Θεοῦ is εἶδος Θεοῦ in John v. 37 (comp. Plat. *Rep.* p. 380 D; Plut. *Mor.* p. 1013 C), which the Son also essentially possessed in His prehuman δόξα (John xvii. 5). The explanation of φύσις was promoted among the Fathers by the opposition to Arius and a

---

[1] Bengel well says: "Ipsa natura divina decorem habebat infinitum, in se, etiam sine ulla creatura illum decorem intuente."—What Paul here designates simply by ἐν μορφῇ Θεοῦ ὑπάρχων is pompously expressed by Clement, *Cor.* I. 16: τὸ σκῆπτρον τῆς μεγαλωσύνης τοῦ Θεοῦ. The *forma mentis aeterna,* however, in Tacitus, *Agric.* 46, is a conception utterly foreign to our passage (although adduced here by Hitzig), and of similar import with Propertius, iii. 1, 64: "ingenio stat sine morte decus."

number of other heretics, as Chrysostom adduces them in triumph ; hence, also, there is much polemical matter in them. For the later controversy with the Socinians, see Calovius. — ὑπάρχων] designating more expressly than ὤν the relation of the *subsisting state* (iii. 20 ; Luke vii. 25, xvi. 23 ; 2 Pet. iii. 11) ; and hence not at all merely *in the decree of God*, or in the divine *self-consciousness* (Schenkel). The *time* is that of the *pre-human* existence. See above on ὅς. Those who under-stand it as referring to His *human* existence (comp. John i. 14) think of the divine majesty, which Jesus manifested both *by word and deed* (Ambrosiaster, Luther, Erasmus, Heinrichs, Krause, *Opusc.* p. 33, and others), especially by His *miracles* (Grotius, Clericus) ; while Wetstein and Michaelis even suggest that the *transfiguration on the mount* is intended. It would be more in harmony with the context to understand the pos-session of the complete divine image (without arbitrarily limiting this, by preference possibly, to the *moral* attributes alone, as de Wette and Schneckenburger do)—a possession which Jesus ("as the God-pervaded man," Philippi) had (*poten-tialiter*) *from the* very *beginning* of His earthly life, but in a *latent* manner, without manifesting it. This view, however, would land them in difficulty with regard to the following ἑαυτ. ἐκένωσε κ.τ.λ., and expose them to the risk of insert-ing limiting clauses at variance with the literal import of the passage ; see below. — οὐχ ἁρπαγμὸν ἡγήσατο τὸ εἶναι ἴσα Θεῷ] In order to the right explanation, it is to be ob-served : (1) that the emphasis is placed on ἁρπαγμόν, and therefore (2) that τὸ εἶναι ἴσα Θεῷ cannot be something essen-tially different from ἐν μορφῇ Θεοῦ ὑπάρχειν, but must in sub-stance denote the same thing, namely, the divine *habitus* of Christ, which is expressed, as to its *form of appearance*, by ἐν μορφῇ Θεοῦ ὑπάρχ., and, as to its internal *nature*, by τὸ εἶναι ἴσα Θεῷ ;[1] (3) lastly, that ἁρπαγμός does not mean *praeda*, or

---

[1] An entirely groundless objection has been made (even by Lünemann) against the view which takes τὸ εἶναι ἴσα Θεῷ as not essentially different from ἐν μορφῇ Θεοῦ εἶναι, viz. that Paul would, instead of τὸ εἶναι ἴσα Θεῷ, have written merely τοῦτο, or even nothing at all. He *might* have done so, but there was no *neces-sity* for his taking that course, least of all for *Paul!* He, on the contrary, distinguishes very precisely and suitably between the two ideas representing

that which is seized on (which would be ἀρπάγιμον, Callim.
Cer. 9 ; Pallad. *ep.* 87 ; Philop. 79 ; or ἅρπαγμα or ἅρπασμα,
and might also be ἀρπαγή), or *that which one forcibly snatches
to himself* (Hofmann and older expositors) ; but actively :
robbing, making booty. In this sense, which is *à priori* probable
from the termination of the word which usually serves to
indicate an *action*, it is used, beyond doubt, in the only profane
passage in which it is extant, Plut. *de pueror. educ.* 15 (*Mor.*
p. 12 A) : καὶ τοὺς μὲν Θήβησι καὶ τοὺς Ἠλίδι φευκτέον ἔρωτας
καὶ τὸν ἐκ Κρήτης καλούμενον ἀρπαγμόν, where it denotes the
Cretan kidnapping of children. It is accordingly to be explained : *Not as a robbing did He consider*[1] *the being equal with
God, i.e.* He did not place it under the point of view of making
booty, as if it was, with respect to its exertion of activity, to
consist *in His seizing what did not belong to Him.* In opposition to Hofmann's earlier logical objection (*Schriftbew.* I.
p. 149) that one cannot consider the *being* as a *doing*, comp.
1 Tim. vi. 5 ; and see Hofmann himself, who has now recognised the linguistically correct explanation of ἀρπαγμός, but
leaves the object of the ἀρπάζειν indefinite, though the latter
must necessarily be something that belongs to *others*, consequently a *foreign* possession. Not otherwise than in the
active sense, namely *raptus*, can we explain Cyril, *de adorat.* I.
p. 25 (in Wetstein) : οὐχ ἀρπαγμὸν[2] τὴν παραίτησιν ὡς ἐξ
ἀδρανοῦς καὶ ὑδαρεστέρας ἐποιεῖτο φρενός ; further, Eus. *in
Luc.* vi. in Mai's *Nov. Bibl. patr.* iv. p. 165, and the passage
in Possini *Cat. in Marc.* x. 42, p. 233, from the Anonym.
Tolos. : ὅτι οὐκ ἔστιν ἀρπαγμὸς ἡ τιμή ;[3] as also the entirely
synonymous form ἀρπασμός in Plut. *Mor.* p. 644 A, and λήϊσμος

the same state, by saying that Christ, in His divine pre-human *form of life*,
did not venture to use this His God-equal *being* for making booty. Both, therefore, express the very same divine *habitus ;* but the εἶναι ἴσα Θεῷ is the general
element, which presents itself in the divine μορφή as its *substratum* and lies at
its basis, so that the two designations *exhaust* the idea of divinity. Comp.
also Liebner, p. 328.

[1] On ἡγεῖσθαι, in this sense of the *mode of regarding*, which places the
object under the point of view of a qualitative category, comp. Krüger on *Thuc.*
ii. 44. 3.

[2] Lot did not let the refusal of the angels be a *making of profit* to himself.

[3] Where, according to the connection, the sense is : Not a *seizing to oneself*

in Byzantine writers; also σκυλευμός in Eustathius; comp. Phryn. *App.* 36, where ἁρπαγμός is quoted as equivalent to ἅρπασις. The passages which are adduced for ἅρπαγμα ἡγεῖσθαι or ποιεῖσθαί τι (Heliod. vii. 11. 20, viii. 7; Eus. *H. E.* viii. 12; *Vit. C.* ii. 31)—comp. the Latin *praedam ducere* (Cic. *Verr.* v. 15; Justin, ii. 5. 9, xiii. 1. 8)—do not fall under the same mode of conception, as they represent the relation in question as something *made a booty of,* and not as the *act of making booty.* We have still to notice (1) that this οὐχ ἁρπαγμὸν ἡγήσατο corresponds exactly to μὴ τὰ ἑαυτῶν σκοποῦντες (ver. 4), as well as to its contrast ἑαυτὸν ἐκένωσε in ver. 7 (see on ver. 7); and (2) that the *aorist* ἡγήσατο, indicating a definite point of time, undoubtedly, according to the connection (see the contrast, ἀλλ᾿ ἑαυτὸν ἐκένωσε κ.τ.λ.), transports the reader to *that moment, when the pre-existing Christ was on the point of coming into the world with the being equal to God.* Had He then thought: " When I shall have come into the world, I will seize to myself, by means of my equality with God, power and dominion, riches, pleasure, worldly glory," then He would have acted the part of ἁρπαγμὸν ἡγεῖσθαι τὸ εἶναι ἴσα Θεῷ; to which, however, He did not consent, but consented, on the contrary, to self-renunciation, etc. It is accordingly self-evident that the supposed case of the ἁρπαγμός is not conceived as an action of the pre-existing Christ (as Richard Schmidt objects), but is put as connecting itself with His appearance on earth. The *reflection,* of which the pre-existent Christ is, according to our passage, represented as capable, even in presence of the will of God (see below, γενόμ. ὑπήκοος), although the apostle has only conceived it as an abstract possibility and expressed it in an anthropopathic mode of presentation, is decisive in favour of the *personal* pre-existence; but in this pre-existence the Son appears as *subordinate* to the Father, as He does throughout the entire New Testament, although this is not (as Beyschlag objects) at variance with the Trinitarian equality of essence in the Biblical sense. By the ἁρπαγμὸν ἡγεῖσθαι κ.τ.λ., if it had taken place, He would have wished to *relieve* Himself from this

is the position of honour, as among the *heathen,* but a *renouncing and serving* after the example of *Christ.*

subordination.—The linguistic correctness and exact apposite correlation of the whole of this explanation, which harmonizes with 2 Cor. viii. 9,[1] completely exclude the interpretation, which is traditional but in a linguistic point of view is quite incapable of proof, that ἁρπαγμός, either in itself or by metonymy (in which van Hengel again appeals quite inappropriately to the analogy of Jas. i. 2, 2 Pet. iii. 15), means *praeda* or *res rapienda*. With this interpretation of ἁρπαγμός, the idea of εἶναι ἴσα Θεῷ has either been rightly taken as practically *identical* with ἐν μορφῇ Θεοῦ ὑπάρχειν, or *not*. (A) In the *former* case, the point of comparison of the figurative *praeda* has been very differently defined : *either*, that Christ regarded the existence equal with God, not as a something usurped and illegitimate, but as something *natural* to Him, and that, therefore, He did not fear to lose it through His humiliation (Chrysostom, Oecumenius, Theophylact, Augustine, and other Fathers ; see Wetstein and J. B. Lightfoot) ; comp. Beza, Calvin, Estius, and others, who, however, give to the conception a different turn ;[2] *or*, that He did not desire *pertinaciously to retain for Himself* this equality with God, as a robber his booty, or as an unexpected gain (Ambrosiaster, Castalio, Vatablus, Kesler, and others ; and recently, Hoelemann, Tholuck, Reuss,

---

[1] Räbiger and Wetzel, and also Pfleiderer, *l.c.*, have lately adopted this view ; likewise Kolbe in the *Luther. Zeitschr.* 1873, p. 311 f. Hofmann also now explains the passage in a way not substantially different. But Grimm, *l.c.* p. 38, very unjustly describes the retention of ἁρπαγμός in the sense which it has in Plutarch, as petty grammatical pedantry. The ideas, *spoil, booty*, occur in countless instances in all Greek authors, and in the LXX., and are very variously expressed (ἁρπαγή, ἅρπαγμα, ἅρπασμα, ληῖς, σκύλευμα, σῦλον, λεία), but never by ἁρπαγμός, or any other form of word ending with μος. It is true that various substantives ending in μος may denote the result of the action ; not, however, as we may be pleased to assume, but solely in accordance with evidence of *empirical usage*, and this is just what is wanting for this sense in the case of ἁρπαγμός. Its rejection, therefore, in our passage, is not *pedantic*, but is simply *linguistically demanded*. Weiss, *bibl. Theol.* p. 426, ed. 2, erroneously objects to our view of ἁρπαγμός, that, in that case, it would be impossible to conceive of *any object*, and that thus an utterly empty antithesis to the giving up of Christ's own possession is the result. As if there were not given in the very notion of ἁρπαγμός its object, viz. that which does not belong to the subject of the action, and this, indeed, in its unrestricted and full compass, just because nothing special is added as an object.

[2] Beza : "Non ignoravit, se in ea re (*i.e.* quod Deo Patri coaequalis esset)

Liebner, Schmid, Wiesinger, Gess, Messner, Grimm ; comp. also
Usteri, p. 314) ;[1] *or*, that He did not *conceal it*, as a prey
(Matthies) ; *or*, that He did not desire *to display it triumphantly*,
as a conqueror his spoils (Luther, Erasmus, Cameron, Vatablus,
Piscator, Grotius, Calovius, Quenstedt, Wolf, and many others,
including Michaelis, Zachariae, Rosenmüller, Heinrichs, Flatt,
Rheinwald) ;[2] whilst others (Wetstein the most strangely, but
also Usteri and several) *mix up* very *various* points of comparison.
The very circumstance, however, that there exists so much
divergence in these attempts at explanation, shows how arbitrarily men have endeavoured to supply a *modal definition* for
ἁρπ. ἡγήσ., which is not at all suggested by the text.—(B) In
the *second* case, in which a *distinction is made* between τὸ εἶναι
ἴσα Θεῷ and ἐν μορφῇ Θεοῦ ὑπάρχειν, it is explained : *non
rapinam duxit*, i.e. *non rapiendum sibi duxit*, or directly, *non
rapuit* (Musculus, Er. Schmidt, Elsner, Clericus, Bengel, and
many others, including am Ende, Martini, Krause, *Opusc.* p. 31,
Schrader, Stein, Rilliet, van Hengel, Baumgarten-Crusius, de
Wette, Ernesti, Raebiger, Schneckenburger, Ewald, Weiss, Schenkel, Philippi, Thomasius, Beyschlag, Kahnis, Rich. Schmidt, and
others) ; that Christ, namely, though being ἐν μορφῇ Θεοῦ, did
not desire to seize to Himself the εἶναι ἴσα Θεῷ, to grasp eagerly

nullam injuriam cuiquam facere, sed suo jure uti ; *nihilominus tamen* quasi *jure
suo cessit.*" So also Calvin, substantially, only that he erroneously interprets
ἡγήσατο as *arbitratus esset*, "Non fuisset injuria, si aequalis Deo apparuisset."
Estius : "that He had not recognised the equality with God as an *usurped*
possession, and *therefore* possibly desired to lay it aside, but had renounced
Himself," etc.

[1] In this class we must reckon the interpretation of Theodoret (comp.
Origen, *ad Rom.* v. 2, x. 7, Eusebius, and others) : that Christ, being God by
nature, did not hold His equality with God as something specially great, as
those do who attain to honours παρ᾽ ἀξίαν ; but that He, τὴν ἀξίαν κατακρύψας,
chose humiliation. To this comes also the view of Theodore of Mopsuestia :
μορφὴν γὰρ δούλου λαβὼν τὴν ἀξίαν ἐκείνην ἀπέκρυψεν, τοῦτο τοῖς ὁρῶσιν εἶναι νομιζόμενος,
ὅπερ ἐφαίνετο.—Tholuck compares the German expression : *als ein gefundenes
Essen* (*einen guten Fund*) *ansehen*. According to him, the idea of the whole
passage is, "Tantum aberat, ut Christus, quatenus λόγος est, in gloria atque
beatitate sua acquiescere sibique soli placere vellet, ut amore erga mortales
ductus servi formam induere ac vel infimam sortem subire sine ulla haesitatione
sustineret."

[2] To this belongs also Pelagius, "Quod erat, humilitate *celavit*, dans nobis
exemplum, ne in his *gloriemur*, quae forsitan non habemus."

the possession of it.[1] In this view expositors have understood the *ἴσα εἶναι Θεῷ* as the divine *plenitudinem et altitudinem* (Bengel) ; the *sessionem ad dextram* (L. Bos) ; the divine *honour* (Cocceius, Stein, de Wette, Grau) ; the *vitam vitae Dei aequalem* (van Hengel) ; the *existendi modum cum Deo aequalem* (Lünemann) ; the *coli et beate vivere ut Deus* (Krause) ; the *dominion on earth as a visible God* (Ewald) ; the divine *autonomy* (Ernesti) ; the *heavenly dignity and glory* entered on after the ascension (Raebiger, comp. Thomasius, Philippi, Beyschlag, Weiss), corresponding to the *ὄνομα τὸ ὑπὲρ πᾶν ὄνομα* in ver. 9 (Rich. Schmidt) ; the *nova jura divina*, consisting in the *κυριότης πάντων* (Brückner) ; the divine *δόξα* of universal *adoration* (Schneckenburger, Lechler, comp. Messner) ; the *original blessedness of the Father* (Kahnis) ; indeed, even the *identity* with the Father consisting in *invisibility* (Rilliet), and the like, which is to sustain to the *μορφὴ Θεοῦ* the relation of a *plus*, or *something separable*, or only to be obtained *at some future time* by humiliation and suffering[2] (ver. 9). So, also, Sabatier, *l' apôtre Paul*, 1870, p. 223 ff.[3] In order to meet the *οὐχ ἁρπ. ἡγ.* (comparing Matt. iv. 8 ff.), de Wette (comp.

---

[1] So also Lünemann, who, in the sense of the divine pre-existence of Christ, paraphrases thus : " Christus, etsi ab aeterno inde dignitate creatoris et domini rerum omnium frueretur, ideoque divina indutus magnificentia coram patre consideret, nihilo tamen minus haud arripiendum sibi esse autumabat existendi modum cum Deo aequalem, sed ultro se exinanivit." In a sense *opposed* to the divine pre-existence, however, Beyschlag says, *Christol.* p. 236 f. : " Christ *possessed* the *μορφὴ Θεοῦ* (that is, 'the inner form of God') ; He *might* have but *stretched out His hand* towards the *ἴσα Θεῷ εἶναι* ; He disdained, however, to *seize* it for Himself, and chose quite the opposite ; therefore it was given Him as the reward of His obedience, etc." Hilgenfeld, in his *Zeitschrift*, 1871, p. 197 f., says : the Pauline Christ is indeed the *heavenly man*, but no divine being ; the *equality with God* was attained by Him only through the renunciation, etc.

[2] The lead in this mode of considering the passage was taken by Arius, whose party, on the ground of the proposition *ἐκεῖνο ἁρπάζει τις, ὃ οὐκ ἔχει*, declared : *ὅτι Θεὸς ὢν ἐλάττων οὐχ ἥρπασε τὸ εἶναι ἴσα τῷ Θεῷ τῷ μεγάλῳ κ. μείζονι.* See Chrysostom.

[3] He thinks that the divine *μορφή* of Christ stands to the *ἴσα εἶναι Θεῷ* in the relation of *potentia* to *actus*. "Christ était des l'origine *en puissance* ce qu' à la fin il devint *en réalité ;*" the *μορφὴ Θεοῦ* denotes the general form of being of Christ, but "une forme vide, qui doit être remplie, c'est-à-dire spirituellement réalisée." This higher position He had not wished to usurp, but had attained to it "réellement par le libre développement de sa vie morale."

Hofmann, *Schriftbew.* p. 151) makes the thought be supplied, that it was not in the aim of the work of redemption befitting that Christ should at the very outset receive divine honour, and that, if He *had taken* it to Himself, it would have been a *seizure*, an usurpation.   But as ἐν μορφῇ Θεοῦ ὑπ. already involves the divine essence,[1] and as ἴσα εἶναι Θεῷ has no distinctive more special definition in any manner climactic (comp. Pfleiderer), Chrysostom has estimated this whole mode of explanation very justly : εἰ ἦν Θεός, πῶς εἶχεν ἁρπάσαι ; καὶ πῶς οὐκ ἀπερινόητον τοῦτο ; τίς γὰρ ἂν εἴποι, ὅτι ὁ δεῖνα ἄνθρωπος ὤν οὐχ ἥρπασε τὸ εἶναι ἄνθρωπος ; πῶς γὰρ ἄν τις ὅπερ ἐστὶν, ἁρπάσειεν.   Moreover, in harmony with the thought and the state of the case, Paul must have expressed himself conversely : ὃς ἴσα Θεῷ ὑπάρχων οὐχ ἁρπ. ἡγ. τὸ εἶναι ἐν μορφῇ Θεοῦ, so as to add to the idea of the equality of *nature* (ἴσα), by way of climax, that of the same *form of appearance* (μορφή), of the divine δόξα also.—With respect to τὸ εἶναι ἴσα Θεῷ, it is to be observed, (1) that ἴσα is *adverbial : in like manner*, as we find it, although less frequently, in Attic writers (Thuc. iii. 14 ; Eur. *Or.* 880 *al.* ; comp. ὁμοῖα, Lennep. *ad Phalar.* 108), and often in the later Greek, and in the LXX. (Job v. 14, x. 10, xi. 12, xiii. 12 ; Wisd. vii. 3, according to the usual reading). This adverbial use has arisen from the frequent employment, even so early as Homer (*Il.* v. 71, xv. 439; *Od.* xi. 304, xv. 519 *al.*), of ἴσα as the case of the object or predicate (see Ellendt, *Lex. Soph.* I. p. 847 ; Krüger, II. § xlvi. 6. 8).   But as εἶναι, as the abstract substantive verb, does not suit the *adverbial* ἴσα, *pari ratione*, therefore (2) τὸ εἶναι must be taken in the sense of *existere ;* so that τὸ εἶναι ἴσα Θεῷ does not mean *the being equal to God* (which would be τὸ εἶναι ἴσον Θεῷ), but *the God-equal existence*, existence in the way of parity with God.[2]   Paul might have written ἴσον (as mascul.) Θεῷ (John v. 18), or ἰσόθεον ; but, as it stands, he has more distinctly expressed the *metaphysical* relation, the *divine mode of*

---

[1] Not merely the *similarity*, from which is there distinguished the *equality* by εἶναι ἴσα (in opposition to Martini and others).

[2] [The German is : nicht *das Gotte gleich sein*, sondern *das gottgleiche Sein*, das Sein auf gottgleiche Weise, *die gottgleiche Existenz.*]

existence,[1] of the pre-human Christ. (3) The *article* points back to ἐν μορφῇ Θεοῦ ὑπάρχων, denoting the God-equal existence *manifesting itself in that* μορφή; for the μορφὴ Θεοῦ is the *appearance*, the adequate subsisting *form*, of the God-equal *existence*. (4) Ernesti (in controversy with Baur), who is followed by Kähler, Kahnis, Beyschlag, and Hilgenfeld, entertains the groundless opinion that our passage alludes to Gen. ii. f., the ἴσα εἶναι Θεῷ pointing in particular to Gen. iii. 5. In the text there is no trace[2] of any comparison of Christ with the first human beings, not even an echo of like expression; how different from the equality with God in our passage is the ἔσεσθε ὡς θεοί in Gen. iii. 5! Certainly, any such comparison lay very remote from the sublime idea of the divine glory of the pre-existent Christ, which was something quite different from the image of God in the first human beings. Comp. also Rich. Schmidt, p. 172; Grimm, p. 42 f.

Ver. 7. Ἀλλ' ἑαυτὸν ἐκένωσε] The emphatically prefixed ἑαυτόν is correlative to the likewise emphatic ἁρπαγμόν in ver. 6. Instead of the ἁρπάζειν, by which he would have entered upon a *foreign* domain, He has, on the contrary, emptied *Himself*, and that, as the context places beyond doubt, of *the divine* μορφή, which He possessed but now exchanged for a μορφὴ δούλου; He renounced the divine glorious form which, prior to His incarnation, was the form of appearance of His God-equal existence, took instead of it the form of a servant, and became as a man. Those who have already taken ver. 6

---

[1] Which, therefore, was not essentially different from that of the Father. The ἴσα εἶναι Θεῷ is the Pauline Θεὸς ἦν ὁ λόγος. Hofmann erroneously, although approved by Thomasius, makes the objection (*Schriftbew.* p. 150) that an existence *equal* to divine existence can only be predicated of Him, who is not God. It may be predicated also of Him who is not the very same person, but of equal divine nature. Thus it might also be asserted of the Holy Spirit. The appeal by Hofmann to Thuc. iii. 14 is here without any bearing whatever.

[2] Ritschl indeed also, *Altkath. Kirche*, p. 80, requires, for the understanding of our passage, a recognition that Christ, as ἐν μορφῇ Θεοῦ ὑπάρχων, is put in comparison with the earthly Adam. But why should Paul, if this comparison was before his mind, not have written, in accordance with Gen. i. 26, κατ' εἰκόνα Θ., or καθ' ὁμοίωσιν Θ., instead of ἐν μορφῇ Θ.? This would have been most natural for himself, and would also have been a hint to guide the readers.—The passages quoted by Hilgenfeld from the Clementine Homilies affirm the μορφὴ Θεοῦ of the *body* of man, and are therefore irrelevant.

as referring to the *incarnate* Christ (see on ὅς, ver. 6) are at
once placed in a difficulty by ἐκένωσε, and explain away its
simple and distinct literal meaning; as, for instance, Calvin:
"*supprimendo . . .* deposuit;" Calovius (comp. *Form. Conc.*
pp. 608, 767): "*veluti* (?) deposuit, quatenus eam (gloriam div.)
non perpetuo manifestavit atque exseruit;" Clericus: "non magis
ea *usus est, quam si* ea destitutus fuisset;" comp. Quenstedt,
Bos, Wolf, Bengel, Rheinwald, and many others. Beyschlag
also finds expressed here merely the idea of the *self-denial* exercised on principle by Christ in His earthly life, consequently
substituting the N. T. idea of ἀπαρνεῖσθαι ἑαυτόν. De Wette,
in accordance with his distinction between μορφὴ Θεοῦ and εἶναι
ἴσα Θεῷ (comp. Schneckenburger, p. 336), referring it only to
the latter (so also Corn. Müller, Philippi, Beyschlag, and others),
would have this εἶναι ἴσα Θεῷ meant merely *in so far* as it
would have *stood* in Jesus' *power*, not *in so far* as He *actually
possessed* it, so that the ἑαυτ. ἐκέν. amounts only to a *renunciation* of the εἶναι ἴσα Θεῷ, which He *might* have appropriated
to Himself; while *others*, like Grotius, alter the *signification* of
κενοῦν itself, some making it mean: *He led a life of poverty*
(Grotius, Baumgarten - Crusius), and others: *depressit* (van
Hengel, Corn. Müller, following Tittmann, *Opusc.* p. 642 f.,
Keil, comp. Chrysostom, Theodoret, and others). Augustine:
"Non amittens quod erat, sed accipiens quod non erat; forma
servi *accessit*, non forma Dei *discessit.*" But ἐκένωσε means
nothing but *exinanivit* (Vulgate) (see Rom. iv. 14; 1 Cor.
i. 17, ix. 15; 2 Cor. ix. 3; and the passages in the LXX.
cited by Schleusner; Plat. *Conv.* p. 197 C, *Rep.* p. 560 D,
Phil. p. 35 E; Soph. *O. R.* 29; Eur. *Rhes.* 914; Thuc. viii.
57. 1; Xen. *Oec.* 8. 7),[1] and is here *purposely selected*, because
it corresponds with the idea of the ἁρπαγμός (ver. 6) all the
more, that the latter also falls under the conception of κενοῦν
(as *emptying* of that which is affected by the ἁρπαγμός; comp.

[1] Comp. Hasse in the *Jahrb. f. Deutsche Theol.* 1858, p. 394 f. (in opposition
to Dorner's reference of the idea to that of ἐξουθενεῖν). Dorner, in the same
Jahrb. 1856, p. 395, is likewise driven to reduce the idea of the κένωσις merely to
that of the renunciation of the appearance of majesty, which would have been
befitting the divine form and parity, this inner greatness and dignity of Jesus
Christ.

LXX. Jer. xv. 9; Plat. *Rep.* p. 560 D; Ecclus. xiii. 5, 7).
The specific reference of the meaning to *making poor* (Grotius)
must have been suggested by the context (comp. 2 Cor. viii. 9;
Ecclus. *l.c.*), as if some such expression as ἐν πλούτῳ Θεοῦ ὑπάρχ.
had been previously used. *Figuratively*, the renunciation of
the divine μορφή might have been described as a *putting it off*
(ἐκδύεσθαι).—The *more precise*, positive *definition* of the *mode*
in which He emptied Himself, is supplied by μορφὴν δούλου
λαβών, and the latter then receives through ἐν ὁμ. ἀνθρ. γενόμενος καὶ σχήμ. εὑρ. ὡς ἄνθρ. its specification of mode, correlative to εἶναι ἴσα Θεῷ. This specification is not co-ordinate (de
Wette, Baumgarten-Crusius, Weiss, Schenkel), but subordinate
to μορφὴν δούλ. λαβών, hence no connecting particle is placed
before ἐν ὁμ., and no punctuation is to be placed before καὶ
σχήματι, but a new topic is to be entered upon with ἐταπείνωσεν in ver. 8 (comp. Luther). The division, by which a stop is
placed before καὶ σχήματι . . . ἄνθρωπος, and these words are
joined to ἐταπείνωσεν κ.τ.λ. (Castalio, Beza, Bengel, and others;
including Hoelemann, Rilliet, van Hengel, Lachmann, Wiesinger, Ewald, Rich. Schmidt, J. B. Lightfoot, Grimm), is at variance
with the purposely-chosen expressions σχήματι and εὑρεθείς,
both of which correspond to the idea of μορφή, and thereby show
that κ. σχ. εὑρ. ὡς ἄνθρ. is still a portion of the modal definition of μορφὴν δούλου λαβών. Nor is the σχήμ. εὑρ. ὡς ἄνθρ.
something following the κένωσις (Grimm), but the empirical
appearance, which was an integral part of the manner in
which the act of self-emptying was completed. Besides,
ἐταπείνωσεν ἑαυτόν has its own more precise definition *following;* hence by the proposed connection the symmetry of
structure in the two statements, governed respectively by
ἑαυτὸν ἐκένωσε and ἐταπείνωσεν ἑαυτόν, would be unnecessarily
disturbed. This applies also in opposition to Hofmann, who
(comp. Grotius) even connects ἐν ὁμοιώματι ἄνθρ. γενόμ. with
ἐταπείνωσεν ἑαυτόν, whereby no less than three participial
definitions are heaped upon the latter. And when Hofmann
discovers in ἐν ὁμοιώματι κ.τ.λ. a second half of the relative
sentence attached to Χριστῷ Ἰησοῦ, it is at variance with the
fact, that Paul does not by the intervention of a particle (or

by ὃς καί, or even by the bare ὅς) supply any warrant for such
a division, which is made, therefore, abruptly and arbitrarily,
simply to support the scheme of thought which Hofmann
groundlessly assumes: (1) that Jesus, when He was in the
divine μορφή, *emptied Himself;* and (2) when He *had become
man, humbled* Himself. Comp. in opposition to this, Grimm,
p. 46, and Kolbe in the *Luther. Zeitschr.* 1873, p. 314. —
μορφὴν δούλου λαβών] so that *He took slave-form,* now making
this lowly form of existence and condition His own, instead of
the divine form, which He had hitherto possessed. *How* this
was done, is stated in the sequel. The *aorist participle* denotes, not what was *previous* to the ἑαυτ. ἐκέν., but what was
contemporaneous with it. See on Eph. i. 9. So also do the
two following participles, which are, however, *subordinated* to
the μορφὴν δούλου λαβών, as definitions of manner. That
Paul, in the word δούλου, thought not of the relation of *one
serving in general* (with reference to God and men, Matthies,
Rheinwald, Rilliet, de Wette, comp. Calvin and others), or
that of a servant of *others,* as in Matt. xx. 28 (Schneckenburger, Beyschlag, *Christol.* p. 236, following Luther and
others), or, indefinitely, that of one subject to the will of
another (Hofmann), but of a slave of *God* (comp. Acts iii. 13 ;
Isa. lii.), as is self-evident from the relation to *God* described
in ver. 6, is plain, partly from the fact that subsequently the
assumption of the slave-form is more precisely defined by ἐν
ὁμοιώμ. ἀνθρ. γενόμ. (which, regarded in itself, puts Jesus only
on the *same* line with *men,* but in the relation of *service* towards
God), and partly from ὑπήκοος in ver. 8. To generalize the
definite expression, and one which corresponds so well to the
connection, into " *miseram sortem, qualis esse servorum solet* "
(Heinrichs, comp. Hoelemann ; and already, Beza, Piscator,
Calovius, Wolf, Wetstein, and others), is pure caprice, which
Erasmus, following Ambrosiaster (comp. Beyschlag, 1860, p.
471), carries further by the arbitrary paraphrase: "servi *nocentis,*
cum ipsa esset innocentia," comp. Rom. viii. 3. — ἐν ὁμοιώμ.
ἀνθρ. γενόμ. κ.τ.λ.] the manner of this μορφ. δούλου λαβεῖν : *so
that He came in the likeness of man, that is, so that He entered
into a form of existence, which was not different from that which*

men have.   In opposition to Hofmann, who connects ἐν ὁμοιώματι κ.τ.λ. with ἐταπείνωσεν κ.τ.λ., see above.   On γίνεσθαι ἐν,
in the sense, *to come into a position, into a state,* comp. 2 Cor.
iii. 7; 1 Tim. ii. 14; Luke xxii. 44; Acts xxii. 17; 1 Macc. i. 27;
2 Macc. vii. 9; Ecclus. xliv. 20; and frequently in Greek authors
after Homer (Xen. *Anab.* i. 9. 1; Herodian, iii. 7. 19, ii. 13. 21);
see Nägelsbach, *zur Ilias,* p. 295 f. ed. 3.   This entrance into
an existence like that of men was certainly brought about by
human *birth ;* still it would not be appropriate to explain γενόμ.
by *natus* (Gal. iv. 4; Rilliet; comp. Gess, p. 295 ; Lechler, p. 66),
or as an expression for the *"beginning of existence"* (Hofmann),
since this fact, in connection with which the miraculous *conception* is, notwithstanding Rom. i. 3, also thought to be
included, was really human, as it is also described in Gal. iv. 4.
Paul justly says: ἐν ὁμοιώματι ἀνθρ., because, in fact, Christ,
although certainly perfect man (Rom. v. 15 ; 1 Cor. xv. 21 ;
1 Tim. ii. 5), was, by reason of the divine nature (the ἴσα
εἶναι Θεῷ) present in Him, not *simply and merely* man, not
a *purus putus homo,* but the *incarnate Son of God* (comp. Rom.
i. 3 ; Gal. iv. 4 ; and the Johannine ὁ λόγος σὰρξ ἐγένετο), ὃς
ἐφανερώθη ἐν σαρκί (1 Tim. iii. 16), so that the power of the
higher divine nature was united in Him with the human appearance, which was not the case in other men.   The nature of
Him who had become man was, so far, not fully *identical* with,
but substantially *conform* (ἐν ὁμοιώμ.) to, that which belongs
to man.[1]   Comp. on Rom. viii. 3, i. 3 f., and respecting the
idea of ὁμοίωμα, which does not convey merely the conception

Our passage contains no trace of *Docetism,* even if Paul had, instead of
ἀνθρώπων, used the singular, which he might just as well have written here as
ὡς ἄνθρωπος in the sequel, in place of which he might also have used ὡς ἄνθρωποι.
This applies in opposition to Lange, *apost. Zeitalt.* I. p. 131, and Lechler, p. 66.
Even Philippi, *Glaubensl.* IV. 1, p. 472, is of opinion that the above-named interpretation amounts to Docetism.   But Christ was in fact, although perfect
man, nevertheless something so much more exalted, that the phrase ἐν ὁμοιώμ.
ἀνθρ. must have vindicated itself to the believing consciousness of the readers
without any misconception, and especially without that of Docetism, which Baur
introduces into it (*neutest. Theol.* p. 269), particularly when we consider the
thoroughly *ethical* occasion and basis of the passage as an exhibition of the
loftiest example of humility (comp. Rich. Schmidt, p. 178).   Nevertheless,
Beyschlag has repeated that objection.

of *analogy*, see on Rom. i. 23, v. 14, vi. 5, viii. 3.   The expression is based, not upon the conception of a *quasi-man*, but upon
the fact that in the man Jesus Christ (Rom. v. 15) there was
the superhuman life-basis of divine ἰσότης, the εἶναι ἴσα Θεῷ
not indwelling in other men.   Justice, however, is not done to
the intentionally used ὁμοιώματι (comp. afterwards σχήματι),
if, with de Wette, we find merely the sense that He (not
appearing as divine Ruler) was *found in a human condition*,—
a consequence of the fact that even ver. 6 was referred to the
time *after* the incarnation.   This drove also the ancient dogmatic expositors to adopt the gloss, which is here out of place,
that Christ assumed the *accidentales infirmitates corporis* (yet
without sin), not *ex naturae necessitate*, but *ex οἰκονομίας
libertate* (Calovius).[1]   By others, the characteristic of *debile et
abjectum* (Hoelemann, following older expositors) is obtruded
upon the word ἀνθρώπων, which is here to be taken in a purely
generic sense ; while Grotius understood ἀνθρ. as referring to
the *first* human beings, and believed that the *sinlessness* of
Jesus was meant.   It is not at all specially *this* (in opposition also to Castalio, Lünemann, Schenkel, and others), but
the *whole divine nature* of Jesus, the μορφή of which He laid
aside at His incarnation, which constitutes the *point of difference* that lies at the bottom of the expression ἐν ὁμοιώματι (διὰ
τὸ μὴ ψιλὸν ἄνθρωπον εἶναι, Theophylact, comp. Chrysostom),
and gives to it the definite reference of its meaning.   The
explanation of the expression by the unique position of Christ
as the *second Adam* (Weiss) is alien from the context, which
presents to us the relation, not of the second man to the first
man, but of the *God-man* to *ordinary* humanity. — καὶ σχήμ.
εὑρ. ὡς ἄνθρωπ.] to be closely connected with the preceding
participial affirmation, the thought of which is *emphatically
exhausted* : "*and in fashion was found as a man*," so that the
divine nature (the Logos-nature) was not perceived in Him.

---

[1] To this also amounts the not so precisely and methodically expressed
explanation of Philippi : Since Christ remained in the divine form, His
assumption of the slave-form consisted "*in the withdrawal of the rays of the
divine glory which continued to dwell in His flesh, and which He only veiled and
subdued with the curtain of the flesh.*"   Thus also does Calvin depict it : the
carnis humilitas was *instar veli, quo divina majestas tegebatur.*

σχῆμα, *habitus*, which receives its more precise reference from the context (Pflugk, *ad Eur. Hec.* 619), denotes here the entire outwardly perceptible mode and form, the whole shape of the phenomenon apparent to the senses, 1 Cor. vii. 31 ; comp. τὸ τῆς θεοῦ σχῆμα κ. ἄγαλμα, Plat. *Crit.* p. 110 B ; τύραννον σχῆμα, Soph. *Ant.* 1154; Eur. *Med.* 1039; Plat. *Polit.* p. 267 C : σχῆμα βασιλικόν, p. 290 D : τῶν ἱερέων σχῆμα; *Dem.* 690. 21 : ὑπηρέτου σχῆμα ; Lucian, *Cyn.* 17 : τὸ ἐμὸν σχῆμα τὸ δ' ὑμέτερον; also, in the plural, Xen. *Mem.* iii. 10. 7 ; Lucian, *D. M.* xx. 5. Men saw in Christ a human form, bearing, language, action, mode of life, wants and their satisfaction, etc., in general the *state and relations* of a human being, so that in the entire mode of His appearance He made Himself known and was recognised (εὑρεθ.) *as a man*. In His external character, after He had laid aside the divine *form* which He had previously had,[1] there was observed no difference between His appearance and that *of a man*, although the subject of His appearance was at the same time essentially *divine*. The ὡς with ἄνθρ. does not simply indicate *what* He was recognised to be (Weiss); this would have been expressed by ἄνθρ. *alone;* but He was found *as a man, not invested with other qualities.* The Vulgate well renders it, " inventus *ut* homo." This included, in particular, that He presented and manifested in Himself the human σάρξ, human weakness and susceptibility of death (2 Cor. xiii. 4 ; Rom. vi. 9 ; Acts xxvi. 23).

Ver. 8. Ἐταπείνωσεν] is placed with great emphasis at the head of a new sentence (see on ver. 7), and without any connecting particle: He has *humbled* Himself. Ἑαυτόν is not prefixed as in ver. 7 ; for in ver. 7 the stress, according to the object in view, was laid on the *reflexive reference* of the action, but here on the reflexive *action itself.* The relation to ἐκένωσε is climactic, not, however, as if Paul did not regard the self-*renunciation* (ver. 7) as being also self-*humiliation*, but in so far as the former manifested in the most extreme way the cha-

---

[1] Comp. *Test. XII. Patr.* p. 644 f. : ὄψισθε Θεὸν ἐν σχήματι ἀνθρώπου. Comp. p. 744 : τὸν βασιλέα τῶν οὐρανῶν, τὸν ἐπὶ γῆς φανέντα ἐν μορφῇ ἀνθρώπου ταπεινώσεως. How these passages agree with the Nazaraic character of the book, is not a point for discussion here.

racter of ταπείνωσις in the shameful death of Jesus. It is a climactic *parallelism* (comp. on iv. 9) in which the two predicates, although the former in the nature of the case already includes the latter (in opposition to Hofmann), are kept apart as respects the essential points of their appearance in historical development. Bengel well remarks : " Status exinanitionis gradatim profundior." Hoelemann, mistaking this, says : " He humbled Himself *even below His dignity as man.*" — γενόμ. ὑπήκοος] The aorist participle is quite, like the participles in ver. 7, simultaneous with the governing verb : *so that He became obedient.* This ὑπήκοος is, however, not to be defined by " *capientibus se, damnantibus et interficientibus*" (Grotius); nor is it to be referred to the *law*, Gal. iv. 4 (Olshausen), but to *God* (Rom. v. 19 ; Heb. v. 8 f.), whose will and counsel (comp. *e.g.* Matt. xxvi. 42) formed the ground determining the obedience. Comp. ver. 9 : διὸ καὶ ὁ Θεός κ.τ.λ. The expression itself glances back to μορφ. δούλου ; " obedientia servum decet," Bengel. — μέχρι θανάτου] belongs to ὑπήκ. γενόμ., not to ἐταπ. ἑαυτ. (Bengel, Hoelemann)— which latter connection is arbitrarily assumed, dismembers the discourse, and would leave a too vague and feeble definition for ἐταπ. ἑαυτ. in the mere ὑπήκ. γενόμ. By μέχρι death is pointed out as the *culminating point*, as the highest degree, up to which He obeyed, not merely as the *temporal* goal (van Hengel). Comp. 2 Tim. ii. 9 ; Heb. xii. 4 ; Acts xxii. 4 ; Matt. xxvi. 38. This extreme height reached by His obedience was, however, just the extreme *depth* of the humiliation, and thereby at the same time its *end ;* comp. Acts viii. 33 ; Isa. liii. 8. Hofmann groundlessly takes ὑπήκ. γίνεσθαι in the sense of *showing* obedience (comp. on Gal. iv. 12). The obedience of Christ was an ethical *becoming* (Heb. v. 8). — θανάτου δὲ σταυρ.] τουτέστι τοῦ ἐπικαταράτου (comp. Gal. iii. 13 ; Heb. xii. 2), τοῦ τοῖς ἀνόμοις ἀφωρισμένου, Theophylact. The δέ, with the repetition of the same word (comp. Rom. iii. 22, ix. 30), presents, just like the German *aber*, the more precisely defined idea in contradistinction to the idea which is previously left without this special definition : *unto death, but* what kind of death ? unto the most shameful and most painful, unto the *death of the cross;* see Klotz, *ad Devar.* p. 361, and Baeumlein, *Partik.* p. 97; and the examples in Hartung, *Partikell.* I. p. 168 f.; Ellendt, *Lex. Soph.* I. p. 388.

REMARK 1.—According to our explanation, vv. 6–8 may be thus paraphrased: *Jesus Christ, when He found Himself in the heavenly mode of existence of divine glory, did not permit Himself the thought of using His equality with God for the purpose of seizing possessions and honour for Himself on earth: No, He emptied Himself of the divine glory, inasmuch as, notwithstanding His God-equal nature, He took upon Him the mode of existence of a slave of God, so that He entered into the likeness of men, and in His outward bearing and appearance manifested Himself not otherwise than as a man. He humbled Himself, so that He became obedient unto God,* etc. According to the explanation of our dogmatic writers, who refer vv. 6–8 to the *earthly* life of Christ, the sense comes to this: " *Christum jam inde a primo conceptionis momento divinam gloriam et majestatem sibi secundum humanam naturam communicatam plena usurpatione exserere et tanquam Deum se gerere potuisse, sed abdicasse se plenario ejus usu et humilem se exhibuisse, patrique suo coelesti obedientem factum esse usque ad mortem crucis*" (Quenstedt). The most thorough exposition of the passage and demonstration in this sense, though mixed with much polemical matter against the Reformed and the Socinians, are given by Calovius. The point of the orthodox view, in the interest of the full Deity of the God-man, lies in the fact that Paul is discoursing, not *de humiliatione* INCARNATIONIS, but *de humiliatione* INCARNATI. Among the Reformed theologians, Calvin and Piscator substantially agreed with our [Lutheran] orthodox expositors.

REMARK 2.—On a difference in the dogmatic understanding of vv. 6–8, when men sought to explain more precisely the doctrine of the Church (*Form. Conc.* 8), was based the well-known controversy carried on since 1616 between the theologians of *Tübingen* and those of *Giessen.* The latter (Feuerborn and Menzer) assigned to Jesus Christ in His state of humiliation the κτῆσις of the divine attributes, but denied to Him their χρῆσις, thus making the κένωσις a renunciation of the χρῆσις. The Tübingen school, on the other hand (Thummius, Luc. Osiander, and Nicolai), not separating the κτῆσις and χρῆσις, arrived at the conclusion of a hidden and imperceptible use of the divine attributes, and consequently made the κένωσις a κρύψις τῆς χρήσεως. See the account of all the points of controversy in Dorner, II. 2, p. 661 ff., and especially Thomasius, *Christi Pers. u. Werk*, II. p. 429 ff. The Saxon *Decisio*, 1624, taking part with the Giessen divines, rejected the κρύψις, without thoroughly refuting it, and even without avoiding unnecessary concessions to it according to the *Formula Concordiae* (pp. 608, 767), so that the disputed questions remained open and the controversy itself only came to a close through final weariness. Among the dogmatic writers of the present day, Philippi is decidedly on the side of the Giessen school. See his *Glaubensl.* IV. 1, p. 279 ff. ed. 2. It is certain that, according to our passage, the idea of the κένωσις is clearly and decidedly to be maintained, and the reducing of it to a κρύψις rejected. But, since Paul expressly refers the ἑαυτὸν ἐκένωσε to the μορφὴ Θεοῦ, and consequently to the divine mode of appearance, while he makes the εἶναι ἴσα Θεῷ to subsist with the assumption of the μορφὴ δούλου, just as subsequently the Incarnate One appears only as ἐν ὁμοιώματι ἀνθρ. and as σχήματι ὡς ἀνθρ.; and since, further, in the case of the κτῆσις of the divine attributes thus laid down, the non-use of them—because as divine they necessarily cannot remain dormant (John v. 17, ix. 4)—is in itself inconceivable and incompatible with the Gospel history; the κτῆσις and the χρῆσις must therefore be inseparably kept together. But, setting aside the conception of the κρύψις as foreign to the N. T., this possession and use of the divine attributes are to be conceived as having, by the renunciation of the μορφὴ Θεοῦ in virtue of the incarnation, entered upon a human development, consequently as conditioned, not as absolute, but as theanthropic. At the same time, the *self-consciousness* of Jesus Christ necessarily remained the self-consciousness of the Son of God developing Himself humanly, or (according to the Johannine phrase) of the Logos that had become flesh, who was the μονογενὴς παρὰ πατρός; see the numerous testimonies in John's Gospel, as iii. 13, viii. 58, xvii. 5, v. 26. "Considered from a purely exegetical point of view, there is no clearer and more certain result of the interpretation of Scripture than the proposition, that the *Ego* of Jesus on earth was identical with the *Ego* which was previously in glory with the Father; any division of the Son speaking on earth into two *Egos*, one of whom was the eternally glorious Logos, the other the humanly humble Jesus, is rejected by clear testimonies of Scripture, however intimate we may seek to conceive the marriage of the two during the earthly life of Jesus;" Liebner in the *Jahrb. f. Deutsche Theol.* 1858, p. 362. That which the divine Logos laid aside in the incarnation was, according to our passage, the μορφὴ Θεοῦ, that is, the divine δόξα as a form of existence, and not the εἶναι ἴσα Θεῷ essentially and necessarily constituting His nature, which He retained,[1] and to which belonged, just as essentially and necessarily, the divine—and consequently in Him who had become man the divine-human—self-consciousness.[2] But as this cannot find its adequate explanation either in the *absolute consciousness of God,* or in the *archetypal character* which Schleiermacher assigned to Christ, or in the idea of the *religious genius* (Al. Schweizer), or in that of the *second Adam* created free from original sin, whose personal development proceeds as a gradual incarnation of God and deification of man (Rothe), so we must by no means say, with Gess, *v. d. Pers. Chr.* p. 304 f., that in becoming incarnate the Logos had laid aside His self-consciousness, in order to get it back again only in the gradual course of development of a human soul, and that merely in the form of a *human* self-consciousness. See, in opposition to this, Thomasius, *Christi Pers. u. Werk,* II. p. 198 f.; Schoeberlein in the *Jahrb. f. D. Th.* 1871, p. 471 ff., comp. the latter's *Geheimnisse des Glaubens,* 1872, 3. The various views which have been adopted on the part of the more recent Lutheran Christologists,[3] diverging from the doctrine of the *Formula Concordiae* in setting forth Christ's humiliation (Dorner: a gradual *ethical blending into one another* of the divine and human life in immanent development; Thomasius: *self-limitation, i.e.*

---

[1] Comp. Düsterdieck, *Apolog. Abh.* III. p. 67 ff.

[2] Paul agrees *in substance* with the Logos doctrine of John, but has not adopted the form of Alexandrine speculation. That the latter was *known* to him in its application to the Christology, may at least be regarded as probable from his frequent and long intercourse with Asia, and also from his relation to Apollos. His conception, however, is just as little Apollinarian as that of John; comp. on Rom. i. 3 f.; Col. i. 15.

[3] Schenkel's ideal transference of Christ's pre-existence simply into the *self-consciousness* of God, which in the person of Christ found a perfect self-manifestation like to humanity, boldly renounces all the results of historical exegesis during a whole generation, and goes back to the standpoint of Löffler and others, and also further, to that of the Socinians. Comp. on John xvii. 5. Yet even Beyschlag's Christology leads no further than to an ideal pre-existence of Christ as archetype of humanity, and that not as a person, but merely as the principle of a person;—while Keerl (*d. Gottmensch. das Ebenbild Gottes,* 1866), in unperceived direct opposition to our passage and to the entire N. T., puts the Son of God already as Son of man in absolute (not earthly) corporeality as pre-existent into the glory of heaven. From 1 Cor. xv. 47 the conception of the pre-existence of Christ as *a heavenly, pneumatic man* and archetype of humanity (Holsten, Biedermann, and others) can only be obtained through misapprehension of the meaning. See on 1 Cor. *l.c.,* and Grimm, p. 51 ff.

partial self-renunciation of the divine Logos; Liebner: the entrance of the Logos *into a process of becoming*, that is, into a divine-human development), do not fall to be examined here in detail; they belong to the province of Dogmatics. See the discussions on the subject by Dorner, in the *Jahrb. f. Deutsche Theol.* 1856, 2, 1857, 2, 1858, 3; Broemel, in the *Kirchl. Zeitschr.* of Kliefoth and Mejer, 1857, p. 144 ff.; Liebner, in the *Jahrb. f. Deutsche Theol.* 1858, p. 349 ff.; Hasse, *ibid.* p. 336 ff.; Schoeberlein, *l.c.* p. 459 ff.; Thomasius, *Chr. Pers. u. Werk,* II. pp. 192 ff., 542 ff.; Philippi, *Dogmat.* IV. 1, p. 364 ff. —According to Schoeberlein, the Son of God, when He became man, did not give up His *operation in governing the world* in conjunction with the Father and the Holy Spirit, but continued to exercise it with *divine* consciousness *in heaven.* Thus the dilemma cannot be avoided, either of supposing a *dual personality of Christ,* or of assuming, with Schoeberlein, that *heaven is not local.* Not only the former, however, but the latter view also, would be opposed to the entire N. T.

Ver. 9. The exaltation of Christ,—by the description of which, grand in its simplicity, His example becomes all the more *encouraging* and *animating.* — διό] *for a recompense,* on account of this self-denying renunciation and humiliation in obedience to God (καί, *also,* denotes the accession of the corresponding *consequence,* Luke i. 35; Acts x. 29; Rom. i. 24, iv. 22; Heb. xiii. 12). Comp. Matt. xxiii. 12; Luke xxiv. 26. Nothing but a dogmatic, anti-heretical assumption could have recourse to the interpretation which is at variance with linguistic usage: *quo facto* (Calvin, Calovius, Glass, Wolf, and others). The conception of *recompense* (comp. Heb. ii. 9, xii. 2) is justified by the *voluntariness* of what Christ did, vv. 6–8, as well as by the ethical nature of the *obedience* with which He did it, and only excites offence if we misunderstand the Subordinatianism in the Christology of the apostle. Augustine well says: "Humilitas claritatis est *meritum,* claritas humilitatis *praemium.*" Thus Christ's saying in Matt. xxiii. 12 was gloriously fulfilled in His own case. — ὑπερύψωσε] comp. Song of Three Child. 28 ff.; LXX. Ps. xxxvi. 37, xcvi. 10; Dan. iv. 34; Synes. *Ep.* p. 225 A; it is not found elsewhere among Greek authors, by whom, however, ὑπερύψηλος, *exceed-*

ingly high, is used. *He made Him very high, exceedingly exalted,* said by way of superlative contrast to the previous ἐταπείνωσεν, of the exaltation to the *fellowship of the highest glory and dominion,* Rom. viii. 17; 2 Tim. ii. 12; Eph. i. 21, *al.;* John xii. 32, xvii. 5.[1] This exaltation has *taken place* by means of the ascension (Eph. iv. 10), by which Jesus Christ attained to the right hand of God (Mark xvi. 19; Acts vii. 55 f.; Rom. viii. 34; Eph. i. 20 f.; Col. iii. 1; Heb. i. 3, viii. 1, x. 12, xii. 2; 1 Tim. iii. 16; 1 Pet. iii. 22), although it is not this *local mode,* but the exaltation viewed *as a state* which is, according to the context, expressed by ὑπερύψ. It is quite unbiblical (John xvii. 5), and without lexical authority, to take ὑπέρ as intimating: more *than previously* (Grotius, Beyschlag). — ἐχαρίσατο] *He granted* (i. 29), said from the point of view of the subordination, on which also what follows (κύριος . . . εἰς δόξαν Θεοῦ πατρός) is based. Even Christ receives the recompense as God's *gift of grace,* and hence also He *prays* Him for it, John xvii. 5. The glory of the *exaltation* did not stand to that possessed *before the incarnation* in the relation of a *plus,* but it affected the *entire divine-human* person, that entered on the *regnum gloriae.* —— τὸ ὄνομα] is here, as in Eph. i. 21, Heb. i. 4, to be taken in the strictly literal sense, not as *dignitas* or *gloria* (Heinrichs, Hoelemann, and many others), a sense which it might have *ex adjuncto* (see the passages in Wetstein and Hoelemann), but against which here the following ἐν τῷ ὀνόματι Ἰησοῦ is decisive. The honour and dignity of the name of Jesus are expressed by τὸ ὑπὲρ πᾶν ὄνομα, but are not implied in τὸ ὄνομα of itself. Nor is it to be understood of an *appellative name,* as some have referred it to κύριος in ver. 11 (Michaelis, Keil, Baumgarten-Crusius, van Hengel, Schneckenburger, Weiss, Hofmann, Grimm); others to υἱὸς Θεοῦ (Theophylact, Pelagius, Estius); and some even to Θεός (Ambrosiaster, Oecumenius, and again

---

[1] In the conception of the "*exaltation*" Paul agrees with John, but does not convey expressly the notion of the *return* to the Father. This is not an *inconsistency* in relation to the doctrine of pre-existence (in opposition to Pfleiderer, *l.c.* p. 517), but a consequence of the more dialectically acute distinction of ideas in Paul, since that change of condition affected the *entire* Christ, the *God-man,* whereas the subject of the pre-existence was the *Logos.*

Schultz; but see on Rom. ix. 5). In accordance with the context—ver. 11, comp. with ver. 6—the thought is: "*God has*, by His exaltation, *granted to Him that the name ' Jesus Christ' surpasses all names in glory.*" The expression of this thought in the form: *God has granted to Him the name*, etc., cannot seem strange, when we take into account the highly poetic strain of the passage.

Ver. 10 f. "*Iva*] This exaltation, ver. 9, was to have, in accordance with the divine purpose, general adoration and confession as its result,—a continuation of the contrast with the previous state of self-renunciation and humiliation. In the mode of expression there may be detected a reminiscence of Isa. xlv. 23 (Rom. xiv. 11). — The ἐν τῷ ὀνόμ. 'Ι., emphatically prefixed, affirms that, in the *name of Jesus, i.e.* in what is involved in that most glorious name " Jesus Christ," and is present to the conception of the subjects as they bend their knees, is to be found the moving *ground* of this latter action (comp. Ps. lxiii. 5 ; 1 Kings xviii. 24 ; 1 Chron. xvi. 10, *al. ;* 1 Cor. vi. 11 ; Eph. v. 20 ; Col. iii. 17 ; 1 Pet. iv. 14, 16 ; Jas. v. 14). The *bowing of the knee* represents *adoration,* of which it is the symbol (Isa. xlv. 23 ; Rom. xiv. 11, xi. 4 ; Eph. iii. 14 ; 3 Esdr. viii. 73 ; 3 Macc. ii. 1 ; and in Greek writers from Homer onward), and the subject to be adored is, according to the context (ἐν τῷ ὀνόμ. 'Ι., and comp. ver. 11), none other than *Jesus*, the adoring worship of whom has its warrant in the fellowship of the divine government and of the divine δόξα to which He is exalted (comp. the habitual ἐπικαλεῖσθαι τὸ ὄνομα κυρίου, Rom. x. 12 f. ; 1 Cor. i. 2 ; 2 Tim. ii. 22 ; Acts vii. 59, ix. 14, 21, xxii. 16), but has also at the same time its peculiar character, not absolute, but *relative, i.e.* conditioned by the relation of the exalted Son to the Father (see Lücke, *de invocat. Jes. Ch.* Gott. 1843, p. 7 f. ; comp. Ernesti, *Urspr. d. Sünde*, I. p. 218),—a peculiarity which did not escape the observation of Pliny (*Ep.* x. 97 : " Christo *quasi* Deo"), and was, although only very casually and imperfectly, expressed by him. *This* adoration (comp. ver. 11, εἰς δόξαν Θεοῦ πατρός) does not infringe that strict monotheism, which could ascribe absolute deity to the Father only

Father
Son
Spirit

(John xvii. 3 ; Eph. iv. 5 ; 1 Cor. xii. 6, viii. 6 ; 1 Tim.
vi. 15 f.) ; the Father only is ὁ ὢν ἐπὶ πάντων Θεός, Rom.
ix. 5 (comp. Ignat. *Tars.* interpol. 5), ὁ Θεός absolutely, God
also of Christ (see on Eph. i. 17), the Θεὸς ὁ παντοκράτωρ
(2 Cor. vi. 18 ; Rev. i. 8, iv. 8, *al.*) ; and the Son, although of
like nature, as σύνθρονος and partaker of His δόξα, is subordinate to Him (1 Cor. xi. 3, xv. 27 f.), as in turn the Spirit
is to the Son (2 Cor. iii. 18) ; the honour which is to be paid
to the Son (Rev. v. 8 ff.) has its principle (John v. 22 f.) and
aim (ver. 11) in the Father, and therefore the former is to be
honoured *as* the Father, and *God in Christ* fills and moves
the consciousness of him who prays to Christ.   According to
van Hengel, it is not the adoration *of Jesus* which is here intended, but that of *God* under *application of the name of Jesus ;*
and de Wette also thinks it probable that Paul only intended
to state that every prayer should be made in the name of
Jesus as the Mediator (κύριος).   Comp. also Hofmann : " the
praying *to God, determined* in the person praying *by the consciousness of his relation to Jesus as regulating his action.*"
Instead of this we should rather say: the praying *to Jesus,*
determined by the consciousness of the relation *of Jesus to
God* (of the Son to the Father), as regulating the action of
the person praying.   All modes of explaining away the
adoration as offered *to Jesus Himself* are at variance not only
with the context generally, which has to do with the honour
of *Jesus,* making Him the *object* of the adoration, but also with
the word ἐπουρανίων which follows, because the *mediatorship*
of Jesus, which is implied in the *atonement,* does not affect
the *angels* as its objects (comp., on the contrary, Heb. i. 4, 6).
The two sentences may not be separated from one another (in
opposition to Hofmann) ; but, on the contrary, it must be
maintained that the personal object, to whom the bowing of
the knee as well as the confession with the tongue applies,
is *Jesus.*   Linguistically erroneous is the view which makes ἐν
τῷ ὀνόμ. equivalent to εἰς τὸ ὄνομα, *for the glorification of
His dignity* (Heinrichs, Flatt, and others), or as *a paraphrase
for* ἐν Ἰησοῦ (Estius ; Rheinwald leaves either of the two to
be chosen) ; while others, by the interpretation " *quoties auditur*

Certainly

nomen,[1] brought out a sense which is altogether without analogy in the N. T. See, in opposition to this, Calvin : " quasi vox (the word *Jesus*) esset *magica,* quae totam in *sono* vim haberet inclusam."—ἐπουρανίων κ.τ.λ.] every knee of *heavenly* beings (those to be found in heaven), *and those on earth, and those under the earth,* is to bow, none is to remain unbent; that is, every one from these three classes shall bow his knees (plural). ἐπουρ. includes the *angels* (Eph. i. 20 f., iii. 10 ; Heb. i. 4, 6 ; 1 Pet. i. 12, iii. 22) ; ἐπιγ. the *human beings on earth* (comp. Plat. *Ax.* p. 368 B : ἐπίγειος ἄνθρωπος) ; and καταχθ. the *dead in Hades* (comp. Hom. *Il.* ix. 457 : Ζεὺς καταχθόνιος, Pluto : καταχθόνιοι δαίμονες, the Manes, *Anthol.* vii. 333). Comp. Rev. v. 13 ; Ignat. *Trall.* 9, and the similar classical use of ὑποχθόνιος, ὑπὸ γαῖαν (Eur. *Hec.* 149, and Pflugk *in loc.*). The adoration on the part of the latter, which Grotius and Hofmann misinterpret, presupposes the *descensus Ch. ad inferos,*[2] Eph. iv. 9, in which He presented Himself to the spirits in Hades as the κύριος. Our passage, however, does not yield any further particulars regarding the so-called descent into hell, which Schweizer has far too rashly condemned as " *a myth without any foundation in Scripture.*" Chrysostom, Theophylact, Oecumenius, Erasmus, and many others, including Baumgarten-Crusius and Wiesinger, have

---

[1] Erasmus, Castalio, Beza, Bretschneider, and others, arrived at this interpretation simply by understanding ἐν τῷ ὀνόμ. as *ad nomen* (comp. Grotius : "*nuncupato* nomine ") ; but Hoelemann, with forced subtilty, by the analysis : "quasi *circumsonitum* appellatione nominis."

[2] To transfer, with Grotius, Hofmann, and Grimm, the genuflexion of the dead to the period *after the resurrection,* so that, according to Hofmann, the καταχθόνιοι "*sleep below and await their resurrection* and *shall then* adore and confess," would be entirely erroneous, mixing up with the direct, poetically plastic description of the apostle a remotely suggested reflection. He views the bowing of the knee, as it has been done and is continuously being done, and not as it *will be* done by an entire class only *in the future, after the* Parousia. Wiesinger, however, has also placed the realization of the ἵνα πᾶν γόνυ κάμψῃ κ.τ.λ. at the end of the world, when the knees, which hitherto had not willingly bent, would be forced to do so (1 Cor. xv. 25 f.). On this point he appeals to Rom. xiv. 11, where, however, the whole text is dealing with the last judgment, which is not the case here. Besides, ἐν τῷ ὀνόματι is far from leading us to the idea of an adoration partially *forced ;* it rather presupposes the *faith,* of which the bowing of the knee and the confession which follows are the free living action ; comp. Rom. x. 9.

incorrectly understood by καταχθ. the *Daemones*, which is an erroneous view, because Paul does not regard the Daemones as being in Hades (see, on the contrary, at Eph. ii. 2, vi. 12). There is an arbitrary rationalizing in Heinrichs, who takes the words as *neuters: " omnes rerum creatarum complexus "* (comp. Nösselt and J. B. Lightfoot), and already in Beza : " *quaecunque* et supra mundum sunt et in mundo." We meet with the right view as early as Theodoret. The Catholics referred καταχθ. to those who are in *purgatory ;* so Bisping still, and Döllinger, *Christenth. u. Kirche,* p. 262, ed. 2.—As regards the *realization* of the divine purpose expressed in ἵνα κ.τ.λ., respecting the ἐπιγείων, it was still in progress of *development,* but its completion (Rom. xi. 25) could not but appear to the apostle near at hand, in keeping with his expectation of the near end of the αἰὼν οὗτος. Observe, moreover, how he emphasizes the *universality* of the divine purpose (ἵνα) with regard to the bowing the knees and confession with the tongue so strongly by πᾶν γόνυ and πᾶσα γλῶσσα, that the arbitrary limitation which makes him mean *only those who desire to give God the glory* (Hofmann) is out of the question.

Ver. 11 appends the express *confession* combined with the adoration in ver. 10, in doing which the *concrete form* of representation is continued, comp. Rom. xiv. 11 ; Isa. xlv. 23 ; hence γλῶσσα is *tongue,* correlative to the previous γόνυ, not *language* (Theodoret, Beza, and others). — ἐξομολ.] a strengthening compound. Comp. on Matt. iii. 6. Respecting the *future* (see the critical remarks) depending on ἵνα, see on Gal. ii. 4 ; Eph. vi. 3 ; 1 Cor. ix. 18. — κύριος] predicate, placed first with strong emphasis : that *Lord* is Jesus Christ. This is the *specific confession* of the apostolic church (Rom. x. 9 ; 2 Cor. iv. 5 ; Acts ii. 36), whose antithesis is : ἀνάθεμα Ἰησοῦς 1 Cor. xii. 3. The κύριον εἶναι refers to the fellowship of the *divine* dominion (comp. on Eph. i. 22 f., iv. 10 ; 1 Cor. xv. 27 f.) ; hence it is not to be *limited* to the *rational creatures* (Hoelemann, following Flatt and others), or to the *church* (Rheinwald, Schenkel). — εἰς δόξ. Θεοῦ πατρ.] may be attached to the *entire* bipartite clause of purpose (Hofmann). Since, however, in the *second* part a modification of the expression is introduced by the *future*, it is more probably to be joined to *this* portion, of which the *telic* destination, *i.e.* the *final cause*, is specified. It is not to be connected merely with κύριος 'I. X., as Bengel wished : " J. Ch. esse dominum, *quippe qui sit in gloria Dei patris*," making εἰς stand for ἐν, for which the Vulgate, Pelagius, Estius, and others also took it. Schnecken-burger also, p. 341 (comp. Calvin, Rheinwald, Matthies, Hoelemann), joins it with κύριος, but takes εἰς δόξαν rightly : *to the honour*. But, in accordance with ver. 9, it was self-evident that the κυριότης of the Son tends to the honour of the Father ; and the point of importance for the full conclusion was not this, but to bring into prominence that the universal *confessing recognition* of the κυριότης of Jesus Christ glorifies the Father (whose will and work Christ's entire work of salvation is ; see especially Eph. i. ; Rom. xv. 7–9 ; 2 Cor. i. 20), whereby alone the exaltation, which Christ has received as a recompense from the Father, appears in its fullest splendour. Comp. John xii. 28, xvii. 1. The whole contents of ver. 9 f. is parallel to the ἐν μορφῇ Θεοῦ, namely, as the recompensing re-elevation to this original estate, now accorded to the *divine-human* person after the completion of the work of humiliation. Complicated and at variance with the words is the view of van Hengel, that ἐξομολ. εἰς δόξαν Θεοῦ is equivalent to ἐξομολ. Θεῷ, *to praise God* (Gen. xxix. 34, *al.*; Rom. xv. 9 ; Matt. xi. 25; Luke x. 21), and that ὅτι is *quod;* hence : " laudibus celebrarent, quod hunc filium suum principem fecerit regni divini."

REMARK.—From vv. 6–11, Baur, whom Schwegler follows, derives his arguments for the assertion that our epistle moves in the circle of *Gnostic* ideas and expressions,[1] and must therefore belong to the post-apostolic period of Gnostic speculation. But with the true explanation of the various points these arguments[2] fall to pieces of themselves. For (1) if τὸ εἶναι ἴσα Θεῷ be related

---

[1] Its idea is, that Christ " divests Himself of that which He already is, in order to receive back that of which He has divested Himself, with the full reality of the idea filled with its absolute contents," Baur, *Neutest. Theol.* p. 265.

[2] Hinsch, *l.c.* p. 76, does not adopt them, but yet thinks it un-Pauline that the incarnation of Christ is represented *detached from its reference to humanity.* This, however, is not the case, as may be gathered from the connection of the passage in its practical bearing with ver. 4 (τὰ ἑτέρων).

to ἐν μορφῇ Θεοῦ εἶναι as the essence to its adequate manifestation, and if our explanation of ἁρπαγμός be the linguistically correct one, then must the Gnostic conception of the Aeon *Sophia*—which vehemently desired to penetrate into the essence of the original Father (Iren. *Haer.* i. 2. 2), and thus before the close of the world's course (*Theol. Jahrb.* 1849, p. 507 ff.) wished to usurp forcibly something not *de jure* belonging to it (*Paulus*, II. p. 51 ff.) —be one entirely *alien* and *dissimilar* to the idea of our passage. But this conception is just as inconsistent with the orthodox explanation of our passage, as with the one which takes the εἶναι ἴσα Θεῷ as something future and greater than the μορφὴ Θεοῦ; since in the case of the μορφή, as well as in that of the ἴσα, the full fellowship in the divine nature is already the relation assumed *as existing.* Consequently (2) the ἑαυτὸν ἐκένωσε cannot be explained by the idea, according to which the Gnostics made that Aeon, which desired to place itself in unwarranted union with the Absolute, fall from the *Pleroma* to the κένωμα—as to which Baur, in this alleged basis for the representation of our passage, lays down merely the distinction, that Paul gives a moral turn to what, with the Gnostics, had a purely speculative signification (" Whilst, therefore, in the Gnostic view, that ἁρπαγμός indeed actually takes place, but as an unnatural enterprise neutralizes itself, and has, as its result, merely something negative, in this case, in virtue of a moral self-determination, matters cannot come to any such ἁρπαγμός; and the negative, which even *in this case* occurs, not in consequence of an act that has failed, but of one which has not taken place at all, is the voluntary self-renunciation and self-denial by an act of the will, an ἑαυτὸν κενοῦν instead of the γενέσθαι ἐν κενώματι "). (3) That even the notion of the μορφὴ Θεοῦ arose from the language used by the Gnostics, among whom the expressions μορφή, μορφοῦν, μόρφωσις, were very customary, is all the more arbitrarily assumed by Baur, since these expressions were very prevalent *generally*, and are not specifically Gnostic designations; indeed, μορφὴ Θεοῦ is not once used by the Gnostics, although it is current among other authors, including philosophers (*e.g.* Plat. *Rep.* p. 381 C : μένει ἀεὶ ἁπλῶς ἐν τῇ αὑτοῦ μορφῇ, comp. p. 381 B : ἥκιστ᾽ ἂν πολλὰς μορφὰς ἴσχοι ὁ Θεός). Further, (4) the erroneousness of the view, which in the phrases ἐν ὁμοιώματι ἀνθρώπων and σχήματι εὑρεθεὶς ὡς ἄνθρ. discovers a *Gnostic Docetism*, is self-evident from the explanation of these expressions in accordance with the context (see on the passage); and Chrysostom and his successors have rightly brought out the essential difference between what the apostle says in ver. 7 and the Docetic conceptions (Theophylact :

οὐκ ἦν δὲ τὸ φαινόμενον μόνον, namely, man, ἀλλὰ καὶ Θεός, οὐκ ἦν ψιλὸς ἄνθρωπος. Διὰ τοῦτο φησιν· ἐν ὁμοιώματι ἀνθρώπων· ἡμεῖς μὲν γὰρ ψυχὴ καὶ σῶμα, ἐκεῖνος δὲ ψυχὴ καὶ σῶμα καὶ Θεός κ.τ.λ. Theodoret: περὶ τοῦ λόγου ταῦτα φησιν, ὅτι Θεὸς ὢν οὐχ ἑωρᾶτο Θεὸς τὴν ἀνθρωπείαν περικείμενος φύσιν κ.τ.λ.). Comp. on Rom. viii. 3. Lastly, (5) even the three categories ἐπουρανίων καὶ ἐπιγ. καὶ καταχθ., and also the notion of the *descensus ad inferos* which the latter recalls, are alleged by Baur to be genuinely Gnostic. But the idea of the descent to Hades is not distinctively Gnostic; it belongs to the N. T., and is a necessary presupposition lying at the root of many passages (see on Luke xxiii. 43; Matt. xii. 40; Acts ii. 27 ff.; Rom. x. 6 ff.; Eph. iv. 8 ff.); it is, in fact, the premiss of the entire belief in Christ's resurrection ἐκ νεκρῶν. That threefold division of all angels and men (see also Rev. v. 13) was, moreover, so appropriate and natural in the connection of the passage (comp. the twofold division, καὶ νεκρῶν καὶ ζώντων, Rom. xiv. 9, Acts x. 42, 1 Pet. iv. 5 f., where only *men* are in question), that its derivation from Gnosticism could only be justified in the event of the Gnostic character of our passage being demonstrated on other grounds. The whole hypothesis is engrafted on isolated expressions, which only become violently perverted into conceptions of this kind by the *presupposition* of a Gnostic atmosphere. According to the Gnostic view, it would perhaps have been said of the Aeon Sophia: ὃς ἐν μορφῇ Θεοῦ ὑπάρχων οὐ προάλλεσθαι ἡγήσατο εἰς τὸ πλήρωμα τοῦ Θεοῦ κ.τ.λ. The *apostle's* expressions agree entirely with the Christology of his other epistles; it is from these and from his own genuine Gnosis laid down in them, that his words are to be understood fully and rightly, and not from the theosophic phantasmagoria of any subsequent Gnosis whatever.

Ver. 12.[1] To this great example of Jesus Paul now annexes another general admonition, which essentially corresponds with that given in i. 27, with which he began all this hortatory portion of the epistle (i. 27–ii. 18). — ὥστε] *itaque*, draws an

[1] Linden, in the *Stud. u. Krit.* 1860, p. 750, attempted a new explanation of vv. 12–14. According to this, μὴ ὡς is to stand for ὡς μή, κατεργάζ. to be *indicative*, μὴ ὡς . . . κατεργ. to belong to the protasis, ver. 13 to be treated as a parenthesis, and, finally, the apodosis to follow in πάντα κ.τ.λ. Against this view may be simply urged the fact, that μὴ ὡς (2 Thess. iii. 15 ; Philem. 14 ; 2 Cor. ix. 5) cannot be equivalent to ὡς μή, and that there must have been used not even ὡς μή, but, on account of the negation of a purely actual relation, ὡς οὐκ ; to say nothing of the involved construction, and of the so special tenor of the alleged apodosis after a preparation of so grand and general a nature by the alleged protasis.

inference from the example of Christ (vv. 6–11), who by the
path of self-renunciation attained to so glorious a recompense.
Following this example, the readers are, just as they had always
been obedient, etc., to work out their own salvation with the
utmost solicitude. ὑπηκούσατε is not, indeed, correlative with
γενόμ. ὑπήκοος in ver. 8 (Theophylact, Calovius, Bengel, and
others), as the latter was in what preceded only an accessory
definition; but the σωτηρία is correlative with the exaltation
of Christ described in ver. 9, of which the future salvation of
Christians is the analogue, and, in fact, the joint participation
(Rom. viii. 17; Eph. ii. 6; Col. ii. 12 f., iii. 3 f.). Since, therefore,
ὥστε has its logical basis in what immediately precedes, it must
not be looked upon as an inference *from all the previous admoni-*
tions, i. 26 ff., from which it draws the general result (de Wette).
It certainly introduces the recapitulation of all the previous
exhortations, and winds them up (on account of the new exhortation which follows, see on ver. 14) as in iv. 1; 1 Thess.
iv. 18; Rom. vii. 12; 1 Cor. iii. 21, iv. 5, v. 8, xi. 33, xiv. 39,
xv. 58, but in such a way that it *joins on to what was last*
discussed. It is least of all admissible to make, with Hofmann,
ὥστε point backwards to πληράσατέ μου τ. χαράν in ver. 2,
so that this prayer "*is repeated in a definitive manner*" by
the exhortation introduced with ὥστε. In that case the
apostle, in order to be understood, must at least have inserted
a resumptive οὖν after ὥστε, and in the following exhortation
must have again indicated, in some way or other, the element
of the *making joy.* — καθὼς πάντοτε ὑπηκούσατε] whom? is
neither a question to be left unanswered (Matthies), nor one
which does not require an answer (Hofmann). The context
yields the supplement here, as well as in Rom. vi. 16, Philem.
21, 1 Pet. i. 14; and the right supplement is the *usual* one,
viz. *mihi*, or, more definitely, *meo evangelio*, as is plain, both
from the words which follow μὴ ὡς ... ἀπουσίᾳ μου, and also
from the whole close personal relation, in which Paul brings
home to the hearts of his readers his admonitions (from i. 27
down till ii. 18) as their teacher and friend. On πάντοτε,
comp. ἀπὸ πρώτης ἡμέρας ἄχρι τοῦ νῦν (i. 5). We cannot
infer from it a reference to *earlier epistles which have been lost*

(Ewald). — μὴ ὡς . . . ἀπουσίᾳ μου] belongs not to ὑπηκούσατε
(Luther, Wolf, Heumann, Heinrichs, and others), as is evident
from μὴ ὡς and νῦν, but to κατεργάζεσθε, so that the comma
before μετὰ φόβου is, with Lachmann, to be deleted.   Comp.
Grotius.—ὡς had to be inserted, because Paul would not and
could not give an admonition for a time when he would be
present.   Not perceiving this, B, min., vss., and Fathers have
omitted it.   If ὡς were *not* inserted, Paul would say : that they
should not merely in his presence work out their salvation.
But *with* ὡς he says : *that they are not to work out their own
salvation in such a way as if they were doing it in His
presence*[1] *merely* (neglecting it, therefore, in His absence); *nay,
much more now, during His absence from them, they are to work it
out with fear and trembling.*   There is nothing to be supplied
along with ὡς, which is the simple modal *as*, since μὴ ὡς is
connected with the governing verb that follows in the antithesis (τ. ἑαυτ. σωτ. κατεργάζεσθε) as its prefixed negative
modal definition : *not as in my presence only* (not as limiting
it to this only) *work out your salvation.*   And the ἀλλά
is the antithetic *much more, on the contrary, nay.*   Erasmus,
Estius, Hoelemann, Weiss, Hofmann, and others, incorrectly
join μόνον with μή, and take ὡς in the sense of the degree :
not merely so, as ye have done it, or would do it, in my absence ;
comp. de Wette, who assumes a blending of two comparisons,
as does also J. B. Lightfoot.   It is arbitrary not to make
μόνον belong to ἐν τ. παρ. μου, beside which it stands ; comp.
also Rom. iv. 16 (where τῷ ἐκ τοῦ νόμου forms *one* idea),
iv. 23 ; 1 Thess. i. 5.   Still more arbitrary is it to hamper
the flow of the whole, and to break it up in such a way as to
insert the imperative ὑπακούετε after ὑπηκούσατε, and then
to make μετὰ φόβου κ.τ.λ. a sentence by itself (Hofmann).
Moreover, in such a case the arrangement of the words in the
alleged apodosis would be illogical ; νῦν (or, more clearly, καὶ
νῦν) must have begun it, and μόνον must have stood immediately after μή. — πολλῷ μᾶλλον] than if I were present ; for

---

[1] The word παρουσία does not contain, any more than in i. 26, a reference to
the Parousia of Christ, which Kähler (" ye know what this word would properly
tell us ") reads between the lines.

now (νῦν), when they were deprived of the personal teaching,
stimulus, guidance, and guardianship of the apostle, moral
diligence and zealous solicitude were necessary for them *in a
far higher measure,* in order to fulfil the great personal duty of
working out their own salvation. Tha⁺ ἑαυτῶν, therefore, cannot
be equivalent to ἀλλήλων (Flatt, Matthies, and older expositors),
is self-evident. — μετὰ φόβου κ. τρόμου] that is, with such
earnest solicitude, that ye shall have a lively fear of not doing
enough in the matter.   Comp. on 1 Cor. ii. 3 ; 2 Cor. vii. 15 ;
Eph. vi. 5.   Δεῖ γὰρ φοβεῖσθαι κ. τρέμειν ἐν τῷ ἐργάζεσθαι τὴν
ἰδίαν σωτηρίαν ἕκαστον, μή ποτε ὑποσκελισθεὶς ἐκπέσῃ ταύτης,
Oecumenius. *Awe before the presence of God* (Chrysostom,
Theophylact, Oecumenius), before the future *Judge* (Weiss),
the feeling of *dependence on God* (de Wette), a reverential
devotion to God (Matthies, comp. van Hengel), and similar ideas,
must be implied in the case, but do not constitute the *sense* of the
expression, in which also, according to the context, we are not
to seek a contrast to spiritual pride (Schinz, Rilliet, Hoelemann,
Wiesinger), as Augustine, Calvin, Bengel, and others have
done. — κατεργάζεσθε] *bring about, peragite* (Grotius), " *usque
ad metam* " (Bengel), expressing, therefore, more than the
simple verb (comp. Eph. vi. 13 ; Dem. 1121. 19 ; Plat. *Legg.*
vii. p. 791 A ; Eur. *Heracl.* 1046 : πόλει σωτηρίαν κατεργά-
σασθαι ; and see on Rom. i. 26).   The *summons itself* is not
at variance with the principle that salvation is God's gift of
grace, and is prepared for, predestined, and certain to believers ;
but it justly claims the exercise of the new moral power bestowed
on the regenerate man, without the exertion of which he
would fall away again from the state of grace to which
he had attained in faith, and would not actually become
partaker of the salvation appropriated to him by faith, so that
the final reception of salvation is so far the result of his
moral activity of faith in the καινότης ζωῆς.   See especially
Rom. vi. 8, 12 ff., and 2 Cor. vi. 1.   Our passage stands
in contrast, *not* to the *certitudo salutis,* but to the moral
securitas, into which the converted person might relapse, if he
do not stand fast (iv. 1 ; 1 Cor. x. 12), and labour at his
sanctification (1 Thess. iv. 3, 7 ; 2 Cor. vii. 1 ; 1 Tim. ii. 15),

etc. Comp. Wuttke, *Sittenl.* II. § 266. The demand is
expressed all the *more earnestly*, the more that the readers have
conflict and suffering to endure (i. 27–30).

Ver. 13. *Ground of encouragement* to the fulfilment of this
precept, in which it is not their own, but God's *power*, which
works in them, etc. Here Θεός is placed first as the subject,
not as the predicate (Hofmann): *God* is the agent. It is,
however, unnecessary and arbitrary to assume before γάρ (with
Chrysostom, Oecumenius, Theophylact, Erasmus, and others)
an unexpressed thought (" be not terrified at my having said :
with fear and trembling"). Bengel gratuitously supplies with
Θεός the thought : " *praesens vobis etiam absente me*" (comp.
also van Hengel), while others, as Calvin, Beza, Hoelemann,
Rilliet, Wiesinger, who found in μετὰ φόβ. κ. τρ. the antithesis of pride (see on ver. 12), see in ver. 13 the *motive to
humility ;* and de Wette is of opinion that what was expressed
in ver. 12 under the aspect of *fear* is here expressed under
the aspect of *confidence.* In accordance with the *unity* of the
sense we ought rather to say : that the great moral demand
μετὰ φόβ. κ. τρ. τὴν ἑαυτῶν σωτ. κατεργάζεσθαι, containing as
it did the utmost incentive to personal activity, needed for the
readers the support of a *confidence* which should be founded
not on *their own*, but on the *divine* working. According to
Ewald, the μετὰ φόβου κ. τρόμου is to be made good by
pointing to the fact that they *work before God*, who is even
already producing in them the right tendency of will. But
the idea of the ἐνώπιον τοῦ Θεοῦ was so familiar to the apostle,
that he would doubtless have here also directly *expressed* it.
Kähler (comp. Weiss) imports a hint of the divine *punishment*,
of which, however, nothing is contained in the text. So also
Hofmann : with fear *in presence of Him who is a devouring
fire* (Heb. xii. 28 f.), who will not leave unpunished him who
does not subordinate his own will and working to the divine.
As if Paul had hinted at such thoughts, and had not, on
the contrary, himself excluded them by the ὑπὲρ τῆς εὐδοκίας
which is added! The thought is rather " *dulcissima* sententia
omnibus piis mentibus," *Form. Conc.* p. 659.——Calvin (comp.
Calovius) rightly observes on the *subject-matter :* " intelligo

gratiam supernaturalem, quae provenit ex spiritu regenerationis; nam quatenus sumus homines, jam in Deo sumus et vivimus et movemur, verum hic de alio motu disputat Paulus, quam illo universali." Augustine has justly (in opposition to the Pelagian rationalizing interpretation of a mediate working: "velle operatur *suadendo et praemia promittendo*"), in conformity with the words, urged the *efficaciter operari*, which Origen, *de Princ.* iii. 1, had obliterated, and the Greeks who followed qualified with synergistic reservations. — ἐν ὑμῖν] not *intra coetum vestrum* (Hoelemann), but *in animis vestris* (1 Cor. xii. 6; 2 Cor. iv. 12; Eph. ii. 2; Col. i. 29; 1 Thess. ii. 13), in which He produces the self-determination directed to the κατεργάζεσθαι of their own σωτηρία, and the activity in carrying out this Christian-moral volition.[1] This activity, the ἐνεργεῖν, is the *inner moral* one, which has the κατεργάζεσθαι as its *consequence*, and therefore is not to be taken as equivalent to the latter (Vulgate, Luther, and others, including Matthies and Hoelemann). Note, on the contrary, the climactic selection of the two cognate verbs. The regenerate man brings about his own salvation (κατεργάζεται) when he does not resist the divine working (ἐνεργῶν) of the willing and the working (ἐνεργεῖν) in his soul, but yields steady obedience to it in continual conflict with the opposing powers (Eph. vi. 10 ff.; Gal. v. 16; 1 Thess. v. 8, *al.*); so that he περιπατεῖ, not κατὰ σάρκα, but κατὰ πνεῦμα (Rom. viii. 4), is consequently the child of God, and as child becomes *heir* (Rom. viii. 14, 17, 23). According, therefore, as the matter is viewed from the standpoint of the *human* activity, which yields obedience to the divine working of the θέλειν and ἐνεργεῖν, or from that of the *divine* activity, which works the θέλειν and ἐνεργεῖν, we may say with equal justice, either that *God* accomplishes the good which He has begun in man, up to the day of Christ; or, that *man* brings about his own salvation. "*Nos* ergo volumus, sed *Deus* in nobis operatur et velle; *nos* ergo operamur, sed *Deus* in nobis operatur et operari," Augus-

---

[1] "*Velle* quidem, quatenus est *actus* voluntatis, nostrum est ex *creatione:* bene velle etiam nostrum est, sed quatenus *volentes facti per conversionem bene volumus*," Calovius.

tine. How wholly is it otherwise with the unregenerate in Rom. vii. ! — The repetition by Paul of the *same* word, ἐνεργῶν . . . τὸ ἐνεργεῖν, has its ground in the encouraging design which he has of making God's agency felt *distinctly* and *emphatically;* hence, also, he specifies the *two* elements of all morality, not merely the ἐνεργεῖν, but also its premiss, the θέλειν, and keeps them apart by using καί twice : *God* is the worker in you, as of the *willing,* so of the *working.* From *His* working comes man's working, just as already his willing.[1] — ὑπὲρ τῆς εὐδοκίας] *for the sake of goodwill,* in order to satisfy His own benignant disposition. On the causal ὑπέρ, which is not *secundum,* comp. Rom. xv. 8 ; Kühner, II. 1, p. 421 ; Winer, p. 359 [E. T. p. 480]; and on εὐδοκία, which is not, with Ewald, to be taken in a deterministic sense, comp. i. 15 ; Rom. x. 1. Theodoret aptly says : εὐδοκίαν δὲ τὸ ἀγαθὸν τοῦ Θεοῦ προσηγόρευσε θέλημα· θέλει δὲ πάντας ἀνθρώπους σωθῆναι κ.τ.λ. The explanation : " for the sake of the *good pleasure,* which He has in such willing and working" (Weiss), would amount to something self-evident. Hofmann erroneously makes ὑπὲρ τ. εὐδοκ. belong to πάντα ποιεῖτε, and convey the sense, that they are to do everything *for the sake of the divine good pleasure,* about which they must necessarily be concerned, etc. In opposition to this view, which is connected with the misunderstanding of the previous words, the fact is decisive, that τῆς εὐδοκίας only obtains its reference to *God* through its belonging to ὁ ἐνεργῶν κ.τ.λ. ; but if it be joined with what follows, this reference must have been *marked,*[2] and that, on account of the *emphasized* position which ὑπ. τ. εὐδοκ. would have, with emphasis (as possibly by ὑπὲρ τῆς αὐτοῦ εὐδοκίας).

Ver. 14. With ver. 13 Paul has closed his exhortations, so far as the *matter* is concerned. He now adds a requisition in respect to the mode of *carrying out* these admonitions, namely, that they shall do *everything* (which, according to the admonitions previously given, and summarily comprised in ver. 12,

[1] This is God's *creative* moral action in salvation, Eph. ii. 10. Comp. Thomasius, *Chr. Pers. u. Werk,* I. p. 287. Incorrectly, however, the Reformed theologians add : " quae *prohiberi non potest.*"

[2] Hofmann groundlessly compares Luke ii. 14 (but see on that passage) and even Ecclus. xv. 15, where Fritzsche, *Handb.* p. 74 f., gives the right view.

they have to do, 1 Cor. x. 31) *willingly* and *without hesitation,*
—an injunction for which, amidst the temptations of the present (i. 27–30), there was sufficient cause. — χωρὶς γογγυσμ.]
without (far removed from) *murmuring.*   The γογγυσμός
(Lobeck, *ad Phryn.* p. 358), that fault already prevalent in
ancient Israel (Ex. xvi. 7 ff.; Num. xiv. 2), is to be conceived as directed *against God,* namely, on account of what He
imposed upon them both to do and to suffer, as follows from
the context in vv. 13 and 15; hence it is not to be referred
to their *fellow-Christians* (Calvin, Wiesinger, Schneckenburger), or to their *superiors* (Estius), as Hoelemann also
thinks.   Comp. on 1 Cor. x. 10. — διαλογισμῶν] not: without *disputes* (Erasmus, Beza, and many others, including
Schneckenburger), *de imperatis cum imperatoribus* (Hoelemann,
comp. Estius), or *among themselves* (Calvin, Wiesinger), and
that *upon irrelevant questions* (Grotius), and similar interpretations, which, although not repugnant to Greek usage generally
(Plut. *Mor.* p. 180 C; Ecclus. ix. 15, xiii. 35), are at variance
with that of the N. T. (even 1 Tim. ii. 8), and unsuitable to
the reference of γογγυσμ. to God.   It means: without *hesitation,* without your first entering upon *scrupulous considerings*
as to whether you are under any obligation thereto, whether
it is not too difficult, whether it is prudent, and the like.
Comp. Luke xxiv. 38, and on Rom. xiv. 1; Plat. *Ax.* p. 367 A:
φροντίδες . . . καὶ διαλογισμοί, *Tim.* p. 59 C: οὐδὲν ποικίλον
ἔτι διαλογίσασθαι. Ecclus. xl. 2.   The Vulgate renders it
rightly, according to the essential sense: "*haesitationibus.*"
The γογγυσμοί would presuppose *aversion* towards God; the
διαλογισμοί, *uncertainty in the consciousness of duty.*

— Ver. 15. If to their obedience of the admonitions given
down to ver. 13 there is added the *manner* of obedience
prescribed in ver. 14, *they shall be blameless,* etc.   This, therefore, must be the high *aim,* which they are to have in view in
connection with what is required in ver. 14. — ἄμεμπτοι κ.
ἀκέραιοι] *blameless and sincere;* the former represents moral
integrity *as manifesting itself to the judgment of others;* the
latter represents the same as respects its *inner nature* (comp. on
Matt. x. 16 and Rom. xvi. 19). — τέκνα Θεοῦ ἀμώμ.] com-

prehending epexegetically the *two* former predicates. *Children of God* (in virtue of the νἱοθεσία that took place in Christ, Rom. viii. 15, 23 ; Gal. iv. 5 ; Eph. i. 5) they *are* (Rom. viii. 16, ix. 8). They are *to become* such children of God, *as have nothing with which fault can be found ;* which in children of God presupposes the inward moral ἀκεραιότης, since they are led by the Spirit of God (Rom. viii. 14). This *ethical* view of the νἱοθεσία, prominent throughout the N. T., and already implied in the mode of contemplating Israel as the people of adoption (Rom. ix. 4) in the O. T. and Apocrypha, necessarily involves, in virtue of the *ideal* character of the relation, the moral *development* towards the lofty aim—implies, therefore, in the *being* the constant task of the *becoming ;* and hence the sense of *showing themselves* is as little to be given, with Hofmann, to the γένησθε here as in Matt. x. 16, John xv. 8, *et al. ;* comp. also on Gal. iv. 12. Ἀμώμητος, *qui vituperari non potest,* occurring elsewhere in the N. T. only at 2 Pet. iii. 14 (not equivalent to ἄμωμος or ἄμεμπτος), but see Hom. *Il.* xii. 109 ; Herod. iii. 82 ; frequently in the Anthol. Its opposite is : τέκνα μώμητα, Deut. xxxii. 5 ; the recollection of this latter passage has suggested the subsequent words, which serve as a *recommendation* of the condition to be striven for by *contrasting it with the state of things around.* — μέσον (see the critical remarks) is adverbial, *in the midst of* (Hom. *Il.* xii. 167 ; *Od.* xiv. 300 ; Eur. *Rhes.* 531 (μέσα) ; LXX. Num. xxxv. 5). — σκολιᾶς κ. διεστραμμ.] *crooked and perverted,* a graphic figurative representation of the great *moral abnormity* of the generation. Comp. on σκολιός, Acts ii. 40 ; 1 Pet. ii. 18 ; Prov. iv. 24 ; Wisd. i. 3 ; Plat. *Legg.* xii. p. 945 B, *Gorg.* p. 525 A ; and on διεστρ., Matt. xvii. 17 ; Deut. xxxii. 20 ; Polyb. viii. 24. 3, v. 41. 1, ii. 21. 8 ; also διάστροφος, Soph. *Aj.* 442. — ἐν οἷς] *i.e.* among the people of this γενεά ; see Buttmann, *Neut. Gr.* p. 242 [E. T. p. 282] ; Bremi, *ad Isocr.* I. p. 213 f. ; Kühner, II. 1, p. 49 f. — φαίνεσθε] not *imperative* (Cyprian, Pelagius, Ambrosiaster, Theophylact, Erasmus, Vatablus, Calvin, Grotius, and others, including Storr, Flatt, Rheinwald, Baumgarten-Crusius), but the *existing* relation, which constitutes the essential distinctive *character* of the Christian state as con-

trasted with the non-Christian, Eph. v. 8, *al.* The *aim* of the
ἐν οἷς φαίνεσθε κ.τ.λ. is, by means of an appeal to the true
Christian sense of honour (the consciousness of their high
Christian position towards them that are without), to assist
the attainment of the end in view; this is misunderstood
by Bengel, when he suggests the addition of "*servata hac
admonitione,*" a view in which he is followed by Hofmann.
The *meaning* is not *lucetis* (so usually), but (comp. also
Weiss, Schenkel, and J. B. Lightfoot): *ye appear,*[1] *come into
view, apparetis* (Matt. ii. 7, xxiv. 27; Jas. iv. 14; Rev.
xviii. 23; Hom. *Il.* i. 477, xxiv. 785, 788, *Od.* ii. 1, *Il.* ix.
707; Hes. *Oper.* 600; Plat. *Rep.* p. 517 B; Xen. *Hell.* iv. 3.
10; Polyb. ix. 15. 7; Lucian, *D. D.* iv. 3; also Xen. *Symp.* i.
9, *Anab.* vii. 4. 16; hence τὰ φαινόμενα, *the heavenly appearances*).   *Lucetis* (Vulgate) would be φαίνετε, John i. 5, v. 35;
1 John ii. 8; 2 Pet. i. 19; Rev. i. 16, xxi. 23; 1 Macc. iv.
40; Plat. *Tim.* p. 39 B; Arist. *Nub.* 586; Hes. *Oper.* 528;
Theoc. ii. 11. — φωστῆρες] *light-givers* (Rev. xxi. 11), here
a designation, not of *torches* (Beza, Cornelius a Lapide) or
lamps (Hofmann), which would be too weak for ἐν τῷ κόσμῳ,
and without support of linguistic usage; but, in accordance
with the usage familiar to the apostle in the LXX., Gen. i. 14,
16, of the *shining heavenly bodies;* Wisd. xiii. 2; Ecclus. xliii.
7; Heliod. 87; *Anthol.* xv. 17; Constant. Rhod. *ep. in Paralip.* 205. — ἐν κόσμῳ] is to be taken in reference to the
physical world, and closely connected with φωστ. As *light-
bearers in the world* (which shine in the world, by day the sun,
by night the moon and stars), *the Christians appear in the
midst of a perverted generation.*   Comp. Matt. v. 14; also
classical expressions like πάτρας φέγγεα (*Anthol.* vi. 614, 2),
etc.   If φαίνεσθε be rightly interpreted, ἐν κόσμῳ cannot be
joined with it (de Wette, Weiss, who takes κόσμῳ in the
ethical sense), or be supplemented by φαίνονται (Hoelemann,

---

[1] So also Homer, *Il.* i. 200, which Hofmann compares and brings out for our
passage the sense : "*stand in the light proper to them.*" Comp., however, *Il.*
xix. 16, xxii. 28, and *l.c.;* Duncan, *Lex.* ed. Rost. p. 1148 f. In the former
passage, i. 200, the sense is: her eyes (Athene's) *appeared* terrible. Comp.
Nägelsbach, p. 87, ed. 3. The same sense, according to another explanation, is
found in Faesi.

Rilliet, van Hengel). It is erroneous, further, to make ἐν κόσμῳ mean *in heaven* (Clericus, Rheinwald[1]), and also erroneous to attach a pregnant force to ἐν, making it mean " *within* the world," in contrast to the lights of heaven shining *from above*; thus Hofmann, connecting it with λόγον ζωῆς ἐπέχ. and bringing out with emphasis something quite self-evident. On κόσμος *without the article,* see Winer, p. 117 [E. T. p. 153]. On the whole passage, comp. *Test. XII. Patr.* p. 577 : ὑμεῖς οἱ φωστῆρες τοῦ οὐρανοῦ ὡς ὁ ἥλιος καὶ ἡ σελήνη· τι ποιήσουσι πάντα τὰ ἔθνη, ἐὰν ὑμεῖς σκοτισθήσεσθε ἐν ἀσεβείᾳ κ.τ.λ. Paul, however, has put φωστῆρες *without the article,* because he has conceived it *qualitatively.*

Ver. 16. *Λόγον ζωῆς ἐπέχοντες*] a definition giving the reason for φαίνεσθε ὡς φωστ. ἐν κ. : *since ye possess the word of life.* This is *the Gospel,* ἐπειδὴ τὴν αἰώνιον προξενεῖ ζωήν, Theodoret. See Rom. i. 16 ; comp. John vi. 68 ; Acts v. 20 ; it is the divinely efficacious vehicle of the πνεῦμα τῆς ζωῆς which frees from sin and death (see on Rom. viii. 2), and therefore not merely " the word *concerning* life" (Weiss). Christ Himself is the *essential* λόγος τῆς ζωῆς (1 John i. 1), His servants are ὀσμὴ ζωῆς εἰς ζωήν (2 Cor. ii. 16), therefore the *word preached* by them must be λόγος ζωῆς in the sense indicated. Paul does not elsewhere use the expression. As to ζωή without the article, of eternal life in the Messiah's kingdom (iv. 3), see Kaeuffer, *de ζωῆς αἰ. not.* p. 73 f. As possessors of this word, the Christians appear like φωστῆρες in a world otherwise dark; without this possession they would not so present themselves, but would be homogeneous with the perverted generation, since the essence of the gospel is *light* (Eph. v. 8 ; Col. i. 12 ; 1 Thess. v. 5 ; 1 Pet. ii. 9 ; Luke xvi. 8 ; Acts xxvi. 18, *al.*), just as Christ Himself is the principal light (John i. 4, 5, iii. 19, viii. 12, xii. 35, *al.*) ; but the element of the unbelieving γενεά, whose image is the κόσμος in itself devoid of light, is *darkness* (2 Cor. iv. 6, vi. 14 ; Eph. v. 8, vi. 12 ; Col. i. 13 ; John i. 5, iii. 19). *Ἐπέχειν, to possess,*[2]

---

[1] The designation of the *heavens* by κόσμος, first used by Pythagoras (see Bremi, ad *Isoc. Paneg.* p. 90), did not enter into the Biblical *usus loquendi.*

[2] Hofmann erroneously pronounces against this, representing that ἐπέχειν could

to have in possession, at disposal, and the like ; see Herod. i. 104, viii. 35 ; Xen. *Symp.* viii. 1 ; Thuc. i. 48. 2, ii. 101. 3 ; *Anth. Pal.* vii. 297. 4 ; Polyb. iii. 37. 6, 112. 8, v. 5, 6 ; Lucian, *Necyom.* 14. Not : *holding fast* (Luther, Estius, Bengel, and others, including Heinrichs, Hoelemann, Baumgarten-Crusius, de Wette, Ewald, Schneckenburger) ; nor yet : *sustinentes* (Calvin), so that the conception is of a light fixed on a candlestick. Others understand it similarly : *holding forth* (Beza, Grotius, and others, including Rheinwald, Matthies, Wiesinger, Lightfoot), namely, " that those, who have a longing for life, may let it be the light which shall guide them to life," as Hofmann explains more particularly ; comp. van Hengel. This would be linguistically correct (Hom. *Il.* ix. 489, xxii. 43 ; Plut. *Mor.* p. 265 A ; Pind. *Ol.* ii. 98 ; *Poll.* iii. 10), but not in harmony with the image, according to which the *subjects themselves* appear as shining, as *self-shining*. Linguistically incorrect is Theodoret's view : τῷ λόγῳ προσέχοντες (*attendentes*), which would require the *dative* of the object (Acts iii. 5 ; 1 Tim. iv. 16 ; Ecclus. xxxi. 2 ; 2 Macc. ix. 25 ; Job xxx. 26 ; Polyb. iii. 43. 2, xviii. 28. 11). Chrysostom, Oecumenius, Theophylact take ἐπέχ. correctly, but understand λόγον ζωῆς as equivalent to σπέρμα ζ. or ἐνέχυρα ζ., and indicate, as the purpose of the words : ὅρα, πῶς εὐθέως τίθησι τὰ ἔπαθλα (Chrysostom). This view is without sanction from the *usus loquendi*. Linguistically it would in itself be admissible (see the examples in Wetstein), but at variance with the N. T. mode of expression and conception, to explain with Michaelis, Storr, Zachariae, and Flatt : *supplying the place* of life (in the world otherwise dead), so that λόγον ἐπέχειν would mean : to hold *the relation*. Comp. Syr. — εἰς καύχημα κ.τ.λ.] the result which the γίνεσθαι ἀμέμπτους κ.τ.λ. on the part of the readers was to have *for the apostle ;* it was to become for him (and what an incitement this must have been to the Philippians !) a matter of glorying (i. 26) for the day of Christ (see on i. 10), when he should have reason to glory, that he, namely (ὅτι), had not laboured in

only be thus used in the sense of *having under one's control.* Compare, in opposition to this, especially such passages as Thuc. iii. 107. 4, where the word is quite synonymous with the parallel simple ἔχειν ; also *Anth. Pal.* vii. 276. 6.

vain, of which the excellent quality of his Philippian converts would afford practical evidence, ὅτι τοιούτους ὑμᾶς ἐπαίδευσα, Theophylact. Comp. 1 Thess. ii. 19 f. ; 2 Cor. i. 14. Thus they were to be to him on that day a στέφανος καυχήσεως (1 Thess. *l.c.*). Paul cannot mean a *present* καυχᾶσθαι *in prospect* of the day of Christ (Hofmann), for εἰς καύχημα κ.τ.λ. cannot be the result accruing for him from the ἐν οἷς φαίνεσθε κ.τ.λ. (since by it the position *of the Christians generally* is expressed), but only the result from the *ethical development* indicated by ἵνα γένησθε ἄμεμπτοι κ.τ.λ. Hence also ὅτι cannot be *a statement of the reason* (Hofmann) ; it is *explicative : that.* — The *twofold*[1] yet climactic, figurative description of his apostolical exertions (on ἔδραμ., comp. Gal. ii. 2 ; Acts xx. 24 ; on ἐκοπίασα, comp. 1 Cor. xv. 10 ; Gal. iv. 11), as well as *the repetition* of εἰς κενόν (see on Gal. ii. 2 ; 2 Cor. vi. 1 ; Polyc. *Phil.* 9), is in keeping with the emotion of joy, of triumph.

Ver. 17. The connection of ideas is this : What Paul had said in ver. 16 : εἰς καύχημα κ.τ.λ., presupposed, in the first place, that *he himself would live to see* the further development described in ver. 15 : ἵνα γένησθε ἄμεμπτοι. Now, however, he puts the opposite case, so as to elevate his readers to the right point of view for this also, and says : "*But even if I should be put to death* in my vocation dedicated to your faith," etc. Van Hengel finds in these words the contrast to the hope *of living to see the Parousia*. But *this* hope is not expressed in what precedes, since the result εἰς καύχημα κ.τ.λ. was conditioned, not by the apostle's living to see the *Parousia*, but only by his living to see the described *perfection of his readers*; inasmuch as, even when *arisen* at the Parousia, he might glory in what he had lived to see in the Philippians. Many others are satisfied with making these words express merely a *climax* (in relation to ἐκοπίασα) (see especially Heinrichs and Matthies); but this is erroneous, because ἐκοπίασα in the preceding verse is neither the main idea, nor specially indicative of tribulation. Arbitrary and entirely unnecessary is, further, the assumption of an opponent's *objection* (" at *vero imminent tristissima !*") to which Paul replies ;

---

[1] Comp. *Anthol. Pal.* xi. 56. 2 : μὴ τρίχε, μὴ κοπία.

or the explanation of ἀλλά by the intervening thought: " *non,
ie n'ai pas travaillé en vain, mais au contraire,*" etc., Rilliet;
comp. also Erasmus, *Paraphr.*   In a similar but direct way
Hofmann gains for ἀλλά the explanation, *but on the contrary,* by
connecting it antithetically with the preceding negative clauses
ὅτι οὐκ εἰς κενόν κ.τ.λ., which, with the right explanation
of the following words, is impossible.   According to de Wette
(comp. also Storr and Flatt), ver. 17 connects itself with i. 26,
so that ἀλλά forms a contrast to ver. 25, and all that intervenes is a digression.   But how could any reader guess at
this?   The suggestion is the more groundless, on account of
the χαίρω in ver. 17 corresponding so naturally and appositely
with the καύχημα in ver. 16. — εἰ καὶ κ.τ.λ.] *if I even* (which
I will by no means call in question) *should be poured out,* etc.
On the concessive sense of εἰ καί (1 Cor. iv. 7; 2 Cor. iv
3, 16, v. 16, vii. 8, *al.*), see Herm. *ad Viger.* p. 832; Klotz,
ad Devar. p. 519.   The case supposed is thus rendered more
probable than by the reading of E G, καὶ εἰ (*even assuming that
I*).   Stallbaum, *ad Plat. Ap. S.* p. 32 A; *Gorg.* p. 509 A;
Schmalf. *Syntax d. Verb.* sec. 99 f.   The protasis beginning
with ἀλλ' εἰ καί extends to τ. πίστ. ὑμῶν.   As in ver. 12,
so also here Hofmann makes the violent assumption that the
apodosis already begins at ἐπὶ τ. θυσίᾳ κ.τ.λ. with σπένδομαι
again to be supplied, whilst at the same time there is imputed
to this ἐπὶ τ. θυσίᾳ κ.τ.λ., in order to give an appropriate turn
to the assumed antithesis for ἀλλά, a tenor of thought which
the words do not bear; see below.— σπένδομαι] *I become offered
as a libation, poured out* as a drink-offering (2 Tim. iv. 6,
frequently in all classical writers; see also Schleusner, *Thes.*
V. p. 79; Suicer, *Thes.* II. p. 993).   The sense stripped of
figure is: if even *my blood is shed,* if even *I should be put to
death.*[1]   Paul represents his apostolic exertions for the faith of
the Philippians as an *offering* (comp. Rom. xv. 16); if he is
therein *put to death,* he is, by means of the shedding of his

---

[1] This (since the time of Chrysostom) unanimous interpretation of the figurative expression has been abandoned by Otto, *Pastoralbr.* p. 214 f., who explains
it as referring, not to the shedding of blood, but to the *severance of the apostle's
life in his vocation from intercourse with the world* by his *imprisonment.* An
abortive suggestion, the forced result of incorrect assumptions.

blood in this sacrifice, *made a libation,* just as among the Jews
(Num. xxviii. 7, xv. 4 ff.; Joseph. *Antt.* iii. 9. 4; see generally, Ewald, *Alterth.* p. 46 f.; Saalschütz, *M. R.* p. 314 f.) in
the sacrifices, together with meat-offerings, *libations of wine* were
made, which were poured upon the ground from sacred vessels
($\sigma\pi o\nu\delta\epsilon\hat{\imath}a$) at the altar.   As to the *Hellenic* sacrificial libations,
see Hermann, *Gottesd. Alterth.* § 25, 15 f.   On the figurative
representation of the shedding of blood as a $\sigma\pi o\nu\delta\dot{\eta}$, comp.
Anthol. ix. 184. 6: $\xi\dot{\imath}\phi o\varsigma$ $a\hat{\imath}\mu a$ $\tau\nu\rho\dot{a}\nu\nu\omega\nu$ $\ddot{\epsilon}\sigma\pi\epsilon\iota\sigma\epsilon\nu$, Ignatius,
Rom. 2; $\sigma\pi o\nu\delta\iota\sigma\theta\hat{\eta}\nu a\iota$ $\Theta\epsilon\hat{\omega}$ $\dot{\omega}\varsigma$ $\ddot{\epsilon}\tau\iota$ $\theta\nu\sigma\iota a\sigma\tau\dot{\eta}\rho\iota o\nu$ $\dot{\epsilon}\tau o\iota\mu\dot{o}\nu$ $\dot{\epsilon}\sigma\tau\dot{\iota}$.
—The *present* tense is used, because Paul has strongly in view
his *present* danger (i. 20 ff.); Kühner, II. 1, p. 119 f.   Rilliet
(comp. Wetstein) takes the *passive* erroneously : *I am besprinkled*
(which also does not correspond with the *present* tense), making
Paul say, " que la libation préparatoire du sacrifice a coulé sur
sa tête."   Confusion with $\kappa a\tau a\sigma\pi\dot{\epsilon}\nu\delta\epsilon\sigma\theta a\iota$, Plut. *Alex.* 50, *de
def. orac.* 46; Strabo, iv. p. 197; Eur. *Or.* 1239; Antip. Sid.
73 (*Anthol.* vii. 27). — $\dot{\epsilon}\pi\dot{\iota}$ τ. $\theta\nu\sigma$. κ. $\lambda\epsilon\iota\tau$. τ. π. $\dot{\nu}\mu$.] *at the
sacrifice and priestly service of your faith,* that is, whilst I present
your faith as a sacrifice and perform priestly service in respect
to it; the sense of this, *stripped of the figure,* is : *whilst I,
by furtherance of your faith in Christ, serve God,* as by the
offering and priestly ministration of a sacrifice. $\tau\hat{\eta}\varsigma$ $\pi\dot{\iota}\sigma\tau$.
is the object which is conceived as sacrificed and undergoing
priestly ministration; $\theta\nu\sigma\dot{\iota}a$ and $\lambda\epsilon\iota\tau o\nu\rho\gamma\dot{\iota}a$ have one article
in common, and are thereby joined so as to form one concep-
tion.   But $\lambda\epsilon\iota\tau o\nu\rho\gamma\dot{\iota}a$ (*priestly function,* comp. Luke i. 23;
Heb. viii. 6, ix. 21, and frequently in the LXX.; see Schleus-
ner, *Thes.;* comp. also Diod. Sic. i. 21, and, for the figurative
use of the word, Rom. xv. 16, 27) is added by the apostle as
a *more precise definition,* because the mere $\theta\nu\sigma\dot{\iota}a$ would leave it
uncertain whether he was to be considered as a *priest,* whereas
Paul desires expressly to describe himself as such. $\theta\nu\sigma\dot{\iota}a$, as
always in the N. T., is *sacrifice,* so that the idea is: at the
sacrifice and priestly service of your faith; hence there is no
necessity for taking it as *sacrificing,* or the *act of sacrifice*
(Herod. iv. 60, viii. 99; Herodian, viii. 3. 5, i. 36. 12, *al.*).
The $\dot{\epsilon}\pi\dot{\iota}$, however, is simply to be taken as *at,* as in i. 3 and

frequently; not as *to, in addition to* (Beza, Raphel, Matthies, de Wette, Weiss, and many others; comp. also Hofmann), or with the Vulgate as *supra* (Heinrichs, Hoelemann, van Hengel), in the sense of the (heathen) *mode*[1] of the libation, an interpretation which should have been precluded by the addition of the abstract κ. λειτουργ. Finally, although Paul's official activity concerned the faith of all his churches, he says ὑμῶν with the same right of *individualizing* reference as in δι᾽ ὑμᾶς at i. 24 and many other passages. The passage is peculiarly misunderstood by Hofmann, who holds that ἐπί has the sense *in association with ;* that τῆς πίστεως ὑμ. is the genitive of *apposition* to θυσίᾳ and λειτουργ.; that the sacrificing and ministering *subject* is not the apostle, but the Philippian *church,* which, when it became *believing,* had presented its own *sacrifice* to God, and has been *constantly honouring* Him with its own *work of service.* Accordingly Paul says that, even though his labours should end in a violent death, yet *the shedding of his blood would not be an isolated drink-offering, but would associate itself with their sacrifice.* But this would only make him say, with artificial mysteriousness, something which is perfectly self-evident (namely : after that ye became believers, and whilst ye are believers). Moreover, ἐπί would thus be made to express two very different relations, namely, with τῇ θυσίᾳ *after, after that,* and with the λειτουργίᾳ *at, during.* And how could a reader discover from the mere ἐπί κ.τ.λ. the alleged antithetical reference of an *isolated* drink-offering, especially as no *antithesis of the persons* is even indicated by ὑμῶν being placed first (immediately after ἐπί) ? The entire explanation is a forced artificial expedient in consequence of the mistaken assumption that an apodosis begins after σπένδομαι, and a new section sets in with χαίρω.[2] —

---

[1] On this *mode* of libation rests the expression ἐπισπένδειν, to pour a libation *over* something (Herod. ii. 39, iv. 60. 62, vii. 167 ; Aesch. *Ag.* 1395 ; Plut. *Rom.* 4).

[2] In which χαίρω κ. συγχαίρω πᾶσιν ὑμῖν are supposed to serve merely *as an introduction* for the exhortation which follows ; thus Paul would be made to say, that even for that supposed case of the σπένδεσθαι he is in a joyful mood, *and he rejoices with any person in the church whose heart is joyful* (all this is supposed to be implied in πᾶσιν ὑμῖν !).

χαίρω] Apodosis down to ὑμῖν : I rejoice, not at the θυσία κ.
λειτουργία τῆς πίστ. ὑμ. (Chrysostom, who connects ἐπὶ τ. θυσ.
κ.τ.λ. with χαίρω; comp. Oecumenius; so also Rilliet), for
it is mere arbitrariness to separate the sacrificial expressions
σπένδομαι and ἐπὶ τ. θυσίᾳ κ.τ.λ. and attach them to different
parts of the sentence, and because χαίρω, as the point of the
apodosis, would have been placed before ἐπὶ τ. θυσ. κ.τ.λ.; but
at the σπένδεσθαι : I rejoice to be employed for so sacred a destination. Theophylact appropriately remarks: οὐχ ὡς ὁ ἀπο-
θανούμενος λυποῦμαι, ἀλλὰ καὶ χαίρω ... ὅτι σπονδὴ γίνομαι,
and Theodoret: ταῦτα δὲ λέγει ψυχαγωγῶν αὐτοὺς κ. διδάσκων
τοῦ μαρτυρίου τὸ μέγεθος. Comp. Grotius, Heinrichs. The
ground of the apostle's joy, assumed by many (including Flatt,
Hoelemann, Matthies, de Wette): because my death will tend
to the advantage of the gospel (i. 20), and also the interpretation
of Weiss: that joy at the progress of the Philippians towards
perfection is intended, are both quite gratuitously imported into
the passage. The explanation of it as referring generally to
inward joyfulness of faith (Wiesinger) or divine serenity (Ewald),
does not correspond with the protasis, according to which it
must be joyfulness in the prospect of death. "Even if I am
compelled to die in this sacrificial service, I rejoice therein,"
and that, indeed, now for the case supposed; hence not
future. — καὶ συνχ. πᾶσιν ὑμῖν] is wrongly explained by most
commentators: "and I rejoice with you all" (so Chrysostom,
Theophylact, Luther, Calvin, Heinrichs, Matthies, van Hengel,
Rilliet, de Wette, Wiesinger, Ewald, Schneckenburger, Weiss,
Hofmann, and many others); along with which explanation
Chrysostom, Theophylact, and various of the older expositors,
bring forward another ground for this joint joy than for the
χαίρω (Chrysostom: χαίρω μὲν, ὅτι σπονδὴ γίνομαι· συγχαίρω δὲ, ὅτι θυσίαν προσενεγκών; comp. Schneckenburger).
Decisive against this interpretation is the χαίρετε which follows
in ver. 18,—a summons which would be absurd, if συγχ. ὑμ.
meant: "I rejoice with you." The Vulgate already rightly
renders: congratulor (comp. Jerome, Beza, Castalio, Grotius,
Storr, Flatt, Rheinwald, Hoelemann, Bisping, Ellicott, Lightfoot), I congratulate you all, namely, on the fact that I am

poured out *in the service of your faith.* *Such* a martyrdom, namely, *for the sake of their faith,* how it must have *elevated and honoured* the readers, their whole church; for such a martyr death concerned them all! Comp. on Eph. iii. 13; it redounds to their *glory,* if the apostle sheds his blood on account of their Christian standing established by him. It is *in this light* that Paul wishes his σπένδεσθαι, should it occur, to be regarded by his readers, and therefore gracefully and ingeniously represents it (though Hofmann holds this to be impossible) as something on which he must *congratulate* them all. Pauline linguistic usage is not to be urged in objection to this view (Weiss), as Paul employs συγχαίρω elsewhere only in the passages 1 Cor. xii. 26, xiii. 6, and these are balanced by vv. 17 and 18 here. Van Hengel and de Wette have erroneously objected that it would have been συγχαίρομαι (3 Macc. i. 8). The *active* as well as the *middle* may convey *either* meaning, *to rejoice along with,* or *gratulari* (Polyb. xxix. 7. 4, xxx. 10. 1; Plut. *Mor.* p. 231 B; 3 Macc. i. 8). See Valckenaer, *Schol.* I. p. 54.

Ver. 18. *And upon the same* (upon my possibly occurring σπένδεσθαι ἐπὶ τ. θυσ. κ.τ.λ., ver. 17) *rejoice ye also* (because it takes place for the sake of your faith), *and congratulate me thereon* (on such a sacred destination). The verbs are *imperatives.* "Postulat enim Paulus parem συμπάθειαν a Philipp.," Beza. The *ground* of the χαίρετε may not be arbitrarily introduced (Hofmann : whatever untowardness may occur), but must by logical necessity be the same which, in ver. 17, suggested the συγχαίρω ὑμῖν; and that of the συγχαίρετέ μοι must be the same as caused Paul to say χαίρω in ver. 17.[1] The expositors, who do not take συγχαίρειν as *gratulari,* are here placed in the awkward position of making the apostle summon his readers to a joy which, according to ver. 17, they would *already possess.* By this impossibility

---

[1] The difficulty which van Hengel (comp. Hofmann) urges, that the readers "vix aut ne vix quidem induci potuerunt de hujus viri morte violenta gaudentes vel gavisuri," entirely mistakes the lofty standpoint of the apostle, who looks death in the face with a holy joy (comp. the frequent corresponding sentiments in the epistles of Ignatius), and also attributes to his readers a corresponding mode of looking at the possibility of his death.

Weiss, in spite of the τὸ αὐτό, allows himself to be driven
into taking the joy in ver. 18, not as in ver. 17, but (comp.
also Hofmann) quite *generally*, of a *joyful frame of mind.* — τὸ
αὐτό] *in the same* (on the *accusative*, comp. Matt. ii. 10)
rejoice ye also; see also on i. 25. Hence it is not to be taken
as equivalent to ὡσαύτως (Beza, Storr, Flatt, Heinrichs, Rheinwald, Rilliet, de Wette, Wiesinger, Weiss, Hofmann) (comp.
on i. 6), in order thereby to avoid identifying it with the joy
mentioned in ver. 17. As to χαίρειν with the accusative in
classical authors, see generally Lobeck, *ad Aj.* 131; Kühner,
II. 1, p. 255 f.

Ver. 19. The apostle now, down to ver. 24, speaks of sending Timothy[1] to them, and states that he himself trusted to
visit them shortly. — ἐλπίζω δὲ κ.τ.λ.] The progress of thought
attaching itself to ver. 17 (not to ver. 12) is: However
threatening, according to ver. 17 f., and dangerous to life my
situation is, nevertheless I hope soon to send Timothy to you,
etc. He hopes, therefore, for such a change in his situation,
as would enable him soon to spare that most faithful friend
for such a mission. Here also, as in i. 21–26, there is an
immediate change from a presentiment of death to a confidence
of his being preserved in life and even liberated (ver. 24). The
right view of vv. 17, 18 debars us from construing the progress of the thought thus: *for the enhancement of my joy, however,* etc. (Weiss). Others take different views, as *e.g.* Bengel:
although I can write *nothing definite* regarding the issue of my
case,—an imported parenthetic thought, which is as little
suggested in ver. 17 f. as is the antithetical relation to χαίρετε
κ. συγχαίρ. μοι discovered by Hofmann, viz. that the apostle
is anxious as to whether all is well in the church. — ἐν κυρίῳ]
making the hope causally *rest in Christ.* Comp. on 1 Cor.
xv. 19. — ὑμῖν] not equivalent to the local πρὸς ὑμᾶς (van
Hengel), nor yet the dative *commodi* ("vestros in usus,

[1] Hofmann's hypothesis, that the church had expressed a desire that the apostle
would send them one who should aid them, with word and deed, in their affairs,
has no hint of it given at all in the text; least of all in ἵνα κἀγὼ εὐψυχῶ κ.τ.λ.
Why should Paul not have mentioned, in some way or another, the wish of the
church?—Baur and Hinsch find *no motive* mentioned for the mission of Timothy.
As if the motive of love conveyed by ἵνα κἀγώ κ.τ.λ. were not enough!

vestra in gaudia," Hoelemann, comp. de Wette and Hofmann), whereby too special a sense is introduced ; but the dative of *reference* (1 Cor. iv. 17 ; Acts xi. 29), indicating the persons concerned as those for whom the mission generally is *intended.* — καγώ] *I also,* as *ye* through the accounts[1] to be received *of me,* namely, those which ye shall receive through this epistle, through Epaphroditus, and through Timothy. — εὐψυχεῖν] *to be of good courage,* occurs here only in the N. T. See Poll. iii. 135 ; Joseph. *Antt.* xi. 6. 9. Comp the εὐψύχει in epitaphs (like χαῖρε) in Jacobs, *ad Anthol.* xii. p. 304. — τὰ περὶ ὑμ.] *the things concerning you,* quite generally, your circumstances. Eph. vi. 22 ; Col. iv. 8. See Heindorf, *ad Plat. Phaed.* p. 58 A.

Ver. 20. Reason why *Timothy* is the person sent. Hofmann erroneously takes it as : the reason why he sends no one *at the time.* As if νῦν γὰρ or ἄρτι γὰρ οὐδένα κ.τ.λ. were written. — ἰσόψυχον] *like-minded,* namely, *with me ;* in what respect, is stated in the sequel. Castalio, Beza, Calvin, Rilliet, Weiss, J. B. Lightfoot, wrongly interpret it : no one who would be so minded *as he* (Rheinwald combines the two references). As αὐτῷ is not added, the text gives no other reference for ἴσος (in ἰσόψυχ.) than to the subject of ἔχω (see also ver. 22) ; as, indeed, Paul could not give a better reason for the choice of Timothy, and could not more effectively recommend him to his readers, than by setting forth his likemindedness *with himself ;* comp. Deut. xiii. 6 : φίλος ἴσος τῇ ψυχῇ μου. The word occurs only here in the N. T. ; see LXX. Ps. lv. 14 ; Aesch. *Agam.* 1470. Comp. on the subjectmatter, 1 Cor. xvi. 10. — ὅστις κ.τ.λ.] the emphasis is laid on γνησίως, and ὅστις, *quippe qui, ita comparatum ut,* introduces the *character* of an ἰσόψυχος, such as is not at his disposal. —

---

[1] There is a delicate compliment implied in this καγώ ; for Timothy was to *come back* again to the apostle (but not Epaphroditus, ver. 25), and thus he hopes to receive the desired news about them which shall make him be of good courage. Hofmann introduces the comparative sense : *fresher* courage, under the assumption which he reads between the lines, that the apostle is *concerned* about various things in the church, *which Timothy would succeed in settling and arranging.* Paul's cordial, loving interest in the welfare of the Philippians is quite sufficient to explain the εὐψυχᾶ.

γνησίως] *in genuine, sincere fashion*, with *one* care without
guile (Dem. 1482, 14; Polyb. iv. 30. 2; 2 Macc. xiv. 8),
the selfish contrast to which is described in ver. 21.　Comp.
2 Cor. viii. 8.—μεριμνήσει] namely, *when I shall have sent him.*
The *caring* is not to be more precisely defined; it necessarily
manifested itself according to the circumstances in watching,
correction, encouragement, counsel, and action.　Comp. 1 Cor.
xii. 25; 2 Cor. xi. 28.

Ver. 21.　Οἱ πάντες] all (except Timothy), of those whom
I now have with me and at my disposal for sending; see
ver. 20.　We have the less warrant to modify this judgment
in any way, expressed, as it is, so very clearly and decidedly
by the absolute antithesis τὰ ἑαυτῶν ζητοῦσιν, οὐ τὰ ’Ι. Χ.,
seeing that we are unacquainted with the circle surrounding
the apostle *at that particular time*, and do not know to what extent the anti-Pauline tendency, i. 15, 17, had then spread in
the immediate neighbourhood of the apostle.　The only limitation of the general expression, which is in accordance with
the text, lies in the fact that Paul does not mean the Christians generally in Rome, but such *assistant teachers* as would
otherwise, if they had been pure and honest, have been *qualified* for such a mission.　The trustworthy ones among these
otherwise qualified fellow-labourers must have been *absent* at
the time, especially *Luke*, who could by no means have been
included among οἱ πάντες (in opposition to Wieseler, *Chronol.
d. apost. Zeitalt.* p. 427); hence the Philippians are not *saluted
specially* either by Luke or by any other, and the omission of
such salutations by name at the end of this epistle receives
in part its explanation from this passage.　Consequently, οἱ
πάντ. cannot be understood as *many* or the *most* (Beza, Wolf,
Hammond, Drusius, Estius, Grotius, Cornelius a Lapide, and
others, including Heinrichs, Rheinwald, Flatt); nor is it:
"all, *whom I can spare*" (Erasmus), or: "*who are known to
you*" (van Hengel).　Neither is the negation to be taken *relatively:* they seek *more* their own interest, etc. (Erasmus,
Calvin, and many others, also Flatt, Hoelemann, comp. the
reservations of Weiss), to which Hofmann's view[1] also ulti-

---

[1] The latter says: they allow themselves *to be influenced in the direction of*

mately comes; nor is it to be explained by assuming an intention of *distinguishing Timothy* (Matthies); nor yet is the judgment to be restricted, with Chrysostom, Oecumenius, and Theophylact, to the hardships *of the long journey*, to which they preferred *their own repose*. Bengel rightly defends the full seriousness of the utterance, and adds: "subtilissima erat αἴσθησις, qua hoc percepit Paulus." But Baur erroneously discovers here merely an *exaggeration*, which arose from the subjectivity of a later author. What an uncalled-for fiction that would have been!

Ver. 22. Contrast, not of the *person* (which would have run τὴν δὲ αὐτοῦ δοκ. or αὐτοῦ δὲ τὴν δοκ.), but of the *qualification*, in order further to *recommend* him, whom he hopes soon to be able to send; not to *make up for the disadvantage*, that they can in the first instance *only hope*, etc. (as Hofmann artificially explains). *But the approved character* (*indoles spectata*, comp. Rom. v. 4; 2 Cor. ii. 9, ix. 13) *of him ye know;* for Timothy had himself been in Philippi (Acts xvi. 1, 3, xvii. 14); hence γινώσκ. is not the *imperative* (Vulgate, Pelagius, Castalio, Cornelius a Lapide, Clericus, Rheinwald, Hoelemann). — ὅτι κ.τ.λ.] *that he, namely*, etc. — ὡς πατρὶ τέκνον] Comp. 1 Cor. iv. 17. The apostle had here ἐδούλευσεν before his mind, but *alters* the conception in such a way, that he thinks upon the service as rendered no longer *to him*, but *with him*, in a humble glance at Christ (ver. 21), whom he himself also serves, so that the apostle's servant is at the same time his σύνδουλος. See Winer, pp. 393, 537 [E. T. pp. 525, 722]. Hofmann labours without success to remove the incongruity, which cannot be got rid of unless, with Vatablus, we were at liberty to supply σύν before πατρί. But, however frequently the Greeks put the preposition only once in comparisons (see Bernhardy, p. 204 f.; Kühner, II. 1, p. 479), its omission does not occur in the clause placed *first*. The poetical use of such an omission in the case of words which are connected by

---

their activity, even though it be consecrated to the kingdom of God (?), *by special personal aims, instead of devoting themselves* ALWAYS ONLY (? οὐ τὰ 'Ι. Χ.) *to that which is* MOST ADVANTAGEOUS *for the cause of Christ* (οὐ τὰ 'Ι. Χ.!). Thus there is imported into the passage what is not at all to be found in it.

καί, τέ, or ἤ (Dissen, *ad Pind. Nem.* x. 38; Lobeck, *ad Aj.* 397 ff.) does not concern us here. — εἰς] *in respect to the gospel* (comp. i. 5), the serving in question having reference to the preaching, defence, etc., thereof.

Ver. 23. *Μὲν οὖν*] οὖν resumes ver. 19, and to the μέν corresponds the δὲ in ver. 24. — ὡς ἂν ἀπίδω κ.τ.λ.] *when* (of the *time*, see Klotz, *ad Devar.* p. 759, that is, *as soon as*, comp. on 1 Cor. xi. 34; Rom. xv. 24) *I anyhow* (by ἄν the matter is left to *experience*) ~~shall have seen to the end~~ (Jonah iv. 5). The latter, which expresses the perceiving from a distance (Herod. viii. 37; Dem. 1472. 15; Lucian, *D. D.* vi. 2), denotes the *knowledge of the final course* of matters *to be expected*,—only after which could it be decided whether or not he could spare the faithful Timothy for a time. The form ἀφίδω (Lachmann and Tischendorf) in A B* D* F G ‭א‬ is, on account of this weighty evidence, to be considered not as a copyist's error, but as the original, and to be derived from the pronunciation of ἰδεῖν (with the digamma). Comp. on Acts iv. 29, and see Winer, p. 44 [E. T. p. 48]; J. B. Lightfoot *ad loc.*; Buttmann, *Neut. Gr.* p. 7 [E. T. p. 7]. — τὰ περὶ ἐμέ] *the things about me,* that is, the state of my affairs. Substantially not different from τὰ περὶ ἐμοῦ (ver. 19 f.). See Kühner, *ad Xen. Mem.* i. 1. 20; Winer, p. 379 [E. T. p. 506].

Ver. 24. *Καὶ αὐτός*] *also myself* personally. *What* Paul shall see, therefore, is, as he confidently trusts (not merely *hopes*), his *liberation* (comp. i. 25 f.); that it will make it possible for him to come soon.[1] The *terminus a quo* of the ταχέως is, as in ver. 19, the *then present* time, although the sending of Timothy and his return (ver. 19) are to precede his own coming. The ταχέως as a *relative* definition of the time is not opposed to this view. But that καὶ αὐτός includes also the case of his *coming at the same time with* Timothy (Hofmann), is, according to ver. 19 ff., not to be assumed.

Ver. 25 f. About *Epaphroditus;* the sending him home,

---

[1] How could this confidence, which the result did not justify, have been put by any later author into the apostle's mouth? Only Paul himself could have written in such a way as here and in i. 25 f. See, in opposition to Hinsch, Hilgenfeld, 1873, p. 185 f.

and recommendation of him, down to ver. 30. — ἀναγκ. δὲ
ἡγ.] *I have, however, judged it necessary*, although Epaphroditus, namely, according to vv. 19–24, might have remained
here still, in order to have made his return-journey to you
later, either in company with Timothy, or eventually with
myself.   For *the special reason*, which Paul had for not
keeping him longer with himself in Rome, see vv. 26, 28.
— Ἐπαφρόδιτον] otherwise not further known. The name
(signifying *Venustus*) was a common one (Tac. *Ann.* xv. 55 ;
Suet. *Domit.* 14 ; Joseph. *Vit.* 76 ; Wetstein *in loc.*), also
written Ἐπαφρόδειτος (Boeckh, *Corp. inscr.* 1811, 2562); but
to regard the man as identical with Ἐπαφρᾶς (Col. i. 7,
iv. 12 ; Philem. 23) (Grotius, Paulus, and others) is all the
more arbitrary, since Epaphras was a *Colossian* teacher.—The
grouping together of *five predicates* which follows, has arisen
out of loving and grateful *regard* for Epaphroditus, as an
honourable testimony to him in his relation to the apostle as
well as to the church. — ἀδελφ., συνεργ., συστρατ.] a climactic
threefold description of *companionship*, advancing from the
most general category, that of Christian brotherhood (ἀδελφός),
to a twofold more special relation. On συστρατ., which sets
forth the joint working (συνεργ.) in relation to the *hostile*
powers, comp. Philem. 2 ; 2 Tim. ii. 3. — ὑμῶν δὲ ἀπόστ. κ.
λειτουργ. τ. χρ. μου.] still belonging to τόν ; hence ὑμῶν, placed
in contrast to the μου, belongs to λειτουργ. τ. χ. μ. as well (in
opposition to de Wette and others). Ἀπόστολος here means
delegate (2 Cor. viii. 23), and not *apostle* (Vulgate, Hilarius,
Theodoret, Luther, Erasmus, Calovius, Wetstein : " mei muneris
vicarium apud vos," am Ende, and others), which would necessitate the genitive ὑμῶν being taken as in Rom. xi. 13, against
which the context, by the union with λειτουργ. τ. χ. μ., is
decisive ; as, indeed, Paul uses ἀπόστ. as an official designation only in the sense of the actual apostolic rank, based
upon a direct call by Christ, in its narrower and wider reference (comp. on Gal. i. 19 ; Rom. xvi. 7 ; 1 Cor. xv. 7), and
hence there is no necessity to seek even an allusion to his
" quasi"-apostolic position towards the Philippians (Matthies).
— κ. λειτουργ. τ. χ. μ.] *the sacrificial minister of my need, ὡς*

τὰ παρ᾽ αὐτῶν ἀποσταλέντα κομίσαντα χρήματα, Theodoret.
By sending aid they had cared for the apostle's need (iv. 16);
and that gift of love being regarded as a sacrifice offered to
God, Epaphroditus, who had been entrusted by them with the
conveying of it, was the λειτουργός in the matter, that is, he
who performed the priestly service in the bringing of this
offering (comp. ver. 17). Such is also the conception in
2 Cor. ix. 12. On τῆς χρείας μ. comp. iv. 16; Rom. xii. 13.—
πέμψαι] as also in Greek authors frequently, in the sense of
dimittere domum, to send home,[1] consequently equivalent to
ἀποπέμπειν or ἀναπέμπειν (Philem. 12); Xen. *Hell.* ii. 7. 9;
Sop. *O. R.* 1518; Polyb. v. 100. 10; and frequently in
Homer. See especially *Od.* xv. 74: χρὴ ξεῖνον παρεόντα
φιλεῖν, ἐθέλοντα δὲ πέμπειν.

Ver. 26. *State of mind* (ἦν with participle) of Epaphroditus,
which supplied the motive for the ἀναγκ. ἡγησ. κ.τ.λ.[2] — The
imperfect is used (ἦν), because Paul transports himself to the
time when the readers shall receive this epistle. Then is
Epaphroditus again among them; but he *was* previously longing,
etc. — ἀδημονῶν] *in anxiety.* Comp. on Matt. xxvi. 37. —
ὅτι ἠσθ.] *that he was sick.* How the Philippians received this
information, remains an open question, as also *how* Epaphroditus learned that they had heard it.

Ver. 27. Confirmation of that ἠκούσατε, ὅτι ἠσθ. — καὶ γὰρ
κ.τ.λ.] *for he has also* (really, see Hartung, *Partikell.* I. p. 132;
Baeumlein, p. 150) *been sick.* — παραπλ. θανάτῳ] adds the
specification *of the mode: in a way almost equivalent to death.*
There is neither an *ellipsis* (de Wette: ἀφίκετο or some such

[1] That Paul, however, here writes πέμψαι πρὸς ὑμᾶς, and, on the other hand,
π. ὑμῖν in ver. 19, is an accidental and undesigned variation. Hofmann thinks
that by π. ὑμῖν is meant the sending of *a representative of the apostle to the
Church*, and by π. πρὸς ὑμᾶς the sending of *a representative of the Church to the
apostle.* This distinction is involved in the state of the case, but has nothing to
do with the difference between the ὑμῖν and πρὸς ὑμᾶς. Comp. 1 Cor. iv. 17;
Eph. vi. 22; Col. iv. 8; Tit. iii. 12; 2 Cor. xii. 17.

[2] The supposition that Paul, in specifying this ground, wished to prevent the
so speedy return of the man *from being interpreted to his disadvantage* (Hofmann), assumes the existence of a certain distrust, for which there is no basis in
the text. Besides, Epaphroditus had in fact *accomplished* the purpose of his
mission.

word is to be understood before παραπλ.; comp. van Hengel)
nor a *solecism* (van Hengel); παραπλ. is *adverbial* (equivalent to παραπλησίως, see Polyb. iv. 40. 10, iii. 33. 17;
Lucian, *Cyn.* 17; comp. παραπλησιαίτερον, Plat. *Polit.* p.
275 C), and the *dativus congruentiae* (instead of which the
genitive might also have been used, Bernhardy, p. 148) is
governed by it. — λύπην ἐπὶ λύπην] *grief upon grief* (super-
added). LXX. Ezra vii. 26; Ps. lxix. 27; Isa. xxviii. 10.
Comp. expressions with the *dative* (as Ecclus. xxvi. 15) in
classic Greek, *e.g.* ὄγχνη ἐπὶ ὄγχνῃ (Hom. *Od.* vii. 120), ἐσλὰ ἐπ'
ἐσλοῖς (Pind. *Ol.* viii. 84), φόνος ἐπὶ φόνῳ (Eur. *Iph.* T. 197);
Polyb. i. 57. 1. See also Eur. *Hec.* 586: λύπη τις ἄλλη
διάδοχος κακῶν κακοῖς, Soph. *El.* 235: ἄταν ἄταις, Eur.
Troad. 175: ἐπ' ἄλγεσι δ' ἀλγυνθῶ. The *first* λύπην refers to
the dreaded death of his friend; the *second,* to the apostle's
affliction *over the painful position* in which he found himself, as a prisoner, and also through the doings of the adversaries (ver. 20 f., i. 15, 17, 30), not over *the sickness of Epaphroditus* (Chrysostom, Oecumenius, Theophylact, Erasmus,
Estius, and others, also Weiss), to which would be added that
for his *death.* Ἀλυπότερος in ver. 28 is fatal to the latter
view, for it appears that, even after Epaphr. had been sent
away, a λύπη still remained, which, therefore, could not be
referred to the latter's sickness. Van Hengel errs in understanding the affliction as pain concerning this sickness, and the
first λύπην as "cogitatio anxietatis vestrae." See, in opposition, on ver. 28. Calvin's remark suffices to justify the double
λύπη: "Non jactat Stoicorum ἀπάθειαν, quasi ferreus esset et
immunis ab humanis affectibus." Comp. John xi. 35 f. —
σχῶ] not optative. See Winer, p. 270 [E. T. p. 359].

Ver. 28. *The more urgently, therefore* (in consequence of
this sickness which he had had and recovered from, of which
ye received tidings, vv. 26, 27), I have brought about his
return, which otherwise I would still have delayed. — πάλιν]
belongs to χαρῆτε, as Paul usually places it *before* the verb, or,
at least, makes it follow *immediately* after. See Gersdorf,
Beitr. p. 491 f., and van Hengel. And the context affords no
ground for departing from the usual mode, and for joining it

with ἰδόντες αὐτόν (Beza, Grotius, and others, also Baumgarten-
Crusius and de Wette). — κἀγὼ ἀλυπότ. ὡ̣] Ἐὰν γὰρ ὑμεῖς
χαρῆτε, καὶ ἐγὼ χαίρω, Oecumenius.   He is not ἄλυπος, for he
is in captivity and surrounded by adversaries; but the joy
which he is aware is already prepared for his beloved Philippians by the return of Epaphroditus, *lessens* his λύπη.   This
tender interweaving of his own alleviation with the rejoicing
of his readers is lost, if we refer ἀλυπότ. to the removal of *the*
vexation *of seeing the recovered one so full of longing and so un-
easy* (Hofmann), which, regarded as λύπη, would be sentimental.
According to Weiss, Paul intends to say : *still more* ἄλυπος,
than I have already become in consequence of Epaphroditus'
recovery.   An unsuitable idea, because the comparative necessarily presupposes a certain degree of the λύπη still remaining.
In the consciousness of this Paul has written ἀλυπότ.; if it
had been otherwise, he would perhaps have used, as in ver. 19,
κἀγὼ εὐψυχῶ or κἀγὼ χαίρω.

Ver. 29 f. Οὖν] Let, then, the *reception* which he meets
with among you be in accordance with my purpose in accelerat-
ing his return (ἵνα ἰδόντες κ.τ.λ.) ; receive him *with all joy.* —
ἐν κυρίῳ] denotes, as in Rom. xvi. 2, the *Christian character* of
the προσδέχεσθαι, the nature and action of which have their
distinctive quality in Christ, in whose fellowship Christians live
and move. — μετὰ πάσ. χαρ.] excludes *every* kind of sullen or
indifferent temper and expression : " *with all* joyfulness." — καὶ
τοὺς τοιούτους κ.τ.λ.] *and the people of such a sort,* etc.   Ἵνα μὴ
δόξῃ αὐτῷ μόνῳ χαρίζεσθαι, κοινῶς παραινεῖ πάντας τοὺς τὴν
αὐτὴν ἀρετὴν ἐπιδεικνυμένους τιμᾶν, Theophylact.   But Epaphroditus is *in his view,* as in the given case, the person
belonging to the class thus to be held in honour.[1]

Ver. 30. διὰ τὸ ἔργ.] emphatically prefixed : on account
of nothing else than for this great sacred aim.   The *work* (see
the critical remarks) is, according to the context (comp. Acts

---

[1] There is no ground for the reference, which Hofmann discovers here, to an
assumed inclination, on the part of the Philippians, to hold in honour people *of
another sort* (such as are described in chap. iii.) *more* than the τοιούτους.   For
this assumption there would, at the most, be occasion only if Paul had used the
comparative instead of ἐντίμους.   Besides, the emphasis is not on τοὺς τοιούτους
(Hofmann), but on ἐντίμους, correlative to the preceding μετὰ πάσ. χαρᾶς.

xv. 38), obvious, namely, that of *labour for the gospel;* the
addition in the *Rec.* τοῦ Χριστοῦ is a correct gloss, and it is
this ἔργον κατ᾽ ἐξοχήν (comp. ὑπὲρ τοῦ ὀνόματος, Acts v. 41)
in the service of which Epaphroditus incurred so dangerous
an illness, namely, when he, according to the testimony of
the predicates in ver. 25, as the συνεργός and συστρατιώτης
of the apostle, with devotedness and self-sacrifice, united his
exertions for the gospel and his striving against the movements of its adversaries (i. 15, 17, 30, ii. 20) with a similar
activity on the part of the apostle. The interpretation which
refers ἔργον to *the business of conveying the bounty* (de Wette,
following older expositors, comp. Weiss), does not suffice for
the more special characteristic description ; and the reference to the *enmity of Nero* against Paul, the dangers of
which Epaphroditus had shared, in order to reach the apostle
and to serve him, finds no warrant either in the context or in
Acts xxviii. (in opposition to Chrysostom, Oecumenius, Theophylact, comp. Theodoret). — μέχρι θαν. ἤγγ.] as in Ps. cvii. 18 :
ἤγγισαν ἕως τῶν πυλῶν τοῦ θανάτου, Ecclus. li. 6 : ἕως θανάτου, Rev. xii. 11. The expression with μέχρι is more definite
than the dative would be (as in Ps. lxxxviii. 3 : ἡ ζωή μου τῷ
ᾅδη ἤγγισε), or εἰς θάνατ. (Job xxxiii. 22) ; he came *near even
unto death.* — παραβουλ. τῇ ψυχ.] Such is the *Text. Rec.,* which
Bengel, Matthaei (vehement in opposition to Wetstein and
Griesbach), Rinck, van Hengel, Reiche, and others defend,
and Tischendorf still follows in the 7th ed. Justly, however,
Scaliger, Casaubon, Salmasius, Grotius, Mill, Wetstein, and
others, including Griesbach, Lachmann, Scholz, Tischendorf,
ed. 8, Rheinwald, Matthies, Rilliet, Winer, Ewald, Weiss,
J. B. Lightfoot, Hofmann, and others, have preferred παραβολ.
τ. ψ. The latter has the authority of A B D E F G ℵ, 177,
178, 179 in its favour, as well as the support of the Itala by
"*parabolatus est de anima sua,*" and of Vulgate, Aeth., Pelagius,
by " *tradens* (Ambrosiaster : *in interitum tradens) animam
suam.*" Since βολεύεσθαι was unknown to the copyists, whilst
βουλεύεσθαι was very current, instead of the one ἅπαξ λεγόμ.
another crept in, the form of which, on account of the pre-
valence of the simple word, had nothing offensive. παρα-

βολεύεσθαι, which is nowhere certainly preserved (in opposition to Wetstein's quotations from the Fathers, see Matthiae, ed. min. p. 341 f., and Reiche, *Comment. crit.* p. 220 f.), is formed from the very current classical word παράβολος, *putting at stake, venturesome,* and is therefore equivalent to παράβολον εἶναι, *to be venturous,* to be an adventurer, as περπερεύεσθαι equivalent to πέρπερον εἶναι (1 Cor. xiii. 4), ἀλογεύεσθαι equivalent to ἄλογον εἶναι (Cic. *Att.* vi. 4), ἀποσκοπεύειν and ἐπισκοπεύειν (see Lobeck, *ad Phryn.* p. 591), κωμικεύεσθαι (Luc. *Philop.* 22). See more such verbs in Lobeck, *ad Phryn.* p. 67, and comp. generally Kühner, I. p. 695, II. 1, p. 98. Hence the παραβολευσάμενος κ.τ.λ., which is to be regarded as a modal definition to μ. θαν. ἤγγισε, means : *so that he was venturesome with his soul* (dative of the more definite reference), *i.e. he hazarded his life,*[1] in order to supply, etc. In this sense παραβάλλεσθαι is current among Greek authors, and that not merely with accusative of the object (Hom. *Il.* ix. 322 ; so usually, as in 2 Macc. xiv. 38), but also with dative of reference (Polyb. ii. 26. 6, iii. 94. 4; Diod. Sic. iii. 35: ἔκριναν παραβαλλέσθαι ταῖς ψυχαῖς), in the sense of ῥιψοκινδυνεῖν (Schol. Thuc. iv. 57) and παραρρίπτειν (Soph. *fr.* 499. Diud.). Comp. παραβάλλομαι τῇ ἐμαυτοῦ κεφαλῇ in Phryn. *ed. Lob.* p. 238. Hence, also, the name *parabolani* for those who waited on the sick (Gieseler, *Kirchengesch.* I. 2, p. 173, ed. 4). Taking the reading of the *Text. Rec.,* παραβουλεύεσθαι would have to be explained : *male consulere* vitae (Luther aptly renders : since he *thought light* of his life). See especially Reiche. This verb, also, does not occur in profane Greek authors ; but for instances from the Fathers, especially Chrysostom, and that in the sense specified, see Matthiae, *l.c.;* Hase in *Steph. Thes.* VI. p. 220. — ἵνα ἀναπλ. κ.τ.λ.] *The object,* to attain which he hazarded his life. We have to notice (1) that ὑμῶν belongs to ὑστέρημα ; and (2) that τῆς πρός με λειτουργ. can denote nothing else but the function,—well known and defined

---

[1] The matter is conceived as *staking a price* or *forfeit.* Comp. παραβόλιον in Poll. viii. 63, Phrynich. p. 238. On the subject-matter comp. also προΐεσθαι τὰς ψυχάς (Pausanias, iv. 10. 3) ; the *animae magnae prodigus* of Horace (*Od.* i. 12. 37) ; and the *vitam profundere pro patria* of Cicero (*de Off.* i. 24).

by the context (ver. 25), and conceived of as a sacrificial service,—with which Epaphroditus had been commissioned by the Philippians in respect to Paul (πρός με). All explanations are therefore to be rejected, which either expressly or insensibly connect ὑμῶν with λειτουργ., and take the latter in the general sense of rendering service (διακονεῖν). We must reject, consequently, Chrysostom's explanation (comp. Theophylact, Theodoret, Pelagius, Castalio, Vatablus, and others): τὸ οὖν ὑστέρημα τῆς ὑμετέρας λειτουργίας ἀνεπλήρωσεν· ... ὅπερ ἐχρῆν πάντας ποιῆσαι, τοῦτο ἔπραξεν αὐτός;[1] also the similar view taken by Erasmus and many others (comp. Grotius, Estius, Heinrichs, Rheinwald, van Hengel, Rilliet): "quo videlicet pensaret id, quod ob absentiam *vestro erga me officio videbatur deesse;*" the arbitrary explanation of Matthies: "in order that he *might perfect the readiness of service which you have shown on various occasions;*" and several other interpretations. Hoelemann, also, in opposition to the simple literal sense, takes τὸ ὑμῶν ὑστέρ. as *defectus cui subvenistis,* and τῆς πρός με λειτουργ. as: *rerum necessariarum ad me subministrando deferendarum.* No; of the two genitives, referring to different things (comp. ver. 25, and see Winer, p. 180 [E. T. p. 239]), by which τὸ ὑστέρημα is accompanied, the first conveys *who* were wanting (ὑμῶν, *ye* were wanting, *ye yourselves* were not there, comp. 1 Cor. xvi. 17), and the second *to what* this want applied. Consequently the passage is to be explained: *in order to compensate for the circumstance, that ye have been wanting at the sacrificial service touching me;* that is, *for the circumstance, that this sacrificial service, which has been made through your love-gifts in my support, was completed, not jointly by you, but without you,* so that only your messenger Epaphroditus was here, and not ye yourselves in person. How delicate and winning, and at the same time how enlist-

---

[1] Hofmann substantially reverts to this. He takes ὑμῶν as the *subject,* which *had allowed something to remain lacking* in the service, namely, in so far as the church had *only collected* the aid, but not *conveyed* it. How *indelicate* would such a thought have been! Besides, it was, in fact, an *impossibility* for the church to have come personally. Hence the church *was wanting,* indeed, at the transmission of the bounty, but it did not thereby *allow* anything *to be wanting* in the latter.

ing their grateful sympathy in the fate of Epaphroditus, was it to represent the absence of the Philippians as something that *had been lacking* in that λειτουργία, and therefore, as something which Paul had *missed,* to supply which, as *representative* of the church, the man had (as his deadly sickness had actually shown) hazarded his life !   He did not therefore contract the illness *on his journey to Rome* (de Wette, Weiss, and older expositors), as Hofmann thinks, who represents him as arriving there *in the hot season of the year ;* but through his exertions διὰ τὸ ἔργον *in Rome itself* during his sojourn there, when his sickness showed that he had risked his life in order to bring the offering of the Philippians, and thus compensate the apostle for the absence of the church. On ἀναπλ. τὸ ὑμ. ὑστέρ., comp. 1 Cor. xvi. 17.   The compound verb is appropriately explained by Erasmus : " accessione implere, quod plenitudini perfectae deerat."   See on Gal. vi. 2. —It was a foolish blunder of Baur to hold the entire passage respecting Timothy and Epaphroditus as merely an *imitation* of 2 Cor. viii. 23 f.   Hinsch very erroneously, because misconceiving the delicate courtesy of the grateful expression, thinks that in ver. 30 the aid is described as a *duty* incumbent on the readers,—which would be un-Pauline ; iv. 10 is far from favouring this idea.

CHAPTER III.

VER. 3. Instead of Θεοῦ Elz. has Θεῷ, against decisive testimony, although again defended by Reiche. A clumsy emendation in order to complete the λατρ. — Ver. 6. ζῆλον] Lachm. and Tisch. read ζῆλος, following A B D* F G ℵ*. A copyist's error; comp. the exeg. remarks on 2 Cor. ix. 2. — Ver. 8. Instead of μὲν οὖν Elz. and Tisch. 8 have μενοῦνγε, which, although supported by A P ℵ, is opposed by very preponderating testimony. — The second εἶναι is wanting in B D* F G ℵ*, 17, Arm. Vulg. It. Lucif., et al. Suspected by Griesb., omitted by Lachm. and Tisch. 8. But how readily may it, otherwise superfluous, have been left out before the similar ἵνα! — Ver. 10. The second τήν is wanting in A B ℵ*; omitted by Lachm.; overlooked as unnecessary.—Instead of συμμορφιζόμενος (so Lachm. and Tisch.), which Griesb. approves, Elz. and Scholz have συμμορφούμενος. But the former has in its favour A B D* P ℵ*, min. Or. ms. Bas. Macar., as also συνφορτιζόμενος in F G It. Lucif. Ir. The Recepta substitutes an analogous form more familiar. — Ver. 11. τῶν νεκρ.] A B D E P ℵ, min., and many vss. and Fathers, have τὴν ἐκ νεκρ., which is recommended by Griesb. and adopted by Scholz, Lachm., and Tisch. But Paul always uses ἀνάστασις with merely the genitive τῶν νεκρῶν, or only νεκρ. The ἐκ was written on the margin here to explain the word ἐξαναστ., which does not occur elsewhere in the N. T., and subsequently the erroneous insertion of this ἐκ after τῶν (so still F G) produced the reading τὴν ἐκ νεκρ. — Ver. 12. The Χριστοῦ alone (Elz. gives τοῦ Χ. Ἰησοῦ) has preponderant evidence. — Ver. 14. ἐπί] Lachm. and Tisch. read εἰς, following A B ℵ, min. Clem. Aeth. Rightly; ἐπί is explanatory. — Ver. 16. After στοιχεῖν, Elz., Scholz have κανόνι, τὸ αὐτὸ φρονεῖν, which is wanting in A B ℵ*, min. Copt. Sahid. Aeth. Hilar. Aug., et al. There are, besides, several variations, and differences in the arrangement of the words. The Recepta has arisen from glosses (following Gal. vi. 16; Phil. ii. 2), and has far too little homogeneousness in a critical point of view, to enable it to be defended on the ground of homoioteleuton (so Matth. and Rinck). — Ver. 21. After ἡμῶν, Elz. has εἰς τὸ γενέσθαι αὐτό, which (although defended by Matth.) is omitted by decisive authorities. An ancient supplement. —

ἑαυτῷ] Following A B D* F G K P ℵ*, min. Eus. Theophyl., αὐτῷ is, with Lachm. and Tisch., to be read; ἑαυτῷ is a more precise definition.

In iii. 1 Paul seems already preparing to close his epistle; but at this point his attention is directed, perhaps by some special momentary occasion, to the party of anti-Pauline teachers, against which he at once breaks forth with vehemence and irony in ver. 2, warning his readers against them; and thereafter, from ver. 4 to 14, he sets forth in detail his own bearing as contrasted with the character of those false teachers.

Ver. 1. Τὸ λοιπόν] introduces what is *still* to be done by the readers *in addition* to what has been hitherto communicated; see on Eph. vi. 10. Hence it is of frequent occurrence towards the close of the epistles, as bringing in a further request, exhortation, etc. Comp. iv. 8; 2 Cor. xiii. 11; 1 Thess. iv. 1; 2 Thess. iii. 1. To the closing address thus introduced, but at once abandoned again in ver. 2, Paul would have attached his giving of thanks for the aid sent to him (comp. iv. 8, 10 ff.). This is contrary to the view of Schinz and van Hengel, who, from the fact that Paul has not yet expressed his thanks, conclude that he did not at this point desire to proceed to the closing of the letter. We need not search for a connection with what precedes (Chrysostom: ἔχετε Ἐπαφρόδιτον, δι' ὃν ἠλγεῖτε, ἔχετε Τιμόθεον, ἔρχομαι κἀγώ, τὸ εὐαγγέλιον ἐπιδίδωσι· τί ὑμῖν λείπει λοιπόν; comp. Oecumenius, Theophylact, Erasmus, Estius, Cornelius a Lapide, Michaelis, and others). The preceding topic is *closed*, and the exhortation beginning with τὸ λοιπ. which now follows stands by itself; so that we are not even justified in saying that Paul here passes from *the particular to the general* (Schinz, Matthies), but must simply assume that he is proceeding to *the conclusion*, which he desired to commence with this general encouragement. — χαίρετε ἐν κυρίῳ] is a summons to *Christian* joyfulness, which is not κατὰ κόσμον (see Chrysostom), but has its ground *in Christ*, and is thereby specifically defined, inasmuch as Christ—through the Holy Spirit—rules in the believing heart; hence the χαρὰ πνεύματος ἁγίου (1 Thess.

i. 6) or ἐν πνεύματι ἁγίῳ (Rom. xiv. 17) are in substance not
different from this (comp. Gal. v. 22). The subsequent
double repetition of this encouragement (iv. 4) is the result of
the apostle's special love for his readers, and of the whole
tone of feeling pervading the epistle.   Moreover, in ἐν κυρίῳ
we are not to seek for a *new special* element, preparing the
way for the transition to the explanations which follow
(Weiss, Hofmann); for Paul could not in what went before
mean any *other* joy, either on his own part (i. 18) or on the
part of his readers (ii. 17 f., 28), and in other passages also
he does not add to χαίρετε the self-evident definition ἐν
κυρίῳ (2 Cor. xiii. 11; 1 Thess. v. 16).   *Another* joy in
the Christian life he *knew* not at all. — τὰ αὐτὰ γράφειν]
"Hic incipit de pseudo-apostolis agere," Calvin. After χαίρ.
ἐν κ. there is a *pause;* Paul *breaks off.* τὰ αὐτά has been
erroneously referred to χαίρ. ἐν κ., and in that case the retrospective reference which Paul had in view is either not
explained at all (Bengel, Zachariae), or is believed to be found
in ii. 18 (van Hengel, Wiesinger), or in i. 27 f. (Matthies,
Rilliet), or in i. 27–ii. 16 (Storr). This view is at variance,
not indeed with the plural τὰ αὐτά (see, on the contrary,
Stallbaum, *ad Plat. Apol.* p. 19 D; Mätzner, *ad Antiph.* p.
153; Kühner II. 1, p. 60), but with the facts, first, that there is
no express summons whatever to *Christian joyfulness generally,*
given in the previous portion of the epistle (not even in ii.
18); secondly, that so simple and natural a summons—which,
moreover, occurs again twice in iv. 4—would certainly have
least of all given rise to an apology for repetition; and
lastly, that ἀσφαλές, in accordance with its idea (*without
danger*), points not to the repetition of a summons *of this kind,*
but to a *warning,* such as follows immediately in the context.[1]
The accusation of *poverty of thought* (Baur) is therefore all the
more groundless here. And as the altogether vague reference of Theodoret and Erasmus (*Annotat.*) to the *numerous*

---

[1] The expedient to which Wiesinger has recourse is gratuitously introduced,
when he connects the χαίρετε ἐν κ. more closely with the warning that follows by
imagining that, in χαίρ. ἐν κ., he detects already the idea on which the sequel is
based, namely the στήκετε ἐν κυρίῳ, iv. 1.

exhortations contained in the epistle generally, or to the *funda-mental tone* of the letter hitherto (Weiss), is simply at variance with the literal import of the words, τὰ αὐτά cannot be inter-preted as applicable to anything but the *subsequent warning against the false teachers.* This warning, however, has not occurred previously, either at i. 15 f., or indirectly in i. 27, as Lünemann thinks, or in i. 27–ii. 18, as Ewald assumes. Hence many have caught at the explanation : " eadem repetere, *quae praesens dixeram* " (Pelagius, Theodore of Mop-suestia, so also Erasmus, *Paraphr.*, Calvin, Beza, Balduin, Estius, Calovius, Wolf, Schrader, and others ; de Wette unde-cidedly). But this *quae praesens dixeram* is quite gratuitously imported; it must at least have been indicated by τὰ αὐτὰ καὶ γρ. ὑμ. or in some other way. The same objection applies against Wieseler (*Chronol. d. apost. Zeitalt.* p. 458 f.), who takes τὰ αὐτά as contrasted with the oral communications, which would be made to the readers *by Epaphroditus* and especially by *Timothy.* The only correct explanation, there-fore, that remains is the assumption (which, however, is expressly rejected already by Theodoret) that Paul had already written what follows *in an earlier epistle to the Philippians* [1] which is not preserved, and that he here repeats the same. So Aegidius Hunnius, Haenlein, Bertholdt, Flatt, Köhler, in the *Annal. d. ges. Theol.* 1834, III. 1, p. 18 f.; Feilmoser, Bleek, Jatho, Schenkel, Bisping, Hilgenfeld, Hofmann ; de Wette undecidedly. It must remain uncertain, however, whether this repetition covers ver. 2 only, or ver. 3 also, or a still larger portion of the sequel; as also, how far the repetition is a *literal* one, which seems to be the case with ver. 2 from its peculiar character. — ὀκνηρόν] *irksome, matter of scruple* (Dem. 777. 5 ; Theocr. xxiv. 35; Pind. *Nem.* xi. 28; Herodian vi. 9, 7 ; Soph. *O. R.* 834), comp. οὐκ ὀκνητέον, Polyb. i. 14. 7, also Plat. *Ep.* II. 310 D : τἀληθῆ λέγειν οὔτε ὀκνήσω οὔτε αἰσχυνοῦμαι. — ἀσφαλές] *safe,* so that ye will the more firmly rely thereon for the determination of your conduct. Comp. Acts xxv. 26 ; Heb. vi. 19 ; Wisd. vii. 23 ; Plat. *Rep.* 450 E ; *Phaed.* p. 100 D E ; Dem. 372. 2, 1460. 15. Hofmann,

---

[1] Comp. also Credner, *Einl.* I. p. 333.

without any precedent of usage, assigns to ὀκνηρόν the sense
of *indolent cowardice,* and takes ἀσφαλές as *prudent,* which
linguistically is admissible (Heind. *ad Plat. Soph.* p. 231 A),
but would be unsuitable to the ὑμῖν. The apostle wishes to
say, that the repetition is *for himself* not irksome (ὄκνος,
haesitatio), and is *for his readers* an ἀσφαλὲς τεκμήριον (Eur.
Rhes. 94.) to be attended to.

NOTE.—This exegetical result, *that, previously to our epistle,
Paul had already written another to the Philippians,*[1] is confirmed
by Polycarp,[2] who, *ad Phil.* 3, says: τοῦ μακαρίου κ. ἐνδόξου
Παύλου, ὃς γενόμενος ἐν ὑμῖν κατὰ πρόσωπον τῶν τότε ἀνθρώπων ἐδίδαξεν
ἀκριβῶς κ. βεβαίως τὸν περὶ ἀληθείας λόγον, ὃς καὶ ἀπὼν ὑμῖν ἔγραψεν
ἐπιστολὰς, εἰς ἃς ἐὰν ἐγκύπτητε, δυνήσεσθε οἰκοδομεῖσθαι κ.τ.λ. It is
true that the *plur.* in this passage (ἐπιστολὰς, εἰς ἃς) is usually
explained as referring to *one* epistle (see Cotelerius *in loc.;* and
Fabricius, *Cod. Apocr.* II. p. 914 f.; Hilgenfeld, *Apost. Väter,* p.
210; J. B. Lightfoot, p. 138 f.), just as it is well known that
also in profane authors ἐπιστολαί (comp. *literae*) is used of *one*
despatch (Thuc. i. 132. 6, viii. 39. 2), sometimes generally in a
generic sense as plural of the *category,* and sometimes specially
of *commissions* and *orders.* See Schaefer, *Plut.* VI. p. 446;
Blomf. and Stanl. *ad Aesch. Prom.* 3; Rettig, *Quaest. Phil.* II.
p. 37 f. But there is the less ground for assuming this construction here, since *doctrinal epistles,* both in the N. T. and
also in the apostolic Fathers, are always described by the
singular when only one epistle is intended, and by the plural
(as in 1 Cor. xvi. 3; 2 Cor. x. 9–11; 2 Pet. iii. 16; comp. Acts
ix. 2, xxii. 5) if more than one are meant,—a practice from which
there is no exception (not even in 1 Cor. xvi. 3), as, in fact,
Polycarp, in regard to ἐπιστολή, elsewhere very definitely distin-

---

[1] Ewald also acknowledges the composition of more than one epistle to the
Philippians, but finds traces of them not here, but at ii. 12, iii. 18.

[2] I cannot at once accept the view that the passages in question, ch. iii. and
xi., are *interpolated* (Ritschl, *altkath. Kirche,* p. 588 ff.). The interpolations
in the Ignatian epistles are at any rate of another kind. Besides, we have from
Polycarp only the one epistle; and we have therefore no sufficient objective standard of comparison, in the absence of which a judgment founded on
taste is very uncertain. But even assuming the interpolation, we should still
have the result that the *interpolator* was acquainted with *several* epistles of Paul
to the Philippians. Otherwise he would have had no reason for using the *plural,*
especially as it was already distinction enough for the church to have had *one*
epistle addressed to it by the apostle.

guishes between the singular and plural.   See ch. xiii.: τὰς ἐπιστολὰς Ἰγνατίου τὰς πεμφθείσας ἡμῖν ὑπ᾽ αὐτοῦ καὶ ἄλλας ὅσας εἴχομεν παρ᾽ ἡμῖν, ἐπέμψαμεν ὑμῖν, καθὼς ἐνετείλασθε· αἵτινες ὑποτεταγμέναι εἰσὶ τῇ ᾽πιστολῇ ταύτῃ.   In order to prove that Polycarp in ch. iii. did not mean *more than one* epistle to the Philippians, an appeal has been made to ch. xi., where, in the Latin version, which alone has been preserved, it is said: "Ego autem nihil tale sensi in vobis vel audivi, in quibus laboravit beatus Paulus, qui estis (non-genuine addition: *laudati*) in principio *epistolae ejus;* de vobis enim gloriatur in omnibus ecclesiis, quæ Deum solae tunc cognoverant, nos autem nondum noveramus."   But *epistolae ejus* cannot here be the epistle to the Philippians, for the idea: "ye are in the beginning of his epistle," would be simply absurd; *epistolae* is, on the contrary, the nominative plural, and the sense is: "Ye are originally *his epistles*," that is, his *letters of recommendation*, in which phrase allusion is made to 2 Cor. iii. 1 ff.[1]   The correctness of this explanation, which Wieseler has substantially adopted, is corroborated by the sequel: *de vobis enim gloriatur*, etc.—It is, moreover, *à priori* intelligible and likely enough that Paul should have corresponded with this church—which enjoyed his most intimate confidence, and the founding of which marked his entrance on his European labours—at an earlier period than merely now, almost at the close of his life.   And Polycarp was sufficiently close to the time of the apostle, not merely to have *inferred* such a correspondence from our passage,

---

[1] Hofmann also explains the expression from 2 Cor. iii. 1 ff., but errs in taking *epistolae* as the *genitive;* he makes this epistle to be *the whole of the Christians gathered by Paul,* and thus represents Polycarp as declaring, in reference to the Philippian church, that *it stands first* in this epistle, *because it is reckoned among his earliest acquisitions.*   According to this interpretation, a vast *aggregate* of churches would be depicted as *one* epistle, in which one church would stand written *first,* and others *after it,* each therefore being *marked by name* in the order of its *date.*   What a different picture this would yield from that presented in 2 Cor. iii., and one, too, delineated singularly enough!   And how unsuitable would such a precedence, as to time, be for the church at Philippi!   By how long a period had the establishment of all the churches of Asia preceded it!   Hofmann's objection to our view, viz. that the present *estis* would be unsuitable, does not apply, since Polycarp *realizes* the state of matters as it stood with the church *in principio* (ἐν ἀρχῇ, *i.e.* in the earliest times of the gospel), *as present;* hence also he subsequently says *gloriatur* (not *gloriabatur*).   The conception is this : Paul in all the churches of that early Christian age boasts of the excellent Philippian church, and so this church serves him as so many letters of recommendation, which by his *gloriari* he communicates, and as it were reads before, those other churches.

but to have had a *historical knowledge* of it (in opposition to Hofmann).

Ver. 2. This is now the τὰ αὐτά which he had previously written, and probably in the very same *words*. At least this seems to be indicated by the *peculiar* expressions *in themselves;* and not only so, but it serves also to explain the relation of *contrast,* which this vehement " fervor pii zeli " (Calvin) presents to the tender and cordial tone of *our* epistle. That lost epistle had probably expressed the apostle's mind at length, and with all the warmth of controversy, for the warning of his readers as to the Judaizing false teachers. How entirely different is the tone in which, in the *present* epistle, he speaks (i. 15 ff.) of teachers likewise of an anti-Pauline type, and labouring, indeed, at that time in his immediate neighbourhood ! Comp., moreover, the remark after i. 18. Those who refer τὰ αὐτά to the χαίρετε ἐν κυρίῳ, labour in very different ways to establish a connection of thought with βλέπετε κ.τ.λ. ; as, for instance, Wiesinger : that Paul wished to *suggest, as a ground* for the reiterated summons to joy in the Lord, *the danger* which was threatening them from the men described ; Weiss : that the readers were to learn *e contrario,* on what the true Christian joy was, and on what it was not, based. — βλέπετε] not : *be on your guard against,* etc. (which would be βλ. ἀπό, Mark viii. 15, xii. 38), but as a *calling attention to : behold !* (1 Cor. i. 26, x. 18), with a view, however, to *warn* the readers against these men as pernicious, by pointing to the forbidding shape in which they present themselves. — τοὺς κύνας] a term of reproach among the Jews and the Greeks (frequently in Homer, who, however, also uses it *without* any dishonourable reference ; see Duncan, *Lex. ed. Rost.* p. 674) ; used by the latter specially to denote impudence, furious boldness (Hom. *Il.* viii. 289 ; *Od.* xvii. 248 ; *Anth. Pal.* ix. 302), snappishness (Pollux, *On.* v. 65), low vulgarity (Lucian, *Nigr.* 22), malice and cunning (Jacobs, *ad Anthol.* VI. p. 18), and the like, see generally Wetstein ; used also among the Jews in similar special references (Isa. lvi. 10 f. ; Deut. xxiii. 18 ; Rev. xxii. 15, *et al.*), and, because dogs were *unclean* animals, generally to denote the *profane, impure, unholy* (Matt. vii. 6 ; Ps. xxii. 17 ; Rev. xxii. 15 ; Schoettgen, *Hor.* I. p. 1145) ; hence the Gentiles were so designated (see on Matt. xv. 26). In this passage also the *profane* nature and demeanour of the false teachers, as contrasted with the holy character of true Christianity, is to be adhered to as the point of comparison (Chrysostom : οὐκέτι τέκνα Ἰουδαῖοι . . . ὥσπερ οἱ ἐθνικοὶ καὶ τοῦ Θεοῦ καὶ τοῦ Χριστοῦ ἀλλότριοι ἦσαν, οὕτω καὶ οὗτοι γεγόνασι νῦν). Any more special reference of the term—as to *shamelessness* (Chrysostom and many others, including Matthies, Baumgarten-Crusius, Ewald), *covetousness* (both combined by Grotius), *snappishness* (Rilliet, and older expositors, following Ambrosiaster, Augustine, and Pelagius), *envy,* and the like ; or to the *disorderly wandering about* in selfishness and animosity towards those who were living peaceably in their Christian calling (Hofmann), to which Lange fancifully adds *a loud howling* against Paul,—is not furnished by the context, which, on the contrary, follows it up with yet another *general* designation, subjoining, namely, to that of the low, unholy *character* (κύνας) that of the *evil working :* τοὺς κακοὺς ἐργάτ. Comp. 2 Cor. xi. 13. The opposite: 2 Tim. ii. 15 ; Xen. *Mem.* i. 2. 57. Ἐργάζονται μέν, φησιν, ἀλλ᾽ ἐπὶ κακῷ, καὶ ἀργίας πολλῷ χεῖρον ἔργον, ἀνασπῶντες τὰ καλῶς κείμενα, Chrysostom ; comp. Theodoret, Oecumenius, Theophylact. They, in fact, *laboured* in *opposition* to the fundamental doctrine of justification by faith. — τὴν κατατομήν] *the cutting in pieces* (Theophr. *H. pl.* iv. 8. 12), a word formed after the analogy of περιτομή, and, like the latter in ver. 3, used in a *concrete* sense : *those who are cut in pieces !* A bitter *paronomasia,* because these men were circumcised merely *as regards the body,* and placed their confidence in this fleshly circumcision, but were wanting in the *inner, spiritual* circumcision, which that of the body typified (see ver. 3 ; Rom. ii. 28 f. ; Col. ii. 11 ; Eph. ii. 11 ; Acts vii. 51). Comp. Gal. v. 11 f. In the absence of this, their characteristic consisted simply in the bodily mutilation, and that, from the ideal point of view which Paul here occupies, was not *circum*cision, but *conc*ision ; whilst, on the other hand, *circ*umcision, as respected its moral idea, was entirely independent of the corporeal operation, ver. 3. Comp. Weiss, *bibl. Theol.* p. 439, ed. 2. This *qualitative* distinction between περιτ. and κατατ. has been misunderstood by Baur, who takes the climax as *quantitative*, and hence sees in it a warped and unnatural antithesis, which is only concocted to give the apostle an opportunity of speaking of his own person. Chrysostom, Oecumenius, and Theophylact justly lay stress on the *abolition of the legal circumcision as such* brought about through Christ (the end of the law, Rom. x. 4),—a presupposition which gives to this antinomistic sarcasm its warrant.[1] A description of *idolatry*, with allusion to Lev. xxi. 5, 1 Kings xviii. 28, *et al.* (Storr, Flatt, J. B. Lightfoot; comp. Beza), is quite foreign to the context. It is erroneous also to discover here any indication of a *cutting off of hearts from the faith* (Luther's gloss), or a *cutting in pieces of the church* (Theodoret, Calvin, Beza, Grotius, Hammond, Clericus, Michaelis, Zachariae, and others), against which the necessary (comp. ver. 3) *passive* signification of the word (not *cutters in pieces*, but *cut in pieces*) is decisive.—The *thrice repeated* βλέπετε belongs simply to the ἐπιμονὴ of earnest *emotion* (Dissen, *ad Dem. de cor.* p. 315; Buttmann, *Neut. Gr.* p. 341 [E. T. 398]), so that it points to the *same* dangerous men, and does not, as van Hengel misconceives, denote *three different classes* of Jewish opponents, viz. *the apostate, the heretical*, and the *directly inimical.* The passage quoted by him from Philostr., *Vit. Soph.* ii. 1, does not bear upon the point, because in it the three repetitions of ἔβλεψε are divided by μὲν ... δέ. Weiss also refers the three designations to three different categories, namely: (1) the unconverted *heathen*, with their immoral life; (2) the self-seeking *Christian* teachers, i. 15-17; and (3) the *unbelieving*

---

[1] Luther's works abound in sarcastic *paronomasiae.* Thus, for instance, in the preface to his works, instead of *D*ecret and *D*ecretal, he has written "*Drecket*" and "*Drecketal*" [Germ. Dreck = dregs, filth]; the *Legenden* he calls *Lügenden*, the *Jurisperitos* he terms *Jurisperditos;* also in proper names, such as Schwenkfeld, whom he called "*Stenkfeld.*" In ancient authors, comp. what Diog. L. vi. 2, 4 relates of Diogenes: τὴν Εὐκλείδου σχολὴν ἔλεγε χολήν, τὴν δὲ Πλάτωνος διατριβὴν κατατριβήν. Thuc. vi. 76. 4: οὐκ ἀξυνετωτέρου, κακοξυνετωτέρου δέ. See also Ast, *ad Plat. Phaedr.* p. 276; Jacobs, *Delect. epigr.* p. 188. For the Latin, see Kühner, *ad Cic. Tusc.* p. 291, ed. 3.

Jews, with their carnal conceit. But the first and third categories introduce alien elements, and the third cannot be
identified with those mentioned at i. 15–17, but must mean
persons much more dangerous. In opposition to the whole
misinterpretation, see Huther in the *Mecklenb. Zeitschr.* p.
626 ff. All the *three* terms must characterize *one* class of
men as in three aspects deserving of detestation, namely the
Judaizing false teachers. As is evident from τ. κατατομήν and
ver. 3 ff., they belonged to the same fundamentally hostile party
against which Paul contends in the Epistle to the Galatians.
At the same time, since the threefold repetition of the article
pointing them out may be founded upon the very *notoriety*
of these men, and yet does not of necessity presuppose a
personal acquaintance with them, it must be left an open
question, whether they had already come to Philippi itself, or
merely threatened danger from some place in its vicinity.
It is certain, however, though Baur still regards it as doubtful,
that Paul did not refer to his opponents *in Rome* mentioned
in i. 15 ff. (Heinrichs), because in the passage before us a
line of teaching must be thought of which was expressly and
in principle anti-Pauline, leading back into Judaism and to
legal righteousness ; and also because the earnest, demonstra-
tive βλέπετε, as well as ἀσφαλές (ver. 2), can only indicate a
danger which was visibly and closely threatening the readers.
It is also certain that these opponents could not as yet have
succeeded in finding adherents among the Philippians ; for if
this had been the case, Paul would not have omitted to censure the readers themselves (as in the Epistle to the Galatians
and Second Corinthians), and he would have given a very different shape generally to his epistle, which betrays nothing but
a church as yet undivided in doctrine. His language directed
against the false teachers is therefore merely *warning* and
precautionary, as is also shown in ver. 3.

Ver. 3. Justification of the preceding τ. κατατομήν ; not,
however, " *an evident copy*" *of* 2 Cor. xi. 18 f. (Baur), but very
different from the latter passage amidst the corresponding
resemblances which the similarity of subject suggested ; in both
cases there is Pauline originality. — ἡμεῖς] with emphasis : *we,*

not they.   The κατατομή being not the unconverted Jews, but
Christian Judaizers, the contrasted ἡμεῖς cannot mean *the Christians generally* (Weiss), but only those who, in the apostle's
sense, were *true and right* Christians, whose more definite
characterization immediately follows.   The ἡμεῖς are the
Ἰσραὴλ τοῦ Θεοῦ of Gal. vi. 15 f., the members of the people
of God in the sense of *the Pauline gospel*, and not merely *Paul
and the true teachers* of the gospel (Hofmann),—a restriction
which the exclusiveness of the predicate, especially furnished
as it is with the article, does not befit; in iii. 17 the context
stands otherwise. — ἡ περιτομή] If this predicate belongs to *us*,
not to *those men*, then, in regard to the point of circumcision,
nothing remains for the latter but the predicate κατατομή!
As the ἡμεῖς, among whom the readers also were included,
were for the most part *uncircumcised* (Gal. ii. 9, iii.; Eph.
ii. 11), it is clear that Paul here takes περιτομή purely in
the antitypical *spiritual* sense, according to which the *circumcised* are those who, since the reception of baptism, *are
regenerated by the Holy Spirit*, and therefore members of the
true people of God; the investiture with their new moral
condition is typically *prefigured* by the legal bodily περιτομή
of the Jewish theocracy.   Comp. Rom. ii. 29, iv. 10 f.; Eph.
ii. 11; Col. ii. 11; Acts vii. 51.   Whether the bodily circumcision *was present* or not, and whether, therefore, the subjects
were Jewish or Gentile Christians, was in that case matter of indifference, 1 Cor. vii. 19; Gal. iii. 28, v. 6.   Comp. the further
amplification of the thought in Barnab. *Ep.* 9. — οἱ πνεύματι
Θεοῦ κ.τ.λ.] *We who serve through the Spirit of God*, in contrast to the external, legal λατρεία (Rom. ix. 4).[1]   Comp. Heb.
ix. 10, 14; Rom. xii. 1 f.   With this λατρεία, wrought by
the Holy Spirit,[2] there takes place on the part of man
(comp. Rom. i. 9), but in virtue of that very working of the
Holy Spirit, the worship which is required in John iv. 24.

---

[1] True Christianity is, according to Paul also, the true continuation of Judaism,
and that not merely of the promise given in it, but also of the law; the latter,
however, according to the idea of the πλήρωσις, Matt. v. 17, in which the letter
has yielded to the spirit.

[2] If we adopt the reading πνεύματι Θεῷ, πνεύματι must be understood as in Rom.
i. 9.   See Reiche, *Comment. crit.* p. 229 ff.

The *article* οἱ extends also to the two participles which follow ;
and the *arthrous* participles (*quippe qui* colimus, etc.) contain
the *experimental* proof that the ἡμεῖς are the περιτομή. The
dative πνεύματι denotes neither the standard (van Hengel) nor
the object (Hilgenfeld), which latter view would amount to
the conception, foreign to the N. T., of a worship of the Holy
Spirit—but is *instrumental,* expressing the inward *agent* (Rom.
v. 5, viii. 14 f., *et al.*) : *vi spiritus divini* (Rom. viii. 13, *et al.*).
On the *absolute* λατρεύειν, *to render divine worship,* comp. Luke
ii. 37 ; Acts xxvi. 7 ; Heb. ix. 9, x. 2 ; Rom. ix. 4 ; 3 Esdr.
iv. 54. — καυχώμ. ἐν Χ. Ἰ.] and who *glory in Christ Jesus* (as
Him through whom alone we have attained righteousness, etc.,
see ver. 9 ; comp. Gal. vi. 14), not in our own privileges and
legal performances, as those false teachers do, who place their
confidence in what is *fleshly, i.e.* in that which belongs to
material human nature and has nothing in common with the
divine blessings of the Christian (such as circumcision, descent,
outward observance of the law, comp. vv. 4–6).   Hence the
contrast : καὶ οὐκ ἐν σαρκὶ πεποιθότες, with which the *disposition of mind* contrary to the καυχᾶσθαι ἐν Χ. Ἰ. (from which
disposition the καυχᾶσθαι, opposed to that Christian καυχᾶσθαι,
of itself results) is negatived ; so that this contrast is *pregnant,*
belonging, however, by way of antithesis, to the second statement, and not containing a separate third one (Hofmann).
If κ. οὐκ ἐν σ. πεπ. were merely a more precise *definition of
purport* added to καυχ. ἐν Χ. Ἰ. (Weiss), it must have been
added without καί.   As to οὐκ in the passage, referring to
concrete persons and a definite fact, and negativing not merely
the ἐν σαρκί (Hofmann), but the actual position ἐν σ. πεποιθ.,
see Winer, p. 451 f. [E. T. 609] ; Baeumlein, *Partik.* p.
276 f.

Ver. 4. By the οὐκ ἐν σαρκὶ πεποιθ., which he had just
used, Paul finds himself led to *his own personal position ;* for
he was, in fact, the proper organ of the anti-Judaizing tendency expressed in ver. 3, and the real object against which
the whole conflict with it was ultimately directed.   Hence, by
the words οὐκ ἐν σαρκὶ πεποιθ. he by no means intends to
concede that he is destitute of that πεποίθησις which was

founded on externals;[1] no, in this respect also he has more to show than others, down to ver. 6.[2] So no one might say that he was despising what he himself *did not possess.* — The classical καίπερ with the participle (only used here by Paul; and elsewhere in the N. T. only in Heb. v. 8, *et al.*; 2 Pet. i. 12), adds to the adversative sentence a limiting concessive clause (Baeumlein, *Partik.* p. 201 f.), and that in such a way, that from the collective subject of the former the apostle now with emphasis singles out partitively his own person (ἐγώ).[3] If, following the Homeric usage, he had *separated* the two particles, he would have written : καὶ ἐγώ περ.; if he had expressed himself *negatively*, he would have said : οὐδέπερ ἐγώ οὐκ ἔχων. — The confidence *also in flesh, i.e.* in such circumstances as belong to the sphere of the materially human, is in ἔχων (comp. 2 Cor. iii. 4) conceived as a *possession;* he *has* this confidence, namely, from his personal position as an *Israelite*—a standpoint which, laying out of view for the moment his Christian transformation, he boldly adopts, in order to measure himself with his Judaistic opponents on their own ground of proud confidence, and thereupon in ver. 7 ff. yet again to abandon this standpoint and to make those Israelitish advantages vanish into nothing before the light of his vital position as a Christian. Hence the πεποίθησις, his *possession* of which he in the first instance urges, is not *fiduciae argumentum* (Beza, Calvin, Grotius, Estius, and others, including Flatt, Hoelemann, and Weiss); nor is the *possession* of it to be viewed as something which he *might* have (Storr, Rilliet, Matthies, Ewald); nor is it to be referred to the *pre-Christian* period of the apostle's life (van Hengel). The latter is also the view of Hofmann, who holds ἔχων (and then διώκων also) as the *imperfect* participle, and gives to the whole passage the involved misinterpretation : *that καίπερ introduces a protasis, the apodosis*

---

[1] καὶ ἐν σαρκί, namely, in addition to the higher Christian relations, on which I place my confidence.

[2] Only a comma is to be placed after πεποιθότες in ver. 3 ; but after ἐν σαρκί in ver. 4 a full stop ; and after ἄμεμπτος in ver. 6 another full stop. So also Lachmann and Tischendorf. In opposition to Hofmann's confusing construction of the sentence, see below.

[3] Comp. Kühner, II. 1, p. 246. 8.

of which follows with ἀλλά *in ver.* 7.   In accordance with this view, ver. 4 is supposed to mean : " *Although I possessed a confidence, and that, indeed, based on such matters as are flesh, if any other ventures to trust in such things, I for my part possessed confidence in a higher degree.*" This is erroneous ; first, because the familiar ἀλλά of the apodosis is used indeed after καίτοι (with *finite tense ;* Stallbaum, *ad Plat. Phaed.* p. 68 E ; *Parm.* p. 128 C), but not after the common καίπερ with participle, attaching itself to a governing verb ; secondly, because καί before ἐν σαρκί means nothing else than *also*, which does not suit the interpretation of Hofmann, who desires to force upon it the here inappropriate sense, *and that indeed ;* thirdly, because the present δοκεῖ presupposes the *present* sense for ἔχων also ; and lastly, because with ἐγὼ μᾶλλον the *present* (in accordance with the preceding δοκεῖ), and not the imperfect, again suggests itself as to be supplied.   And how awkward would be the whole form of expression for the, after all, very simple idea ! — τις . . . ἄλλος] quite generally : *any other person,* but the intended *application* to the above-mentioned *Judaizers* was obvious to the reader.   See the sequel.   The separation by δοκεῖ lays all the stronger stress on the τίς. — δοκεῖ] not : " *thinks to be able* to confide" (de Wette and many others) ; nor yet : " si quis alius *videtur*" (Vulgate), since it is a matter depending not upon the judgment of others, but upon his own *fancy,* according to the connection.   Hence : if any one *allows himself to think,* if he *presumes.*   Just in the same way, as in the passage parallel also in substance, Matt. iii. 9. Comp. 1 Cor. xi. 16. — ἐγὼ μᾶλλον] sc. δοκῶ πεπ. ἐν σαρκί, I for my part presume it still more.   This mode of expression implies a certain boldness, defiance ; comp. 2 Cor. xi. 21.

    Vv. 5, 6. Predicates of the ἐγώ, by which that ἐγὼ μᾶλλον is justified.—If those Judaizers were, as may be inferred from our passage, partly *proselytes* (to these the περιτ. ὀκταήμ. stands in contrast), partly persons whose *Jewish descent* was not so noble and pure as that implied in ἐκ γένους. . . . Ἑβραίων, and if they could not boast of any such *law-strictness, zealous activity, and righteousness,* as is described in κατὰ νόμον . . . ἄμεμπτος ; and if, on the other hand, there were found conjoined in the case of Paul the elements here adduced of ancient theocratic legitimacy and perfection ; the ἐγὼ μᾶλλον in ver. 4 was completely made good. — περιτομῇ ὀκταήμ.] *in respect to circumcision an eighth-day-one,* not older, as were the *proselytes* who were only circumcised at a later period of life. The *eighth-day character* in the relation specified by περιτομῇ is conceived as a *quality* of the persons concerned, which distinguishes them from those circumcised later.[1] The reading περιτομή as *nominative* (some min. and Fathers, Erasmus, Vatablus, Cornelius a Lapide, Mill, Bengel, Matthies, Heinrichs, and others, also Elz. 1624, 1633, not 1641), so that it would stand in the concrete sense (*circumcisus*), is erroneous, because this usage occurs only *collectively.* — ἐκ γένους Ἰσρ.] that is, a *descendant of Jacob,* not, therefore, possibly of *Idumaean* blood. The *theocratic* name Ἰσρ. corresponds entirely with the design of the passage. Comp. on Eph. ii. 12. On what follows, comp. 2 Cor. xi. 22 ; Rom. xi. 1. — φυλῆς Βενιαμ.] therefore not, possibly, an *Ephraimite* (Ezra iv. 1) ; a climactic more precise definition of the εὐγένεια ; εὐγενὴς γὰρ ἡ φύσις κἀξ εὐγενῶν, Soph. *Phil.* 862 (874). For its fuller exhibition Paul finally specifies the last feature of his lineage : Ἐβραῖος ἐξ Ἐβρ., that is, *a Hebrew born of Hebrew parents,* so that his mother also was a Hebrew woman. His lineage is not carried further back in respect to *both* parents, because it was not the custom to trace back the genealogy of the wives. Inappropriate to the context is the rendering of Michaelis, following Chrysostom, Oecumenius, and Theophylact : " one *speaking* Hebrew, born of Hebrew-*speaking* parents." It is also erroneous, following the Greek Fathers, to take ἐξ Ἐβρ. of the *tota majorum series* (Beza, Grotius, Storr, Matthies, Baumgarten-Crusius, and others), because this was after the two previously specified points self-evident. If, among his ancestors, Paul had had one who was a non-Hebrew, he would not have been descended from Jacob and Benjamin, but from the non-Hebrew and his forefathers. For instances of expressions quite similar to Ἐβρ. ἐξ Ἐβρ., used to denote the

---

[1] For instances of the personal use of such *nomina dialia,* see especially Wetstein on John xi. 39 ; comp. generally Kühner, II. 1, p. 234 f.

identity, as conditioned by birth, of a man's position with that
of his parents, see Wetstein and Kypke; they occur very
frequently in classic authors. — κατὰ νόμον κ.τ.λ.] After his
Jewish εὐγένεια there now follows his distinguished *personal
position* in Judaism, set forth in a threefold climactic grada-
tion: (1) *In respect of the law* (of Moses) *a Pharisee.* Comp.
Acts xxvi. 5, xxii. 6. The Pharisees stood in the closest and
strictest relation to the law, as they with their traditions
were regarded as the most orthodox expositors, defenders, and
observers of it. The interpretation of νόμον, not in its habitual
historic sense, but generally as *regular rule* (Beza) or *dis-
ciplina* (αἵρεσις) (Castalio, Wolf, Grotius, Storr, Heinrichs,
Rheinwald, Hoelemann, and others), is all the more erroneous,
since the validity of the *Mosaic* law in Christianity was the very
principle upheld by those Judaizers; see also below, δικαιοσ.
τ. ἐν νόμῳ. (2) *In respect of zeal* (zealous maintenance and
championship of the law-religion, 1 Macc. ii. 58; Acts xxi. 20;
Gal. i. 14), *a persecutor of the church.* Comp. Gal. i. 13 f.
The *present* participle is used as a *substantive,* comp. on Gal. i.
23. What Paul, to his deep grief, *had been* (1 Cor. xv. 8 f.;
1 Tim. i. 13), he, with a bitter *recalling* of his former distinction in Judaism, throws, by way of confronting the Jewish
zealots, into the scale, as a characteristic predicate not yet
extinct. And precisely thus, unaccompanied by any ποτέ as in
Gal. i. 23, it carries from the standpoint to which he has now
attained very strong weight (in opposition to Hofmann, who
holds the present sense to be impossible here). (3) *In respect
to righteousness, which is grounded on the law, having become
blameless* (ii. 15), *having carried it so far* (not: having *borne
myself so,* as Hofmann renders it; comp. on ii. 15), that
human judgment *finds nothing in me to blame* in this respect!
That which is here denoted by δικ. ἡ ἐν νόμῳ is not substantially different from δικ. ἡ ἐκ νόμου in ver. 9; comp. Rom.
x. 5. It has its basis *in the law,* so far as it consists in the
accordance of its nature with the character and the rules of
that institute (Gal. iii. 11, v. 4), and proceeds *from the law,*
so far as it is produced by the precepts of the latter which
man follows. In opposition to the correlation with ver. 9

de Wette interprets: "the righteousness *valid* in the *state* of law (comp. Rom. ii. 12)." Calvin appropriately observes that Paul means "*totam* justitiam legis," but "*communi hominum existimatione;*" that it is not, therefore, the real moral *fulfilment* of the law, but its justitia *externa literalis.* Comp. J. Müller, *v. d. Sünde,* I. p. 59, ed. 5.

Ver. 7. Now, with the antithetic ἀλλά, the apostle comes again to his real standpoint, far transcending any πεποιθέναι ἐν σαρκί, and says: *No! everything that was gain to me,* etc. — ἅτινα] *quaecunque,* the *category* of the matters specified in vv. 5 and 6.[1] The emphasis is to be placed on this word; comp. ταῦτα subsequently. — ἦν μοι κέρδη] μοι is not the dative of *opinion* (Erasmus, Beza, and many others, including Heinrichs, Rheinwald, Hoelemann, Matthies, de Wette, Hofmann; comp. van Hengel, who takes κέρδη as lucra *opinata*); but such things were to the apostle in his pre-Christian state *really* gain (κατὰ σάρκα). By means of them he was within the old theocracy put upon a path which had already brought him repute and influence, and promised to him yet far greater honours, power, and wealth in the future; *a career rich in gain* was opened up to him. The *plural* κέρδη denotes the various advantages dependent on such things as have been mentioned. Frequently used also in the classical writers. — ταῦτα] emphatically: *these very things.* — διὰ τὸν X.] *for the sake of Christ,* who had become the *highest* interest of my life. Paul explains himself more particularly in vv. 8, 9, explanations which are not to be here anticipated. — ζημίαν] *as harm,* that is, as *disadvantageous* (the contrast to κέρδος; comp. Plat. *de lucri cup.* p. 226 E, *Leg.* viii. p. 835 B), because, namely, they had been impediments to the conversion to Christ, and that owing to the false moral judgment and confidence attaching to them. Comp. *Form. Conc.* p. 708; Calvin on ver. 8. This *one* disadvantage he has seen in *everything* of which he

---

[1] The later heretical enemies of the law appealed to this passage, in which also, in their view, the *law* was meant to be included. On the other hand, Chrysostom and his successors asserted that the law was meant *only in comparison with Christ.* Estius, however, justly observes: "non de *ipsa lege* loquitur, sed de *justitia,* quae in lege est."

is speaking; hence the *plural* is not again used here as previously in κέρδη. The ἥγημαι (*perfect*), however, has occurred, and is an accomplished fact since his *conversion*, to which the apostle here glances back. On ἡγεῖσθαι ζημίαν, comp. Sturz, *Lex. Xen.* II. p. 454; Lucian, *Lexiph.* 24; on the relation of the *singular* to the plural κέρδη, Eur. *Cycl.* 311: πολλοῖσι κέρδη πονηρὰ ζημίαν ἡμείψατο.

Ver. 8. Ἀλλά is the climactic *but, still, much more*, giving a *corrective* reference of the sense, signifying that with the previous ἅτινα ... ζημίαν there has not yet been enough said. Comp. on 2 Cor. vii. 11. In the μὲν οὖν it is implied, that " μὲν rem praesentem confirmet, οὖν autem conclusionem ex rebus ita comparatis conficiat," Klotz, *ad Devar.* p. 663. Hence ἀλλὰ μὲν οὖν: *at quidem igitur*. The καί before ἡγοῦμαι (after ἀλλὰ μ. οὖν) serves also to help the *climactic* sense, *outbidding* what has been said previously: *etiam*, i.e. *adeo*. It is consequently to be explained: *but, accordingly, I am even of opinion that everything* (not merely what was meant by ἅτινα in ver. 7) *is a disadvantage*. It is clear, withal, from the following διὰ τὸ ὑπερέχον κ.τ.λ. that πάντα is meant indeed *without restriction*, of *all* things, goods, honours, etc. (comp. also Hofmann), but *in so far as they are not made subordinate to the knowledge of Christ*. The explanation of others, according to which ἀλλὰ μὲν οὖν is intended to oppose the *present* ἡγοῦμαι by way of correction to the *perfect* ἥγημαι (Calvin and others, including Winer, p. 412 [E. T. 552], and the explanation hitherto given by me), is incorrect, because ἥγημαι, and not the aorist ἡγησάμην, was employed previously, and the perfect already involves the continuance of the opinion in the present, so that no contrast of the *tenses* would logically be elicited. The climactic contrast lies rather in the fact that the second ἡγεῖσθαι ζημίαν is a much *more comprehensive* one than the first, in fact, *one without exception* (πάντα). — διὰ τὸ ὑπερέχον κ.τ.λ.] *on account of the surpassingness of the knowledge of Christ;* that is, because this knowledge, to which I have attained, is a possession which excels in value everything else; the eminent quality of a possession attained is the *ground* (διά) for estimating other possessions according to their relation to

that one, and consequently, if they stand to the latter in a relation hindersome to us, for looking upon them no longer as something advantageous, but as hurtful.   As to the *neuter adjective*
used as a substantive with the genitive, in order to the more
prominent setting forth of the attribute, see Bernhardy, p.
155 f.; Winer, p. 220 [E. T. 294]. — Χριστὸς Ἰησοῦς ὁ κυριός
μοῦ; this is the fundamental *sum of the whole contents* of
Christian knowledge.   This saving knowledge is the necessary
intelligence of faith (comp. on John viii. 32), and grows with
the *experience* of faith (ver. 10; Eph. iii. 16 ff.). — δι᾽ ὅν] *for
the sake of whom, i.e.* for the sake of possessing *Him;* comp.
afterwards ἵνα Χριστὸν . . . αὐτῷ. — τὰ πάντα] *the whole*, not
general like πάντα previously (Hofmann), but: *which I
possessed*, vv. 5–7.   This more precise definition by the *article*
results from ἐζημιώθην, in connection with which the *aorist*
is to be noted, by which Paul denotes that great historical
turning-point in his life, the event of his *conversion;* through
that event he *has lost* all his (pre-Christian) valued possessions,[1]
and thenceforth *he has them no more.*   Luther erroneously
interprets : " *considered as harm ;*" and the emotion and force
of the expression are only weakened by the frequently given
reflexive sense (see Beza, Calvin, Heinrichs, Flatt, Hoelemann,
van Hengel, and many): *I have made myself lose,*—a meaning,
besides, which cannot be shown to belong to the passive form
of the aorist of this verb (not even in Luke ix. 25).   The future
passive form ζημιωθήσομαι (see Kühner, *ad Xen. Mem.* iii. 9.
12, *Thuc.* iii. 40. 2) is invariably *damno afficiar.* — καὶ ἡγοῦμαι
κ.τ.λ.] not to be taken as independent (de Wette, Baumgarten-
Crusius, Weiss), but, in keeping with the climactic flow of the
discourse, as still in continuous connection with δι᾽ ὃν κ.τ.λ. ;
hence δι᾽ ὃν τ. π. ἐζημ. is not, with van Hengel, to be put in a
parenthesis.   Paul *had become loser* of all these things for
Christ's sake, and he *holds* them as not worthy of possession,

---

[1] Observe here, also, the shrewdly contrived correspondence of ζημίαν in ver.
7 f., and ἐζημιώθην in ver. 8, in which the former expresses the idea of *damnum,
detrimentum,* and the latter : *I have become loser of.*   It might be reproduced
in Latin : "etiam censeo omnia *detrimentum* (*i.e.* detrimentosa) *esse* . . . propter
quem *omnium detrimentum* (*i.e.* jacturam) *passus sum* censeoque ea esse quis-
quilias."

but as *rubbish!* σκύβαλον,[1] *refuse* (such as sweepings, dung, husks, and the like) ; Ecclus. xxvii. 4 ; Plut. *Mor.* p. 352 D ; and see Wetstein *ad loc.;* frequently in the *Anthol.*, see Jacobs, *Ach. Tat.* p. 522, *ad Anthol.* VII. p. 173, IX. p. 208. Comp. the similar figurative expressions περικάθαρμα and περίψημα, 1 Cor. iv. 13. — ἵνα Χ. κερδ.] The design in the ἡγοῦμαι σκύβ. εἶναι : *in order to gain Christ,* not the aim of τὰ πάντα ἐζημιώθην (Hofmann), there being no reason for such a retrospective reference. The *gaining* of Christ, *i.e.* the appropriation of Him by means of the fellowship brought about through faith, is that, which for him is to take the place of those former κέρδη which he has *lost,* and so he looked to *this gain* in his ἡγοῦμαι σκύβαλα εἶναι ; it is present to his view as the one and highest gain at which he has to aim. It is true that Paul *has* Christ already long ago (Gal. ii. 20 ; Eph. iii. 17 ; 2 Cor. xiii. 3) ; nevertheless, this κερδαίνειν is from its nature a development, the completion of which still lies before him. Comp. ver. 12 ff.

Ver. 9. Καὶ εὑρεθῶ ἐν αὐτῷ] *and to be found in Him.* The emphasis, which previously lay upon Χριστόν, is laid not upon ἐν αὐτῷ (Hofmann), but upon the εὑρεθῶ placed first for that reason, and introducing a new feature of the relation aimed at, annexing to the (subjective) gaining of Christ the (objective) *moulding of life* corresponding to it. The apostle desires *to be found* in Christ, as in the element of his life ; by this he means (comp. Ignatius, *Eph.* 11) the whole perceptible *manifestation* of his Christian being and nature ; so that εὑρ. must neither be limited to the *judicium Dei* (Beza, comp. Flatt), nor taken as *sim* (Grotius and others). Calvin erroneously makes εὑρεθῶ *active :* Paulum renuntiasse omnibus quae habebat, *ut recuperaret in Christo.* — μὴ ἔχων κ.τ.λ.] Specific modal definition to εὑρ. ἐν αὐτῷ : *so that I,* in accordance with this design, *may not have,* etc. Van Hengel erroneously connects (Lachmann, also, and Tischendorf have omitted the comma after αὐτῷ) μὴ ἔχων κ.τ.λ. immediately with εὑρ. ἐν αὐτῷ· et deprehendar *in communione ejus non meam qualem-*

---

[1] Not to be derived from τοῖς κυσὶ βάλλειν, *quod* canibus projicitur, but from σκῶρ (σκάς). See Lobeck, *Pathol.* p. 92.

cunque habere probitatem. Thus, indeed, ἐν αὐτῷ would be utterly superfluous! The *subjective* negation μή flows from the conception of design (ἵνα), see Baeumlein, *Partik.* p. 295; Buttmann, *Neut. Gr.* p. 302 [E. T. 351]; and ἔχων is the simple *habens, possessing,* not: *holding fast* (am Ende, Rheinwald, Baumgarten-Crusius). — ἐμὴν δικ. τὴν ἐκ νόμου] See on ver. 6; comp. Rom. x. 3. It is the righteousness acquired as a self-achievement (ἐμήν), which proceeds from the law by means of a justifying compliance with it (Rom. ii. 13). As to the nature of this righteousness, and the impossibility of attaining it, comp. Gal. ii. 16, iii. 10; Rom. iii. 19 f., iv. 4, vii. 7 ff., ix. 31, *et al.* — τὴν διὰ πίστ. Χριστοῦ] contrast to ἐμήν: *that procured by faith in Christ*[1] (as the *causa apprehendens*). The *causa efficiens* is *God* (His grace, see Eph. ii. 8); hence, for the complete exhaustion of the matter, τὴν ἐκ Θεοῦ δικ. is added, in which ἐκ Θεοῦ, correlative to the preceding ἐκ νόμου, expresses the causal issuing from God. As to the *way* in which this ἐκ Θεοῦ takes place, namely, by God's imputing faith as righteousness,[2] see Rom. i. 17, iii. 24 f., iv. 3 ff.; 2 Cor. v. 19; Gal. iii. 6. — ἐπὶ τῇ πίστει] *on the ground of faith* (Acts iii. 16), added at the end with solemn emphasis, and dependent on ἔχων, which is again to be supplied after ἀλλά. So also Weiss. The repetition of ἔχων after ἐπὶ τ. πίστει, which Hofmann feels the want of in this explanation, would be simply superfluous and clumsy. Ἐπὶ τ. π. is usually attached to δικαιοσύνην (" justitiam superstructam fidei," Hoelemann, Wiesinger), some having taken ἐπί as " *in* fide" (Vulgate, Calvin), or *in fide sitam* (Castalio); others as "*per* fidem" (Beza, Grotius); others, *for the sake* of faith (de Wette); others, *upon the condition* of faith (Storr, Flatt, Matthies, Rilliet, van Hengel, J. B. Lightfoot). But it may be urged against this connection, first, that, in accordance with the previous definitions, we could not but expect the repeti-

---

[1] On the genitive *of the object* with πίστις, comp. i. 27. Against taking it as the genitive *auctoris*, see on Rom. iii. 22.

[2] In this passage also, therefore, justification by *faith* is the basis and presupposition of further Christian development up to the blessed consummation, ver. 11. Comp. Köstlin, in the *Jahrb. f. Deutsche Theol.* 1856, p. 121 f.

tion of the article; secondly, that δικαιοῦσθαι with ἐπί nowhere
occurs in the N. T.; and lastly, that δικαιοσύνη in its quality
as righteousness *of faith* was already distinctly designated by
τὴν διὰ πίστ. X., so that the same attribute of it would be
expressed *twice*, and, on the other hand, the ἔχων which is
to be repeated after ἀλλά (the basis of which is still ἐπὶ τ.
π.) would be *without* any more precise definition. In opposition to Hofmann, who makes ἐπὶ τ. πίστει belong to the
following infinitive clause, see on ver. 10.

Ver. 10. Telic definition of the relation expressed by μὴ
ἔχων κ.τ.λ. in ver. 9. Paul has not the righteousness of the
law, but the righteousness of faith, *in order to know*, etc. This
knowledge would fail him if, on the contrary, instead of the
righteousness of faith, he had that of the law. So he reverts
to a more detailed illustration of τὸ ὑπερέχον τῆς γνώσεως X.,
ver. 8, expressing, in the first place, again generally the great
personal contents of the knowledge accruing from the righteousness of faith (τοῦ γνῶναι αὐτόν), and next, more particularly,
the most important—especially to the apostle in his position
infinitely important—*matters* which were its objects (τὴν δύναμιν κ.τ.λ.), developing them from his own richest experience,
which had thus brought home to his deepest consciousness the
ὑπερέχον τῆς γνώσεως X. The τοῦ γνῶναι might also be conceived as dependent on εὑρεθῶ ἐν αὐτῷ (Wiesinger, Schneckenburger, Schenkel); but the more precise definition of this
εὑρεθῶ ἐν αὐτῷ by μὴ ἔχων κ.τ.λ. is so important, earnest, and
solemn, that it most naturally carries with it also the statement of aim which follows. Chrysostom joins ἐπὶ τῇ πίστει
to ver. 10: τί δέ ἐστιν ἐπὶ τῇ πίστει τοῦ γνῶναι αὐτόν; ἄρα
διὰ πίστεως ἡ γνῶσις, καὶ πίστεως ἄνευ γνῶναι αὐτὸν οὐκ ἔστι.
So also Theodoret and Erasmus, and recently Hofmann (comp.
also his *Schriftbew.* I. p. 618), who, in doing so, takes ἐπί in
and by itself correctly as *on the ground* of faith. But such
cases of emphatic prefixing, while they are certainly found
with ἵνα (see on Gal. ii. 10; Eph. iii. 18), are not found
before the genitive of the infinitive with the article, which
represents the expression with ἵνα, but in such infinitive
clauses only *between* article and infinitive; hence Paul would

have written τοῦ ἐπὶ τῇ πίστει γνῶναι. Comp. Rom. viii. 12 ;
1 Cor. xvi. 4. Hofmann improperly appeals, not any longer
indeed to Rev. xii. 7, but, doing violence to the position of the
words in the LXX., to 2 Sam. vi. 2 ; Isa. x. 32. According
to Castalio, Calvin, Grotius, Bengel, and others, the genitive
τοῦ γν. is meant to depend on τῇ πίστει; " describit *vim et
naturam fidei*, quod scilicet sit Christi cognitio" (Calvin). But
πίστις is never joined with the genitive of the *infinitive* with
the article ; and, besides, not the nature, but the object of
the faith (ver. 9) would be denoted by the genitive (Col.
ii. 12 ; 2 Thess. ii. 13, *et al.*). Nor is τοῦ γνῶναι αὐτόν to be
regarded as parallel with ἵνα Χ. κερδήσω κ. εὐρ. ἐν αὐτῷ
(Estius, Storr, Heinrichs, and others, including Rheinwald,
Hoelemann, Rilliet, de Wette, Winer), since it is in itself
arbitrary to despise the appropriate dependence on what immediately precedes, and to go back instead to ἡγοῦμαι σκύβαλα εἶναι; and since in ἵνα Χριστὸν κερδ. κ. εὑρεθῶ ἐν αὐτῷ
two elements are given, a subjective and an objective one, so
that thus there would be presented no parallel *corresponding*
with the subjective τοῦ γνῶναι κ.τ.λ. Moreover, Paul is in the
habit of introducing two parallel clauses of design *with a
double* ἵνα (Rom. vii. 13 ; Gal. iii. 14; 2 Cor. ix. 3). — The
γνῶναι, which both conditions the faith and also in fuller
development follows it (see on ver. 8), is not the discursive,
or generally theoretical and speculative knowing, but the
inwardly salutary, *experimental* becoming - acquainted - with
(" qui *expertus* non fuerit, non *intelliget*," Anselm), as is plain
from τὴν δύναμιν κ.τ.λ. Comp. 1 Cor. ii. 8, viii. 2 ; Gal. iv. 9,
et al. ; frequently so used in John. See also Weiss, *bibl. Theol.*
p. 421, ed. 2. — καὶ τὴν δύναμιν τῆς ἀναστ. αὐτοῦ καὶ τ.
κοινων. τ. παθ. αὐτ.] *and* (that is, and especially) *the power of
His resurrection and the fellowship of His sufferings.* The
δύναμ. τ. ἀναστ. αὐτ. is not the power *by which He has been
raised* (Vatablus, Grotius ; comp. Matthies), which would be
quite unsuitable to the context, but the power *which the resurrection of Christ has*, its *vis et efficacia* in respect to believers.
The special point that Paul has in view, is supplied by the
context through what is said immediately before of the

righteousness of faith, to which τοῦ γνῶναι κ.τ.λ. refers.   He
means the *powerful guarantee of justification and salvation* which
the resurrection of Christ affords to believers ; see Rom. iv. 25,
v. 10 ; 1 Cor. xv. 17 ; Acts xiii. 37, 38.   This power of the
resurrection is experienced, not by him that is righteous
through the law, but by him that is righteous through faith,
to whom the resurrection of the Lord brings the constant
energetic certainty of his reconciliation procured by Jesus'
death and the completion of eternal life (Rom. viii. 11 ;
1 Cor. vi. 14 ; Col. iii. 1 ff.; Phil. iii. 21).   Comp. also Rom.
viii. 34, where this δύναμις τῆς ἀναστ. *is triumphant* in the
apostle.   As a matter of course, this power, in virtue of which
the resurrection of Christ, according to 1 Cor. xv. 17, Rom.
iv. 25, might be described as "complementum redemtionis"
(Calvin), is already in regeneration experimentally known,
as is Christ generally (αὐτόν) ; but Paul speaks from the consciousness that every element of the regenerate life, which
has τὴν ἐκ Θεοῦ δικαιοσύνην ἐπὶ τῇ πίστει, is an ever *new*
perception of this power.   The view which understands it of
the *moral* power of *awakening* (Beza and others, also van
Hengel; comp. Rilliet), according to Rom. vi. 4, Col. ii. 12,
or the *living power of victory*, which lies for the believer in
the resurrection of Christ, according to 2 Cor. iv. 10, Gal.
ii. 20, Phil. iv. 13,—by means of which the Christian,
"through his glorified Lord, himself also possesses an infinite
new power of acquiring victory over the world and death"
(Ewald, comp. de Wette, Schneckenburger, Wiesinger, Schenkel;
substantially also Hofmann),—does not accord either with the
words themselves (for so understood it would be *the power of
the risen Christ*, not the power *of His resurrection*), or with the
following κ. τὴν κοινωνίαν τῶν παθημ. αὐτοῦ, which, in a
logical point of view (comp. 2 Cor. iv. 10–12), must either
have gone before, or have been expressed by ἐν τῇ κοινωνίᾳ κ.τ.λ.   The *certainty of our own resurrection and glory*
(Estius, Cornelius a Lapide, Storr, Heinrichs, Hoelemann, and
others ; comp. Pelagius, Theodore of Mopsuestia, Theodoret, and
Theophylact) is necessarily *included* also in the δύναμις, without, however, being exclusively meant.   By the *series ser-*

monis Bengel (comp. Samuel Crell) has allowed himself to be misled into explaining ἀνάστασις, not of the resurrection at all, but of the *exortus* or *adventus* of the Messiah. References *of various kinds* are mixed up by Rheinwald, Flatt, Schinz, Usteri, and others. — καὶ τὴν κοινων. τῶν παθημ. αὐτοῦ] In these words Paul intends to express—and he does so by the repetition of the article with a certain solemnity —a second, highly valuable relation, conditioned by the first, to the experimental knowledge of which the possession of the righteousness of faith was destined to lead him, namely, *the fellowship of the sufferings of Christ*, in which he sees a high proof of divine grace and distinction (i. 29, ii. 17 f.). Comp. Col. i. 24. Suffering for the sake of Christ's cause is a *participation in Christ's sufferings* (a συμπάσχειν, Rom. viii. 17), because, as respects the characteristic kind and way of suffering, one suffers the same that Christ suffered (according to the ethical category, drinks of the same cup which Christ drank, Matt. xx. 22). Comp. 1 Pet. iv. 13, and see on 2 Cor. i. 5, Col. i. 24; also on τὴν νέκρωσιν τοῦ Ἰησοῦ, 2 Cor. iv. 10. The explanation which makes it: suffering *with such a disposition of mind as He* suffered (as stedfastly, etc.), given by Flatt and others, is imported from a rationalistic point of view; and the view which takes it in the sense of: the *believing appropriation of the merit of Christ* (Calovius, Rheinwald, and others), is opposed to the words, and at variance with the habitual conception of a real συμπάσχειν with Christ, under which the sufferings of Christian martyrs were regarded. Chrysostom, Theodoret, Theophylact, have already in substance the correct view. Observe, moreover, that Paul has not written τὴν δύναμιν τῆς κοινωνίας κ.τ.λ. (Hoelemann: "vim ac pondus;" de Wette: "all that this fellowship involves;" comp. Corn. a Lapide: "dulcedinem ac sanctitatem"); the γνῶναι, on the contrary, relates to the *matter itself*, to the knowledge of which only those righteous by faith can attain, whilst to those righteous by the law it remains an unknown element; the subjectivity for it is wanting to the latter, though the objective suffering is present. It was otherwise with the previous element; for the resurrection of Christ in itself—the fact as such—is known also by him who is righteous through the law, but not so its δύναμις, of which only the righteous through faith is aware. The knowledge of this δύναμις, in virtue of which he experiences in the resurrection of Christ the abiding divinely effectual guarantee of his justification and eternal life, makes him capable also of recognising in his sufferings for the sake of the gospel a fellowship in the sufferings of Christ; the latter knowledge is conditioned by the former; he would not have it *without* the former, because he would be driven to look upon his faith as vain and idle, and upon himself, so far as he suffers, as ἐλεεινότερον πάντων ἀνθρώπων (1 Cor. xv. 14, 17, 19). The enthusiastic feeling of drinking the cup of Christ is not possible, unless a man bears in his heart the mighty assurance of salvation through the resurrection of the Lord. — συμμορφι-ζόμενος τῷ θανάτῳ αὐτοῦ] denotes the *corresponding situation* (comp. 2 Cor. iv. 10), in which Paul was conscious that he should know, as one righteous by faith, the κοινωνίαν τῶν παθ. Χριστοῦ: *inasmuch as I am made like to His death;* for his position then was such that he saw himself threatened with *martyrdom*, consequently (comp. ii. 17) his state of suffering developed itself into similarity to the death of Christ. This present *state of development* of the being made like to Christ is indicated by the *present* participle. The interpretation, which takes it of the *fellowship in suffering generally,* which is here more precisely described (Calvin, Estius, and others; also Wiesinger and Weiss), does not satisfy the progression from the general παθημάτων to the definite θανάτῳ. And the sense: " *non detrectando* mortem ejus morti similem" (Vatablus; comp. Matthies and de Wette) is imported into the words, which by Grotius, van Hengel, Rilliet, Schneckenburger, and others, are interpreted quite in opposition to the context, as referring to the *ethical* dying to the world, its lusts, etc. (Rom. vi.; Gal. ii. 19). The nominative συμμορφ., which is to be explained as dependent, not in a clumsily complicated fashion on εὑρεθῶ (Grotius, Hoelemann, Hofmann, and others), but on τοῦ γνῶναι κ.τ.λ., refers to its *logical* subject. See Eph. iv. 2.

Ver. 11. Εἴ πως] *if possibly,* designating the *aim,* the attain-

ment of which is before the apostle's mind in the συμμορφιζόμενος τῷ θαν. αὐτοῦ.   In this case, however, the *deliberative*
form of expression (comp. Rom. i. 10, xi. 14; Kühner, II. 2,
p. 1034) bears the impress, not of *doubt that* he will attain to
the resurrection of the dead (in case, namely, he should not live
to see the Parousia), but of *humility* under the conception of
the *greatness of the bliss*, and of the *moral condition* to which, on
man's part, it is subject; οὐ θαρρῶ γάρ, φησιν, οὔπω· οὕτως
ἐταπεινοφρόνει, ὅπερ ἀλλαχοῦ λέγει· ὁ δοκῶν ἑστάναι, βλεπέτω
μὴ πέσῃ, Theophylact : comp. Chrysostom.   This suffices also
in opposition to Baur's doubt (*Paulus*, II. p. 79 f.) whether
Paul could have expressed himself in this way at all.   The
expression excludes moral *security*, but not the *certitudo
salutis* in itself, as, following Estius and other Catholic expositors, Bisping still thinks.   The certainty of salvation is
founded on God's decree, calling (Rom. viii. 29 f.), promise,
and attestation by the Spirit (Rom. viii. 10), in faith on
the saving facts of redemption (Rom. viii. 32 ff.).   Comp.
Calovius.—The reader could not feel any doubt as to *what*
ἐξανάστασις τῶν νεκρῶν Paul means, namely, the *first*, in which
οἱ τοῦ Χριστοῦ ἐν τῇ παρουσίᾳ αὐτοῦ (1 Cor. xv. 23) shall
arise.[1]   Comp. 1 Thess. iv. 16.   It is the resurrection of the
dead κατ᾽ ἐξοχήν, not different from the ἀνάστασις τῶν δικαίων.
See on Luke xiv. 14.   Nevertheless, we must not find this
resurrection *denoted* by the double compound ἐξανάστ., the
ἐξ in it conveying the idea ἐκ τῆς γῆς εἰς τὸν ἀέρα (Theophylact).   This ἐξ is simply to be explained by the conception
ἐκ τῆς γῆς, so that neither in the substantial meaning nor even
in style (Bengel: "Paulinus enim *stylus* Christo adscribit
ἀνάστασιν, ἐξανάστασιν Christianis ") is ἐξανάστ. to be dis-

---

[1] It is incorrect to ascribe to the apostle the idea that none but believers will
rise at the resurrection, and that unbelievers will remain in Hades (Weiss).   The
resurrection *of all*, as Christ Himself unquestionably taught it (see on John
v. 28 f. ; Luke xiv. 14), is also in Paul's view the necessary premiss of the *judgment* of all, of believers and also of unbelievers (of the κόσμος, Rom. iii. 6 ; 1 Cor.
vi. 2, xi. 32).   That view, moreover, is at variance with the apostle's distinct
declaration in Acts xxiv. 15 , comp. xvii. 31.   Gerlach properly declares himself
(*Letzte Dinge*, p. 147 ff.) opposed to Weiss, but still limits the final judgment,
at p. 101 ff., as regards the persons subjected to it, in a way that is exegetically
altogether unjustifiable.

tinguished from ἀνάστ.; but the former is to be explained
solely from the more vividly imaginative view of the event
which the apostle has before him. Comp. on 1 Cor. vi. 14.
The double compound *substantive* does not occur elsewhere in
the N. T. (the *verb*, Mark xii. 19; Luke xx. 28; Acts xv. 5);
but see Polyb. iii. 55. 4, ii. 21. 9, ii. 35. 4; Gen. vii. 4.
Compl. We may add, that while it has been explained, at
variance with the context, as referring to the *ethical* resurrection, Rom. vi. 4 f. (Flacius, Balduin, Coccejus, and others;
comp. Schrader), it is also erroneous to find in it the sense:
" if perchance *I should remain alive until the resurrection of the
dead* " (van Hengel, Hilgenfeld); since, on the contrary,
essentially the same meaning is expressed as in Luke xx. 34
by οἱ καταξιωθέντες . . . τῆς ἀναστάσεως, and it is conceived
as a possible case (comp. i. 20 ff., ii. 17) that Paul will *not*
remain alive until the Parousia.[1] καταντ. εἰς (comp. Eph.
iv. 13) denotes the attaining to a *goal* (frequently in Polybius,
see Schweighäuser, *Lex.* p. 332; see also the passages from the
LXX. and Apocr. in Schleusner, III. p. 234 f.), which, however, is here not a *point of time*, but a *bliss* which is to be
attained. Comp. Acts xxvi. 7.

Vv. 12–14. Protest, that in what he had said in vv. 7–11
he had not expressed the fanciful idea of a Christian perfection
already attained; but that, on the contrary, his efforts are
still ever directed forward towards that aim — whereby a
mirror for self-contemplation is held up before the Philippians
in respect to the moral conceit which disturbed their unity
(ii. 2–4), in order to stir them up to a like humility and
diligence as a condition of Christian perfection (ver. 15).

Ver. 12. Οὐχ ὅτι] *By this I do not mean to say that,* etc.
See on 2 Cor. i. 24, iii. 5; John vi. 46. Aken, *Lehre v.
Temp. u. Mod.* p. 91 ff. He might encounter such a misconception on the part of his opponents; but " in summo fervore
sobrietatem spiritualem non dimittit apostolus," Bengel. — ἤδη
ἔλαβον] that *I have already grasped it.* The *object* is not
named by Paul, but left to be understood of itself from the

---

[1] This also applies against the view of Otto, *Pastoralbr.* p. 233, who has
altogether misunderstood vv. 11 and 12.

context. The latter represents a prize-runner, who at the goal of the σταδιοδρομία grasps the βραβεῖον (ver. 14). This βραβεῖον typifies the *bliss of the Messiah's kingdom* (comp. 1 Cor. ix. 24; 2 Tim. iv. 7, 8), which therefore, and that *as βραβεῖον*, is here to be conceived as the object, the attainment of which is denied to have already taken place. And accordingly, ἔλαβον is to be explained of the having attained in *ideal* anticipation, in which the individual is as sure and certain of the future attainment of the βραβεῖον, as if it were already an accomplished fact. What therefore Paul here denies of himself is the same imagination with which he reproaches the Corinthians in 1 Cor. iv. 8 (see *in loc.*). The reference to the βραβεῖον (so Chrysostom, Oecumenius, Theophylact, Erasmus, Bengel, Heinrichs, Rilliet, and others) is not proleptic;[1] on the contrary, it is *suggested* by the idea of the *race* just introduced in ver. 12, and is *prepared for* by the preceding καταντήσω εἰς τὴν ἐξανάστασιν τ. νεκρ., in which the Messianic σωτηρία makes its appearance, and the grasping of the βραβεῖον is realized; hence it is so accordant with the context that all other references are excluded. Accordingly, we must neither supply *metam* generally (Beza, comp. Ewald); nor τὴν ἀνάστασιν (Rheinwald); nor τὸν Χριστόν (Theodoret; comp. Weiss); nor *moral perfection* (Hoelemann, following Ambrosiaster and others); nor the *right of resurrection* (Grotius); nor even " the *knowledge of Christ* which appropriates, imitates, and strives to follow Him " (de Wette; comp. Ambrosiaster, Calvin, Vatablus, van Hengel, Wiesinger); nor yet the καταντᾶν of ver. 11 (Matthies). — ἢ ἤδη τετελείωμαι] or—in order to express without a figure that which had been figuratively denoted by ἤδη ἔλαβον—*were already perfected*.[2] For only the ethically *perfected* Christian, who has entirely become and is (observe the *perfect*) what he was intended to become and be, would

---

[1] As also Hofmann objects, who finds the notion of the verb alone sufficient for expressing what is to be negatived, but yet likewise ultimately comes to *eternal life* as a supplement; for that which is not yet attained is one and the same with that which is one day to be attained.

[2] This being perfected is not the *result* of the ἔλαβον (Wiesinger, Weiss), but the *moral condition* of him who can say ἔλαβον. Note that ἤ is used, and not καί; καί might have been taken as annexing the *result*.

be able to say with truth that he had already grasped the βραβεῖον, however infallibly certain might be to him, looking at his inward moral frame of life, the future σωτηρία. He who is not yet perfect has still always *to run* after it; see the sequel. The words ἢ ἤδη δεδικαίωμαι, introduced in considerable authorities before ἤ, form a correct gloss, when understood in an *ethical* sense. For instances of τελειοῦσθαι—which is not, with Hofmann, to be here taken in the indefinite generality of *being ready*—in the sense of *spiritual perfection* (comp. Heb. ii. 10, v. 9, xii. 23), see Ast, *Lex. Plat.* III. p. 369; comp. Philo, *Alleg.* p. 74 C, where the βραβεῖα are adjudged to the soul, when it is *perfected*. *To be at the goal* (Hammond, Wolf, Loesner, Heinrichs, Flatt, Rilliet, and others), is a sense, which τετελ. might have according to the context. In opposition to it, however, we may urge, not that the figure of the race-contest only comes in distinctly in the sequel, for it is already introduced in ver. 12, but that Paul would thus have expressed himself quite tautologically, and that τέλειοι in ver. 15 is correlative with τετελείωμαι. — διώκω δέ] *but I pursue it, i.e.* I strive after it with strenuous running; see ver. 14. The idea of urgent *haste* is conveyed (Abresch, *ad Aesch. Sept.* 90; Blomfield, *Gloss. Pers.* 86). The δέ has the force of an ἀλλά in the sense of *on the other hand;* Baeumlein, *Partik.* p. 95, and comp. on Eph. iv. 15. We must understand τὸ βραβεῖον as *object* to διώκω, just as in the case of ἔλαβον and καταλάβω; hence διώκω is not to be taken *absolutely* (Rilliet; comp. Rheinwald, de Wette, Hofmann), although this in itself would be linguistically admissible (in opposition to van Hengel), see on ver. 14. Phavorinus: διώκειν ἐνίοτε τὸ ἁπλῶς κατὰ σπουδὴν ἐλαύνειν; also Eustathius, *ad Il.* xxiii. 344. — εἰ καὶ καταλάβω] This εἰ is, as in εἴ πως, ver. 11, deliberative: *if* I also, etc., the idea of σκοπεῖν or some similar word being before his mind; the compound καταλάβω is more (in opposition to Weiss) than ἔλαβον, and denotes the *a*pprehension which takes possession; comp. on Rom. ix. 30, 1 Cor. ix. 24, where we have the same progression from λαμβ. to καταλαμβ.; Herod. ix. 58: διωκτέοι εἰσὶ ἐς ὃ καταλαμφθέντες; and καί implies: I not merely *grasp* (ἔλαβον), but *also actually appre-*

hend.[1] — ἐφ᾿ ᾧ καὶ κατελήφθην ὑπὸ X.] Comp. Plat. *Tim.* p.
38 D : ὅθεν καταλαμβάνουσί τε καὶ καταλαμβάνονται, 1 Cor.
xiii. 12 : ἐπιγνώσομαι καθὼς καὶ ἐπεγνώσθην, Ignatius, *Rom.*
8 : θελήσατε, ἵνα καὶ ὑμεῖς θεληθῆτε, *Trall.* 5 : πολλὰ γὰρ
ἡμῖν λείπει, ἵνα Θεοῦ μὴ λειπώμεθα : *because I was also apprehended by Christ.* This is the *determining ground* of the διώκω,
and of the thought thereto annexed, εἰ καὶ καταλάβω. Theophylact (comp. Chrysostom and Theodoret) aptly remarks :
δεικνὺς, ὅτι ὀφείλη ἐστὶ τὸ πρᾶγμα, φησί· διότι καὶ κατελήφθ.
ὑπὸ X. Otherwise, in fact, this having been apprehended
would not have been responded to on my part.[2] Respecting
ἐφ᾿ ᾧ, *on the ground of this, that,* i.e. *propterea quod,* see on
Rom. v. 12 ; 2 Cor. v. 4. The interpretation : *for which, on
which behalf* (Oecumenius, Beza, Grotius, Rheinwald, Rilliet,
Weiss, and others), just as in iv. 10, is indeed linguistically
correct and simple ; but it assigns the conversion of Paul,
not to the general object which it had (Gal. i. 16), but to a
personal object. In this case, moreover, Rilliet, de Wette,
Wiesinger supply τοῦτο previously, which is not in accordance
with the objectless ἔλαβον. More artificial are the explanations : *whereunto,* in the sense of *obligation* (Hoelemann) ;
under which condition (Matthies) ; *in so far as* (Castalio,
Ewald) ; *in the presupposition, that* (Baur) ; *which is certain
from the fact, that* (subjective ground of knowledge ; so Ernesti,
Urspr. d. Sünde, II. p. 217). According to Hofmann, Paul
desires to give the reason *why, and for what purpose, he con-
templates an apprehension.* But thus the reference of ἐφ᾿ ᾧ κ.τ.λ.
would be limited to εἰ κ. καταλάβω, although the positive
leading thought has been introduced in διώκω δέ. Ἐφ᾿ ᾧ κ.τ.λ.
serves this *leading* thought *along with* that of its accessory
definition εἰ κ. καταλάβω. — καί] *also, subjoins* to the active
καταλάβω the ingeniously corresponding passive relation
κατελήφθην. And by κατελήφθ. Paul expresses what *at his*

---

[1] 2 Tim. iv. 7 does not conflict with our passage, but is the confession at *the
end* of the course, "exemplum *accipientis* jam jamque," Bengel.

[2] Paul is conscious that, being apprehended by Christ, he may not and cannot
do otherwise. Comp. Bengel : *quoniam ;* sensus virtutis Christi accendit
Christianum.

conversion he experienced from Christ (hence the *aorist*) ; there is no need for suggesting the idea, foreign to the context, of an apprehended *fugitive* (Chrysostom, Theophylact, Theodoret, and others, including Flatt and van Hengel). The fact that at that time Christ *laid hold of* him on his pre-Christian career, and took him into His power and gracious guidance as His own, is vividly illustrated by the figure, to which the context gave occasion, κατελήφθ. ὑπὸ X.

Vv. 13, 14. Once more, and with loving earnestness (ἀδελφοί), Paul says what he had already said in ver. 12 with οὐχ ὅτι ... καταλάβω ; and in doing so, he brings more into relief in the first portion the element of *self*-estimation, which in his own case he denies ; and, in the second part, he sets forth more in detail the idea : διώκω δὲ εἰ κ. καταλ. — ἐγὼ ἐμαυτόν] *ego me ipsum*, an emphatic mode of indicating one's own estimation, in which one is both subject and object of the judgment. Comp. John v. 30 f., vii. 17, viii. 54 ; Acts xxvi. 9, *et al.* A reference to the judgment of *others* about him (Bengel, Weiss, and others ; comp. also Hofmann) is here out of place. — λογίζομαι] *I judge*, I am of opinion,[1] Rom. iii. 28, viii. 18, xiv. 14 ; 2 Cor. xi. 5, *et al.;* Xen. *Anab.* ii. 2. 13 ; Dem. lxiii. 12. — ἐν δέ] Comp. Anthol. Pal. vii. 455 : ἐν δ' ἀντὶ πάντων, also the frequent ἐν μόνον ; see Stallbaum, *ad. Plat. Symp.* p. 184 C, *Rep.* p. 548 C. It is here usually supplemented by ποιῶ (Chrysostom appears to have understood ποιῶν). So also Winer, Buttmann, de Wette, Wiesinger, Ellicott. But how arbitrarily, seeing that the context by what immediately precedes suggests simply the supplying of λογίζομαι (not λογίζ. κατειληφέναι, Oecumenius, Weiss), and this is in perfect harmony with the sense ! Hence we take it thus : " but one thing *I think, unum censeo.*" This one thing which Paul thinks regarding the matter in question, in contrast to the previous negative (δέ, as in ver. 12), is then directly expressed by all that follows from τὰ μὲν ὀπίσω to ἐν X. ʼI. Nearest to this contextual supplement comes the Syriac, which has added οἶδα, and Luther, who has added λέγω. The supplying of

---

[1] Οὐ belongs to λογίζομαι. The erroneous reference to κατειληφέναι produced the reading οὕτω (A D ℵ min. vss. and Fathers), which Tischendorf 8. has adopted.

λογίζομαι is confirmed by the cognate φρονῶμεν, ver. 15.
Without supplying anything, ἐν δέ has either been connected
with διώκω (thus Augustine, *Serm. de divers.* i. 6, Pierce,
Storr, van Hengel, and others), or has been taken *absolutely :*
" *unum contra !* " see Hoelemann, comp. Rheinwald. But the
former is to be rejected, because the subsequent διώκω carries
its own complete definiteness ; and the *latter* would render
the discourse abrupt without reason, since it is not written
under emotional excitement, and would, withal, require a
supplement, such as Beza gives by ἐστί. Hofmann also comes
at length in substance to this latter supplement, mixing up an
imaginary contrast to that which the *adversaries* imputed to the
apostle : over-against this, his conduct subsequently described
was the only thing which was quite right (?). — τὰ μὲν ὀπίσω]
what is behind, cannot be referred to what *has been mentioned*
in *vv.* 5 *and* 6 and the *category* of those pre-Christian advantages generally (so in substance, Pelagius ; τινὲς in Theodoret,
Vatablus, Zeger, Wolf, and others, also Ewald and Hofmann) ;
this would be at variance with the context, for τὰ μὲν ὀπίσω
ἐπιλανθ. corresponds to the negation of the having already attained or being perfect in ver. 12, and must therefore apply to
the *previous achievements of the Christian life,* to the degrees
of *Christian* moral perfection already reached, which are
conceived as the spaces already left behind in the *stadium*
of the runner still pressing forward ; and not to what had
belonged to his *pre-Christian* conduct (Hofmann). Comp.
Chrysostom, Oecumenius, Theophylact. — ἐπιλανθαν.] *forgetting,* like the runner who dismisses from his mind the space
already traversed, and fixes his thoughts only on what still
lies before him. This is surely no break in the internal connection (as Hofmann objects) ; on the contrary, like the runner
pressing forward, Paul in his continuous restless striving *overlooks* the degree of moral perfection already attained, which he
would not do, if he reckoned it already as itself perfection.
ἐπιλανθάνεσθαι is joined with the genitive and accusative ;
the simple verb, on the contrary, only with the genitive. See
Kühner, II. 1, p. 313.   On the use of the word in the sense of
intentional forgetting, comp. Herod. iii. 75, iv. 43 ; 1 Macc. i. 49.

It thus amounts to the sense of *nullam rationem habere* (Sturz, *Lex. Xen.* II. p. 294). — τοῖς δὲ ἔμπροσθεν ἐπεκτεινόμ.] *but stretching myself out towards that which is before.* The *dative* is governed by the verb compounded with ἐπί (Krüger, § 48. 11. 5 ; Nägelsbach, *zur Ilias*, p. 30, ed. 3), the ἐπί intimating the *direction.* In the case of such an one running "prono et quasi praecipiti corpore" (Beza), " oculus manum, manus pedem praevertit et trahit," Bengel. On the verb, comp. Strabo, xvii. p. 800 ; Aristot. *Poet.* 21 ; Plut. *Mor.* p. 1147 A. Τὰ ἔμπρ. represent the higher stages of Christian perfection not yet attained.[1] — κατὰ σκοπὸν διώκω] *I hasten towards the goal,* therefore in a straight course towards the prize of victory. The opposite : ἀπὸ σκοποῦ, Hom. *Od.* xi. 344, xxii. 6 ; Plat. *Theaet.* p. 179 C, *Tim.* p. 25 E ; Xen. *Conv.* ii. 10 ; Lucian, *Icarom.* 2 ; and παρὰ σκοπόν, Pind. *Ol.* xiii. 144. On διώκω *without an accusative of the object* (in opposition to van Hengel), comp. Xen. *Anab.* vii. 2. 20, vi. 5. 25 (δρόμῳ διώκειν) ; Aesch. *Sept.* 89 ; Buttmann, *Lexil.* p. 219 ; Jacobs, *ad Anthol.* IX. p. 213. Comp. on ver. 12. The *prize of victory* (τὸ βραβεῖον, see on 1 Cor. ix. 24 ; Clem. Cor. I. 5 ; Schol. min. *ad Soph. El.* 680 ; Oppian, *Cyneg.* iv. 196 ; Lycophr. 1154) represents *the salvation of the Messiah's kingdom* (see on ver. 12), to which God has called man. Hence : τῆς ἄνω κλήσεως, a *genitive* which is to be taken not as appositional (de Wette, Schenkel), but as the genitive of the *subject :* the βραβεῖον, *to which the calling relates.* Comp. Luther : " which the heavenly calling holds out." This is therefore the object of the ἐλπὶς τῆς κλήσεως (Eph. i. 18, iv. 4 ; comp. the Platonic καλὸν τὸ ἆθλον καὶ ἡ ἐλπὶς μεγάλη, *Phaed.* p. 114 C). — ἡ ἄνω κλῆσις τοῦ Θεοῦ is *the calling which issued from God above in heaven* (on ἄνω, comp. Col. iii. 2, Gal. iv. 26 ; and on the subject-matter, Heb. iii. 1), by which He has called us to the σωτηρία of His kingdom. The general form of expression, not even limited

---

[1] Τὰ ἔμπροσθεν is thus conceived by the apostle as *that which still lies further in prospect after every advance in the ethical course ;* not as that *which lay before him in consequence of his conversion* (contrasting with his *pre-Christian* efforts), as Hofmann thinks. It is the ever new, greater, and loftier task which he sees before him, step after step.

by a pronoun (such as τῆς ἐμῆς), does not allow us to think only
of the miraculous calling *of the apostle himself;* this is rather
included under the general category of the ἄνω κλῆσις τοῦ
Θεοῦ, which in the individual cases may have taken historically
very different forms.   The ἄνω, which in itself is not necessary, is added, because Paul is thoroughly filled with the consciousness of the divine nature of the κλῆσις in its exaltedness
above everything that is earthly.   Lastly, the κλῆσις itself is,
as always (even in 2 Thess. i. 11), the *act* of calling; not *that
whereto one is called* (de Wette), or "le bonheur céleste même"
(Rilliet); and the general currency of the idea and expression
forbids us also, since no indication of the kind is given, to
conceive of God as βραβευτής or βραβεύς, as the judge of the
contest (Pollux, iii. 145; Blomf. *Gloss. ad Aesch. Pers.* 307),
who through the herald summons the runners to the race
(Grotius, Wolf, Rosenmüller, am Ende, Hoelemann, van Hengel,
Wiesinger); τῆς ἄνω κλ. τ. Θ. serves to define more accurately
that which is figuratively denoted by βραβεῖον, but does not
itself form a part of the allegory. — ἐν X. 'I.] is rightly (so
also Weiss) joined by Chrysostom to διώκω: ἐν Χριστῷ Ἰησοῦ
τοῦτο ποιῶ, φησίν. οὐ γὰρ ἔνι χωρὶς τῆς ἐκείνου ῥοπῆς τοσοῦτον
διελθεῖν διάστημα.   Comp. Theodoret and Oecumenius.   This
thought, that the διώκειν just described is done by him *in
Christ,* as the great upholding and impelling element of life in
which amidst this activity he moves, is emphatically placed
at the end as that which regulates all his efforts.   The *usual*
connection of these words with τ. ἄνω κλήσεως τ. Θεοῦ, in
which the calling is understood as *brought about through Christ*
(rather: *having its causal ground in Christ*), yields a superfluous
and self-obvious definition of the κλῆσις already so accurately defined; although the connecting article would not be
necessary, since, according to the construction καλεῖν ἐν X.
(1 Cor. vii. 22; 1 Pet. v. 10), ἐν X. 'I. might be joined with
κλήσεως so as to form one idea; comp. Clem. Cor. I. 46.   A
contrast to the calling issued to *Israel* to be God's people *on
earth,* is groundlessly suggested by Hofmann.

Ver. 15. Application of the passage vv. 12–14 for the
benefit of the Philippians, down to ver. 17. — τέλειοι] denotes

not *perfection*, like τετελείωμαι in ver. 12, but the *moral ripeness* which, with differences of degree in the case of individuals, belongs to the true Christian state that has advanced beyond the novitiate—that Christian *maturity* in which one is no longer νήπιος ἐν Χριστῷ; comp. on 1 Cor. ii. 6, iii. 1; Eph. iv. 13. The τετελείωμαι is the ideal goal of the development of this τέλειον εἶναι, contradistinguished from the νηπιότης. The special aspect of this maturity, which Paul had in view in using τέλειοι, is to be regarded, not as *theoretical knowledge*,— the doctrine of *righteousness by faith* being conceived to be specially referred to (Erasmus, Wolf, Rheinwald, and others),— but as the *moral* character and striving of believers, as appears from ver. 13 f., along with which the corresponding relation of practical insight is self-evident as a necessary presupposition (comp. Col. iv. 12, i. 28); although there is no reason to suppose that particular questions in this domain (such as those relating to sacrificial flesh, fasts, feasts, and the like) had arisen in Philippi and occasioned division, of which no trace exists. The jealousy and partial disunion in the church arose from a *moral conceit*, which was prejudicial to mutual humility (ii. 3 ff.) and to personal genuine striving after holiness (ii. 12 ff.). In using ὅσοι—with which we are to supply *sumus* simply, and not *volumus esse*—Paul leaves it to the conscientious judgment of every reader whether he, on his part, belongs to the number of the τέλειοι; but by including *himself* in this predicate, and yet having previously negatived the ἤδη τετελείωμαι in his own case (ver. 12), the apostle removes all idle misunderstanding and abuse of his words which might tend to moral pride, and then by τοῦτο φρονῶμεν leaves room only for the consciousness: ὡς τελείου τὸ μὴ νομίζειν ἑαυτὸν τέλειον εἶναι, Chrysostom. A tone of *irony* (Schenkel) is utterly alien to the heartfelt character of the whole discourse, which is, moreover, in this application, ver. 15, so expressed as to include the apostle in common with his readers. To the Catholic fictions of a state of perfection the passage is in direct opposition. — τοῦτο φρονῶμεν] *let us have this frame of mind*, namely, which I, in ver. 13 f., have just expressed as mine; the frame of humble self-estimation, and at the same time incessant pressing forward. Grotius holds quite arbitrarily that Paul reverts to what he had said in ver. 3. But it is also wrong to seek the reference of τοῦτο φρον. in the passage from ver. 4 onwards: "renunciandum esse splendidis virtutibus Judd. (vv. 4–7), contra in solo Christo acquiescendum (vv. 8–10) et ad victricem palmam studio indefesso annitendum (vv. 12–14)," Hoelemann; comp. Calvin, Wolf, Heinrichs, and others, including Matthies, Baumgarten-Crusius, Rilliet, and Reiche; similarly Hofmann, who makes it refer to the entire presentation—joining on to ver. 3 — of a frame of mind which is opposed to the disposition of those against whom they are to be on their guard. Vv. 4–11 are certainly said by way of warning against the *false teachers*, and are opposed *to these;* but this opposition is of a *dogmatic* nature, for the upholding of the Pauline fundamental doctrine against Judaism, and it is only ver. 12 that begins what has regard to the *moral progress of the Church* in the right way pressing onward to the goal, in which respect Paul desires to serve for their *model* (ver. 17), —as which he has sketched himself in ver. 13 f., when he begins with ἀδελφοί and introduces his ἐγώ. Besides, the φρονῶμεν, which is correlative with the λογίζομαι, does not point back beyond ver. 13 f. Therefore, not even the appropriation of Christ, vv. 8–11, is to be included in the reference of the τοῦτο (in opposition to de Wette and Wiesinger). Van Hengel is inclined to refer τοῦτο to τὸ βραβεῖον; but the readers needed the exhortation *to the right mode of striving* after the βραβεῖον, and not *the* summons generally, that they should have the βραβ. in view. This applies also against the similar, although more exact, interpretation of Fritzsche (*Diss. II. in 2 Cor.* p. 92): " *hac mente simus* sc. *ut* τὸ βραβ. τῆς ἄνω κλήσεως *consectemur.*" — καὶ εἴ τι ἑτέρως φρον.] *and if as to any point* (τὶ, accusative of the object) *ye be otherwise minded,* take up another way of thinking, varying, namely, from that specified in τοῦτο φρονῶμεν. A man may, forsooth, have in general the same frame of mind which Paul has represented in himself, and to which he has summoned his readers; but at the same time an isolated concrete case (τἰ) may occur, which a man cannot fit into the φρονεῖν in question, and regarding which he is of opinion that he ought to be differently minded, so that in such a state of things he becomes *morally inconsistent* in his frame of mind, inasmuch as he lacks the befitting ἐπίγνωσις and αἴσθησις εἰς τὸ δοκιμάζειν κ.τ.λ., i. 9, in the moral judgment which determines the φρονεῖν. Hofmann arbitrarily limits the τἰ to some matter *independent of the essential disposition of the Christian life*. This sense would have required a more precise definition, in order to be found. And the hope which is uttered in the apodosis, is in perfect harmony with the prayer in i. 9 f.; hence Hofmann's objection, that the readers *must have themselves corrected* the fault which according to our view here emerges, is quite groundless. The *subject addressed* is the *readers generally* (see ver. 17), not the νήπιοι (Hunnius, Wolf, Bengel, Storr, and others, including Flatt, Rheinwald, Hoelemann, Rilliet, Reiche), whom several expositors have regarded as those who had not yet raised themselves to the pure righteousness of faith excluding the law (see Rheinwald and Reiche), or who had allowed themselves to be led away by false teachers (see Hunnius, Grotius, Storr). But setting aside the arbitrariness generally with which this contrast is introduced, it is opposed by the fact, that Paul does not assume any thorough and essential diversity in the φρονεῖν, but only such a variation as might affect some one or other isolated point (τἰ), and that not in the doctrinal, but in the moral province of Christian conduct. Moreover, if *persons led astray* were here in question, nothing would be less in harmony with the character of the apostle than the hopeful tolerance which is expressed in the words καὶ τοῦτο . . . ἀποκαλύψει. Lastly, the change of person (in opposition to Bengel) was necessary, because Paul, speaking of a partial ἑτέρως φρονεῖν, *could* not include himself. — In ἑτέρως, *otherwise* (not occurring elsewhere in the N. T.), there is implied, according to the context, an *unfavourable* sense, the notion of *incorrectness, secius quam oportet*. Comp. Hom. *Od.* i. 234; Dem. 298. 22, 597. 3; Eustath. *ad Od.* p. 1448. 2; Soph. *Phil.* 503; Valckenaer, *Diatr.* p. 112; just as ἕτερος (comp.

on ἄλλο, Gal. v. 10) may denote even that which is bad or
hostile (Wisd. xix. 3; Dissen. *ad Pind. Nem.* viii. 3, *Pyth.*
iii. 54; Wyttenbach, *ad Plat. Phaed.* p. 321). It is here the
ἑτεροδοξεῖν (Plat. *Theaet.* pp. 190 E, 193 D), as *frame of mind.*
This has not been attended to by van Hengel, when he takes
with equal unsuitableness τὶ in an emphatic sense, and φρονεῖν
as to *strive for :* " si *quid boni* per aliam viam *expetitis*, quam
ego persequor." — καὶ τοῦτο ὁ Θεὸς ὑμ. ἀποκ.] Expression of
the *hope* that such variations will not fail to be rectified, on the
part of God, by His revealing operation. Certainly, therefore,
the variations, which Paul so forbearingly and confidently and
without polemical handling commits to revealing correction
on the part of God, were not on matters of principle or of an
anti-Pauline character. — καὶ τοῦτο] *this also*, like other things
which He has already revealed unto you; so that in καὶ is
contained the idea *also still* (Hartung, *Partikell.* I. p. 135).
Hofmann erroneously says that καὶ implies: *there, where the
disposition is present, which I require.* It in fact belongs to
τοῦτο. This τοῦτο, however, is not: *that* ye (Oecumenius,
Grotius, Cornelius a Lapide, Fritzsche, *l.c.* p. 93), but *what* ye
wrongly think; *the frame of mind in question*, as it *ought to be*
instead of the ἑτέρως φρονεῖν, not: " whether you are right or
I" (Ewald). Calvin aptly says: " Nemo ita loqui jure posset,
nisi cui certa constat suae doctrinae ratio et veritas." The
passage is very far from betraying uncertainty or want of
firmness (Baur). — The ἀποκαλύψει, which is to be taken as
purely future, is conceived by Paul as taking place *through the
Holy Spirit* (see Eph. i. 17; Col. i. 10), not by human instruction (Beza). He might also have written διδάξει (comp. θεοδί-
δακτοι, 1 Thess. iv. 9; also John vi. 45), by which, however,
the special *kind* of instruction which he means would not
have been indicated. This is the inward divine unveiling of
ethical truth, which is needed for the practical reason *of him*
who in any respect otherwise φρονεῖ than Paul has shown
in his own example; for οὐ περὶ δογμάτων ταῦτα εἴρηται, ἀλλὰ
περὶ βίου τελειότητος καὶ τοῦ μὴ νομίζειν ἑαυτοὺς τελείους εἶναι,
Chrysostom. Wherever in this moral respect the right frame of
mind is not yet completely present in one or the other, Paul

trusts to the disclosing operation of God Himself, whose Spirit rules and works in the Church and its individual members (1 Cor. ii. 14, iii. 16 ; Eph. i. 17, ii. 21 f. ; Rom. viii. 9, 15, 26 ; Gal. v. 22, 25, *et al.*).

Ver. 16. A caution added to the precept given in ver. 15, and the promise coupled with it : Only let there be no devia-tion in the prosecution of the development of your Christian life from the point to which we have attained ! Neither to the right nor to the left, but forward in the same direction ! This warning Paul expresses briefly and precisely thus : " *Only whereto we have attained,—according to the same to direct your walk !*"—that is, " however ye may be in some point otherwise minded and, therefore, may have to await further revelation, at all events *ye ought not to deviate*—this must in every case be your fundamental rule—*from that whereto we have already attained in the Christian life ; but, on the contrary, should let the further direction of your moral walk be determined by that same.*" *Such* a general precept addressed to the Philippians conveys an honourable testimony to the state of their moral constitution on the whole, however different in individuals we may con-ceive the point to be from which Paul says εἰς ὃ ἐφθ., as is evident from the very fact that he includes himself in the εἰς ὃ ἐφθ., which could not but honour and stimulate the readers. On πλήν, *nisi quod,* comp. i. 18 ; on φθάνειν εἰς, *to attain to anything,* comp. Matt. xii. 28 ; Luke xi. 26 ; 1 Thess. ii. 16 (ἐπί); Rom. ix. 31 ; Dan. iv. 19 ; Tob. v. 18 ; Plut. *Mor.* p. 338 A ; Apollod. xii. 242. It denotes the having come *forward,* the having *advanced.* Ewald takes it : if we *had the advantage* (see 1 Thess. iv. 15, and the common classical usage), that is : " in what we already possess much better and higher than Judaism." But this reference to Judaism is not given in the text, which aims to secure generally their further pro-gress in the development of Christian life. On στοιχεῖν with the dative *of the rule : to advance* (march) *according to something,* that is, to direct oneself in one's constant conduct by some-thing, see on Gal. v. 16, 25. The *infinitive,* however, as the expression of a briefly measured wish or command, without supplying λέγω, δεῖ, or the like (which Buttmann requires,

PHIL. M

Neut. Gr. p. 233 [E. T. 272]), stands in place of the *impera-tive,* as in Rom. xii. 15 ; see Hom. *Il.* i. 20, and Nägelsbach *in loc.;* Stallbaum, *ad Plat. Rep.* p. 473 A; Pflugk, *ad Eur. Heracl.* 314 ; Fritzsche, *ad Rom.* III. p. 86. Fritzsche, how-ever, *Diss.* II. 2 *Cor.* p. 93, has erroneously made the infinitive dependent on ἀποκαλύψει : " praeterea instituet vos, ut, quam ego consecutus sum τῷ βραβείῳ τῆς ἄνω κλήσεως intentam mentem, ejusdem participes fieri ipsi annitamini." Comp. Oecumenius. Decisive against this view is the plural ἐφθά-σαμεν, which, according to the context (ver. 15), cannot apply merely to Paul, as well as the fact that the antithesis of persons (*ego . . . ipsi*) is gratuitously introduced. Michaelis, who is followed by Rilliet, closely unites ver. 16 with the sequel,[1] but in such a way that only an awkward arrangement of the sentences is attained, and the nervous vigour of the concise command is taken away.—The εἰς ὃ ἐφθάσ.—which cannot in accordance with the context denote the having attained to *Christianity,* to the *being Christian* (Hofmann's view, which yields a meaning much too vague and general)—has been rightly explained by Chrysostom and Theophylact as relating to the *attainments in the Christian life,* which are to be maintained, and in the further development of which constant progress is to be made (ὃ κατωρθώσαμεν, κατέχωμεν, Theophylact). Comp. Schinz and van Hengel. This view is corroborated by the sequel, in which Paul represents himself as model of the *walk ;* and therefore it is not to be referred merely to the measure of the right *frame of mind* attained (Weiss). Most expositors understand the words as signifying the measure of *Christian knowledge* acquired (so also Heinrichs, Flatt, Rheinwald, Matthies, Hoelemann, de Wette, Wiesinger), in conformity with which one ought to live. In connection with this, various arbitrary definitions of the *object* of the know-ledge have been suggested, as, for instance, by Grotius : " de cir-

---

[1] This is thrown out as a suggestion also by Hofmann, according to whom the infinitive clause ought "perhaps more correctly" to be coupled with συμμιμηταὶ κ.τ.λ., and taken as a prefixed designation of that *in doing which they are to be his imitators and to have their attention directed to those,* etc. Thus the infinitive would come to stand as infinitive of *the aim.* But even thus the whole attempt would be an artificial twisting of the passage without reason or use.

cumcisione et ritibus;" Heinrichs and de Wette: concerning
the main substance of the Christian faith apart from secondary
matters; Schneckenburger: "that man is justified by faith,
and not by the works of the law;" along with which de Wette
lays stress on the point that it is not the *individual* more or
less perfect knowledge (so usually; see Flatt, Rheinwald,
Matthies) that is meant, but the *collective conviction*, the
truths *generally* recognised. But the whole interpretation
which refers it to *knowledge* is not in keeping with the text;
for ἐφθάσαμεν, correlative with στοιχεῖν, presents together
with the latter a *unity* of figurative view, the former denoting the point of the way already attained, and τῷ αὐτῷ
στοιχεῖν, perseverance in the direction indicated by that
attainment. Therefore, if by στοιχεῖν there is clearly (see
ver. 17) intended the moral conduct of life, this also must be
denoted by εἰς ὃ ἐφθ. as respects its quality attained up to the
present time. Moreover, if εἰς ὃ ἐφθ. is to be understood as
referring to *knowledge*, there would be no motive for the prominence given to the identity by τῷ αὐτῷ.

REMARK.—What Paul means in ver. 16 may be illustrated thus:

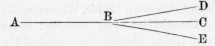

Here B is the point of the development of Christian life εἰς ὃ
ἐφθάσαμεν, which, in the case of different individuals, may be more
or less advanced. The τῷ αὐτῷ στοιχεῖν takes place, when the
path traversed from A to B is continued in the direction of C.
If any one should move from B in the direction of either D or
E, he would not τῷ αὐτῷ στοιχεῖν. The reproach of *uncertainty*
which Wiesinger brings against this canon, because a ἑτέρως
φρονεῖν may take place which does not lie in the same direction,
and generally because the power of sin might hinder the following out of this direction, would also apply in opposition to every
other explanation of the εἰς ὃ ἐφθ., and particularly to that of the
knowledge attained; but it is altogether unfounded, first, because
the ἑτέρως φρονεῖν only refers to one or another concrete *single
point* (τι), so that the *whole* of moral attainment—the collective development—which has been reached is not thereby disturbed; and, secondly, because Paul in this case has to do with a

church already *highly advanced* in a moral point of view (i. 5 ff.), which he might, at all events generally, enjoin to continue in the same direction as the path in which they had already travelled. Very groundless is also the objection urged by Hofmann, that the εἰς ὃ ἐφθ. must necessarily be *one and the same for all*. This is simply to be denied ; it is an utterly arbitrary assumption.

Ver. 17. In carrying out this command they are to follow his example, which he has previously held up to their view, especially from ver. 12 onwards. — συμμιμηταί] *co-imitators*, is a word not elsewhere preserved. Comp., however, συμμι-μούμενοι, Plat. *Polit.* p. 274 D. σύν is neither *superfluous* (Heinrichs, comp. Hofmann), nor does it refer to the imitation *of Christ* in common with the apostle (Bengel, Ewald),—a reference which cannot be derived from the remote i. 30–ii. 8, and which would be expressed somewhat as in 1 Cor. xi. 1 ; 1 Thess. i. 6. Neither does it refer to the obligation of his readers *collectively* to imitate him (Beza, Grotius, and others, including Matthies, Hoelemann, van Hengel, de Wette), so that "*omnes uno consensu et una mente*" (Calvin) would be meant ; but it means, as is required by the context that follows: "*una cum aliis, qui me imitantur* (Estius ; comp. Erasmus, *Annot.*, Vatablus, Cornelius a Lapide, Wiesinger, Weiss, Ellicott, and others). Theophylact aptly remarks : συγκολλᾷ αὐτοὺς τοῖς καλῶς περιπατοῦσι, whereby the weight of the exhortation is *strengthened*. — σκοπεῖτε] *direct your view* to those who, etc., namely, in order to become imitators of me in like manner as they are. *Other* Christians, not Philippians, are meant, just as ver. 18 also applies to those of other places. — καθώς] does not correspond to the οὕτω, as most expositors think, but is the *argumentative* "*as*" (see on i. 7), by which the two previous requirements, συμμιμηταί κ.τ.λ. and σκοπεῖτε κ.τ.λ., are estab-lished : *in measure as* ye have us for an example. This interpretation (which Wiesinger and Weiss adopt) is, notwith-standing the subtle distinction of thought which Hofmann suggests, required both by the second person ἔχετε (not ἔχουσι) and by the plural ἡμᾶς (not ἐμέ). This ἡμᾶς refers not to *the apostle alone* (so many, and still de Wette ; but in this case, as before, the *singular* would have been used), nor yet generally to the apostle *and his companions* (van Hengel, Baumgarten-Crusius, Lightfoot), especially *Timothy* (Hofmann), or to all *tried Christians* (Matthies); but to *him and those* οὕτω *(in this manner, imitative of me)* περιπατοῦντας. This view is not at variance with τύπον in the *singular* (de Wette); for the several τύποι of individuals are conceived *collectively* as τύπος. Comp. 1 Thess. i. 7 (Lachmann, Lünemann); see also 2 Thess. iii. 9; comp. generally, Bernhardy, p. 58 f.; Kühner, II. 1, p. 12 f. This predicative τύπον, which is therefore placed *before* ἡμᾶς, is emphatic.

Ver. 18. Admonitory confirmation of the injunction in ver. 17. — περιπατοῦσιν] is not to be defined by κακῶς (Oecumenius), or *longe aliter* (Grotius; comp. Syr.); nor is it to be taken as *circulantur* (comp. 1 Pet. v. 8) (Storr, Heinrichs, Flatt), which is at variance with the context in ver. 17. Calvin, unnaturally breaking up the plan of the discourse, makes the connection: "*ambulant terrena cogitantes*" (which is prohibited by the very article before ἐπίγ. φρον.), and puts in a parenthesis what intervenes (so also Erasmus, Schmid, and Wolf); whilst Estius quite arbitrarily overleaps the first relative clause, and takes περιπ. along with ὧν τὸ τέλος κ.τ.λ. Erasmus (see his *Annot.*) and others, including Rheinwald, van Hengel, Rilliet, de Wette, Wiesinger, and Weiss, consider the discourse as broken off, the introduction of the relative clauses inducing the writer to leave out the modal definition of περιπ. Hofmann transforms the simple λέγειν (comp. Gal. i. 9) into the idea of *naming*, and takes τοὺς ἐχθρούς as its *object - predicate*, in which case, however, the *mode* of the περιπατεῖν would not be stated. On the contrary, the construction is a genuine Greek mode of attraction (see Wolf, *ad Dem. Lept.* 15; Pflugk, *ad Eur. Hec.* 771; Kühner, II. 2, p. 925; Buttm. *Neut. Gr.* p. 68 [E. T. 77]), so framed, that instead of saying: *many walk as the enemies of the cross*, this predicative definition of mode is drawn into the relative clause οὓς πολλάκις κ.τ.λ.[1] and *assimilated* to the relative; comp. Plat. *Rep.*

---

[1] Hence also the conjecture of Laurent (*Neut. Stud.* p. 21 f.), that οἵ; πολλάκις ... ἀπώλεια is a *supplementary marginal note* inserted by the apostle, is unwarranted.

p. 402 c., and Stallbaum *in loc.* It is therefore to be interpreted:
*Many, of whom I have said that to you often, and now tell you
even weeping, walk as the enemies,* etc. The πολλάκις, emphatically corresponding with the πολλοί (2 Cor. viii. 22), refers to
the apostle's *presence* in Philippi; whether, at an earlier date
in an epistle (see on iii. 1), he had thus characterized these
enemies of the cross (Flatt, Ewald), must be left undecided.
But it is incorrect to make these words include a reference
(Matthies) to ver. 2, as in the two passages *different* persons
(see below) must be described. — νῦν δὲ καὶ κλαίων] διὰ τί;
ὅτι ἐπέτεινε τὸ κακὸν, ὅτι δακρύων ἄξιοι οἱ τοιοῦτοι . . . οὕτως
ἐστὶ συμπαθητικὸς, οὕτω φροντίζει πάντων ἀνθρώπων, Chrysostom. The deterioration of these men, which had in the
meanwhile increased, now extorts *tears* from the apostle on
account of their own ruin and of their ruinous influence. —
τοὺς ἐχθρ. τ. στ. τ. Χ.] The article denotes the class of men
characteristically defined. We must explain the designation
as referring, not to enemies of the *doctrine* of the cross (Theodoret: ὡς διδάσκοντας ὅτι δίχα τῆς νομικῆς πολιτείας ἀδύνατον
σωτηρίας τυχεῖν, so in substance Luther, Erasmus, Estius,
Calovius, Cornelius a Lapide, Wolf, and many others; also
Heinrichs, Rheinwald, Matthies), so that passages such as Gal.
v. 11, vi. 12, would have to be compared; but, as required
by the context which follows, to *Christians of Epicurean
tendencies* (ἐν ἀνέσει ζῶντες κ. τρυφῇ, Chrysostom; comp. Theophylact and Oecumenius), who, as such, are hostile to the
fellowship of the cross of Christ (comp. iii. 10), whose maxims
of life are opposed to the παθήματα τοῦ Χριστοῦ (2 Cor. i. 5),
so that it is hateful to them *to suffer with Christ* (Rom.
viii. 17). Comp. ver. 10, also Gal. vi. 14. In opposition to
the context, Rilliet and Weiss understand *non-Christians,* who
reject Christianity with hostile disdain, because its founder
was crucified (comp. 1 Cor. i. 18, 23), or because the preaching of the cross required the crucifixion of their own lusts
(Weiss); Calvin interpreted it generally of hypocritical *enemies
of the gospel.* This misunderstanding ought to have been precluded by the very use of the tragic πολλοί, the melancholy
force of which lies in the very fact that they are *Christians,* but

Christians whose conduct is the deterrent contrast to that
which is required in ver. 17. See, besides, in opposition to
Weiss, Huther in the *Mecklenb. Zeitschr.* 1862, p. 630 ff.—
We have still to notice that the persons here depicted are
not the same as those who *were described in ver.* 2 (contrary
to the usual view, which is also followed by Schinz and Hilgenfeld); for *those* were *teachers,* while these πολλοί are *Christians generally.* The *former* might indeed be characterized
as ἐχθροὶ τ. σταυροῦ τ. X., according to Gal. vi. 12, but their
Judaistic standpoint does not correspond to the Epicureanism
which is affirmed of the *latter* in the words ὧν ὁ Θεὸς ἡ κοιλία,
ver. 19. Hoelemann, de Wette, Lünemann, Wiesinger,
Schenkel, and Hofmann have justly pronounced against the
identity of the two; Weiss, however, following out his wrong
interpretation of κύνες in ver. 2 (of the *heathen*), maintains the
identity to a certain extent by assuming that the conduct of
those κύνες is here described; while Baur makes use of the
passage to deny freshness, naturalness, and objectivity to the
polemic attack here made on the false teachers.

Ver. 19. A more precise deterrent delineation of these
persons, having the most *deterrent* element put *foremost,* and
then those points by which it was brought about.— ὧν τὸ
τέλος ἀπώλ.] By this is meant *Messianic* perdition, eternal
condemnation (comp. i. 28), which is the *ultimate destiny* appointed (τό) for them (τέλος is not: *recompense,* see Rom. vi. 21 ;
2 Cor. xi. 15 ; Heb. vi. 8). For corresponding Rabbinical
passages, see Wetstein and Schoettgen, *Hor.* p. 801. — ὧν ὁ
Θεὸς ἡ κοιλία] λατρεύουσι γὰρ ὡς Θεῷ ταύτῃ καὶ πᾶσαν θερα-
πείαν προσάγουσι, Theophylact. Comp. Rom. xvi. 18; Eur. *Cycl.*
334 f.; Senec. *de benef.* vii. 26 ; and the maxim of those whose
highest good is eating and drinking, 1 Cor. xv. 32. It is the
γαστριμαργία (Plat. *Phaed.* p. 81 E; Lucian, *Amor.* 42) in its
godless nature; they were κοιλιοδαίμονες (Eupolis in Athen. iii.
p. 100 B), τὰς τῆς γαστρὸς ἡδονὰς τιθέμενοι μέτρον εὐδαιμονίας
(Lucian, *Patr. enc.* 10) ; τῇ γαστρὶ μετροῦντες καὶ τοῖς αἰσχίσ-
τοις τὴν εὐδαιμονίαν (Dem. 524. 24).—καὶ ἡ δόξα κ.τ.λ.] also
dependent on ὧν: *and whose honour is in their shame,* that is,
who find their honour in that which redounds to their shame,

as for instance, in revelling, haughty behaviour, and the like, in which the immoral man is fond of making a show. ἡ δόξα is *subjective*, viewed from the opinion of those men, and τῇ αἰσχύνῃ is *objective*, viewed according to the reality of the ethical relation. Comp. Polyb. xv. 23. 5 : ἐφ᾿ οἷς ἐχρῆν αἰσχύνεσθαι καθ᾿ ὑπερβολὴν, ἐπὶ τούτοις ὡς καλοῖς σεμνύεσθαι καὶ μεγαλαυχεῖν, and also Plat. *Theaet.* p. 176 D ; ἀγάλλονται γὰρ τῷ ὀνείδει. On εἶναι ἐν, *versari in*, to be found in, to be contained in something, comp. Plat. *Gorg.* p. 470 E : ἐν τούτῳ ἡ πᾶσα εὐδαιμονία ἐστίν, Eur. *Phoen.* 1310 : οὐκ ἐν αἰσχύνῃ τὰ σά. The view, foreign to the context, which refers the words to *circumcision*, making αἰσχ. signify the *genitals* (*Schol. Ar. Equ.* 364 ; Ambrosiaster ; Hilary ; Pelagius ; Augustine, *de verb. apost.* xv. 5 ; Bengel ; Michaelis ; Storr), is already rejected by Chrysostom and his successors. — οἱ τὰ ἐπίγεια φρονοῦντες] who *bear the earthly* (that which is on the earth ; the opposite in ver. 20) *in their mind* (as the goal of their interest and effort). Comp. Col. iii. 2. Thus Paul closes his delineation with a *summary* designation of their fundamental immoral tendency, and he put this, not in the *genitive* (uniformly with the ὧν), but more independently and emphatically in the *nominative*, having in view the *logical* subject of what precedes (comp. on i. 30), and that with the individualizing (*ii, qui*) article of apposition. Comp. Winer, p. 172 [E. T. 228] ; Buttmann, *Neut. Gr.* p. 69 [E. T. 79].

Ver. 20. After Paul has, by way of confirmation and warning, subjoined to his exhortation given in ver. 17 the deterrent example of the enemies of the cross of Christ in ver. 18 f., he now sketches by the side of that deterrent delineation—in outlines few, but how clear !—the *inviting picture of those* whom, in ver. 17, he had proposed as τύπος. — γάρ] The train of thought runs thus : " Justly I characterize their whole nature by the words οἱ τὰ ἐπίγεια φρονοῦντες ; for it is the direct opposite of *ours ;* our πολίτευμα, the goal of *our* aspiration, is not on earth, but in heaven." γάρ therefore introduces a *confirmatory reason,* but not for his having said that the earthly *mind* of the πολλοί necessarily *involves* such a *walk* (Hofmann) ; for he has not said this, and what follows would not be a proof of it. The apostle gives, rather, an *experimental proof e contrario*, and that for what immediately precedes, not for the remote ὧν τὸ τέλος ἀπώλεια (Weiss). — ἡμῶν] emphatically placed first; contrast of the persons. These ἡμεῖς, however, are the same as the ἡμᾶς in ver. 17, consequently Paul himself and the οὕτω περιπατοῦντες. — τὸ πολίτευμα] *the commonwealth*, which may bear the sense either of: *the state* (2 Macc. xii. 7; Polyb. i. 13. 12, ii. 41. 6 ; Lucian, *Prom.* 15 ; Philo, *de opif.* p. 33 A, *de Jos.* p. 536 D); or *the state-administration* (Plat. *Legg.* 12, p. 945 D ; Aristot. *Pol.* iii. 4; Polyb. iv. 23. 9; Lucian, *Dem. enc.* 16), or its *principles* (Dem. 107. 25, 262. 27; Isocr. p. 156 A); or the *state-constitution* (Plut. *Them.* 4; Arist. *Pol.* iii. 4. 1; Polyb. v. 9. 9, iv. 25. 7), see generally Raphel, *Polyb. in loc.;* Schweigh. *Lex. Polyb.* p. 486; Schoemann, *ad Plut. Cleom.* p. 208. Here, in the first sense : *our commonwealth,* that is, the *state* to which *we* belong, *is in heaven.* By this is meant the *Messiah's kingdom which had not yet appeared,* which will only at Christ's Parousia (comp. ἐξ οὗ κ.τ.λ. which follows) come down from heaven and manifest itself in its glory on earth. It is the state of the *heavenly Jerusalem* (see on Gal. iv. 26 ; comp. Usteri, *Lehrbegr.* p. 190; Ritschl, *altkath. Kirche,* p. 59), of which true Christians are citizens (Eph. ii. 19) even now before the Parousia in a proleptic and ideal sense (ἐπ᾽ ἐλπίδι τῆς δόξης, Rom. v. 2 ; comp. viii. 24), in order that one day, at the ἐπιφάνεια τῆς παρουσίας τοῦ κυρίου (2 Thess. ii. 8), they may be so in complete reality (comp. Heb. xii. 22 f., xiii. 14), as κοινωνοί τῆς μελλούσης ἀποκαλύπτεσθαι δόξης (1 Pet. v. 1 ; Col. iii. 4), nay, as συμβασιλεύοντες (2 Tim. ii. 12 ; comp. Rom. viii. 17 ; 1 Cor. iv. 8). Hence, according to the necessary psychological relation, " where your treasure is, there will your heart be also" (Matt. vi. 21), they φρονοῦσιν, not τὰ ἐπίγεια, but τὰ ἄνω (Col. iii. 1 f.), which serves to explain the logical correctness of the γάρ in its relation to οἱ τὰ ἐπίγ. φρον. Others, following the Vulgate (*conversatio*), render it : our *walk,* making the sense, " tota *vita nostra* quasi jam nunc apud Deum naturasque coelestes puriores versatur, longe remota a τοῖς ἐπιγείοις eorumque captatione" (Hoelemann). So Luther (who up till 1528 rendered it "citizenship"), Castalio, Erasmus, Calvin, Grotius, and many others, including Matthies, van Hengel, de Wette; while Rheinwald mixes up interpretations of various kinds.   This rendering is not justified by linguistic usage, which indeed vouches for πολιτεύεσθαι (i. 27) in this sense, and for πολιτεία (Clem. *Cor.* I. 54: πολιτεύεσθαι πολιτείαν Θεοῦ, Ep. ad Diogn. 5), but not for πολίτευμα, not even in Eus. *H. E.* v. *prooem.*   Nor does linguistic usage even permit the interpretation: *citizenship.*   So Luther, in the *Postil. Epist. D.* 3, *post f. pasch.:* "Here on earth we are in fact not citizens …; *our citizenship* is with Christ in heaven …, there we are to remain for ever citizens and lords;" comp. Beza, Balduin, Erasmus Schmid, Zachariae, Flatt, Wiesinger, Ewald, Weiss, and others.   This would be πολιτεία, Acts xxii. 28 ; Thuc. vi. 104. 3 ; Dem. 161. 11 ; Polyb. vi. 2. 12 ; 3 Macc. iii. 21. Theophylact's explanation, τὴν πατρίδα (which is used also for *heaven* by Anaxagoras in Diog. L. ii. 7), must be referred to the correct rendering *state* (comp. Hammond, Clericus, and others[1]), while Chrysostom gives no decided opinion, but Theodoret (τὸν οὐρανὸν φανταζόμεθα) and Oecumenius (στρατευόμεθα) appear to follow the rendering *conversatio.* — ἐξ οὗ καὶ κ.τ.λ.] And what a happy change is before us, in consequence of our thus belonging to the heavenly state ! From the heaven (scil. ἥξοντα, comp. 1 Thess. i. 10) we expect, etc.   The neuter οὗ, which is certainly to be taken in a strictly *local* sense (in opposition to Calovius), is not to be referred to πολίτ. (Wolf, Schoettgen, Bengel, Hofmann) ; but is correctly rendered by the Vulgate: "*unde.*"   Comp. on ἐξ οὗ, Col. ii. 19, and Bornemann, *ad Xen. Anab.* i. 2. 20 : ἡμέρας τρεῖς, ἐν ᾧ. — καί, *also,* denotes the relation *corresponding* to the foregoing (namely, that our πολίτευμα is to be found in heaven), not a *second one to be added* (Hofmann). — σωτῆρα] placed first with great emphasis, and that not as the accusative of the *object* (Hofmann), but—hence without the article—as *predicative* accusative: *as Saviour,* namely, from all the sufferings and conflicts involved in our fellowship with the cross of Christ (ver. 18), not from the ἀπώλεια (Weiss),

---

[1] The Gothic Version has : "unsara *báuáins*" (that is, *building, dwelling*).

which, indeed, the ἡμεῖς have not at all to fear. Comp. on the subject - matter, Luke xviii. 7 f., xxi. 28; Tit. ii. 13; 2 Tim. iv. 18. — ἀπεκδεχ.] comp. 1 Cor. i. 7; Tit. ii. 13. As to the signification of the word: *perseveranter expectare*, see on Rom. viii. 19; Gal. v. 5.

Ver. 21. As a special feature of the Lord's saving activity at His Parousia, Paul mentions the *bodily transfiguration* of the ἡμεῖς, in significant relation to what was said in ver. 19 of the enemies of the cross. The latter now lead an Epicurean life, whilst the ἡμεῖς are in a condition of bodily humiliation through affliction and persecution. But at the Parousia—what a change in the state of things! what a glorification of these bodies now so borne down! — μετασχηματ.] *shall transform.*[1] What is meant is the ἀλλάσσειν of the body (1 Cor. xv. 51 f.) at the Parousia, which in this passage, just as in 1 Cor. xv. 52, Paul assumes that the ἡμεῖς will *live to see.* To understand it at the same time of the resurrection of the dead (so most expositors, including de Wette, Wiesinger, Weiss), is inappropriate both to ἀπεκδεχόμεθα and to the definition of the quality of the body to be remodelled: τῆς ταπειν. ἡμῶν, both these expressions being used under the conviction of being still alive in the present state when the change occurs. Moreover, the resurrection is something more than a μετασχημάτισις; it is also an investiture with a new body out of the germ of the old (1 Cor. xv. 36–38, 42-44. — τῆς ταπεινώσ. ἡμῶν] Genitive of the *subject.* Instead of saying ἡμῶν merely (*our* body), he expresses it with more specific definition: the body *of our humiliation,* that is, the body *which*

---

[1] As to the nature of this transformation, see 1 Cor. xv. 53. The older dogmatic exegetes maintained in it the identity of substance. Calovius: "Ille μετασχηματισμός non *substantialem* mutationem, sed *accidentalem*, non ratione *quidditatis* corporis nostri, sed ratione *qualitatum* salva quidditate importat." This is correct only so far as the future body, although an organism without σάρξ and αἷμα, 1 Cor. xv. 50, will not only be again specifically *human*, but will also belong to the identity of the *persons*. See 1 Cor. xv. 35 ff. Comp. Ernesti, *Urspr. d. Sünde*, I. p. 127 f. More precise definitions, such as those in Delitzsch's *Psychol.* p. 459 ff., lose themselves in the misty region of hypothesis. The inappropriateness of the expression employed in the *Confession:* Resurrection *of the flesh*, has been rightly pointed out by Luther in the Larger Catechism, p. 501.

is the vehicle of the state *of our humiliation*, namely, through
the privations, persecutions, and afflictions which affect the
body and are exhibited in it, thereby reducing us into our present oppressed and lowly position; πολλὰ πάσχει νῦν τὸ σῶμα,
δεσμεῖται, μαστίζεται, μυρία πάσχει δεινά, Chrysostom. This
definite reference of τ. ταπ. ἡμ. is required by the context
through the contrast of the ἡμεῖς to the ἐχθροὺς τοῦ σταυροῦ
τ. Χ., so that the sufferings which are meant by the *cross of
Christ* constitute the ταπείνωσις of the ἡμεῖς (comp. Acts viii.
33); in which case there is no ground for our taking ταπείνωσις, contrary to Greek usage (Plat. *Legg.* vii. p. 815 A;
Polyb. ix. 33. 10; Jas. i. 10), as equivalent to ταπεινότης,
lowliness, as in Luke i. 48 (Hofmann). On this account, and
also because ἡμῶν applies to subjects *distinctly defined* in conformity with the context, it was incorrect to explain ταπειν.
generally of *the constitution of our life* (Hofmann), of *weakness
and frailty* (Luther, Calvin, Grotius, Estius, and many others;
including Rheinwald, Matthies, Hoelemann, Schrader, Rilliet,
Wiesinger, Weiss); comparison being made with such passages
as Col. i. 22; Rom. vii. 24; 1 Cor. xv. 44. The contrast
lies in the *states*, namely, of humiliation on the one hand and
of δόξα on the other; hence ἡμῶν and αὐτοῦ are neither to be
joined with σῶμα (in opposition to Hoelemann), nor with τ.
σῶμα τ. ταπ. and τ. σ. τῆς δόξης as ideas forming an unity
(Hofmann), which Paul would necessarily have marked by separating the genitives in position (Winer, p. 180 [E. T. 239]). —
σύμμορφον] Result of the μετασχημ., so that the reading εἰς
τὸ γενέσθαι αὐτό is a correct gloss. See on Matt. xii. 13 and
1 Cor. i. 8; Fritzsche, *Diss. II. in 2 Cor.* p. 159; Lübcker,
grammat. Stud. p. 33 f. The thing itself forms a part of the
συνδοξάζεσθαι, Rom. viii. 17. Comp. also 1 Cor. xv. 48 f.;
Rom. viii. 29. We may add Theodoret's appropriate remark: οὐ κατὰ τὴν ποσότητα τῆς δόξης, ἀλλὰ κατὰ τὴν
ποιότητα. — τῆς δόξ. αὐτοῦ] to be explained like τῆς ταπ. ἡμ.:
in which His heavenly glory is shown forth. Comp. ἐγείρεται
ἐν δόξῃ, 1 Cor. xv. 44. — κατὰ τ. ἐνέργ. κ.τ.λ.] removes every
doubt as to the possibility; *according to the working of His
being able* (comp. Eph. i. 19) *also to subdue all things unto*

Himself; that is, in consequence of the *energetic efficacy which belongs to His power of also subduing all things to Himself.* Comp. κατὰ τ. ἐνέργ. τῆς δυνάμ. αὐτοῦ, Eph. iii. 7, also Eph. i. 19 ; as to the subject-matter, comp. 1 Cor. xv. 25 f. ; as to the expression *with the genitive of the infinitive,* Onosand. I. p. 12 : ἡ τοῦ δύνασθαι ποιεῖν ἐξουσία. — καί] adds the general element ὑποτάξαι αὐτῷ τὰ π. to the μετασχημάτ. κ.τ.λ.[1] Bengel aptly says : " non modo conforme facere corpus nostrum suo." — τὰ πάντα] *all things collectively,* is not to be limited ; *nothing* can withstand His power; a statement which to the Christian consciousness refers, as a matter of course, to *created* things and powers, not to God also, from whom Christ has *received* that power (Matt. xxviii. 18 ; 1 Cor. xv. 27), and to whom He will ultimately deliver up again the dominion (1 Cor. xv. 24, 28). Chrysostom and Theophylact have already with reason noticed the argumentum *a majori ad minus.*

[1] Hoelemann takes καί as *and,* so that the sense would be, " that Christ can *do* all things, and *subdues* all things to Himself." The very aorist ὑποτάξαι should have withheld him from making this heterogeneous combination, as it betrays itself to be dependent on δύνασθαι.

CHAPTER IV.

VER. 3. Instead of ναί Elz. has καί, against decisive witnesses.—
Instead of σύζυγε γνήσιε, γνήσιε σύζυγε should be written, with
Lachm. and Tisch., upon preponderating evidence.—On decisive
testimony, in ver. 12, instead of οἶδα δὲ ταπ. (Elz.), οἶδα καὶ ταπ.
is to be received. The δὲ has taken its rise from the last syllable of οἶδα; hence we also find the reading δὲ καί. — Ver. 13.
After με Elz. has Χριστῷ, in opposition to A B D* ℵ, vss.
(also Vulgate) and Fathers. Defended by Reiche, but it is an
addition from 1 Tim. i. 12, from which passage also are found
the amplifications in Or., X. Ἰησοῦ and X. Ἰ. τῷ κυρίῳ ἡμῶν.—Ver.
16. εἰς] wanting in A D* E**, min. vss. and Fathers. Bracketed
by Lachm. But after δΙΣ, ἑΙΣ might the more readily be
omitted, as it seemed superfluous, and might, indeed, on account
of the absence of an object for ἐπέμψ., appear offensive. — Ver.
19. With Lachm. and Tisch., the form τὸ πλοῦτος is to be adopted
upon decisive testimony. See on 2 Cor. viii. 2. — Ver. 23.
πάντων ὑμῶν] A B D E F G P ℵ**, min. Copt. Sahid. Aeth. Arm.
Vulg. It. Damasc. Ambrosiast. Pel. have τοῦ πνεύματος ὑμῶν.
So Lachm. and Tisch. Taken from Gal. vi. 18, whence also in
Elz. ἡμῶν has likewise crept in after κυρίου.

Ver. 1. Conclusion drawn from what precedes, from ver.
17 onwards. We are not justified in going further back (de
Wette refers it to the whole exhortation, iii. 2 ff., comp. also
Wiesinger, Weiss, Hofmann), because the direct address to the
readers in the second person is only introduced at ver. 17, and
that with ἀδελφοί, as in the passage now before us; secondly,
because the predicates ἀγαπητοί . . . στέφανός μου place the
summons in that close personal relation to the apostle, which
entirely corresponds with the words συμμιμηταί μου γίνεσθε
in ver. 17; thirdly, because ὥστε finds its logical reference in
that which immediately precedes, and this in its turn is connected with the exhortation συμμιμηταί κ.τ.λ. in ver. 17; and
lastly, because οὕτω in ver. 1 is correlative to the οὕτω in

iii. 17.[1] — ὥστε] *accordingly;* the ethical actual result, which
what has been said of the ἡμεῖς in. iii. 20 f. ought to have
with the readers. Comp. ii. 12 ; 1 Cor. xv. 58. — ἀγαπητοί
κ.τ.λ.] " blandis appellationibus in eorum affectus se insinuat,
quae tamen non sunt adulationis, sed sinceri amoris," Calvin.—
How might they disappoint and grieve such love as this by
non-compliance ! — ἐπιπόθητοι] *longed for,* for whom I yearn
(comp. i. 8); not occurring elsewhere in the N. T. ; comp.
App. *Hisp.* 43 ; Eust. *Opusc.* p. 357. 39 ; Aq. Ez. xxiii. 11
(ἐπιπόθησις) ; Ps. cxxxix. 9 (ἐπιπόθημα) ; Ael. *N. A.* vii. 3
(ποθητός). — στέφανος] comp. 1 Thess. ii. 19 ; Ecclus. i. 9,
vi. 31, xv. 6 ; Ez. xvi. 12, xxiii. 42 ; Prov. xvi. 31, xvii. 6 ;
Job xix. 9. The *honour,* which accrued to the apostle from
the excellent Christian condition of the church, is represented by him under the figure of a *crown of victory.* Comp.
στέφανον εὐκλείας μέγαν, Soph. *Aj.* 465 ; Eur. *Suppl.* 313 ;
Iph. A. 193, *Herc. F.* 1334 ; Thuc. ii. 46 ; Jacobs, *ad Anthol.*
IX. p. 30 ; Lobeck *ad Aj. l.c.;* also στεφανοῦν (Wesseling, *ad
Diod. Sic.* I. p. 684), στεφάνωμα, Pind. *Pyth.* i. 96, xii. 9,
στεφανηφορεῖν, Wisd. iv. 2, and Grimm *in loc.* The reference of χαρά to the present time, and of στέφ. to the future
judgment (Calvin and others, comp. Pelagius), introduces arbitrarily a reflective distinction of ideas, which is not in keeping
with the fervour of the emotion. — οὕτω] corresponding to the
τύπος that has just been set forth and recommended to you
(iii. 17 ff.). Chrysostom, Theophylact, Oecumenius, Erasmus,
Calvin, Bengel, and others, interpret : so, *as ye stand,* so that
Paul " praesentem statum laudando ad perseverantiam eos
hortetur," Calvin. This is at variance with the context, for
he has just adduced *others* as a model for his readers ; and the
exhortation would not agree with συμμιμ. μ. γίνεσθε, iii. 17,
which, notwithstanding all the praise of the morally advanced
community, still does not presuppose the existence already of
a normal Christian state. — ἐν κυρίῳ] Comp. 1 Thess. iii. 8.

[1] In opposition to which Hofmann quite groundlessly urges the objection,
that Paul in that case would have written περιπατεῖτε instead of στήκετε. As if
he must have thought and spoken thus mechanically ! The στήκετε is in fact
substantially just a περιπατεῖν which maintains its ground.

Christ is to be the element *in which* the standing fast required of them is to have its specific character, so that in no case can the moral life ever act *apart from* the fellowship of Christ. — ἀγαπητοί] "περιπαθὴς haec vocis hujus ἀναφορά," Grotius. In no other epistle so much as in this has Paul multiplied the expressions of love and praise of his readers ; a strong testimony certainly as to the praiseworthy condition of the church, from which, however, Weiss infers too much. Here, as always (Rom. xii. 19 ; 2 Cor. vii. 1, xii. 19 ; Phil. ii. 12 ; 1 Cor. x. 14 ; Heb. vi. 9, *et al.*), moreover, ἀγαπητοί stands as an address without any more precise self-evident definition, and is not to be connected (as Hofmann holds) with ἐν κυρίῳ.

Ver. 2 f. After this general exhortation, ver. 1, the apostle, still deeply concerned for the community that is so dear to him, finds it requisite to give a special admonition to and for *two meritorious women*,[1] through whose disagreement, the details of which are unknown to us, but which probably turned on differences of their working in the church, a scandal had occurred, and the στήκειν ἐν κυρίῳ might more or less be imperilled. Whether they were *deaconesses* in Philippi (as many conjecture), must remain undecided. Grotius has erroneously considered both names, Hammond and Calmet only the second, to be *masculine*,[2] and in that case αὐταῖς in ver. 3 is made to apply to others (viz. αἵτινες κ.τ.λ.). For the two *feminine* names on inscriptions, see Gruter and Muratori. With Tischendorf and Lipsius (*Gramm. Unters.* p. 31), Συντυχή is to be treated as oxytone. Comp. generally Kühner, I. p.

---

[1] According to Baur, indeed, they are alleged to be two *parties* rather than two *women ;* and Schwegler (*nachapostol. Zeitalt.* II. p. 135) makes out that *Euodia* represents the *Jewish-Christian,* and *Syntyche* the *Gentile-Christian* party, and that γνήσιος σύζυγος applies to *Peter !* On the basis of *Constitutt. ap.* vii. 46. 1 (according to which Peter appointed an *Euodius,* and Paul Ignatius, as Bishop of Antioch), this discovery has been amplified with further caprice by Volkmar in the *Theol. Jahrb.* 1857, p. 147 ff. But exegetical fiction in connection with the two feminine names has been pushed to the utmost by Hitzig, *z. Krit. Paulin. Br.* p. 5 ff., according to whom they are supposed to have their origin in Gen. xxx. 9 ff. ; he represents our author as having changed *Asher* and *Gad* into *women* in order to represent figuratively two parties, and both of them *Gentile-Christian.*

[2] Theodore of Mopsuestia quotes the opinion that the two were *husband and wife.*

256. The *twice used* παρακ.: "quasi coram adhortans seorsum utramvis, idque summa cum aequitate," Bengel. An earnestly individualizing ἐπιμονή (Bremi, *ad Aeschin.* p. 400). — τὸ αὐτὸ φρον.] see on ii. 2. — ἐν κυρ.] characterizes the specifically *Christian* concord, the moral nature and effort of which are grounded on Christ as their determining vital principle. Paul does not desire a union of minds *apart from* Christ.—Whether the disunion, which must be assumed, had its deeper root in *moral pride* on account of services in the cause of the gospel (Schinz), is not clear.

Ver. 3. *Indeed, I entreat thee also,* etc. This bringing in of a third party is a *confirmation* of the previous admonition as regards its necessity and urgency; hence the ναί; comp. Philem. 20. See also on Matt. xv. 27. — σύζυγε is erroneously understood by Clemens Alexandrinus, Isidorus, Erasmus, Musculus, Cajetanus, Flacius, and others, as referring to the *wife* of the apostle; an idea which, according to 1 Cor. vii. 8, compared with ix. 5, is at variance with history (see, already, Chrysostom, Theodoret, Oecumenius, Theophylact), and at the same time at variance with grammar, as the adjective must in that case have stood in the feminine (*Test. XII. Patr.* p. 526; Eur. *Alc.* 314, 342, 385). Others understand the *husband of one of the two women* (so, although with hesitation, Chrysostom, also Theophylact, according to whom, however, he might have been a *brother*, and Camerarius; not disapproved by Beza); but what a strangely artificial designation would "genuine *conjux*" be! Weiss prefers to leave *undecided* the nature of the bond which connected the individual in question with the two women. But if, in general, a relation to the *women* were intended, and that apart from the bond of matrimony, by the term σύζυγε Paul would have expressed himself very awkwardly; for the current use of the word σύζυγος, and also of συζυγής (3 Macc. iv. 8) and σύζυξ (Eur. *Alc.* 924), in the sense of *conjux* (comp. συζευγνύναι, Xen. *Oec.* 7. 30; Herodian, iii. 10. 14), must have been well known to the reader. The usual mode of interpreting this passage (so Flatt, Rheinwald, Hoelemann, Matthies, de Wette, following Pelagius and Theodoret) has been to refer it to some dis-

tinguished *fellow - labourer of the apostle*, well known, as a
matter of course, to the readers of the epistle, who had his
abode in Philippi and deserved well of the church there
by special services.   Some have arbitrarily fixed on *Silas*
(Bengel), and others quite unsuitably on *Timothy* (Estius),
and even on *Epaphroditus* (Vatablus, Grotius, Calovius,
Michaelis, van Hengel, and Baumgarten-Crusius), whom Hofmann also would have us understand as referred to, inasmuch
as he regards him as the *amanuensis* of the epistle, who had
therefore heard it dictated by the apostle, and then heard it
again when it came to be read in the church, so that *he knew
himself to be the person addressed*.   What accumulated invention, in order to fasten upon Epaphroditus the, after all,
unsuitable confession before the church that he was himself
the person thus distinguished by the apostle !   According to
Luther's gloss, Paul means " *the most distinguished bishop* in
Philippi."   Comp. also Ewald, who compares συμπρεσβύτερος,
1 Pet. v. 1.   But how strange would such a nameless designation be in itself !   How easily might the preferential
designation by γνήσιος have seemed even to slight other fellow-
labourers in Philippi !   Besides, Paul, in describing his
official colleagues, never makes use of this term, σύζυγος,
which does not occur elsewhere in the N. T., and which would
involve the assumption that the unknown individual stood
in quite a special relation to the apostle corresponding to this
purposely-chosen predicate.   Laying aside arbitrariness, and
seeing that this address is surrounded by proper names
(vv. 2, 3), we can only find in σύζυγε a *proper name*, in
which case the attribute γνήσιε corresponds in a delicate
and winning way to the *appellative* sense of the name (comp.
Philem. 11) ; *genuine Syzygus*, that is, thou who art in
reality and substantially that which thy name expresses :
" *fellow-in-yoke*," *i.e. yoke-fellow*, fellow-labourer.   We may
assume that Syzygus had rendered considerable services to
Christianity in Philippi in joint labour with the apostle, and
that Paul, in his appellative interpretation of the name, followed the figurative conception of *animals in the yoke* ploughing
or thrashing (1 Cor. ix. 9 ; 1 Tim. v. 18), a conception which

was suggested to him by the very *name itself.* The opposite of γνήσιος would be: οὐκ ὄντως ὤν (comp. Plat. *Polit.* p. 293 E), so that the man with his name *Syzygus* would not be ἐπώνυμος (Eur. *Phoen.* 1500 ; Soph. *Aj.* 430), Jacobs, *ad Del. Epigr.* p. 272 f. He bore this his name, however, as ὄνομα ἐτήτυμον (*Del. Epigr.* v. 42). This view of the word being a proper name—to which Wiesinger inclines, which Laurent decidedly defends [1] in his *Neut. Stud.* p. 134 ff. and Grimm approves of in his *Lexicon,* and which Hofmann, without reason, rejects [2] simply on account of the *usus loquendi* of γνήσιος not being proved—was already held by τινές in Chrysostom; comp. Niceph. Call. ii. p. 212 D ; Oecumenius permits a choice between it and the explanation in the sense of the *husband* of one of the two women. It is true that the name is not preserved elsewhere ; but with how many names is that the case ? Hence it was unwarranted to assume (Storr) a translation of the name Κολληγᾶς (Joseph. *Bell.* vii. 3. 4), in connection with which, moreover, it would be hard to see why Paul should have chosen the word σύζυγος elsewhere not used by him, and not συνεργός, or the like.[3] To refer the word to *Christ,* who helps every one to bear his yoke (Wieseler), was a mistake. — συλλαμβ. αὐταῖς] *lay hold along with them,* that is, *assist them* (Luke v. 7 ; Herod. vi. 125 ; Xen. *Ages.* 2. 31 ; Wunder, *ad Soph. Phil.* 280 ; *Lex. Plat.* III. p. 294), namely, for their reconciliation and for restoring their harmonious action. — αἵτινες] *utpote quae,* giving the motive, comp. i. 28 ;

[1] In doing so, Laurent takes the reference of σύν contained in the name as *general:* "helper of *all* labour in the vineyard of the Lord." More thoughtful, however, is the reference to *the apostle himself,* whose true yoke-fellow is to supply his place with *his former female fellow-strivers* (συνήθλ. μοι) ; comp. also subsequently συνεργῶν μου.

[2] According to our view, γνήσιος is, in fact, taken in no other sense than that which is current in all Greek authors, viz. ἀληθινός, *verus,* as Hofmann himself takes it. Whether we refer it thus to σύζυγι as an *appellative* word, or as the *appellative* contents of a *name*—is a matter which leaves the linguistic use of γνήσιος altogether untouched. As is well known, νόθος has the same general linguistic usage in the *opposite* sense (see *e.g.* Plat. *Rep.* p. 536 A ; Jacobs, *ad Del. Epigr.* i. 103. 3).

[3] This holds at the same time against the view of Pelagius : "*Germanus* dictus est *nomine,* qui erat compar *officii.*" He is followed by Lyra.

see on Rom. i. 25, ii. 15, vi. 2, *et al.*—ἐν τῷ εὐαγγ.] the domain, *in which they,* etc.   Comp. Rom. i. 9 ; 1 Thess. iii. 2.   It was among *women* that the gospel had first struck root in Philippi (Acts xvi. 13), and it is to be assumed that the two women named had rendered special service in the spread and con- firmation of Christianity among their sex, and therein had shared the conflict of affliction and persecution with Paul (1 Thess. ii. 2).   On συνήθλησαν, comp. i. 27. — μετὰ καὶ Κλήμεντος κ.τ.λ.] and in what *fellowship, so honourable to them,* have they shared my conflict for Christ's sake ? *in association also with Clement and,* etc.   The reference of the καί is to μοι; their joint-striving with Paul had been a fellowship in striving also with Clement, etc. ; they had therein stood *side by side with these men also.*   On καὶ . . . καί, the first καὶ meaning *also,* comp. Ellendt, *Lex. Soph.* I. p. 891 ; on its rarer position, however, between preposition and noun, see Schaefer, *Ind. ad Gregor. Cor.* p. 1064 ; Hartung, *Partikell.* I. p. 143 ; Kühner, II. 1, p. 480 f.   The connection of μετὰ κ. Κλ. κ.τ.λ. with συλλαμβ. αὐταῖς (Coccejus, Michaelis, Storr, Flatt, J. B. Lightfoot, Hofmann) is opposed by the facts, that Paul has committed the service of mediation to an *individual,* with which the general impress now given to this commission is not in keeping, and that the subsequent ὧν τὰ ὀνόματα κ.τ.λ., in the absence of any specification of the churches, would neither be based on any motive nor intelligible to the readers, and would be strangest of all in the event of Paul's having intended, as Hofmann thinks, to indicate here *the presbyters and deacons* mentioned in i. 1.   The λοιποὶ συνεργοί, as well as generally the more special circumstances of which Paul here reminds his readers, were—if μετὰ καὶ κ.τ.λ. be joined with συνήθλησάν μοι, beside which it stands—*historically* known to these readers, although unknown to us.—That Clement was a teacher in *Philippi* (so most modern expositors ; according to Grotius, a *presbyter* in Philippi, but " Romanus aliquis in Macedonia negotians "), must be maintained in accordance with the con- text, seeing that with him those two *Philippian women* laboured as sharing the conflict of the apostle ; and of a *travelling com- panion* of this name, who had laboured with the apostle in

Macedonia, there is no trace to be found; and seeing that the
λοιποὶ συνεργοί also are to be regarded as *Philippians*, because
thus only does the laudatory expression ὧν τὰ ὀνόματα κ.τ.λ.
appear in its vivid and direct set purpose of bespeaking for
the two women the esteem of the *church*. The more frequent,
however, in general the name of Clement was, the more
arbitrary is the old view, although not yet known to Irenaeus
(iii. 3. 3), that Clement *of Rome* is the person meant.[1] So
most Catholic expositors (not Döllinger), following Origen,
ad Joh. i. 29 ; Eusebius, *H. E.* iii. 15 ; Epiphanius, *Haer.*
xxvii. 6 ; Jerome, Pelagius, and others ; so also Francke, in
the *Zeitschr. f. Luth. Theol.* 1841, iii. p. 73 ff., and van Hengel,
who conjectures Euodia and Syntyche to have been Roman
women who had assisted the apostle *in Rome*, and had travelled
with Epaphroditus to Philippi. See generally, besides Lünemann and Brückner, Lipsius, *de Clem. Rom. ep.* p. 167 ff. ;
J. B. Lightfoot, p. 166 ff. ; and Hilgenfeld, *Apost. Väter*, p.
92 ff. — ὧν τὰ ὀνόμ. κ.τ.λ.] refers merely to τῶν λοιπῶν κ.τ.λ.,
whom Paul does not adduce *by name*, but instead of this
affirms of their names something so great and honourable.
God has recorded their names in His book, in which are
written down the future partakers of the everlasting Messianic
life ; so *surely and irrevocably is this life assigned to them.*
What Paul thus expresses by this solemn figure, he *knew*
from their whole Christian character and action, in which he
recognised by experience " *quasi electionis* [2] *absconditae sigilla* "

---

[1] Nevertheless, upon this hypothesis Baur builds up a whole fabric of combinations, which are intended to transfer the date of our epistle to the post-
apostolic age, when the *Flavius Clemens* known in Roman history, who was a
patruelis of Domitian (Suet. *Dom.* 15), and a Christian (Lami, *de erud. apost.*
p. 104 ; Baur, II. p. 68), had already become the well-known Clement of Roman
tradition. Comp. Volkmar in the *Theolog. Jahrb.* 1856, p. 309, according to
whom the Roman Clement is to be here already assumed as a *martyr.* Indeed,
according to Schwegler and Hitzig, *z. Krit. paulin. Br.* p. 13, a first attempt
is made here to connect this Clement also with *Peter* (for no other in their view
is the σύζυγος). Thus, no doubt, the way is readily prepared for bringing down
our epistle to the days of Trajan. Round the welcome name of Clement all
possible fictions crystallize.

[2] The detailed discussion of the question as to the *ground* of the divine *electio*
here portrayed (the Reformed theologians, "the *decretum absolutum ;*" the
Lutherans, "the *praevisa fides ;*" the Catholics, "the *praevisa opera*") is out of

(Calvin). See, moreover, on Luke x. 20, and Wetstein on our passage ; it is different in Heb. xii. 23 (see Lünemann *in loc*). ἐστί must be supplied, not the *optative*, as Bengel thinks ; and it must remain an open question, whether the persons referred to (among whom Ewald reckons Clement) are to be regarded as already dead (Bengel, Ewald), which is not to be inferred from ὧν τὰ ὀνόματα κ.τ.λ. ; see Luke x. 20 ; Hermas, *Pastor* i. 1. 3.   It is at all events certain that this predicate, which Paul nowhere else uses, is an *especially honourable* one, and does not simply convey what holds true of *all Christians* (so Hofmann in connection with his erroneous reference of μετὰ καὶ κ.τ.λ.).   At Luke x. 20, and Rev. xiii. 8 also, it is a *mark of distinction.*

Ver. 4 f. Without any particle of transition, we have once more *general* concluding admonitions, which begin by taking up again the encouraging address broken off in iii. 1, and now strengthened by πάντοτε—the key-note of the epistle.   They extend as far as ver. 9 ; after which Paul again speaks of the assistance which he had received. — πάντοτε] not to be connected with πάλιν ἐρῶ (Hofmann), which would make the πάλιν very superfluous, is an essential element of the Christian χαίρειν; comp. 1 Thess. v. 16 ; 2 Cor. vi. 10.   Just at the close of his epistle the apostle brings it in significantly. Paul desires joyfulness *at all times* on the part of the believer, to whom even tribulation is grace (i. 7, 29) and glory (Rom. v. 3), and in whom the pain of sin is overcome by the certainty of atonement (Rom. viii. 1); to whom everything must serve for good (Rom. viii. 28 ; 1 Cor. iii. 21 f.), and nothing can separate him from the love of God (Rom. viii. 38 f.). — πάλιν ἐρῶ] *once more I will say.*   Observe the *future*, which exhibits the *consideration* given to the matter by the writer ; consequently not equivalent to πάλιν λέγω, 2 Cor. xi. 16 ; Gal. i. 9.   Καλῶς ἐδιπλασίασεν, ἐπειδὴ τῶν πραγμάτων ἡ φύσις λύπην ἔτικτε, διὰ τοῦ διπλασιασμοῦ δείκνυσιν, ὅτι πάντως δεῖ χαίρειν, Chrysostom. — Τὸ ἐπιεικὲς ὑμῶν] *your mildness*

place here. Flacius, *Clav. s.v.* "liber," justly observes that it is not *fatalis quaedam electio* which is pointed to, but *ob veram justitiam, qualis Christi est, credentes eo referri et inscribi.*

[*Lindigkeit*, Luther], that is, *your gentle character*, as opposed to undue sternness (Polyb. v. 10. 1 : ἡ ἐπιείκεια καὶ φιλαν-θρωπία, Lucian, *Phal. pr.* 2 : ἐπιεικὴς κ. μέτριος, Herodian, ii. 14. 5, ix. 12 ; 1 Tim. iii. 3 ; Tit. iii. 2 ; Jas. iii. 17 ; 1 Pet. ii. 18 ; Ps. lxxxv. 5 ; Add. to Esth. vi. 8 ; 2 Macc. ix. 27). Comp. on 2 Cor. x. 1. The opposite : ἀκριβοδίκαιος, Arist. *Eth. Nic.* v. 10. 8, σκληρός. As to the neuter of the adjective taken as a substantive, see on iii. 8 ; comp. Soph. *O. C.* 1127. It might also mean : your *becoming* behaviour ; see *e.g.* the passages from Plato in Ast, *Lex.* I. p. 775. But how indefinite would be such a requirement as this ! The *general duty of the Christian walk* (which Matthies finds in the words) is not set forth till ver. 8. And in the N. T. ἐπιεικ. always occurs in the above-named special sense. — γνωσθήτω πᾶσιν ἀνθρ.] *let it be known by all men,* through the acquaintance of experience with your conduct. Comp. Matt. v. 16. The *universality* of the expression (which, moreover, is to be taken *popularly :* "let no man come to know you in a harsh, rigorous aspect") prohibits our referring it to their rela-tion to the *enemies of the cross of Christ,* against whom they should not be hatefully disposed (Chrysostom, Oecumenius, Theophylact), or to the *enemies of Christianity* (Pelagius, Theodoret, Erasmus, and others), or to the *Judaists* (Rhein-wald), although none of these are excluded, and the *motive* for the exhortation is in part to be found in the outward circum-stances full of tribulation, face to face with an inclination to moral pride.—The *succession* of exhortations without any outward link may be psychologically explained by the fact, that the disposition of Christian joyfulness must elevate men quite as much above strict insisting upon rights and claims as above solicitude (ver. 6). Neither with the former nor with the latter could the Christian fundamental disposition of the χαίρειν ἐν κυρίῳ subsist, in which the heart enlarges itself to yielding love and casts all care upon God. — ὁ κύριος ἐγγύς] points to the *nearness of Christ's Parousia,* 1 Cor. xvi. 22. Comp. on ἐγγύς, Matt. xxiv. 32 f.; Luke xxi. 31 ; Rev. i. 3, xxii. 10 ; Rom. xiii. 11. The reference to *God,* by which Paul would bring home to their hearts, as Calvin expresses it, " *divinae providentiae fiduciam*" (comp. Ps. xxxiv. 18, cxix. 151, cxlv. 18; so also Pelagius, Luther, Calovius, Zanchius, Wolf, Rheinwald, Matthies, Rilliet, Cornelius Müller, and others), is not suggested in vv. 1, 2, 4 by the context, which, on the contrary, does not refer to *God* until ver. 6.   Usually and rightly, following Chrysostom and Erasmus, the words have been attached to *what precedes*.[1]   If the Lord is at hand, who is coming as the *Vindex* of every injustice endured and as the σωτήρ of the faithful, how should they not, in this prospect of approaching victory and blessedness (iii. 20), willingly and cheerfully renounce everything opposed to Christian ἐπιείκεια ! The words therefore convey an *encouragement* to the latter. What follows has its complete reference, and that to God, pointed out by the antithesis ἀλλ' ἐν παντὶ κ.τ.λ.

Ver. 6. The μεριμνᾶτε is not to be limited in an arbitrary way (as by Grotius, Flatt, Weiss, and others, to *anxious* care); *about nothing* (neither want, nor persecution, nor a threatening future, etc.) are they at all to give themselves concern, but on the contrary, etc.; μηδέν, which is emphatically prefixed, is the accusative of the *object* (1 Cor. vii. 32 ff., xii. 25 ; Phil. ii. 20).   Comp. Xen. *Cyrop.* viii. 7. 12 : τὸ πολλὰ μεριμνᾶν καὶ τὸ μὴ δύνασθαι ἡσυχίαν ἔχειν.   Caring is here, as in Matt. vi., the contrast to full confidence in God.   Comp. 1 Pet. v. 7. " Curare et orare plus inter se pugnant quam aqua et ignis," Bengel. — ἐν παντί] opposed to the μηδέν; hence : *in every case* or *affair* (comp. Eph. v. 24; 2 Cor. iv. 8; 1 Thess. v. 18; Plat. *Euthyd.* p. 301 A), not : *at all times* (Syriac, Grotius, Bos, Flatt, Rheinwald). — τῇ προσευχῇ κ. τῇ δεήσει] *by prayer and supplication.*   On the distinction between the two (the former being *general*, the latter *supplicating* prayer), see on Eph. vi. 18.   The *article* indicates the prayer, *which ye make;*

---

[1] They do not belong, by way of *introduction*, to *what follows*, as Hofmann thinks, who understands " the helpful nearness of the Lord" (Matt. xxviii. 20 ; Jas. iv. 8) *in the present*, and consequently the assurance *of being heard in the individual case.*   Comp., rather, on the ἐγγύς habitually used of the future *final coming*, in addition to the above passages, Matt. iii. 2, iv. 17, x. 7 ; Mark i. 15 ; Luke xxi. 8, 28 ; Rom. xiii. 12 ; Heb. x. 25 ; Jas. v. 8 ; 1 Pet. iv. 7 ; and the ἔρχομαι ταχύ of the Apocalypse.   The simply correct rendering is given after Chrysostom by Erasmus ("*instat enim adventus Christi*"), Grotius, and others.

and the *repetition* of the article, otherwise not required, puts
forward the two elements the more emphatically (Kühner, II. 1,
p. 529). — μετὰ εὐχαρ.] belongs to γνωριζ. κ.τ.λ., which, excluding all *solicitude* in the prayer, should never take place (comp.
1 Thess. v. 18 ; Col. iii. 17) without *thanksgiving* for the
proofs of divine love already received and continually being
experienced, of which the Christian is conscious *under all circumstances* (Rom. viii. 28). In the thanksgiving of the sup-
pliant there is expressed entire surrender to God's will, the very
opposite of solicitude. — τὰ αἰτήματα ὑμ.] *what ye desire* (Plat.
Rep. viii. p. 566 B ; Dionys. Hal. *Antt.* vi. 74 ; Luke xxiii.
24), that is, in accordance with the context : your *petitions*
(1 John v. 15 ; Dan. vi. 7, 13 ; Ps. xix. 6, xxxvi. 4, *et al.;*
Schleusner, *Thes.* I. p. 100). — γνωριζέσθω πρὸς τ. Θεόν] *must
be made known towards God;* πρός, *versus;* it is the *coram*
of the direction. Comp. Bernhardy, p. 265 ; Schoem. *ad Is.*
iii. 25. The expression is more *graphic* than the mere dative
would be ; and the conception itself (γνωριζ.) is popularly
anthropopathic ; Matt. vi. 8. Bengel, moreover, aptly remarks
on the subject-matter : " qui desideria sua praepostero pudore
ac diffidenti modestia . . . velant, suffocant ac retinent, curis
anguntur ; qui filiali et liberali fiducia erga Deum expromunt,
expediuntur. Confessionibus ejusmodi scatent Psalmi."

Ver. 7. The blessed *result*, which the compliance with
ver. 6 will have for the inner man. How independent is this
blessing of the concrete granting or non-granting of what is
prayed for ! — ἡ εἰρήνη τ. Θεοῦ] the *peace of soul* produced by
God (through the Holy Spirit ; comp. χαρὰ ἐν πνεύματι ἁγίῳ,
Rom. xiv. 17), the repose and satisfaction of the mind in God's
counsel and love, whereby all inward discord, doubt, and
variance are excluded, such as it is expressed *e.g.* in Rom.
viii. 18, 28. So in substance most expositors, including
Rheinwald, Flatt, Baumgarten-Crusius, Hoelemann, Rilliet, de
Wette, Wiesinger, Ewald, Weiss, Hofmann, and Winer. This
view—and not (in opposition to Theodoret and Pelagius) that
explanation of peace in the sense of *harmony with the brethren*
(Rom. xv. 33, xvi. 20 ; 2 Cor. xiii. 11 ; 1 Thess. v. 23 ;
2 Thess. iii. 16), which corresponds to the ordinary use of the

correlative ὁ Θεὸς τῆς εἰρήνης in ver. 9—is here required on the part of the context, both by the contrast of μεριμνᾶτε in ver. 6, and by the predicate ἡ ὑπερέχουσα πάντα νοῦν. The latter, if applicable to the *peace of harmony*, would express too much and too general an idea; it is, on the other hand, admirably adapted to the holy peace of the soul which God produces, as contrasted with the μέριμνα, to which the feeble νοῦς by itself is liable; as, indeed, in the classical authors also (Plat. *Rep.* p. 329 C, p. 372 D), and elsewhere (Wisd. iii. 3), εἰρήνη denotes the *tranquillitas* and *securitas*, the mental γαλήνη (Plat. *Legg.* vii. p. 791 A) and ἡσυχία—a rest, which here is invested by τοῦ Θεοῦ with the consecration of divine life. Comp. εἰρήνη τοῦ Χριστοῦ, Col. iii. 15; John xiv. 33; and, on the other hand, the false εἰρήνη κ. ἀσφάλεια, 1 Thess. v. 3. It is therefore not to be understood, according to Rom. v. 1, as "pax, *qua reconciliati estis Deo*" (Erasmus, *Paraphr.*; so Chrysostom, ἡ καταλλαγὴ, ἡ ἀγάπη τ. Θεοῦ; and Theophylact, Oecumenius, Beza, Estius, Wetstein, and others, including Storr, Matthies, and van Hengel), which would be too general and foreign to the context. The peace of reconciliation is the *presupposition* of the divinely produced moral feeling which is here meant; the former is εἰρήνη πρὸς τὸν Θεόν, the latter εἰρήνη τοῦ Θεοῦ.—ἡ ὑπερέχουσα πάντα νοῦν] *which surpasses every reason*, namely, in regard to its salutary power and efficacy; that is, *which* is able *more than any reason to elevate above all solicitude*, to comfort and to strengthen. Because the reason in its moral thinking, willing, and feeling is of itself too weak to confront the power of the σάρξ (Rom. vii. 23, 25; Gal. v. 17), *no* reason is in a position to give this clear holy elevation and strength against the world and its afflictions. This can be effected by nothing but the agency of the divine peace, which is given by means of the Spirit in the believing heart, when by its prayer and supplication with thanksgiving it has elevated itself to God and has confided to Him all its concerns, 1 Pet. v. 7. Then, in virtue of this blessed peace, the heart *experiences* what it could not have experienced by means of its own thinking, feeling, and willing. According to de Wette, the *doubting* and heart-disquieting νοῦς is meant, which is surpassed by the peace of God, because the latter is based upon faith and feeling. In opposition to this, however, stands the πάντα, according to which not merely all *doubting* reason, but *every* reason is meant. *No one*, not even the believer and regenerate, has through his reason and its action what he has through the peace of God. Others have explained it in the sense of the *incomprehensibleness* of the peace of God, "the greatness of which the understanding cannot even grasp" (Wiesinger). So Chrysostom, Oecumenius, Theophylact, Erasmus, Luther, Calvin, Grotius, also Hoelemann and Weiss. Comp. Eph. iii. 20. But the context, both in the foregoing μηδὲν μεριμνᾶτε and in the φρουρήσει κ.τ.λ. which follows, points only to the blessed *influence*, in respect of which the peace of God surpasses every kind of reason whatever, and consequently is *more efficacious* than it. It is a ὑπερέχειν τῇ δυνάμει; Paul had no occasion to bring into prominence the *incomprehensibleness* of the εἰρήνη Θεοῦ. — On ὑπερέχειν with the *accusative* (usually with the genitive, ii. 3), see Valckenaer, *ad Eur. Hippol.* 1365; Kühner, II. 1, p. 337. — φρουρήσει κ.τ.λ.] not *custodiat* (Vulgate, Chrysostom, Theodoret, Theophylact: ἀσφαλίσαιτο, Luther, Calovius, Cornelius a Lapide, and others, including Storr, Heinrichs, Flatt), but *custodiet* (Castalio, Beza, Calvin), whereby *protection against all injurious influences* (comp. 1 Pet. i. 5) is *promised.* Comp. Plat. *Rep.* p. 560 B: οἱ . . . ἄριστοι φρουροί τε καὶ φύλακες ἐν ἀνδρῶν θεοφιλῶν εἰσὶ διανοίαις. Eur. *Suppl.* 902: ἐφρούρει (πολλοὺς) μηδὲν ἐξαμαρτάνειν. "*Animat* eos hac fiducia," Erasmus, *Annot.* This protecting vigilance is more precisely defined by ἐν Χ. 'Ι., which expresses its specific character, so far as this peace of God is *in Christ* as the element of its nature and life, and therefore its influence, protecting and keeping men's hearts, is not otherwise realized and carried out than in this its holy sphere of life, which is Christ. The φρουρά which the peace of God exercises implies in Christ, as it were, the φρουραρχία (Xen. *Mem.* iv. 4. 17). Comp. Col. iii. 15, where the εἰρήνη τοῦ Χριστοῦ βραβεύει in men's hearts. Others consider ἐν Χ. 'Ι. as that which takes place on the part of the *readers, wherein* the peace of God would *keep*

them, namely " *in unity with Christ*, in His divinely-blessed,
holy life," de Wette ; or ὥστε μένειν καὶ μὴ ἐκπεσεῖν αὐτοῦ,
Oecumenius, comp. Chrysostom, Theophylact, Luther, Zanchius,
and others, including Heinrichs, Storr, Flatt, Rheinwald, van
Hengel, Matthies, Rilliet, Wiesinger, Weiss. But the words
do not affirm *wherein* watchful activity is to *keep* or *preserve*
the readers (Paul does not write τηρήσει ; comp. John xvii. 11),
but wherein it will *take place ;* therefore the inaccurate rendering *per Christum* (Erasmus, Grotius, Estius, and others) is so
far more correct. The artificial suggestion of Hoelemann
("Christo fere cinguli instar τὰς καρδίας ὑμῶν κ.τ.λ. circum-
cludente," etc.) is all the less warranted, the more familiar
the idea ἐν Χριστῷ was to the apostle as representing the
element in which the life and action, as Christian, move.——The
pernicious influences themselves, the withholding and warding off
of which are meant by φρουρήσει κ.τ.λ., are not to be arbitrarily limited, *e.g.* to *opponents* (Heinrichs), or to *Satan* (Beza,
Grotius, and others), or *sin* (Theophylact), or *pravas cogitationes*
(Calvin), or "*omnes insultus et curas*" (Bengel), and the like ;
but to be left quite general, comprehending all such special
aspects. Erasmus well says (*Paraphr.*) : "adversus omnia,
quae hic possunt incidere formidanda."—— τὰς καρδ. ὑμ. κ. τὰ
νοήμ. ὑμῶν] emphatically kept apart. It is enough to add
Bengel's note : "cor sedes cogitationum." Comp. Roos, *Fun-
dam. psychol. ex sacr. script.* III. § 6 : "causa cogitationum
interna eaque libera." The heart is the organ of self-consciousness, and therefore the moral seat of the activity of thought
and will. As to the νοήματα (2 Cor. iii. 14) as the internal
products of the theoretical and practical reason, and therefore
including purposes and plans (Plat. *Polit.* p. 260 D ;
2 Cor. ii. 11), comp. Beck, *bibl. Seelenl.* p. 59, and Delitzsch,
Psychol. p. 179. The distinction is an arbitrary one, which
applies τ. καρδ. to the emotions and will, and τ. νοήμ. to the
intelligence (Beza, Calvin).

Ver. 8 f. A *summary closing summons* to a Christian mode
of thought and (ver. 9) action, compressing everything closely
and succinctly into a few pregnant words, introduced by τὸ
λοιπόν, with which Paul had already, at iii. 1, wished to pass

on to the conclusion. See on iii. 1. This τὸ λοιπόν is not, however, resumptive (Matthies, Ewald, following the old expositors), or concluding the exhortation begun in iii. 1 (Hofmann), for in that passage it introduced quite a *different* summons; but, without any reference to iii. 1, it conveys the transition of thought: "what over and above all the foregoing I have to urge upon you in general still is: *everything that*," etc. According to de Wette, it is intended to bring out what remained for *man* to do, in addition to that which *God* does, ver. 7. But in that case there must have been *expressed*, at least by ὑμεῖς before ἀδελφοί or in some other way, an antithetic statement of that which had to be done on the *part of man.* — ὅσα] nothing being excepted, expressed asyndetically six times with the emphasis of an earnest ἐπιμονή. Comp. ii. 1, iii. 2 ; Buttmann, *Neut. Gr.* p. 341 [E. T. 398]. — ἀληθῆ] The thoroughly *ethical* contents of the whole summons requires us to understand, not *theoretical* truth (van Hengel), but that which is *morally true ;* that is, *that which is in harmony with the objective standard of morality contained in the gospel.* Chrysostom: ἡ ἀρετή· ψεῦδος δὲ ἡ κακία. Oecumenius : ἀληθῆ δέ φησι τὰ ἐνάρετα. Comp. also Theophylact. See 1 John i. 6 ; John iii. 21 ; Eph. v. 9 ; 1 Cor. v. 8. To limit it to truth in *speaking* (Theodoret, Bengel) is in itself arbitrary, and not in keeping with the general character of the predicates which follow, in accordance with which we must not even understand specially *unfeigned sincerity* (Erasmus, Grotius, Estius, and others; comp. Eph. iv. 21 ; Plat. *Phil.* p. 59 C: τὸ ἀληθὲς καὶ ὃ δὴ λέγομεν εἰλικρινές), though this essentially belongs to the morally true. — σεμνά] *worthy of honour,* for it is in accordance with *God.* Comp. 1 Tim. ii. 2 : εὐσεβείᾳ καὶ σεμνότητι. Plat. *Soph.* p. 249 A: σεμνὸν καὶ ἅγιον νοῦν. Xen. *Oec.* vi. 14 : τὸ σεμνὸν ὄνομα τὸ καλόν τε κἀγαθόν. Dem. 385. 11 ; Herodian, i. 2. 6 ; Ael. *V. H.* ii. 13, viii. 36 ; Polyb. ix. 36. 6, xv. 22. 1, xxii. 6. 10. — δίκαια] *upright,* as it ought to be ; not to be limited to the relations "erga alios" (Bengel, Heumann, and others), so that justice in the narrower sense would be meant (so Calvin : "ne quem laedamus, ne quem fraudemus ;" Estius, Grotius, Calovius, and others),

Comp., on the contrary, Theogn. 147 : ἐν δικαιοσύνῃ συλλήβδην πᾶσ᾽ ἀρετή ἐστι. — ἀγνά] *pure, unstained,* not : *chaste* in the narrower sense of the word (2 Cor. xi. 2 ; Dem. 1371. 22 ; Plut. *Mor.* p. 268 E, 438 C, *et al.*), as Grotius, Calovius, Estius, Heumann, and others would explain it. Calvin well says : "castimoniam denotat in omnibus vitae partibus." Comp. 2 Cor. vi. 6, vii. 11 ; 1 Tim. v. 22 ; Jas. iii. 17 ; 1 Pet. iii. 2 ; 1 John iii. 3 ; often so used in Greek authors. Comp. Menand. in Clem. *Strom.* vii. p. 844 : πᾶς ἀγνός ἐστιν ὁ μηδὲν ἑαυτῷ κακὸν συνιδών. — προσφιλῆ] *dear, that which is loved.* This is just once more *Christian morality,* which, in its whole nature as the ethical καλόν, is *worthy of love ;*[1] Plat. *Rep.* p. 444 E ; Soph. *El.* 972 : φιλεῖ γὰρ πρὸς τὰ χρηστὰ πᾶς ὁρᾶν. "Nihil est *amabilius* virtute, nihil quod magis alliciat ad diligendum, Cic. *Lael.* 28. Comp. *ad Famil.* ix. 14 ; Xen. *Mem.* ii. 1. 33. The opposite is the αἰσχρόν, which deserves hate (Rom. vii. 15). Chrysostom suggests the supplying τοῖς πιστοῖς κ. τῷ Θεῷ ; Theodoret only τῷ Θεῷ. Others, as Calovius, Estius, Heinrichs, and many : "amabilia *hominibus.*" But there is no necessity for any such supplement. The word does not occur elsewhere in the N. T., although frequently in classical authors, and at Ecclus. iv. 8, xx. 13. Others understand *kindliness,* benevolence, friendliness, and the like. So Grotius ; comp. Erasmus, *Paraphr.* : " quaecumque ad alendam concordiam accommoda." Linguistically faultless (Ecclus. *l.c. ;* Herod. i. 125 ; Thuc. vii. 86 ; Polyb. x. 5. 6), but not in keeping with the context, which does not adduce any *special* virtues. — εὔφημα] not occurring elsewhere either in the N. T., or in the LXX., or Apocrypha ; it does not mean : "quaecumque *bonam famam conciliant*" (Erasmus ; comp. Calvin, Grotius, Cornelius a Lapide, Estius, Heinrichs, and others, also Rheinwald) ; but : *that which sounds well* (Luther), *which has an auspicious* (faustum) *sound, i.e.* that which, when it is named, sounds significant of happiness, as, for instance, *brave, honest, honourable,* etc. The opposite would be : δύσφημα. Comp. Soph. *Aj.* 362 ; Eur. *Iph. T.* 687 :

---

[1] Luther well renders it : "*lieblich,*" and the Gothic : "*liubaleik ;*" the Vulgate : "*amabilia.*"

εὔφημα φώνει. Plat. *Leg.* vii. p. 801 A : τὸ τῆς ᾠδῆς γένος εὔφημον ἡμῖν. Aesch. *Suppl.* 694, *Agam.* 1168 ; Polyb. xxxi. 14. 4; Lucian, *Prom.* 3. Storr, who is followed by Flatt, renders it : " *sermones, qui bene aliis precantur.*" So used in later Greek authors (also Symmachus, Ps. lxii. 6) ; but this meaning is here too special. — εἴ τις κ.τ.λ.] *comprehending* all the points mentioned : *if there be any virtue, and if there be any praise;* not if there be yet another, etc. (de Wette).—ἀρετή used by Paul here only, and in the rest of the N. T. only in 1 Pet. ii. 9, 2 Pet. i. 3, 5,[1] in the ethical sense : *moral aptitude in disposition and action* (the opposite to it, κακία : Plat. *Rep.* 444 D, 445 C, 1, p. 348 C). Comp. from the Apocrypha, Wisd. iv. 1, v. 13, and frequent instances of its use in the books of Macc. — ἔπαινος] not : *res laudabilis* (Calvin, Grotius, Estius, Flatt, Matthies, van Hengel, and many others; comp. Weiss), but *praise* (Erasmus : " laus virtutis comes"), which the reader could not understand in the apostle's sense otherwise than of a laudatory judgment actually corresponding to the moral value of the object. Thus, for instance, Paul's commendation of love in 1 Cor. xiii. is an ἔπαινος ; or when Christ pronounces a blessing on the humble, the peacemakers, the merciful, etc., or the like. " Vera laus uni virtuti debetur," Cic. *de orat.* ii. 84. 342 ; virtue is καθ᾽ αὑτὴν ἐπαινετή, Plat. *Def.* p. 411 C. Mistaken, therefore, were such additions as ἐπιστήμης (D* E* F G) or *disciplinae* (Vulg., It., Ambrosiaster, Pelagius). — ταῦτα λογίζεσθε] *consider these things,* take them to heart, in order (see ver. 9) to determine your conduct accordingly. " Meditatio praecedit, deinde sequitur opus," Calvin. On λογίζεσθαι, comp. Ps. lii. 2 ; Jer.

---

[1] We are not entitled to assume (with Beza) as the reason why Paul does not use this word elsewhere, that it is "verbum nimium humile, si cum donis Spiritus Sancti comparetur." The very passage before us shows the contrary, as it means no other than *Christian* morality. Certainly in Paul's case, as with the N. T. authors generally and even Christ Himself, the *specific* designations of the idea of virtue, which correspond more closely to the sphere of theocratic O. T. ideas, such as δικαιοσύνη, ὑπακοή, ἁγιότης, ἁγιωσύνη, ὁσιότης, κ. τ. λ., too necessarily suggested themselves to his mind to allow him to use the general term for morality, ἀρετή, as familiar, however worthily and nobly the Platonic doctrine, in particular, had grasped the idea of it (εἰς ὅσον δυνατὸν ἀνθρώπῳ ὁμοιοῦσθαι Θεῷ, Plat. *Rep.* p. 613 A, 500 C, *et al.*).

xxvi. 3 ; Nah. i. 9 ; Ps. xxxv. 4, xxxvi. 4 ; 3 Macc. iv. 4 ;
Soph. *O. R.* 461 ; Herod. viii. 53 ; Dem. 63, 12 ; Sturz, *Lex.
Xen.* III. p. 42 ; the opposite : θνητὰ λογίζεσθαι, *Anthol. Pal.*
xi. 56. 3.—Ver. 9. The Christian morality, which Paul in
ver. 8 has commended to his readers by a series of predicates,
he now again urges upon them in special reference to their
relation to himself, their teacher and example, as that *which
they had also learned,* etc.   The first καί is therefore *also,* prefixing to the subsequent ταῦτα πράσσετε an element corresponding to this requirement, and *imposing an obligation* to its
fulfilment.   " Whatsoever also has been the object and purport
of your instruction, etc., that do."   To take the four times
repeated καί as a double *as well . . . as also* (Hofmann and
others), would yield an inappropriate formal scheme of separation.   *Καί* in the last three cases is the simple *and,* but so
that the whole is to be looked upon as *bipartite :* " Duo priora
verba ad *doctrinam* pertinent, reliqua duo ad *exemplum*"
(Estius). — ἅ] not ὅσα again ; for no further *categories* of
morality are to be given, but what they are bound to do
generally is to be described under the point of view of what
is *known to the readers,* as that *which they also have learned,* etc.
— παρελάβετε] *have accepted.*   Comp. 1 Cor. xv. 1 ; John
i. 11 ; Polyb. xxxiii. 16. 9.   The interpretation : " *have
received*" (Vulgate, Erasmus, Luther, Beza, and most expositors, including Rheinwald, Rilliet, Hoelemann, de Wette,
Weiss, Hofmann), which makes it denote the *instruction* communicated (1 Thess. ii. 13, iv. 1 ; 2 Thess. iii. 6 ; 1 Cor.
xi. 23 ; Gal. i. 9, 12 ; Col. ii. 6 ; comp. Plat. *Theaet.* p. 198 B :
παραλαμβάνοντα δὲ μανθάνειν), would yield a *twofold* designation for the *one* element,[1] and on the other hand would *omit*
the point of the *assensus,* which is so important as a motive ;
moreover, from a logical point of view, we should necessarily
expect to find the position of the two words reversed (comp.

---

[1] *Real distinctions* have, indeed, been made, but how purely arbitrary they
are ! Thus Grotius (comp. Hammond) makes ἐμάθ. apply to the *primam in-
stitutionem,* and παρελάβ. to the *exactiorem doctrinam.* Rilliet explains it differently, making the former denote : " *son enseignement direct,*" and the latter :
" *les instructions, qu'il leur a transmises sous une forme quelconque.*"

Gal. i. 12). — ἠκούσατε] does not refer to the proper *preaching and teaching* of the apostle (Erasmus, Calvin, Elsner, Rheinwald, Matthies), which is already fully embraced in the two previous points ; nor does it denote : " audistis *de me absente* " (Estius and others, including Hoelemann, Rilliet, Hofmann), for all the other points refer to the time of the apostle's *presence*, and consequently not merely the " *de me*," but also the " *absente* " would be purely imported. No, by the words ἠκούσατε and εἴδετε, to *both* of which ἐν ἐμοί belongs, he represents to his readers *his own example of Christian morality*, which he had given them when he was present, *in its two portions*, in so far as they had perceived it in him (ἐν ἐμοί, comp. i. 30) partly by *hearing*, in his whole *oral* behaviour and intercourse with them, partly by *seeing*, in his *manner of action* among them ; or, in other words, his example both in *word* and *deed*. — ταῦτα πράσσετε] *these things do*, is not related to ταῦτα λογίζεσθε, ver. 8, as excluding it, in such a way that for what is said in ver. 8 the λογίζεσθαι merely would be required, and for what is indicated in ver. 9 the πράσσειν ; on the contrary, the two operations, which *in substance* belong jointly to the contents of both verses, are *formally* separated in accordance with the mode of expression of the parallelism. Comp. on ii. 8 and Rom. x. 10. — καὶ ὁ Θεός κ.τ.λ.] in substance the same promise as was given in ver. 7. *God, who works peace* (that holy peace of soul, ver. 7), *will be with you*, whereby is meant the help given through the Holy Spirit ; and His *special* agency, which Paul here has in view, is unmistakeably indicated by the very predicate τῆς εἰρήνης.

REMARK.—It is to be noticed that the predicates in ver. 8, ἀληθῆ ... εὔφημα, do not denote different *individual virtues*, but that each represents *the Christian moral character generally*, so that in reality the *same thing* is described, but *according to the various aspects which commended it*. Comp. Diog. Laert. ii. 106 : ἓν τὸ ἀγαθὸν πολλοῖς ὀνόμασι καλούμενον. Cic. *de fin.* iii. 4. 14 : " *una virtus unum istud, quod honestum appellas, rectum, laudabile, decorum.* " That it is *Christian* morality which Paul has in view, is clearly evident from ver. 9 and from the whole preceding context. Hence the passage cannot avail for placing the morality of the moral law of nature (Rom. ii. 14 f.) on an equality with the gospel field of duty, which has its specific definition and consecration—as also, for the reconciled whom it embraces, the assurance of the divine keeping (vv. 7, 9)—in the revealed word (ver. 9), and in the enlightening and ethically transforming power of the Spirit (comp. Rom. xii. 2).

Ver. 10. Carrying on his discourse with δέ, Paul now in conclusion adds, down to ver. 20, some *courteous expressions*, as dignified as they are delicate, *concerning the aid which he had received*. Hitherto, indeed, he had only mentioned this work of love briefly and casually (ii. 25, 30). In the aid itself Baur discovers a contradiction of 1 Cor. ix. 15, and conjectures that the author of the epistle had 2 Cor. xi. 9 in view, and had inferred too much from that passage. But, in fact, Baur himself has inferred too much, and incorrectly, from 1 Cor. ix. 15 ; for in this passage Paul speaks of *payment for his preaching*, not of loving gifts from persons at a distance, which in point of fact put him in the position to preach gratuitously in Achaia, 2 Cor. xi. 8 ff. There is, besides, in our passage no mention of regular sendings of money. — ἐν κυρίῳ] as in iii. 1, iv. 4. It was, indeed, not a joy felt *apart from Christ ;* οὐ κοσμικῶς ἐχάρην, φησὶν, οὐδὲ βιωτικῶς, Chrysostom. — μεγά- λως] *mightily.* Comp. LXX., 1 Chron. xxix. 9 ; Neh. xii. 42 ; Polyb. iii. 87. 5 ; Polyc. *Phil.* 1. The position at the end is emphatic. See on Matt. ii. 10 ; and Stallbaum, *ad Plat. Phaedr.* p. 256 E, *Menex.* p. 235 A. — ὅτι ἤδη ποτέ κ.τ.λ.] is to be rendered : " *that ye have at length once again come into the flourishing condition of taking thought for my benefit, in behalf of which ye also* TOOK *thought, but had no favourable opportunity.*" — ἤδη ποτέ] taken in itself may mean : *already once ;* or, as in Rom. i. 10 : *tandem aliquando.* The latter is the meaning here, as appears from ἐφ' ᾧ κ.τ.λ. Chrysostom justly observes (comp. Oecumenius and Theophylact) that it denotes χρόνον μακρόν, when namely that θάλλειν had not been present, which has now again (comp. ver. 15 f.) set in. Comp. Baeumlein, *Partik.* p. 140. This view of ἤδη ποτέ is the less to be evaded, seeing that the *reproach* which some have discovered in the passage (ἐπιτίμησις, Chrysostom) is not by any means conveyed in it, as indeed from the delicate feeling of the apostle we might expect that it would not, and as is apparent from the correct explanation of the sequel. — ἀνεθάλετε] *ye have again become green* (*refloruistis*, Vulgate), like a tree or an orchard which had been withered, and has again budded and put forth new shoots (θαλλούς).[1] It cannot be the *revival* of their *care-taking love* which is meant, so that the readers would have previously been ἀπομαρανθέντες ἐν τῇ ἐλεημοσύνῃ (Oecumenius, also Chrysostom, Theophylact, Pelagius, Erasmus, Luther, Calvin, Beza, Estius, Cornelius a Lapide, Bengel, Flatt, Wiesinger, Ewald, and most expositors, who rightly take ἀνεθάλ. as *intransitive*, as well as all who take it *transitively*; see below); for how indelicate would be such an utterance, which one could not, with Weiss, acquit from implying an assumption that a different disposition previously existed; and how at variance with the ἐφ' ᾧ ἐφρονεῖτε κ.τ.λ. which immediately follows, and by which the continuous care previously exercised is attested! No, it is the *flourishing anew of their prosperity* (comp. Rheinwald, Matthies, van Hengel, Baumgarten-Crusius, Schenkel, Hofmann, and others), the opposite of which is afterwards expressed by ἠκαιρεῖσθε, that is denoted, as prosperous circumstances are so often represented under the figure of becoming green and blooming. Comp. Ps. xxviii. 7: ἀνέθαλεν ἡ σάρξ μου, Wisd. iv. 3 f.; Hes. *Op.* 231: τέθηλε πόλις, Pind. *Isth.* iii. 9: ὄλβος . . . θάλλων, *Pyth.* vii. 22: θάλλουσαν εὐδαιμονίαν. Plat. *Legg.* xii. p. 945 D: ἡ πᾶσα οὕτω θάλλει τὲ καὶ εὐδαιμονεῖ χώρα κ. πόλις. Of frequent occurrence in the tragedians; comp. also Jacobs, *ad Del. Epigr.* viii. 97. It is therefore inconsistent, both with delicate feeling and with the context, to take ἀνεθάλ. *transitively*: "*revirescere sivistis* solitam vestram rerum mearum procurationem" (Hoelemann; comp. Coccejus, Grotius, Hein-

---

[1] The conjecture, on the ground of this figurative expression, that the Philippians might have sent to the apostle in *spring*, and that ἠκαιρεῖσθε δέ applies to the *winter season* (Bengel), is far-fetched and arbitrary. The figurative ἀνεθάλ. does not even need to be an image of *spring*, as Calvin, Estius, Weiss, and others understand it.

richs, Hammond, and others, including Rilliet, de Wette, Weiss),
although the transitive use of ἀναθάλλειν in the LXX. and
also in the Apocrypha is unquestionable (Ezek. xvii. 24 ; Ecclus.
i. 16, xi. 20, l. 10 ; see generally Schleusner, *Thes.* I. p.
220 f.) ; and that of θάλλειν is also current in classical authors
(Pind. *Ol.* iii. 24 ; Aesch. *Pers.* 622 (608) ; Jacobs, *ad Anthol.*
VII. p. 103 ; Kühner, II. 1, p. 265). An unfounded objection is brought against the view which explains it of the
revival *of prosperity*, that it is inappropriate as a subject of joy
in the Lord (see Weiss) ; it is appropriate at all events, when
such a *use* is made of the revived prosperity. — τὸ ὑπὲρ ἐμοῦ
φρονεῖν] is usually, with the correct intransitive rendering of
ἀνεθάλ.,[1] so understood that τὸ is taken together with φρονεῖν,
and this must be regarded as the *accusative of more precise
definition*, which is only distinguished by its greater emphasis
from the mere epexegetical infinitive.   See Bernhardy, p. 356 ;
Schmalfeld, *Syntax d. Griech. Verb.* p. 401 f. ; Ellendt, *Lex.
Soph.* II. p. 222. Comp. van Hengel : "negotium volo mihi
consulendi."   But the whole view which takes τό with
φρονεῖν is set aside by the following ἐφ' ᾧ κ. ἐφρονεῖτε ; seeing
that ἐφ' ᾧ, unless it is to be rendered at variance with linguistic usage by *although* (Luther, Castalio, Michaelis, Storr),
or *just as* (Vulgate, van Hengel), could only convey in its ᾧ
the previous τὸ ὑπὲρ ἐμοῦ φρονεῖν, and would consequently
yield the logically absurd conception : ἐφρονεῖτε ἐπὶ τῷ ὑπὲρ
ἐμοῦ φρονεῖν, whether ἐφ' ᾧ be taken as equivalent to οὗ ἕνεκα
(Beza) or *qua de re* (Rheinwald, Matthies, de Wette, Wiesinger,
Ewald, and others), or *in eo quod* (Erasmus), *in qua re* (Cornelius a Lapide, Hoelemann), or *et post id* (Grotius), and the
like.   Recourse has been had, by way of helping the matter,
to the suggestion that φρονεῖν ἐπί is a thinking *without action*,
and φρονεῖν ὑπέρ a thinking *with action* (de Wette, Wiesinger ;
comp. Ewald) ; but how purely arbitrary is this view ! Less
arbitrarily, Calvin and Rilliet ("vous pensiez bien à moi")
have referred ᾧ to ἐμοῦ, by which, no doubt, that logical

---

[1] In the *transitive* interpretation (see, against it, *supra*) the τὸ φρονεῖν, which
would likewise be taken together, would be the accusative forming *the object* of
ἀνεθάλ.   See Buttmann, *Neut. Gr.* p. 226 [E. T. 263] ; Kühner, II. 2, p. 603.

awkwardness is avoided; but, on the other hand, the objection arises, that ἐφ᾽ ᾧ is elsewhere invariably used by Paul as *neuter* only, and that it is difficult to see why, if he desired to take up ὑπὲρ ἐμοῦ in a relative form, he should not have written ὑπὲρ οὗ, since otherwise in ἐπί, if it merely went back to ἐμοῦ, the more precise and definite reference which he must have had in view would not be expressed, and since the progress of the thought suggested not a change of *preposition*, but only the change of the *tenses* (καὶ ἐφρονεῖτε). Weiss, interpreting ἐφ᾽ ᾧ as: *about which* to take thought, refers it back to ἀνεθάλετε—a reference, however, which falls to the ground with the active interpretation of that word. Upon the whole, the only right course seems to be to *take* τὸ ὑπὲρ ἐμοῦ *together* (comp. τὰ περὶ ὑμῶν, ii. 20; also τὰ παρ᾽ ὑμῶν, ver. 18; and see generally, Krüger, § 50. 5. 12; Kühner, II. 1, p. 231 f.), *and that as the accusative of the object to* φρονεῖν (comp. Bengel, Schenkel, J. B. Lightfoot, Hofmann): "*to take into consideration that which serves for my good*," to think of my benefit; on ὑπὲρ, comp. i. 7. Only thus does the sequel obtain its literal, logical, and delicately-turned reference, namely, when ἐφ᾽ ᾧ applies to τὸ ὑπὲρ ἐμοῦ. Taking this view, we have to notice: (1) that ἐπί is used in the sense of the aim (Lobeck, *ad Phryn.* p. 475; Kühner, II. 1, p. 435): *on behalf of which, for which*, comp. Soph. *O. R.* 569; (2) that Paul has not again written the mere *accusative* (ὁ καὶ ἐφρ.), because ἐφ᾽ ᾧ is intended to refer not alone to κ. ἐφρονεῖτε, but also to the antithesis ἠκαιρεῖσθε δέ, consequently to the entire κ. ἐφρ., ἠκαιρ. δέ;[1] (3) that the emphasis is placed on ἐφρον. as *the*

---

[1] All the more groundless, therefore, is Hofmann's objection, that φρονεῖν ἐπί τινι means: *to be proud about something*. This objection, put thus generally, is even in itself incorrect. For φρονεῖν ἐπί τινι does not in itself mean: *to be proud about something*, but only receives this signification through the addition of μέγα, μεγάλα, or some similar more precise definition (Plat. *Theaet.* p. 149 D, *Alc.* I. p. 104 C, *Prot.* p. 342 D, *Sympos.* p. 217 A: Dem. 181. 16, 836. 10), either expressly specified or directly suggested by the context. Very artificial, and for the simple reader hardly discoverable, is the view under which Hofmann takes the fact expressed by καὶ ἐφρονεῖτε as the *ground*, "*upon, or on account of, which their re-emergence from an unfavourable position has been a revival unto care for him.*" If the reference of ἐφ᾽ ᾧ to τὸ ὑπὲρ ἐμοῦ were not directly given in the text, it would be much simpler to take ἐφ᾽ ᾧ as in Rom. v. 12, Phil. iii. 12, 2 Cor. v. 4, in

imperfect, and καί indicates an element *to be added* to the
φρονεῖν which has been just expressed; hence καὶ ἐφρ. intimates: " in behalf of which ye not only *are* taking thought
(that is, *since* the ἀνεθάλετε), but also *were* taking thought
(namely, πρόσθεν, *before* the ἀνεθάλετε) ;" lastly, (4) that after
ἐφρ. there is no μέν inserted, because the antithesis is meant
to emerge unprepared for, and so all the more vividly. —
ἠκαιρεῖσθε] *ye had no favourable time;* a word belonging to
the later Greek. Diod. *exc. Mai.* p. 30 ; Phot., Suid. The
opposite: εὐκαιρεῖν, Lobeck, *ad Phryn.* p. 125. Unsuitably
and arbitrarily this is explained : " deerat vobis *opportunitas
mittendi*" (Erasmus, Estius, Grotius, Bengel, Rosenmüller, and
others). It refers, in keeping with the ἀνεθάλετε, not without
delicacy of description, to the *unfavourable state of things as
regards means* (Chrysostom : οὐκ εἴχετε ἐν χερσὶν, οὐδὲ ἐν
ἀφθονίᾳ ἦτε ; so also Theophylact; while Oecumenius adduces
this interpretation *alongside* of the previous one) which had
occurred among the Philippians, as Paul might have learned
from Epaphroditus and otherwise. Comp. εὐκαιρεῖν τοῖς βίοις
in Polyb. xv. 21. 2, xxxii. 21. 12 ; and also the mere εὐκαιρεῖν
in the same sense, iv. 60. 10 ; εὐκαιρία: xv. 31. 7, i. 59. 7 ;
ἀκαιρία: Plat. *Legg.* iv. p. 709 A; Dem. 16. 4; Polyb. iv.
44. 11.

Ver. 11. Obviating of a misunderstanding. — οὐχ ὅτι] as in
iii. 12 : *my meaning is not, that I say this in consequence of
want*, that is, this my utterance of joy in ver. 10 f. is not
meant as if it were the expression of felt want, from which
your aid has delivered me. On κατά, *secundum*, in the sense
of *propter*, see Kühner, II. 1, p. 413, and *ad Xen. Mem.* i. 3.
12. According to van Hengel's interpretation: " *ut more
receptum est penuriae,* s. hominibus penuria oppressis," κατά
could not have been united with an *abstract noun* (Rom. iii. 5,
et al.). — ἐγὼ γὰρ ἔμαθον κ.τ.λ.] *for I, as regards my part*
(although it may be different with others), *have learned in the*

___

the sense of *propterea quod*, and that as a graceful and ingenious specification of
the reason for the *great joy* of the apostle, that they had flourished again to
take thought for his benefit; for their previous omission had been caused not
by any lack of the φρονεῖν in question, but by the unfavourableness of the times.

circumstances, in which I find myself, to be self-contented, that is, to have enough independently without desiring aid from others. It is evident from the reason thus assigned that in οὐχ. ὅτι καθ' ὑστ. λ. he has meant not the objective, but the *subjective* state of need. —ἐγώ] with noble self-consciousness, there being no need to supply, with Bengel, "in tot adversis." — ἔμαθον] signifies the having learned *by experience* (comp. Plat. *Symp.* p. 182 C: ἔργῳ δὲ τοῦτο ἔμαθον καὶ οἱ ἐνθάδε τύραννοι), and all that accordingly he *can,* he owes to the strengthening influence *of Christ,* ver. 13. — ἐν οἷς εἰμι] *in the situation, in which I find myself.* See examples in Wetstein and Kypke; comp. also Mätzner, *ad Antiph.* p. 131. Not merely his position *then,* but, generally, *every* position in which he finds himself, is meant, although it is not exactly to be taken as: "*in quocunque statu sim*" (Raphel, Wetstein, and others), which would be ungrammatically expressed. In opposition to the context (see ver. 12), Luther: *among whom* (οἷς, masculine) *I am.* As to αὐτάρκεια as applied to persons, the *subjective* self-sufficing, by means of which a man does not make the satisfaction of his needs dependent upon others, but finds it in himself, comp. Ecclus. xl. 18; Xen. *Mem.* iv. 7. 1; Dem. 450. 14; Stob. v. 43; and see on 2 Cor. ix. 8.

Ver. 12. Paul now *specifies* this his αὐτάρκεια (in Plat. *Def.* p. 412 B, termed τελειότης κτήσεως ἀγαθῶν). — οἶδα] *I understand how* (1 Thess. iv. 4; Col. iv. 6; 1 Tim. iii. 5; Matt. vii. 11; Soph. *Aj.* 666 f.; Anth. Pal. vii. 440. 5 ff.);[1] result of the ἔμαθον. — καὶ ταπειν.] *also to be abased,* namely, by want, distress, and other allotted circumstances which place the person affected by them in the condition of abasement. Paul *understands* this, inasmuch as he knows how to bear himself in the right attitude to such allotted circumstances, namely, in such a way that, independently thereof, he finds his sufficiency in himself, and does not seek it in that which he lacks. We find a commentary on this in 2 Cor. iv. 8, vi. 9, 10. οἶδα καὶ περισσεύειν is to be understood analogously, of the right attitude to the matter, so that one is not led away by

[1] It is the *moral* understanding, having its seat in the *character.* Comp. Ameis, *Anh. z. Hom. Od.* ix. 189.

abundance to find his satisfaction in the latter instead of in
himself.   Pelagius well says : " ut nec abundantia *extollar*, nec
frangar inopia." — The first καί adds to the general ἐν οἷς εἰμι
the *special* statement on the one side, to which thereupon the
second "*also*" adds the counterpart.   The *contrast*, however, is
less *adequate* here than subsequently in περισσεύειν καὶ ὑστε-
ρεῖσθαι, for ταπεινοῦσθαι is a *more comprehensive* idea than the
counterpart of περισσεύειν, and also contains a *figurative* conception.   Some such expression as ὑψοῦσθαι would have been
adequate as the contrast of ταπειν. (Matt. xxiii. 12 ; 2 Cor. xi. 7 ;
Phil. ii. 8, 9 ; Polyb. v. 26. 12).   There is a lively versatility
of conception, from not perceiving which some have given to
this περισσεύειν (*to have a superfluity*) the explanation *excellere*
(Erasmus, Vatablus, Calvin), or to ταπειν. the meaning *to be
poor, to be in pitiful plight*, ὀλίγοις κεχρῆσθαι, Theophylact
(Estius and others; comp. also Cornelius a Lapide, Grotius,
Rheinwald, Matthies, Baumgarten-Crusius, de Wette, Hofmann), which even the LXX., Lev. xxv. 39, does not justify. —
In what follows, ἐν παντὶ κ. ἐν πᾶσι is not to be regarded as
belonging to ταπεινοῦσθαι and περισσεύειν (Hofmann), but is
to be joined with μεμύημαι.   We are dissuaded from the
former connection by the very repetition of the οἶδα ; and the
latter is recommended by the great emphasis, which rests upon
ἐν παντὶ κ. ἐν πᾶσι heading the last clause, as also by the
correlative πάντα at the head of ver. 13.   Further, *no comma
is to be placed after* μεμύημαι, nor is ἐν παντὶ … μεμύημαι to be
explained as meaning: "*into everything I am initiated*," and
then καὶ χορτάζεσθαι κ.τ.λ. as elucidating the notion of "*everything*" : "cum re qualicunque omnibusque, tam saturitate et
fame, quam abundantia et penuria, tantam contraxi familiari-
tatem, ut rationem teneam iis bene utendi," van Hengel ;
comp. de Wette, Rilliet, Wiesinger; so also, on the whole,
Chrysostom, Erasmus, Estius, and many others, but with
different interpretations of παντί and πᾶσιν.   This view is at
variance with the fact, that μυεῖσθαι has that into *which* one
is initiated expressed not by means of ἐν, but—and that most
usually—in the *accusative* (Herod. ii. 51 ; Plat. *Gorg.* p. 497 C,
Symp. p. 209 E ; Aristoph. *Plut.* 845 (ἐμμυεῖσθαι) ; Lucian,

Philop. 14), or in the *dative* (Lucian, *Demon.* 11), or *genitive* (Heliod. i. 17; Herodian, i. 13. 16); hence πᾶν κ. πάντα, or παντὶ κ. πᾶσιν, or παντὸς κ. πάντων must have been written (in 3 Macc. ii. 30 it has κατά with the accusative). No; Paul says that *in everything and in all,* that is, under every relation that may occur and in all circumstances, *he is initiated into,* that is, made completely familiar with, *as well the being satisfied as the being hungry, as well the having superfluity as want;* in all situations, without exception, he quite understands how to assume and maintain the right attitude to these different experiences, which in ver. 11 he characterizes by the words αὐτάρκης εἶναι. Ἐν παντὶ κ. ἐν πᾶσι is accordingly to be taken after the analogy of ἐν οἷς εἰμι, ver. 11, and therefore as *neuter.* It was purely arbitrary to render ἐν παντί: *ubique* (Vulgate, Castalio, Beza, Calvin, and many others), or to refer it to *time* (Chrysostom, Grotius), or to *time and place* (Theophylact, Erasmus, and others, also Matthies). Luther and Bengel explain παντί correctly as neuter, but make πᾶσιν (as in 2 Cor. xi. 6) *masculine* (Bengel: "respectu omnium hominum"). It is not necessary to supply anything to either of the two words; and as to the alternation of the singular and plural, which only indicates the total absence of any exception (comp. analogous expressions in Lobeck, *Paral.* p. 56 ff.), there is no occasion for artificial explanation. — In German we say: *in Allem und Jedem* [in all and each]. Comp. on ἐν πᾶσι on Col. i. 18. With strange arbitrariness Hofmann makes ἐν παντὶ κ. ἐν πᾶσι denote everything *that is a necessary of life* (in detail and in whole). In that case certainly the contrast of χορτάζ. and πεινᾶν is unsuitable!— μεμύημαι] the proper word for the various grades of initiation into the mysteries (Casaubon, *Exerc. Baron.* p. 390 ff.; Lobeck, *Aglaoph.* I. p. 38 ff.) is here used in a figurative sense, like *initiatum esse,* of a special, unusual, not by every one attainable, *familiar acquaintance* with something. See Munthe, *Obss.* p. 383; Jacobs, *ad Anthol.* III. p. 488. The opposite is ἀμύητος. — The climax should here be noticed, ἔμαθον ... οἶδα ... μεμύημαι. Ver. 13 places beyond doubt to whom the apostle owes this lofty spiritual superiority over all outward circumstances. As

to the later form πεινᾶν instead of πεινῆν, see Lobeck, *ad*
Phryn. p. 61; Jacobs, *ad Ael.* II. p. 261.

Ver. 13. After the *special* statement, the consciousness of
the αὐτάρκεια now finds fresh utterance *generally*; and in the
grand brevity of the latter how marked is the assurance, and,
at the same time, the humility!— ἰσχύω] of *moral* strength,
homogeneous as to category with ἔμαθον in ver. 11, and with
οἶδα and μεμύημαι in ver. 12, because these predicates also were
dynamically meant, of the understanding of ethical practice.
There is therefore the less reason for limiting πάντα in any
way (van Hengel: " omnia memorata ;" comp. Weiss); there
is *nothing* for which Paul did not feel himself morally strong ;
for *every* relation he knew himself to be morally adequate.
πάντα is the accusative of the *object*.   Gal. v. 6 ; Jas. v. 16.
The opposite to it: μηδὲν ἰσχύωσιν, Plat. *Crit.* p. 50 B, Ael.
V. H. xii. 22, *et al.* — ἐν τῷ ἐνδυν. με] Not in his own human
ability does Paul feel this power, but it has its basis *in Christ*,
whose δύναμις the apostle experiences in his fellowship of life
with Him (2 Cor. xii. 9).   Comp. 1 Tim. i. 12 ; 2 Tim. ii. 1,
iv. 17.   Thus he is able to do all things ἐν τῷ κράτει τῆς
ἰσχύος αὐτοῦ, Eph. vi. 10.

Ver. 14. Πλήν] *Nevertheless* (1 Cor. xi. 11 ; Eph. v. 33),
apart from the fact that with such moral power I am equal to
all emergencies, and therefore, as far as want is concerned, do
not need aid (comp. ver. 11).   "Cavet, ne fortiter loquendo
contemsisse ipsorum beneficium videatur," Calvin.   Comp.
Chrysostom and Theophylact. — καλῶς] in the *moral* sense. —
συγκοιν. μου τῇ θλίψ.] characterizes the work according to its
high *ethical value* (ὅρα σοφίαν, πῶς ἐπαίρει τὸ πρᾶγμα, Theophylact) : *that ye became partakers with me in my affliction.*   He
who renders the aid enters into the relation of a participant in
the position of the afflicted one, inasmuch as by his very work
of love he, in common with the latter, shares and bears his
θλῖψις.   Comp. Rom. xii. 13.   It is a *practical* participation,
and not merely that of feeling and emotion.   Comp. Eph. v.
11 ; Rev. xviii. 4, i. 9.   By τῇ θλίψ., Paul means his position
at the time as a whole, not : *want* (which also in 2 Cor. viii.
13 it does not mean).   The *dative* is governed by συγκοιν.

(Eph. v. 11; Rev. xviii. 4; Rom. xii. 13, xv. 27, *et al.*); and
μου is, in accordance with the well-known usage, to be taken
as if μοι were in the text (comp on ii. 2; and Stallbaum,
ad Plat. Rep. p. 518 C, *Symp.* p. 215 C). The *aorist* participle
coincides as to time with ἐποιήσατε (see on Eph. i. 9); as to the
participle with καλῶς ποιεῖν, see Winer, p. 323 f. [E. T. 434].

Ver. 15 f. A courteous recalling of the fact, *that in the
very beginning of the gospel the Philippians had distinguished
themselves by such manifestation of love towards Paul.* — δέ]
carrying the discourse onward: But what ye have done connects itself with a relation into which, as ye also know, no
other church, but yours only, placed itself to me at the very
first! — οἴδατε δὲ κ.τ.λ.] *but it is known also to you, Philippians,
that,* etc. Hofmann very erroneously derives the *object* of
οἴδατε from what *precedes,* and takes ὅτι in the sense of
because. He makes the apostle say, namely, to the Philippians:
That they had done well in helpfully taking part in his affliction *they knew also,* as *other* churches knew that it was well
done; by *experience* they knew it, because it was *not the first
time* that they had sent similar gifts to him, etc. This explanation is erroneous, because invariably where οἶδα (οἴδαμεν,
οἴδατε, κ.τ.λ.) is accompanied, not with an accusative of the
object, but with ὅτι, the latter conveys the contents (*that*), and
not the reason or the cause (*because*), of the οἶδα (comp. i. 19,
25; Rom. iii. 2; 1 Cor. iii. 16, xii 2; Gal. iv. 13, and in-
numerable other passages); secondly, because the previously
attested καλῶς ἐποιήσατε, while perfectly suitable to be expressed *by the grateful apostle,* was not so suited to be transferred
to the consciousness of the donors, to which it was self-evident,
and to be appealed to by them; thirdly, because the καί in
the alleged reference to other churches would be very unsuitable, since the question here concerns merely a work of love
of the Philippians, but other churches could only know
generally that it was well done to aid the apostle, into which
general idea, therefore, Hofmann insensibly transforms the
object of οἴδατε, instead of abiding strictly by the concrete
καλῶς ἐποιήσατε as its object; finally, it would be strange and
not in keeping with the *thoughtful* manner of the apostle, to

furnish the idea: "ye know that ye did well therein" (which οἴδατε is supposed to convey) with the altogether external specification of a ground for it: "because ye have already formerly and repeatedly supported me." The contents attributed by Hofmann to οἴδατε needed no assignment of a causal ground, or—if any—one internal, ethical, and in harmony with the subtle delicacy of the apostle. — Observe, moreover, in connection with οἴδατε κ. ὑμεῖς, that in that which the readers also know (consequently in ὅτι κ.τ.λ.) the stress lies upon the *negative* οὐδεμία κ.τ.λ. — καὶ ὑμεῖς] *ye also*, as I.[1] — Φιλιππήσιοι] addressing them by name, not because he desires to assert something of them which no other church had done (Bengel: for in this case Paul would have written ὅτι ὑμεῖς, Φιλιππ.), but in his *increasing earnestness*. Comp. 2 Cor. vi. 11. — ἐν ἀρχῇ τ. εὐαγγ.] glancing back, certainly, to the second missionary journey (Weiss); but the *relative* expression is used from the standpoint of the *time then present*, behind which lay the founding of the Macedonian churches about ten years back; a long past which seemed, *in relation to the present* and to the *wider development* of the church now attained, as still belonging to the period of the *beginning* of the gospel. Comp. Clement. *Cor.* I. 47. An epexegetical more precise definition of this expression—which does not betray the hand of a later author (Hinsch)—for the date intended is: ὅτε ἐξῆλθον ἀπὸ Μακεδ., *when I departed from Macedonia*, Acts xvii. 14. Paul, therefore, *immediately on leaving that country*, received aid from the infant church, when the brethren τὸν Παῦλον ἐξαπέστειλαν πορεύεσθαι ὡς ἐπὶ τὴν θάλασσαν and ἤγαγον ἕως Ἀθηνῶν, Acts *l.c.* Doubtless the money which Paul subsequently received in Corinth (see 2 Cor. xi. 9) through Macedonian delegates was sent, if not exclusively, at least *jointly* by the Philippians, so that they thereby gave *continued* active proof of the fellowship εἰς λόγον δόσ. κ. λήψ., into which they had *entered* with the apostle at

---

[1] To express this, Paul was not at all under the necessity of writing οἴδατε αὐτοί, as Hofmann objects. The latter would convey a *different* conception, namely: ye know *without my reminding you* (Acts ii. 22; 1 Thess. ii. 1, iii. 3; 2 Thess. iii. 7).

his very departure. But this receipt of money *at Corinth* is not the fact meant by ἐκοινώνησεν κ.τ.λ., in which case ἐξῆλθον would have to be taken, with Estius, Flatt, van Hengel, de Wette, Wiesinger, Weiss, Hofmann, and others, in the sense of the pluperfect (Winer, p. 258 [E. T. 343]); for the latter would be the more unwarranted in the context, seeing that Paul himself by ἐν ἀρχῇ τοῦ εὐαγγ. carries them back to the earliest time possible, and indeed afterwards (ver. 16) to a period even antecedent to the ὅτε ἐξῆλθον. The *aorist*, however, has its justification in this purely historical statement of fact, although the imperfect also, but following a different conception, *might*—not, however (in opposition to Hofmann's objection), *must*—have been used. — ἐκοινώνησεν εἰς λόγον δόσεως κ. λήψ.] *entered into fellowship* with me *in reference to account of giving and receiving*,—a euphemistic indication, calculated to meet the sense of delicacy in the readers, of the thought : " *has entered into the relation of furnishing aid towards me.*" On κοινωνεῖν εἰς, comp. on i. 5. The *analysis* of the figurative description is this : The *Philippians* keep an account of *expenditure* on Paul and *income* from him ; and *the apostle* likewise keeps account of his *expenditure* on the Philippians and *income* from them. This *mutual* account-keeping, in which the δόσις on the one part, agrees with the λῆψις on the other, is the κοινωνία εἰς λόγον κ.τ.λ. It is true that in this case no *money*-amount is entered in the account of the Philippians under the heading of λῆψις, or the account of the apostle under the heading of δόσις ; instead of this, however, comes in the *blessing*, which the readers were to receive *from their gifts of love*, according to ver. 17, as if it were an income corresponding to this expenditure, and coming in from it. We are therefore not justified in adopting *the* view, that δόσ. and λῆψ. apply *to Paul alone* (Schrader), or that δόσεως applies to the *Philippians* and λήψ. to *Paul* (" Ego sum in *vestris expensi* tabulis, vos in *meis accepti*," Grotius ; comp. Erasmus, Camerarius, Casaubon, Castalio, and others, including Heinrichs, Storr, Flatt, Matthies, van Hengel, Rilliet, Ewald) ; for the words require the idea of an account under *both* headings on the side of *both* parties. Others, maintaining indeed this reciprocity, but arbitrarily introducing ideas from 1 Cor. xi. 11, comp. Rom. xv. 27, consider that the δόσις on the part of the apostle, and the λῆψις on the part of the Philippians, consisted in the *spiritual benefits* brought about *by the preaching of the gospel* (so Chrysostom, Oecumenius, Theophylact, Pelagius, Calvin, Cornelius a Lapide, Zanchius, Zeger, Estius, Hammond, Wiesinger, Weiss, Hofmann, and others); whilst others, again, import into the words the thought : " Quae a Philippensibus accepit *in rationes Dei remuneratoris* refert Paulus" (Wetstein, Rosenmüller; comp. Wolf, Schoettgen, and already Ambrosiaster). Rheinwald finds the λῆψις of the Philippians and the δόσις of the apostle even in the assumption that *he* also had assisted *them*, namely, out of the sums of money collected in the churches,—an error which is at variance with the context, and which ought to have been precluded both by the prominence given to the statement of the date, and also by the exclusion of all other churches, as well as by the inappropriateness of the mention just in *this* passage of such a λῆψις on the part of the Philippians.—On λόγος, *ratio, account,* comp. Matt. xii. 36 ; Luke xvi. 2 ; Rom. xiv. 12 ; 1 Macc. x. 40 ; Dem. 227. 26 ; Diod. Sic. i. 49 ; Polyb. xv. 34. 2. The rendering which takes εἰς λόγον : *in respect to* (Bengel, Heinrichs, Storr, Matthies, van Hengel, Rilliet, Lünemann), would no doubt be linguistically correct (Dem. 385. 11 ; 2 Macc. i. 14 ; and see Krüger *on Thuc.* iii. 46. 3), but is to be rejected on account of the context, as expressions *of accounting* follow (comp. Cic. *Lael.* 16 : "*ratio acceptorum et datorum*"). For instances from Greek writers of δόσις καὶ λῆψις (Ecclus. xli. 14, xlii. 7) as *expenditure and income,* see Wetstein. Comp. Plat. *Rep.* p. 332 A B: ἡ ἀπόδοσις κ. ἡ λῆψις. As to the corresponding משא ומתן, see Schoettgen, *Hor.* p. 804.

Ver. 16. Ὅτι] *since, indeed, ye also already in Thessalonica,* etc. It is *argumentative,* namely, outbidding the *early* definition of date ἐν ἀρχῇ ... Μακεδονίας, in ver. 15, by one even *antecedent,* and thus serving more amply to justify that specification of time,[1] for which purpose the ὅτι specifying the

---

[1] If Baur had noticed this correct logical connection, he would not have made an improper use of our passage to fortify his opinion of the affair of the aid

reason was quite sufficient, and (in opposition to Hofmann's objection) no γάρ was necessary. The opinion of Wiesinger, that ὅτι κ.τ.λ. is intended to explain that it was only with the aid sent after Paul at a distance that the readers had entered into such a connection with the apostle as is previously mentioned, is bound up with the untenable interpretation of ἐξῆλθον as pluperfect. The rendering of ὅτι by *that* (Rheinwald, Matthies, Hoelemann, van Hengel, Rilliet, de Wette, Lünemann, Weiss) is to be set aside, because, while the emphatic οἴδατε καὶ ὑμεῖς, ver. 15, accords doubtless with the exclusion of other churches in ver. 15, it does not accord with ver. 16 ("*ye also* know that ye have sent ... to me !"), to which it would stand in an illogical relation, even apart from the uncalled-for *inversion of the order of time*, which would result. Hofmann's explanation, which makes ὅτι in ver. 16 parallel to the ὅτι in ver. 15 and places it in causal relation to οἴδατε, falls with his erroneous view of ver. 15. — The καί before ἐν Θεσσαλ., for which Hinsch, following Baur, thinks that he finds a reference in 2 Cor. xi. 9, is the simple *also* in the sense of *also already;* a climax as regards *time;* see Hartung, *Partik.* I. p. 135 ; Kühner, II. 2, p. 797. — ἐν Θεσσαλ.] is not used, in the sense of the bearers having arrived, for εἰς, for there is no certain instance of ἀποστέλλειν or πέμπειν with ἐν in this sense (Thuc. vii. 17 must, with Becker and Krüger, be read : ἐς τὴν Σικελίαν) ; but the preposition is used from the standpoint of the *receiver :* "*also at Thessalonica* (when I was there) ye sent to me." Thus this sending took place *in Thessalonica.* Comp. on Matt. x. 16 ; Poppo and Krüger *on Thuc.* iv. 27. 1. — καὶ ἅπαξ καὶ δίς] Comp. 1 Thess. ii. 18. The conception is : "when the first *aid* arrived, the ἐπέμψατε had taken place *once;* when the second arrived, it had taken place *both once and twice.*" Paul has not written δίς merely, nor yet ἅπαξ κ. δίς (1 Macc. iii. 30 ; Xen. *Anab.* iv. 7. 10), but by καὶ ἅπ. κ.

being *an invented incident.*—The *same* assistance which is meant in ver. 15 cannot be meant in ver. 16, as some not attending to the καί (comp. Luther, Castalio, and others) have thought. This view is also at variance with the specification of time ὅτε ἐξῆλθον, ver. 15 ; for Paul abode several weeks in Thessalonica (Acts xvii. 2), and then there still followed his sojourn in Beroea (Acts xvii. 10 ff.), ere he quitted Macedonia and travelled to Athens.

δίς he sets forth the repetition of the matter *more emphatically*, to the praise of his readers (Hartung, *Partikell.* I. p. 144). Comp. καὶ δὶς καὶ τρίς, Plat. *Phaed.* p. 63 D, *Phil.* p. 59 E; Herod. ii. 121, iii. 148. The opposite: οὐχ ἅπαξ οὐδὲ δίς, Plat. *Clit.* p. 410 B. — εἰς τ. χρείαν] on behalf of *the necessity*, in order to satisfy it; comp. ii. 15. The article indicates the necessity that had been *existing* in Paul's case. On πέμψαι, used absolutely, comp. Acts xi. 29. *What* they sent, they knew.

Ver. 17. Just as in ver. 11 Paul anticipated a possible misunderstanding in respect to ver. 10, so here in reference to the praises contained in ver. 14 ff. This, he would say, is not the language of material desire, but, etc. — οὐχ ὅτι κ.τ.λ.] as in ver. 11: I do not mean by this to convey that my desire is directed towards *the gift* (the emphasis being laid on τὸ δόμα)—this, namely, taken in and by itself—in which case the *article* means the donation *accruing to him as the case occurred*, and the *present* ἐπιζητῶ denotes the *constant* and *characteristic* striving after (Bernhardy, p. 370): it is not my business, etc. The *compound* verb indicates by ἐπί the *direction*. Comp. on ἐπιποθῶ, i. 8, and on Matt. vi. 33; Rom. xi. 7. The view which regards it as *strengthening* the simple verb (*studiose quaero*, so Hoelemann and others) is not implied in the context any more than the sense: *insuper quaero* (Polyb. i. 5. 3); so van Hengel, who indelicately, and notwithstanding the article, explains τὸ δόμα as *still more gifts.* — ἀλλ᾽ ἐπιζητῶ] The repetition of the verb after ἀλλά makes the contrast stand out independently with special emphasis; comp. Rom. viii. 15; 1 Cor. ii. 7; Fritzsche, *ad Rom.* II. p. 137. — τὸν καρπὸν κ.τ.λ.] This is what Paul desires, towards which his wishes and endeavours are directed: *the fruit which abounds to your account;* not, therefore, a gain which he wishes to have for himself, but gain for the Philippians. So completely is his ἐπιζητεῖν devoid of any selfish aim,—which, however, would not be the case, if the ἐπιζητῶ τὸ δόμα were true. This applies against Hofmann's objection, that the καρπός must be something which Paul *himself desires to have;* the notion of ἐπιζητῶ is *anquiro, appeto,* and this indeed applies to personal possession in the *negative* half of the sentence; but then the second half expresses the *real* state of the case, which *does away with* the notion of selfishness.—The καρπός itself cannot be the fruit *of the gospel* (Ewald), or of the *labour of the apostle* (Weiss); but, in accordance with the context, only the fruit of the δόμα, that is, *the blessing which accrues from the gift to the givers;* comp. on ver. 15. By this is meant [1] *the divine recompense at the judgment* (2 Cor. ix. 6), which they will then receive, as if it were the product of their account, for their labour of love (Matt. xxv. 34 ff.). This produce of their δόμα is figuratively conceived as *fruit,* which is largely placed to the credit of their account, in order to be drawn by them at the day of harvest (comp. also Gal. vi. 7 ff.). Comp. ver. 19. In substance it is the *treasure in heaven* that is meant (Matt. xix. 21, vi. 20), which will be received at the Parousia. Comp. on Col. i. 5. The figurative εἰς λόγον ὑμῶν, which here also is not to be understood, with Bengel, Storr, Flatt, Rilliet, and others, as equivalent to εἰς ὑμᾶς, is the completion of the figure in ver. 15; although there is no need to explain καρπός as *interest* (Salmasius, Michaelis, who thinks in πλεονάζ. of *compound interest,* Zachariae, Heinrichs), because it is difficult to see why Paul, if he used *this* figure, should not have applied to it the proper term (τόκος), and because the idea of *interest* is quite alien to that of the δόμα (*a present*). — τ. πλεονάζ. εἰς λόγον ὑμῶν] to be taken together (see above); εἰς states the *destination* of the πλεονάζ. Van Hengel and de Wette needlessly break up the passage by coupling εἰς λόγ. ὑμ. with ἐπιζητῶ, because πλεονάζειν with εἰς is not used elsewhere by Paul (not even 2 Thess. i. 3). The preposition is in fact not determined by the word in itself, but by its logical reference, and may therefore be *any one* which the reference requires.

Ver. 18. Δέ] The train of thought is: "not the gift do I

---

[1] Not the *active manifestation of the Christian life* (Matthies, Rilliet, Hofmann; comp. Vatablus, Musculus, Piscator, Zanchius; Flatt and Rheinwald mingle together heterogeneous ideas); for only the fruit *of the* δόμα can be meant, not the δόμα itself *as* fruit, which is produced *in the shape of the love-gift* (Hofmann).

seek, but the fruit (ver. 17); and as regards what has been received from you in the present instance, I have everything already, and need nothing further." That this refers to the desire of the church to know what he possibly still needed (Hofmann), is a very unnecessary assumption. — ἀπέχω δὲ πάντα] not: *habeo autem omnia* (Vulgate); not a mere *acknowledgment of receipt* (Erasmus, Beza, Grotius, Cornelius a Lapide, Heinrichs, and others); nor yet equivalent to περισσεύω (Rheinwald); but, in keeping with the sense of the *compound*: *I have everything away*, so that I have nothing left to desire at your hands. Comp. Philem. 15; Matt. vi. 2, 5, 16; Luke vi. 24; Callim. *ep.* 22; Arrian. *Epict.* iii. 2. 13, iii. 24. 17; Jacobs, *ad Anthol.* VII. pp. 276, 298. Πάντα, therefore, according to the context (ἐπιζητῶ τ. δόμα, ver. 17), is: *everything which I could desire*, although there is no necessity for introducing specially, with Chrysostom and Oecumenius, τὰ ἐλλειφθέντα ἐν τῷ παρελθόντι χρόνῳ. The *emphasis*, moreover, is laid, not on πάντα, but on ἀπέχω, in contrast to ἐπιζητεῖν. — καὶ περισσεύω] and my wants are thus so fully satisfied, that *I have over*. — πεπλήρωμαι] forms a climax to περισσ.: *I am full*, I have abundance. The gift must have been ample; but gratitude sets this forth in all the stronger a light. To πεπλήρ. is attached δεξάμενος κ.τ.λ. — ὀσμὴν εὐωδίας κ.τ.λ.] This apposition to τὰ παρ' ὑμῶν, expressing a judgment as to the latter (see on Rom. xii. 1), sets forth, to the honour of the givers, the relation in which the gifts received stand *towards God*, by whom they are esteemed *as a sacrifice well-pleasing to Him*. As to ὀσμὴ εὐωδίας, *smell of a sweet savour*, רֵיחַ נִיחֹחַ (genitive of quality), which is used of *free-will* offerings, see on Eph. v. 2. It describes the thing according to its *effect* on God, namely, that it is *acceptable* to Him; θυσίαν κ.τ.λ., however, describes it according to what it *is*. — δεκτὴν, εὐάρεστ.] *acceptable, well-pleasing*, a vividly asyndetic climax (on the former, comp. Ecclus. xxxii. 7); τῷ Θεῷ, however, applies to the whole apposition ὀσμὴν . . . εὐαρ. The asyndetic juxtaposition of several epithets is frequent also in classical authors, from Homer onward (Ameis *z. Od.* iv., *Anh.*). As to the view, originating in the O. T., which regards works well-

pleasing to God as ethical *sacrifices,* see the expositors on Rom.
xii. 1; 1 Pet. ii. 5; Heb. xiii. 16.   Comp. Philo, *de vit. Mos.*
II. p. 151: ἡ γὰρ ἀληθὴς ἱερουργία τίς ἂν εἴη πλὴν ψυχῆς
θεοφιλοῦς εὐσέβεια; passages from the Rabbins in Schoettg.
Hor. p. 1006.

Ver. 19. The thought starts from τῷ Θεῷ. But *God,* to
whom your gift stands in the relation of such a sacrifice, will
recompense you.—Paul says ὁ δὲ Θεός μου (comp. i. 3), because
he himself had been the recipient of that which they had
brought as a sacrifice pleasing to God; as *his* God (to whom
he belongs and whom he serves, comp. on Rom. i. 8), therefore, will God carry out the recompense. — πληρώσει] used
with significant reference to πεπλήρ., ver. 18, according to the
idea of recompense.   Not, however, a *wish* (hence also in
Codd. and in the Vulgate the reading πληρῶσαι), as Chrysostom, Luther, and others take it, but a *promise.* — πᾶσαν χρείαν
ὑμῶν] likewise corresponding to the service which the readers
had *rendered;* for they had sent εἰς τὴν χρείαν (ver. 16) of the
apostle.   To be understood as: *every need which ye have,* not
merely *bodily* (so usually, following Chrysostom, who explains
it as the fulfilment of the *fourth petition,* also van Hengel, de
Wette, Wiesinger), and not merely *spiritual* (Pelagius, Rilliet,
also mainly Weiss), but as it stands: *every* need.   It is not,
however, an *earthly* recompense which is meant (Hofmann),
but (comp. on ver. 17) the recompense *in the Messiah's kingdom,* where, in the enjoyment of the σωτηρία, the highest
satisfaction of every need (comp. on πληρ. χρείαν, Thuc. i. 70.
4, and Wetstein *in loc.*) shall have set in amidst the full,
blessed sufficiency of the eternal ζωή (comp. Rom. viii. 17 f.;
Rev. xxi. 4).[1]   There are specifications of this satisfaction in
the beatitudes of the Sermon on the Mount, Matt. v.; comp.
especially the χορτασθήσεσθε and γελάσετε, Luke vi. 21, also

---

[1] Hofmann very irrelevantly objects that it is out of place to speak of *want* in
that kingdom.   But just, in fact, *on that account* is the bliss of the kingdom
the complete *satisfaction of every need.*   Comp. Rev. vii. 16 f.; 2 Tim. iv. 7 f.
Thus also is the perfect then put in the place of that which is in part.   Consequently the idea of the satisfaction of every χρεία in eternal life, where man
even beholds God, and where He is all in all, is anything but a "monstrous
thought."

the οὐ μὴ διψήσῃ εἰς τὸν αἰῶνα in John iv. 14, and the sarcastic κεκορεσμένοι in 1 Cor. iv. 8. That it is the *Messianic* satisfaction in the ἐλευθερία τῆς δόξης τῶν τέκνων τοῦ Θεοῦ (Rom. viii. 21), in the possession of the πλοῦτος τῆς δόξης τῆς κληρονομίας αὐτοῦ (Eph. i. 18), which is to be thought of, Paul himself states by ἐν δόξῃ, which is to be taken as *instrumental* (Eph. i. 23, v. 18) and dependent on πληρ.: *with glory,* whereby the *Messianic* is indicated. Hofmann also, though he rejects the instrumental view, comes ultimately to it : " *Therewith and thus* will God fulfil all their need, *in that He gives them glory.*"[1] *Others,* who also correctly join the words with πληρ., take them as a *modal definition :* in a glorious *way,* that is, *amply, splendide,* and the like. See Castalio, Beza, Calvin, and many others, including Hoelemann, van Hengel, Rilliet, de Wette, Wiesinger, Weiss. But what an indefinite yet peculiarly affected, and withal—by its so habitual reference elsewhere to the final judgment—misleading expression would this be for so simple an idea ! And how far would it be from the apostle's mind, considering his expectation of the nearness of the Parousia (comp. 1 Cor. vii. 29, 31), to promise *on this side of it* a hearty recompense, which was to take place, moreover, ἐν Χριστῷ Ἰησοῦ ! An appeal is wrongly made to 2 Cor. ix. 8, where an increase of means for further welldoing, to be granted through God's blessing, and not the *recompense,* is the point under discussion. Others erroneously join ἐν δόξῃ with τὸ πλοῦτος αὐτοῦ (Grotius, Storr, Flatt, Rheinwald, and others) : "*pro amplissimis suis divitiis,* id est, potestate sua omnia excedente," Heinrichs. It is true that ἐν δόξῃ *might* be attached without a connecting article (according to the combination πλουτεῖν ἐν τινι, 1 Tim. vi. 8 ; comp. 1 Cor.

[1] In order, however, to bring out of the passage, notwithstanding this ἐν δόξῃ, the idea of a recompense *in this life,* Hofmann makes δόξα mean the glory of the children of God *which is hidden from the world,* and which is the fulfilment of every want only in proportion " *as there is lacking in us what, either corporally or spiritually, is necessary for the completion of our divine sonship.*" Instead of such arbitrary inventions, let us keep clearly before us how great a weight in the very word of *promise,* which forms the *conclusion* of the epistle, lies *in the fact* that *the grand aim of all promise and hope, i.e.* the glory of eternal life (Rom. v. 2, viii. 18, 21, ix. 23 ; 1 Cor. xv. 43 ; 2 Cor. iv. 17 ; Col. iii. 4 ; and many other passages), is once more presented to the reader's view.

i. 5 ; 2 Cor. ix. 11); but Paul always connects πλοῦτος with the *genitive* of the thing, and πλοῦτος τῆς δόξης in particular, said of God, is so constantly used by him, that it seems altogether unwarranted to assume the expression πλοῦτος ἐν δόξῃ in this passage. See Rom. ix. 23 ; Eph. i. 18, iii. 16 ; Col. i. 27. He would have written : κατὰ τὸ πλοῦτος τῆς δόξης αὐτοῦ, comp. Rom. ix. 23. — κατὰ τὸ πλοῦτος αὐτοῦ] that is, *in conformity with His being so rich,* and consequently having so much to give. Comp. Rom. x. 12, xi. 33. This *assures* what is promised. — ἐν Χριστῷ ᾽Ιησοῦ] definition annexed to πληρώσει ... δόξῃ; that which is promised has its causal ground *in Christ,* who by His work has acquired for believers the eternal δόξα. Christ is, in fact, ἡ ἐλπὶς τῆς δόξης, Col. i. 27.

Ver. 20. The conception of the superabundant salvation, which Paul has just promised from God, forces from his heart a *doxology.* — πατρί] through Christ, in virtue of our υἱοθεσία, Rom. viii. 15 ; Gal. iv. 5. As to τ. Θεῷ κ. πατρὶ ἡμ. comp. on Gal. i. 5. — ἡ δόξα] *sc.* εἴη, the *befitting* glory. See on Eph. iii. 21 ; Rom. xi. 36, xvi. 27, *et al.* — εἰς τοὺς αἰῶν. τῶν αἰών.] Gal. i. 5 ; 1 Tim. i. 17 ; 2 Tim. iv. 18 ; Heb. xiii. 21 ; 1 Pet. iv. 11, v. 11, and frequently in Rev. As to the analysis of the expression, see on Eph. iii. 21.

Vv. 21–23. Πάντα ἅγιον] *every one,* no one in the church being excepted,—a point which is more definitely expressed by the singular.[1] — ἐν Χ. ᾽Ι.] is not to be joined to ἅγιον (so usually, as by Rheinwald, Hoelemann, Matthies, van Hengel, de Wette, Ewald, Weiss, Hofmann), but belongs to ἀσπάσ. (comp. Rom. xvi. 22 ; 1 Cor. xvi. 19), denoting the specifically *Christian* salutation, in conveying which the consciousness lives *in Christ.* This is the connection adopted by Ambrosiaster, Estius, Heinrichs, Rilliet, Wiesinger, Schenkel, and J. B. Lightfoot, and it is the right one, since with ἅγιον it is self-evident that *Christians* are meant, and there would be no motive for

---

[1] Since Paul does not here express, as in other cases (Rom. xvi. 17 ; 1 Cor. xvi. 20 ; 2 Cor. xiii. 12), the conception of *mutual* salutation (ἀλλήλους), he has in ἀσπάσασθε had in view the immediate recipients of the epistle (presbyters and deacons, i. 1). So also 1 Thess. v. 26.

specially expressing this here, as there was, for instance, in the
address i. 1, where τοῖς ἁγίοις ἐν Χ. Ἰ. bears a certain *formal*
character. — οἱ σὺν ἐμοὶ ἀδελφ.] is the narrower circle of
those Christians who were round the apostle in Rome, including
also the *official colleagues* who were with him, though there is
no ground for understanding these *alone* (Chrysostom, Oecumenius, Theophylact, and many others), Grotius even pointing
distinctly to *Timothy, Linus,* and *Clement.* The difficulty,
which has been raised in this case by a comparison of ii. 20,
is unfounded, since, in fact, the expression in ii. 20 excludes
neither the giving of a salutation nor the mention of brethren ;
groundless, therefore, are the attempted solutions of the
difficulty, as, for example, that of Chrysostom, that either
ii. 20 is meant οὐ περὶ τῶν ἐν τῇ πόλει, or that Paul οὐ
παραιτεῖται καὶ τούτους ἀδελφοὺς καλεῖν (comp. Oecumenius,
who brings forward the latter as a proof of the σπλάγχνα of
the apostle). Misapprehending this second and in itself correct
remark of Chrysostom, van Hengel insists on a distinction
being drawn between two classes of companions in office,
namely, *travelling companions,* such as Luke, Mark, Titus, Silas,
and those *who were resident in the places where* the apostle
sojourned (among whom van Hengel reckons in Rome, Clement,
Euodia, Syntyche, and even Epaphroditus), and holds that only
the latter class is here meant. The limits of the narrower circle
designated by οἱ σὺν ἐμοὶ ἀδ. are not at all to be definitely
drawn. Estius well says : " Qui . . . mihi vincto ministrant,
qui me visitant, qui mecum hic in evangelio laborant." —
πάντες οἱ ἅγιοι] generally, *all Christians* who are here ; comp.
on 2 Cor. xiii. 12 ; 1 Cor. xvi. 20. — μάλιστα δέ] but *most
of all, pre-eminently ;* they have requested the apostle to give
special prominence to their salutation. Comp. Plat. *Critias,*
p. 108 D : τούς τε ἄλλους κλητέον καὶ δὴ καὶ τὰ μάλιστα
Μνημοσύνην. Whether these persons stood in any personal
relations to the Philippians, remains uncertain. It is enough
to assume that Paul had said to them much that was honourable concerning the church to which he was about to write.
— οἱ ἐκ τῆς Καίσαρος οἰκίας] sc. ἅγιοι, as is plain from the
connection with the preceding (in opposition to Hofmann) :

those from the emperor's house (from the *Palatium*, see Böttger, *Beitr.* II. p. 49) who belong to the saints. We have to think of probably inferior *servants* of the emperor (according to Grotius, Hitzig, and others : *freedmen*), who *dwelt*, or at least *were employed, in the palace.* In this way there is no need for departing from the immediate meaning of the word, and taking it in the sense of *household* (Hofmann). In no case, however, can we adopt as the direct meaning of οἰκία the sense of *domestic servants*, a meaning which it does not bear even in Xen. *Mem.* ii. 7. 6 ; Joseph. *Antt.* xvi. 5. 8 ; and Tac. *Hist.* ii. 92 ;[1] *domestic servants* would be οἰκετεία. Others have taken οἰκία, in accordance with current usage, as *family* (1 Cor. xvi. 15, and frequently), and have understood *kinsmen of the emperor*, a meaning which in itself seems by no means shown by Philo *in Flacc.* p. 190 A to be at variance with linguistic usage[2] (in opposition to Hofmann). So recently Baur, who needed this point for his combinations against the genuineness of the epistle, and van Hengel.[3] But apart from the fact that through Nero himself this family was greatly diminished, and that conversions among those related to the emperor were *à priori* (comp. also 1 Cor. i. 26 ff.) very improbable, doubtless some historical traces of such a striking success would have been preserved in tradition.[4] Matthies, quite

---

[1] Where it is said of those who entered the service of the emperor : "in *domum Caesaris* transgressi." Comp. Herodian, iii. 10. 9 : πρὶν εἰς τὸν βασίλειον οἶκον παρελθεῖν.

[2] For in Philo *l.c.* it is said regarding Herod Agrippa : "Even though he were not king, but only one of the emperor's kinsmen (ἐκ τῆς Καίσαρος οἰκίας), it would still be necessary to prefer and honour him."

[3] Whether Chrysostom and his successors understood here *members of the imperial family*, is a matter of doubt. At all events Chrysostom does not take the word itself, οἰκία, as *family*, but explains it by τὰ βασίλεια, *palace*, and finds in the salutation a purpose *of encouragement* : εἰ γὰρ οἱ ἐν τοῖς βασιλείοις πάντων κατεφρόνησαν διὰ τὸν βασιλέα τῶν οὐρανῶν, πολλῷ μᾶλλον αὐτοὺς χρὴ τοῦτο ποιεῖν. Comp. Theodoret, Oecumenius, Theophylact.

[4] Certainly Baur believes that he has found these traces in sufficient number. *Flavius Clemens*, namely, was a kinsman of Domitian (see on ver. 3). Now, since out of *this* Clement grew the Clemens *Romanus* of Christian tradition, the latter also must have been a kinsman of the imperial family, as indeed the *Homil. Clement.* iv. 7, comp. xiv. 10, designate him as ἀνὴρ πρὸς γένους Τιβερίου Καίσαρος. He, therefore, would be exactly the man, in whom Christianity was

arbitrarily, understands the *Praetorians*, as if Paul had written : οἱ ἐκ τοῦ πραιτωρίου (i. 13). This also applies, in opposition to Wieseler, *Chronol. d. apostol. Zeitalt.* p. 420, who, considering the Praetorium to be a portion of the palace (see remark on i. 13), thinks the apostle alludes *especially* to the Praetorians. Those who transfer the epistle to Caesarea (see Introduction, § 2), suppose the *Praetorium of Herod in that place* to be intended, and consequently also think of *Praetorians,* Acts xxiii. 35 (Paulus, Böttger) ; or (so Rilliet) taking οἰκία as *familia,* of administrators of the imperial private domain, called *Caesariani* or *Procuratores*—a view against which the plural should have warned them ; or even of " the family of the imperial freedman *Felix*" (Thiersch). What *persons,* moreover, were meant (various of the older expositors have even included *Seneca*[1] among them), is a point just as unknown to us, as it was well known to the Philippians or became known to them through Epaphroditus. The general result is, that people from the imperial palace were Christians, and that those could obtain access to the apostle probably

represented in the circle of the imperial house itself. " *Concluding from one that there were several, the author of the epistle might make his apostle write earnest salutations to the church in Philippi from believing members of the imperial house in the plural,*" etc. Thus does criticism, departing from the solid ground of history, lose itself in the atmosphere of subjective inventions, where hypothesis finds no longer either support or limit. Indeed, Baur now goes further beyond all bounds (II. p. 69), and discovers that the mention of Clement even throws *a new light over the whole plan of the epistle.* With this Clement, namely, and the participation, as attested by him, of the imperial house in the gospel, is given the προκοπὴ τοῦ εἰαγγ. (i. 12), and with the latter the feeling of *joyfulness,* which expresses itself throughout the epistle as the ground-tone of the apostle (ii. 17 f., comp. iii. 1, iv. 1, 4, 10), and which is again and again the refrain of each separate section. Only by the preponderance of this feeling is it to be explained that the author makes his apostle even express the hope of a speedy liberation (ii. 24). But with this joy there is also blended, with a neutralizing effect, the idea of a nearly approaching death, i. 20-24, and this divided state of mind between life and death betrays an author "*who had already before his eyes as an actual fact the end of the apostle, which was so far from harmonizing with all these presuppositions.*"

[1] See generally on "*Paul and Seneca,*" and the apocryphal fourteen Latin letters exchanged between them, Baur in Hilgenfeld's *Zeitschr.* 1858, 2. 3 ; Reuss in Herzog's *Encyklop.* XIV. p. 274 ff. ; J. B. Lightfoot, *Exc.* II. p. 268 ff., 327 ff. ; latest edition of the text of these epistles in the *Theol. Quartalschr.* 1867, p. 609 ff.

with special ease and frequency ; hence their *especial* salutation.   The question also, whether one or another of the persons
saluted in Rom. xvi. should be understood as included here
(see especially J. B. Lightfoot, p. 173 ff.), must remain entirely
undecided.   Calvin, moreover, well points to the working of
the divine mercy, in that the gospel " in illam scelerum
omnium et flagitiorum abyssum penetraverit."— ἡ χάρις τ. κυρ.
'I. X.] see on Gal. i. 6.— μετὰ πάντων ὑμ.] Comp. Rom.
xvi. 24; 1 Cor. xvi. 24; 2 Cor. xiii. 13 ; 2 Thess. iii. 18;
Tit. iii. 15.

THE

EPISTLE OF PAUL TO THE COLOSSIANS.

INTRODUCTION.[1]

§ 1. THE CHURCH.

WITH the exception of the Epistle to the Romans, the letter now before us is the only one of all the epistles of Paul that have been preserved, which is addressed to a *church* that was neither founded by Paul himself nor even subsequently visited by him in person (see on i. 7, ii. 1), although the Colossian Philemon was his immediate disciple (Philem. 19), and the Book of Acts relates that the apostle passed through Phrygia on two occasions (Acts xvi. 6, xviii. 23). There, in Phrygia Magna on the Lycus, was situate *Kolossae*, or *Kolassae* (see the critical remarks on i. 2). It is designated by Herodotus, vii. 30, as πόλις μεγάλη, and by Xenophon, *Anab.* i. 2. 6, as εὐδαίμων κ. μεγάλη; but, subsequently, as compared with the cities of Apamea and Laodicea which had become great (μεγίσται . . . πόλεις, Strabo xii. 8, p. 576), it became so reduced, that it is placed by Strabo, *l.c.*, only in the list of the Phrygian πολίσματα, and by Pliny, *N. H.* v. 41, only among the *oppida*, although *celeberrima*. According to the Eusebian Chronicle and Oros. vii. 7, it also was visited by

---

[1] See Hofmann, *Introduct. in lectionem ep. P. ad Col.* Lips. 1749; Böhmer, *Isagoge in ep. ad Col.* Berol. 1829; Mayerhoff, *Der Brief an d. Kol. kritisch geprüft*, Berlin, 1838; Wiggers, *d. Verh. d. Ap. P. zu d. christl. Gem. in Kol.* in the *Stud. u. Krit.* 1838, p. 165 ff.; Leo Montet, *Introd. in ep. ad Col.* 1841; Klöpper, *De orig. ep. ad Eph. et Col.* 1853; Weiss in Herzog's *Encykl.* XIX. p. 717 ff.; Schenkel in his *Bibellex.* III. p. 565 ff.; Holtzmann, *Krit. der Epheser- und Kolosserbriefe*, 1872.

the earthquake which, according to Tacit. *Ann.* xiv. 27, devastated Laodicea. This took place not so late as the tenth year of Nero's reign (Eus. Chron.), or even the fourteenth (Orosius), but, according to Tacitus, in the seventh—about the same time with the composition of our epistle, perhaps shortly afterwards, as the earthquake is not mentioned in it. In the Middle Ages the city was again flourishing under the name *Chonae* (Theophylact and Oecumenius on i. 2; Constant. Porphyr. *Them.* i. 3); it is in the present day the village of *Chonus* (see Pococke, *Morgenl.* III. p. 114; and generally, Mannert, *Geogr.* VI. 1, p. 127 f.; Böhmer, *Isag.* p. 21 ff.; Steiger, p. 13 ff.).

By whom the church—which consisted for the most part of Gentile Christians, i. 21, 27, ii. 13—was *founded,* is not unknown; Epaphras is indicated by i. 7 f. as its *founder,* and not merely as its specially faithful and zealous *teacher.* See the remark after i. 7 f. That it had received and accepted the *Pauline* gospel, is certain from the whole tenor of the epistle. It may be also inferred as certain from ii. 1 compared with Acts xviii. 23, that the *time* of its being founded was subsequent to the visit to Phrygia in Acts xviii. 23. From the address (i. 2) we are not warranted to infer (with Bleek), that the body of Christians there had not yet been constituted into a formal church; comp. on Rom. i. 7. It was so numerous, that it had a section assembling in the house of Philemon (Philem. 2).

§ 2. OCCASION, AIM, TIME AND PLACE OF COMPOSITION, CONTENTS.

The apostle had received through Epaphras, who had come to him (i. 7 f., iv. 12; Philem. 23), detailed accounts of the condition of the church, and of its perils and needs at that time, whereby he found himself *induced*—and the removal of Epaphras from the church at the moment certainly made the matter appear all the more urgent—to despatch *Tychicus,* an inhabitant of Asia Minor (Acts xx. 4), to Colossae, and to send with him this epistle (iv. 7 f., comp. Eph. vi. 21 f.).

Tychicus was also to visit the Ephesians, and to convey the letter written at the same time to them (see on Eph. Introd. § 2). Tychicus was despatched at the same time with *Onesimus*, the Colossian slave (iv. 9), who had to deliver to his master Philemon the well-known letter from the apostle (Philem. 11 f.). Doubtless Onesimus also—who had come, although still as a heathen, from Colossae to Paul—brought with him accounts as to the state of matters there, as he had been a servant in a Christian household amidst lively Christian intercourse (Philem. 2).

In accordance with these circumstances giving *occasion* to the letter, the *aim* of the apostle was not merely *to confirm* the church generally *in its Christian faith and life*, but also *to warn it against heretical perils* by which it was threatened. The *false teachers* whom he had in view were *Jewish-Christians;* not, however, such as those who, as in Galatia and in the neighbourhood of Philippi (Phil. iii. 2 ff.), restricting themselves to the sphere of legal requirement and especially of the necessity of circumcision, did away with Christian freedom, the foundation of which is justification by faith,—but such *as had mixed up Christian Judaism with theosophic speculation*. While they likewise adhered to circumcision (ii. 11), and to precepts as to meats and feasts (ii. 16), to the prejudice of Christ's atoning work (ii. 13 ff.), they at the same time—and this forms their distinctive character—put forward *a philosophy as to the higher spirit-world*, with the fancies and subtleties of which (ii. 18) were combined, as practical errors, a conceited *humility, worship of angels*, and unsparing *bodily asceticism* (ii. 20–23)— extravagances of an unhealthy *Gnosis*, that could not fail to find a fruitful soil in the mystico-fanatical character of the Phrygian people, which served as an appropriate abode formerly for the orgiastic cultus of Cybele, and subsequently for Montanism.[1] These theosophists, however, came most keenly into conflict with the exalted rank and the redeeming work of Christ, to whom they did not leave His full divine dignity (as εἰκὼν τοῦ Θεοῦ κ.τ.λ., i. 15 ff.), but preferred to assign to

---

[1] The *theosophic* tendency, which haunted Colossae, may help to explain the fact that Paul does not make use, as in the Epistle to the Galatians, of arguments *derived from the O. T.* The epistle contains no quotation from Scripture.

Him merely a rank in the higher order of spirits, while they ascribed to the angels a certain action in bringing about the Messianic salvation, entertaining, probably, at the same time, *demiurgic* ideas as to the creation of the world. We must not conclude from i. 18, ii. 12, that they also rejected the resurrection of Christ; into such an important point as this Paul would have entered directly and at length, as in 1 Cor. xv. But that in dualistic fashion they looked on matter as evil, may be reasonably inferred from their adoration of spirits, and from their asceticism mortifying the body, as well as from the at all events kindred phenomenon of later Gnosticism.

Attempts have been made in very different ways to ascertain more precisely the *historical* character of the Colossian false teachers, and on this point we make the following remarks : (1) They appear as Jewish-*Christians,* not as *Jews* (in opposition to which see ii. 19), which they were held to be by Schoettgen, Eichhorn, and others, some looking on them as *Pharisees* (Schoettgen ; comp. Schulthess, *Engelwelt,* p. 110 f.) ; others, as *indirect opponents* of Christianity through the semblance of more than earthly sanctity (Eichhorn) ; others, as adherents of the *Alexandrine Neo-Platonism* (doctrine of the Logos) (so Juncker, *Kommentar,* Introd. p. 43 ff.) ; others, as *Chaldaeans* or Magians (Hug); others, as *syncretistic universalists,* who would have allowed to Christ a subordinate position in their doctrinal structure and passed Christianity off as a stage of Judaism (Schneckenburger, last in the *Stud. u. Krit.* 1832, p. 840 f.; in opposition to him, Rheinwald, *de pseudodoct. Coloss.* Bonn, 1834). Just as little were they *adherents of a heathen philosophy,* whether they might be looked upon as of the *Epicurean* (Clemens Alexandrinus), or of the *Pythagorean* (Grotius), or of the *Platonic and Stoic* (Heumann) *school,* or of *no definite school* at all (Tertullian, Euthalius, Calixtus). (2) The right view of these false teachers, in accordance with history, necessarily carries us back to *Essenism.* In opposition to the opinion that they were Christian *Essenes* (so Chemnitz, Zachariae, Storr, Flatt, Credner, Thiersch, *histor. Ständp.* p. 270 f., Ritschl, Ewald, Holtzmann, *et al.*), it is not to be urged that the Essene *washings,* and various other peculiarities of Essenism,

remain unnoticed in the epistle; or that the secluded and
exclusive character peculiar to this society, and the limitation
of their abode to Syria and Palestine, do not suit the case of
the Colossian heretics; or that the hypocrisy, conceit, and
persuasiveness which belonged to the latter do not harmonize
with the character of the Essenes, as it is otherwise attested.
These difficulties are got rid of by comparison with the Roman
ascetics (Rom. xiv.), who likewise were Essene Jewish-Christians, only more unprejudiced and inoffensive than these
Asiatics, whose peculiar character, which had already received
a more Gnostic development and elaboration, was of a philosophic stamp, addicted to rhetorical art, full of work - piety
and hypocrisy, and therefore fraught with more danger to
Pauline Christianity, the greater the opportunity they had, just
then whilst the great apostle was himself far away and in
bonds, of raising their head. Now, if at that time the
Essene influence was not at all unfrequent among the Jews,
and thence also among Jewish-Christians (see Ritschl, *altkath. Kirche*, p. 232 ff., and in the *Theolog. Jahrb.* 1855,
p. 355), and if, beyond doubt, the theosophy of the Essenes
—kindred with the Alexandrine philosophy, although in origin
Jewish—and their asceticism (see Joseph. *Bell.* ii. 8; Philo,
Quod omnis probus liber, p. 876 ff.; Euseb. *Praep. ev.* viii. 11 ff.),
as well as their adherence to their tradition (Joseph. *l.c.* ii.
8. 7; comp. Credner, *Beitr.* I. p. 369), are very much in
accord with the characteristic marks of our heretics (comp.
generally Keim, *Gesch. Jesu*, I. p. 286 ff.), the latter are with
justice designated as Jewish-Christian *Gnostics*, or more accurately, as *Gnostics* addicted to an *Essene* tendency.[1] This
designation, however, is not to be taken in the sense of any
subsequently elaborated system, but must be understood as
intimating that in the doctrines of our theosophists there were
apparent the widely-spread, and especially in Essenism strongly-
asserted, *elements* of Gnosticism, out of which the formal
Gnostic systems were afterwards gradually and variously developed (comp. Böhmer, *Isag.* p. 56 ff.; Neander, *Gelegenheitsschr.*

[1] Comp. Grau, *Entwickelungsgesch. d. n. t. Schriftth.* II. p. 145 ff.; Lipsius
in Schenkel's *Bibel-Lexic.* II. p. 498.

p. 40 ff. ; Schott, *Isag.* p. 272 ; Weiss, *l.c.* p. 720 ; Grau, *l.c.* ;
Holtzmann, p. 296 ff. ; Clemens in Hilgenfeld's *Zeitschr.* 1871,
p. 418 ff.).   Among the latter, the *Cerinthian* doctrine in particular is, in various points, closely allied with that combated
in our epistle (comp. F. Nitzsch on Bleek, *Vorles.* p. 15 f. ;
Lipsius, *d. Gnosticismus*, 1860, p. 81 f.), although we are not
justified in considering with Mayerhoff that this polemic was
already directed against Cerinthus and his adherents, and
thence arguing against the genuineness of the epistle.   A
similar judgment is to be formed regarding their relation to the
Valentinians, who often appealed to the Epistle to the Ephesians ; and Baur leaps much too rapidly to a conclusion,
when he thinks (*Paulus,* II. p. 4 ff.) that in the Colossian false
teachers are to be found the *Gnostic Ebionites* (who no doubt
originated from Essenism)—thereby making our epistle a product of the fermentation of the post-apostolic age, and connecting it as a spurious twin-letter with that to the Ephesians.
Holtzmann forms a much more cautious judgment, when he
takes his stand at a *preliminary stage* of Gnosticism ; but even
this he places in the post-apostolic age,—a position which the
less admits of proof, seeing that we have no other letter from
the later period of the apostle's life before the letters of the
captivity and subsequent to that to the Romans, and possess
for comparison no letter of Paul at all addressed to those
regions where the Gnostic movements had their seat.   The false
teachers have, moreover, been designated as *Cabbalistic* (Herder,
Kleuker, Osiander in the *Tüb. Zeitschr.* 1834, 3, p. 96 ff.) ;
but this must likewise be restricted to the effect that the
theosophic tendency generally, the special Essene-Christian
shape of which Paul had to combat, may have probably been
at bottom akin to the subsequently developed Cabbala, although
the origin of this Jewish metaphysics is veiled in obscurity.
(3) We must decidedly set aside, were it only on account of
the legal strictness of the men in question, the assumption of
Michaelis, that they were *disciples of Apollos,* to whom Heinrichs adds also *disciples of John,* as well as Essenes and other
Judaistic teachers, and even a *malevolum hominum genus ex
ethnicis*—of which, in itself extremely improbable, medley the

epistle itself contains no trace. (4) In contrast to all previous attempts to classify the Colossian false teachers, Hofmann prefers to abide by the position that they were Jewish Christians, " who, starting from the presupposition that the Gentile Christians, in their quality as belonging to Ethnicism, were subject to the spirits antagonistic to God which ruled therein, recommended—with a view to complete their state of salvation, which, it was alleged, in this respect needed supplement—a sanctification of the outward life, based partly on the Sinaitic law, partly on dogmas of natural philosophy." But this cannot be made good as an adequate theory by the explanation of the characteristic individual traits, since, on the contrary, that theosophico - Judaistic false teaching presents sufficient evidences of its having its historical root in Essenism, and its further development and diversified elaboration in the later Gnosticism, provided that with unprejudiced exegesis we follow the apostle's indications in regard to the point; see especially on ii. 16–23.

In *date* and *place of composition* our epistle coincides with that to the Ephesians, and is, like the latter, to be assigned not, in conformity with the usual opinion, to the *Roman*, but to the *Caesarean* captivity of the apostle. See on Eph. *Introd.* § 2. In opposition to this view,[1] de Wette, Bleek, and others attach decisive importance specially to two points : (1) That what Paul says in Col. iv. 3, 11 of his labours for the gospel harmonizes with Acts xxviii. 31, but not with his sojourn in Caesarea, Acts xxiv. 23. But iv. 11 contains no special statement at all as to the labours of the apostle in captivity, and as to iv. 3 we must observe that he there expresses the longing for *future* free working. The latter remark applies also in opposition to Wieseler (*Chronol. des apostol. Zeitalt.* p. 420) and Hofmann, who likewise regard iv. 3 f. as decisive in favour of the Roman captivity, while Hofmann finds the statement as to Mark and Jesus contained in iv. 11 incompatible with the situation in Caesarea (but see *in loc.*). In assuming that

---

[1] Which, with Hausrath, Laurent, and others, Sabatier also (*l'apôtre Paul,* 1870, p. 193 ff.) prefers, while Weiss leaves the point undecided. Hofmann rejects our view, and Holtzmann does not find it the more probable.

the conversion of the *Gentile* Onesimus (Philem. 10) is incompatible with the statement in Acts xxiv. 23, Wieseler infers *too much* from the words τῶν ἰδίων αὐτοῦ (Acts xxiv. 23), especially as the intention of a *liberal* custody is obvious in the arrangement of Felix.   (2) That *in Rome* Paul might have thought of the journey to Phrygia hoped for at Philem. 22, but not *in Caesarea* (comp. Hofmann, p. 217), where, according to Acts xix. 21, Rom. i. 13, xv. 23 ff., Acts xxiii. 11, he had the design of going to Rome, but a return to Asia Minor would have been, after his language in Acts xx. 25, far from his thoughts.   But although certainly, when he spoke the words recorded in Acts xx. 25, a return to Asia was far from his thoughts, nevertheless this idea might subsequently occur to him just as easily at *Caesarea* as at *Rome ;* indeed more easily, for, if Paul had been set free at Caesarea, he could *combine* his intended journey to Rome with a passage through Asia. There is no doubt that when at Rome he expressed the hope (Phil. ii. 24) of again visiting the scene of his former labours ; but why should he not have done the same when at Caesarea, so long, namely, as his appeal to the emperor had not taken place ?   See also on Philem. 22.—If our epistle was written in Caesarea, the *time* of its composition was the year 60 or 61, while the procuratorship was still in the hands of Felix.

As regards the *contents* of the epistle, after the salutation (i. 1 f.), a thanksgiving (i. 3–8), and intercessory prayer (i. 9–12), Paul passes on (ver. 12) to the blessedness of the redemption which his readers had obtained through Christ, whose dignity and work are earnestly and very sublimely set before their minds with reference to the dangers arising from heresy (i. 13–23).   Next Paul testifies to, and gives the grounds for, the joy which he now felt in his sufferings as an apostle (i. 24–29).   By way of preparation for his warnings against the false teachers, he next expresses his great care for his readers and all other Christians who do not personally know him, as concerns their Christian advancement (ii. 1–3), and then subjoins the warnings themselves in detail (ii. 4–23). Next follow moral admonitions (iii. 1–iv. 6) ; a commendatory mention of Tychicus and Onesimus (iv. 7–9); salutations with commendations and injunctions (iv. 10–17); and the conclusion appended by the apostle's own hand (ver. 18).

§ 3. GENUINENESS.

Even if it be allowed that the apparent allusions to our Epistle which one might find in the apostolic Fathers (Clement, Barnabas, Ignatius) are uncertain, and that even the mention of πρωτότοκος πάσης κτίσεως in Justin Mart. c. Tryph. p. 311 (comp. p. 310, 326), and Theophil. ad Autol. ii. 31, may be independent of Col. i. 15, still the *external* attestation of our Epistle is so ancient, continuous, and general (Marcion, the school of Valentinus; Irenaeus, *Haer.* iii. 14. 1 and v. 14. 2, who first cites it by name; Canon Murat.; Clem. Al. *Strom.* i. p. 277, iv. p. 499, v. p. 576, vi. p. 645; Tert. *Praescr.* 7, *de resurr.* 23; Origen, *c. Cels.* v. 8, etc.), that no well-founded doubt can from this quarter be raised.

But modern criticism has assailed the Epistle on *internal* grounds; and the course of its development has been as follows. Mayerhoff (*d. Brief an die Kol. mit vornehml. Berücksicht. d. Pastoralbr. kritisch geprüft*, Berl. 1838) assumed the genuineness of the Epistle to the Ephesians, to the prejudice of our Epistle (de Wette inverts the procedure to the prejudice of the Ephesian Epistle); Baur, on the other hand (*Paulus*, II. p. 8 ff.), rejected both the cognate Epistles; comp. also Schwegler, *nachapost. Zeitalt.* II. p. 325 ff. According to Weisse (*philos. Dogmat.* I. p. 146), our Epistle, like most of the Pauline letters, is pervaded by interpolations. Hitzig also (*zur Kritik paulin. Briefe*, 1870, p. 22 ff.) asserts their presence, and ascribes them to the author of the (un-Pauline) Ephesian Epistle, who, after the composition of his own work, had manipulated afresh a Pauline letter to the Colossians, the genuine text of which he misunderstood. In assigning his reasons for this view, Hitzig does not go beyond the bounds of bare assertions and misunderstandings on his own part. Hoenig (in Hilgenfeld's *Zeitschr.* 1872, p. 63 ff.), after comparing the two kindred letters, propounds the view that all those passages of the Epistle to the Colossians are to be regarded as interpolations, regarding which it can be shown that the author of the (not genuine) Epistle to the Ephesians did not know them. But Hoenig has reserved to a future time the exhibition of the detailed grounds for this bold view, and has consequently for the present withdrawn it from criticism. After thorough investigation, Holtzmann (*Kritik d. Epheser- u. Kolosserbriefe*, 1872) has arrived at the hypothesis of a great series of interpolations, the author of which was none other than the author of the Epistle to the Ephesians written, according to Holtzmann, somewhere about the year 100, who, with the help of this writing of his own, had worked up the short and genuinely Pauline letter to the Colossians, which he found in existence, into a new and amplified form, and thereby rescued it in a second enlarged edition from oblivion. But neither can the course of interpolation thus set forth be exegetically verified, nor can it—seeing that all the witnesses from the beginning prove only the present shape of the letter, and no trace has been left of any earlier one —be without arbitrariness rendered critically intelligible, as in fact such a procedure on the part of an interpolator, who had withal so much mastery of free movement in the sphere of Pauline thought and language that he could write the Epistle to the Ephesians, would yield a laborious and—as overlaying and obscuring the given nucleus—somewhat clumsy mosaic patchwork, which, from a psychological point of view, would be hardly conceivable.

Mayerhoff, in order to characterize the Epistle as a production of possibly the second century epitomized from the Epistle to the Ephesians with the addition of some controversial matter, lays stress on (a) differences in language and style, (b) deviations from the Pauline character both of conception and of representation, (c) the comparison with the Epistle to the Ephesians, and (d) the supposed reference of the polemics to Cerinthus. But, first, the stamp of language and the style are so entirely Pauline, that particular expressions, which we are accustomed to in Paul's writings but do not find here (δικαιοσύνη κ.τ.λ., σωτηρία κ.τ.λ., ἀποκάλυψις, ὑπακοή, ἄρα, διό, διότι, ἔτι, et al.), or ἅπαξ λεγόμενα which occur (as ἐθελοθρησκεία, πιθανολογία, et al.), cannot furnish any counter argument, since, in fact, they are fully outweighed by similar phenomena in epistles which are indubitably genuine. There is the less ground for urging the occurrence only six times of γάρ (*Text. Rec.*), as even in the larger Epistle to the Ephesians it occurs only eleven times, and in the Second Epistle to the Thessalonians only five times. And how little are such mechanical standards of comparison at all compatible with a mind so free in movement and rich in language as was that of Paul! In his case even the order of the words Ἕλλην καὶ Ἰουδαῖος (iii. 11) cannot seem surprising, nor can the combining of designations similar in meaning (as i. 6, 10, ii. 18, 23) appear as a strange hunting after synonyms. See, besides, Huther, *Schlussbetracht.* p. 420 ff.; Hofmann, p. 179 f. Secondly, un-Pauline conceptions are only imported into the Epistle by incorrect interpretations; and the peculiar developments of doctrine, which Paul gives only here, but which are in no case without their preliminary conditions and outlines in the earlier Epistles, were suggested to him by the special occasion of the letter (as, in particular, the development of the relation of Christ to the angel-world). And if the Epistle is said to lack in its dogmatic portion the logical arrangement which is found in the hortatory portion (the reverse being the case in the genuine Epistles); if Pauline freshness and vigour are said to be wanting, and poverty of thought to prevail; these are judgments which in some cases are utterly set aside by a right exegesis, and in others are of a partisan character and aesthetically incorrect. The complaint, in particular, of " poverty of thought" is characteristic of the procedure of such criticism towards its victims, no matter how precarious a subjective standard must ever be in such questions, or how various may be the judgments which are put forth as based on taste (according to Böhmer, *Isag.* p. 160, our Epistle is " *viva, pressa, solida, nervis plena, mascula*"). Thirdly, the affinity of our Epistle with that to the Ephesians in style and contents is explained by their composition at the same time,

—as respects which, however, the priority lies with our letter, —and by the analogy of the circumstances giving occasion to write, which in either case the apostle had in view.[1] See on Eph. Introd. § 3.   Lastly, the assertion that Cerinthus is assailed is erroneous—a critical *prothysteron ;* see § 2.

Baur,[2] who describes the Epistle to the Ephesians and that to the Colossians, which are held at any rate to stand or fall together, as un-Pauline, and places the former in a secondary relation to the latter, looks upon this latter as combating an Ebionitism, which would have nothing to do with a recognition of the universalism of Christianity at the cost of renouncing everything that was incompatible with the absoluteness of the Christian principle. He holds, however, that this universalism was not that based on the Pauline anthropology, but only the external universalism, which consisted in the coalition between Gentiles and Jews effected by the death of Christ, and in which, alongside of the forgiveness of sin, the Clementines placed the aim of Christ's death. Thus, according to Baur, the Epistles to the Ephesians and Colossians are to be placed in the post-apostolic period of a conciliation between Jewish and Gentile Christianity. The highest expression of this conciliatory destination is the Christology of the Epistles, in so far, namely, as Christ appears as the primordial principle of all being, and His whole work onward to His exaltation as the self-realization of this idea, according to which the pre-existence is the main point of the Christology. The arguments of Baur are mostly derived from the Epistle to the Ephesians ; those that particularly affect our Epistle, and are supposed to attest a *Gnostic* stamp impressed on it (such as the idea of Christ as the central point of the whole kingdom of spirits, the notion of the πλήρωμα, etc.), will be shown by the exposition to be a homogeneous development of elements of

---

[1] The assertion is being constantly repeated, that Paul could not have copied himself. But, in fact, we have not among the apostle's letters any other two, which were written so immediately at the same time, and to churches whose wants were similar. If we had had two such, who knows but that they would have presented an analogous resemblance ?

[2] Planck, Köstlin, Hilgenfeld, Höckstra (in the *Theolog. Tijdschrift,* 1868), as well as Schwegler, agree in substance with Baur.

doctrine already presented in the earlier Epistles.[1] Concerning these Christological doubts, see, moreover, especially Raebiger, *Christol. Paul.* p. 42 ff., and generally Klöpper, *de orig. epp. ad Eph. et Coloss.* Gryphisw. 1853; Hofmann, p. 181 ff.; Rich. Schmidt, *Paul. Christol.* p. 196 ff.; Sabatier, *l'apôtre Paul,* p. 207 ff.[2] It may be observed in general, that if our Epistle (and that to the Ephesians) is nothing more than a pseudo-apostolic movement of Gnosis against Ebionitism, then every other Epistle is so also, since every other writing in the N. T. may, with almost equal justice, be brought under some such category of subjective presupposition; and that it is in reality inconsistent, if the whole N. T. is not (and for the most part it has already been) made out to be a collection of later books written with some set purpose, which, by means of their pseudo-epigraphic names, have succeeded in deceiving the vigilance of centuries. The *fabrication* of such an epistle *as that to the Colossians* would be more marvellous than its originality. "Non est cujusvis hominis, Paulinum pectus effingere; tonat, fulgurat, meras flammas loquitur Paulus," Erasmus, *Annot. ad* iv. 16.

Ewald has modified the theory of its composition by the apostle in a peculiar way. In his view, the Epistle is indeed planned and carried out quite after the manner of the apostle; but after the contents had been settled by preliminary discussion, Paul committed the composition to Timothy (i. 1), again, however, towards the end, dictating the words more in person, and adding the final salutation (iv. 18) with his own hand. But, first, this hypothesis is already rendered doubtful

---

[1] The exegesis of the Epistle will also dispose of what Hilgenfeld, who rejects the genuineness of the Ephesian and Colossian letters, adduces by way of establishing his assertion, that "the new and characteristic feature of the Colossian Epistle consists simply in this, that it represents Paulinism no longer merely in contradistinction to Jewish Christianity, but also in contradistinction to Gnosticism (proper);" see Hilgenfeld's *Zeitschr.* 1870, p. 245 f. We see, he says, Paulinism in this case not merely *repelling*, but even in part *adopting*, Gnostic elements.—For Baur's Gnostic interpretation of the πλήρωμα, see especially his *Paulus,* II. p. 12 ff., and *Neutest. Theol.* p. 257 ff.

[2] Compare, also generally, in opposition to the hypothesis of a positive influence of Gnosis on N. T. doctrinal ideas, Heinrici, *d. Valent. Gnosis u. d. heil. Schr.* 1871.

by the fact that it is not made to extend uniformly to chap. iv. Secondly, it may be urged against it, that a Timothy himself, even after preliminary discussion with the apostle, could hardly have appropriated or imitated the completely Pauline stamp in such measure, as in this Epistle it recurs at every sentence and in every turn.   Thirdly, the conjectured course of pro-cedure does not appear in any other of Paul's Epistles, and yet the present was one of the shortest and the easiest to be dictated.   Fourthly, such a procedure can scarcely be recon-ciled with the high value and authority, well understood by the apostle, which an Epistle from him could not but possess for any Christian church, especially for one not founded by him-self.   Fifthly, we cannot but naturally regard the concluding salutation by his own hand (iv. 18) as simply the token of his own, and not of a merely indirect, composition (2 Thess. iii. 17).   Sixthly, according to iv. 16, a similar merely indirect composition on his part would have to be attributed also to the Epistle to the Laodiceans, since the two Epistles, as they were to be read in both churches, must have been, as it were, cast in the same mould, and of essentially the same import.   Lastly, the peculiar dangerous character of the spiritualistic Judaism, which had to be opposed in the Epistle, was precisely such as to claim the undivided personal action of the apostle, which was certainly, even in the enforced leisure of his imprisonment, sufficiently within his power for the purpose of his epistolary labours.   The grounds on which the foregoing hypothesis is based[1]—and in the main the assailants of the genuineness

---

[1] Ewald appeals (presupposing, moreover, the non-genuineness of the Epistle to the Ephesians) to the longer compound words, such as ἀνταναπληρόω, ἀπο-καταλλάσσω, ἀπαλλοτρίόω, παραλογίζομαι, ἐθελοθρησκεία, ὀφθαλμοδουλεία ; to un-usual modes of expression, such as θέλω ὑμᾶς εἰδέναι (ii. 1), ὅ ἐστιν for the explanatory *that is* (i. 24 [27], ii. 10, iii. 14), in connections capable of being easily misunderstood ; to the circumstances, that in the progress of the discourse and in the structure of sentences we entirely miss " the exceedingly forcible flow and the exultant ebullition, and then, again, the quick concentration and the firm collocation of the thoughts ;" that the words δέ, γάρ, and ἀλλά are less frequently found, and that the sentences are connected more by simple little rela-tional words and in excessively long series, like the links of a chain, alongside of which is also frequently found the merely rhetorical accumulation of sen-tences left without links of connection (such as i. 14, 20, 25 f., 27, ii. 8, 11, 23,

have already used them—are in part quite unimportant, in part framed after a very subjective standard, and far from adequate in the case of a letter-writer, who stands so high and great in many-sided wealth both of thought and diction and in its free handling as Paul, and who, according to the diversity of the given circumstances and of his own tone of feeling, was capable of, and had the mastery over, so ample and manifold variety in the presentation of his ideas and the structure of his sentences.   Nor do those linguistic difficulties, which Holtzmann, p. 104 ff., has brought forward more discreetly than Mayerhoff, and to some extent in agreement with Ewald, with a view to separate the portions of the letter pertaining to the genuine Paul from those that belong to the manipulator and interpolator, suffice for his object.[1]   They could only be of weight, in the event of their exhibiting modes of expression beyond doubt un-Pauline, or of the interpolated character of the passages in question being already established on other grounds.

iii. 5) ; that we meet delicate but still perceptible distinctions of thought, such as the non-mention of δικαιοσύνη and δικαιοῦν, and the description of the Logos by the word πλήρωμα itself (i. 19, ii. 9) ; that we find a multitude of words and figures peculiarly Pauline, but that we miss all the more the whole apostle in his most vivid idiosyncrasy throughout the main portions of the Epistle ; and that many a word and figure, in fact, appears imitated from the Epistles of Paul, especially that to the Romans.

[1] When we take fully into account the singularly ample storehouse of the Greek language, from which the apostle knew how to draw his materials with so much freedom and variety in all his letters, we shall not be too hastily ready to hold that such expressions, phrases, or turns, as have no parallels in the undisputed letters, at once betray another author ; or, on the other hand, to reckon that such as are characteristic of, and currently used by, the apostle, are due to an assumption of the Pauline manner.

Παύλου ἐπιστολὴ πρὸς Κολοσσαεῖς.

A B K min. Copt. have the superscription πρὸς Κολ.ασσαεῖς. So Matth. Lachm. and Tisch. Comp. on ver. 2.

CHAPTER I.

Ver. 1. The arrangement Χριστοῦ Ἰησοῦ (Lachm. Tisch.) has preponderant testimony in its favour, but not the addition of Ἰησοῦ after Χριστοῦ in ver. 2 (Lachm.). — Ver. 2. Κολοσσαῖς] K P, also C and ℵ in the subscription, min. Syr. utr. Copt. Or. Nyss. Amphiloch. Theodoret, Damasc. *et. al.* have Κολασσαῖς. Approved by Griesb., following Erasm. Steph. Wetst. ; adopted by Matth. Lach. Tisch. 7. The *Recepta* is supported by B D E F G L ℵ, min. Vulg. It. Clem. Chrys. Theophyl. Tert. Ambrosiast. Pelag. The matter is to be judged thus : (1) The name in itself correct is undoubtedly Κολοσσαί, which is supported by coins of the city (Eckhel, *Doctr. num.* III. p. 107) and confirmed by Herod. vii. 30 (see Wessel. and Valck. *in loc.*) ; Xen. *Anab.* i. 2. 6 (see Bornem. *in loc.*) ; Strabo, xii. 8, p. 576 ; Plin. *N. H.* v. 32. (2) But since the form Κολασσαί has so old and considerable attestation, and is preserved in Herodotus and Xenophon as a various reading, as also in Polyaen. viii. 16, and therefore a mere copyist's error cannot be found in the case—the more especially as the copyists, even apart from the analogy which suggested itself to them of the well-known κολοσσός, would naturally be led to the *prevalent* form of the name Κολοσσαί,—we must assume that, although Κολοσσαί was the more formally correct name, still the name Κολασσαί was also (vulgarly) in use, that this was the name which Paul himself wrote, and that Κολοσσαῖς is an ancient *correction.* If the latter had originally a place in the text, there would have been no occasion to alter the generally known and correct form of the name.—After πατρὸς ἡμῶν, Elz. (Lachm. in brackets) has καὶ κυρίου Ἰησοῦ Χριστοῦ, in opposition to B D E K L, min. vss. and Fathers. A complementary addition in accordance with the openings of other epistles, especially as no ground for intentional omission suggests itself (in opposition to Reiche, *Comm. crit.* p. 351 f.). — Ver. 3. καὶ πατρί] Lachm. and Tisch. 7 :

πατρί. So B C*, vss. and Fathers, while D* F G, Chrys. have
τῷ πατρί. Since, however, Paul always writes ὁ Θεὸς καὶ πατὴρ
τοῦ κυρίου (Rom. xv. 6; 2 Cor. i. 3, xi. 31; Eph. i. 3; also 1 Cor.
xv. 24; Eph. v. 20), and never ὁ Θεὸς ὁ πατὴρ τ. κ. or ὁ Θεὸς πατὴρ
τ. κ., the *Recepta*, which has in its favour A C** D*** E K L P א,
min. Vulg. and Fathers, is with Tisch. 8 to be retained. The
καί was readily omitted in a mechanical way after the immediately preceding Θεοῦ πατρός. — Instead of περί, Lachm. reads
ὑπέρ, which is also recommended by Griesb., following B D* E*
F G, min. Theophyl. Not attested by preponderating evidence,
and easily introduced in reference to ver. 9 (where ὑπέρ stands
without variation). — Ver. 4. Instead of ἣν ἔχετε (which is recommended by Griesb., adopted by Lachm. and Tisch.), Elz.
Matth. Scholz have τήν merely, but in opposition to A C D*
E* F G P א, min. vss. (including Vulg. It.) Fathers. If τήν were
originally written, why should it have been exchanged for ἣν
ἔχετε? On the other hand, ἣν ἔχετε, as it could be dispensed
with for the sense, might easily drop out, because the word
preceding concludes with the syllable ΗΝ, and the word following (εἰς), like ἔχετε, begins with Ε. The grammatical gap
would then, following Eph. i. 15, be filled up by τήν. — Ver. 6.
καὶ ἔστι] καί is wanting in A B C D* E* P א, min. and some vss.
and Fathers; condemned by Griesb., omitted by Lachm. and
Tisch. 8. But, not being understood, this καί, which has the
most important vss. and Fathers in its favour, was omitted in
the interest of simplicity as disturbing the connection. — καὶ
αὐξανόμενον] is wanting in Elz. Matth., who is of opinion that
Chrys. introduced it from ver. 10. But it is so decisively
attested, that the omission must be looked upon as caused by
the *homoeoteleuton*, the more especially as a similar ending and a
similar beginning here came together (ΟΝΚΑ). — Ver 7. καθὼς
καί] καί is justly condemned by Griesb. on decisive evidence,
and is omitted by Lachm. and Tisch. A mechanical repetition
from the preceding. — ὑμῶν] A B D* G F א*, min.: ἡμῶν; approved
by Griesb., adopted by Lachm. But since the first person both
precedes and follows (ἡμῶν . . . ἡμῖν), it was put here also by care-
less copyists. — Ver. 10. After περιπατῆσαι, Elz. Tisch. 7 have
ὑμᾶς, against decisive testimony; a supplementary addition. —
εἰς τὴν ἐπίγνωσιν] Griesb. Lachm. Scholz. Tisch. 8 have τῇ ἐπιγνώσει.
So A B C D* E* F G P א, min. Clem. Cyr. Maxim. But it lacks
the support of the vss., which (Vulg. It. *in scientia Dei*) have
read the *Recepta* εἰς τ. ἐπίγν. attested by D*** E** K L and
most min., also Theodoret, Dam. Theophyl. Oec., or with א**
and Chrys. ἐν τῇ ἐπιγνώσει. The latter, as well as the mere τῇ

ἐπιγν., betrays itself as an explanation of the difficult εἰς τ. ἐπίγν., which, we may add, belongs to the symmetrical structure of the whole discourse, the participial sentences of which all conclude with a destination introduced by εἰς. — Ver. 12. ἱκανώσαντι] Lachm.: καλέσαντι καὶ ἱκανώσαντι, according to B, whilst D* F G, min. Arm. Aeth. It. Didym. Ambrosiast. Vigil. have καλέσαντι merely. Looking at the so isolated attestation of καλ. κ. ἱκαν., we must assume that καλέσαντι was written on the margin by way of complement, and then was in some cases inserted with καί, and in others without καί substituted for ἱκανώσ.—Instead of ἡμᾶς, Tisch. 8 has ὑμᾶς; but the latter, too weakly attested by B ℵ, easily slipped in by means of the connection with εὐχαρ. — Ver. 14. After ἀπολυτρ. Elz. has διὰ τοῦ αἵματος αὐτοῦ, against de- cisive testimony; from Eph. i. 7. — Ver. 16. τὰ ἐν τοῖς οὐρανοῖς καὶ τά] Lachm. has erased the first τά and bracketed the second. In both cases the τά is wanting in B ℵ*, Or.; the first τά only is wanting in D* E* F G P and two min. But how easily might TA be absorbed in the final syllable of πάνTA; and this would then partially involve the omission of the second τά! The assump- tion that the final syllable of πάντα was written twice would only be warranted, if the omitting witnesses, especially in the case of the second τά, were stronger. — Ver. 20. The second δι' αὐτοῦ is wanting in B D* F G L, min. Vulg. It. Sahid. Or. Cyr. Chrys. Theophyl. and Latin Fathers. Omitted by Lachm. It was passed over as superfluous, obscure, and disturbing the sense. — Ver. 21. Instead of the Recepta ἀποκατήλλαξεν, Lachm., following B, has ἀποκατηλλάγητε. D* F G, It. Goth. Ir. Am- brosiast. Sedul. have ἀποκαταλλαγέντες. Since, according to this, the passive is considerably attested, and the active ἀποκατήλλαξεν, although most strongly attested (also by ℵ), may well be sus- pected to be a syntactic emendation, we must decide, as between the two passive readings ἀποκατηλλάγητε and ἀποκαταλλαγέντες, in favour of the former, because the latter is quite unsuitable. If the Recepta were original, the construction would be so entirely plain, that we could not at all see why the passive should have been introduced. — Ver. 22. After θανάτου, A P ℵ, min. vss. Ir. have αὐτοῦ, which Lachm. has admitted in brackets. It is attested so weakly, as to seem nothing more than a familiar addition. — Ver. 23. τῇ before κτίσει is, with Lachm. and Tisch., to be omitted, following A B C D* F G ℵ, min. Chrys.—Instead of διάκονος, P ℵ have κήρυξ κ. ἀπόστολος. A gloss; comp. 1 Tim. ii. 7. In A all the three words κήρυξ κ. ἀπ. κ. διακ. are given. — Ver. 24. νῦν] D* E* F G, Vulg. It. Ambrosiast. Pel. have ὅς νῦν. Rightly; the final syllable of διάκονος in ver. 23, and the beginning of a

church-lesson, co-operated to the suppression of ὅς, which, however, is quite in keeping with the connection and the whole
progress of the discourse. — After παθήμ. Elz. has μου, against
decisive testimony. — ὅ ἐστιν] C D* E, min.: ὅς ἐστιν. So Lachm.
in the margin. A copyist's error. — Ver. 27. The neuter τί τὸ
πλοῦτος (Matth. Lachm. Tisch.) is attested by codd. and Fathers
sufficiently to make the masculine appear as an emendation:
comp. on 2 Cor. viii. 2. — ὅς ἐστιν] A B F G P, min. (quod in Vulg.
It. leaves the reading uncertain): ὅ ἐστιν. So Lachm. A grammatical alteration, which, after ver. 24, was all the more likely.
— Ver. 28. After διδάσκ., πάντα ἄνθρωπον is wanting in D* E* F G,
min. vss. and Fathers. Suspected by Griesb., but is to be
defended. The whole καὶ διδάσκ. πάντα ἄνθρωπ. was omitted owing
to the homoeoteleuton (so still in L, min. Clem.), and then the
restoration of the words took place incompletely. — After Χριστῷ
Elz. has Ἰησοῦ, against decisive testimony.

Vv. 1, 2. Διὰ θελήμ. Θεοῦ] see on 1 Cor. i. 1. Comp. 2
Cor. i. 1; Eph. i. 1. — καὶ Τιμόθ.] see on 2 Cor. i. 1; Phil.
i. 1. Here also as subordinate joint-author of the letter, who
at the same time may have been the amanuensis, but is not
here jointly mentioned as such (comp. Rom. xvi. 22). See on
Phil. i. 1. — ὁ ἀδελφός] see on 1 Cor. i. 1; referring, not to
official (Chrys.: οὐκοῦν καὶ αὐτὸς ἀπόστολος), but generally to
Christian brotherhood. — τοῖς ἐν Κολ. ἁγ. κ.τ.λ.] to the saints
who are in Colossae. To this theocratic designation, which in
itself is not as yet more precisely defined (see on Rom. i. 7), is
then added their distinctively Christian character: and believing brethren in Christ. Comp. on Eph. i. 1. ἁγίοις is to be
understood as a substantive, just as in all the commencements
of epistles, where it occurs (Rom. i. 7; 1 Cor.; 2 Cor.; Eph.;
Phil.); and ἐν Χριστῷ is closely connected with πιστ. ἀδ., with
which it blends so as to form one conception (hence it is not
τοῖς ἐν X.), expressly designating the believing brethren as
Christians, so that ἐν X. forms the element of demarcation,
in which the readers are believing brethren, and outside of
which they would not be so in the Christian sense. Comp.
on 1 Cor. iv. 17; Eph. vi. 21; in which passages, however,
πιστός is faithful,—a meaning which it has not here (in opposition to Baumgarten-Crusius, Ewald, Dalmer), because every-

where in the superscriptions of the Epistles it is only the
Christian standing of the readers that is described.   No doubt
ἐν Χριστῷ was in itself hardly necessary ; but the addresses
have a certain *formal* stamp.   If ἁγίοις is taken *as an adjective :* " the holy and believing brethren " (de Wette), ἐν Χριστῷ
being made to apply to the whole formula, then πιστοῖς coming
after ἁγίοις (which latter word *would* already *have*, through
ἐν X., its definition in a *Christian* sense, which, according to
our view, it still has *not*) would be simply a superfluous and
clumsy addition, because ἁγίοις would already *presuppose* the
πιστοῖς. — The fact that Paul does not expressly describe the
church to which he is writing *as a church* (as in 1 Cor. ;
2 Cor. ; Gal. ; 1 and 2 Thess.) has no special motive (comp.
Rom., Eph., Phil.), but is purely accidental.   If it implied
that he had not founded the church and stood in no kind of
relation to it *as such*, and especially to its rulers (de Wette,
by way of query), he would not have written of a Λαοδικέων
ἐκκλησία (iv. 16).   Indeed, the principle of addressing *as
churches* those communities only which he had himself
founded, is not one to be expected from the apostle's disposition of mind and wisdom ; and it is excluded by the inscription
of the Epistle to the Ephesians (assuming its genuineness and
destination for the church at Ephesus), as also by Phil. i. 1
(where the mention of the bishops and deacons would not
compensate for the formal naming of the church).   It is also
an accidental matter that Paul says ἐν Χριστῷ merely, and
not ἐν X. Ἰησοῦ (1 Cor. ; Eph. ; Phil. ; 2 Thess.), although
Mayerhoff makes use of this, among other things, to impugn
the genuineness of the epistle ; just as if such a mechanical
regularity were to be ascribed to the apostle ! — χάρις ὑμῖν
κ.τ.λ.] See on Rom. i. 7.

Ver. 3 f. Thanksgiving for the Christian condition of the
readers, down to ver. 8. — εὐχαριστοῦμεν] I and Timothy ;
plural and singular *alternate* in the Epistle (i. 23, 24, 28,
29 ff., iv. 3) ; but not without significant occasion. — καὶ πατρὶ
κ.τ.λ.] who is at the same time the Father, etc.   See on Eph.
i. 3. — πάντοτε] belongs to εὐχαρ., as in 1 Cor. i. 4 ; 1 Thess.
i. 2 ; 2 Thess. i. 3 ; Philem. 4, and not to περὶ ὑμ. προσευχ.

(Chrysostom, Oecumenius, Theophylact, Erasmus, Luther, Castalio, Beza, Calvin, Grotius, Bengel, and many others, including Böhmer, Olshausen, Dalmer)—a connection opposed to the parallel Eph. i. 16, as well as to the context, according to which the thanksgiving is the main point *here*, and the prayer merely a concomitant definition; and it is not till ver. 9 that the latter is brought forward as the object of the discourse, and that as *unceasing*. This predicate belongs here to the *thanking*, and in ver. 9 to the *praying*, and περὶ ὑμῶν προσευχ. —words which are not, with Bähr, to be separated from one another (whereby προσευχ. would unduly stand without relation)—is nothing but a more precise definition of πάντοτε: "*always* (each *time*, Phil. i. 4; Rom. i. 10 [1]), *when we pray for you.*" — ἀκούσαντες κ.τ.λ.] with reference to time; *after having heard*, etc. Comp. ver. 9. In *that, which* Paul had heard of them, lies the *ground* of his thanksgiving. The πίστις is *faith* (Rom. i. 8; 1 Thess. i. 3; 2 Thess. i. 3) not *faithfulness* (Ewald), as at Philem. 5, where the position of the words is different. That Paul has heard their faith *praised*, is self-evident from the context. Comp. Eph. i. 15; Philem. 5. — ἐν X. 'I.] *on Christ*, in so far, namely, as the faith *has its basis in Christ.* See on Mark i. 15; Gal. iii. 26; Eph. i. 13, 15. As to the non-repetition of τήν, see on Gal. iii. 26.—ἣν ἔχετε] Paul so writes,—not by joining on immediately (τὴν ἀγάπην εἰς πάντας κ.τ.λ.), nor yet by the mere repetition of the article, as in Eph. i. 15 (so the *Recepta*, see the critical remarks),—because he has it in view to enter more fully upon this point of ἀγάπη, and indeed definitely upon the reason *why they cherished it.*

Ver. 5. Διὰ τὴν ἐλπίδα κ.τ.λ.] *on account of the hope*, etc., does not belong to εὐχαρ. ver. 3 (Bengel, " ex *spe* patet, quanta sit causa *gratias agendi* pro dono fidei et amoris ;" comp. Bullinger, Zanchius, Calovius, Elsner, Michaelis, Zachariae, Storr, Rosenmüller, Hofmann, and others), because the ground for the apostolic thanksgiving at the beginnings of the Epistles, as also here at ver. 4, always consists in the Christian character of the readers (Rom. i. 8; 1 Cor. i. 4 ff.; Eph. i. 15; Phil. i. 5; 1 Thess. i. 3; 2 Thess. i. 3; 2 Tim. i. 5; Philem. 5),

[1] For a like use of ἀεί, see Stallbaum, *ad Plat. Rep.* p. 360 A.

and that indeed as a *ground in itself*,[1] and therefore not merely on account of what one has in future to hope from it; and, moreover, because εὐχαριστεῖν with διά and the accusative does not occur anywhere in the N. T.   It is connected with ἣν ἔχετε κ.τ.λ., and thus specifies the motive ground of the *love;* for love guarantees the realization of the salvation hoped for.   So correctly, Chrysostom, Theodoret, Oecumenius, Theophylact, Erasmus, Calvin, Estius, Steiger, Bleek, and others.   The more faith is active through love, the richer one becomes εἰς Θεόν (Luke xii. 21), and this riches forms the contents of hope.   He who does not love remains subject to death (1 John iii. 14), and his faith profits him nothing (1 Cor. xiii. 1–3).   It is erroneous to refer it *jointly* to πίστις, so as to make the hope appear here as ground of the *faith and* the love; so Grotius and others, including Bähr, Olshausen, and de Wette; comp. Baumgarten-Crusius and Ewald.   For ἣν ἔχετε (or the *Rec.* τήν) indicates a further statement merely as regards τὴν ἀγάπην; and with this accords the close of the whole outburst, which in ver. 8 emphatically reverts to τὴν ὑμῶν ἀγάπην. — The ἐλπίς is here conceived *objectively* (comp. ἐλπ. βλεπομένη, Rom. viii. 24): our hope *as to its objective contents*, that *which* we hope for.   Comp. Job vi. 8; 2 Macc. vii. 14, and see on Rom. viii. 24 and Gal. v. 5; Zöckler, *de vi ac notione voc.* ἐλπίς, Giss. 1856, p. 26 ff. — τὴν ἀποκειμ. ὑμῖν ἐν τ. οὐρ.] What is meant is the *Messianic salvation* forming the contents of the hope (1 Thess. v. 8; Rom. v. 2, viii. 18 ff.; Col. iii. 3 f.), which remains *deposited*, that is, *preserved, laid up* (Luke xix. 20), in heaven for the Christian until the Parousia, in order to be then given to him.[2]   On ἀποκ. comp. 2 Tim. iv. 8; 2 Macc. xii. 45; Kypke, II. p. 320 f.; Loesner, p. 360; Jacobs, *ad Ach. Tat.* p. 678. Used of death, Heb. ix. 27; of punishments, Plat. *Locr.*

---

[1] In opposition to the view of Hofmann, that Paul names the reason *why* the news of the faith and love of the readers had become to him a cause of thanksgiving.

[2] It is erroneous to say that the Parousia no longer occurs in our Epistle.   It is the substratum of the ἐλπὶς ἀποκ. ἐν τ. οὐρ.   Comp. iii. 1 ff. (in opposition to Mayerhoff, and Holtzmann, p. 203 f.).

p. 104 D, 4 Macc. viii. 10. As to the idea, comp. the conception
of the treasure in heaven (Matt. vi. 20, xix. 21 ; 1 Tim. vi. 19),
of the reward in heaven (see on Matt. v. 12), of the πολίτευμα
in heaven (see on Phil. iii. 20), of the κληρονομία τετηρημένη
ἐν οὐραν. (1 Pet. i. 4), and of the βραβεῖον τῆς ἄνω κλήσεως
(Phil. iii. 14). — ἣν προηκούσατε κ.τ.λ.] *Certainty* of this hope,
which is not an unwarranted subjective fancy, but is objectively conveyed to them through the word of truth previously
announced. The πρό in προηκούσατε (Herod. viii. 79 ; Plat.
Legg. vii. p. 797 A ; Xen. *Mem.* ii. 4. 7 ; Dem. 759. 26, 955. 1 ;
Joseph. *Antt.* viii. 12. 3) does not denote *already formerly,*
whereby Paul premises *se nihil allaturum novi* (Calvin and
many), but must be said with reference to the *future,* to which
the hope belongs ; hence the sense imported by Ewald : *wherewith the word of truth began among you* (Mark i. 15), is the
less admissible. The conception is rather, that the contents
of the ἐλπίς, the heavenly salvation, is the great *future* blessing, the infallible *pre-announcement* of which *they have heard.*
As previously *announced,* it is also previously *heard.* — τῆς
ἀληθείας is the *contents* of the λόγος (comp. on Eph. i. 13) ;
and by τοῦ εὐαγ., the ἀλήθεια, that is, the absolute truth, is
specifically defined as that *of the gospel,* that is, as that *which
is announced in the gospel.* Both genitives are therefore to be
left in their *substantive* form (Erasmus, Heinrichs, Baumgarten-
Crusius, and many others understand τῆς ἀληθ. as adjectival :
sermo verax; comp. on the contrary, on ἀλήθ. τοῦ εὐαγγ., Gal.
ii. 5, 14), so that the expression advances to greater definiteness. The circumstantiality has something *solemn* about it
(comp. 2 Cor. ix. 4) ; but this is arbitrarily done away, if we
regard τοῦ εὐαγγ. as the genitive of apposition to τῷ λόγῳ τῆς
ἀληθ. (Calvin, Beza, and many others, including Flatt, Bähr,
Steiger, Böhmer, Huther, Olshausen, de Wette, Hofmann) ;
following Eph. i. 13, Paul would have written τῷ εὐαγγελίῳ.

Ver. 6. In what he had just said, ἣν προηκούσατε . . .
εὐαγγελίου, Paul now desires to make his readers sensible of
the *great and blessed fellowship* in which, through the gospel,
they are placed, in order that they may by this very consciousness feel themselves aroused to faithfulness towards the

COL. R

gospel, in presence of the heretical influences; ἐπειδὴ μάλιστα οἱ πολλοὶ ἐκ τοῦ κοινωνοὺς ἔχειν πολλοὺς τῶν δογμάτων στηρίζονται, Chrysostom. Comp. Oecumenius : προθυμοτέρους αὐτοὺς περὶ τὴν πίστιν ποιεῖ ἐκ τοῦ ἔχειν πάντας κοινωνούς. — εἰς ὑμᾶς] not ἐν ὑμῖν, because the conception of the previous *arrival* predominates ; 1 Macc. xi. 63. Often so with παρεῖναι in classical authors (Herod. i. 9, vi. 24, viii. 60; Polyb. xviii. 1. 1; comp. Acts xii. 20). See Bornemann and Kühner, *ad Xen. Anab.* i. 2. 2 ; Bremi, *ad Aeschin.* p. 320 ; and generally, Nägelsbach, *z. Ilias*, p. 158 f., ed. 3. Observe, moreover, the emphasis of τοῦ παρόντος: *it is there!* it has not remained away ; and to the *presence* is then added the *bearing fruit.*— καθὼς καὶ ἐν παντὶ τ. κόσμῳ] A popular hyperbole. Comp. Rom. i. 8; Acts xvii. 6, and see ver. 23. The expression is neither arbitrarily to be restricted, nor to be used against the genuineness of the Epistle (Hilgenfeld), nor yet to be rationalized by "as regards the *idea*" (Baumgarten-Crusius) and the like; although, certainly, the idea of the catholicity of Christianity is expressed in the passage (comp. Rom. x. 18 ; Mark xiv. 9, xvi. 15 ; Matt. xxiv. 14).—καὶ ἔστι καρποφ. κ.τ.λ.] Instead of continuing : καὶ καρποφορουμένου κ.τ.λ., Paul carries onward the discourse with the finite verb, and thus causes this element to stand out more independently and forcibly :[1] "*and it is fruit-bearing and growing*" (see Maetzner, *ad Lycurg. Leocr.* p. 108 ; Heindorf, *ad Plat. Soph.* p. 222 B ; Winer, p. 533 [E. T. 717]), by which is indicated the fact, that the gospel, wherever it is present, is also in course of living dynamical *development*, and this *state* of development is expressed by ἔστι with the participle. This *general* proposition based on experience : καὶ ἔστι καρποφ. κ. αὐξαν., is then by καθὼς κ. ἐν

---

[1] If καί is not genuine, as Bleck, Hofmann, and others consider (see the critical remarks), the passage is to be translated : *as it also in the whole world is fruit-bearing*, by which Paul would say that the gospel is present among the readers in the same fruit-bearing quality which it developes on all sides. But in that case the following καθὼς καὶ ἐν ὑμῖν would necessarily appear as very superfluous. No doubt we might, after the preceding παρόντος, take the ἐστί with F. Nitzsch, as equivalent to πάρεστι (see Stallb. *ad Plat. Phaed.* p. 59 B) ; and to this comes also the punctuation in Tisch. 8, who puts a comma after ἐστίν. But how utterly superfluous would this ἐστί then be!

ὑμῖν confirmed through the experience found *also among the readers ;* so that Paul's view passes, in the first clause (τοῦ παρόντος . . . κόσμῳ), from the special to the general aspect, and in the second, from the general to the special. With καρποφορ. (not occurring elsewhere in the *middle*) is depicted the blissful *working in the inward and outward life* (comp. Gal. v. 22; Eph. v. 9) ; and with αὐξανόμ. the continuous *diffusion*, whereby the gospel is obtaining more and more adherents and local extension. Comp. Theodoret : καρποφορίαν τοῦ εὐαγγ. κέκληκε τὴν ἐπαινουμένην πολιτείαν αὔξησιν δὲ τῶν πιστευόντων τὸ πλῆθος. Huther and de Wette groundlessly refrain from deciding whether αὐξ. is intended to refer to the *outward* growth or to the *inward* (so Steiger), or to *both.* See Acts vi. 7, xii. 24, xix. 20. Comp. Luke xiii. 19 ; Matt. xiii. 32. The μᾶλλον στηρίζεσθαι, which Chrysostom finds *included* in αὐξ., is not *denoted,* but *presupposed* by the latter. Comp. Theophylact. The *figure* is taken from a *tree,* in which the καρποφορία does not exclude the continuance of growth (not so in the case of cereals). — ἀφ' ἧς ἡμέρ. κ.τ.λ.] since the first beginning of your conversion which so happily took place (through true knowledge of the grace of God), that development of the gospel proceeds among you ; how could ye now withdraw from it by joining yourselves to false teachers ? — τὴν χάριν τοῦ Θεοῦ] *contents* of the gospel, which they have heard ; the object of ἠκούσ. is the gospel, and τ. χάριν τ. Θεοῦ belongs to ἐπέγνωτε ; and by ἐν ἀληθείᾳ (2 Cor. vii. 14), equivalent to ἀληθῶς (John xvii. 8), the *qualitative character* of this knowledge is affirmed : it was a *true* knowledge, corresponding to the nature of the χάρις, *without* Judaistic and other *errors.* Comp. on John xvii. 19. Holtzmann hears in ἠκούσατε . . . ἀληθῶς "the first tones of the foreign theme," which is then in vv. 9, 10 more fully entered upon. But how conceivable and natural is it, that at the very outset the danger which threatens the right knowledge of the readers should be present to his mind !

Ver. 7 f. Καθώς] not *quandoquidem* (Flatt, comp. Bähr), but the *as* of the *manner in which.* So, namely, as it had just been affirmed by ἐν ἀληθείᾳ that they had *known* the divine grace, had they *learned* it (comp. Phil. iv. 9) *from Epaphras.*

Notwithstanding this appropriate connection, Holtzmann finds
in this third καθώς a trace of the interpolator. — Nothing
further is known from any other passage as to *Epaphras* the
Colossian (iv. 12) ; according to Philem. 23, he was συναιχμάλωτος of the apostle. That the latter circumstance is *not
mentioned* in our Epistle is not to be attributed to any special
design (Estius : that Paul was unwilling to make his readers
anxious). See, on the contrary, on iv. 10. Against the
identity of Epaphras with *Epaphroditus*, see on Phil. ii. 25.
The *names* even are not alike (contrary to the view of Grotius
and Ewald, who look upon *Epaphras* as an abbreviation) ;
'Επαφρᾶς and the corresponding feminine name 'Επαφρώ are
found on Greek inscriptions. — συνδούλου] namely, of *Christ*
(comp. Phil. i. 1). The word, of common occurrence, is used
elsewhere by Paul in iv. 7 only. — ὅς ἐστιν κ.τ.λ.] This
faithfulness towards the readers, and also, in the sequel, the
praise of their love, which Epaphras expressed to the apostle,
are intended to stir them up " ne a doctrina, quam ab eo didi-
cerant, per novos magistros abduci se patiantur," Estius. The
emphasis is on πιστός. — ὑπὲρ ὑμῶν] for, as their teacher, he
is the servant of Christ *for them, for their benefit.* The interpretation, *instead of you* (" in prison he serves me in the
gospel," Michaelis, Böhmer), would only be possible in the
event of the service being designated as rendered *to the apostle*
(διάκονός μου ἐν Χριστῷ, or something similar). Comp.
Philem. 13. Even with Lachmann's reading, ὑπ. ἡμῶν
(Steiger, Olshausen, Ewald), it would not be necessary to take
ὑπέρ as *instead ;* it might equally well be taken as *for* in
the sense of interest, as opposite of the *anti-Pauline* working (comp. Luke ix. 50). The *present* ἐστί (Paul does not put
ἦν) has its just warrant in the fact, that the merit, which the
founder of the church has acquired by its true instruction, is
living and continuous, reaching in its efficacy down to the
present time. This is an *ethical* relation, which is quite independent of the circumstance that Epaphras was himself a
Colossian (in opposition to Hofmann), but also makes it unnecessary to find in ἐστι an *indirect continuance* of Epaphras'
work for the Colossians (in opposition to Bleek).— ὁ καὶ δηλώσας

κ.τ.λ.] *who also* (in accordance with the interest of this faithful service) *has made us to know;* comp. 1 Cor. i. 11. The ἀγάπη is here understood either of the love of the Colossians *to Paul* (and Timothy), as, following Chrysostom, most, including Huther, Bleek, and Hofmann,[1] explain it, or of the *brotherly love* already commended in ver. 4 (de Wette, Olshausen, Ellicott, and others). But both these modes of taking it are at variance with the emphatic position of ὑμῶν (comp. 1 Cor. ix. 12 ; 2 Cor. i. 6, vii. 7, viii. 13, *et al.*), which betokens the love of the readers to *Epaphras* as meant. There had just been expressed, to wit, by ὑπὲρ ὑμῶν, the faithful, loving position of this servant of Christ *towards the Colossians,* and correlative to this is now the love *which he met with from them,* consequently *the counter-love* shown to him, of which he has informed the apostle. A delicate addition *out of courtesy* to the readers. — ἐν πνεύματι] attaches itself closely to ἀγάπην, so as to form one idea, denoting the love as truly *holy*—not conditioned by anything outward, but divinely upheld—which is *in the Holy Spirit* as the element which prompts and animates it ; for it is the fruit of the Spirit (Gal. v. 22 ; Rom. xv. 30), οὐ σαρκική, ἀλλὰ πνευματική (Oecumenius). Comp. χαρὰ ἐν πν., Rom. xiv. 17.

REMARK.—Since ἀφ᾽ ἧς ἡμέρας ἠκούσατε κ.τ.λ.., ver. 6, refers the readers back to the first commencement of their Christianity, and καθὼς ἐμάθετε ἀπὸ Ἐπαφρᾶ κ.τ.λ., ver. 7, cannot, except by pure arbitrariness, be separated from it as regards time and regarded as something later, it results from our passage that Epaphras is to be considered as the *first* preacher of the gospel at Colossae, and consequently as *founder of the church.* This exegetical result remains even if the *Recepta* καθὼς καί is retained. This καί would not, as Wiggers thinks (in the *Stud. u. Krit.* 1838, p. 185), place the preaching of Epaphras in contradistinction to an earlier one, and make it appear as a continuation of the latter (in this case καθὼς καὶ ἀπὸ Ἐπαφρ. ἐμάθετε or καθὼς ἐμάθετε καὶ ἀπὸ Ἐπαφρ. would have been employed) ; but it is to be taken as *also, not otherwise,* placing the ἐμάθετε on a parity with the ἐπέγνωτε. This applies also in opposition to Vaihinger, in Herzog's *Encykl.* iv. p. 79 f.

[1] Who, at the same time, makes the ἐν πνεύματι suggest the reference, that the ἀγάπη took place *in a manner personally unknown*—which must have been conveyed in the context.

Ver. 9. *Intercession*, down to ver. 12.— διὰ τοῦτο] on
account of all that has been said from ἀκούσαντες in ver. 4
onward: *induced* thereby, *we also cease not*, etc.   This reference
is required by ἀφ᾽ ἧς ἡμέρας ἠκούσαμεν, which cannot correspond to the δηλώσας ἡμῖν, belonging as that does merely to
an accessory thought, but must take up again (in opposition to
Bleek and Hofmann) the ἀκούσαντες which was said in ver. 4.
This resumption is *emphatic*, not tautological (Holtzmann). —
καὶ ἡμεῖς] *are to be taken together*, and it is not allowable to join
καί either with διὰ τοῦτο (de Wette), or even with προσευχ.
(Baumgarten-Crusius).   The words are to be rendered: *We also*
(I and Timothy), like *others*, who make the same intercession for
you, and among whom there is mentioned by name the founder
of the church, who stood in closest relation to them.—προσευχ.]
"*Precum* mentionem *generatim* fecit, ver. 3; nunc exprimit, *quid*
precetur" (Bengel). — καὶ αἰτούμενοι] adds the special (*asking*)
to the general (*praying*).   Comp. 1 Macc. iii. 44; Matt. xxi.
22; Mark xi. 24; Eph. vi. 18; Phil. iv. 6.   As to the popular
form of hyperbole, οὐ πανόμ., comp. on Eph. i. 16.   On ὑπὲρ
ὑμῶν, so far as it is also to be taken with κ. αἰτούμ., comp.
Lys. c. Alc. p. 141. — ἵνα πληρωθ.] Contents of the asking in
the form of its *purpose*.   Comp. on Phil. i. 9.   The emphasis
lies not on πληρωθ. (F. Nitzsch, Hofmann), but on the object
(comp. Rom. xv. 14, i. 29, *al.*), which gives to the further elucidation in vv. 9, 10 its specific definition of contents. — τὴν
ἐπίγν. τοῦ θελ. αὐτοῦ] *with the knowledge of His will*, accusative, as in Phil. i. 11; αὐτοῦ applies to God as the subject,
to whom prayer and supplication are addressed.   The context
in ver. 10 shows that by the θέλημα is meant, not the *counsel
of redemption* (Eph. i. 9; Chrysostom, Oecumenius, Theophylact, and many others, including Huther and Dalmer), but,
doubtless (Matt. vi. 10), that which God wills *in a moral respect*
(so Theodoret, who makes out a contrast with the νομικαῖς
παρατηρήσεσιν).   Comp. Rom. ii. 18, xii. 2; Eph. v. 17, vi. 6;
Col. iv. 12.   The distinction between γνῶσις and ἐπίγνωσις,
which both here and also in ver. 10, ii. 2, iii. 10, is the knowledge which *grasps and penetrates into* the object, is incorrectly
denied by Olshausen.   See on Eph. i. 17. — ἐν πάσῃ κ.τ.λ.]

instrumental definition of manner, how, namely, this πληρωθῆναι τὴν ἐπίγν. τ. θελ. αὐτοῦ (a knowledge which is to be
the product not of mere *human* mental activity, but of objectively *divine* endowment by the Holy Spirit) must be brought
about : *by every kind of spiritual wisdom and insight*, by the
communication of these from God ; comp. on Eph. i. 8. A
combination with the following περιπατῆσαι (comp. iv. 5 : ἐν
σοφίᾳ περιπ.), such as Hofmann suggests, is inappropriate,
because the two parts of the whole intercession stand to one
another in the relation of the divine *ethical foundation*
(ver. 9), and of the corresponding *practical conduct of life*
(ver. 10 f.) ; hence the latter portion is most naturally and
emphatically headed by the expression of this Christian practice, the περιπατῆσαι, to which are then subjoined its modal
definitions in detail. Accordingly, περιπατῆσαι is not, with
Hofmann, to be made dependent on τοῦ θελήμ. αὐτοῦ and
taken as its contents, but τ. θελ. τ. Θ. is to be left as an *absolute* idea, as in iv. 12. On πνευματικός, *proceeding from the
Holy Spirit*,[1] comp. Rom. i. 11 ; 1 Cor. ii. 13, xii. 1 ; Eph.
i. 3, v. 19, *et al.* The σύνεσις is the *insight*, in a theoretical
and (comp. on Mark xii. 33) practical respect, depending upon
judgment and inference, Eph. iii. 4 ; 2 Tim. ii. 7. For the
opposite of the *pneumatic* σύνεσις, see 1 Cor. i. 19. It is
related to the σοφία as the *special* to the *general*, since it is
peculiarly the expression of the *intelligence* in the domain of
truth,[2] while the σοφία concerns the *collective* faculties of the
mind, the activities of knowledge, willing, and feeling, the
tendency and working of which are harmoniously subservient to
the recognised highest aim, if the wisdom is πνευματική ; its
opposite is the σοφία σαρκική (2 Cor. i. 12 ; Jas. iii. 15),
being of man, and not of God, in its aim and efforts. According as φρόνησις is conceived subjectively or objectivized, the
σύνεσις may be considered either as synonymous with it

---

[1] Hence ἡ ἄνωθεν σοφία, Jas. iii. 15, 17. The predicate, although in the case
of divine endowment with σοφία and σύνεσις obvious of itself (as Hofmann
objects), was yet all the more apposite for expressly bringing the point into prominence, the greater the danger which threatened Colossae from non-divine,
fleshly wisdom ; comp. ii. 23.

[2] Comp. Dem. 269. 24 : σύνεσις, ᾗ τὰ καλὰ καὶ αἰσχρὰ διαγινώσκεται.

(Eph. i. 8; Dan. ii. 21; Plat. *Crat.* p. 411 A), or as an attribute of it (Ecclus. i. 4: σύνεσις φρονήσεως).

Ver. 10. The practical *aim*[1] which that πληρωθῆναι κ.τ.λ.
is to accomplish; ἀεὶ τῇ πίστει συζεύγνυσι τὴν πολιτείαν,
Chrysostom.   The Vulgate renders correctly: *ut ambuletis* (in
opposition to Hofmann, see on ver. 9). — ἀξίως τοῦ κυρίου] so
that your behaviour may stand in morally appropriate relation
to your belonging to Christ.   Comp. Rom. xvi. 2; Eph. iv. 1;
Phil. i. 27; 1 Thess. ii. 12; 3 John 6.   The *genitive* (and in
the N. T. such is always used with ἀξίως) does not even
" perhaps " (Hofmann) belong to the following εἰς π. ἀρεσκ.,
especially as ἀρεσκεία, in the Greek writers and in Philo
(see Loesner, p. 361), stands partly with, partly without, a
genitival definition, and the latter is here quite obvious of
itself.   Such a combination would be an unnecessary artificial
device.   Comp. Plat. *Conv.* p. 180 D: ἀξίως τοῦ Θεοῦ. — εἰς
πᾶσαν ἀρεσκείαν] *on behalf of every kind of pleasing*, that is,
in order to please Him in every way.   The word only occurs
here in the N. T., but the apostle is not on that account to be
deprived of it (Holtzmann); it is found frequently in Polybius,
Philo, *et al.*; also Theophr. *Char.* 5; LXX. Prov. xxix. 30
(xxx. 30); Symmachus, Ps. lxxx. 12.   On πᾶσαν ἀρ. comp.
Polybius, xxxi. 26. 5: πᾶν γένος ἀρεσκείας προσφερόμενος.
Among the Greeks, ἀρεσκεία (to be accentuated thus, see
Winer, p. 50 [E. T. 57]; Buttmann, *Neut. Gr.* p. 11 [E. T.
12]) bears, for the most part, the sense of *seeking to please.*
Comp. Prov. xxix. 30: ψευδεῖς ἀρεσκείαι. — ἐν παντὶ ἔργῳ
κ.τ.λ.] There now follow *three expositions*, in order to define
more precisely the nature and mode of the περιπατῆσαι ἀξίως
κ.τ.λ.   We must, in considering these, notice the homogeneous
plan of the three clauses, each of which commences with a
prepositional relation of the participial idea, viz. (1) ἐν παντὶ
ἔργῳ κ.τ.λ., (2) ἐν πάσῃ δυνάμει, (3) μετὰ χαρᾶς, and ends

---

[1] Not to be attached as object of the request immediately to προσευχόμενοι, and
all that intervenes to be assigned to the interpolator (Holtzmann, p. 85).   Yet,
according to Holtzmann, p. 123, ἐν παντὶ ἔργῳ down to τοῦ Θεοῦ is alleged to be
simply an interpolated duplicate of ver. 6; in which case, however, it would not
be easy to see why καρποφορούμενοι was not written, after the precedent of ver. 6,
but on the contrary καρποφοροῦντες.

with a relation expressed by εἰς, viz. (1) εἰς τ. ἐπίγν. τ. Θεοῦ, (2) εἰς πᾶσ. ὑπομ. κ. μακροθυμ., (3) εἰς τὴν μερίδα κ.τ.λ. The construction would be still more symmetrical if, in the third clause, ἐν πάσῃ χαρᾷ (Rom. xv. 32) had been written instead of μετὰ χαρᾶς—which was easily prevented by the versatility of the apostle's form of conception. — ἐν παντὶ ἔργῳ ἀγαθῷ καρποφ. is to be taken together (and then again, αὐξανόμ. εἰς τὴν ἐπίγν. τ. Θεοῦ), inasmuch as ye by every good work (by your accomplishing every morally good action) bear fruit, as good trees, comp. Matt. vii. 17. But not as if the καρποφορεῖν and the αὐξάνεσθαι were separate things; they take place, as in ver. 6, jointly and at the same time, although, after the manner of parallelism, a special more precise definition is annexed to each. Moreover, ἐν παντὶ ἔργ. ἀγ. is not to be connected with εἰς πᾶσαν ἀρεσκ. (Oecumenius, Theophylact, Erasmus, and others, also Steiger); otherwise we mistake and destroy the symmetrical structure of the passage. — καὶ αὐξανόμ. εἰς τ. ἐπίγν. τ. Θ.] and, inasmuch as with this moral fruit-bearing at the same time ye increase in respect to the knowledge of God, that is, succeed in knowing Him more and more fully. The living, effective knowledge of God, which is meant by ἐπίγν. τ. Θεοῦ (ver. 6, iii. 10, ii. 2), sustains an ethically necessary action and reaction with practical morality. Just as the latter is promoted by the former, so also knowledge grows through moral practice in virtue of the power of inward experience of the divine life (the ζωὴ τοῦ Θεοῦ, Eph. iv. 18), by which God reveals Himself more and more to the inner man. The fact that here τοῦ Θεοῦ generally is said, and not τοῦ θελήματος Θεοῦ repeated, is in keeping with the progressive development set forth; there is something of a climax in it. On εἰς, used of the telic reference, and consequently of the regulative direction of the growth, comp. on Eph. iv. 15; 2 Pet. i. 8. The reading τῇ ἐπιγνώσει τ. Θ. would have to be taken as instrumental, with Olshausen, Steiger, Huther, de Wette, Bleek, who follow it, but would yield after ver. 9 something quite self-evident. We may add that αὐξάν., with the dative of spiritual increase by something, is frequent in Plato and classic writers.—As to the nominatives of the participles, which are not to be taken with πληρωθ. (Beza, Bengel, Reiche, and others), but relate to the logical subject of περιπατ. ἀξίως, comp. on Eph. iv. 2 ; 2 Cor. i. 7.

Ver. 11 *is co-ordinate* with the foregoing ἐν παντὶ ἔργῳ . . . Θεοῦ. — ἐν πάσῃ δυν. δυναμ.] ἐν is instrumental, as in ver. 9 (Eph. vi. 10 ; 2 Tim. ii. 1) ; hence not designating that, in *the acquiring of which* the invigoration is supposed *to consist* (Hofmann), but : *by means of every* (moral) *power* (by its bestowal on God's part) *becoming empowered.* δυναμόω (Lobeck, *ad Phryn.* p. 605) does not occur in Greek authors, and is only found here and at Heb. xi. 34, Lachm. in the N. T. ; in the LXX. at Eccles. x. 10 ; Dan. ix. 27 ; Ps. lxvii. 31 ; in Aquila ; Job xxxvi. 9 ; Ps. lxiv. 4. Paul elsewhere uses ἐνδυναμοῦν. — κατὰ τὸ κράτος τῆς δόξ. αὐτ.] *according to the might of His majesty ;* with this divine might (see as to κράτος on Eph. i. 19), through the powerful influence of which that strengthening is to be imparted to them, it is also to be *correspondent*—and thereby *its* eminent *strength and efficacy* are characterized (κατά in Eph. i. 19 has another sense). Comp. 2 Thess. ii. 9 ; Phil. iii. 21. And τὸ κράτος τ. δόξ. αὐτ. is not *His glorious power* (Luther, Castalio, Beza, and others ; also Flatt and Bähr), against which αὐτοῦ should have been a sufficient warning ; but τὸ κράτος is the appropriate *attribute* of the divine majesty (of the glorious nature of God). Comp. Eph. iii. 16 ; Ecclus. xviii. 5. The κράτος therefore *is* not the glory of God (Böhmer), but the latter *has* the former,—and the δόξα is not to be referred to a single aspect of the divine greatness (Grotius : *power ;* Huther : *love*), but to its glorious *whole.* Comp. on Rom. vi. 4. — εἰς πᾶσαν ὑπομ. κ. μακροθ.] *in respect to every endurance* (in affliction, persecution, temptation, and the like, comp. Rom. v. 3 ; 2 Cor. i. 6, vi. 4 ; Jas. i. 3 f. ; Luke viii. 15 ; Rom. ii 7, *et al.*) *and long-suffering* (towards the offenders and persecutors), that is, so as to be able to exercise these virtues in every way by means of that divine strengthening. The distinction of Chrysostom : μακροθυμεῖ τις πρὸς ἐκείνους οὓς δυνατὸν καὶ ἀμύνασθαι· ὑπομένει δὲ, οὓς οὐ δύναται ἀμύνασθαι, is arbitrary. See, on the contrary, for instance, Heb. xii. 2, 3. Others understand it variously ;

but it is to be observed, that ὑπομονή expresses the more
general idea of endurance, and that μακροθυμία, the opposite
of which is ὀξυθυμία (Eur. *Andr.* 729 ; Jas. i. 19) and
ὀξυθύμησις (Artem. iv. 69), always refers in the N. T. to the
relation of patient tolerance towards offenders. Comp. iii. 12 ;
Gal. v. 22 ; Rom. ii. 4 ; Eph. iv. 2 ; also Heb. vi. 12 ; Jas.
v. 10. — μετὰ χαρᾶς] is joined with πᾶσαν ὑπομ. κ. μακροθ.
by Theodoret, Luther, Beza, Castalio, Calvin, Grotius, Calovius,
Bengel, Heinrichs, and many others, including Olshausen,
Bähr, Steiger, de Wette, Baumgarten-Crusius, Dalmer, so that
the true, *joyful* patience (comp. ver. 24) is denoted. But the
symmetry of the passage (see on ver. 10), in which the two
previous participles are also preceded by a prepositional definition, points so naturally to the connection with what follows
(Syr., Chrysostom, Oecumenius, Theophylact, Erasmus, Estius,
and others, including Lachmann, Tischendorf, Böhmer, Huther,
Ewald, Ellicott, Bleek, Hofmann), that it cannot be abandoned
without arbitrariness. Even in that case, indeed, the thought
of *joyful* patience, which is certainly apostolic (Rom. v. 3 ; 1 Pet.
i. 6 ; Rom. xii. 12 ; comp. Matt. v. 12), is not lost, when the
intercession rises from patience to *joyful thanksgiving.* Observe
also the deliberate juxtaposition of μετὰ χαρᾶς εὐχαριστ.

Ver. 12. *While ye give thanks with joyfulness,* etc.,—a *third*
accompanying definition of περιπατῆσαι ἀξίως κ.τ.λ. (ver. 10),
co-ordinate with the two definitions preceding, and not to be
connected with οὐ παυόμεθα κ.τ.λ. (Chrysostom, Theophylact,
Calvin : " iterum redit ad gratulationem," Calovius, Böhmer,
Baumgarten-Crusius). — τῷ πατρί] of Jesus Christ ; comp.
ver. 13, and τοῦ Κυρίου in ver. 10, not : " the Father *absolutely* "
(Hofmann). It is always in Paul's writings to be gathered
from the context, *whose* Father God is to be understood as
being (even at Eph. i. 17) ; never does he name God absolutely
(*in abstracto*) ὁ πατήρ. Comp. ver. 3, which, however, is held
by Holtzmann to be the original, suggesting a repetition by
the editor at our passage, in spite of the fact that the two
passages have different subjects. Just as little does εἰς τὴν
μερίδα κ.τ.λ. betray itself as an interpolation from Eph. i. 18
and i. 11 (Holtzmann), seeing that, on the one hand, the

expression at our passage is so wholly peculiar, and, on the
other hand, the idea of κληρονομία is so general in the N. T.
Comp. especially Acts xxvi. 18.[1] — τῷ ἱκανώσαντι κ.τ.λ.]
Therein lies the ground of the thanksgiving, *quippe qui*, etc.
God *has made us fit* (ἡμᾶς applies to the letter-writers and
readers, so far as they are *Christians*) for a share in the Messianic salvation *through the light*, inasmuch as, instead of the
darkness which previously prevailed over us, He has by means
of the gospel brought to us the ἀλήθεια, of which light is the
distinctive element and the quickening and saving principle
(Eph. v. 9) of the Christian constitution both in an intellectual
and ethical point of view (Acts xxvi. 18) ; hence Christians are
children of the light (Eph. v. 8 ; 1 Thess. v. 5 ; Luke xvi. 8).
Comp. Rom. xiii. 12 ; 2 Cor. vi. 14 ; 1 Pet. ii. 9. In Christ the
light had attained to personal manifestation (John i. 4 ff., iii. 9,
viii. 12 ; Matt. iv. 16, *et al.*), as the personal revelation of the
divine nature itself (1 John i. 5), and the gospel was the means
of its communication (Eph. iii. 9 ; Heb. vi. 4 ; 2 Cor. iv. 4 ;
Acts xxvi. 23, *et al.*) to men, who *without* this enlightenment
were *unfit* for the Messianic salvation (Eph. ii. 1 ff., iv. 18,
v. 11, vi. 12 ; 1 Thess. v. 4, *et al.*). The instrumental definition ἐν τῷ φωτί is placed *at the end,* in order that it may stand
out with special *emphasis;* hence, also, the relative sentence
which follows refers to *this* very element. An objection has
been wrongly urged against our view (which is already adopted
by Chrysostom, Oecumenius, Theophylact ; comp. Estius and
others, including Flatt and Steiger), that Paul must have used
πνεῦμα instead of φῶς (see Olshausen). The ἱκανοῦν ἐν τῷ
φωτί is, indeed, nothing else than the καλεῖν εἰς τὸ φῶς
(1 Pet. ii. 9) conceived in respect of its moral efficacy, and
the result thereof on the part of man is the εἶναι φῶς ἐν κυρίῳ
(Eph. v. 8), or the εἶναι υἱὸν τοῦ φωτός (1 Thess. v. 5 ; John
xii. 36), ὡς φωστῆρες ἐν κόσμῳ (Phil. ii. 15). But the light

---

[1] The mode in which Acts xxvi. 18 comes into contact as regards thought and
expression with Col. i. 12-14, may be sufficiently explained by the circumstance
that in Acts xxvi. also *Paul* is the speaker. Holtzmann justly advises caution
with reference to the apparent echoes of the Book of Acts in general, as Luke
originally bears the Pauline stamp.

is a *power;* for it is τὸ φᾶς τῆς ζωῆς (John viii. 12), has its
armour (Rom. xiii. 12), produces its fruit (Eph. v. 9), effects
the Christian ἐλέγχειν (Eph. v. 13), endurance in the conflict
of affliction (Heb. x. 32), etc. Ἐν τῷ φωτί is usually connected with τοῦ κλήρου τῶν ἁγίων, so that this κλῆρος is described as *existing* or *to be found* in light, as the *kingdom of
light;* in which case we may think either of its *glory* (Beza
and others, Böhmer, Huther), or of its *purity and perfection*
(Olshausen, de Wette, and Dalmer) as referred to. But
although the connecting article τοῦ might be wanting, and the
κλῆρος τ. ἁγ. ἐν τῷ φωτί might thus form a single conception, it
may be urged as an objection that the heritage meant cannot
be the *temporal* position of Christians, but only the *future
blessedness of the Messianic glorious kingdom;* comp. ver. 13,
τὴν βασιλ. τοῦ υἱοῦ. Hence not ἐν τῷ φωτί, but possibly ἐν
τῇ δόξῃ, ἐν τῇ ζωῇ, ἐν τοῖς οὐρανεῖς, or the like, would be a
fitting definition of κλῆρος, which, however, already *has* in
τῶν ἁγίων its definite description (comp. Eph. i. 18; Acts
xx. 32, xxvi. 18). Just as little—for the same reason, and
because τ. μερίδα already carries with it its own definition
(share *in the* κλῆρος)—is ἐν τῷ φωτί to be made dependent on
τὴν μερίδα, whether ἐν be taken locally (Bengel: " Lux est
regnum Dei, habentque fideles *in* hoc regno *partem* beatam")
or as in Acts viii. 21 (Ewald), in which case Hofmann finds
the *sphere* expressed (comp. also Bleek), *where the saints have
got their peculiar possession assigned to them,* so that the being
in light stands related to the future glory as that which is still
in various respects *conditioned* stands to *plenitude*—as if κλῆρος
(comp. on Acts xxvi. 18) had not already the definite and full
eschatological sense of the possession of eternal glory. This
κλῆρος, of which the Christians are *possessors* (τῶν ἁγίων), ideally
before the Parousia, and thereafter really, is the theocratic designation (נחלה) of the *property of the Messianic kingdom* (see
on Gal. iii. 18; Eph. i. 11), and the μερὶς (חלק) τοῦ κλήρου is
the *share of individuals*[1] in the same. Comp. Ecclus. xliv. 23.

[1] Comp. also Bleek. Hofmann incorrectly says that τοῦ κληροῦ serves only to
designate the μερίς as *destined for special possession.* In that case, at least, the
qualitative genitive of the *abstract* must have been put (τῆς κληρονομίας, as in

Ver. 13. A more precise elucidation of the divine benefit previously expressed by τῷ ἱκανώσαντι . . . φωτί. This verse forms the transition, by which Paul is led on to the instructions as to Christ, which he has it in view to give down to ver. 20.[1] — ἐκ τῆς ἐξουσ. τοῦ σκοτ.] τοῦ σκοτ. is not genitive *of apposition* (Hofmann), but, corresponding to the εἰς τὴν βασιλείαν that follows, genitive *of the subject: out of the power, which darkness has.* The latter, as the influential power of non-Christian humanity (of the κόσμος, which is ruled by the devil, Eph. ii. 2), is *personified ;* its *essence* is the negation of the intellectual and ethical divine ἀλήθεια, and the affirmation of the opposite. Comp. Luke xxii. 53; Matt. iv. 16; Acts xxvi. 18; Rom. xiii. 12; Eph. v. 8, vi. 12, *et al.* The act of the ἐρρύσατο *has taken place* by means of the conversion to Christ, which is the work *of God,* Rom. viii. 29 f.; Eph. ii. 4 ff. It is to be observed, that the expression ἐκ τ. ἐξουσ. τ. σκότους is chosen as the correlative of ἐν τῷ φωτί in ver. 12. — καὶ μετέστησεν] The matter is to be conceived *locally* (εἰς ἕτερον τόπον, Plat. *Legg.* vi. p. 762 B), so that the deliverance from the power of darkness appears to be united with the *removing away* into the kingdom, etc. Comp. Plat. *Rep.* p. 518 A: ἔκ τε φωτὸς εἰς σκότος μεθισταμένων καὶ ἐκ σκότους εἰς φῶς. — εἰς τὴν βασιλ. κ.τ.λ., that is, *into the kingdom of the Messiah,* Eph. v. 5; 2 Pet. i. 11; for this and nothing else is meant by ἡ βασιλεία Χριστοῦ (τοῦ Θεοῦ, τῶν οὐρανῶν) *in all passages of the N. T.* Comp. iv. 11; and see on Rom. xiv. 17; 1 Cor. iv. 20; Matt. iii. 2, vi. 10. The *aorist*

Ps. xvi. 5). But the concrete τοῦ κλήρου τ. ἁγ. is, as the literal sense of μερίς, *portio,* most naturally suggests, the genitivus *partitivus* (G. *totius),* so that the individual is conceived as μερίτης of the κλῆρος of the saints, in which he for his part συμμετέχει.

[1] This Christological outburst runs on in the form of purely positive statement, although having already in view doctrinal dangers of the kind in Colossae. According to Holtzmann, the Christology belongs to the *compiler ;* the whole passage, vv. 14–20, is *forced and without motive,* and it is only in ver. 21 that we find the direct sequel to ver. 13. The latter statement is incorrect. And why should this excursus, as a grand basis for all the exhortations and warnings that follow, be held *without due motive?* Holtzmann forms too harsh a judgment as to the whole passage i. 9–23, when he declares it incompatible with any strict exegetical treatment.

μετέστ. is to be explained by the matter being conceived proleptically (τῇ γὰρ ἐλπίδι ἐσώθημεν, Rom. viii. 24), as something already *consummated* (comp. on ἐδόξασε, Rom. viii. 30). Thus the kingdom which is nigh is, by means of their fellowship of life with their Lord (Eph. ii. 6), as certain to the redeemed as if they were already translated into it. The explanation which refers it to the *Christian church* (so still Heinrichs, Bähr, Huther, and most expositors) as contrasted with the κόσμος, is just as unhistorical as that which makes it the invisible *inward, ethical* kingdom (see especially Olshausen, following an erroneous view of Luke xvii. 21), to which also Bleek and Hofmann ultimately come. Certainly all who name Christ their Lord are under this king (Hofmann); but this is not yet his βασιλεία; *that* belongs to the *future* αἰών, Eph. v. 5; 1 Cor. vi. 9 f., xv. 24, 50; Gal. v. 21, *et al.*; John xviii. 36.— τῆς ἀγάπης αὐτοῦ] in essential meaning, indeed, nothing else than τοῦ υἱοῦ αὐτοῦ τοῦ ἀγαπητοῦ (Matt. iii. 17, xvii. 5, *et al.*), or τοῦ υἱοῦ τοῦ ἀγαπητοῦ αὐτοῦ (Matt. xii. 18; Mark xii. 6), but more prominently singling out the attribute (Buttmann, *Neut. Gr.* p. 141 [E. T. 162]): *of the Son of His love*, that is, of the Son who is the object of His love, genitive of the *subject*. Comp. Gen. xxxv. 18 : υἱὸς ὀδύνης μου. Entirely parallel is Eph. i. 6 f.: ἐν τῷ ἠγαπημένῳ, ἐν ᾧ ἔχομεν κ.τ.λ. Augustine, *de Trin.* xv. 19, understood it as genitive *of origin*, making ἀγάπη αὐτοῦ denote the divine *substantia*.[1] So again Olshausen, in whose view the expression is meant to correspond to the Johannine μονογενής. This is entirely without analogy in the N. T. mode of conception, according to which not the procreation (ver. 15), but the *sending* of the Son is referred to the divine love as its act; and the love is not the *essence* of God (in the metaphysical sense), but His essential *disposition* (the essence in the ethical sense), even in 1 John iv. 8, 16. Consequently it might be explained : " of the Son, whom His love *has sent*," if this were suggested by the context; so far, however, from this being the case, the language refers to the *exalted* Christ who *rules* (βασι-

---

[1] Theodore of Mopsuestia finds in the expression the contrast that Christ was the Son of God οὐ φύσει, ἀλλ᾽ ἀγάπη τῆς υἱοθεσίας.

λείαν). The expression itself, ὁ υἱὸς τῆς ἀγάπ. αὐτοῦ, is found
in the N. T. only here, but could not be chosen more suitably
or with deeper feeling to characterize the opposite of the
God-hated element of σκότος, which in its nature is directly
opposed to the divine love. The view, that it is meant to be
intimated that the sharing in the kingdom brings with it the
υἱοθεσία (Huther, de Wette), imports what is not expressed,
and anticipates the sequel. Holtzmann without ground, and
unfairly, asserts that in comparison with Eph. i. 6 our passage
presents " stereotyped modes of connection and turns of an
ecclesiastical orator," under which he includes the Hebraizing ὁ
υἱὸς τῆς ἀγάπης αὐτ. as being thoroughly *un-Pauline*—as if the
linguistic resources of the apostle could not even extend to an
expression which is not indeed elsewhere used by him, but is
in the highest degree appropriate to a specially vivid sense of
the divine act of love ; something sentimental in the best sense.

Ver. 14. Not a preliminary condition of the υἱοθεσία (de
Wette), nor the benefit of which Christians become partakers
in the kingdom of the Son of God (Huther ; against which it
may be urged that the βασιλεία does not denote the kingdom
of the *church*) ; nor yet a mark of the deliverance from darkness having taken place (Ritschl in the *Jahrb. f. Deutsche
Theol.* 1863, p. 513), since this deliverance necessarily
coincides with the translation into the kingdom ; but it is the
abiding (ἔχομεν, *habemus*, not *accepimus*) relation, *in which that
transference into the kingdom of God has its causal basis.* The
ransoming (from the punishment of sin, see the explanatory
τὴν ἄφεσιν τῶν ἁμαρτ.) we have *in Christ*, inasmuch as He,
by the shedding of His blood as the purchase-price (see on
1 Cor. vi. 20 ; Gal. iii. 13, iv. 5), has given Himself as a
λύτρον (Matt. xx. 28 ; Mark x. 45 ; 1 Tim. ii. 6) ; and this
redemption, effected by His ἱλαστήριον (Rom. iii. 21 ff.),
remains continually in subsistence and efficacy. Hence : ἐν ᾧ,
which specifies wherein the subjective ἔχομεν is objectively
based, as its *causa meritoria* (Rom. iii. 24). Comp., moreover,
on Eph. i. 7, whence διὰ τοῦ αἵματος αὐτοῦ has found its way
hither as a correct gloss. But the deleting of this addition
by no means implies that we should make τῶν ἁμαρτιῶν also

belong to τὴν ἀπολύτρωσιν (Hofmann), as in Heb. ix. 15,
especially as Paul elsewhere only uses ἀπολύτρωσις either
absolutely (Rom. iii. 24; 1 Cor. i. 30; Eph. i. 7, iv. 30) or
with the genitive of *the subject* (Rom. viii. 23; Eph. i. 14).
The expression ἄφεσις τ. ἁμαρτ. is not used by him elsewhere
in the epistles (comp., however, Rom. iv. 7), but at Acts xiii.
38, xxvi. 28.   Holtzmann too hastily infers that the writer
had read the Synoptics.

Ver. 15. As to vv. 15–20, see Schleiermacher in the *Stud.
u. Krit.* 1832, p. 497 ff. (*Werke z. Theol.* II. p. 321 ff.), and,
in opposition to his *ethical* interpretation (of Christ as the
moral Reformer of the world), Holzhausen in the *Tüb. Zeitschr.*
1832, 4, p. 236 ff.; Osiander, *ibid.* 1833, 1, 2; Bähr, appendix to *Komment.* p. 321 ff.; Bleek on Heb. i. 2.   See
generally also Hofmann, *Schriftbew.* I. p. 153 ff., II. 1, p.
357 ff.; Beyschlag in the *Stud. u. Krit.* 1860, p. 446 f.—
After having stated, in ver. 14, what we *have* in Christ (whose
state of *exaltation* he has in view, see ver. 13, τὴν βασιλείαν),
Paul now, continuing his discourse by an epexegetical relative
clause, depicts what Christ *is*, namely, as regards His divine
dignity—having in view the influences of the false teachers,
who with Gnostic tendencies depreciated this dignity.   The
plan of the discourse is not tripartite (originator of the physical creation, ver. 15 f.; maintainer of everything created,
ver. 17; relation to the new moral creation, ver. 18 ff.,—so
Bähr, while others divide differently[1]), but *bipartite*, in such a
way that vv. 15–17 set forth the exalted metaphysical relation of Christ *to God and the world*, and then ver. 18 ff., His
historical relation of dignity *to the church*.[2]   This division,
which in itself is *logically* correct (whereas ver. 17 is not
suited, either as regards contents or form, to be a separate,
co-ordinate part), is also *externally* indicated by the two confirmatory clauses ὅτι ἐν αὐτῷ κ.τ.λ. in ver. 16 and ver. 19, by

---

[1] *e.g.* Calovius: "Redemptoris descriptio *a Deitate:* ab opere *creationis,*" and
"quod *caput ecclesiae* sit."   Comp. Schmid, *Bibl. Theol.* II. p. 299 f.

[2] Olshausen brings the two divisions under the exegetically erroneous point of
view that, in vv. 15–17, Christ is described *without* reference to the incarnation,
and in vv. 18–20, *with* reference to the same.

which *the two preceding*[1] *affirmations in ver.* 15 *and ver.* 18
are shown to be the proper *parts* of the discourse. Others
(see especially Bengel, Schleiermacher, Hofmann, comp. also
Gess, *Pers. Chr.* p. 77) have looked upon the twice-expressed
ὅς ἐστιν in ver. 15 and ver. 18 as marking the beginning of the
two parts. But this would not be justifiable as respects the
second ὅς ἐστιν; for the main idea, which governs the *whole*
effusion, vv. 15–20, is the *glory of the dominion of the Son of
God*, in the description of which Paul evidently begins the
second part with the words καὶ αὐτός, ver. 18, passing over
from the general to the special, namely, to His government
over the church to which He has attained by His resurrection. On the details, see below. — ὅς ἐστιν κ.τ.λ.] It is to be
observed that Paul has in view Christ as regards His *present*
existence, consequently as regards the presence and continuance of His state of *exaltation* (comp. on. vv. 13, 14); hence
he affirms, not what Christ *was*, but what He *is*. On this
ἐστίν, comp. vv. 17, 18, and 2 Cor. iv. 4. Therefore not
only the reference to *Christ's temporal manifestation* (Calvin,
Grotius, Heinrichs, Baumgarten-Crusius, and others), but also
the limitation to Christ's *divine nature* or the *Logos* (Calovius,
Estius, Wolf, and many others, including Bähr, Steiger, Olshausen, Huther) is incorrect. The only correct reference is
to His *whole person*, which, in the divine-human state of its
present heavenly existence, *is* continually that which its divine
nature—this nature considered in and by itself—*was* before
the incarnation; so that, in virtue of the identity of His
divine nature, the same predicates belong to the exalted Christ
as to the Logos. See Phil. ii. 6; John xvii. 5. — εἰκὼν τοῦ
Θεοῦ τοῦ ἀοράτου] *image of God the invisible.* Comp. on 2 Cor.
iv. 4. As, namely, Christ in His pre-existence[2] down to His

---

[1] In conformity with the *confirmatory* function of the ὅτι, according to which
not the clause introduced by ὅτι, but the clause which it is to confirm, contains
the leading thought, to which ὅτι κ.τ.λ. is logically subordinated. Hence the
two parts are not to be begun with the two clauses ὅτι ἐν αὐτῷ themselves (so
Rich. Schmidt, *Paulin. Christol.* p. 182), in which case, moreover, ver. 15 is
supposed to be quite aloof from this connection—a supposition at variance with
its even verbally evident association with ver. 16.

[2] Sabatier, p. 290, without reason represents the apostle as in a state of indis-

incarnation already possessed the essential divine glory, so that He was as to nature ἴσα Θεῷ, and as to form of appearance ἐν μορφῇ Θεοῦ ὑπάρχων (see on Phil. ii. 6); so, after He had by means of the incarnation divested Himself, not indeed of His God-equal nature, but of His divine δόξα, and had humbled Himself, and had in obedience towards God died even the death of the cross, He has been exalted again by God to His original glory (Phil. ii. 9; John xvii. 5), so that the divine δόξα now exists (comp. on ii. 9) in His glorified corporeal manifestation (Phil. iii. 21); and He—the exalted Christ—in this His glory, which is that of His Father, represents and brings to view by exact image God, who is in Himself invisible. He is ἀπαύγασμα τῆς δόξης καὶ χαρακτὴρ τῆς ὑποστάσεως Θεοῦ (Heb. i. 3),[1] and, in this majesty, in which He is the exactly similar visible revelation of God, He will present Himself to all the world at the Parousia (Matt. xvi. 27, xxv. 31; Phil. iii. 20; 2 Thess. i. 7; 1 Pet. iv. 13; Tit. ii. 13, *et al.*). The predicate τοῦ ἀοράτου, placed as it is in its characteristically significant attributive position (Bornemann, *Schol. in Luc.* p. xxxvi.; Bernhardy, p. 322 f.) behind the emphatic τοῦ Θεοῦ, posits for the conception of the exact image *visibility* (Heb. xii. 14; 2 Cor. iii. 18; Acts xxii. 11); but the assumption that Paul had thus in view the Alexandrian doctrine of the *Logos*, the doctrine of the hidden and manifest God (see Usteri, *Lehrbegr.* p. 308; comp. Bähr, Olshausen, Steiger, Huther), the less admits of proof, because he is not speaking here of the *pre-existence*, but of the *exalted* Christ,

tinct suspense in regard to his conception of this pre-existence. And Pfleiderer (in Hilgenfeld's *Zeitschr.* 1871, p. 533) sees in the pre-existence a subjective product, the consequence, namely, of the fact that Christ is the *ideal of the destiny of the human mind*, hypostasized in a single person, to which is transferred the eternity and unchanged self-equality of the idea.

[1] This is the chief point of agreement between our Epistle and the Epistle to the Hebrews; and it is explained by the Pauline basis and footing, on which the author of the latter stood. The subsequent πρωτότοκος πάσ. κτίσ., however, has nothing to do with πρωτότοκος, Heb. i. 6, where the absolute word is rather to be explained in accordance with Rom. viii. 29. We make this remark in opposition to Holtzmann, according to whom "the *autor ad Ephesios* as to his Christology walks in the track opened by the Epistle to the Hebrews." Other apparent resemblances to this letter are immaterial, and similar ones can be gathered from all the Pauline letters.

including, therefore, His human nature; hence, also, the comparison with the angel *Metatron* of Jewish theology (comp. Hengstenberg, *Christol.* III. 2, p. 67) is irrelevant. The Fathers, moreover, have, in opposition to the Arians, rightly laid stress upon the fact (see Suicer, *Thes.* I. p. 415) that, according to the entire context, εἰκὼν τοῦ Θεοῦ is meant in the eminent sense, namely of the *adequate*, and consequently consubstantial, image of God (μόνος ... καὶ ἀπαραλλάκτως εἰκών, Theophylact), and not as man (Gen. i. 26; comp. also 1 Cor. xi. 7; Col. iii. 10) or the creation (Rom. i. 20) is God's image. In that case, however, the *invisibility* of the εἰκών is not at all to be considered as presupposed (Chrysostom, Calovius, and others); this, on the contrary, pertains to the Godhead *in itself* (1 Tim. i. 17; Heb. xi. 27), so far as it does *not* present itself in its εἰκών; whereas the notion of εἰκών necessarily involves *perceptibility* (see above); "Dei inaspecti aspectabilis imago," Grotius. This visibility—and that not merely mental (Rom. i. 20)—had been experienced by Paul himself at his conversion, and at Christ's Parousia will be fully experienced by all the world. Different from this is the (discursive) *cognoscibility* of God, which Christ has brought about by His appearance and working. John i. 18, xiv. 9. This applies against the view of Calvin, Clericus, and many others, including de Wette: "in His person, appearance, and operation ... God has made Himself *as it were visible;*" comp. Grotius: "Adam imago Dei fuit, sed valde tenuis; in Christo perfectissime apparuit, quam Deus esset sapiens, potens, bonus;" Baumgarten-Crusius: "the affinity to God (which is held to consist in the destination of ruling over the spirit-world) as Christ showed it upon earth." Thus the substantiality of the exact image is more or less turned into a *quasi* or *quodammodo*, and the text is thus laid open to every kind of rationalizing caprice. We may add that Christ was already, as λόγος ἄσαρκος, necessarily the image of God, but ἐν μορφῇ Θεοῦ, in *purely divine* glory; not, as after His exaltation, in *divine-human* δόξα; consequently, the doctrine of an eternal humanity of Christ (Beyschlag) is not to be based on εἰκὼν τοῦ Θεοῦ. Comp. Wisd. vii. 26, and Grimm, *Handb.* p. 161 f. The idea, also, of the *prototype of humanity*, which

is held by Beyschlag here to underlie that of the image
of God (comp. his *Christol.* p. 227), is foreign to the context.
Certainly God has in eternity *thought of* the humanity which
in the fulness of time was to be assumed by His Son (Acts xv.
18) ; but this is simply an *ideal* pre-existence (comp. Delitzsch,
Psychol. p. 41 ff.), such as belongs to the entire history of salvation, very different from the real antemundane existence of
the personal Logos. — πρωτότοκος πάσης κτίσεως] After the
relation of Christ to *God* now follows His relation to *what is
created*, in an apologetic interest of opposition to the Gnostic false
teachers ; βούλεται δεῖξαι, ὅτι πρὸ πάσης τῆς κτίσεώς ἐστιν ὁ
υἱός· πῶς ὤν ; διὰ γενήσεως· οὐκοῦν καὶ τῶν ἀγγέλων πρότερος,
καὶ οὕτως ὥστε καὶ αὐτὸς ἔκτισεν αὐτούς, Theophylact. The
false teachers denied to Christ the supreme unique rank in the
order of spirits. But he is *first-born of every creature*, that
is, born before every creature—*having come to personal existence*,[1] entered upon subsistent being, *ere yet anything created
was extant* (Rom. i. 25, viii. 39 ; Heb. iv. 13). Analogous,
but not equivalent, is Prov. viii. 22 f. It is to be observed
that this predicate also belongs to the *entire* Christ, inasmuch
as by His exaltation His entire person is raised to that state in
which He, as to His divine nature, had already existed before
the creation of the world, corresponding to the Johannine
expression ἐν ἀρχῇ ἦν ὁ λόγος, which in substance, although
not in form, is also Pauline ; comp. Phil. ii. 6. Philo's term
πρωτόγονος, used of the Logos, denotes the same *relation ;* but
it is not necessary to suppose that Paul appropriated from
him this *expression*, which is also current among classical
authors, or that the apostle was at all dependent on the Alexandrian philosophic view. The mode in which he conceived

---

[1] According to Hofmann (*Schriftbew.*), the expression is also intended to imply
that the existence of all created things was brought about through Him. But
this is only stated *in what follows*, and is not yet contained in πρωτότοκος *by
itself*, which only posits the origin of Christ (as λόγος προφορικός) in His *temporal*
relation to the creature ; and this point is the more purely to be adhered to,
seeing that Christ Himself does not belong to the category of the κτίσις. Calvin
also has understood it as Hofmann does ; comp. also Gess, *v. d. Pers. Chr.* p.
79, and Beyschlag, p. 446, according to whom Christ is at the same time to be
designated as the *principle* of the creature, whose origin bears in itself that of
the latter.

of the personal pre-existence of Christ before the world as regards (timeless) origin, is not defined by the figurative πρωτότοκος more precisely than as *procession* from the divine nature (Philo illustrates the relation of the origin of the Logos, by saying that the Father ἀνέτειλεν Him), whereby the premundane Christ became subsistent ἐν μορφῇ Θεοῦ and ἴσα Θεῷ (Phil. ii. 6). The genitive πάσης κτίσεως, moreover, is not the *partitive* genitive (although de Wette still, with Usteri, Reuss, and Baur, holds this to be indubitable), because the anarthrous πᾶσα κτίσις does not mean *the whole creation*, or *everything which is created* (Hofmann), and consequently cannot affirm the *category* or *collective whole*[1] to which Christ belongs as its first-born individual (it means: *every creature;* comp. on πᾶσα οἰκοδομή, Eph. ii. 21[2]); but it is the genitive *of comparison*, corresponding to the superlative expression: " *the first-born in comparison with every creature*" (see Bernhardy, p. 139), that is, born *earlier than* every creature. Comp. Bähr and Bleek, Ernesti, *Urspr. d. Sünde*, I. p. 241; Weiss, *Bibl. Theol.* p. 424; Philippi, *Glaubensl.* II. p. 214, ed. 2. In Rev. i. 5, πρωτότοκ. τῶν νεκρῶν, the relation is different, τ. νεκρῶν pointing out the category; comp. πρωτότοκ. ἐν πολλοῖς ἀδ., Rom. viii. 29. The genitive here is to be taken quite as the comparative

---

[1] Comp. Stallb. *ad Plat. Rep.* p. 608 C. The article would necessarily be added, as πᾶσα ἡ κτίσις, Judith xvi. 14, or ἡ πᾶσα κτίσις, 3 Macc. vi. 2, or ἡ κτίσις πᾶσα. Comp. also ὅλη ἡ κτίσις, Wisd. xix. 6.

[2] Hofmann, *Schriftbew.* I. p. 156: "In relation to all that is created, Christ occupies the position which a first-born has towards the household of his father." Essentially similar is his view in his *Heil. Schr. N. T.*, p. 16, where π. κτίσ. is held to mean "all creation," and to signify "*all that is created in its unity*," which is also the opinion of Rich. Schmidt, *Paul. Christol.* p. 211. The interpretation of Hofmann (comp. Gess, *Pers. Chr.* p. 79) is incorrect, because there would thereby be necessarily affirmed a *homogeneous* relation of origin for Christ and all the κτίσις. The κτίσις would stand to Christ in the relation of the μετατεχθείς to the πρωτότοκος, of the ἐπίγονος to the πρωτόγονος. Hofmann indeed (*Heil. Schr. in loc.*) opines that πάσης κτίσεως is simply genitive "of the definition of relation." But this, in fact, explains *nothing*, because the question remains, *What* relation is meant to be defined by the genitive? The πρωτότοκος πάσης κτίσεως is not at all to be got over so easily as it is by Hofmann, namely, with a grammatically erroneous explanation of the anarthrous πᾶσα κτίσις, and with appeal to Ps. lxxxix. 28 (where, in fact, πρωτότοκος stands without *genitive*, and בְּכוֹר in the sense of the first *rank*).

genitive with πρῶτος; see on John i. 15, and generally, Kühner, II. 1, p. 335 f. The element *of comparison* is the relation of *time* (πρὸ τοῦ τὸν κόσμον εἶναι, John xvii. 5), and that in respect of *origin*. But because the latter in the case of every κτίσις is *different* from what it is in the case of Christ, neither πρωτόκτιστος nor πρωτόπλαστος is made use of,[1]—terms which would indicate for Christ, who is withal *Son* of God, a similar mode of origin as for the creature—but the term πρωτότοκος is chosen, which, in the comparison as to time of origin, points to the peculiar *nature* of the origination in the case of *Christ*, namely, that He was not *created* by God, like the other beings in whom this is implied in the designation κτίσις, but *born*, having come forth homogeneous from the nature of God. And by this is expressed, not a relation homogeneous with the κτίσις (Holtzmann), a relation *kindred to the world* (Beyschlag, *Christol.* p. 227), but that which is absolutely *exalted above* the world and unique. Theodoret justly observes: οὐχ ὡς ἀδελφὴν ἔχων τὴν κτίσιν, ἀλλ᾽ ὡς πρὸ πάσης κτίσεως γεννηθείς. At variance with the words, therefore, is the Arian interpretation, that Christ is designated as the *first creature;* so also Usteri, p. 315, Schwegler, Baur, Reuss. With this view the sequel also conflicts, which describes Christ as the accomplisher and aim of creation ; hence in His case a mode of origin higher and different from *the being created* must be presupposed, which is, in fact, characteristically indicated in the purposely-chosen word πρωτότοκος. The Socinian interpretation is also incorrect[2] (Grotius, Wetstein, Nösselt, Heinrichs, and others), that κτίσις denotes the *new* ethical creation, along with which there is, for the most part, associated the reference of πρωτότοκ. to the highest *dignity* (Pelagius, Melanch-

---

[1] How much, however, the designations πρωτόκτιστος, κτίσμα, κτίζειν κ.τ.λ., as applied to the origin of the Son, were in use among the Alexandrians (following Prov. viii. 22, where Wisdom says : κύριος ἔκτισέ με, comp. Ecclus. i. 4, xxiv. 8 f.), may be seen in Gieseler, *Kirchengesch.* I. 1, p. 327, ed. 4.

[2] The Socinian doctrine argues thus : "primogenitum unum ex eorum numero, quorum primogenitus est, esse necesse est ;" but Christ could not be "unus e rebus conditis creationis *veteris*,"—an assumption which would be Arian ; He must consequently belong to the *new* creation, from which it follows, at the same time, that He does not possess a divine nature. See *Catech. Racov.* 167, p. 318, ed. Oeder.

thon, Cameron, Hammond, Zachariae, and others, including
Storr and Flatt; comp. de Wette), which is assumed also by
many who understand it of the physical creation.   It is
decisive against this interpretation, that κτίσις would necessarily require for the moral notion a more precise definition,
either by a predicate (καινή, 2 Cor. v. 17; comp. Barnabas,
ep. c. xvi.: λαβόντες τὴν ἄφεσιν τῶν ἁμαρτιῶν καὶ ἐλπίσαντες
ἐπὶ τῷ ὀνόματι τοῦ κυρίου, ἐγενόμεθα καινοί, πάλιν ἐξ ἀρχῆς
κτιζόμενοι), or at least by a context which admitted of no
doubt; also, that πρωτότοκος never means *the most excellent*,
and can only have this sense *ex adjuncto* (as at Ps. lxxxix. 28;
Rom. viii. 29), which in this passage is not by any means the
case, as the context (see ver. 16, and πρὸ πάντων in ver. 17;
comp. also πρωτότοκος ἐκ τῶν νεκρῶν in ver. 18) brings prominently forward the relation of *time*.   Chrysostom justly says:
οὐχὶ ἀξίας κ. τιμῆς, ἀλλὰ χρόνου μόνον ἐστὶ σημαντικόν, and
already Theophilus, *ad Autol.* ii. 31, p. 172: ὅποτε δὲ ἠθέλησεν
ὁ Θεὸς ποιῆσαι ὅσα ἐβουλεύσατο, τοῦτον τὸν λόγον ἐγέννησε
προφορικόν, πρωτότοκον πάσης κτίσεως.   This πρωτότοκον
εἶναι *belongs* to the high dignity of Christ (comp. Rev. iii. 14:
ἡ ἀρχὴ τῆς κτίσεως τοῦ Θεοῦ), but it does not *signify* it.   Comp.
Justin, *c. Tr.* 100: πρωτότοκον μὲν τοῦ Θεοῦ κ. πρὸ πάντων τῶν
κτισμάτων.   The ethical[1] interpretation of the passage appears
all the more mistaken, since according to it, even if πρωτότοκ. is understood temporally (Baumgarten-Crusius: " κτίσις
is that which is *remodelled*, and πρωτότοκος, He who has come
first under this category, has first received this higher spiritual
dignity "), Christ is made *to be included under the* κτίσις,
which is at variance both with the context in ver. 16 f.,
and with the whole N. T. Christology, especially the sinlessness of Christ.   If, however, in order to obviate this ground
of objection, πρωτότοκος is combined as an adjective with
εἰκών, we not only get a complicated construction, since both

[1] Both errors of the Socinians, etc., are already present in Theodore cf Mopsuestia, namely, that πρωτότοκος πάσ. κτίσ. does not stand ἐπὶ χρόνου, but ἐπὶ
προτιμήσεως, and signifies παρὰ πᾶσαν τὴν κτίσιν τιμώμενος; and that the following
ἐν αὐτῷ κ.τ.λ. does not denote τὴν πρώτην, but τὴν ἐν αὐτῷ γενομένην ἀνάκτισιν.
Comp. also Photius, *Amphil.* 192.

words have their genitival definition, but πρωτότοκος (instead of πρωτότυπος) would be an *inappropriate* predicate for εἰκών. This applies against Schleiermacher, who, taking κτίσις as "disposition and arrangement of human things," educes the rationalizing interpretation, that Christ is in the whole compass of the spiritual world of man the first-born image, *the original copy of God;* that all believers ought to be formed in the image of Christ, and thence the image of God would likewise necessarily arise in them—an image of the second order. In the interest of opposition to heresy, some, following Isidore of Pelusium, *Ep.* iii. 31, p. 237, and Basil the Great, *c. Eunom.* iv. p. 104, have made the first-*born* even into the first-*bringer-forth* (πρωτοτόκος, as paroxytone, according to the classical usage, Hom. *Il.* xvii. 5 ; Plat. *Theaet.* p. 161 A, 151 C; Valckenaer, *Schol.* II. p. 389), as, with Erasmus in his *Annot.* (but only permissively) Erasmus Schmid and Michaelis did, although πρωτοτόκος in an active sense occurs only of the female sex, and the very πρωτότοκος ἐκ τ. νεκρ. of ver. 18 ought to have dissuaded from such an idea, to say nothing of the unfitness and want of delicacy of the figure[1] as relating to Christ's agency in the creation of the world, and of the want of reference in the πρῶτον to the idea of a δεύτερον—an idea which, with the usual interpretation, is implied in κτίσεως. —Ver. 15 f. is, moreover, strikingly opposed to that assumption of a world *without beginning* (Schleiermacher, Rothe).

Ver. 16. *For in Him were all things created,*—the logically correct confirmation of πρωτότοκος πάσ. κτίσεως. For if the *creation* of all things took place in Christ, it is evident that He must stand *before* the series of created things, and be πρωτό-τοκος πάσης κτίσεως. — ἐν αὐτῷ] is not equivalent to δι᾿ αὐτοῦ (Chrysostom, Oecumenius, Theophylact, Erasmus, Beza, Bleek, and many others), but : *on Christ depended* (causally) the act of creation, so that the latter was not done independently of Him—in a causal connection apart from Him—but it had in Him the ground essentially conditioning it. In Him lay, in fact, the potency of life, from which God made the work of creation proceed, inasmuch as He was the personal principle of the divine self-revelation, and therewith the accomplisher of the

---

[1] πρῶτον αὐτὸν τετοκέναι, τοῦτ᾿ ἐστι πεποιηκέναι τὴν κτίσιν, Isidore, *l.c.*

divine idea of the world. A well - known classical usage
to denote the dependence of a state of things, *the causality
of which* is contained *in any one.* See Bernhardy, p. 210 ;
Kühner, II. 1, p. 403 f.; from the N. T., Winer, p. 364 [E. T.
521]. Not as if the " causa *principalis* " of the creation
lay in Christ, but the *organic* causality of the world's becoming created was in Him ; hence the following δι' αὐτοῦ
affirms not a different *state of things,* but the same thing under
a varied *form of conception* and designation, by which it is
brought out in greater definiteness. The *primary ground* of
creation is ever God, Rom. xi. 36 ; 1 Cor. viii. 6 ; Heb. xi. 3.
The speculative interpretation of scholastic theology, which
found here the " causa *exemplaris,*" according to which the *idea
omnium rerum* was in Christ, is indeed followed in the main
again by Beyschlag, as earlier by Kleuker, Böhmer, Bähr,
Neander, Schleiermacher, Steiger, Julius Müller, Olshausen (the
latter saying : " the Son of God is the intelligible world, the
κόσμος νοητός, that is, things in their very idea ; He bears their
essence in Himself "), but is destitute of confirmation from
the modes of conception and expression elsewhere in the
N. T., and, as ἐκτίσθη denotes the *historical* fact of the having
been created, it would require not ἐν αὐτῷ, but ἐξ αὐτοῦ, by
which the coming forth of the real from the ideal existence in
Christ might be expressed. Huther finds the inward connection
indicated by ἐν αὐτῷ in the idea, that the eternal essence of
the universe is the divine essence itself, which in Christ became
man. This idea in itself has no biblical ground ; and Paul is
speaking here, not of the existence and essence of the universe
in Christ, but of the becoming created, which *took place* in
Christ (ἐν αὐτῷ ζωὴ ἦν, John i. 4), consequently of a divine
act depending on Christ; comp. John i. 3 : χωρὶς αὐτοῦ
ἐγένετο οὐδὲ ἓν ὃ γέγονεν ; Heb. i. 2 ; and Bleek *in loc.* Lastly,
de Wette finds in ἐν besides the instrumental agency at
the same time something of a *telic* idea (comp. also Ewald and
Weiss, *Bibl. Theol.* p. 424 f.) ; but this blending together of
two heterogeneous references is not justified by the δι' αὐτοῦ
καὶ εἰς αὐτόν that follows. — ἐκτίσθη] *physical* act of creation ;
Schleiermacher ought not to have called in question the

linguistic usage to this effect, with a view to favour the *ethical* interpretation of the founding of the *church*. See Wisd. i. 14, x. 1, xi. 18 ; Deut. iv. 32 ; comp. Gen. vi. 7 ; Ecclus. xxiv. 9, comp. xv. 14 ; Judith xiii. 18 ; comp. Gen. i. 1 ; 1 Cor. xi. 9 ; Eph. iii. 9 ; Rom. i. 25 ; Rev. x. 6, comp. xiv. 7. The word *may* have the meaning adopted by Schleiermacher : *to obtain its arrangement and constitution* (Herod. i. 149, 167, 168 ; Thuc. i. 100 ; Aesch. *Choeph.* 484 ; Soph. *Ant.* 1101 ; Pind. *Ol.* vi. 116 ; 3 Esdr. iv. 53), and that according to the relative nature of the notion implied in the word *condere* (comp. Blomf. *Gloss. in Aesch. Pers.* 294) ; but not here, where it is correlative with πάσης κτίσεως, and where the quite general and in no way to be restricted τὰ πάντα follows. Throughout the N. T., in general κτίζω, κτίσις, κτίσμα, denote the *original* bringing forth, never merely the arrangement of that which exists ; and even in such passages as Eph. ii. 10, 15, iv. 24, the relation is conceived, only in a popular manner, as actual *creation*.—Observe, moreover, the *distinction of the tenses :* ἐκτίσθη, which denotes *the act* that *took place ;* and then ἔκτισται, which denotes the creation *which has taken place and now subsists.* See Winer, p. 255 [E. T. 340] ; Kühner, II. 1, p. 143 f., and *ad Xen. Mem.* iii. 1. 4, iii. 7. 7. — τὰ πάντα] the *collective whole,* namely, of what is created. This is then specified in a twofold way, as well in regard to place as in regard to nature. — τὰ ἐν τοῖς οὐρανοῖς κ.τ.λ.] *the things to be found in the heavens and those to be found on earth.* This is certainly a less exact designation of all created things than that in Rev. x. 6 (τὸν οὐρανὸν καὶ τὰ ἐν αὐτῷ κ.τ.λ. ; comp. Neh. ix. 6 ; Gen. ii. 1, *et al.*), but does not differ from it, as it does not exclude heaven and earth themselves, the constituent elements of which, in the popular view, are included in these two categories. Comp. 1 Chron. xxx. 11. It is incorrect, therefore, to press this expression in opposition to the explanation which refers it to the creation of the world (Wetstein : "non dicit ὁ οὐρανὸς καὶ ἡ γῆ ἐκτίσθη sed τὰ πάντα, etc., quo *habitatores* significantur, qui reconciliantur," comp. Heinrichs and others, also *Catech. Racov.* 132, p. 214, ed. Oeder), and to think, with Schleiermacher, of the *kingdom of heaven;* but it is arbitrary also, especially after τὰ πάντα, to make the apostle mean primarily the living (Bähr, de Wette) or rational creatures. The expression embraces *everything;* hence there was neither need for the mention of the *lower world,* nor, looking at the bipartite form of enumeration, occasion for it (it is otherwise in Phil. ii. 10 ; Rev. v. 3). The idea that Paul could not have adduced *those under the earth* as a special class of created beings, because God had not created them with the view of their being under the earth (de Wette), would imply a reflection alien to the vivid flow of the passage before us. — τὰ ὁρατὰ κ. τὰ ἀόρατα] By the latter is meant the *heavenly world of spirits,* the angelic commonwealth, as is evident from the more precise enumeration which follows, and not the *souls of men* (Chrysostom, Theophylact, and others), which, on the contrary, as animating a portion of the ὁρατά, are *included among* the latter. Theodoret erroneously asserts that even τὰ ὁρατά applies to *heavenly* things (sun, moon, and stars) ; it applies to *everything* visible, as in Plat. *Phaed.* p. 79 A : θῶμεν οὖν, εἰ βούλει, ἔφη, δύο εἴδη τῶν ὄντων τὸ μὲν ὁρατόν, τὸ δὲ ἀειδές. — The ἀόρατα are now more precisely specified disjunctively by εἴτε, *sive . . . sive* (put *more than twice;* comp. Plat. *Rep.* p. 612 A, 493 D ; Ecclus. xli. 4). As to the *four denominations of angels* which follow—whose difference of *rank* Hofmann groundlessly denies,[1] understanding thereby merely " *spirits collectively, of whatever name they may be* "—see on Eph. i. 21 ; Rom. viii. 38. In accordance with Eph. i. 21, where the grades of angels are mentioned in descending order, the arrangement here must be understood so, that the θρόνοι are the highest and the κυριότητες the lowest class, the ἀρχαί and the ἐξουσίαι being two middle orders lying between these two extremes. At Eph. *l.c.* Paul names also *four* grades of the angelic hierarchy ; but neither there nor here has he intended to give a *complete* enumeration of them, for in the former case he omits the θρόνοι, and in the latter the δυνάμεις. The θρόνοι are not mentioned elsewhere in the N. T. (nor yet in Ignat. *ad Trall.* 5), but they occur in the *Test. Levi,* p. 548, in

---

[1] See, on the other hand, Hahn, *Theol. d. N. T.* I. p. 292 f. ; Philippi, *Glaubensl.* II. p. 308 f. ; Kahnis, *Dogm.* I. p. 559.

which they are placed in the seventh heaven (ἐν ᾧ ἀεὶ ὕμνοι τῷ θεῷ προσφέρονται), also in Dionys. Areop. *Hier. coel.* 6 ff., and in the Rabbins (Buxtorf, *Lex. Talm.* p. 1097; Schoettgen, *Hor.* p. 808). As regards the *expression*, the last three denominations are to be taken as *abstracts*, which represent the respective *concretes*, and analogously the concrete noun θρόνοι is used for *those to be found on the thrones* (for *those enthroned*); comp. Kühner, II. 1, p. 11; Ruhnken, *ad Tim.* p. 190. In this case the very natural supposition that *the* angels, whose designation by the term θρόνοι must have been *in current use*, were, in the imagery which gave sensuous embodiment to religious ideas, conceived as *on thrones*, is not to be called in question (in opposition to Fritzsche, *ad Rom.* II. p. 226). They were probably conceived as enthroned round the throne of God (comp. Rev. iv. 4, xx. 4). It is to be observed, moreover, generally that Paul presupposes the various classes of angels, which he names, as *well known;* although we are unacquainted with the details of the case, *this much* is nevertheless certain, that the apostle was far removed from the dreamy fancies indulged in on this point by the later Rabbins (see Eisenmenger, *entdeckt. Judenth.* II. p. 374). But very soon *after* the apostolic age (comp. Hermas, *Past.* vis. iii. 4), instruction as to τοποθεσίας τὰς ἀγγελικάς was regarded as teaching for the *more perfect.* See Ignatius, *ad Trall.* 5. For the Christian faith there remains and suffices the testimony as to different and distinctively designated stages and categories in the angelic world, while any attempt to ascertain more than is written in Scripture passes into the fanciful domain of theosophy.—With ἐξουσίαι is *concluded the confirmatory sentence* (ὅτι), so that a full stop is to be placed after ἐξουσ. With τὰ πάντα begins a *new* sentence, in which τὰ πάντα and αὐτός correspond to one another; hence a comma only must stand after ἔκτισται. There is no reason for placing (with Lachmann) τὰ πάντα down to ἐκκλησ. in a parenthesis. — τὰ πάντα δι' αὐτοῦ κ.τ.λ.] *a solemn recapitulation,*[1] but in such a way that, instead of the *act* of crea-

[1] Ewald well says: "Just at this point the discourse breaks forth as if with fresh force, so as once more to express as clearly as possible the whole in all conceivable temporal relations."

tion previously mentioned, there is now presented the finished
and ready *result* (ἔκτισται) ; the causal relation which was previously denoted by ἐν is now more precisely indicated as a
relation of *mediate agency* (δι' αὐτοῦ, comp. 1 Cor. viii. 6) ; then
in εἰς αὐτόν a new element is added, and the *emphasis* which in
ver. 16 lay on ἐκτίσθη, is now laid on τὰ πάντα which stands
at the head of the sentence.   We cannot say with Hofmann,
that by δι' αὐτοῦ and εἰς αὐτόν the Son comes to stand in contradistinction to what has been created *as Creator*, after by ἐν
αὐτῷ the creative act has been presented as one *that had taken
place only not without the Son*.   By the latter, ἐν αὐτῷ would
become too general and indefinite a thought ; while δι' αὐτοῦ
in fact leaves the Father as the Creator, which He is, and predicates of the Son merely the "causa *medians*" of the execution of
the work, just as εἰς αὐτόν predicates the "causa *finalis*" of the
same.—εἰς αὐτόν] *in reference to Him, for Him,* as the aim and
end, "in quo Pater acquiescit," Beza.   Comp. Rom. xi. 36 ; 1 Cor.
viii. 6 ; Barnab. *Ep.* 12 : ἐν αὐτῷ τὰ πάντα καὶ εἰς αὐτόν.
The more exact purport of this relation is apparent from all
that follows down to ver. 20.   Everything, namely, is created,
in order to be dependent on Christ and to serve His will and aim.[1]
Comp. on Eph. i. 23, iv. 10 ; Phil. ii. 9 ff.   The final cause
of the world, referred in Rom. xi. 36 to *God*, is here affirmed
of *Christ*, and with equal right ; for He, as He was the organ
of God in creation, is the *commissioned ruler* to whom the
κυριότης τῶν πάντων is *committed* (Matt. xxviii. 18 ; Phil. ii. 9 ;
1 Cor. xv. 27 ; Heb. ii. 8), in order that everything created
may have the ethical telic destination of serving *Him*.[2]   *More*

---

[1] And, if the world was created not merely δι' αὐτοῦ, but also εἰς αὐτόν, conse-
sequently *in telic reference to Him*, it is certain that with the counsel of *creation* there was also posited, in prospect of the entry of sin, the counsel of
redemption.   Comp. Thomasius, *Christi Pers. u. Werk*, I. p. 196 f. ; Julius
Müller, *Dogm. Abhand.* p. 121 ff.

[2] This εἰς αὐτόν is wrongly found incompatible with 1 Cor. viii. 6 (see, after
Mayerhoff, Baur, and others, especially Holtzmann, p. 219), where, in fact, it is
said of the *ethical existence of Christians* that they exist for God through Christ,
inasmuch as the subject of εἰς αὐτόν (for God) and of δι' αὐτοῦ (through Christ)
is not the universe, but the ἡμεῖς.   The relation of subordination between Father
and Son would be only done away with at our passage, in the event of its being

special definitions of the meaning of εἰς αὐτόν are without due
warrant, and in particular, the often-repeated one: *to His glorification* (Beza, Flatt, Böhmer, and others); it lays down Christ
in general as the *legitimus finis* (Calvin). — The expositors,
who explain the words as referring to the *new moral* creation,
have summoned to their aid all kinds of arbitrary conjectures
in detail — a remark which applies not merely to Nösselt,
Heinrichs, and others, but also to Schleiermacher, who holds
(comp. Baumgarten-Crusius) that τὰ ἐν τ. οὐρ. is everything
that belongs to the kingdom of heaven, and τὰ ἐπὶ τ. γῆς
everything which belongs to civil order in earthly kingdoms;
that τὰ ὁρατά and τὰ ἀόρατα apply only to the latter; that
the θρόνοι κ.τ.λ. are *magisterial offices*, and the like.

Ver. 17. Καὶ αὐτός] which is to be separated from the
preceding by a comma only (see on ver. 16), places, in contradistinction to the created objects in ver. 16 (τὰ πάντα), the
subject, the creating *self*: "*and He Himself, on His part,* has
an earlier existence than all things, and the collective whole
subsists in Him." Never is αὐτός in the nominative[1] the
mere unemphatic "*he*" of the previous subject (de Wette),
either in Greek authors or in the N. T., not even in
passages such as Buttmann (*Neut. Gr.* p. 94 [E. T. 107])
brings forward; see Fritzsche, *ad Matth.* p. 47; Winer, p.
141 f. [E. T. 187]; Kühner, II. 1, p. 563. — πρὸ πάντων] like
πρωτότοκος, referring to *time*, not to rank (as the Socinians,
Nösselt, Heinrichs, Schleiermacher, Baumgarten-Crusius, and

said of Christ that τὰ πάντα were created ἐξ αὐτοῦ. But by ἐν αὐτῷ, and by the
more precise definition δι' αὐτοῦ, it is guarded; and the subordination remains
unaffected by the circumstance that the εἰς αὐτόν is laid down by God for the
world as its telic aim. This εἰς αὐτόν ἔκτισται is the necessary preliminary condition, on God's part, to the universal dominion which he has destined for Christ,
and which the latter shall one day, at the goal of consummation, hand over to
the Father (1 Cor. xv. 24, 28). Moreover, what Paul says of the κτίσις in Rom.
viii. is essentially connected with that εἰς αὐτόν, which does not go beyond Paul
or come at all into opposition to him. The resemblance of our passage to ὁ
πρῶτος καὶ ὁ ἔσχατος, Rev. i. 17, xxii. 13, rests upon the Christological basis of
their common faith, not upon a dependence of our epistle on the Apocalypse,
which would doubtless imply a post-Pauline date (in opposition to Holtzmann,
p. 247).

[1] Bengel correctly observes on ver. 16: "*Ipse* hic saepe positum magnam sig-
nificat majestatem et omnem excludit creaturam."

others hold) ; Paul thus *repeatedly and emphatically lays stress*
on the pre-existence of Christ.   Instead of ἐστί, he *might*
have written ἦν (John i. 1) ; but he makes use of the former,
because he has in view and sets forth the *permanence* of
Christ's existence, and does not wish to narrate about Him
historically, which is done only in the auxiliary clauses with
ὅτι, vv. 16 and 19.   On the present, comp. John viii. 58.
His existence is more ancient than that of all things (πάντων,
not masculine, as the Vulgate and Luther translate). — ἐν
αὐτῷ] as in ver. 16, referring to the *causal dependence* of the
subsistence of all existing things *on Christ.* — συνέστηκε] denotes *the subsistence* of the whole, the *state of lasting inter-
dependence and order,*—an idea which is not equivalent to
that of creation, but presupposes it.   Reiske, *Ind. Dem.* ed.
Schaef. p. 481 : " Corpus unum, integrum, perfectum, secum
consentiens esse et permanere."   Comp. 2 Pet. iii. 5 ; Plat.
Rep. p. 530 A : ξυνεστάναι τῷ τοῦ οὐρανοῦ δημιουργῷ αὐτόν
τε καὶ τὰ ἐν αὐτῷ, *Tim.* p. 61 A : γῆν ... ξυνεστηκυῖαν, *Legg.*
vii. p. 817 B : ἡ πολιτεία ξυνέστηκε μίμησις τοῦ καλλίστου ...
βίου.   Herod. vii. 225 ; Philo, *quis rer. div. haer.* p. 489 :
ὁ ἔναιμος ὄγκος, ἐξ ἑαυτοῦ διαλυτὸς ὢν καὶ νεκρὸς, συνέστηκε
κ. ζωπυρεῖται προνοίᾳ Θεοῦ κ.τ.λ.   It expresses that there is
in Christ not merely the creative cause, but also the cause
which brings about organic *stability and continuance* in unity
(preserving and governing) for the whole of existing things.
Comp. Heb. i. 3.   Of attempts at explanation under the *moral*
interpretation, we may note that of Schleiermacher : the *con-
solidating of earthly relations* and institutions ; and that of
Baumgarten - Crusius : " in this *new* world He is *Lord in
recognition and in sway.*"

REMARK.—The intentional prominence given to the fact of
the creation of all things through Christ, and in particular of
the creation of the angels in their various classes, justifies
the supposition that the false teachers disparaged Christ in
this respect, and that they possessed at least elements of the
Gnostic-*demiurgic* doctrine which was afterwards systematically
elaborated.   There is no evidence, however, of their particular
views, and the further forms assumed by the Gnostic elements,

as they showed themselves according to the Fathers in *Simon Magus* (Iren. *Haer.* i. 20 : "Eunoiam . . . generare angelos et potestates, a quibus et mundum hunc factum dixit;" comp. Epiph. *Haer.* xxi. 4), *Cerinthus*, etc., and especially among the *Valentinians*, while certainly to be recognised as fundamentally akin to the Colossian doctrinal errors (comp. Heinrici, *Valentinian. Gnosis*, 1871), are not to be identified with them; nor are those elements to be made use of as a proof of the post-apostolic origin of the epistle, as still is done by Hilgenfeld (see his *Zeitschr.* 1870, p. 246 f.), and more cautiously by Holtzmann. Of Ebionitism only *Essene* elements are to be found in Colossae, mingled with other Gnostic doctrines, which were not held by the later Ebionites. In particular, the πρὸ πάντων εἶναι, on which Paul lays so much stress, must have been doubted in Colossae, although a portion of the Ebionites expressly and emphatically taught it (λέγουσιν ἄνωθεν μὲν ὄντα πρὸ πάντων δὲ κτισθέντα, Epiph. *Haer.* xxx. 3). Moreover, the opinion that Paul derived the appellations of the classes of angels in ver. 16 from the language of the heretics themselves (Böhmer, comp. Olshausen) is to be rejected, because in other passages also, where there is no contrast to the Gnostic doctrine of Aeons, he makes use in substance of these names (Rom. viii. 38; 1 Cor. xv. 24 ; comp. Eph. i. 20 ff., iii. 10, vi. 11 ff.). They are rather to be regarded as well-known and generally-current appellations, which were derived from the terminology of later Judaism, and which heretics made use of in common with the orthodox. The anti-Gnostic element is contained, not in the technical expressions, but in the doctrinal contents of the passage; and it was strong enough to induce Marcion, who took offence at it, to omit vv. 15–17 (Tertullian, *c. Marcion*, v. 19). See, besides, Räbiger, *Christol. Paul.* p. 51 f.; Lechler, *apost. Zeit.* p. 55 f.; Klöpper, *l.c.*

Ver. 18. *Second* part (see on ver. 15) of the exhibition of the exaltedness of Christ. To that which Christ is as πρωτότοκος πάσης κτίσεως (vv. 16, 17) is now added what He is as πρωτότοκος ἐκ τῶν νεκρῶν, namely, the Head of the Church, and thus His πρωτεύειν has its consummation (ἐν πᾶσιν). The latter, namely, ἵνα γένηται . . . πρωτεύων, *embraces* also a retrospect to that πρωτότοκος πάσης κτίσεως, and includes it in ἐν πᾶσιν, without its being necessary, however, to attach ver. 18 to the carrying out of the relation to the world expressed in πρωτότοκ. π. κτίσ. (Hofmann, comp. Rich. Schmidt). The perspective proceeds from the dignity of the *original state* of our Lord to that of His *state as Saviour*, from His *cosmical* to His *soteriological* glory, and so at length exhibits Him to view as the ἐν πᾶσι πρωτεύων. — That ver. 18, with its confirmation in ver. 19 f., has an *apologetic* reference to the Gnostic false teaching, must be assumed from its connection with what goes before. The passage is to be looked upon as antagonistic to the *worship of angels* (ii. 18), which disparaged Christ in His dignity as Head of the Church, but not (in opposition to Bähr and Huther) as antagonistic to a theological dogma, such as is found in the Cabbala, according to which the body of the Messiah (the Adam Kadmon) is the aggregate of the emanations. For the emphasis of the passage and its essential point of doctrine lie in the fact that Christ is the *Head* of the church, and not in the fact that He is the head of the *church*; it is not the doctrine of another σῶμα, but that of any other πρωτεύων, which is excluded. — καὶ αὐτός] stands again, as κ. αὐτός in ver. 17, in significant reference to τὰ πάντα : *et ipse, in quo omnia consistunt, est caput, etc.*, so that the passage continues to divide itself as into the links of a chain. — τοῦ σώματος τῆς ἐκκλησ.] to be taken together; the second genitive is that of apposition (Winer, p. 494 [E. T. 666]), which gives to the word governing it concrete definiteness ; comp. Müller in the *Luther. Zeitschr.* 1871, p. 611 ff. On the familiar Pauline mode of considering the church of believers, livingly and actively ruled by Christ as the head (Eph. iii. 10 ; Phil. iii. 6 ; Acts ix. 31), as His *body*,[1] comp. 1 Cor. x. 17, xii. 12 ff., 27 ; Eph. i. 23, iv. 12, v. 23, 30 ; Rom. xii. 5. — ὅς ἐστιν κ.τ.λ.] epexegetical relative clause (as in ver. 15), the contents of which are related by way of confirmation to the preceding statement (Matthiae, p. 1061 f. ; Kühner, *ad Xen. Mem.* i. 2. 64 ; Stallbaum, *ad Phil.* p. 195 f.),

---

[1] In which is expressed the idea of the invisible church. Comp. Julius Müller, *Dogmat. Abh.* p. 316 ff. And this conception and representation belong quite to the apostle's general sphere of ideas, not specially to that of the Epistle to the Ephesians, into which the interpolator is supposed by Holtzmann again to enter here, after he has manifested a comparative independence in vv. 15-18.

like our: *he, who, etc.*, which *might* be expressed, but not *neces-sarily*, by ὅστις (or ὅσγε). Comp. on Eph. i. 14. If Christ had not risen, He would not be *Head* of the church (Acts ii. 24–36 ; 1 Cor. xv. ; Rom. i. 4, *et al.*). — ἀρχή] *beginning;* which, however, is not to be explained either as " initium *secundae* et novae *creationis*" (Calvin), progenitor of the re-generate (Bisping), or " *author of the church*" (Baumgarten-Crusius), or even " *ruler of the world*" (Storr, Flatt) ; but agreeably to the context in such a way, as to make it have with the appositional πρωτότοκος its definition in ἐκ τῶν νεκρῶν, just as if the words ran : ἀρχὴ τῶν νεκρῶν, πρωτότοκος ἐξ αὐτῶν, although Paul did *not* express himself thus, because at once upon his using the predicate ἀρχή in and by itself the exegetical πρωτότοκος suggested itself to him. Accordingly Christ is called ἀρχὴ (τῶν νεκρῶν), inasmuch as He *is among all the dead the first arisen to everlasting life.* It is arbitrary to discover in ἀρχή an allusion to the *offering of first-fruits* sanctifying the whole mass (Chrysostom, Beza, Ewald, and others) ; especially as the term ἀπαρχή, which is elsewhere used for the first portion of a sacrifice (Rom. xi. 16), is not here employed, although it has crept in from 1 Cor. xv. 20, 23, in a few *minusculi* and Fathers, as in Clement also, *Cor.* I. 24, Christ is termed ἀπαρχὴ τῆς ἀναστάσεως. To assume a re-miniscence of 1 Cor. xv. (Holtzmann) is wholly unwarranted, especially as ἀπαρχή is not used. On ἀρχή, used of *persons,* denoting the one who begins the series, as the first in order of time, comp. Gen. xlix. 3, where ἀρχὴ τέκνων μου is equivalent to πρωτότοκος μου, as also Deut. xxi. 17. *In what respect* any one is ἀρχή of those concerned, must be yielded by the con-text, just as in this case it is yielded by the more precisely defining πρωτότοκος ἐκ τ. νεκρῶν ; hence it has been *in sub-stance* correctly explained, following the Fathers : ἀρχή, φησίν, ἐστι τῆς ἀναστάσεως, πρὸ πάντων ἀναστάς,[1] Theophylact.

---

[1] The Fathers have already correctly judged that even in regard to the isolated cases of rising from the dead, which have taken place through Christ and before Him, Christ remains the first-risen. Theophylact : εἰ γὰρ καὶ ἄλλοι πρὸ τούτου ἀνέστησαν, ἀλλὰ πάλιν ἀπέθανον· αὐτὸς δὲ τὴν τελείαν ἀνάστασιν ἀνέστη. Comp. on 1 Cor. xv. 20.

Only τῆς ἀναστάσεως is not to be *mentally supplied*, nor is
it to be conjectured (de Wette) that Paul had intended to
write ἀρχὴ τ. ἀναστάσεως, but, on account of the word πρωτότοκος presenting itself to him from ver. 15, did not complete
what he had begun. It follows, moreover, from the use of
the word πρωτότοκος, that ἀρχή is to be taken in the *temporal*
sense, consequently as equivalent to *primus*, not in the sense
of *dignity* (Wetstein), and not as *principle* (Bähr, Steiger,
Huther, Dalmer, following earlier expositors). — πρωτότοκος ἐκ
τ. νεκρ.] ἐκ τ. νεκρ. is conceived in the same way as in ἀναστῆναι
ἐκ τ. νεκρ. (Eph. v. 14), so that it is the dead in Hades
among whom the Risen One was, but *from* whom He *goes
forth* (*separates* Himself from them, hence also ἀπὸ τ. νεκρ.,
Matt. xiv. 2, xxvii. 64, xxviii. 7), and returning into the body,
with the latter rises from the tomb. Comp. πρῶτος ἐξ ἀναστάσεως νεκρῶν, Acts xxvi. 23, also 1 Cor. xv. 22 f. This
living exit from the grave is figuratively represented as *birth ;*
comp. Rev. i. 5, where the partitive genitive τῶν νεκρ. (not ἐκ
τ. ν.) yields a form of conceiving the matter not materially
different. Calvin takes πρωτότοκος ἐκ. τ. ν. as specifying the
ground for ἀρχή : "*principium* (absolutely), *quia primogenitus
est ex mortuis ;* nam in resurrectione est rerum omnium in-
stauratio.*" Against this it may be urged, that ἀρχή has no more
precise definition ; Paul must have written either ἀρχὴ τῆς
καινῆς κτίσεως, or at least ἧς instead of ὅς. Calvin was likewise
erroneously of opinion (comp. Erasmus, Calovius) that Christ
is called *Primogenitus ex mortuis*, not merely because He was
the first to rise, but also "*quia restituit aliis vitam.*" This
idea is not conveyed either by the word or by the context,
however true may be the thing itself ; but a belief in the
subsequent general resurrection of the dead is the *presupposition* of the expression πρωτότοκος (αἰνίττεται δὲ ὁ λόγος καὶ
τὴν πάντων ἡμῶν ἀνάστασιν, Theodoret). This expression is
purposely chosen in significant reference to ver. 15, as is intimated by Paul himself in the following ἵνα γένηται ἐν πᾶσιν
κ.τ.λ. But it is thus all the more certain, that πρωτότοκος ἐκ
τ. νεκρ. is to be taken independently, and not adjectivally
together with ἀρχή (Heinrichs, Schleiermacher, Ewald), which

would only amount to a tautological verboseness (*first-born beginning*); and, on the other hand, that ἐκ τῶν νεκρῶν may not be separated from πρωτότοκος in such a way as to emphasize the *place, issuing forth from which* Christ is what He is, namely, ἀρχή, πρωτότοκος ; *the former,* " as the personal beginning of what commences with Him ;" *the latter,* " in the same relation to those who belong to the world therewith coming into life as He held to the creation" (Hofmann). In this way the specific more precise definition, which is by means of ἐκ τ. νεκρῶν in significant reference to ver. 15 *attached* to the predicates of Christ, ἀρχή and πρωτότοκος, would be groundlessly *withdrawn* from them, and these predicates would be left in an indefiniteness, in which they would simply be open vessels for receiving a gratuitously imported supplement. — ἵνα γένηται κ.τ.λ.] not to be restricted to the affirmation ἐκ τῶν νεκρῶν (Hofmann),[1] but to be referred to the whole sentence that Christ is ἀρχή, πρωτότοκος ἐκ τ. νεκρ., expressing the *divine teleology* of this position of Christ as the Risen One : *in order that He may become,* etc. ; not : in order " that He *may be held as*" (Baumgarten-Crusius), nor yet " that He *may be*" (Vulgate, and so most expositors), as γίγνεσθαι and εἶναι are *never* synonymous. The ἐν πᾶσιν αὐτὸς πρωτεύει is looked upon by Paul as something which is still in course of development (comp. Steiger and Huther), and is only to be completed in the future, namely, when the Risen One shall have conquered all the power of the enemy (1 Cor. xv. 25 f.) and have erected the kingdom of the Messiah—but of this result His resurrection itself was the necessary *historical basis*, and hence the future universal πρωτεύειν is the divinely intended *aim* of His being risen. — ἐν πᾶσιν] *in all points*, without excepting any relation, not, therefore, merely in the relation of creation (vv. 15–17). Comp. Phil. iv. 12 ; 1 Tim. iii. 11, iv. 15 ; 2 Tim. ii. 7, iv. 5 ; Tit. ii. 9 ; Heb. xiii. 4, 18. Ἐν παντί is more commonly used by Paul (1 Cor. i. 5 ; 2 Cor. iv. 8, *et al.*). According to Beza, πᾶσιν is *masculine :* "inter *omnes*, videlicet *fratres*, ut Rom. viii. 29." So also

[1] So that it would express the design, which *Christ Himself* had in His coming forth from the dead.

Kypke and Heinrichs.   But this would be here, after the
universal bearing of the whole connection, much too narrow
an idea, which, besides, is self-evident as to the Head of the
church.   According to Pelagius, it denotes: " tam in visi-
bilibus quam in invisibilibus *creaturis*."   At variance with
the text; this idea was conveyed by vv. 16, 17, but in ver.
18 another relation is introduced which does not refer to
created things as such. — αὐτός] emphatic, as in vv. 17, 18.
— πρωτεύων] *having the first rank*, not used elsewhere in the
N. T., but see Esth. v. 11 ; 2 Macc. vi. 18, xiii. 15 ; Aquila,
Zech. iv. 7 ; Plat. *Legg.* iii. p. 692 D, *Dem.* 1416. 25 :
πρωτεύειν ἐν ἅπασι κράτιστον.   Xen. *Cyr.* viii. 2. 28 ;
Mem. ii. 6. 26.   This precedence in rank is to be the final
result of the condition which set in with the πρωτότοκον
εἶναι ἐκ τ. νεκρ. ; but it is not contained in this πρωτότοκον
εἶναι itself,—an idea against which the very ἵνα γένηται
is logically decisive (in opposition to de Wette's double
signification of πρωτότοκ.).

Ver. 19.[1] Ὅτι] Confirmatory of the ἵνα γένηται κ.τ.λ., just
said : " about which divinely intended γίγνεσθαι ἐν πᾶσιν αὐτὸν
πρωτεύοντα *there can be no doubt, for it has pleased*, that *in Him*,
etc."   How could He, who was thus destined to be possessor of
the divine fulness and reconciler of the world, have been destined otherwise than to become ἐν πᾶσιν πρωτεύων !   This confirmation, therefore, does not refer to the statement that Christ
is the Head of the church (Steiger, Huther, comp. Calovius),
which has already its confirmation by means of ὅς ἐστιν ἀρχὴ
κ.τ.λ, nor at all to ἐκ τῶν νεκρῶν (Hofmann, following up his
incorrect explanation of these words), as if the reason were
specified why Christ should have gone to His high dignity as
beginner of a new world *by the path of deepest abasement*—a
thought which Paul would have known how to express quite
differently (comp. Phil. ii. 7 f.) than by the bare ἐκ τῶν νεκρ.,

---

[1] Holtzmann, after having rejected vv. 14–18 entirely as an interpolation,
allows to stand as original in vv. 19, 20 only the words: ὅτι ἐν αὐτῷ εὐδόκησεν
καταλλάξαι, to which καταλλ. there is then attached in ver. 21, as object, καὶ
ἡμᾶς, *also you*, with reference to ἡμᾶς in ver. 13.   How daring and violent, and
yet how paltry (rescuing merely the καὶ ὑμᾶς), would the procedure of the author
thus have been !

which is currently used everywhere of resurrection from death, and without conveying any special significance of humiliation. Nor yet does Paul move *in a circle,* by putting forward in ver. 19 as ground of proof that from which in ver. 15 (ὅς ἐστιν εἰκὼν κ.τ.λ.) he had started (de Wette); for ver. 19 is a *historical* statement (observe the *aorists*), whereas ver. 15 expressed what Christ *is,* His *habitual being.* — ἐν αὐτῷ] although belonging to κατοικ., is prefixed in emphatic transposition (Kühner, II. 2, p. 1101). — εὐδόκησε] *He was pleased, placuit ei,* that, etc. As to this use of εὐδοκεῖν in the later Greek (1 Cor. i. 21; Gal. i. 15, *et al.*), for which, in the classical language, δοκεῖν merely was employed, see Fritzsche, *ad Rom.* II. p. 370. On the *accusative with infinitive,* comp. 2 Macc. xiv. 35; Polyb. i. 8. 4. The *subject,* whose pleasure it is, is not expressed; but that it is God, is obvious from the context, which in ἵνα γένηται κ.τ.λ. has just stated the *divine* purpose. Among Greek authors also ὁ Θεός is not unfrequently omitted, where it is self-evident as the subject. See Kühner, II. 1, p. 30 c. According to Ewald and Ellicott (also Weiss, *Bibl. Theol.* p. 428, ed. 2, and Rich. Schmidt, *Paul. Christol.* p. 208), πᾶν τὸ πλήρωμα is the subject; and *the whole fulness* is a new expression for the Godhead, inasmuch as, going as it were out of itself, it fills something separate and thus becomes visible (=כבוד יהוה, δόξα, λόγος, πνεῦμα). Without support from N. T. usage; πᾶν, too, would be unsuitable for the *subject* of εὐδόκησε; and εἰς αὐτόν in ver. 29 clearly shows that Θεός is conceived as subject, to which εἰρηνοποιήσας then refers. According to Hofmann (comp. also his *Schriftbew.* II. 1, p. 357 f.), *Christ* is meant to be the subject of εὐδόκ. Ver. 20 itself, and Eph. i. 9, ought to have precluded this error. Throughout the whole of the N. T. it is never Christ, but always *the Father,* who in respect to the work of redemption to be executed gives the decree, while Christ executes it *as obedient* to the Father; hence also Paul, "beneficium Christi commemorans, nunquam dimittit memoriam Patris," Bengel. Comp. Reiche, *Comment. crit.* p. 263. — πᾶν τὸ πλήρωμα κατοικ.] that in Him *the whole fulness was to take up its abode.* The more precise definition of the absolute πᾶν τὸ πλήρωμα is placed beyond doubt by the subject to be mentally supplied with εὐδόκησε,[1] namely, τὸ πλήρωμα τοῦ Θεοῦ (Eph. iii. 19 ; comp. τὸ πλήρ. τῆς θεότητος, Col. ii. 9). Τὸ πλήρωμα, the signification of which is not to be defined *actively : id quod rem implet* (in opposition to Storr, *Opusc.* I. p. 144 ff., Bähr, Steiger), but *passively : id quo res impletur* (see generally on Eph. i. 10, iii. 19, Fritzsche, *ad Rom.* II. p. 469), has here, as in Eph. iii. 9, the derivative general notion of *copia*, πλοῦτος, like the German *Fülle.* What is meant, namely, is the whole *charismatic riches of God,* His whole *gracious fulness* of εὐλογία πνευματική (Eph. i. 3), of which Christ became permanent (κατοικῆσαι) possessor and bearer, who was thereby capable of fulfilling the divine work of reconciliation (see the following καὶ δι' αὐτοῦ ἀποκαταλλάξαι κ.τ.λ.). The case is otherwise in ii. 9, where the divine *essence* (τῆς θεότητος) is indicated as the contents of the πλήρωμα, and the κατοικεῖν of the same in Christ is affirmed as *present* and with reference to His *state of exaltation.* It would be an utterly arbitrary course *mentally to supply* here the τῆς θεότητος, ii. 9, and to regard both passages as an echo of Eph. i. 23, where the notion of πλήρωμα is a very different one (in opposition to Holtzmann). Inasmuch as the charismatic πλήρωμα of *God,* meant in our passage, dwelt in *Christ,* and consequently Christ was the possessor and disposer of it, this divine fulness is not in substance different from the πλήρωμα Χριστοῦ, out of which grace passed over to men (John i. 16 ; Eph. iv. 13). The thought and expression in 1 Cor. xv. 28 are different from our passage, and different also from Eph. i. 23. Beza aptly observes : " cumulatissima omnium divinarum rerum copia, quam scholastici *gratiam habitualem* ... appellant, ex qua in Christo, tanquam inexhausto fonte, omnes gratiae in nos pro cujusque membri modulo deriventur ;" comp. also Bleek. Observe, at the same time, the stress lying on the πᾶν, in contrast to a merely *partial* imparting out of this fulness, which would have been inadequate to the object of reconciling the universe. The *ontological* interpretation of the " fulness of

---

[1] Hence not : "*la totalité de l'être* qui doit être realisée dans le monde," Sabatier, *l'apôtre Paul,* p. 209.

the *nature* of God" (Huther, Dalmer, Weiss; Oecumenius, and Theodoret: the nature of the Θεὸς λόγος; Calovius and others: of the *communicatio hypostatica,* that is, of the absolute immanence of God in Him, comp. Ernesti, *Urspr. d. Sünde,* I. p. 222; Rich. Schmidt, *Paul. Christol.* p. 201) does not correspond to the idea of εὐδόκησεν, for doubtless the *sending* of the Son, and that with the *whole treasure* of *divine grace,* into the world (John iii. 17) for behoof of its reconciliation and blessedness, was the act of the divine *pleasure and resolve;* but not so the *divine nature* in Christ, which was, on the contrary, *necessary* in Him,[1] although by His incarnation He emptied Himself of the divine *mode of appearance* (δόξα or μορφή, Phil. ii. 6 ff.). The divine *nature* is *presupposed* in what is here said of Christ. Comp. Gess, *v. d. Pers. Christi,* p. 85. Some (see especially Steiger, Bähr, and Reuss) have regarded τὸ πλήρωμα as derived *from the Gnostic terminology of the false teachers,* who might perhaps, like Valentinus, have given this name to the aggregate of the Aeons (see Baur, *Gnosis,* p. 157),[2] and in opposition to whom

[1] As in the *Son* of God in the metaphysical sense; hence the original being of God in Him cannot be conceived merely as *ideal,* which was to develope itself into reality, and the realization of which, when it at length became perfect, made Him the absolute abode of the fulness of Godhead. So Beyschlag, *Christol.* p. 232 f., according to whom Christ would be conceived as "*man drawing down upon himself*" this indwelling of God. He is conceived as the incarnate *Son* (comp. ver. 13 fi.), who, in accordance with the Father's decree, has appeared as bearer of the whole fulness of salvation. For He was its dwelling not merely *in principle,* but in *fact* and *reality,* when He appeared, and He employed it for the work, which the Father desired to accomplish by Him (ver. 20). Comp. Gal. iv. 4; Rom. viii. 3. The indwelling of the πᾶν τὸ πλήρωμα He had not, indeed, to achieve by his own effort; but He had, in obedience towards the Father, to preserve (comp. Heb. iv. 15), apply, communicate it; and so this indwelling is—not merely in the risen One, but in His very work on the cross—the presupposition of the universal reconciliation, ver. 20.

[2] Baur himself (*Paulus,* II. p. 12 ff.) likewise explains πλήρωμα from the technical language of the Gnostics, especially of the Valentinian doctrine of Aeons, but finds the Gnosticism to belong to the (post-apostolic) *writer of the epistle.* According to Baur (see his *Neutest. Theol.* p. 258), Christ is the πλήρωμα of God as He "*in whom that which God is in Himself, according to the abstract idea of His nature, is filled with its definite concrete contents.*" Comp. also Hilgenfeld in his *Zeitschr.* 1870, p. 247, according to whom our passage is intended to affirm that the Pleroma of divine nature is to be sought *not in the prolix series of the Aeons of the Gnostics, but in Christ alone.* Holtzmann, with

Paul maintains that in Jesus there dwells the *totality* of all divine powers of life, and not merely a single emanated spirit ; but this view is all the more unwarranted, because Paul himself does not intimate any such polemical destination of the word ; on the contrary, in Eph. iii. 19 also he uses πᾶν τὸ πλήρωμα τ. Θεοῦ evidently without any reference of the kind. And if he had wished to place the whole fulness of the efflux of divine power in contrast to an asserted single emanation, he must have prefixed, not ἐν αὐτῷ (*in Him and in none other*), but πᾶν (*the whole* πλήρωμα, *not merely a single constituent element* of it) with the main emphasis, and have logically said : ὅτι πᾶν τὸ πλήρωμα εὐδόκησεν ἐν αὐτῷ κατοικῆσαι. Hofmann (comp. his *Schriftbew.* p. 29, 359), who in general has quite misunderstood ver. 19 f. (comp. above on εὐδόκησεν), takes πᾶν τὸ πλήρωμα as "*the one-like totality of that which is ;*" and holds that the will of Christ (to which εὐδοκ. applies) can only have been, "*that that may come to dwell in Him, which otherwise would not be in Him, consequently not what is in God, but what is out of God.*" This idea of the immanent indwelling of the universe in Christ, repeated by Schenkel in the sense of Christ being the *archetype,* would be entirely alien to the N. T. view of the relation of Christ to the world, and is not indicated either at Eph. i. 10 or here in the context by τὰ πάντα ἐν αὐτῷ συνέστηκεν. Christ is not the place *for the world,* so that ultimately all comes to dwell in Him, as all has been created in Him and has in Him its subsistence ; but the world originated and maintained through Him, which He was to redeem, is the place *for Him.*[1] If Paul had really entertained the obscure paradoxical conception attributed to him by Hofmann, he would have known how to express it simply by τὸ πᾶν (or τὰ πάντα) κατοικῆσαι, or by τὸ πλήρωμα τοῦ παντὸς (or τῶν πάντων) κατοικῆσ. Lastly, at utter variance with both the word and the context, some have based on Eph. i.

more caution, adheres to the view that the idea of the πλήρωμα forms a *first step* towards the extended use which the Gnostics make of the word ; whereas Hilgenfeld (*Zeitschr.* 1873, p. 195) finds the idea here already *so firmly established,* " that the πλήρωμα emerges as in a certain measure holding an *independent* position between God and Christ."

[1] Comp. Rich. Schmidt, *l.c.* p. 208.

22 f, the interpretation of πλήρωμα as *the church.* So already Theodoret: πλήρ. τὴν ἐκκλησίαν ἐν τῇ πρὸς Ἐφεσίους ἐκά- λεσεν, ὡς τῶν θείων χαρισμάτων πεπληρωμένην. Ταύτην ἔφη εὐδοκῆσαι τὸν Θεὸν ἐν τῷ Χριστῷ κατοικῆσαι, τουτέστιν αὐτῷ συνῆφθαι, and recently in substance Heinrichs, Baumgarten- Crusius, and others ; comp. also Schleiermacher, who, in accord- ance with Rom. xi. 12, 25, understands " *the fulness of the Gentiles and the collective whole of Israel,*" the *dwelling* of whom in Christ is the " definitive abiding state," which the total reconciliation (see the sequel) must necessarily have preceded, as this reconciliation is conditioned by the fact that both parties must have become peaceful. — κατοικῆσαι] The πλή- ρωμα is personified, so that the *abiding presence,* which it was to have according to the divine εὐδοκία in Christ, appears conceived under the form of *taking up its abode;* in which, however, the idea of the *Shechinah* would only have to be presupposed, in the event of the πλήρωμα being represented as *appearance* (כבוד יהוה). See on Rom. ix. 5. Comp. John i. 14. Analogous is the conception of the dwelling of Christ (see on Eph. iii. 17) or of the Spirit (see Theile on Jas. iv. 5) in believers. Comp. also 2 Pet. iii. 13. In point of *time,* the indwelling of the divine fulness of grace according to God's pleasure in Christ refers to the *earthly life of the Incarnate One,* who was destined by God to fulfil the divine work of the ἀποκαταλλάξαι τὰ πάντα, and was to be empowered thereto by the dwelling in Him of that whole divine πλήρωμα. Without having completed the performance of this work, He could not become ἐν πᾶσιν πρωτεύων; but of this there could be no doubt, for God has caused it to be completed through Him (ὅτι, ver. 19). Ernesti, *Urspr. d. Sünde,* I. p. 215 f. (comp. also Weiss, *Bibl. Theol.* p. 428, ed. 2), refers εὐδόκησε κ.τ.λ. to the *heavenly* state of Christ, in which God, by way of reward for the completion of His work, has made Him the organ of His glory (Phil. ii. 9); he also is of opinion that ἀποκαταλλάξαι in ver. 20 does not apply to the reconciliation through His blood, but to the reunion of all created things through the exalted Lord, as a similar view is indicated in Phil. ii. 10. But this idea of the ἀποκαταλλάξαι

is just the point on which this view breaks down. For ver. 21 clearly shows that ἀποκαταλλάξαι is to be taken in the usual sense of the work of reconciliation completed through the ἱλαστήριον of Christ. Moreover, that which Christ received through His exaltation was not the divine πλήρωμα, but the divine δόξα.

Ver. 20.[1] " Haec inhabitatio est fundamentum reconciliationis," Bengel. Hence Paul continues: καὶ δι᾿ αὐτοῦ ἀποκαταλλάξαι τὰ πάντα, and through Him to reconcile the whole. As to the double compound ἀποκαταλλ., prorsus reconciliare,[2] see on Eph. ii. 16. The considerations which regulate the correct understanding of the passage are: (1) that τὰ πάντα may not in any way be restricted (this has been appropriately urged by Usteri, and especially by Huther); that it consequently cannot be referred either merely to intelligent beings generally (the usual view), or to men (Cornelius a Lapide, Heinrichs, Baumgarten-Crusius, and others), especially the Gentiles (Olshausen), or to the " universam ecclesiam" (Beza), but is, according to the context (see ver. 16 ff.), simply to be

---

[1] According to Holtzmann, p. 92, the author is assumed to have worked primarily with the elements of the fundamental passage 2 Cor. v. 18 f., which he has taken to apply to the cosmical ἀποκαταλλαγή. But, instead of apprehending this as the function of the risen Christ, he has by διὰ τοῦ αἵματος κ.τ.λ. occasioned the coincidence of two dissimilar spheres of conception, of which, moreover, the one is introduced as form for the other. The interpolator reproduces and concentrates the thought of Eph. i. 7, 10, ii. 13–17, bringing the idea of a cosmical reconciliation (Eph. i. 10) into expression in such a way " that he, led by the sound of the terminology, takes up at the same time and includes the thought of the reconciliation of the Jews and Gentiles." In opposition to this view, the exegesis of the details in their joint bearing on the whole will avail to show that the passage with all its difficulty is no such confused medley of misunderstanding and of heterogeneous ideas, and contains nothing un-Pauline. The extension of the reconciliation to the celestial spheres, in particular, has been regarded as un-Pauline (see, especially, Holtzmann, p. 231 ff.). But even in the epistles whose genuineness is undisputed it is not difficult to recognise the presuppositions, from which the sublime extension of the conception to an universality of cosmic effect in our passage might ensue. We may add, that Eph. i. 10 is not " the leading thought of the interpolation" at ver. 16 ff. (Holtzmann, p. 151); in ver. 16 ff. much more is said, and of other import.

[2] As if we might say in German, abversöhnen, that is : to finish quite the reconciliation. Comp. ἀφιλάσκισθαι, Plat. Legg. ix. p. 873 A.

taken as quite *general : the whole of that which exists* (has been created); (2) that the *reconciling subject* is here not Christ (Hofmann, in accordance with his incorrect reference of εὐδό-κησε in ver. 19), but *God,* who *through Christ* (δι᾽ αὐτοῦ) reconciled all things; (3) that consequently ἀποκαταλλάξαι cannot be meant of *the transforming of the misrelation between the world and Christ into a good relation* (Hofmann), and just as little of the reconciliation of all things *with one another,* of the removal of *mutual* hostility among the *constituent elements* composing τὰ πάντα, but only of the universal reconcilia-tion *with the God who is hostile to sin,*[1] as is clearly evident from the application to the readers in ver. 21. The only correct sense therefore is, *that the entire universe has been re-conciled with God through Christ.* But *how far ?* In answer-ing this question, which cannot be disposed of by speculation beyond the range of Scripture as to the having entered into the finite and having returned again to the infinite (Usteri), nor by the idea imported into ἀποκαταλλ. of *gathering up into the unity of absolute final aim* (Baur, *neut. Theol.* p. 257), the follow-ing considerations are of service : (*a*) The original harmony, which in the state of innocence subsisted between God and the whole creation, was annulled by sin, which first obtained mastery over a portion of the angels, and in consequence of this (2 Cor. xi. 3), by means of the transgression of Adam, over all mankind (Rom. v. 12). Comp. on Eph. i. 10. (*b*) Not only had sinful mankind now become alienated from God by sin and brought upon themselves His hostility (comp. ver. 21), but also the whole of the non-rational creation (Rom. viii. 19 ff.) was affected by this relation, and given up by God to ματαιό-της and δουλεία τῆς φθορᾶς (see on Rom. *l.c.*). (*c*) Indeed, even the world of heavenly spirits had lost its harmony with

[1] *God* is the *subject, whose hostility* is removed by the reconciliation (comp. on Rom. v. 10) ; τὰ πάντα is the *object,* which was affected by this hostility grounded of necessity on the holiness and righteousness of God. If the hostile disposition of *men* towards *God,* which had become removed by the reconciliation, were meant (Ritschl in the *Jahrb. f. Deutsche Theol.* 1863, p. 515), the universal τὰ πάντα would not be suitable ; because the whole universe might, indeed, be affected by the hostility of God against sin, but could not itself be hostilely disposed towards Him. See, moreover, on ver. 21.

God as it originally existed, since a portion of the angels—those that had fallen—formed the kingdom of the devil, in antagonism to God, and became forfeited to the wrath of God for the everlasting punishment which is prepared for the devil and his angels. (*d*) But in Christ, by means of His ἱλαστήριον, through which God made peace (εἰρηνοποιήσας κ.τ.λ.), the reconciliation of the whole has taken place, in virtue of the blotting out, thereby effected, of the curse of sin. Thus not merely has the *fact* effecting the reconciliation as its *causa meritoria* taken place, but the realization of the *universal reconciliation itself* is also *entered upon*, although it is not yet *completed*, but down to the time of the Parousia is only in course of *development*, inasmuch, namely, as in the present αἰών the believing portion of mankind is indeed in possession of the reconciliation, but the unreconciled unbelievers (the tares among the wheat) are not yet separated; inasmuch, further, as the non-intelligent creation still remains in its state of corruption occasioned by sin (Rom. viii.); and lastly, inasmuch as until the Parousia even the angelic world sees the kingdom of the devil which has issued from it still—although the demoniac powers have been already vanquished by the atoning death, and have become the object of divine triumph (ii. 15)—not annulled, and still in dangerous operation (Eph. vi. 12) against the Christian church. But through the Parousia the reconciliation of the whole which has been effected in Christ will reach its consummation, when the unbelieving portion of mankind will be separated and consigned to Gehenna, the whole creation in virtue of the Palingenesia (Matt. xix. 28) will be transformed into its original perfection, and the new heaven and the new earth will be constituted as the dwelling of δικαιοσύνη (2 Pet. iii. 13) and of the δόξα of the children of God (Rom. viii. 21); while the demoniac portion of the angelic world will be removed from the sphere of the new world, and cast into hell. Accordingly, in the whole creation there will no longer be anything alienated from God and object of His hostility, but τὰ πάντα will be in harmony and reconciled with Him; and God Himself, to whom Christ gives back the regency which He has hitherto exercised, will become the only

Ruler and All in All (1 Cor. xv. 24, 28). This collective
reconciliation, although its consummation will not occur until
the Parousia, is yet justly designated by the *aorist* infinitive
ἀποκαταλλάξαι, because to the telic conception of God in
the εὐδόκησε it was present as *one moment in conception.* —
The angels also are necessarily included in τὰ πάντα (comp.
subsequently, τὰ ἐν τοῖς οὐρανοῖς) ; and in this case—seeing
that a reconciliation of the angels who had not fallen, who
are holy and minister to Christ (Hahn, *Theol. d. N. T.* I. p.
269 ff.), considered in themselves as individuals, cannot be
spoken of, and is nowhere spoken of in the N. T.[1]—it is to
be observed that the angels are to be conceived *according to
category,* in so far, namely, as the hostile relation of God
towards the fallen angels affected the angelic world viewed
as a whole. The original normal relation between God and
this higher order of spirits is no longer existing, so long as
the kingdom of demons in antagonism to God still subsists—
which has had its powers broken no doubt already by the
death of Christ (ii. 14 f; Heb. ii. 14), but will undergo at
length utter separation — a result which is to be expected
in the new transformation of the world at the Parousia. The
idea of reconciliation is therefore, in conformity with the
manner of popular discourse, and according to the variety of the
several objects included in τὰ πάντα, meant partly in an immediate sense (in reference to mankind), partly in a mediate
sense (in reference to the κτίσις affected by man's sin, Rom.
viii., and to the angelic world affected by its partial fall) ;[2]

[1] According to Ignatius, *Smyrn.* 6, the angels also, ἐὰν μὴ πιστεύσωσιν εἰς τὸ
αἷμα Χριστοῦ, incur judgment. But this conception of angels needing reconciliation, and possibly even unbelieving, is doubtless merely an abstraction, just as is
the idea of an angel teaching falsely (Gal. i. 8). It is true that, according to
1 Cor. vi. 3, angels also are judged ; but this presupposes not believing and
unbelieving angels, but various stages of moral perfection and purity in the
angelic world, when confronted with the absolute ethical standard, which in
Christianity must present itself even to the angels (Eph. iii. 10). Comp. on
1 Cor. vi. 3.

[2] The idea of ἀποκαταλλάξαι is not in this view to be altered, but has as its
necessary presupposition the idea of *hostility,* as is clear from εἰρηνοποίησας and from
ἐχθρούς, ver. 21, compared with Eph. ii. 16 ! Compare Fritzsche, *ad Rom.* I.
p. 276 ff. ; Eur. *Med.* 870 : διαλλαγῆναι τῆς ἔχθρας, Soph. *Aj.* 731 (744) :

the idea of ἀποκαταλλάξαι, in presence of the all-embracing τὰ πάντα, is as it were of an *elastic* nature.[1] At the same time, however, ἀποκαταλλ. is not to be made *equivalent* (Melanchthon, Grotius, Cornelius a Lapide, Flatt, Bähr, Bleek, and others) to ἀποκεφαλαιώσασθαι (Eph. i. 10), which is rather the *sequel* of the former; nor is it to be conceived as merely *completing* the harmony of the good angels (who are not to be thought *absolutely* pure, Job iv. 18, xv. 15; Mark x. 18; 1 Cor. vi. 3) with God (de Wette), and not in the strict sense therefore *restoring* it—an interpretation which violates the meaning of the word.   Calvin, nevertheless, has already so conceived the matter, introducing, moreover, the element— foreign to the literal sense—of *confirmation* in righteousness: " quum creaturae sint, *extra lapsus periculum* non essent, nisi Christi gratia fuissent *confirmati.*" According to Ritschl, in the *Jahrb. f. Deutsche Theol.* 1863, p. 522 f., Paul intends to refer to the angels that had been active in the *law-giving on Sinai* (Deut. xxxiii. 2; Ps. lxvii. 18, LXX.), to whom he attributes " a deviation from God's plan of salvation." But this latter idea cannot be made good either by ii. 15, or by Gal. iii. 19, or by Eph. iii. 10, as, indeed, there is nothing in the context to indicate any such reference to the angels *of the law* in particular. The exegetical device traditionally resorted to, that what was meant with respect to the angels was their reconciliation, not *with God*, but *with men*, to whom on

θεοῖσιν ὡς καταλλαχθῇ χόλου, Plat. *Rep.* p. 566 E: πρὸς τοὺς ἔξω ἐχθροὺς τοῖς μὲν καταλλαγῇ, τοὺς δὲ καὶ διαφθείρῃ. This applies also against Hofmann's enervating weakening of the idea into that of *transposition from the misrelation* into a good one, or of "*an action, which makes one, who stands ill to another, stand well to him.*" In such a misrelation (namely, *to Christ,* according to the erroneous view of εὐδόκησις) stand, in Hofmann's view, even the "*spirits collectively,*" in so far as they *bear sway in the world - life* deteriorated by human sin, *instead of in the realization of salvation.*—Richard Schmidt, *l.c.* p. 195, also proceeds to dilute the notion of reconciliation into that of the *bringing to Christ,* inasmuch as he explains the καταλλάσσειν as effected by the fact that Christ has become the head of all, and all has been put in dependence on Him. Hilgenfeld, *l.c.* p. 251 f., justly rejects this alteration of the sense, which is at variance with the following context, but adheres, for his own part, to the statement that here the author *in a Gnostic fashion* has in view disturbances of peace in the heavenly spheres (in the πλήρωμα).

[1] Comp. Philippi, *Glaubensl.* IV. 2, p. 269 f., ed. 2.

account of sin they had been previously inimical (so Chrysostom, Pelagius, Theodoret, Oecumenius, Theophylact, Zanchius, Cameron, Calovius, Estius, Bengel, Michaelis, Böhmer, and others), is an entirely erroneous makeshift, incompatible with the language of the passage. — εἰς αὐτόν] is indeed to be written with the *spiritus lenis*, as narrating the matter from the standpoint of the *author*, and because a *reflexive* emphasis would be without a motive; but it is to be referred, not to *Christ*, who, as mediate agent of the reconciliation, is at the same time its *aim* (Bähr, Huther, Olshausen, de Wette, Reiche, Hofmann, Holtzmann, and others; comp. Estius, also Grotius: "ut ipsi pareant"), but to *God*, constituting an instance of the abbreviated form of expression very usual among Greek writers (Kühner, II. 1, p. 471) and in the N. T. (Winer, p. 577 [E. T. 776]), the *constructio praegnans:* to reconcile *to God-ward*, so that they are now no longer separated from God (comp. ἀπηλλοτρ., ver. 21), but *are to be united with Him in peace.* Thus εἰς αὐτ., although identical in reality, is not in the mode of conception equivalent to the mere *dative* (Eph. ii. 16; Rom. v. 10; 1 Cor. vii. 11; 2 Cor. v. 18, 19, 20), as Beza, Calvin, and many others take it. The reference to *Christ* must be rejected, because the definition of the aim would have been a special element to be added to δι' αὐτοῦ, which, as in ver. 16, would have been expressed by καὶ εἰς αὐτόν, and also because the explanation which follows (εἰρηνο-ποιήσας κ.τ.λ.) concerns and presupposes simply the *mediate agency* of Christ (δι' αὐτοῦ). — εἰρηνοποιήσας, down to σταυροῦ αὐτοῦ, is a modal definition of δι' αὐτοῦ ἀποκαταλλάξαι (not a parenthesis): *so that He concluded peace,* etc., inasmuch, namely, as the blood of Christ, as the expiatory offering, is meant to satisfy the holiness of God, and now His grace is to have free course, Rom. v. 1; Eph. vi. 15. The aorist participle is, as ver. 21 shows, to be understood as *contemporary* with ἀποκα-ταλλ. (see on Eph. i. 9, and Kühner, II. 1, p. 161 f.; Müller in the *Luther. Zeitschr.* 1872, p. 631 ff.), and not *antecedent* to it (Bähr), as has been incorrectly held by Ernesti in consistency with his explanation of ver. 19 (see on ver. 19), who, moreover, without any warrant from the context, in accordance

COL. U

with Eph. ii. 14–16, thinks of the conclusion of peace *between Jews and Gentiles.* The *nominative* refers to the *subject;* and this is, as in the whole sentence since the εὐδόκησεν, not *Christ* (Chrysostom, Theodoret, Oecumenius, Luther, Storr, Heinrichs, Flatt, Steiger, Hofmann, and many others), but *God.* The verb εἰρηνοποιεῖν, occurring only here in the N. T., which has elsewhere ποιεῖν εἰρήνην (Eph. ii. 15 ; Jas. iii. 18), and also foreign to the ancient Greek, which has εἰρηνοποιός, is nevertheless found in Hermes, *ap. Stob. Ecl. ph.* i. 52, and in the LXX. Prov. x. 10. — διὰ τοῦ αἵμ. τ. σταυροῦ αὐτοῦ] that is, *by means of the blood to be shed on His cross,* which, namely, as the sacrificial blood reconciling with God (comp. 2 Cor. v. 21), became the *causa medians* which procured the conclusion of peace between God and the world.   Rom. iii. 25, v. 9 f. ; Eph. i. 7. The reason, which historically induced Paul to designate the blood of Christ with such specific definiteness as *the blood of His cross,* is to be sought in the spiritualism of the false teachers, who ascribed to the angels a mediating efficacy with God. Hence comes also the designation—so intentionally material— of the reconciling sacrificial death, ver. 22, which Hofmann seeks to avoid as such, namely, as respects its definite character of a satisfaction.[1] — δι' αὐτοῦ] not with the *spiritus asper,* equivalent to δι' ἑαυτοῦ, as those take it who refer εἰρηνοποιήσας to Christ as subject (ἑαυτὸν ἐκδούς, Theophylact), since this reference is erroneous.   But neither can δι' αὐτοῦ be in apposition to διὰ τοῦ αἵματος τ. στ. αὐτοῦ (Castalio, " per ejus sanguinem, h. e. *per eum* "), for the *latter,* and not the former, would be the explanatory statement.   It is a *resumption of the above-given* δι' αὐτοῦ, after the intervening definition εἰρηνοποιήσας κ.τ.λ., in order to complete the discourse thereby interrupted,

---

[1] According to Hofmann, *Schriftbew.* II. 1, p. 362 ff., by the blood of the cross, ver. 20, the death of Christ is meant to be presented as a *judicial act of violence,* and " *what befell Him* " as an *ignominy,* which He allowed to be inflicted on Him with the view of establishing a peace, which brought everything out of alienation from Him into fellowship of peace with Him.   Ver. 22 does not affirm the expiation of sin, but the transition of mankind, which had once for all been effected in Christ, from the condition involved in their sin into that which came into existence with His death.   Christ has, in a body like ours, and by means of the death to which we are subject, done that which we have need of in order

and that by once more emphatically bringing forward the δι' αὐτοῦ which stood at the commencement; "*through Him*," I say, to reconcile, whether they be things on earth or whether they be things in heaven. Comp. on Eph. i. 11 ; Rom. viii. 23. — εἴτε τὰ ἐπὶ τ. γ., εἴτε τὰ ἐν τ. οὐρ.] divides, without "affected tautology" (Holtzmann), but with a certain solemnity befitting the close of this part of the epistle, the τὰ πάντα into its two component parts. As to the *quite universal* description, see above on τὰ πάντα; comp. on ver. 16. We have, besides, to notice: (1) that Paul here (it is otherwise in ver. 16, where the *creation* was in question, comp. Gen. i. 1) names the earthly things *first,* because the atonement *took place* on earth, and *primarily* affected things earthly; (2) that the *disjunctive* expression εἴτε . . . εἴτε renders impossible the view of a reconciliation of the *two sections one with another* (Erasmus, Wetstein, Dalmer, and others). To the category of exegetical aberrations belongs the interpretation of Schleiermacher, who understands earthly and heavenly *things,* and includes among the latter all the relations *of divine worship* and the *mental tendencies* of Jews and Gentiles relative thereto : "Jews and Gentiles were at variance as to both, as to the heavenly and earthly things, and were now to be brought together in relation to God, after He had founded peace through the cross of His Son." The view of Baumgarten-Crusius is also an utter misexplanation: that the reconciliation of men (Jews and Gentiles) among themselves, and with the spirit-world, is the thing meant; and that the reconciliation with the latter consists in the consciousness given back to men of being worthy of con-

that we may come to stand holy before Him. Not different in substance are Hofmann's utterances in his *Heil. Schr. N. T.* But when we find it there stated : "*how far* Christ has hereby (namely, by His having allowed Himself to be put to death as a transgressor by men) converted the variance, which subsisted between Him and the world created for Him, into its opposite, *is not here specified in detail,*"—that is an unwarranted evasion ; for the strict idea of reconciliation had so definite, clear, firm, and vivid (comp. ver. 14, ii. 13 f.) a place in the consciousness of the apostle and of the church, which was a Pauline one, that it did not need, especially in express connection with the *blood of the cross,* any more precise mention in detail. Comp. Gal. iii. 13 ; Rom. iii. 25. Calvin well says : "Ideo *pignus* et *pretium* nostrae cum Deo pacificationis sanguis Christi, *quia* in cruce fusus."

nection with the higher spirits.—Lastly, against the reference
to *universal restoration*, to which, according to Olshausen, at
least the *tendency* of Christ's atonement is assumed to have
pointed, see on Eph. i. 10, remark 2.   Comp. also Schmid in
the *Jahrb. f. D. Theol.* 1870, p. 133.

Ver. 21. As far as ver. 23, an application to the readers of
what had been said as to the reconciliation, in order to animate
them, through the consciousness of this blessing, to stedfastness in the faith (ver. 23).—καὶ ὑμᾶς κ.τ.λ.] *you also*, not : *and
you*, so that it would have to be separated by a mere comma
from the preceding verse, and νυνὶ δὲ . . . θανάτου would, notwithstanding its great importance, come to be taken as parenthetical (Lachmann), or as quite breaking off the discourse, and
leaving it unfinished (Ewald).   It begins a new sentence, comp.
Eph. ii. 1 ; but observe, at the same time, that Eph. ii. is much
too rich in its contents to admit of these contents being here
compressed into vv. 20, 21 (in opposition to Holtzmann, p. 150).
As to the way in which Holtzmann gains an immediate connection with what precedes, see on ver. 19.   The *construction*
(following the reading ἀποκατηλλάγητε, see the critical notes)
has become *anacoluthic*, inasmuch as Paul, when he began the
sentence, had in his mind the *active* verb (which stands in the
Recepta), but he does not carry out this formation of the sentence ; on the contrary, in his versatility of conception, he
suddenly starts off and continues in a passive form, as if he
had begun with καὶ ὑμεῖς κ.τ.λ.   See Matthiae, p. 1524 ;
Winer, p. 527 ff. [E. T. 714] ; and upon the aorist, Buttmann,
Neut. Gr. p. 171 [E. T. 197].— ἀπηλλοτρ. κ.τ.λ] *when ye
were once in the state of estrangement*, characterizes their *heathen*
condition.   As to ἀπηλλοτρ., see on Eph. ii. 12 ; from which
passage ἀπὸ τῆς πολιτείας τ. Ἰσρ. is here as unwarrantably
supplied (Heinrichs, comp. Flatt), as is from Eph. iv. 14 τῆς
ζωῆς τοῦ Θεοῦ (Bähr).   In conformity with the context, seeing
that previously God was the subject as author of reconciliation,
the being estranged from *God* (τοῦ Θεοῦ), the being excluded
from His fellowship, is to be understood.   Comp. ἄθεοι ἐν τ.
κόσμῳ, Eph. ii. 12.   On the subject-matter, Rom. i. 21 ff. —
ἐχθρούς] sc. τῷ Θεῷ, in a *passive sense* (comp. on Rom. v. 10,

xi. 28): *invisos Dco*,[1] as is required by the idea of having become reconciled, through which God's enmity against sinful men, who were τέκνα φύσει ὀργῆς (Eph. ii. 3), has changed into mercy towards them.[2] This applies in opposition to the usual *active* interpretation, which Hofmann also justly rejects: hostile *towards* God, Rom. viii. 7; Jas. iv. 4 (so still Huther, de Wette, Ewald, Ritschl, Holtzmann), which is not to be *combined with* the passive sense (Calvin, Bleek). — τῇ διανοίᾳ and ἐν τοῖς ἔργοις τ. π. belong to *both* the preceding elements ; the former as dative of the *cause : on account of their disposition of mind* they were once alienated from God and hateful to Him ; the latter as specification of the overt, *actual sphere of life, in which* they had been so (*in the wicked works,* in which their godless and God-hated behaviour had exhibited itself). Thus information is given, as to ἀπηλλ. and ἐχθρούς, of an internal and of an external kind. The view which takes τῇ διανοίᾳ as dative of the *respect* (comp. Eph. iv. 18): *as respects disposition* (so, following older expositors, Huther, de Wette, Baumgarten-Crusius, Ewald), would no doubt suit the erroneous *active* explanation of ἐχθρ., but would furnish only a *superfluous* definition to it, as it is self-evident that the enmity towards God resides in the *disposition.* Luther incorrectly renders: "through the *reason ;*" for the διάν. is not the reason itself, but its immanent *activity* (see especially, Plato, *Soph.* p. 263 E), and that here viewed under its moral aspect; comp. on Eph. iv. 18. Beza ("mente operibus malis intenta"), Michaelis, Storr, and Bähr attach ἐν τοῖς ἔργοις κ.τ.λ. to τῇ διανοίᾳ.

---

[1] Compare the phrase very current in the classical writers, from Homer onward, ἐχθρὸς θεοῖς, *quem Dii oderunt.*

[2] See Fritzsche, *ad Rom.* I. p. 276 ff., who aptly explains καταλλάσσεσθαί τινι : *in alicujus favorem venire, qui antea succensuerit.* Comp. Philippi, *Glaubensl.* IV. 2, p. 265 ff., ed. 2. The reconciliation of men takes place, when God, instead of being further angry at them, has become gracious towards them,— when, consequently, *He Himself is reconciled.* Comp. Luke xviii. 13 ; 2 Cor. v. 19. So long as His wrath is not changed, and consequently *He* is not reconciled, men remain unreconciled. 2 Macc. vii. 33 : ὁ ζῶν κύριος ... βραχέως ἐπώργισται καὶ πάλιν καταλλαγήσεται τοῖς ἑαυτοῦ δούλοις, comp. viii. 29, i. 5, v. 20 ; Clem. *Cor.* I. 48 : ἱκετεύοντες αὐτόν (God), ὅπως ἵλεως γενόμενος ἐπικαταλλαγῇ ἡμῖν. In *Constt. Apost.* viii. 12. 14, it is said of *Christ* that He τῷ κόσμῳ κατήλλαξε God, and § 17, of *God : σοῦ καταλλαγέντος αὐτοῖς* (with believers).

This is grammatically admissible, since we may say διανοεῖσθαι ἐν, *animo versari in* (Ps. lxxiii. 8; Ecclus. vi. 37; Plato, *Prot.* p. 341 E), and therefore the repetition of the article was not necessary. But the *badness* of the disposition was so entirely self-evident from the context, that the assumed more precise definition by ἐν τοῖς ἔργ. τ. πονηρ. would appear tediously circumstantial.—The articles τῇ and τοῖς denote the disposition *which they have had*, and the works *which they have done*. In the latter case the *subjoined* attributive *furnished with the article* (τοῖς πονηροῖς) is not causal ("*because* they were bad," Hofmann), but *emphatically* brings into prominence the quality, as at Eph. vi. 13; 1 Cor. vii. 14, and often (Winer, p. 126 [E. T. 167]). — νυνὶ δὲ ἀποκατηλλάγητε] as if previously ὑμεῖς κ.τ.λ. were used (see above) : *Ye also ... have nevertheless now become reconciled.* On δέ after participles which supply the place of the protasis, as here, where the thought is: *although* ye formerly, etc., see Klotz, *ad Devar.* p. 374 ff.; Maetzner, *ad Antiph.* p. 136; Kühner, *ad Xen. Mem.* iii. 7. 8, *Anab.* vi. 6. 16. On νυνί, with the aorist following, comp. ver. 26; Rom. vii. 6; Eph. ii. 13; Plat. *Symp.* p. 193 A: πρὸ τοῦ ... ἐν ἦμεν, νυνὶ δὲ διὰ τὴν ἀδικίαν διῳκίσθημεν ὑπὸ τ. θεοῦ. Ellendt, *Lex Soph.* II. p. 176; Kühner, II. 2, p. 672. It denotes the present time, which *has set in* with the ἀποκατηλλ. (comp. Buttmann, *Neut. Gr.* p. 171 [E. T. 197]) ; and the latter has taken place *objectively* through the death of Christ, ver. 22, although realized subjectively in the readers only when they *became believers*—whereby the reconciliation became *appropriated* to them, and there existed now for them a decisive contrast of their νυνί with their ποτέ.[1] The reconciling *subject* is, according to the context (vv. 19, 20), not Christ (as at Eph. ii. 16), *through* whom (comp. Rom. v. 10; 2 Cor. v. 18) the reconciliation has taken place (see ver. 20), but, as at 2 Cor. v. 19, *God* (in opposition to Chrysostom, Theodoret, Oecumenius, Beza, Calvin, Estius, Calovius, Heinrichs, and others, including de Wette and Ewald). For the reference to Christ even the reading ἀποκατήλλαξεν would by no means furnish a reason, far less a

---

[1] Comp. Luthardt, *vom freien Willen*, p. 403.

necessity, since, on the contrary, even this *active* would have, according to the correct explanation of εὐδόκησε in ver. 19, to be taken as referring to *God* (in opposition to Hofmann).

Ver. 22. Ἐν τῷ σώματι κ.τ.λ.] *that, by means of which* they have been reconciled; corresponding to the δι᾽ αὐτοῦ and διὰ τοῦ αἵματος τοῦ σταυροῦ αὐτοῦ of ver. 20 : *in the body of His flesh by means of death.* Since *God* is the reconciling subject, we are not at liberty, with Elzevir, Scholz, and others, to read αὑτοῦ (with the *spiritus asper*), which would not be justified, even though Christ were the subject. We have further to note : (1) διὰ τ. θανάτου informs us *whereby* the being reconciled ἐν τῷ σώματι τ. σ. αὐ. *was brought about*, namely, by the *death* occurring, without which the reconciliation would not have taken place in the body of Christ. (2) Looking to the concrete presentation of the matter, and because the procuring element is subsequently brought forward specially and on its own account by διά, the ἐν is not, with Erasmus and many others, to be taken as *instrumental*, but is to be left as *local ;* not, however, in *the* sense that Christ accomplished the ἀπο-καταλλάσσειν *in* His body, which was fashioned materially like ours (Hofmann, comp. Calvin and others, including Bleek) —which, in fact, would amount to the perfectly self-evident point, that it took place in His corporeally-human form of being,—but, doubtless, especially as διὰ τοῦ θανάτου follows, in *the* sense, that *in the body* of Christ, by means of the death therein accomplished, our reconciliation was objectively realized, which fact of salvation, therefore, *inseparably asso-ciated itself* with His body ; comp. ἐν τῇ σαρκί μου, ver. 24, see also 1 Pet. ii. 24 and Huther *in loc.* The conception of substitution, however, though involved in the *thing* (in the ἱλαστήριον), is not to be sought in ἐν (in opposition to Böhmer and Baumgarten-Crusius). (3) The reason for the *intentional* use of the *material* description : "in the body *which consisted of His flesh*" (comp. ii. 11 ; Ecclus. xxiii. 16), is to be sought in the apologetic interest of antagonism to the *false teachers*, against whom, however, the charge of *Docetism*, possibly on the ground of ii. 23, can the less be proved (in opposition to Beza, Balduin, Böhmer, Steiger, Huther, and Dalmer), as Paul nowhere in the epistle expressly treats of the material *Incarnation,* which he would hardly have omitted to do in contrast to Docetism (comp. 1 John).   In fact, the apostle found sufficient occasion for writing about the reconciliation as he has done here and in ver. 20, in the *faith in angels* on the part of his opponents, by which they ascribed the reconciling mediation with God in part to those higher *spiritual* beings (who are without σῶμα τῆς σαρκός).   Other writers have adopted the view, without any ground whatever in the connection, that Paul has thus written in order to distinguish the real body of Christ from the spiritual σῶμα of the *church* (Bengel, Michaelis, Storr, Olshausen).   The other σῶμα of Christ, which contrasts with His earthly body of flesh (Rom. i. 3, viii. 3), is His glorified heavenly body, Phil. iii. 21; 1 Cor. xv. 47 ff.   References, however, such as Calvin, *e.g.,* has discovered (" humile, terrenum et infirmitatibus multis obnoxium corpus"), or Grotius (" tantas res perfecit instrumento adeo tenui ;" comp. also Estius and others), are forced upon the words, in which the form of expression is selected simply in opposition to *spiritualistic* erroneous doctrines.   Just as little may we import into the simple historical statement of the means διὰ τοῦ θανάτου, with Hofmann, *the ignominy of shedding His blood on the cross,* since no modal definition to that effect is subjoined or indicated. — παραστῆσαι ὑμᾶς κ.τ.λ.] Ethical *definition of the object aimed at* in the ἀποκαταλλ.: ye have been reconciled ... *in order to present you,* etc.   The presenting *subject* is therefore the subject of ἀποκαταλλ., so that it is to be explained : ἵνα παραστήσητε ὑμᾶς, *ut sisteretis vos,* and therefore this continuation of the discourse is by no means awkward in its relation to the reading ἀποκαταλλάγητε (in opposition to de Wette).   We should be only justified in expecting ἑαυτούς (as Huther suggests) instead of ὑμᾶς (comp. Rom. xii. 1) if (comp. Rom. vi. 13 ; 2 Tim. ii. 15) the connection required a reflexive emphasis.   According to the reading ἀποκατήλλαξεν the sense is *ut sisteret vos,* in which case, however, the subject would not be *Christ* (Hofmann), but, as in every case since εὐδόκησε in ver. 19, *God.*—The *point of time* at which the παραστ. is to take place (observe the *aorist*) is that of *the judgment,* in

which *they shall come forth* holy, etc., *before the Judge.* Comp.
ver. 28, and on Eph. v. 27. This reference (comp. Bähr,
Olshausen, Bleek) is required by the context in ver. 23, where
the παραστῆσαι κ.τ.λ. is made dependent on *continuance in the
faith* as its condition ; consequently there cannot be meant *the
result already accomplished by the reconciliation itself,* namely,
the state of δικαιοσύνη entered upon through it (so usually,
including Hofmann). The state of justification sets in at any
rate, and unconditionally, through the reconciliation ; but it
may be lost again, and at the Parousia will be found subsisting only in the event of the reconciled remaining constant
to the faith, by means of which they have appropriated the
reconciliation, ver. 23. — ἁγίους κ.τ.λ.] does not represent the
subjects as *sacrifices* (Rom. xii. 1), which would not consist
with the fact that *Christ* is the sacrifice, and also would not
be in harmony with ἀνεγκλ. ; it rather describes *without* figure
the *moral holiness* which, after the justification attained by
means of faith, is wrought by the Holy Spirit (Rom. vii. 6,
viii. 2, 9, *et al.*), and which, on the part of man, is preserved
and maintained by continuance in the faith (ver. 23). The
three predicates are not intended to represent the relation
" erga *Deum,* respectu *vestri,* and respectu *proximi*" (Bengel,
Bähr), since, in point of fact, ἀμώμους (*blameless,* Eph. i. 4,
v. 27 ; Herod. ii. 177 ; Plat. *Rep.* p. 487 A : οὐδ᾽ ἂν ὁ Μῶμος
τό γε τοιοῦτον μέμψαιτο) no less than ἀνεγκλ. (*reproachless,*
1 Cor. i. 8) points to an *external* judgment : but the moral
condition is intended to be described with exhaustive emphasis
positively (ἁγίους) and *negatively* (ἀμώμ. and ἀνεγκλ.). The
idea of the moral holiness of the righteous through faith
is thoroughly Pauline ; comp. not only Eph. ii. 10, Tit. ii.
14, iii. 8, but also such passages as Rom. vi. 1–23, viii. 4 ff. ;
Gal. v. 22–25 ; 1 Cor. ix. 24 ff. ; 2 Cor. xi. 2, *et al.* — κατενώπιον αὐτοῦ] refers to *Christ,*[1] to His judicial appearance at
the Parousia, just as by the previous αὐτοῦ after σαρκός *Christ*

---

[1] So also Holtzmann, p. 47, though holding in favour of the priority of Eph.
i. 4, that the *sense* requires a reference to *God,* although *syntactically* the reference is made to Christ. But, in fact, the one is just as consistent with the sense
as the other.

also was meant. The *usual* reference to *God* (so Huther, de Wette, Baumgarten-Crusius, Ewald, Bleek) is connected with the reading ἀποκατήλλαξεν taken as so referring; comp. Jude 24; Eph. i. 4. The objection that κατενώπιον elsewhere occurs only in reference to *God*, is without force; for that this is the case in the few passages where the word is used, seems to be purely accidental, since ἐνώπιον is also applied to Christ (2 Tim. ii. 14), and since in the notion itself there is nothing opposed to this reference. The frequent use of the expression "before *God*" is traceable to the theocratically national *currency* of this conception, which by no means excludes the expression "before *Christ*." So ἔμπροσθεν is also used of Christ in 1 Thess. ii. 19. Comp. 2 Cor. v. 10: ἔμπροσθεν τοῦ βήματος τοῦ Χριστοῦ, which is a *commentary* on our κατενώπιον αὐτοῦ; see also Matt. xxv. 32.

REMARK.—The proper reference of παραστῆσαι κ.τ.λ. to the *judgment*, as also the *condition* appended in ver. 23, place it beyond doubt that what is meant here (it is otherwise in Eph. i. 4) is *the* holiness and blamelessness, which is entered upon through justification by faith *actu judiciali* and is positively wrought by the Holy Spirit, but which, on the other hand, *is preserved and maintained* up to the judgment by the *self-active perseverance of faith* in virtue of the new life of the reconciled (Rom. vi.); so that the justitia *inhaerens* is therefore neither meant alone (Chrysostom, Oecumenius, Theophylact, Calvin, and others), nor excluded (Theodoret, Erasmus, Beza, and others), but is included. Comp. Calovius.

Ver. 23. Requirement, with which is associated not, indeed, the being included in the work of reconciliation (Hofmann), but the attainment of its blessed final aim, which would otherwise be forfeited, namely the παραστῆσαι κ.τ.λ. above described : *so far at any rate as ye*, i.e. *assuming, namely, that* ye, etc. A confidence that the readers *will fulfil* this condition is not conveyed by the εἴγε in itself (see on 2 Cor. v. 3; Gal. iii. 4; Eph. iii. 2), and is not implied here by the context; but Paul sets forth the relation purely as a *condition certainly taking place*, which they *have to fulfil*, in order to attain the παραστῆσαι κ.τ.λ. — that " fructus in posterum lae-

tissimus" of their reconciliation (Bengel). — τῇ πίστει]
belonging to ἐπιμέν.: *abide by the faith,* do not cease from it.[1]
See on Rom. vi. 1. The *mode* of this abiding is indicated by
what follows positively (τεθεμ. κ. ἑδραῖοι), and negatively (κ. μὴ
μετακιν. κ.τ.λ.), under the figurative conception of a *building,*
in which, and that with reference to the Parousia pointed at by
παραστῆσαι κ.τ.λ., the hope of the gospel is conceived as the
foundation, in so far as *continuance* in the faith *is based* on
this, and is in fact not possible without it (ver. 27). "Spe
amissa perseverantia concidit," Grotius. On τεθεμελ., which
is not interjected (Holtzmann), comp. Eph. iii. 17; 1 Pet.
v. 10; and on ἑδραῖοι, 1 Cor. xv. 58. The opposite of
τεθεμελ. is χωρὶς θεμελίου, Luke vi. 49; but it would be a
contrast to the τεθεμελ. καὶ ἑδραῖοι, if they were μετακινούμενοι
κ.τ.λ. ; concerning μή, see Winer, p. 443 [E. T. 596];
Baeumlein, *Part.* p. 295. — μετακινούμ.] *passively,* through
the influence of false doctrines and other seductive forces. —
ἀπό] *away . . . from,* so as to stand no longer on hope as the
foundation of perseverance in the faith. Comp. Gal. i. 6. —
The ἐλπὶς τοῦ εὐαγγ. (which is proclaimed through the gospel
by means of its promises, comp. ver. 5, and on Eph. i. 18) is
the hope of eternal life in the Messianic kingdom, which has
been imparted to the believer in the gospel. Comp. vv. 4,
5, 27; Rom. v. 2, viii. 24; Tit. i. 2 f., iii. 7. — οὐ ἠκούσατε
κ.τ.λ.] three definitions rendering the μὴ μετακινεῖσθαι κ.τ.λ.
in its universal *obligation* palpably apparent to the readers ;
for such a μετακινεῖσθαι would, in the case of the Colossians,
be inexcusable (οὗ ἠκούσατε, comp. Rom. x. 18), would set at
naught the universal proclamation of the gospel (τοῦ κηρυχθ.

---

[1] In our Epistle faith is by no means postponed to knowing and perceiving
(comp. ii. 5, 7, 12), as Baur asserts in his *Neut. Theol.* p. 272. The frequent
emphasis laid upon knowledge, insight, comprehension, and the like, is not to
be put to the account of an intellectualism, which forms a fundamental peculiarity betokening the author and age of this Epistle (and especially of that to
the Ephesians), as Holtzmann conceives, p. 216 ff. ; on the contrary, it was
owing to the attitude of the apostle towards the antagonistic philosophical speculations. Comp. also Grau, *Entwickelungsgesch. d. N. T.* II. p. 153 ff. It was
owing to the necessary relations, in which the apostle, with his peculiarity of
being all things to all men, found himself placed towards the interests of the
time and place.

κ.τ.λ.), and would stand in contrast to the personal weight
of the apostle's position as its servant (οὗ ἐγεν. κ.τ.λ.).   If,
with Hofmann, we join τοῦ κηρυχθέντος as an adjective to τοῦ
εὐαγγελίου, οὗ ἠκούσατε, we withdraw from the οὗ ἠκούσατε
that element of practical significance, which it must have, if
it is not to be superfluous.   Nor is justice done to the third
point, οὗ ἐγενόμην κ.τ.λ., if the words (so Hofmann, comp. de
Wette) are meant to help the apostle, by enforcing what he
is thenceforth to write with the weight of his name, *to come
to his condition at that time.*   According to this, they would
be merely destined as a transition.   In accordance with the
context, however, and without arbitrary tampering, they can
only have the same aim with the two preceding attributives
which are annexed to the gospel; and, with this aim, how
appropriately and forcibly do they stand at the close![1]   λοιπὸν
γὰρ μέγα ἦν τὸ Παύλου ὄνομα, Oecumenius, comp. Chrysostom.
Comp. on ἐγὼ Παῦλος, with a view to urge his personal
authority, 2 Cor. x. 1 ; Gal. v. 2 ; Eph. iii. 1; 1 Thess. ii. 18 ;
Philem. 19.   It is to be observed, moreover, that if Paul
himself had been the teacher of the Colossians, this relation
would certainly not have been passed over here in silence. —
ἐν πάσῃ κτίσει (without τῇ, see the critical remarks) is to
be taken as : *in presence of* (*coram,* see Ast, *Lex. Plat.* I. p. 701 ;
Winer, p. 360 [E. T. 481]) *every creature,* before everything
that is created (κτίσις, as in i. 15).   There is nothing created
under the heaven, in whose sphere and environment (comp.
Kühner, II. 1, p. 401) the gospel had not been proclaimed.
The sense of the word must be left in this entire generality,
and not limited to the *heathen* (Bähr).   It is true that the
popular expression of universality may just as little be pressed
here as in ver. 6.   Comp. Herm. *Past.* sim. viii. 3 ; Ignatius,
Rom. 2.   But as in i. 15, so also here πᾶσα κτίσις is not
all creation, according to which the sense is assumed to be :
" *on a stage embracing the whole world*" (Hofmann).   This Paul
would properly have expressed by ἐν πάσῃ τῇ κτίσει, or ἐν
παντὶ τῷ κόσμῳ, or ἐν ὅλῳ τῷ κ. ; comp. ver. 6.   The expression

---

[1] According to Baur, indeed, such passages as the present are among those
which betray the *double personality* of the author.

is more lofty and poetic than in ver. 6, appropriate to the close of the section, not a fanciful reproduction betraying an imitator and a later age (Holtzmann). Omitting even οὗ ἠκούσατε (because it is not continued by οὗ καὶ ἐγώ), Holtzmann arrives merely at the connection between ver. 23 and ver. 25 : μὴ μετακιν. ἀπὸ τοῦ εὐαγγ. οὗ ἐγεν. ἐγὼ Π. διάκ. κατὰ τὴν οἰκον. τ. θεοῦ τὴν δοθεῖσάν μοι εἰς ὑμᾶς, just as he then would read further thus: πληρῶσαι τ. λόγ. τ. θεοῦ, εἰς ὃ καὶ κοπιῶ ἀγωνιζόμ. κατὰ τ. ἐνέργ. αὐτοῦ τὴν ἐνεργουμ. ἐν ἐμοί. — διάκονος] See on Eph. iii. 7. Paul has *become* such through his calling, Gal. i. 15 f.; Eph. iii. 7. Observe the *aorist*.

Ver. 24.[1] A more precise description of this relation of service, and that, in the first place, with respect to the *sufferings* which the apostle is now enduring, ver. 24, and then with respect to his important calling generally, vv. 25–29. — ὅς (see the critical remarks) νῦν χαίρω κ.τ.λ. : *I who now rejoice*, etc. How touchingly, so as to win the hearts of the readers, does this join itself with the last element of encouragement in ver. 23 ! — νῦν] places in contrast with the great element of his *past*, expressed by οὗ ἐγεν. κ.τ.λ., which has imposed on the apostle so many sorrows (comp. Acts ix. 16), the situation as it *now* exists with him in that relation of service on his part to the gospel. This *present* condition, however, he characterizes, in full magnanimous appreciation of the sufferings under which he writes, as joyfulness over them, and as a becoming perfect in the fellowship of tribulation with Christ, which is accomplished through them. It is plain, therefore, that the emphatic νῦν is not transitional (Bähr) or inferential (Lücke : " quae cum ita sint"); nor yet is it to be defined, with Olshausen, by arbitrary importation of the thought : now, *after that I look upon the church as firmly established* (comp. Dalmer), or, with Hofmann, to be taken as standing in contrast to the apostolic *activity*. — ἐν τοῖς παθήμ.] *over* the sufferings; see on Phil. i. 18 ; Rom. v. 3. This joy in suffering is so entirely in harmony with the Pauline spirit,

[1] See upon ver. 24, Lücke, *Progr.* 1833 ; Huther in the *Stud. u. Krit.* 1838, p. 189 ff.

that its source is not to be sought (in opposition to Holtzmann) in 2 Cor. vii. 4, either for the present passage or for
Eph. iii. 13 ; comp. also Phil. ii. 17. — ὑπὲρ ὑμῶν] joins itself
to παθήμασιν so as to form one conception, without connecting article.   Comp. on vv. 1, 4 ; 2 Cor. vii. 7 ; Eph. iii. 13 ;
Gal. iv. 14.   Since ὑπέρ, according to the context, is not to be
taken otherwise than as in ὑπὲρ τοῦ σώμ. αὐτοῦ, it can neither
mean *instead of* (Steiger, Catholic expositors, but not Cornelius
a Lapide or Estius), nor *on account of* (Rosenmüller, Heinrichs, Flatt; comp. Eph. iii. 1 ; Phil. i. 29), but simply : *in
commodum*,[1] namely, ἵνα ὑμᾶς ὠφελῆσαι δυνηθῶ, Oecumenius,
and that, indeed, *by that honourable attestation and glorifying
of your Christian state, which is actually contained in my
tribulations;* for the latter show forth the faith of the readers,
for the sake of which the apostle has undertaken and borne
the suffering, as the holy divine thing which is worthy of
such a sacrifice.   Comp. Phil. i. 12 ff. ; Eph. iii. 13.   The
reference to the *example*, which confirms the readers' faith
(Grotius, Wolf, Bähr, and others), introduces inappropriately
a reflection, the indirect and tame character of which is not
at all in keeping with the emotion of the discourse. — The
ὑμῶν, meaning the *readers*, though the relation in question
concerns *Pauline Christians generally*, is to be explained by
the tendency of affectionate sympathy to individualize (comp.
Phil. i. 25, ii. 17, *et al.*).   It is arbitrary, doubtless, to supply
τῶν ἐθνῶν here from Eph. iii. 1 (Flatt, Huther) ; but that
Paul, nevertheless, has his readers in view *as Gentile Christians*,
and as standing in a special relation to himself as *apostle of
the Gentiles*, is shown by vv. 25–27. — καί] not equivalent to
καὶ γάρ (Heinrichs, Bähr), but the simple *and*, subjoining to
the subjective state of feeling the *objective* relation of suffering, which the apostle sees accomplishing itself in his destiny.
It therefore *carries on*, but not from the special (ὑμῶν) " ad
totam omnino ecclesiam" (Lücke), since the new point to be
introduced is contained in the specific ἀνταναπληρῶ . . .
Χριστοῦ, and not in ὑπὲρ τ. σώμ. αὐτοῦ.   The connection of

---

[1] So also Bisping, who, however, explains it of *the meritoriousness of good
works availing for others.*

ideas is rather : " I *rejoice* over my sufferings, and what a
holy *position* is theirs ! through them *I fulfil,*" etc. Hence
the notion of χαίρω is not, with Huther, to be carried over
also to ἀνταναπληρῶ : and I supplement *with joy,* etc. At
the same time, however, the statement introduced by καί
stands related to χαίρω as *elucidating* and *giving information* regarding it. — ἀνταναπληρῶ] The double compound
is more *graphic* than the simple ἀναπληρῶ, Phil. ii. 30 ;
1 Cor. xvi. 17 (*I fill up*), since ἀντί (*to fill up over against*)
indicates what is *brought in for the making complete* over
against the still existing ὑστερήματα. The *reference* of the ἀντί
lies therefore in the notion of what is lacking ; inasmuch,
namely, as the incomplete is rendered complete by the very
fact, that the supplement corresponding to what is lacking is
introduced in its stead.   It is the reference *of the corresponding adjustment,*[1] of the supplying of what is still wanting.
Comp. Dem. 182. 22 : ἀνταναπληροῦντες πρὸς τὸν εὐπορώτα-
τον ἀεὶ τοὺς ἀπορωτάτους (where the idea is, that the poverty
of the latter is *compensated for* by the wealth of the former) ;
so also ἀνταναπλήρωσις, Epicur. *ap. Diog. L.* x. 48 ; Dio Cass.
xliv. 48 : ὅσον . . . ἐνέδει, τοῦτο ἐκ τῆς παρὰ τῶν ἄλλων συντε-
λείας ἀνταναπληρωθῇ.   Comp. ἀντεμπίπλημι, Xen. *Anab.* iv.
5. 28 ; ἀνταναπλήθειν, Xen. *Hell.* ii. 4. 12 ; and ἀντιπληροῦν,
Xen. *Cyr.* ii. 2. 26.   The distinction of the word from the
simple ἀναπληροῦν does not consist in this, that the latter is
said of *him,* who " ὑστέρημα *a se* relictum *ipse* explet," and
ἀνταναπλ. of *him,* who " alterius ὑστέρημα *de suo* explet " (so
Winer, *de verbor. c. praepos. in N. T. usu,* 1838, III. p. 22) ;
nor yet in the endurance *vieing* with Christ, the author of the
afflictions (Fritzsche, *ad Rom.* III. p. 275) ; but in the circumstance, that in ἀνταναπλ. the filling up is conceived and
described as *defectui respondens,* in ἀναπλ., on the other hand,

---

[1] Many ideas are arbitrarily introduced by commentators, in order to bring
out of the ἀντί in ἀνταναπλ. a *reciprocal relation.* See *e.g.* Clericus : " Ille ego,
qui olim ecclesiam Christi vexaveram, *nunc vicissim* in ejus utilitatem pergo
multa mala perpeti." Others (see already Oecumenius) have found in it the
meaning : for *requital* of that which Christ suffered for us ; comp. also Grimm
in his *Lexicon.* Wetstein remarks shortly and rightly : " ἀντὶ ὑστερήματος suc-
cedit πλήρωμα,"—or rather ἀναπλήρωμα.

only in general as *completio*. See 1 Cor. xvi. 17 ; Phil. ii. 30 ;
Plat. *Legg.* xii. p. 957 A, *Tim.* p. 78 D, *et al.* Comp. also
Tittmann, *Synon.* p. 230. — τὰ ὑστερήματα] The *plural*
indicates those elements yet wanting in the sufferings of
Christ in order to completeness. Comp. 1 Thess. iii. 10 ;
2 Cor. ix. 12. — τῶν θλίψ. τοῦ Χριστοῦ] τοῦ X. is the genitive of the *subject.* Paul describes, namely, *his own sufferings,*
in accordance with the idea of the κοινωνεῖν τοῖς τοῦ Χριστοῦ
παθήμασι (1 Pet. iv. 13 ; comp. Matt. xx. 22 ; Heb. xiii. 13),
as *afflictions of Christ,* in so far as the apostolic suffering in
essential character was the same as Christ endured (the same
cup which Christ drank, the same baptism with which Christ
was baptized). Comp. on Rom. viii. 17 ; 2 Cor. i. 5 ; Phil.
iii. 10. The collective mass of these afflictions is conceived
in the form of a definite *measure,* just as the phrases ἀνα-
πιμπλάναι κακά, ἀναπλῆσαι κακὸν οἶτον, and the like, are
current in classic authors, according to a similar figurative
conception (Hom. *Il.* viii. 34. 354, xv. 132), Schweigh. *Lex.
Herod.* I. p. 42. He only who has suffered *all,* has *filled up*
the measure. That Paul is now, in his captivity fraught
with danger to life, on the point (the *present* ἀνταναπλ.
indicating the being in the act, see Bernhardy, p. 370) of
filling up all that still remains behind of this measure of
affliction, that he is therefore engaged in the final full solution
of his task of suffering, without leaving a single ὑστέρημα in
it,—this he regards as something grand and glorious, and
therefore utters the ἀνταναπληρῶ, which bears the emphasis at
the head of this declaration, with all the sense of *triumph*
which the approaching completion of such a work involves.
" *I rejoice on account of the sufferings which I endure for you,
and*—so highly have I to esteem this situation of affliction—*I am in the course of furnishing the complete fulfilment of what in my case still remains in arrear of fellowship of
affliction with Christ.*" This lofty consciousness, this feeling
of the grandeur of the case, very naturally involved not only
the selection of the most graphic expression possible, ἀνταναπληρῶ, to be emphatically prefixed, but also the description,
in the most honourable and sublime manner possible, of the

apostolic afflictions themselves as the θλίψεις τοῦ Χριστοῦ,[1] since in their kind and nature they are no other than those which Christ Himself has suffered. These sufferings *are*, indeed, sufferings *for Christ's sake* (so Vatablus, Schoettgen, Zachariae, Storr, Rosenmüller, Flatt, Böhmer, and others; comp. Wetstein), but they are not so *designated* by the genitive; on the contrary, the designation follows the idea of *ethical identity*, which is conveyed in the ἰσόμοιρον εἶναι τῷ Χριστῷ, as in Phil. iii. 10. Nor are they to be taken, with Lücke (comp. Fritzsche, *l.c.*), as : " afflictiones, quae Paulo apostolo *Christo auctore et auspice Christo* perferendae erant," since there is no ground to depart from the primary and most natural designation of the suffering subject (θλῖψις, with the genitive of the person, is *always* so used in the N. T., *e.g.* in 2 Cor. i. 4, 8, iv. 17 ; Eph. iii. 12 ; Jas. i. 27), considering how current is the idea of the κοινωνία of the sufferings of Christ. Theodoret's comment is substantially correct, though not exhibiting precisely the relation expressed by the genitive : Χριστὸς τὸν ὑπὲρ τῆς ἐκκλησίας κατεδέξατο θάνατον ... καὶ τὰ ἄλλα ὅσα ὑπέμεινε, καὶ ὁ θεῖος ἀπόστολος ὡσαύτως ὑπὲρ αὐτῆς ὑπέστη τὰ ποικίλα παθήματα. Ewald imports more, when he says that Paul designates his sufferings from the point of view of the continuation and further accomplishment of *the divine aim* in the sufferings of Christ. Quite erroneous, however, because at variance with the idea that Christ has exhausted the suffering appointed to Him in the decree of God for the redemption of the world (comp. also John xi. 52, xix. 30 ; Luke xxii. 37, xviii. 31 ; Rom. iii. 25 ; 2 Cor. v. 21, *et al.*), is not only the view of Heinrichs : " *qualia et Christus passurus fuisset, si diutius vixisset* " (so substantially also Phot. *Amphil.* 143), but also that of Hofmann, who explains it to mean : *the supplementary continuation of the afflictions* which *Christ* suffered in His earthly life—a continuation which belonged to the apostle as apostle *of the Gentiles*, and consisted in a suffering which *could not* have affected Christ,

---

[1] When de Wette describes our view of θλίψ. τ. Χ. as *tame*, and Schenkel as *tautological*, the incorrectness of this criticism arises from their not observing that the stress of the expression lies on ἀνταναπληρῶ, and not on τ. θλ. τ. Χ.

because He was only sent to the lost sheep *of Israel*. As if Christ's suffering were not, throughout the N. T., the one perfect and completely valid suffering *for all mankind*, but were rather to be viewed under the aspect of two quantitative *halves*, one of which He bore Himself as διάκονος περιτομῆς (Rom. xv. 8), leaving the other behind to be borne by Paul as the διδάσκαλος ἐθνῶν; so that *the first*, namely, that which Jesus suffered, consisted in the fact *that Israel brought Him to the cross*, because they would not allow Him to be their Saviour; whilst *the other*, as the complement of the first, consisted in this, that Paul *lay in captivity with his life at stake*, because Israel would not permit him to proclaim that Saviour to the Gentiles. Every explanation, which involves the idea of the suffering endured by Christ in the days of His flesh having been incomplete and needing supplement, is an anomaly which offends against the analogy of faith of the N. T. And how incompatible with the deep humility of the apostle (Eph. iii. 8; 1 Cor. xv. 9) would be the thought of being supposed to *supplement* that, which the highly exalted One (ver. 15 ff.) had suffered for the reconciliation of the universe (ver. 20 ff.)! Only when misinterpreted in this fashion can the utterance be regarded as one *perfectly foreign to Paul* (as is asserted by Holtzmann, pp. 21 f., 152, 226); even Eph. i. 22 affords no basis for such a view. As head of the Church, which is His body, and which He fills, He is *in statu gloriae* in virtue of His *kingly* office. Others, likewise, holding the genitive to be that of the *subject*, have discovered here the conception of the *suffering of Christ in the Church*, His *body*,[1] so that when the *members* suffer, *the head suffers also*. So Chrysostom and Theophylact (who compare the apostle with a lieutenant, who, when the general-in-chief is removed, takes the latter's place and receives his wounds), Theodore of Mopsuestia, Augustine, Erasmus, Luther, Beza, Calvin, Melanchthon, Clarius, Cornelius a Lapide, Vitringa, Bengel, Michaelis, and others, including Steiger, Bähr, Olshausen, de Wette, Schenkel, Dalmer; comp. Grotius and Calovius, and even Bleek. But the idea of *Christ suffering* in the sufferings of His people

[1] Comp. also Sabatier, *l'apôtre Paul*, p. 213.

(Olshausen: " Christ is the suffering God in the world's history!") is nowhere found in the N. T., not even in Acts ix. 4, where Christ, indeed, appears as the One against whom the persecution of Christians is *directed*, but not as *affected by it in the sense of suffering*. He lives in His people (Gal. ii. 20), speaks in them (2 Cor. xiii. 3); His heart beats in them (Phil. i. 8); He is mighty in them (ver. 29), when they are weak (2 Cor. xii. 9), their hope, their life, their victory; but nowhere is it said that He *suffers* in them. This idea, more-over—which, consistently carried out, would involve even the conception of the *dying* of Christ in the martyrs—would be entirely opposed to the victoriously reigning life of the Lord in glory, with whose death all His sufferings are at an end, Acts ii. 34 ff.; 1 Cor. xv. 24; Phil. ii. 9 ff.; Luke xxiv. 26; John xix. 30. Crucified ἐξ ἀσθενείας, He lives ἐκ δυνάμεως Θεοῦ, 2 Cor. xiii. 4, at the right hand of God exalted above all the heavens and filling the universe (Eph. i. 22 f., iv. 10), ruling, conquering, and beyond the reach of further suffering (Heb. iii. 18 ff.). The application made by Cajetanus, Bellar-mine, Salmeron, and others, of this explanation for the pur-pose of establishing the *treasury of indulgences*, which consists of the merits not merely of Christ but also *of the apostles and saints*, is a Jewish error (4 Macc. vi. 26, and Grimm *in loc.*), historically hardly worthy of being noticed, though still de-fended, poorly enough, by Bisping. — ἐν τῇ σαρκί μου] belongs to ἀνταναπλ., as to which it specifies the *more precise mode;* not to τῶν θλίψ. τ. X. (so Storr, Flatt, Bähr, Steiger, Böhmer, Huther), with which it *might* be combined so as to form one idea, but it would convey a more precise description of the Christ-sufferings experienced by the apostle, for which there was no motive, and which was evident of itself. Belong-ing to ἀνταναπλ., it contains with ὑπὲρ τοῦ σώμ. ἀ. a *pointed* definition (σάρξ ... σῶμα) of the mode and of the aim.[1] Paul accomplishes that ἀνταναπληροῦν *in his flesh*,[2] which in its

[1] Steiger rightly perceived that ἐν τ. σαρκί μ. and ὑπὲρ τ. σ. ἀ. belong together; but he erroneously coupled both with τῶν θλ. τ. X (" the sufferings which Christ endures in my flesh for His body"), owing to his incorrect view of the θλίψεις τ. X

[2] Hofmann thinks, without reason, that, according to our explanation of

natural weakness, exposed to suffering and death, receives the
affliction from without and feels it psychically (comp. 2 Cor.
iv. 11; Gal. iv. 14; 1 Pet. iv. 1), for the benefit of the *body*
of Christ, which is the *church* (comp. ver. 18), for the confirmation, advancement, and glory of which (comp. above on
ὑπὲρ ὑμῶν) he endures the Christ - sufferings.   Comp. Eph.
iii. 13.   The significant purpose of the addition of ἐν τῇ σαρκὶ
κ.τ.λ. is to bring out more clearly and render palpable, in
connection with the ἀνταναπληρῶ κ.τ.λ., what *lofty happiness*
he experiences in this very ἀνταναπληροῦν.   He is therein
privileged to step in with his mortal σάρξ for the benefit
of the holy and eternal body of Christ, which is the church.

Ver. 25. That *He* suffers thus, as is stated in ver. 24, for
the good of the *church*, is implied in his special *relation of
service* to the latter; hence the epexegetical relative clause
ἧς ἐγενόμην κ.τ.λ. (comp. on ver. 18): *whose servant I have
become* in conformity with my divine appointment as preacher
to the *Gentiles* (κατὰ τ. οἰκον. κ.τ.λ.).   In this way Paul now
brings this his *specific and distinctive calling* into prominence
after the general description of himself as servant *of the gospel*
in ver. 23, and here again he gives expression to the consciousness of his *individual* authority by the emphasized ἐγώ.   The
relation of the testimony regarding himself in ver. 25 to that
of ver. 23 is *climactic*, not that of a clumsy duplicate (Holtzmann). — κατὰ τὴν οἰκονομ. κ.τ.λ.] *in accordance with the
stewardship of God, which is given to me with reference to you.*
The οἰκονομία τ. Θεοῦ is in itself nothing else than a characteristic designation of the apostolic office, in so far as its
holder is appointed as *administrator of the household of God*
(the οἰκοδεσπότης), by which, in the theocratic figurative conception, is denoted the *church* (comp. 1 Tim. iii. 15).   Comp.
1 Cor. ix. 17, iv. 1; Tit. i. 7.   Hence such an one is, *in consequence of* this office conferred upon him, in his relation to
the church the *servant* of the latter (2 Cor. iv. 5), to which

ἀνταναπληρῶ κ.τ.λ., we ought to join ἐν τῇ σαρκί μου with τῶν θλίψ. τ. X., as the
latter would otherwise be without any reference to the person of the apostle.   It
has, in fact, this reference through the very statement, that the ἀνταναπληροῦν
κ.τ.λ. takes places *in the flesh of the apostle.*

function God has appointed him, just because he is His
steward. This sacred stewardship then receives its more precise distinguishing definition, *so far as it is entrusted to Paul,*
by the addition of εἰς ὑμᾶς κ.τ.λ. It is purely arbitrary, and
at variance with the context (τὴν δοθ. μοι), to depart from the
proper signification, and to take it as *institution, arrangement*
(see on Eph. i. 10, iii. 2). So Chrysostom and his successors
(with much wavering), Beza, Calvin, Estius, Rosenmüller, and
others. It is well said by Cornelius a Lapide : " in domo Dei,
quae est ecclesia, sum oeconomus, ut dispensem . . . bona et
dona Dei domini mei." Comp. on 1 Cor. iv. 1. — εἰς ὑμᾶς]
although the office concerned *Gentile Christians* generally ;
a concrete appropriation, as in ver. 24. Comp. on Phil. i. 24.
It is to be joined with τ. δοθεῖσάν μοι, as in Eph. iii. 2 ; not
with πληρῶσαι κ.τ.λ. (Hofmann), with the comprehensive tenor
of which the individualizing *"for you"* is not in harmony,
when it is properly explained (see below). — πληρῶσαι κ.τ.λ.]
telic infinitive, depending on τὴν δοθεῖσάν μοι εἰς ὑμᾶς, beside
which it stands (Rom. xv. 15 f.) ; not on ἧς ἐγεν. διάκ.
(Huther). Paul, namely, has received the office of *Apostle to
the Gentiles,* in order through the discharge of it *to bring to
completion* the gospel (τὸν λόγον τ. Θεοῦ, 1 Cor. xiv. 36 ;
2 Cor. ii. 17, iv. 2 ; 1 Thess. ii. 13 ; Acts iv. 29, 31, vi. 2,
and frequently), obviously not as regards its contents, but
as regards its universal destination, according to which the
knowledge of salvation had not yet reached its fulness, so long
as it was only communicated to the Jews and not to the
Gentiles also. The latter was accomplished through *Paul,* who
thereby *made full* the gospel—conceived, in respect of its
proclamation in accordance with its destiny, as a measure to be
filled—just because the divine stewardship *for the Gentiles* had
been committed to him. The same conception of πλήρωσις
occurs in Rom. xv. 19. Comp. Erasmus, *Paraphr. ;* also
Calovius.[1] Similarly Bengel : " ad omnes perducere ; P. ubique
ad summa tendit." Partly from not attending to the contextual reference to the element, contained in τ. δοθ. μοι εἰς

[1] Who rightly says : "Nimirum *impletur* ita verbum *non ratione sui* ceu im-
perfectum, sed ratione *hominum,* cum ad plures sese diffundit."

ὑμᾶς, of the πλήρωσις of the gospel which was implied in the *Gentile - apostolic* ministry, and partly from not doing justice to the verbal sense of the selected expression πληρῶ-σαι, or attributing an arbitrary meaning to it, commentators have taken very arbitrary views of the passage, such as, for example, Luther: *to preach copiously;* Olshausen, whom Dalmer follows: "to *proclaim it completely* as respects its whole tenor and compass;" Cornelius a Lapide: "ut compleam praedicationem ev., *quam cocpit Christus;*" Vitringa, Storr, Flatt, Bähr: πληροῦν has after נמר the signification of the simple *docere;* Huther: it means either *to diffuse,* or (as Steiger also takes it) *to "realize,"* to introduce into the life, inasmuch as a doctrine not preached is *empty;*[1] de Wette: *to "execute,"* the word of God being regarded either as a *commission* or (comp. Heinrichs) as a *decree;* Estius and others, following Theodoret: "ut *omnia loca* impleam *verbo Dei*" (quite at variance with the words here, comp. Acts v. 28); Fritzsche, *ad Rom.* III. p. 275: *to supplement,* namely, *by continuing the instruction of your teacher Epaphras.* Others, inconsistently with what follows, have explained the λόγος τ. Θεοῦ to mean the divine *promise* ("partim de Christo in genere, partim de vocatione gentium," Beza, comp. Vatablus), in accordance with which πληρ. would mean *exsequi.* Chrysostom has rightly understood τ. λόγ. τ. Θεοῦ of *the gospel,* but takes πληρῶσαι, to which he attaches εἰς ὑμᾶς, as meaning: *to bring to full, firm faith* (similarly Calvin)—a view justified neither by the word in itself nor by the context.

Ver. 26. Appositional more precise definition of the λόγος τοῦ Θεοῦ, and that as regards its great *contents.* — As to τὸ μυστήριον κ.τ.λ., *the decree of redemption,* hidden from eternity in God, fulfilled through Christ, and made known through the gospel, see on Eph. i. 9. It embraces the *Gentiles* also; and this is a special part of its nature that had been veiled (see Eph. iii. 5), which, however, is not brought into prominence till

---

[1] In a similarly artificial fashion, emptying the purposely chosen expression of its meaning, Hofmann comes ultimately to the bare sense: "*to proclaim* God's word," asserting that the word is a *fact,* and so he who *proclaims* the fact *fulfils* it.

ver. 27. Considering the so frequent treatment of this idea in Paul's writings, and its natural correlation with that of the γνῶσις, an acquaintance with the Gospel of Matthew (xiii. 11) is not to be inferred here (Holtzmann).[1] — ἀπὸ τῶν αἰώνων κ. ἀπὸ τῶν γενεῶν] This twofold description, as also the repetition of ἀπό, has solemn emphasis: *from the ages and from the generations.* The article indicates the ages that *had existed* (since the beginning), and the generations that *have lived.* As to ἀπὸ τῶν αἰώνων, comp. on Eph. iii. 9. Paul could not write πρὸ τῶν αἰών., because while the divine decree was *formed* prior to all time (1 Cor. ii. 7; 2 Tim. i. 9), its *concealment* is not conceivable before the beginning of the times and generations of mankind, *to whom* it remained unknown. Expressions such as Rom. xvi. 25, χρόνοις αἰωνίοις,[2] and Tit. i. 2 (see Huther *in loc.*), do not conflict with this view. ἀπὸ τ. γενεῶν does not occur elsewhere in the N. T.; but comp. Acts xv. 21. The two ideas are not to be regarded as synonymous (in opposition to Huther and others), but are to be kept separate (*times—men*). — νυνὶ δὲ ἐφανερώθη] A transition to the finite tense, occasioned by the importance of the contrast. Comp. on i. 6. Respecting νυνί, see on ver. 21. The φανέρωσις has taken place *differently* according to the different subjects; partly by ἀποκάλυψις (Eph. iii. 5; 1 Cor. ii. 10), as in the case of Paul himself (Gal. i. 12, 15; Eph. iii. 3); partly by preaching (iv. 4; Tit. i. 3; Rom. xvi. 26); partly by both. The *historical realization* (de Wette; comp. 2 Tim. i. 10) was the antecedent of the φανέρωσις, but is not here this latter itself, which is, on the contrary, indicated by τοῖς ἁγίοις αὐτοῦ as a special act of clearly manifesting *communica-*

[1] Just as little ground is there for tracing κατὰ τὰ ἐντάλματα κ.τ.λ., in ii. 22, to Matt. xv. 9; οὐ κρατῶν, in ii. 19, to Matt. vii. 3, 4; ἀπάτη, in ii. 8, to Matt. xiii. 22; and in other instances. The author, who manifests so much lively copiousness of language, was certainly not thus confined and dependent in thought and expression.

[2] According to Holtzmann, indeed, p. 309 ff., the close of the Epistle to the Romans is to be held as proceeding from the post-apostolic *auctor ad Ephesios*,— a position which is attempted to be proved by the tones (quite Pauline, however) which Rom. xvi. 15-27 has in common with Col. i. 26 f.; Eph. iii. 20, iii. 9, 10, v. 21; and in support of it an erroneous interpretation of διὰ γραφῶν προφητικῶν, in Rom. xvi. 26, is invoked.

tion. — τοῖς ἁγίοις αὐτοῦ] *i.e.* not: *to the apostles and prophets
of the N. T.* (Flatt, Bähr, Böhmer, Steiger, Olshausen, Baumgarten-Crusius, following Estius and older expositors, and even
Theodoret, who, however, includes other Christians also),—
a view which is quite unjustifiably imported from Eph. iii. 5,[1]
whence also the reading ἀποστόλοις (instead of ἁγίοις) in F G
has arisen.   It refers to *the Christians generally.*   The mystery
was indeed *announced* to all (ver. 23), but was *made manifest*
only to the believers, who as such are the κλητοὶ ἅγιοι
belonging to God, Rom. i. 7, viii. 30, ix. 23 f.   Huther
wrongly desires to leave τοῖς ἁγίοις *indefinite,* because the
μυστήριον, so far as it embraced the Gentiles also, had not
come to be known to many Jewish-Christians.   But, apart from
the fact that the Judaists did not misapprehend the destination of redemption for the Gentiles in itself and generally,
but only the direct character of that destination (without a
transition through Judaism, Acts xv. 1, *et al.*), the ἐφανερώθη
τοῖς ἁγίοις αὐτοῦ is in fact a *summary* assertion, which is to
be construed *a potiori,* and does not cease to be true on
account of exceptional cases, in which the result was not
actually realized.

Ver. 27. Not *exposition* of the ἐφανερ. τοῖς ἁγ. αὐτοῦ, since
the γνωρίσαι has for its object not the μυστήριον itself, but the
glory of the latter among the Gentiles.   In reality, οἷς subjoins
an *onward movement* of the discourse, so that to the general
τὸ μυστήριον ἐφανερώθη τοῖς ἁγ. αὐτοῦ a *particular* element is
added: "The mystery was made manifest to His saints,—to
them, to whom (*quippe quibus*) God withal desired especially
to make known *that,* which is the riches of the glory of this
mystery among the Gentiles."   Along with the general
ἐφανερώθη τοῖς ἁγίοις αὐτοῦ God had this *special definite
direction* of His will.   From this the reason is plain why Paul
has written, not simply οἷς ἐγνώρισεν ὁ Θεός, but οἷς ἠθέλεσεν
ὁ Θεὸς γνωρίσαι.   The meaning that is usually discovered in

[1] Holtzmann also, p. 49, would have the apostles thought of "*first of all.*"
The resemblances to Eph. iii. 3, 5 do not postulate the similarity of the conception throughout.   This would assume a *mechanical process* of thought,
which could not be proved.

ἠθέλησεν, *free grace,* and the like (so Chrysostom, Theodoret, Calvin, Beza, and many others, including Bähr, Böhmer, de Wette; Huther is, with reason, doubtful), is therefore not the aim of the word, which is also not intended to express the *joyfulness* of the announcement (Hofmann), but simply and solely the idea: "He had a mind." — γνωρίσαι] *to make known,* like ἐφανερώθη, from which it differs in meaning not essentially, but only to this extent, that by ἐφανερ. the thing formerly hidden is designated as openly displayed (Rom. i. 19, iii. 21, xvi. 26; Eph. v. 13, *et al.*), and by γνωρίσαι that which was formerly unknown as *brought to knowledge.* Comp. Rom. xvi. 26, ix. 22; Eph. i. 9, iii. 3, 5, 10, vi. 19; Luke ii. 15, *et al.* The latter is not related to ἐφανερ. either as a something *more* (Bähr: the making fully acquainted with the nature); or as its *result* (de Wette); or as entering more into *detail* (Baumgarten-Crusius); or as *making* aware, namely *by experience* (Hofmann). — τί τὸ πλοῦτος τῆς δόξης κ.τ.λ.] *what is the riches of the glory of this mystery among the Gentiles,* i.e. *what rich fulness of the glory contained in this mystery exists among the Gentiles,*—since, indeed, this riches consists in the fact (ὅς ἐστι), that Christ is among you, in whom ye have the hope of glory. In order to a proper inter- pretation, let it be observed: (1) τί occupies *with emphasis* the place of the indirect ὅ, τι (see Poppo, *ad Xen. Cyrop.* i. 2. 10; Kühner, *ad Mem.* i. 1. 1; Winer, p. 158 f. [E. T. 210]), and denotes "*quae* sint divitiae" as regards *degree:* how great and unspeakable the riches, etc. Comp. on Eph. i. 18, iii. 18. The text yields this definition of the sense from the very connection with the quantitative idea τὸ πλοῦτος. (2) All the substantives are to be left in their full solemn force, without being resolved into adjectives (Erasmus, Luther, and many others: the glorious riches; Beza: "divitiae gloriosi hujus mysterii"). Chrysostom aptly remarks: σεμνῶς εἶπε καὶ ὄγκον ἐπέθηκεν ἀπὸ πολλῆς διαθέσεως, ἐπιτάσεις ζητῶν ἐπιτάσεων. Comp. Calvin: "*magniloquus* est in extollenda evangelii dignitate." (3) As τῆς δόξης is governed by τὸ πλοῦτος, so also is τοῦ μυστηρίου governed by τῆς δόξης, and ἐν τοῖς ἔθν. belongs to the ἐστί which is to be supplied, comp.

Eph. i. 18.   (4) According to the context, the δόξα cannot be anything else (see immediately below, ἡ ἐλπὶς τῆς δόξης) than the *Messianic* glory, the glory of the *kingdom* (Rom. viii. 18, 21 ; 2 Cor. iv. 17, *et al.*), the glorious blessing of the κληρονομία (comp. ver. 12), which before the Parousia (Rom. viii. 30 ; Col. iii. 3 f.) is the ideal (ἐλπίς), but after it is the realized, possession of believers.   Hence it is neither to be taken in the sense of the *glorious effects generally*, which the gospel produces among the Gentiles (Chrysostom, Theophylact, and many others, including Huther, comp. Dalmer), nor in that specially of their *conversion from death to life* (Hofmann), whereby its glory is unfolded.   Just as little, however, is the δόξα *of God* meant, in particular His wisdom and grace, which manifest themselves objectively in the making known of the mystery, and realize themselves subjectively by moral glorification and by the hope of eternal glory (de Wette), or the *splendor internus* of true Christians, or the bliss of the latter combined with their moral dignity (Böhmer). (5) The *genitive of the subject*, τοῦ μυστηρίου τούτου, defines the δόξα as that *contained* in the μυστήριον, previously unknown, but now become manifest with the mystery that has been made known, as the blessed *contents* of the latter.   Comp. ver. 23 : ἐλπίς τοῦ εὐαγγελίου.   To take the δόξα as *attribute of the mystery*, is forbidden by what immediately follows, according to which the idea can be none other than the familiar one of that glory, which is the proposed aim of the saving revelation and calling, the object of faith and hope (in opposition to Hofmann and many others) ; iii. 4.   Comp. on Rom. v. 2. — ἐν τοῖς ἔθνεσιν] φαίνεται δὲ ἐν ἑτέροις, πολλῷ δὲ πλέον ἐν τούτοις ἡ πολλὴ τοῦ μυστηρίου δόξα, Chrysostom. "Qui tot saeculis demersi fuerant in morte, ut viderentur penitus desperati," Calvin. — ὅς ἐστι Χριστὸς ἐν ὑμῖν] "*Christus in gentibus*, summum illis temporibus paradoxon," Bengel. According to a familiar attraction (Winer, p. 157 [E. T. 207]), this ὅς applies to the previous subject τὸ πλοῦτος τῆς δόξης τοῦ μυστ. τ., and introduces *that, in which this riches consists.* Namely : *Christ among you*,—in this it *consists*, and by this information is given at the same time *how great* it is (τί ἐστιν).

Formerly they were χωρὶς Χριστοῦ (Eph. ii. 12) ; now Christ,
who by His Spirit reigns in the hearts of believers (Rom.
viii. 10 ; Eph. iii. 17 ; Gal. ii. 20 ; 2 Cor. iii. 17, *et al.*), *is
present and active among them.* The proper reference of the
relative to τὸ πλοῦτος κ.τ.λ., and also the correct connection of
ἐν ὑμῖν with Χριστός (not with ἡ ἐλπίς, as Storr and Flatt
think), are already given by Theodoret and Oecumenius (comp.
also Theophylact), Valla, Luther, Calovius, and others, including Böhmer and Bleek, whereas Hofmann, instead of closely
connecting Χριστὸς ἐν ὑμῖν, makes this ἐν ὑμῖν depend on
ἐστί, whereby the thoughtful and striking presentation of the
fact "*Christ among the Gentiles*" is without reason put in the
background, and ἐν ὑμῖν becomes superfluous. Following the
Vulgate and Chrysostom, ὅς is frequently referred to τοῦ
μυστηρ. τούτου : "this mystery consists in Christ's being
among you, the Gentiles," Huther, comp. Ewald. The context, however, is fatal to this view ; partly in general, because
it is not the mystery itself, but the riches of its glory,
that forms the main idea in the foregoing ; and partly, in
particular, because the way has been significantly prepared
for ὅς ἐστι through τί, while ἐν ὑμῖν corresponds [1] to the ἐν
τοῖς ἔθνεσιν referring to the πλοῦτος, and the following ἡ ἐλπὶς
τῆς δόξης glances back to the πλοῦτος τῆς δόξης. — Χριστός]
Christ Himself, see above. Neither ἡ τοῦ X. γνῶσις (Theophylact) is meant, nor the *doctrine*, either *of Christ* (Grotius,
Rosenmüller, and others), or *about Christ* (Flatt). On the
individualizing ὑμῖν, although the relation concerns the Gentiles generally, comp. ὑμᾶς in ver. 25. "Accommodat ipsis
Colossensibus, ut efficacius in se agnoscant," Calvin. — ἡ ἐλπὶς
τῆς δόξης] characteristic apposition (comp. iii. 4) to Χριστός,
giving information how the Χριστὸς ἐν ὑμῖν forms the great
riches of the glory, etc. among the Gentiles, since Christ is
the *hope* of the Messianic δόξα, in Him is given the *possession
in hope* of the future glory. The emphasis is on ἡ ἐλπίς, in
which the *probative* element lies. Compare on the subject-

---

[1] Hence also to be rendered not *in vobis* (Luther, Böhmer, Olshausen), but
inter vos. The older writers combated the rendering *in vobis* from opposition to
the Fanatics.

matter, Rom. viii. 24 : τῇ γὰρ ἐλπίδι ἐσώθημεν, and the contrast ἐλπίδα μὴ ἔχοντες in Eph. ii. 12 ; 1 Thess. iv. 13 ; and on the concrete expression, 1 Tim. i. 1 ; Ignat. *Eph.* 21 ; *Magnes.* 11 ; Ecclus. xxxi. 14 ; Thuc. iii. 57. 4 ; Aesch. *Ch.* 236. 776.

Ver. 28. Christ was not proclaimed by *all* in the definite character just expressed, namely, as *" Christ among the Gentiles, the hope of glory ;" other* teachers preached Him in a *Judaistic* form, as Saviour of the Jews, amidst legal demands and with theosophic speculation. Hence the emphasis with which not the simply epexegetic ὅν (Erasmus and others), but the ἡμεῖς, which is otherwise superfluous, is brought forward ;[1] by which Paul has meant himself along with Timothy and other like-minded preachers to the Gentiles (*we, on our part*). This emphasizing of ἡμεῖς, however, requires the ὅν to be referred to Christ regarded in the *Gentile-Messianic* character, precisely as the ἡμεῖς make Him known (comp. Phil. i. 17 f.), thereby distinguishing themselves from others ; not to Christ *generally* (Hofmann), in which case the emphasizing of ἡμεῖς is held to obtain its explanation only from the subsequent clause of purpose, ἵνα παραστ. κ.τ.λ. — The *specification of the mode* of announcement νουθετοῦντες and διδάσκοντες, *admonishing* and *teaching,* corresponds to the two main elements of the evangelical preaching μετανοεῖτε and πιστεύετε (Acts xx. 21, xxvi. 18 ; Rom. iii. 3 ff. ; Mark i. 15). Respecting the idea of νουθετεῖν, see on Eph. vi. 4. It occurs also joined with διδάσκ.[2] in Plato, *Legg.* viii. p. 845 B, *Prot.* p. 323 D, *Apol.* p. 26 A ; Dem. 130. 2. — ἐν πάσῃ σοφίᾳ] belongs to νουθετ. and διδάσκ.: *by means of every wisdom* (comp. iii. 16) which we bring to bear thereon. It is the πῶς of the process of warning and teaching, comp. 1 Cor. iii. 10, in which no sort of wisdom remains unemployed. The fact that Paul, in

---

[1] Without due reason, Holtzmann, p. 153, finds the use of the plural disturbing, and the whole verse tautological as coming after ver. 25. It is difficult, however, to mistake the full and solemn style of the passage, to which also the thrice repeated πάντα ἄνθρωπον belongs.

[2] In iii. 16 the two words stand in the inverse order, because there it is not the μετανοεῖν *preceding* the πίστις which is the aim of the νουθεσία, but mutual improvement on the part of *believers.*

1 Cor. i. 17, comp. ii. 1, 4, repudiates the σοφία λόγου in his
method of teaching, is not—taking into consideration the sense
in which σοφία there occurs—at variance, but rather in keeping,
with the present assertion, which applies, not to the wisdom of
the world, but to *Christian* wisdom in its manifold forms. ——
The *thrice repeated* πάντα ἄνθρωπον (in opposition to the
Judaizing tendency of the false teachers) "maximam habet
δεινότητα ac vim," Bengel. The proud feeling of the apostle of
the *world* expresses itself.[1] — ἵνα παραστήσ. κ.τ.λ.] The purpose of the ὃν ἡμεῖς καταγγέλλομεν down to σοφίᾳ. This
purpose is not in general, that man may so *appear* (Bleek), or
come to stand so (Hofmann), but it refers, as in ver. 22, and
without mixing up the conception of *sacrifice* (in opposition to
Bähr and Baumgarten-Crusius), to the *judgment* (comp. on
2 Cor. iv. 14), at which it is the highest aim and glory
(1 Thess. ii. 19 f.) of the apostolic teachers *to make* every man
come forward τέλειον ἐν X. Ἐν Χριστῷ contains the distinguishing specialty of the τελειότης, as *Christian,* which is not
based on anything outside of Christ, or on any other element
than just on Him. It is perfection in respect of the *whole*
Christian nature; not merely of knowledge (Chrysostom,
Theophylact, and others, including Böhmer), but also of life.
Moreover, this ἐν X. is so essential to the matter, and so current with the apostle, that there is no ground for finding in it
an opposition to a doctrine of the law and of angels (Chrysostom,
Theophylact, and others). Theophylact, however (comp. Chrysostom), rightly observes regarding the entire clause of purpose:
τί λέγεις; πάντα ἄνθρωπον; ναί, φησι, τοῦτο σπουδάζομεν· εἰ
δὲ μὴ γένηται, οὐδὲν πρὸς ἡμᾶς.

Ver. 29. On the point of now urging upon the readers
their obligation to fidelity in the faith (ii. 4), and that from
the platform of the personal relation in which he stood
towards them as one unknown to them by face (ii. 1), Paul

[1] Which Hofmann groundlessly calls in question, finding in πάντα ἄνθρωπον
the idea: "*every one singly and severally.*" This is *gratuitously introduced,*
and would have been significantly expressed by Paul through ἵνα ἕκαστον (Acts
xx. 31), or through the addition of καθ' ἵνα, or otherwise; comp. also 1 Thess.
ii. 11. Calvin hits the thought properly: "*ut sine exceptione totus mundus ex
me discat.*"

now turns from the form of expression *embracing others in
common with himself*, into which he had glided at ver. 28 in
harmony with its contents, back to the *individual* form (the
first person *singular*), and asserts, first of all, in connection
with ver. 28, that for the purpose of the παραστῆσαι κ.τ.λ. (εἰς
ὅ, comp. 1 Tim. iv. 10) he also *gives himself even toil* (κοπιῶ,
comp. Rom. xvi. 6, 12 ; 1 Cor. iv. 12), striving, etc. — καί]
also, subjoins the κοπιᾶν to the καταγγέλλειν κ.τ.λ., in which
he subjects himself *also to the former ;* it is therefore *aug-
mentative*, in harmony with the climactic progress of the discourse ; not a mere equalization of the aim and the striving
(de Wette).   Neither this καί, nor even the transition to the
singular of the verb,—especially since the latter is not emphasized by the addition of an ἐγώ,—can justify the interpretation
of Hofmann, according to which εἰς ὅ is, contrary to its position,
to be attached to ἀγωνιζόμενος, and κοπιῶ is to mean : " *I
become weary and faint*" (comp. John iv. 6 ; Rev. ii. 3, and
Düsterdieck *in loc.*).   Paul, who has often impressed upon others
the μὴ ἐκκακεῖν, and for himself is certain of being more than
conqueror in all things (Rom. viii. 37 ; 2 Cor. iv. 8, *et al.*),
can hardly have borne testimony about himself in *this* sense,
with which, moreover, the ἀγωνίζεσθαι *in the strength of Christ*
is not consistent.   In *his* case, as much as in that of any one, the
οὐκ ἐκοπίασας of Rev. ii. 3 holds good. — ἀγωνιζόμενος] Compare 1 Tim. iv. 10.   Here, however, according to the context,
ii. 1 ff., the *inward* striving (comp. Luke xiii. 24) against difficulties and hostile forces, the striving of solicitude, of watching,
of mental and emotional exertion, of prayer, etc., is meant ; as
respects which Paul, like every regenerate person (Gal. v. 17),
could not be raised above the resistance of the σάρξ to the
πνεῦμα ruling in him.   Comp. Chrysostom : καὶ οὐχ ἁπλῶς
σπουδάζω, φησιν, οὐδὲ ὡς ἔτυχεν, ἀλλὰ κοπιῶ ἀγωνιζόμενος
μετὰ πολλῆς τῆς σπουδῆς, μετὰ πολλῆς τῆς ἀγρυπνίας.   It is
not : " tot me periculis ac malis objicere" (Erasmus, comp.
Grotius, Estius, Heinrichs, Bähr, and others), which *outward*
struggling, according to Flatt, de Wette, Baumgarten-Crusius,
and others, should be understood *along with* that *inward*
striving ; ii. 1 only points to the latter ; comp. iv. 12. — κατὰ

τὴν ἐνέργειαν κ.τ.λ.] for Paul does not contend, amid the labours
of his office, according to the measure of his own strength,
but *according to the effectual working of Christ* (αὐτοῦ is not to
be referred to *God,* as is done by Chrysostom, Grotius, Flatt,
Baumgarten-Crusius, and others), *which worketh in him.* Comp.
Phil. iv. 13.   How must this consciousness, at once so humble
and confident of victory, have operated upon the readers to
stir them up and strengthen them for stedfastness in the faith !
— τὴν ἐνεργουμ.] is *middle;* see on 2 Cor. i. 6; Gal. v. 6;
Eph. iii. 20.   The modal definition to it, ἐν δυνάμει, *mightily*
(comp. on Rom. i. 4), is placed at the end significantly, as in
2 Thess. i. 11; it is groundlessly regarded by Holtzmann as
probably due to the interpolator.

CHAPTER II.

VER. 1. περί] Lachm. and Tisch. 8 read ὑπέρ, following A B C D*
P ℵ min.   But how easily may ὑπέρ have been suggested to the
copyists by i. 24 and iv. 12!—The form ἑώρακαν (Lachm. and
Tisch. 7) or ἑόρακαν (Tisch. 8) is more than sufficiently attested
by A B C D* ℵ*, etc., to induce its reception in opposition to
the usage elsewhere.   Respecting this Alexandrian form see
Winer, p. 73 [E. T. 90]; and on ἑόρ., Fritzsche, *ad Aristoph. Th.*
32. — Ver. 2. Instead of συμβιβασθέντες, Elzevir has συμβιβασθέντων,
in opposition to decisive testimony; an emendation. — πάντα
πλοῦτον] A C min. have πᾶν τὸ πλοῦτος (so Lachm. Tisch. 7), and are
also joined by B ℵ* Clem. with πᾶν πλοῦτος (so Tisch. 8).   Here
also (comp. i. 27) the neuter is the original; in thinking of the
more common ὁ πλοῦτος the ΠΑΝΤΟ became ΠΑΝΤΑ, in accordance with which πλοῦτον also came to be written.   The reading
of Tisch. 8 is a restoration of the neuter form after the article
had been lost. — Instead of the simple τοῦ Θεοῦ (so Griesb.
Scholz, Tisch. 7, Rinck; among modern expositors, Bähr,
Olshausen, de Wette, Ewald), Elzevir has τοῦ Θεοῦ καὶ πατρὸς καὶ
τοῦ Χριστοῦ, while Lachm. reads τοῦ Θεοῦ Χριστοῦ, and Tisch. 8 τοῦ
Θεοῦ, Χριστοῦ.   Among the numerous various readings, τοῦ Θεοῦ
Χριστοῦ (also adopted by Steiger, Huther, Bleek, Hofmann) is
certainly strongly enough attested by B. Hilar. (but without
vss.), while the simple τοῦ Θεοῦ has only 37, 67**, 71, 80*, 116,
Arm. *ed. Venet.* in its favour.   A C ℵ*, 4, Sahid. Vulg. ms. have
τοῦ Θεοῦ πατρὸς (τοῦ) Χ., which Böhmer and Reiche prefer, whilst
ℵ** Syr. p. have τ. Θεοῦ καὶ πατρ. τοῦ Χ., and others still, such as
Syr. Copt. Chrys. read τ. Θ. πατρὸς καὶ τοῦ Χριστοῦ, and consequently come nearest to the *Recepta;* but a few authorities,
after the mention of God, insert ἐν Χριστῷ, as Clem. Ambrosiaster:
τοῦ Θεοῦ ἐν Χ.   Regarding these variations we must judge thus:
(1) the far too weak attestation of the bare τοῦ Θεοῦ is decisive
against it; (2) the reading of Lachm.: τοῦ Θεοῦ Χριστοῦ, is to be
regarded as the original, from which have arisen as glosses the
amplifications τοῦ Θεοῦ πατρὸς τοῦ Χ.,[1] and τοῦ Θεοῦ πατρ. καὶ τοῦ Χ.,

---

[1] If this reading, relatively so strongly attested, were the original one, it
would not be easy to see why it should have been glossed or altered. The

as well as the *Recepta ;* (3) the reading τοῦ Θεοῦ ἐν Χριστῷ arose
out of a gloss (ἐν Χριστῷ) written on the margin at ἐν ᾧ, in accordance with i. 27, which supplanted the original Χριστοῦ; (4) the
ἐν Χριστῷ thus introduced was again subsequently eliminated,
without, however, the original Χριστοῦ being reinserted, and thus
arose the reading of Griesb. τοῦ Θεοῦ, which therefore—and with
this accords its late and weak attestation—appears to be merely
a half completed critical restoration. — Ver. 4. δέ] is wanting in
B א*, Tisch. 8; but it was readily omitted by the copyists before
the syllable ΛΕ. — μή τις] Lachm. and Tisch. read μηδείς, which,
following preponderant codd. (A B C D E P א), is to be preferred. — Ver. 7. ἐν τῇ πίστ.] Lachm. and Tisch. have only τῇ
πίστει, following B D* min. Vulg. It. Archel. Ambrosiast.
Theophyl. Properly ; the ἐν was mechanically introduced from
the adjoining text. — ἐν αὐτῇ] though suspected by Griesb., and
rejected by Tisch. 8 (it is wanting in A C א*, min. Copt. Tol.
Archel.), is to be defended. Its omission was easily occasioned
by the fact that περισσ. was found to be already accompanied by
a more precise definition expressed by ἐν. The ἐν αὐτῷ read by
D* א**, 1, Pel. vss., though only a mechanical repetition of the
preceding ἐν αὐτῷ, testifies indirectly to the fact that originally
ἐν αὐτῇ was in the text. — Ver. 10. ὅς ἐστιν] Lachm. reads ὅ ἐστιν,
following B D E F G Germ. Hilar. A mistaken correction,
occasioned by the reference of the preceding ἐν αὐτῷ to τὸ
πλήρωμα. — Ver. 11. After σώματος Elz. has τῶν ἁμαρτιῶν; an
exegetical addition, in opposition to decisive testimony. Comp.
Rom. vi. 6. — Ver. 13. The second ὑμᾶς is indeed wanting in
Elz., but receives so sufficient attestation through A C K L א*.
min. vss. and Fathers, that its omission must be explained on
the ground of its seeming superfluous. B min. Ambr. have
ἡμᾶς, which is conformed to the following ἡμῖν. Instead of this
ἡμῖν, Elz. has ὑμῖν, in opposition to decisive testimony. — Ver.
17. ἅ] Lachm. reads ὅ, following B F G It. Goth. Epiph. Ambrosiast. Aug. To be preferred, inasmuch as the plural was
naturally suggested to the copyists by the plurality of the
things previously mentioned. — Ver. 18. ἃ μὴ ἑώρακεν] μή is
wanting in A B D* א*, 17, 28, 67**, Copt. Clar. Germ. codd.
in Aug., Or. ed. Tert. ? Lucif. Ambrosiast., while F G have οὐκ.
The negation is with justice condemned by Griesb., Steiger,
Olshausen, Huther, Ewald ; deleted by Tisch. 8 (bracketed by
Lachm.), although defended specially by Reiche, whom Hof-

original expression must have given rise to dogmatic scruples, and only the
description of God as τοῦ Θεοῦ Χριστοῦ could have done so.

mann also follows. An addition owing to misapprehension.
See the exegetical remarks. — Ver. 20. εἰ] Elz. reads εἰ οὖν, in
opposition to decisive testimony. An addition for the sake of
connecting, after the analogy of ver. 16 and iii. 1.

Expressing in a heart-winning way his earnest concern for
the salvation of the souls of his readers, Paul introduces
(vv. 1–3) what he has to urge upon them in the way of
warning against the seduction of false teachers (vv. 4, 5), of
exhortation to faithfulness (vv. 6, 7), and then, again, of warning (ver. 8).   He then supports what he has urged by subjoining the relative soteriological instructions and reminders
(vv. 9–15), from which he finally draws further special
warnings as respects the dangers threatening them on the
part of the false teachers (vv. 16–23).

Ver. 1. Γάρ] The apostle now confirms *in concreto* the εἰς ὃ
κ. κοπ. ἀγωνιζόμενος κ.τ.λ., which has just been affirmed of
himself in general: in *proof* of that assertion I would have
you to know, etc. Hofmann holds erroneously, in consequence
of his mistaken explanation of κοπιῶ in i. 29, that Paul desires
to *explain why* he *has said* that he is *becoming weary* over the
exertion, etc. — Instead of the more frequent οὐ θέλω ὑμᾶς
ἀγνοεῖν (see on Rom. xi. 25, i. 13), Paul uses the θέλω ὑμ.
εἰδέναι, also in 1 Cor. xi. 3 ; comp. Phil. i. 12. — ἡλίκον]
what a *great, vehement* conflict. Paul nowhere else uses this
word, which is classical, but does not occur either in the LXX.
or in the Apocrypha ; in the N. T. it is only found again at Jas.
iii. 5.   That by the *conflict* is meant the *internal pressure of
solicitude and apprehension*, etc. (comp. i. 29, also Rom. xv. 30),
is plain—when we remember the imprisoned condition of the
apostle, who now could not contend outwardly with the false
teachers themselves—from ver. 2.   It is at the same time self-
evident that the wrestling of *prayer* was an eminent *way of con-
ducting* this spiritual conflict, without its being necessary to
regard iv. 12 as a criterion for determining the sense in our
passage.—καὶ τῶν ἐν Λαοδικ.] The neighbouring *Laodiceans*
(Rev. iii. 14 ff.) were without doubt exposed to like heretical
dangers ; hence also the injunction as to the mutual communication of the Epistles, iv. 16.—καὶ ὅσοι κ.τ.λ.] The sense is :

and generally (καί, see Fritzsche, *ad Matth.* p. 786. 870) *for all to whom I am personally unknown.* It adds the *entire category*, to which the ὑμεῖς and those ἐν Λαοδικείᾳ, both regarded as *churches*, were *reckoned to belong.* Comp. Acts iv. 6. It is plain from our passage that Paul had *not* been in Colossae and Laodicea. It is true that Wiggers, in the *Stud. u. Krit.* 1838, p. 176, would have ὅσοι κ.τ.λ. understood as referring to *a portion of the Colossians and Laodiceans,* in which case καί would mean *even;* but the text itself is decisively opposed to this view by the following αὐτῶν, ver. 2, which, if the ὅσοι κ.τ.λ. to which it refers be not the *class* in which the readers and Laodiceans *were included,* would be altogether *unsuitable ;* as, indeed, the bare *even* does not suffice to give special prominence to a particular portion (we should expect μάλιστα δέ or the like), and the comprehensive ὅσοι withal does not seem accounted for. Erroneous also is the view (held already by Theodoret in the *Hypothes.* and in the *Commentary,* though Credner, *Einl.* § 154, erroneously denies this) of Baronius, Lardner, and David Schultz (in the *Stud. u. Krit.* 1829, p. 535 ff.), that the ὅσοι κ.τ.λ. were *other* than the ὑμεῖς and οἱ ἐν Λαοδικ. ; Paul having been personally known to both the latter. The subsequent αὐτῶν is fatal to this theory likewise ; and how singularly without reason would it have been, if Paul had designated as the objects of his anxiety, along with two churches of the district which are supposed to have known him personally, *all* not knowing him personally, without distinction of locality ! With how many of the latter were there no such dangers at all existing, as the Colossians and Laodiceans were exposed to ! To this falls to be added the fact, that in the entire Epistle there is not a single hint of the apostle having been present in Colossae. See, on the contrary, on i. 8 and on i. 23. Comp. Wieseler, *Chronol. des apost. Zeitalt.* p. 440. According to Hilgenfeld, in his *Zeitschr.* 1870, p. 245 f., the intimation that Paul was personally unknown to the Colossians betrays the *composition of the* Epistle at a *later* time, when the recollection of his labours there had been already superseded and had vanished from the memory of the churches. As if such a forgetfulness were even conceivable, in presence of the high esteem in which the apostle was held !—That Paul should have been so concerned about the Colossians and Laodiceans, *as those who did not know him personally*, is natural enough, seeing that they were not in a position to oppose the living impression of the apostle's personal ministry, and his direct authority, to the heretical seductions. Comp. ver. 5. — ἐν σαρκί] not belonging to ἑωράκασι—in which case it would be a contrast to seeing ἐν πνεύματι (Chrysostom, Theophylact, Baumgarten-Crusius)— joins itself, so as to form one idea, with τὸ πρόσωπον μου (Winer, p. 128 [E. T. 169]). See ver. 5. The addition, which might in itself be dispensed with (comp. Gal. i. 22 ; 1 Thess. ii. 17), serves the purpose of *concrete representation*, without its being necessary to import into it a contrast to the " spiritual *physiognomy*" (Olshausen), or to the having made acquaintance *in a spiritual fashion* (Hofmann), in connection with which Estius even discovers a certain ταπείνωσις through a higher estimation of the latter ; although generally the idea of a *spiritual mode of intercourse*, independent of bodily absence, very naturally occasioned the concrete description : my *bodily* face. There is all the less ground for assigning ἐν σαρκί, as an anticipation of ver. 5, to the hand of the manipulator, and that in such a way as to betray an author who knows the apostle to be already snatched away from the flesh and present in heaven (Holtzmann).

Ver. 2. The end aimed at (ἵνα) in this conflict : *in order that their hearts may be comforted*, viz. practically by *the fact, that they are united in love*, etc. Accordingly, συμβιβασθ. κ.τ.λ. contains the *mode* of that comforting, which ensues, when through loving union the evil of heretical division, whether threatening or already rampant, is removed. Most thoughtfully and lovingly Paul designates the concern of his solicitude as παράκλησις τῶν καρδιῶν αὐτῶν, not impeaching them on account of the heretical seductions, but making those temptations to be felt as a *misfortune*, in the presence of which one requires *comfort* (Vulgate : " *ut consolentur*"). Chrysostom remarks aptly (comp. Theophylact): ἤδη λοιπὸν σπεύδει καὶ ὠδίνει ἐμβαλεῖν εἰς τὸ δόγμα, οὔτε κατηγορῶν οὔτε ἀπαλλάττων αὐτοὺς κατηγορίας. The explanation which makes παρακαλ. mean, like יִמֵּץ (LXX. Deut. iii. 28 ; Job iv. 3), *to strengthen*, *confirm* (so Huther, de Wette, Baumgarten-Crusius), is quite opposed to the Pauline usage, according to which it means to exhort (so Luther here), to give consolation (so Hofmann ; comp. Bleek), to entreat, to encourage, to *comfort ;* the latter in particular when, as here, it is joined with καρδία. Comp. iv. 8 ; Eph. vi. 22 ; 2 Thess. ii. 17 (also Ecclus. xxx. 23). — συμβιβασθέντες] referred to the logical subject of the foregoing, *i.e.* to the *persons*, of whom αἱ καρδίαι αὐτῶν was said. See on Eph. iv. 2. It means here not *instructi* (Vulgate ; comp. 1 Cor. ii. 16, and the LXX.), nor yet *introduced*,[1] which linguistic usage does not permit, but *brought together, united, compacti* (ver. 19 ; Eph. iv. 16 ; Thuc. ii. 29. 5 ; Herod. i. 74 ; and see Wetstein and Valckenaer, *Schol.* I. p. 453 f.). In connection therewith, ἐν ἀγάπῃ, which denotes Christian brotherly love, is the moral *element, in which* the union is to subsist ; to which is then added the *telic reference* of συμβιβασθ. by καὶ εἰς κ.τ.λ. : united in love *and for behoof of the full richness,* etc., *i.e.* in order, by that union, to attain the possession of this full richness, which could not be attained, but only hindered, by division and variance. καὶ εἰς is not to be *joined* with παρακλ. (Storr, Flatt), since the καί rather adds to the ἐν-relation of the συμβιβ. its εἰς-relation, and is therefore merely the simple *and*, not *etiam* (Bengel, Hofmann) ; but not to be explained either as *et quidem* (Bähr, Böhmer), or by an ἔλθωσι to be supplied (Olshausen permits a choice between the two). — τῆς πληροφ. τῆς συνέσ.] *The full certainty of Christian insight* is the lofty blessing, the *whole riches* of

---

[1] So Hofmann, who couples it in this sense with εἰς πᾶν τὸ πλοῦτος, taking ἐν ἀγάπη adverbially, and explaining the καί, which stands in the way, in the sense of "*even*," to the effect that this introduction into all riches of the *understanding* has as its presupposition *another* introduction, viz. that into the *faith.* This is a sophistically forced mode of disposing of the καί, suggested by nothing in the context, especially since faith by no means, either of itself or in vv. 5–7, falls to be considered as a *preliminary stage,* as if the πληροφορία κ.τ.λ., like a *new* stadium, had to be entered upon through a *second* introduction ; on the contrary, this πληροφορία is the full rich *development* of faith in the inner life. We may add that συμβιβάζειν = *to introduce* is nothing but a *lexicographical fiction* invented by Hofmann. Chrysostom already says rightly : ἵνα ἑνωθῶσι.

which, *i.e.* its blissful possession as a whole, they are to attain, so that in no element of the σύνεσις and in no mode thereof does there remain any lack of completely undoubting conviction;[1] comp. 1 Thess. i. 5 ; Heb. vi. 11, x. 22 ; Rom. iv. 21, xiv. 5. On the conception of πληροφορεῖν, see Bleek on *Hebr.* II. 2, p. 233 f. As to σύνεσις, *intelligence*, both theoretical and practical, comp. on i. 9 ; that here also what is specifically *Christian* is meant κατ' ἐξοχήν, is plain from the context. See the sequel. The cumulative fulness of the description πᾶν τὸ πλ. τ. πληρ. τ. συνέσ. is naturally and earnestly called forth by the consideration of the dangers which threatened the πληροφ. τ. συνέσ. through the attempts of false teachers (ver. 4). Οἶδα, ὅτι πιστεύετε, ἀλλὰ πληροφορηθῆναι ὑμᾶς βούλομαι· οὐκ εἰς τὸν πλοῦτον μόνον, ἀλλ' εἰς πάντα τὸν πλοῦτον, ἵνα καὶ ἐν πᾶσι καὶ ἐπιτεταμένως πεπληροφορημένοι ἦτε, Chrysostom. — εἰς ἐπίγνωσιν κ.τ.λ.] parallel to the preceding εἰς πᾶν τὸ πλοῦτος κ.τ.λ., and destined to bring in with emphasis the great *object* of the σύνεσις (*the divine counsel of redemption*, τὸ μυστήριον, see on i. 26) ; so that what was previously *set forth at length* by εἰς πᾶν τὸ πλοῦτος τ. πληροφ. τ. συνέσ. is now succinctly *summed up* for the sake of annexing the object by εἰς ἐπίγνωσιν. Thus the distinction between ἐπίγνωσις and γνῶσις (ver. 3) is brought out clearly.[2]   Comp. on i. 9. But τοῦ μυστ. τ. Θ. is not to be attached also to τῆς συνέσεως (Hofmann), so that the τὴν ἐπίγνωσιν would occupy an interrupting position. — τοῦ Θεοῦ] Genitive of the subject ; it is *God*, whose decree the μυστ. is. The reading to be approved, τοῦ Θεοῦ Χριστοῦ (see the critical remarks), means : *of the God of Christ*, i.e. *to whom Christ belongs* in a special way, as to His Father, Sender, Head, etc. ; see on Eph. i. 17 ; comp.

---

[1] Neither Greek authors, nor the LXX., nor the Apocrypha have πληροφορία. In Ptol. *Tetr.* p. 4. 9, πληροφόρησις is found.

[2] According to Holtzmann, p. 303, in the frequent mention of γνῶσις and ἐπίγνωσις, of σοφία and σύνεσις, of γνωρίζειν and φωτίζειν, of μυστήριον ἀποκεκρυμμ. and φανέρωσις τοῦ μυστ., we may detect already the terminology of the Grecian mysteries. As if these ideas and expressions were not sufficiently Pauline, and their intentional application were not sufficiently intelligible in the light of theosophic aberrations. Comp. also on i. 23 ; and Weiss, *Bibl. Theol.* p. 420, ed. 2.

John xx. 17; Matt. xxvii. 46. The separation of Χριστοῦ,
however, from τ. Θεοῦ, and the taking it as apposition to τοῦ
μυστηρ. τοῦ Θεοῦ, so that *Christ Himself* appears as the *personal secret of God*, " because He is personally the truth contained in God and revealed from God" (Hofmann, comp.
Holtzmann, p. 215), must be rejected, because Paul would
thus have expressed himself in a way as much exposed to misapprehension as possible. He would either have inserted an
ὅ ἐστι after τοῦ Θεοῦ (i. 24; 1 Cor. iii. 11), or have omitted
τοῦ Θεοῦ, which would have made τὸ μυστήριον Χριστοῦ,
as in Eph. iii. 4, the mystery contained personally in Christ.
But as the apostle has actually written, the reader could only
understand the mystery *of the God of Christ*. If Christ is
God's (see on 1 Cor. iii. 23; comp. Luke ii. 26, ix. 20; Acts
iv. 26), then God is also the God *of Christ*. After Θεοῦ,
therefore, no comma is to be inserted. Finally, the view of
Hilary (" *Deus Christus* sacramentum est"), that ὁ Θεός is
Christ Himself (so Steiger and Bisping, also Philippi, *Glaubensl.* IV. 1, p. 460, ed. 2), is wholly without Pauline analogy,
and is not to be supported by such passages as Rom. ix. 5;
Tit. ii. 13; Eph. v. 5; in fact, even the lofty predicates employed in i. 15 ff., ii. 9, draw the line of distinction between
God and Christ. Moreover, the expression itself is not harsher
(de Wette), or even more inconceivable (Olshausen), more
unsuitable and obscure (Reiche), than the phrase ὁ Θεὸς τοῦ
κυρίου ἡμ. Ἰησοῦ Χ. in Eph. i. 17; since in connection with
the notion " the God of Christ," the designation of the latter
as our Lord is unessential. The addition Χριστοῦ *finds its
motive* in the connection, because it was just *in Christ* that
God formed the decree of redemption (the μυστήριον), and has
carried it out (Eph. iii. 10 f., *et al.*). Whosoever has known
God as the *God of Christ*, has the divine μυστήριον therewith
unveiled to him.

Ver. 3. Ἐν ᾧ] is to be referred to τοῦ μυστηρίου—a
remark which applies also in the case of every other reading
of the foregoing words—not to *Christ*,[1] as is commonly done

---

[1] Older dogmatic expositors (see especially Calovius) discover here the *omni-
science of Christ*.

with the *Recepta*, and by Böhmer, Dalmer, and Hofmann even
with our reading. The correct reference is given, in connection with the *Recepta*, by Grotius (against whom Calovius
contends), Hammond, Bengel, and Michaelis ; and in connection with our reading, by Huther, Schenkel, and Bleek ; its
correctness appears from the correlation in which ἀπόκρυφοι
stands to τοῦ μυστηρ. The *destination* of this relative clause
is to bring out the high value of the ἐπίγνωσις τοῦ μυστηρίου
(*since in Him*, etc.), and that in contrast to the pretended
wisdom and knowledge of the false teachers ; hence also the
emphatic πάντες οἱ θησ. κ.τ.λ. — The σοφία and γνῶσις are
here conceived *objectively*, and the *genitives* indicate wherein
the treasures *consist*. The *distinction* between the two words
is not, indeed, to be abandoned (Calvin : " duplicatio ad
augendum valet ;" comp. Huther and others), but yet is not
to be defined more precisely than that γνῶσις is more special,
knowledge, and σοφία more general, the whole Christian *wisdom*,
by which we with the collective activity of the mind grasp
divine relations and those of human morality, and apply them
to right practice. Comp. on i. 9. — On θησαυροί, comp.
Plato, *Phil.* p. 15 E: ὥς τινα σοφίας εὑρηκὼς θησαυρόν, Xen.
Mem. iv. 2. 9, i. 6. 14 ; Wisd. vii. 14 ; Ecclus. i. 22 ; Bar.
iii. 15. — ἀπόκρυφοι] is not the predicate to εἰσί (so most
writers, with Chrysostom and Luther), as if it were ἀποκε-
κρυμμένοι εἰσιν instead of εἰσὶν ἀπόκρυφοι ; for, as it stands,
the unsuitable sense would be conveyed : " *in whom all
treasures . . . are hidden treasures.*" But neither is it a description of the qualitative *how* of their *being in Him*,[1] in so far,
namely, as they do not lie open for ordinary perception (Hofmann) ; for this adverbial use of the adjective (see Kühner,
ad Xen. Anab. i. 4. 12, ii. 2. 17 ; Krüger, § 57. 5) would be
without due motive here, seeing that the apostle is concerned,
not about the mode of the ἐν ᾧ εἰσι, but about the characterizing of the treasures themselves, whereupon the *how*
in question was obvious of itself. We must therefore take

---

[1] In connection with which Bähr, Baumgarten-Crusius, and Bleek convert
the notion of *being hidden* into that of being *deposited for preservation* (ἀπο-
κεῖσθαι, i. 5).

ἀπόκρυφοι simply as an attributive adjective to θησαυροί, placed at the end with emphasis: *in whom the collective hidden treasures . . . are contained.* Comp. LXX. Isa. xlv. 3 ; 1 Macc. i. 23 ; Matt. xiii. 44. The treasures, which are to be found in the mystery, are not such as lie open to the light, but, in harmony with the conception of the secret, *hidden* (comp. Matt. *l.c.*), because unattainable by the power of natural discernment in itself, but coming to be found by those who attain εἰς ἐπίγνωσιν τοῦ μυστηρίου, whereby they penetrate into the domain of these secret riches and discover and appropriate them. The objection to this view of ἀποκρ. as the adjective to θησ., viz. that there must then have been written οἱ ἀποκρ. (Bähr, Bleek, Hofmann), is erroneous; the article *might* have been (1 Macc. i. 23), but did not *need* to be, inserted. With the article it would mean : *quippe qui absconditi sunt;* without the article it is simply : *" thesauri absconditi"* (Vulgate), *i.e.* ἀπόκρυφοι ὄντες, not οἱ ὄντες ἀπόκρυφοι.

Ver. 4. After this affecting introduction, testifying to his zealous striving for the Christian development of his readers, and thereby claiming their faithful adherence to his gospel, the warning now follows, for the sake of which Paul has prefixed vv. 1–3 (τοῦτο). That τοῦτο does not refer merely to ver. 3 (so Oecumenius, Theophylact, Calvin, Zanchius, Estius, and others, including Bähr and Böhmer; Huther is undecided) is in itself probable, since vv. 1–3 form a connected sentence admirably preparatory in its entire purport for what follows, and is confirmed by ver. 5, which glances back to ver. 1. Hence: This contained in vv. 1–3, which ye ought to know, I say with the design that, etc. — ἵνα μηδείς (see the critical remarks); comp. Mark v. 43 ; Tit. iii. 12 ; Rev. iii. 11, *et al.* — παραλογίζ.] In N. T., only found elsewhere in Jas. i. 22 (see Theile *in loc.*); frequent in the later Greek writers since Demosthenes (822. 25, 1037. 15). It indicates, by a term borrowed from false reckoning, the deception and overreaching that take place through *false reasoning.* *What* particular sophistries the false teachers, whose agitations at all events tended (see ver. 8 f.) *to the disadvantage of the Pauline gospel,* were guilty of, does not appear. It is certain, however, that they were not those suggested by Böhmer (nothing good can come out of Nazareth; one who was crucified cannot have possessed divine wisdom), since the false teachers were not non-Christians. Hardly did these beguiling sophistries affect *the person of the apostle,* as if he were not concerning himself about the confirming and training of churches not planted by himself, as Hofmann thinks. In that case we should have in vv. 1–3 only a self-testimony to the contrary, which, as assertion against assertion, would neither have been skilful nor delicate; nor do we in what follows find any defence in opposition to personal calumniation. This applies also in opposition to Holtzmann, p. 177. The γάρ in ver. 5 by no means requires this interpretation. — ἐν πιθανολογίᾳ] *by means of persuading speech;* Luther's "with *rational* discourses" misapprehends the meaning. It occurs in this place only in the N. T.; but see Plato, *Theaet.* p. 162 E; comp. Dem. 928. 14: λόγους θαυμασίως πιθανούς, also πιθανολογεῖν, Diog. L. x. 87; Diod. Sic. i. 39; and πιθανῶς λέγειν, Lucian, *Amor.* 7. Hence the art of persuasion: ἡ πιθανολογική, Arr. *Epict.* i. 8. 7.

Ver. 5. A special reason, having reference to his bodily absence, by which his readers are encouraged not to allow themselves to be deceived. — τῇ σαρκί] with respect to the flesh, *i.e. bodily.* Comp. 1 Cor. v. 3. — ἀλλά] *at,* yet am I *on the other hand,* beginning the apodosis; see on Rom. vi. 5 and 1 Cor. iv. 15. — τῷ πνεύματι] with respect to the spirit, *i.e. mentally;* my spirit, translating itself in thought into your midst, is along with you. Erroneously Grotius: "Deus Paulo *revelat,* quae Colossis fierent," so that πνεῦμα would be meant of the *Holy* Spirit. According to Wiggers, in the *Stud. u. Krit.* 1838, p. 181, and Vaihinger, in Herzog's *Encyklop.* IV. p. 79, ἄπειμι takes for granted the apostle's *having been there previously.* A quite groundless assumption; the verb expresses (ἀπό) the *being away from,* but does not indicate whether a person had been previously present or not, which can only be gathered from the connection or other circumstances of the case. In this case the context directly indicates, by ver. 1, that a bodily παρεῖναι had *not* occurred. It

is otherwise in 1 Cor. v. 3; 2 Cor. x. 1, 11, xiii. 2, 10;
Phil. i. 27. From the similar expression in 1 Cor. v. 3.
Theodoret nevertheless infers that Paul ὡς θεασάμενος αὐτοὺς
ἔγραψεν τὴν ἐπιστολήν. — σὺν ὑμῖν] in your society, *among
you.* Comp. Luke viii. 38, xxii. 56; Phil. i. 23; 1 Thess.
iv. 17; 2 Pet. i. 18, *et al.* — χαίρων κ. βλέπων] There is
here no *illogical* prefixing of the χαίρων in the lively feeling
of joy (Huther, comp. de Wette); χαίρων rather expresses
joy *at the fact* that he is with them spiritually, and καὶ βλέπων
ὑμ. τὴν τάξιν κ.τ.λ. then adds *what at this joyful being with
the Colossians he sees in them,* so that the description thus
advances with κ. βλέπ.: in spirit I am along with you,
rejoicing in this mental presence, and *therewith seeing,* etc.
Comp. also Hofmann, who, however, imports into βλέπων the
pregnant meaning not conveyed by the simple verb; it is as
plainly present to my soul, as if I saw it with my eyes. This
would be κ. ὡς βλέπων, or κ. ὡς ἐν ὀφθαλμοῖς βλ. Renderings
blending the ideas, such as *gaudeo videns* (Grotius, Wolf,
Bähr, Baumgarten-Crusius, Bleek, and others), or *beholding
with joy* (Bengel, Heinrichs, Flatt), are at variance with the
words as they stand. Some erroneously cite Josephus, *Bell.*
iii. 10. 2, where χαίρω καὶ βλέπων (not βλέπω) means: I
rejoice, when I even see it. Winer, p. 438 [E. T. 589], and
Fritzsche, *ad Rom.* II. p. 425, supply with χαίρων the words:
concerning you. But the supplying of ἐφ' ὑμῖν is not justified by
the context, which naturally suggests joy *at the being together
with the readers,* for χαίρ. stands *alongside of this* as an
accompanying relation without any other definition of object.
And according to this view there is no ground at all for an
explicative rendering of καί, which Winer still admits (so also
Böhmer and Olshausen). — The testimony, moreover, which is
given to the readers by βλέπων κ.τ.λ. is not inconsistent with
the anxious conflict in ver. 1; but, on the contrary, makes the
latter, in a psychological point of view, all the more conceivable, when the dangers which threatened a state of things
still even now so good are considered.—ὑμῶν τ. τάξιν] The
prefixed pronoun owes this position to the favourable expectation which the Colossians, *more than many others,* have

awakened in the apostle.   The τάξις is *order,* orderly condition.   Its antithesis is ἀταξία, Plato, *Tim.* p. 30 A.   For the
idea see Plato, *Gorg.* p. 504 A : τάξεως ... καὶ κόσμου τυχοῦσα
οἰκία, Polyb. i. 4. 6 : ἡ σύμπασα σχέσις κ. τάξις τῆς οἰκουμένης,
iii. 36. 6 : ἡ ... διαίρεσις κ. τάξις.   It is often used of the
organized condition of the *state,* Dem. 200. 4, Plat. *Crit.*
p. 109 D ; elsewhere also (see Sturz, *Lex. Xen.* IV. p. 245)
of the *army,* sometimes to designate a *section* of it (a company
of two λόχοι), and sometimes to express its regular *arrangement in rank and file* (Thuc. iii. 87. 2, iv. 72. 2, 126. 4,
viii. 69. 1).   Hofmann[1] takes both τάξ. and στερέωμα in a
military sense.   But the two words have not in and of themselves the military sense ; they would receive it from the context, which is not the case here.   Moreover, the meaning
fortress, military bulwark, is expressed not by στερέωμα
generally, but by ἔρυμα or ὀχύρωμα, 2 Cor. x. 4.   Hence, if
we would avoid arbitrariness, we can only abide by the view
that here τάξις means the *orderly state of the Christian church,*
which has hitherto not been disturbed by sectarian divisions
or forsaken by the readers.   Comp. 1 Cor. xiv. 40.   To this
outward condition Paul then subjoins the *inner* one, by which
the former is conditioned : *and the solid hold of your faith in
Christ.*   στερέωμα, *firmamentum,* that which has been *made
firm* (Arist. *partt. an.* ii. 9 ; Theophr. *H. pl.* v. 7. 3), a late
word, often found in LXX., Aquila, Theodotion, Symmachus,
and Apocrypha (see Schleusner, *Thes.* V. p. 102 f.), represents
the stedfastness and immoveableness of faith in such a way,
that the latter appears as protected by a strong work (with
solid foundation, masonry, etc.) from injury (Ezek. xiii. 5 ; Ps.
xviii. 2 ; 3 Esdr. viii. 81).   On the subject-matter, comp. Acts
xvi. 5 : ἐστερεοῦντο τῇ πίστει, 1 Pet. v. 9 : ἀντίστητε στερεοὶ
τῇ πίστει.   The abstract *firmness,* however (Huther, de Wette,
Baumgarten-Crusius, Bleek, and older expositors), which would
be στερεότης, is never designated by the word.   Chrysostom
explains rightly : ὅτε πολλὰ συναγαγὼν συγκολλήσεις πυκνῶς
καὶ ἀδιασπάστως, τότε στερέωμα γίνεται.   The *genitive* τῆς
πίστεως, finally, is not to be taken in such a way as *to make*

---

[1] Whom Holtzmann, p. 177, has too rashly followed.

faith the στερέωμα (Hofmann), which protects the readers, as
if it were τὸ ὑμῶν στερέωμα; but as the genitive of the *subject*, in such a way that their faith *has* the στερέωμα securing
it, which Paul spiritually sees.—To *call in question* the *unse-
ducedness* here attested (Baumgarten-Crusius, who leaves it a
question whether the sense is not merely: " *if* it is so "), or
to refer it to only a *part* of the church (Flatt), is a quite
arbitrary result of unduly pressing the general utterance of
commendation.

Ver. 6 f. From the warning given in ver. 4 and having its
ground assigned in ver. 5, follows (οὖν) the positive obligation
to make Christ, as He had been communicated to them through
the instruction which they had received, the element in which
(ἐν αὐτῷ) their conduct of the inner and outer life moves
(περιπατεῖτε), whereupon the more precise modal definitions
are subjoined by ἐρριζωμένοι κ.τ.λ.—ὡς] *according as.* Observe
that in the protasis παρελάβετε and in the apodosis περιπατεῖτε (not ἐν αὐτῷ, as Hofmann thinks) have the emphasis, in
which case the addition of an οὕτως was not necessary. Their
walk in Christ is to be in harmony with the *instruction*, by
means of which they have through Epaphras *received* Christ.
— παρελάβετε] have *received* (i. 7; Eph. iv. 20), comp. Gal.
i. 9, 12; 1 Thess. ii. 13, iv. 1; 2 Thess. iii. 6; 1 Cor. xi. 23.
Christ was *communicated* to them as the *element of life.*[1] The
rendering: have *accepted* (Luther, Bähr, Böhmer, Huther,
Hofmann), is not contrary to Pauline usage (de Wette; but
see on Phil. iv. 9; 1 Cor. xv. 1); but it is opposed to the
context, in which after ver. 4 (see especially ver. 7: καθὼς
ἐδιδάχθητε, and ver. 8: κατὰ τὴν παράδοσιν τῶν ἀνθρ.) the contrast between true and false Christian *instruction* as regulative
of the walk, and not the contrast between *entrance into the
fellowship of Christ* and the walk therewith given (Hofmann),
predominates.[2] — τὸν Χ. Ἰ. τὸν κύριον] A solemnly complete

[1] To this conception ἐν αὐτῷ refers subsequently. Chrysostom and his followers
take this ἐν so, that Christ is regarded as the *way.* But this Johannine conception nowhere occurs in Paul's writings; nor does it accord with παρελάβετε,
with which, however, the extremely common Pauline idea of the ἐν Χριστῷ εἶναι
is in harmony.

[2] Eph. iii. 17 f., by comparing which Holtzmann discovers in our passage the

designation, *a summary of the whole confession* (1 Cor. xii. 3 ,
Phil. ii. 11), in which τὸν κύριον, conformably with its position and the entire connection, is to be taken in the sense :
as the Lord, consequently *attributively,* not as a mere *apposition*
(de Wette, Bleek, Ellicott, and others), in which Hofmann
includes also Ἰησοῦν, a view which is not warranted by Eph.
iii. 1. — Ver. 7. ἐρριζωμ. κ. ἐποικοδ. ἐν αὐτῷ] introduces the
ethical habitus in the case of the required περιπατεῖν ἐν Χ.
But the vivid conception, in the urgency of properly exhaust-
ing the important point, combines very dissimilar elements ;
for the two figures, of a plant and of a building, are inconsistent as such both with περιπατεῖτε and with one another.
Comp. Eph. iii. 17 f. By beginning a new sentence with
ἐρριζωμένοι κ.τ.λ., and thus construing it in connection with
ver. 8 (Schenkel, Hofmann), we should gain nothing in symmetry, and should only lose without sufficient reason in
simplicity of construction ; while we should leave the ἐν αὐτῷ
περιπατεῖτε in ver. 6 in a disproportionately bald and isolated
position. This conjunction, moreover, of heterogeneous figures
might quite as legitimately have been made by the apostle
himself as by an interpolator, whose hand Holtzmann thinks
that he here discovers. — Observe further the *difference in time*
of the two participles, whereby the *stedfastness of the* ἐν Χριστῷ
εἶναι (figuratively represented by ἐρρίζωμ.) is denoted as a
subsistent state, which must be present in the case of the περιπατεῖν ἐν αὐτῷ, while *the further development of the Christian
condition* (figuratively represented by ἐποικοδ.) is set forth as a
continuing process of training ; comp. Acts xx. 32. — ἐποικοδ.]
becoming built up, in which ἐπί exhibits the building rising *on
the foundation.* Comp. 1 Cor. iii. 10, 12 ; Eph. ii. 20 ; Xen.
Anab. iii. 4. 11 ; Plat. *Legg.* v. p. 736 E. The building up
may in itself be also regarded as an act *accomplished* (through
conversion), as in Eph. ii. 20 : ἐποικοδομηθέντες, which, however, as modal definition of περιπατ., would not have suited
here. The *progress* and *finishing* of the *building* (de Wette,
following Acts xx. 32, where, however, the simple form οἰκοδ.

hand of the interpolator, is both as regards contents and form too diverse for
that purpose.

should be read) are conveyed by the present, not by ἐποικοδ. in itself (comp. Eph. ii. 22). Nor does the latter represent the readers as *stones*, which are built up *on the top of those already laid* (Hofmann); on the contrary, they are in their *aggregate as a church* (comp. on Eph. *l.c.*) represented as an οἰκοδομή in the course of being built (*i.e.* of a more and more full development of their Christian common life), in regard to which the ἐπί in ἐποικοδ. presupposes the *foundation* laid by Epaphras, namely, Christ (1 Cor. iii. 11); and the building *materials*, including the stones, are not the persons, but the *doctrines*, by means of which the builders accomplish their work (see on 1 Cor. iii. 12). — ἐν αὐτῷ] belongs to both participles, so that Christ is to be conceived doubtless as the *soil* for the roots striking downwards (Eph. iii. 17), and as the *foundation* (1 Cor. iii. 11) for the building extending upwards; but the *expression* is determined by the conception of the *thing* signified, namely, the ἐν Χριστῷ εἶναι, as in ἐν αὐτῷ περιπατ., and not by the *figures;* hence Paul has not written ἐπ᾽ αὐτόν (1 Cor. iii. 12), or ἐπ᾽ αὐτῷ (Eph. ii. 20), which would have been in harmony with the latter participle, but he exhibits Christ as the Person, *in whom* that which is meant by the being rooted and becoming built up has its specific being and nature, and consequently the condition of endurance and growth.[1] Comp. on Eph. ii. 21. — καὶ βεβαιούμ. τῇ πίστ.] And to this being rooted and becoming built up there is to be added the *being stablished by the faith*, as the development *of quality* in the case, in order that no loose rooting may take place, nor any slack building be formed. The *dative* τῇ πίστει (see the critical remarks) is to be taken as *instrumental*, not: *with respect to* (in opposition to de Wette), since the following modal definition περισσ. ἐν αὐτῇ specifies, not how they are to be stablished *in respect of* the faith, but how they are to be stablished *by* it, by the fact, namely, that they are *rich* in faith; *poverty* in faith would not be sufficient to bring about that establishment. In like manner we should have to

---

[1] Hofmann inappropriately, since in the case of ἐποικοδ. at any rate we have to think of the *foundation*, takes ἐν αὐτῷ in the sense that Christ *surrounds* the building.

take the reading ἐν τ. πίστει, which Hofmann defends. He,
however, joins this ἐν τ. πίστει not with βεβαιούμ., but with
the following περισσεύοντες,—a connection which is excluded
by the genuineness of ἐν αὐτῇ, but which is, even apart from
this, to be rejected, because Paul would, in order to be fairly
intelligible, have inserted the ἐν αὐτῷ only after βεβαιούμενοι,
to which it would also refer. — καθὼς ἐδιδάχθ.] namely, *to
become stablished by the faith.* For this they have received
(from Epaphras, i. 7) the instructions which are to guide
them. — περισσεύοντες κ.τ.λ.] is subordinate to the βεβαιούμ.,
and that as specifying the *measure* of the faith, which must
be found in them in order that they may be stablished
through faith; while at the same time the requisite *vital
expression, consecrated to God, of the piety* of the believing
heart is brought out by ἐν εὐχαρ.: *while ye are abounding
in the same amidst thanksgiving, i.e.* while ye are truly *rich* in
faith, and at the same time giving thanks to God for this
blessing of fulness of faith. The emphasis is upon περισσ.,
in which lies the more *precisely defining* element; περισσεύειν
ἐν is nothing else than the usual *abundare aliqua re, to have
abundance of something* (Rom. xv. 13; 1 Cor. viii. 7; Phil.
i. 9, *et al.*), and ἐν εὐχαρ. indicates an *accompanying circumstance in the case,* the ethical consecration of grateful piety,
with which the richness in faith must be combined; comp.
iii. 17, i. 12. It is well explained, in substance, by Theophylact: περισσόν τι ἐνδείκνυσθαι ἐν τῇ πίστει, εὐχαριστοῦντες τῷ
θεῷ, ὅτι ἠξίωσεν ἡμᾶς τοιαύτης χάριτος, καὶ μὴ ἑαυτοῖς τὴν
προκοπὴν ἐπιγράφοντας. Rightly also by Oecumenius, who
takes ἐν εὐχαρ. as equivalent to σὺν εὐχαρ. Comp. Castalio,
Erasmus, Beza, Calvin, Estius, Cornelius a Lapide, Bähr,
Steiger, Olshausen, Baumgarten-Crusius, Dalmer, Hofmann,
and others. Others, however, regard ἐν εὐχαρ. as belonging to
περισσ. Such is the view not only of the majority who reject
ἐν αὐτῇ on critical grounds (as Ewald), but also of Luther,
Michaelis, Storr, Flatt, Huther (that the Colossians in their
faith towards God . . . are to show themselves *abundantly grateful*). De Wette favours this rendering on the ground that the
clause is not attached by καί, which, however, is quite in keep-

ing with the circumstance that περισσ. κ.τ.λ. is subordinate
to the βεβαιούμ. κ.τ.λ. In opposition to the combination
περισσ. ἐν εὐχαρ. there may be urged, first, the arrangement
of the words in itself; secondly, the fact that ἐν αὐτῇ would
be superfluous; and thirdly, that all the other elements of the
verse refer to the nature of *faith*, and hence the latter, in
harmony with the context, is to be regarded also in the last
participial clause as the object of the discourse, whereas ἐν
εὐχαρ. is to be treated as a relation *associated with* the
faith.

Ver. 8. *Be upon your guard, lest there shall be some one
carrying you away as a prey.* In that case, how grievously
would what I have just been impressing upon your hearts,
in vv. 6, 7, be rendered fruitless! — The *future* ἔσται after
μή (comp. Heb. iii. 12) has arisen from the apprehension that
the case may yet actually occur. See Stallbaum, *ad Plat.
Rep.* p. 451 A; Hartung, *Partikell.* II. p. 139 f.; Ellendt,
Lex. Soph. II. p. 104. Comp. also on Gal. iv. 11. — As to
the *participle with the article*, comp. on Gal. i. 7: τινές εἰσιν
οἱ ταράσσοντες. — Respecting συλαγωγεῖν, belonging to the
later Greek, see Eustath. *ad Il.* v. p. 393, 52. Very inaccurately rendered by the Vulgate: *decipiat.* In Aristaen. ii. 22,
joined with οἶκον, it means *to rob;* and is so taken here by
Hilary, Chrysostom, Theodoret (ἀποσυλᾶν τὴν πίστιν),
Theophylact (τὸν νοῦν), Luther, Wolf, and many others,
including Baumgarten-Crusius. But the stronger sense of
the word *praedam abigere* (Heliod. x. 35; Nicet. *Ann.* 5, p. 96
D) is in keeping with the verb of the previous exhortation,
περιπατεῖτε, as well as with the purposely chosen peculiar
expression in itself, which is more significant than the classical
συλᾶν or συλεύειν, and serves vividly to illustrate the idea of
the *seduction*, through which one falls under extraneous power,
as respects its *disgracefulness.* — διὰ τῆς φιλοσοφίας κ. κενῆς
ἀπάτης] *through philosophy and empty deceit.* It is to be
observed that neither the preposition nor the article is repeated
before κενῆς (see Kühner, II. 1, pp. 476, 528; Buttmann, *Neut.
Gr.* p. 86 [E. T. 100]), because with καὶ κεν. ἀπατ. there
is added no further element different from τῆς φιλοσοφ. (in

COL. Z

opposition to Hofmann), but only *that which the philosophy in its essence is ;* it is *empty deception,* that is, having no real contents ; the πιθανολογία (ver. 4), with which it is presented, is a κενεαγορία (Plat. *Rep.* p. 607 B), and κενολογία (Plut. *Mor.* p. 1069 C). On the idea of κενός (1 Cor. xv. 14 ; Eph. v. 6), comp. Dem. 821. 11. : κενώτατον πάντων λόγων λέγουσι, and on ἀπάτη, Plat. *Soph.* p. 260 C : ὄντος δέ γε ψεύδους ἔστιν ἀπάτη..., καὶ μὴν ἀπάτης οὔσης εἰδώλων τε καὶ εἰκόνων ἤδη καὶ φαντασίας πάντα ἀνάγκη μεστὰ εἶναι. The φιλοσοφία, however, against which Paul utters his warning, is not *philosophy generally and in itself,*—a view at variance with the addition κ. κενῆς ἀπατ. closely pertaining to it, however much the wisdom of the world in its degeneracy (comp. Herm. *gottesd. Alterth.* § 12 ; and *Culturgesch. d. Griech. u. Röm.* I. p. 236 ff., II. p. 132), as experience was conversant with its phenomena in that age,[1] may have manifested itself to the apostle as foolishness when compared with the wisdom of the gospel (1 Cor. i. 18 ff., ii. 6). Rather, he has in view (comp. ver. 18) the characteristic speculation, *well known to his readers,* which engaged attention in Colossae and the surrounding district,[2] and consisted of a Gnostic theosophy mixed up with Judaism (Essenism). This is, on account of its nature directed to the supersensuous and its ontological character, correctly designated by the term philosophy in general, apart from its relation to the truth, which is signalized by the κ. κενῆς ἀπάτης appended.[3] (Plat. *Def.* p. 414 C : τῆς τῶν

[1] Comp. Luther's frequent denunciations of philosophy, under which he had present to his mind its degeneracy in the Aristotelian scholasticism.

[2] Comp. also Calovius. The latter rightly remarks how ἀφιλοσόφως and ἀθεολόγως men would proceed, who should regard philosophical and theological truth as opposites ; and points out that if Greek philosophy do not teach the doctrine of eternal life and its attainment, it is not a κινὴ ἀπάτη, but an *imperfectio.* Fathers of the Church also, as *e.g.* Clemens Al. (comp. Spiess, *Logos spermat.* p. 341), aptly distinguish philosophy itself from the phenomena of its abuse. The latter are philosophy also, but not in accordance with the truth of the conception.

[3] These words κ. κιν. ἀσ., characterizing the philosophy meant, are therefore all the less to be regarded, with Holtzmann, as a tautological insertion ; and it is mere arbitrariness to claim the words κατὰ τ. παράδ. τῶν ἀνθρώπ. for the Synoptical Gospels (Matt. xv. 2 f.) ; as if παράδοσις (comp. especially Gal. i. 14) were not sufficiently current in the apostle's writings.

ὄντων ἀεὶ ἐπιστήμης ὄρεξις· ἕξις θεωρητικὴ τοῦ ἀληθοῦς, πῶς ἀληθές). Possibly it was also put forward by the false teachers themselves expressly under this designation (comp. the Sophists as the φάσκοντες φιλοσοφεῖν, Xen. *Mem.* i. 2. 19 ; and οἰόμενοι πάντ' εἰδέναι, in i. 4. 1). The latter is the more probable, since Paul uses the word only in this passage. Comp. Bengel : " quod adversarii jactabant esse philosophiam et sapientiam (ver. 23), id Paulus *inanem fraudem* esse dicit." The nature of this philosophy is consequently to be regarded as *Judaistic-Oriental ;* [1] we are under no necessity to infer from the word φιλοσοφία a reference to *Greek* wisdom, as Grotius did, suggesting the *Pythagorean* (Clemens Alexandrinus thought of the *Epicureans,* and Tertullian of such philosophers as Paul had to do with at *Athens*). The idea that the " *sacrarum literarum* earumque recte interpretandarum *scientia* " (Tittmann, *de vestigiis Gnosticor. in N. T. frustra quaesitis,* p. 86 ff.) is meant, is opposed, not to the word in itself, but to the marks of heretical doctrine in our Epistle, and to the usage of the apostle, who never so designates the O. T. teaching and exposition, however frequently he speaks of it; although Philo gives it this name (see Loesner, *Obss.* p. 364), and Josephus (see Krebs, p. 236) applies it to the systems of Jewish sects, and indeed the Fathers themselves apply it to the Christian doctrine (Suicer, *Thes. s.v.*) ; see Grimm on 2 Macc. i. 1, p. 298 f. — κατὰ τ. παράδ. τ. ἀνθρ.] might be — and this is the common view—closely joined with ἀπάτης (Winer, p. 128 f. [E. T. 169]). But the οὐ κατὰ Χριστόν would not suit this connection, since ἀπάτη is already in itself a definite and proper idea, in association with which a κατὰ Χριστόν would be inconceivable ; whereas the *figurative* συλαγωγεῖν still admits also the negative modal statement (οὐ κατὰ Χ.) for greater definiteness. Accordingly κατὰ τ. παράδ. κ.τ.λ. (comp. Steiger, Ellicott) is to be taken as definition of mode to συλαγωγῶν. Paul, namely, having previously announced *whereby* the συλαγωγεῖν takes place, now adds for the still more precise description of that procedure, in order the more

---

[1] The speculations of Essenism are also designated as philosophy in Philo. Comp. Keim, *Gesch. Jesu,* I. p. 292.

effectively to warn his readers against it, *that in accordance with which* it takes place, *i.e.* what is the objective *regulative standard* by which they permit themselves to be guided. He does this *positively* (κατὰ τὴν . . . . κόσμου) and *negatively* (κ. οὐ κατὰ Χριστόν). The genitive τῶν ἀνθρ. is to be explained: ἣν παρέλαβε παρὰ τῶν ἀνθρ. (comp. 2 Thess. iii. 6), and τῶν denotes the *category*, the traditio *humana* as such, opposed to the divine revelation. Comp. Mark vii. 8. What is *meant*, doubtless, is the ritual *Jewish* tradition outside of the Mosaic law (comp. on Matt. xv. 2), the latter being excluded by τῶν ἀνθρ. ; but Paul *designates* the thing quite generally, according to the *genus* to which it belongs, as *human*. — κατὰ τὰ στοιχεῖα τοῦ κόσμου] Parallel of the foregoing : *according to the elements of the world*, i.e. *according to the religious rudiments, with which non-Christian humanity occupies itself.* The expression in itself embraces the ritual observances[1] both of *Judaism and heathenism*, which, in comparison with the perfect religion of Christianity, are only "puerilia *rudimenta*" (Calvin), as it were the A B C of religion, so that Paul therefore in this case also, where he warns his readers against *Judaistic* enticing, characterizes the matter according to its *category*. As to the designation itself and its various interpretations, see on Gal. iv. 3. Among the latest expositors, Bleek agrees with our view, while Hofmann explains : "because it (the philosophy which is described as deceit) permits *the material things, of which the created world consists*, to form its standard." See in opposition to this on Gal. *l.c.* Both expressions, τὴν παράδ. τ. ἀνθρ. and τὰ στοιχ. τ. κόσμου, have it as their aim to render apparent the worthlessness and unsuitableness for the Christian standpoint (comp. Gal. iv. 9). Hence, also, the contrast which, though obvious of itself, is nevertheless emphatic : καὶ οὐ κατὰ Χριστόν. The activity of that συλαγωγεῖν has not *Christ for its objective standard ;* He, in accordance with His divine dignity exalted above everything (see ver. 9), was to be the

---

[1] Calvin well says : "Quid vocat *elementa mundi ?* Non dubium quin *ceremonias ;* nam continuo post exempli loco speciem unam adducit, circumcisionem scilicet."

sole regulative for all activity in Christian teaching, so that
the standard guiding their work should be found in the relation of dependence upon Him; but instead of this the procedure of the συλαγωγῶν allows human tradition, and those
non-Christian rudiments which the Christian is supposed to
have long since left behind, to serve as his rule of conduct!
How unworthy it is, therefore, to follow such seduction!

Ver. 9. *Since indeed in Him dwells,* etc. This is not "a
peg upon which the interpolator hangs his own thoughts"
(Holtzmann). On the contrary, *Paul assigns a reason for the*
οὐ κατὰ Χριστόν *just said,* with a view more effectually to
deter them from the false teachers. The force of the reason
assigned lies in the fact that, if the case stand so with Christ,
as is stated in vv. 9 ff., by every other regulative principle of
doctrine that which is indicated in the words κατὰ Χριστόν
is excluded and negatived. *Others* make the reason assigned
refer to the *warning:* βλέπετε κ.τ.λ., so that ὅτι adduces the
reason why they ought to permit this warning to be addressed
to them (Hofmann, comp. Huther and Bleek); but, in opposition to this view, it may be urged that the ἐν αὐτῷ placed
emphatically first (*in Him* and in no other) points back to the
immediately preceding οὐ κατὰ Χριστόν (comp. Chrysostom
and Calvin); there is therefore nothing to show that the
reference of ὅτι ought to be carried further back (to βλέπετε).
In Christ the whole fulness of Godhead—what a contrast to the
human παράδοσις and the στοιχεῖα of the world! — κατοικεῖ]
The *present,* for it is the *exalted* Christ, in the state of His
heavenly δόξα, that is in view. Comp. i. 15. In Him the
entire πλήρωμα has its κατοικητήριον (Eph. ii. 22), so that He
is the personal bearer of it, the personal seat of its essential
presence. — πᾶν τὸ πλήρωμα (comp. on i. 19) is here more
precisely defined by the "vocabulum *abstractum significantissi-
mum*" (Bengel) τῆς θεότητος, which specifies *what* dwells in
Christ in its entire fulness, *i.e.* not, it may be, partially, but
in its complete entirety. On the *genitive,* comp. Rom. xi. 25,
xv. 29. It is not the genitive *auctoris* (Nösselt: "universa
comprehensio eorum, quae Deus per Christum vellet in homines
transferre"); the very abstract θεότητ. should have been a

sufficient warning against this view, as well as against the interpretation : " id quod inest θεότητι" (Bähr).   ἡ θεότης, the *Godhead* (Lucian, *Icarom.* 9 ; Plut. *Mor.* p. 415 C), the abstract from ὁ Θεός, is to be distinguished from ἡ θειότης, the abstract from θεῖος (Rom. i. 20 ; Wisd. xviii. 19 ; Lucian, *de calumn.* 17).   The former is *Deitas, the being God, i.e.* the divine *essence, Godhead ;* the latter is *divinitas, i.e.* the divine *quality, godlikeness.*   See on Rom. i. 20.   Accordingly, the *essence* of God, undivided and in its whole fulness, dwells in Christ in His exalted state, so that He is the essential and adequate image of God (i. 15), which He could not be if He were not possessor of the divine essence.   The distinction between what is here said about Christ and what is said about Him in i. 19 is, that the πλήρωμα is here meant *metaphysically,* of the divina *essentia,* but in the former passage charismatically, of the divina *gratia,* and that κατοικεῖν is conceived here as in present permanence, but in the former passage historically (namely, of Christ's historical, earthly appearance). See on i. 19.   The erroneous attempts that have been made to explain away the literal meaning thus definitely and deliberately expressed by Paul, are similar to those in i. 19. One of these, in particular, is the mis-explanation referring it to the *church* as the God-filled organ of divine self-revelation (Heinrichs, Baumgarten - Crusius, Schenkel) which has its dwelling-place in Christ.[1]   Already Theodoret (comp. τινές in Chrysostom), indeed, quotes the explanation that *Christ* signifies the church *in which* the πλήρωμα dwells, but on account of σωματικῶς hesitates to agree to it, and rather accedes to the common view, thereby deviating from his interpretation of i. 19.   Theophylact is substantially right (comp. Chrysostom and Oecumenius) : εἰ τί ἐστιν ὁ Θεὸς λόγος, ἐν αὐτῷ οἰκεῖ, so that the fulness of the Godhead in the *ontological,* and not in

[1] Thus, indeed, the *fulness of the Godhead* has been removed from Christ, but there has only been gained instead of it the unbiblical idea that *the church* dwells in Christ.   The church has its support in Christ as the corner-stone (Eph. ii. 20, 21), but it does not *dwell* in Him.   On the contrary, *Christ dwells in the church,* which is His *body,* and the πλήρωμα *filled by Him* (see on Eph. i. 23), namely, in virtue of the Spirit dwelling in the church (see on Eph. ii. 22), which is the Spirit of Christ (Rom. viii. 9 ; Gal. iv. 6 ; Phil. i. 19).

the simply mystical or *morally religious* sense (de Wette) is meant. — But *how* does it dwell in Christ? σωματικῶς, in *bodily* fashion, *i.e.* in such a way that through this indwelling in Christ it is in a bodily form of appearance, *clothed with a body.* Comp. also Hofmann *in loc.*, and *Schriftbew.* II. 1, p. 29 ; Weiss, *Bibl. Theol.* p. 428, ed. 2. It is not in Christ (ἀσωμάτως), as before the Incarnation it was in the λόγος (Θεὸς ἦν ὁ λόγος, John i. 1), but (comp. also Gess, *Pers. Chr.* p. 260 ff.) it is in His glorified body (Phil. iii. 21), so that the ἐν μορφῇ Θεοῦ and ἴσα Θεῷ εἶναι, which already existed in the λόγος ἄσαρκος (Phil. ii. 6), now in Christ's estate of exaltation —which succeeded the state of humiliation, whereby the μορφὴ Θεοῦ was affected—have a *bodily* frame, are *in bodily personality.*[1] Of course the θεότης does not thereby itself come into the ranks of the σωματικαὶ οὐσίαι (Plat. *Locr.* p. 96 A), but is in the exalted Christ after a real fashion σωματικῷ εἴδει (Luke iii. 22), and therefore Christ Himself is the visible divine-human image of the invisible God (i. 15). In this glory, as Possessor of the Godhead dwelling in Him bodily, He will also appear at the Parousia—an appearance, therefore, which will manifest itself visibly (1 John iii. 2) as the actual ἐπιφάνεια τῆς δόξης τοῦ μεγάλου Θεοῦ (Tit. ii. 13). The reference of the whole statement, however, to the *exalted* Christ is placed beyond question by the use of the present κατοικεῖ, which asserts the *presently existing* relation, without requiring a νῦν along with it (in opposition to Huther). The renderings : *essentialiter*, οὐσιωδῶς (Cyril, Theophylact, Calvin, Beza, and others, including Usteri, Steiger, Olshausen, Huther, Bisping), in which case some thought of a contrast to the divine ἐνέργεια in the *prophets* (see Theophylact), and: *realiter* (Augustine, Erasmus, Vatablus, Cornelius a Lapide, Grotius, Schoettgen, Wolf, Nösselt, Bleek, and others), in which was found the opposite of τυπικῶς (ver. 17), are linguistically inappropriate ; for σωματικός never means anything else than *corporeus.* Comp. on the

---

[1] It is now only worth remarking historically, but is almost incredible, how the *Socinians* have twisted our verse. Its sense in their view is : "quod in *doctrina* ipsius tota Dei *voluntas integre* et reapse est *patefacta*," *Catech. Racov.* 194, p. 398, ed. Oeder. Calovius gives a refutation in detail.

adverb, Plut. *Mor.* p. 424 D. The less justifiable is the hypothesis of Rich. Schmidt (*Paul. Christol.* p. 191), that in the term σωματικῶς the contrast of ver. 17 was already present to the apostle's mind. Those who adopt the erroneous explanation of πλήρωμα as referring to the *church*, assign to σωματικῶς the meaning : " so that the church stands related to Him *as His body*" (Baumgarten-Crusius and Schenkel), which issues in the absurdity that the body of Christ is held to dwell in Christ, whereas conversely Christ could not but dwell in His body. It is true that the church is related to Christ as His body, not, however, in so far as *it* dwells *in Him* (and, according to the context, this must have been the case *here*, if the explanation in question be adopted), but either in so far as *He* dwells *in it*, or in so far as He is *its Head*, which latter thought is quite foreign to the connection of the passage ; for even in ver. 10 Christ is not called the Head of the *church*. It is, morever, to be observed, that the adverb is placed emphatically at the end. The special *reason*, however, on account of which the κατοικεῖν κ.τ.λ. is thus prominently set forth as bodily, cannot, indeed, be directly shown to have been supplied by the circumstances of the Colossians, but is nevertheless to be recognised in an apologetic interest of opposition to the false teachers, who by their doctrines concerning the angels (comp. ver. 10 : ἀρχῆς κ. ἐξουσ.) must have broken up, in a spiritualistic sense, the πλήρωμα τῆς θεότητος.

Ver. 10. Καί ἐστε ἐν αὐτῷ πεπληρ.] still depending on ὅτι : *and (since) ye are filled in Him,* i.e. and since the πληρότης which ye possess rests on Him, the bodily Bearer of the divine πλήρωμα. The two are correlative : from the πλήρωμα τῆς θεότητος, which dwells in the exalted Christ, flows the πεπληρωμένον εἶναι of the Christian, which has its basis, therefore, in no other than in Christ, and in nothing else than just in fellowship with Him. Filled *with what ?* was self-evident to the consciousness of the reader. It is the *dynamic, charismatic* πλήρωσις, which Christians, in virtue of their union of life with the Lord, whose Spirit and ζωή are in them, have received, and continuously possess, out of the *metaphysical* πλήρωμα dwelling in Christ, out of the πλήρωμα τῆς θεότητος.—

The emphasis is not upon ἐστέ, but, as shown by the subsequent relative definitions, upon ἐν αὐτῷ. If the πεπληρω- μένον εἶναι depends *on Him*, on nothing and on no one but *on Him*, then everything else which men may teach you, and with which they may wish to seize you and conduct you in leading strings, is οὐ κατὰ Χριστόν. With due attention to this emphasis of ἐν αὐτῷ, we should neither have expected ὑμεῖς (in opposition to de Wette; comp. Estius and others: "*et vos*") nor have explained ἐστέ in an *imperative* sense (in opposition to Grotius, Bos, Heumann); which latter view is to be rejected, because the entire connection is not paraenetic, and generally because, whilst a πληροῦσθε (Eph. v. 18) or γίνεσθε πεπληρ. may, ἐστε πεπληρ. cannot, logically be enjoined.[1] There is, moreover (comp. also Hofmann), nothing to be supplied with πεπληρ. (*usually*: τῆς θεότητος, see Theophylact and Huther; de Wette, Bleek: τοῦ πληρώμ. τ. θεότ.), since the specifically ontological sense of the purposely-chosen θεότητος would not even be consistent with the supposed equalization of the Christians with Christ (οὐδὲν ἔλαττον ἔχετε αὐτοῦ, ἀλλὰ πεπληρωμένοι καὶ ὑμεῖς ἐστε τῆς θεότητος, Theophylact), and this equalization does not exist at all, because Paul has not written καὶ ὑμεῖς. In what their being filled consisted, was known to the readers from their own experience, without further explanation; their thoughts, however, were to dwell upon *the fact* that, since their being full depended *on Christ*, those labours of the false teachers were of quite another character than κατὰ Χριστόν. — ὅς ἐστιν ἡ κεφαλὴ κ.τ.λ.] This, as also ver. 11, now supplies *confirmatory information* regarding the fact that they have their being filled not otherwise than just *in Christ*; namely, neither through ἀρχαὶ κ. ἐξουσίαι, since Christ is the head of every ἀρχή and ἐξουσία; nor yet through *circumcision*, since they have received in Christ the real ethical circumcision. — πάσης ἀρχ. κ. ἐξουσ.] is not more precisely defined as in Eph. iii. 10; hence, in

---

[1] Calovius has well said : " Beneficium Christi, non nostrum officium ;" comp. Wolf. In complete opposition to the context, Grotius brings out the sense : "*illo contenti estote*," which he supports by the remark : "quia quod plenum est, nihil aliud desiderat."

virtue of the *munus regium* of the Lord quite generally : *every principality and power*, but with the tacit apologetic reference : consequently also of the *angelic powers* (i. 16) belonging to these categories and bearing these names, to whose mediation, to be attained through θρησκεία, the false teachers direct you, —a reference which Hofmann, understanding the expressions in the sense of spiritual beings *ruling arbitrarily and in opposition to God* especially *over the Gentile world* (notwithstanding the fact that *Christ* is their *Head !*), groundlessly denies ; see ver. 18. If Christ be the Head of every ἀρχή and ἐξουσία, *i.e.* their governing sovereign, the Christian cannot have anything to expect from any angelic powers subordinate to Christ, —a result involved in the union in which He stands to the Higher, *to Christ Himself.*—With the reading ὅ ἐστιν (see the critical remarks), which is also preferred by Ewald,[1] Lachmann has placed καί ἐστε ἐν αὐτῷ πεπληρ. in a parenthesis. But, while this important thought would neither have motive nor be appropriate as a mere parenthesis, it would also be improper that the neuter subject τὸ πλήρωμα τ. θεότ. should be designated as ἡ κεφαλὴ κ.τλ., which applies rather to the personal possessor of the πλήρωμα, to Christ.

Ver. 11. Respecting the connection and its reference to the false teachers, so far as they "legem evangelio miscebant" (Calvin), see on ver. 10. — ἐν ᾧ] like ἐν αὐτῷ in ver. 10 : on whom it also causally depends that ye, etc. This applies to the point of time of their *entrance* into the union with Christ, as is clear from the historical περιετμ., which took place on them through their *conversion* (comp. ver. 12).—καί] *also circumcised* were ye. The καί is the simple *also*, which, however, does not introduce an element included under πεπληρωμ. ἐστε (Hofmann), but to the previous relative statement (ὅς ἐστιν κ.τλ.) *appends* another ; comp. ver. 12. Hofmann's objection, that the foregoing relative statement *has* indeed *reference* to the readers, but *is made without reference to them*, is an empty subtlety, which is connected with the

---

[1] Inasmuch as he takes ὅ ἐστιν directly as *scilicet, utpote*, and regards this usage as a linguistic peculiarity of this Epistle. But this rendering is not required either in i. 24 or in iii. 17 ; and respecting i. 27, see the critical remarks.

erroneous rendering of πάσης ἀρχῆς κ. ἐξουσ. — περιτομῇ
ἀχειροπ.] is not supplementary and parenthetical (Hofmann),
as if Paul had written περιτομῇ δὲ ἀχειροπ., but appends
immediately to περιετμηθ. its *characteristic,* whereby it is distinguished from what is elsewhere meant by circumcision ;
hence the thought is : " in your union with Christ *there has
also taken place a circumcision upon you* (Gentiles), *which is not*
(like the Jewish circumcision) *the work of hands ;*" comp. Eph.
ii. 11. On the word ἀχειροπ. itself (which is similar to
ἀχειρούργητος, *Poll.* ii. 154), in analogous antithetical reference,
comp. Mark xiv. 58 ; 2 Cor. v. 1 ; and on the idea of the
inner ethical circumcision, of which the bodily is the type,
comp. Deut. x. 16, xxx. 6 ; Ezek. xliv. 7; Acts vii. 51. See
Michaelis *in loc.,* and the expositors on Rom. ii. 29 ; Schoettgen,
Hor. I. p. 815. — ἐν τῇ ἀπεκδύσει κ.τ.λ.] This characteristic
περιετμήθητε περιτ. ἀχειρ. took place *by means of the putting off
of the body of the flesh,* which was accomplished in your case
(observe the *passive* connection), *i.e.* in that *the body, whose
essence and nature are flesh, was taken off and put away from
you by God.*[1] With reference to ἐν τῇ ἀπεκδύσει κ.τ.λ., which
is to be coupled not merely with περιετμήθητε (Hofmann), but
with the entire specifically defined conception of circumcision
περιετμ. περιτ. ἀχειροπ., it is to be noticed : (1) that the genitive τῆς σάρκος is the genitivus *materiae,* as in i. 22 ; (2) that
the σάρξ here is not indifferent, but means the flesh *as the seat
of sin, and of its lusts and strivings* (Rom. vii. 23, 25, viii. 3, 13 ;
Gal. v. 16 ; Eph. ii. 3 ; Col. iii. 5, *et al.*) ; so that Paul (3) might
have conveyed the idea of τὸ σῶμα τῆς σαρκ. also by τὸ
σῶμα τῆς ἁμαρτίας (Rom. vi. 6), but the description by τῆς
σαρκός was suggested to him by the thought of the circumcision
(Rom. ii. 28 ; Eph. ii. 11). (4) The significant and weighty
expression ἀπεκδύσει (the substantive used only here, the verb
also in ver. 15, iii. 9 ; Josephus, *Antt.* vi. 14. 2) is selected in
contrast to the operation of the legal circumcision, which only

---

[1] Compare Hofmann, *Schriftbew.* II. 2, p. 171. The same writer, however,
now objects that ἀπέκδυσις cannot have *passive* significance. But this it *is not*
alleged to have : God is the ἀπεκδύων, *i.e.* He who, as author of regeneration,
puts off from man the body of flesh.

wounded the σῶμα τ. σαρκός and removed a portion of one
member of it; whereas the spiritual circumcision, divinely
performed, consisted in a complete *parting and doing away
with* this body, in so far as God, by means of this ethical circumcision, *has taken off and removed* the sinful body from man
(the two acts are expressed by the double compound), like a
garment which is drawn off and laid aside. Ethically circumcised, *i.e.* translated by conversion from the estate of sin
into that of the Christian life of faith and righteousness (see
ver. 12), consequently born again as καινὴ κτίσις,[1] as a καινὸς
ἄνθρωπος created after God (Eph. iv. 24), *man has no longer
any* σῶμα τῆς σαρκός at all, because the body which he has
is rid of the sinful σάρξ as such, as regards its sinful quality;
he is no longer ἐν τῇ σαρκί as previously, when lust ἐνηργεῖτο
ἐν τοῖς μέλεσιν (Rom. vii. 5; comp. ver. 23); he is no longer
σάρκινος, πεπραμένος ὑπὸ τὴν ἁμαρτίαν (Rom. vii. 14), but is
dead for sin (Rom. vi. 11); he has crucified the σάρξ (Gal.
v. 24), and no longer walks κατὰ σάρκα, but ἐν καινότητι
πνεύματος (Rom. vii. 6); by the law of the Holy Spirit he is
freed from the law of sin and death (Rom. viii. 2), ἐν πνεύματι
(Rom. viii. 9), dead with Christ (Gal. ii. 19; 2 Cor. v. 14;
Col. iii. 3), and risen, so that his members are ὅπλα δικαιοσύνης τῷ Θεῷ (Rom. vi. 13). This Christian transformation is
represented in its *ideal* aspect, which disregards the empirical
imperfection, according to which the σάρξ is still doubtless even
in the regenerate at variance with the πνεῦμα (Gal. v. 17). Our
dogmatists well describe regeneration as *perfecta* a parte *Dei*,
but as *imperfecta* a parte *hominum recipientium*. To take σῶμα
in the sense of *massa* or *aggregate* (Calvin, Grotius, Calovius,
and others, including Steiger and Bähr[2]), is opposed as well to

---

[1] The epoch of this transformation is *baptism* (see Weiss, *Bibl. Theol.* p. 439,
ed. 2; comp. Holtzmann, p. 178), by which, however, the baptism of *Christian
children* is by no means assumed as the antitype of circumcision (Steiger,
Philippi). Comp. on 1 Cor. vii. 14; Acts xvi. 15.

[2] Comp. also Philippi, *Glaubensl.* V. 2, p. 225, who declares my explanation
to be forced, without proof, and contrary to the Scripture; and Reiche, *Comm.
crit.* p. 274, who understands σῶμα of the "toto *quasi* vitiositatis (τ. σαρκός)
corpore," so that the putting away of *all* immorality is denoted. Similarly
Dalmer.

the context, in which the discourse turns upon *circumcision* and (ver. 12) upon *burial* and *resurrection*, as also to the linguistic usage of the N. T. In classic authors it expresses the notion in question in the *physical* sense, *e.g.* Plat. *Tim.* p. 32 C: τὸ τοῦ κόσμου σῶμα (comp. p. 31 B, *Hipp. maj.* p. 301 B), and in later writers may also denote generally a *whole* consisting of parts (comp. Cicero, *ad Att.* ii. 1. 4). In opposition to the erroneous assumption that σῶμα must have a figurative meaning here, as Julius Müller, *v. d. Sünde,* I. p. 459 f., still in the 5th ed., thinks,[1] see on Rom. vi. 6 ; comp. also Hofmann, *Schriftbew.* I. p. 560 f. — ἐν τῇ περιτομῇ τοῦ **X**.] *by means of the circumcision of Christ,* parallel to the previous ἐν τῇ ἀπεκδύσει κ.τ.λ., *naming* specifically (as different from that of the Old Testament) the circumcision *described* previously according to its nature. The genitive τοῦ Χριστοῦ is to be rendered : the circumcision, *which is produced through Christ.* The context requires this by the further explanation of the thing itself in ver. 12. Comp. above, ἐν ᾧ. But Christ is not conceived of as *Himself the circumciser,* in so far, namely, as by *baptism* (Theophylact, Beza, and others), or by His *Spirit* (Bleek), He accomplishes the cleansing and sanctification of man (see on ver. 12); but as the One through whom, in virtue of the effective living union that takes place in conversion between man and Himself, this divine περιτομή, in its character specifically different from the Israelite circumcision, is practically *brought about and rendered a reality,* and *in so far* it is based on Christ as its αἴτιος (Theodoret). It is not, however, *baptism itself* (Hofmann, following older expositors) that is meant by the circumcision of Christ, although the predicate ἀχειροπ. would not be in opposition to this view, but the spiritual transformation, that consecration of a holy state of life, which takes place *in baptism ;* see ver. 12 : ἐν τῷ βαπτίσματι. According to Schneckenburger, in the *Theol. Jahrb.* 1848, p. 286 ff., the ἀπέκδυσις τ. σώμ. τ. σαρκ. is meant of the *death of Christ,* and also the περιτομὴ τοῦ **X**. is meant to denote this *death,* so that

---

[1] Müller also holds that Paul here conceives the old sinful nature as a *body* which, in regeneration, the Christian puts off ; and that σάρξ is to be understood only of the *earthly-human life.*

the latter is an explanation by way of application of the former, in opposition to the heretical recommendation of a bodily or mystical περιτομή. It may be decisively urged against this view, that after τῆς σαρκός there is no αὐτοῦ, (comp. i. 22), which was absolutely necessary, if the reader was to think of another subject than that of περιετμήθητε; further, that τῇ ἀκροβυστίᾳ τῆς σαρκὸς ὑμῶν, in ver. 13, stands in significant retrospective reference to the ἀπέκδυσις τ. σώμ. τῆς σαρκός; and that συνταφέντες κ.τ.λ. in ver. 12 is *synchronous* with περιετμήθητε κ.τ.λ., and represents substantially the *same* thing. Moreover, the description of the *death* of Christ as His *circumcision* would be all the more inappropriate, since, in the case of Christ, the *actual* circumcision was not absent. According to Holtzmann, the entire clause : ἐν τ. ἀπεκδ. τοῦ σώμ. τ. σαρκ., ἐν τ. περιτ. τ. Χ., should be deleted as an addition of the interpolator, because the expression σῶμα τῆς σαρκός has occurred at i. 22 in quite another—namely, an indifferent, genuinely Pauline—reference. This reason is incorrect, because in i. 22 it is not τῆς σαρκός, but τῆς σαρκὸς αὐτοῦ, and this αὐτοῦ makes the great essential difference between the expression in that passage and that employed in our present one.

Ver. 12 supplies further information as to how the περιετμήθητε, so far as it has taken place by means of the circumcision *of Christ*, has been accomplished. — συνταφέντες κ.τ.λ.] synchronous with περιετμ. (comp. on i. 20, εἰρηνοποιήσας): *in that ye became buried with Him in baptism.* The immersion in baptism, in accordance with its similarity to burial, is— seeing that baptism translates into the fellowship of the death of Christ (see on Rom. vi. 3)—a *burial along with* Christ, Rom. vi. 4. Through that fellowship *of death* man dies as to his sinful nature, so that the σῶμα τῆς σαρκός (ver. 11) ceases to live, and by means of the fellowship *of burial* is put off (ver. 11). The subject who effects the joint burial is *God*, as in the whole context. In the burial of Christ this joint burial of all that confess Him as respects their sinful body was objectively completed; but it takes place, as respects each individually and in subjective appropriation, by their baptism, prior to which the realization of that fellowship of burial was, on the part of individuals, still wanting.—ἐν ᾧ καὶ συνηγέρθητε] A new benefit, which has accrued to the readers ἐν Χριστῷ, and which in their case must bring still more clearly to living consciousness their ἐν Χριστῷ πεπληρωμένον εἶναι; so that ἐν ᾧ here is parallel to the ἐν ᾧ in ver. 11, and refers to *Christ*, as does also αὐτόν subsequently.   It is rightly taken thus, following Chrysostom and his successors, by Luther and most others, including Flatt, Bähr, Huther, Ewald.   Others have referred it to ἐν τῷ βαπτ. (Beza, Calixtus, Estius, Michaelis, Heinrichs, and others, including Steiger, Böhmer, de Wette, Baumgarten-Crusius, Hofmann, Dalmer, Bleek); but, in opposition to this may be urged, first, the very symmetry of the discourse (ὅς ... ἐν ᾧ καί ... ἐν ᾧ καί); secondly, and specially, the fact that, if ἐν ᾧ refers to baptism, ἐν could not be the proper preposition, since ἐν τῷ βαπτ., in accordance with the meaning of the word and the figure of burial, refers to the *dipping into* (not *overflowing*, as Hofmann thinks), whilst the spiritual awakening to new life, in which sense these expositors take συνηγέρθ., would have taken place through the *emerging again*, so that we should expect ἐξ οὗ, or, at all events, the non-local δι' οὗ; and, thirdly, the fact that just as συνταφέντες has its own more precise definition by ἐν τῷ βαπτ., so also has συνηγέρθ. through διὰ τῆς πίστεως κ.τ.λ., and therefore the text affords no occasion for taking up again for συνηγέρθ. the more precise definition of the previous point, viz. ἐν τῷ βαπτίσματι.   No, the first benefit received in Christ which Paul specifies, viz. the moral circumcision, accomplished by God through the joint burial in baptismal immersion, has been fully handled in ver. 11 down to βαπτίσματι in ver. 12, and there now follows a second blessing received by the readers in Christ (ἐν ᾧ καί): they have been *raised up also with Christ*, which has taken place *through faith*, etc.   The previous joint burial was the necessary moral preliminary condition of this joint awakening, since through it the σῶμα τῆς σαρκός was put off.   This συνηγέρθ. is to be understood in the sense of *the fellowship of the bodily resurrection of Christ*, into which fellowship man enters by faith in

such a way that, in virtue of his union of life and destiny
with Christ brought about by means of faith, he knows his
own resurrection as having taken place in that of Christ—a
benefit of joint resurrection, which is, indeed, prior to the
Parousia, an *ideal* possession, but through the Parousia
becomes *real* (whether its realization be attained by resurrection proper in the case of the dead, or by the change that shall
take place in those who are still alive).   Usually συνηγέρθ.
is taken in the *ethical* sense, as referring to the *spiritual*
awakening, viz. from moral death, so that Paul, after the
negative aspect of the regeneration (ver. 11 ; βαπτίσματι,
ver. 12), now describes its *positive* character ; comp. also
Huther, Ewald, Bleek, Hofmann.   But in opposition to this
view is the fact that the fresh commencement ἐν ᾧ καί, corresponding with the similar commencement of ver. 11, and
referring to Christ, makes us expect the mention of a *new
benefit*, and not merely that of another aspect of the *previous*
one, otherwise there would have been no necessity for repeating the ἐν ᾧ καί ; as also, that the inference of participation in
the *proper* resurrection of Christ from death lies at the basis of
the following τοῦ ἐγείραντος αὐτὸν ἐκ νεκρῶν.   Comp. on Eph.
ii. 1, and ii. 5, 6.   Chrysostom, Theodoret, and Oecumenius
have already correctly explained it of the *proper* resurrection
(καὶ γὰρ ἐγηγέρμεθα τῇ δυνάμει, εἰ καὶ μὴ τῇ ἐνεργείᾳ), but Theophylact makes it include the ethical awakening also : holding
that it is to be explained κατὰ δύο τρόπους, of the *actual*
resurrection *in spe*, and at the same time ὅτι πνευματικῶς τὴν
νέκρωσιν τῶν ἔργων τῆς ἁμαρτίας ἀπερρίψαμεν. — διὰ τῆς
πίστεως κ.τ.λ.] The τῆς πίστεως is described by Holtzmann,
p. 70, as syntactically clumsy and offensive ; he regards it as
an interpolation borrowed from Eph. i. 19 f.   Groundlessly ;
Paul is describing the *subjective medium*, without which the
joint awakening, though objectively and historically accomplished in the resurrection of Christ, would not be appropriated
individually, the ληπτικόν for this appropriation being wanting.
The unbeliever has not the blessing of having risen with
Christ, because he stands apart from the fellowship of life with
Christ, just as also he has not the reconciliation, although the

reconciliation of all has been accomplished objectively through Christ's death. The genitive τῆς ἐνεργείας τ. Θ. is the *object* of faith ; so Chrysostom, Theodoret, Oecumenius, Theophylact, Erasmus, Castalio, Beza, Calvin, Zeger, Grotius, Estius, Cornelius a Lapide, Michaelis, Rosenmüller, and others, including Baumgarten-Crusius, Ewald, Bleek, and Hofmann, in the 2d ed. of the *Schriftbew.* II. 2, p. 174 f. But others, such as Luther ("through the faith *which God works*"), Bengel, Flatt, Bähr, Steiger, de Wette, Böhmer, Huther, *et al.*, take τῆς ἐνεργ. τ. Θ. as genitivus *causae*, for which, however, Eph. i. 19 is not to be adduced (see *in loc.*), and in opposition to which it is decisive that in *all* passages, where the genitive with πίστις is not the believing subject, it denotes the *object* (Mark xi. 22 ; Acts iii. 16 ; Rom. iii. 22 ; Gal. ii. 16, 20, iii. 22 ; Eph. iii. 12 ; Phil. i. 27, iii. 9 ; 2 Thess. ii. 13 ; Jas. ii. 1 ; Rev. ii. 13, xiv. 12), and that the description of God as the Being *who has raised up Christ from the dead* stands most naturally and directly in significant reference to the divine activity which procures, not the *faith*, but the συνεγείρεσθαι, and which is therefore set forth in a very appropriate manner as the special object[1] of faith (comp. iv. 17, 24, vi. 8, x. 9 ; 2 Cor. iv. 13, 14 ; Eph. i. 19 f. ; 1 Pet. i. 21). At the basis, namely, of the τοῦ ἐγείραντος αὐτ. ἐκ νεκρ. lies the certainty in the believer's consciousness : since God has raised up Christ, His activity, which has produced this *principale* and *majus*, will have included therein the *consequens* and *minus*, my *resurrection with Him*. To the believer the two stand in such essential connection, that in the operation of God which raised up Christ he beholds, by virtue of his fellowship of life with Christ, the assurance of his own resurrection having taken place along with that act ; in the former he has the pledge, the ἐνέχυρον (Theodoret) of the latter. Hofmann now again (as in the first ed. of the *Schriftbeweis*) explains τῆς ἐνεργ. τ. Θ. as in *apposition to* τῆς πίστεως, in such a way that Paul, "*as if correcting himself*," makes the former take the place of the latter, in order to guard against the danger of his readers conceiving to

---

[1] The efficacy of the divine power shown in the resurrection of Christ is the guarantee of the certainty of salvation.

COL. 2 A

themselves faith as a *conduct on man's part* making possible
the participation in the resurrection of Christ by God, while in
reality it is nothing else than the product of the ἐνέργεια *of
God*.   A quite gratuitously invented self-correction, without
precedent, and undiscoverable by the reader; although the
thought, if it had entered the mind of Paul, might have been
indicated with the utmost simplicity and ease (possibly by διὰ
τῆς πίστεως, μᾶλλον δὲ διὰ τῆς ἐνεργ. τ. Θ.).

Ver. 13. Since that συνηγέρθητε was the awaking to *eternal
life*, Paul now goes on to give special prominence to *this* great
blessing, the *making alive*, and that in reference to the *Gentile-*
Christian position of the readers; and to this he annexes, in
ver. 14 f., an anti-Judaistic triumphant statement reminding
them of the cancelling of their debt-bond with the law.——
To attach καὶ ὑμᾶς ... σαρκὸς ὑμῶν still to ver. 12, and to
make it depend on ἐγείραντος (Steiger), is rendered impossible
by the right explanation of τῆς πίστεως τῆς ἐνεργείας τ. Θ.
in ver. 12,[1] to say nothing of the abrupt position in which
συνεζωοπ. would thus appear.   Καὶ ὑμᾶς goes along with
συνεζωοπ., so that ὑμᾶς is then *repeated* (see Fritzsche, *Quaest.
Luc.* p. 14; Bornemann in the *Sächs. Stud.* 1846, p. 66;
Kühner, II. 1, p. 568; Winer, p. 139 [E. T. 184]), the repetition being here occasioned by the emphasis of the συνεζωοπ.:
"You also, when ye were dead ... He made you *alive together*
with Him."   The καί therefore is not the copula *and*, but, in
harmony with the ὑμᾶς placed in the front emphatically: *also*,
as in Eph. ii. 1.   It has its reference in this, that the readers
had been *Gentiles* liable to eternal death, but the συνεζωοπ.
had been extended, as to all believers, so *also to them*.   The

---

[1] This applies also in opposition to Hofmann, who takes ver. 13 likewise as a
continuation of the description of God given in τοῦ ἐγείρ. αὐτὸν ἐκ νεκρ., and
therein makes the apostle guilty of a clumsy change of construction, viz. that he
intended to make συζωοποιήσαντος follow, but, because this word would have been
"*inconvenient*" after νεκροὺς ὄντας κ.τ.λ., exchanged it for an independent sentence.   But συζωοποιήσαντος would have been inserted without any *inconvenience*
whatever : on the contrary, it would only have expressed the alleged idea conformably to the construction *clearly* and *definitely*.   The comparison of i. 26
is unsuitable.   Holtzmann follows substantially the view of Hofmann, but
regards the change of structure as the result of *dictation*.   There is no change of
structure in the passage at all.

correctness of this reference is shown by the context as well through τῇ ἀκροβυστίᾳ τῆς σαρκ. ὑμ., as through the pronoun of the *first* person which is introduced after χαρισάμ. Extremely arbitrary is the view of Olshausen, who thinks that in ver. 11 f. the readers are addressed as *representatives of the collective community*, but by καὶ ὑμᾶς in ver. 13 *personally;* while Baumgarten-Crusius, in complete antagonism to the position of the words, joins καί, not to ὑμᾶς, but to the verb : "*also* He has called you *to the new life that abideth.*"—To arrive at a proper understanding of what follows we must observe : (1) That συνεζωοποίησεν is not to be taken, any more than συνηγέρθητε previously, in an *ethical* sense, as referring to regeneration (so usually since Oecumenius, as *e.g.* Grotius : "sicut Christo novam contulit vitam ex morte corporis, ita et nobis novam *ex morte animorum;*" comp. also Bleek and Hofmann), but in its *proper* sense, and that (comp. Kaeuffer, *de* ζωῆς αἰων. not. p. 94 f.) as referring to the *everlasting life* to which God[1] raised up Christ, and which He has thereby also provided for believers in virtue of their fellowship with Christ (as an ideal possession now, but to be realized at the Parousia). See also Eph. ii. 5. The *reconciliation* (which de Wette understands) is not the ζωοποίησις itself, as is plain from the compound συνεζωοπ., but its precursor and medium. The συζωοποιεῖν stands in the same relation to the συνεγείρειν as the nature of the act to its process ; but the reason why συνηγέρθ. here stands *before* the συζωοποιεῖν (it is different in Eph. ii. 5) is, that the συνηγέρθητε was correlative with the συνταφέντες in ver. 12, hence that word is used first, while in Eph. *l.c.* the being dead preceded, with which the συζωοποιεῖν primarily corresponds. (2) Like συνεζωοπ., so also νεκρούς is not to be taken in an ethical sense (so usually both here

---

[1] *God* is the subject of συνεζωοποίησιν, not *Christ* (Ewald and the older expositors) ; for *God* has raised up Christ, and *God* is, according to the present context (it is different in iii. 13), the forgiver of sins, and has brought about the remission of sins through the ἱλαστήριον of Christ (ver. 14). Hence also it is not to be written σ. αὐτῷ (with the aspirate). Just as God was obviously the acting subject in περιτμήθητε, in συνταφέντες, and in συνηγέρθ., so also He is introduced in the same character emphatically in ver. 12, and remains so till the close of ver. 15.

and in Eph. ii. 1, as *e.g.* Calvin, who thinks that the *alienatio a Deo* is meant), but, with Chrysostom and Theodoret, in its *proper* sense; the readers have been—this is the conception —prior to their conversion to Christ a prey of *death*. This is by no means to be understood, however, in the sense of *physical* death (for that comes from *Adam's* sin, see on Rom. v. 12), but in that of *eternal* death, to which they were liable through their sins, so that they could not have become partakers of the eternal ζωή (comp. on Rom. vii. 9 f.). See also on Eph. ii. 1. What is meant, therefore, is not a death which *would have only become their eternal death* in the absence of the quickening (Hofmann), but *the eternal death itself*, in which they *already lay*, and *out of which* they would not have come without that deliverance, nay, which on the contrary—and here we have a prolepsis of the thought— would only have *completed* itself in the future αἰών.[1] (3) This being dead occurred *in the state* (ἐν) *of their sins* (τοῖς indicates the sins which they had committed) *and of the uncircumcision of their flesh, i.e.* when as respects *their sinful materially-psychical nature* they were still uncircumcised, and had not yet put off by conversion their Gentile *fleshly* constitution.[2] The ἀκροβυστία *in itself* they even now had as Gentile Christians, but according to ver. 11 it was no longer ἀκρόβ. τῆς σαρκός in their case, but was now *indifferent* (iii. 11; 1 Cor. vii. 19; Gal. v. 6, vi. 15), since they had been provided with the ethical circumcision of Christ and emptied of the σῶμα τῆς σαρκός. The ethical reference of the expression does not lie, therefore, in ἀκροβυστία itself, but in the characteristic τῆς σαρκὸς ὑμῶν (genitive of the *subject*); in *this* uncircumcision they were *as Gentiles* prior to their conversion, but were so no longer *as Christians*. Consequently ἀκρόβ. is not to be taken *figuratively* (Deut. x. 16; Ezek. xliv. 7; Jer. iv. 4) as a designation of *vitiositas* (so Theodoret, Beza,

---

[1] Quite correlative is the conception of the ζωή as *eternal* life, which the righteous man already *has*, although he has still *in prospect* the glorious perfection of it in the future αἰών.

[2] The ἐν is not repeated before τῇ ἀκρόβ. because the two elements coupled by καί are conceived together so as to form the single idea of unconversion; Kühner, II. 1, p. 476. This applies also in opposition to Holtzmann, p. 156.

Grotius, Bähr, Bleek, and most expositors), but in its *proper* sense, in which the readers as ἀκρόβυστοι could not but have understood it, and therein withal not as a symbol of *uncleanness* (Huther), or of the *alienatio a Deo* (Calvin, comp. Hofmann), or the like ; on the contrary, the entire ethical stress lies on τῆς σαρκ. ὑμ. The idea of *original sin* (Flacius and other dogmatic expositors, comp. Bengel: "*exquisita* appellatio peccati origin.") is likewise involved, and that according to its N. T. meaning (Rom. vii. 14 ff.), not in ἀκροβυστ., but doubtless in τῆς σαρκ. ὑμῶν. Nevertheless this τῆς σαρκ. ὑμῶν belongs only to τῇ ἀκροβυστίᾳ, and not to τοῖς παραπτώμασι as well (Hofmann) ; comp. Eph. ii. 11. Otherwise we should have, quite unnecessarily, two references heterogeneous in sense for the genitive ; besides, the notion of παράπτωμα presupposes not the σάρξ, but the *Ego* in its relation to the divine law as the subject ; hence also the expression παράπτ. τῆς σαρκ. (or ἁμαρτία τ. σ.) does not occur, while we find ἔργα τῆς σαρκός in Gal. v. 19. Holtzmann, p. 71, ascribes the words καὶ τῇ ἀκροβ. τ. σαρκὸς ὑμ. to the interpolator's love for synonyms and tautological expressions, and wishes to condemn them also in consequence of what in ver. 11 belongs to the latter (p. 155). But they are not at all tautological ; and see on ver. 11. — χαρισάμενος κ.τ.λ.] *after having granted to us*, i.e. *forgiven*, etc. This blotting out of our whole debt of sin was necessarily prior to the συνεζωοπ. ὑμᾶς σὺν αὐτῷ. By the fact, namely, *that He remitted to us all the sins* which we had committed (πάντα τὰ παραπτ.), the *causa efficiens* of the being (eternally) dead was *done away*. Comp. Chrysostom : τὰ παραπτώματα, ἃ τὴν νεκρότητα ἐποίει. This χαρισάμενος κ.τ.λ. is *the appropriation of the reconciliation* on the part of God, which believers experienced *when they believed and were baptized ; the objective expiatory act* through the death of Christ had preceded, and is described in ver. 14. — ἡμῖν] applies to *believers generally*.[1] This extension, embracing himself in com-

---

[1] Not specially to *Jewish Christians* (Hofmann, who discovers here the same idea that is expressed in Heb. ix. 15, and makes a new period begin with χαρισάμενος), since Paul does not express a contrast with the Gentile-Christians, but very often passes from the second person, which refers to the readers, to the

mon with others, is *prepared for* by καὶ ὑμᾶς, but could
not have been introduced, if χαρισάμ. κ.τ.λ. had been conceived as synchronous with συνεζωοπ., in which case Paul
must logically have used ὑμῖν (not ἡμῖν), as the reading
is in B ℵ** Vulg. Hilary. On χαρίζεσθαι, comp. 2 Cor. ii.
10, xii. 13 ; Eph. iv. 32. On the subject-matter : 2 Cor. v.
19 ff.

Ver. 14. The *participle*, which is by no means parallel and
synchronous with χαρισάμενος in ver. 13, or one and the
same with it (Hofmann), is to be resolved as : *after that He
had blotted out*, etc. For it is the historical divine reconciling
act *of the death of Christ* that is meant, with which χαρισάμενος κ.τ.λ. cannot coincide, since that work of reconciliation
had first to be accomplished before the χαρίζεσθαι κ.τ.λ. could
take place through its appropriation to believers. — ἐξαλείφειν]
is to be left quite in its *proper* signification, as in Acts iii. 19,
Rev. iii. 5, vii. 17, xxi. 4, and frequently in LXX. and
Apocrypha, since the discourse has reference to something
written, the invalidating of which is represented in the sensuous
form of *blotting out*, even more forcibly than by διαγράφειν (*to
score out;* see Ruhnken, *ad Tim.* p. 81). Comp. Plat. *Rep.*
p. 386 C, p. 501 B : ἐξαλείφοιεν . . . πάλιν ἐγγράφοιεν, *Ep.*
7, p. 342 C : τὸ ζωγραφούμενόν τε καὶ ἐξαλειφόμενον, Dem.
468. 1 in reference to a *law : εἰ χρὴ τοῦτον ἐξαλεῖψαι*, Xen.
Hell. ii. 3. 51 ; Lucian, *Imag.* 26 ; Eur. *Iph. A.* 1486. Comp.
Valckenaer, *ad Act.* iii. 19. — τὸ καθ᾽ ἡμῶν χειρόγραφον] *the
handwriting existing against us.* What is thus characterized
is not the *burden of debt* lying upon man, which is, as it were,
his debt-schedule (Bleek), but the *Mosaic law.* A χειρόγραφον,
namely, is an obligatory document of debt (Tob. v. 3, ix. 5 ;
Polyb. xxx. 8. 4 ; Dion. Hal. v. 8 ; and the passages in
Wetstein ; also the passages quoted from the Rabbins in
Schoettgen), for which the older Greek writers use συγγραφή

first, in which he, in accordance with the sense and connection, continues the
discourse from the standpoint of the common Christian consciousness.   Comp.
i. 12 ; Gal. iv. 5, 6 ; Eph. ii. 1, 4, *et al.;* Winer, p. 539 [E. T. 725].   Nor does
the idea of the figurative χειρόγραφον, which Hofmann urges, by any means
require such a limitation—which there is nothing to indicate—of the ἡμῖν embracing himself and others.

or γραμματεῖον, Dem. 882. 7, 956. 2 ; see also Hermann, *Privatalterth.* § 49, 12. And the *law* is the χειρόγραφον confronting us, *in so far* as men are bound to fulfil it perfectly, in order to avoid the threatened penal curse ; and consequently because no one renders this fulfilment, it, like a bill of debt, proves them *debtors* (the creditor is God). We are not to carry the figure further, in which case we should come to the halting point in the comparison, that the *man* who is bound has not *himself written* the χειρόγραφον.[1] Hofmann maintains that this element also, namely, man's *having written it with his own hand,* is retained in the conception of the figurative χειρόγραφον. But the apostle himself precludes this view by his having written, not : τὸ ἡμῶν χειρόγρ. (which would mean : *the document of debt drawn by us*), but : τὸ καθ᾽ ἡμῶν χειρόγρ. ; which purposely chosen expression does not affirm that we have *ourselves written* the document, but it does affirm that it *authenticates* us *as arrested for debt,* and is consequently *against* us. The words τοῖς δόγμασιν appended (see below) also preclude the conception of the debt-record being written by man's own hand. Moreover, the law is to be understood as an integral *whole,* and the various limitations of it, either to the *ceremonial law* (Calvin, Beza, Schoettgen, and others), or to the *moral law* (Calovius), are altogether in opposition to the connection (see above, πάντα τὰ παραπτ.), and un-Pauline. The explanation referring it to the *conscience* (Luther, Zwingli, Melanchthon, and

---

[1] The relation of *obligation* and *indebtedness* in which man stands to the law (comp. Gal. iii. 10) is quite sufficient to justify the conception of the latter as the χειρόγραφον, without seeking this specially in the *promise of the people,* Ex. xxiv. 3 (Chrysostom, Oecumenius, Theophylact, and others ; also Hofmann) ; which the reader could not guess without some more precise indication. Indeed, that promise of the people in Ex. xxiv. 3 has by no means the mark of being *self-written,* but contains only the self-*obligation,* and would not, therefore, any more than the *amen* in Deut. xxvii. (which Castalio suggests), suffice for the idea of the χειρόγραφον, if the latter had to contain the debtor's *own handwriting.* In accordance with the apostle's words (τὸ καθ᾽ ἡμῶν χειρόγρ., see above), and with the type of his doctrine regarding the impossibility of legal righteousness, his readers could think only of the γράμμα of *the law itself* as that which proves man a debtor ; comp. Rom. ii. 27, 29, vii. 6 ; 2 Cor. iii. 6. Wieseler, on Gal. p. 258 (appealing to Luke xvi. 5 ff.), Bleek, and Holtzmann, p. 64, also erroneously press the point that the χειρόγρ. must necessarily be written or signed *by the debtor himself.*

others) is also at variance both with the word and with the context.[1] The conscience is the medium for the *knowledge* of the law *as* the handwriting which testifies against us; without the activity of the conscience, this relation, in which the law stands to us, would remain unknown. Exception has been taken to its being explained of the Mosaic law on account of the use of ἡμῶν, seeing that this law existed only for the *Jews*. But without due ground; for it is in fact also the schedule of debt against the *Gentiles*, in so far, namely, as the latter have the knowledge of the δικαίωμα τοῦ Θεοῦ (Rom. i. 32), have in fact τὸ ἔργον τοῦ νόμου γραπτὸν ἐν ταῖς καρδίαις αὐτῶν (Rom. ii. 15), and, consequently, fall likewise under the condemning sentence of the law, though not directly (Rom. iii. 19, ii. 12), but indirectly, because they, having incurred through their own fault a darkening of their minds (Rom. i. 20–23), transgress the "κοινὸν ἀπάντων ἀνθρώπων νόμον" (Dem. 639. 22). The earnest and graphic description of the abrogation of the condemning law in ver. 14 is dictated by an *apologetic* motive, in opposition to the Judaism of the false teachers; hence it is the more inappropriate to understand with Cornelius a Lapide and others *the covenant of God with Adam* in Gen. ii. 16, as was already proposed by Chrysostom, Oecumenius, Theophylact (comp. Iren. *Haer.* v. 17. 3, and Tertullian). — τοῖς δόγμασιν] Respecting δόγμα, command, especially of *legal* decrees, see on Eph. ii. 15 ; Wetstein on Luke ii. 1 ; the *dative* is closely connected with χειρόγραφον, and is instrumental : *what is written with the commands* (therein given), so that the δόγματα, which form the constituent elements of the law, are regarded as that *wherewith it is written*. Thus the tenor of the *contents* of what is written is indicated by the dative of the instrument (*ablativus modi*), just as the *external* constituent elements of writing, *e.g.* γράμμασι in Gal. vi. 11, and τύποις in Plat. *Ep.* 7, p. 343 A, are expressed by the

---

[1] Luther's gloss : "Nothing is so hard against us as our own conscience, whereby we are convinced as by our own handwriting, when the law reveals to us our sin." Melanchthon : "sententia in mente et corde tanquam scripta lege et agnitione lapsus," in connection with which he regards the conscience as "syllogismus practicus ex lege ductus."

same dative. Observe the *verbal* nature of χειρόγραφον, and that the dative is joined to it, as to τὸ γεγραμμένον (comp. Plat. *l.c.*: τὰ γεγραμμένα τύποις). This direct combination of a verbal substantive with a dative of the instrument is such an unquestionable and current phenomenon in classical Greek (see Matthiae, II. p. 890 ; Heindorf, *ad Plat. Cratyl.* p. 131 ; and especially Kühner, II. 1, p. 374), that the connection in question cannot in the least degree appear as harsh (Winer, Buttmann), or even as unnatural (Hofmann) ; nor should it have been regarded as something " *welded on* " by the interpolator (Holtzmann, p. 74), who had desired thereby to give to χειρόγρ. its reference to the law. The explanation given by many writers (Calvin, Beza, Vitringa, Wolf, Michaelis, Heinrichs, and others, comp. Luther), which hits nearly the true sense : the χειρόγραφον, *consisting in the* δόγμασι, is to be corrected grammatically in accordance with what we have said above. It is in complete variance with the arrangement of the words to join τοῖς δόγμ. to τὸ καθ᾽ ἡμῶν by supplying an ὄν (Calovius).[1] Bähr, Huther, and Dalmer (comp. de Wette) regard it as a more precise definition of the entire τὸ καθ᾽ ἡμ. χειρόγρ., so that Paul explains what he means by the χειρόγρ., and, at the same time, how it comes to be a debt-document testifying against us. So also Winer, p. 206 [E. T. 275]. This, however, would have been expressed by τὸ τοῖς δόγμασι καθ᾽ ἡμῶν χειρόγρ., or in some other way corresponding grammatically with the sense assumed. Ewald joins τοῖς δόγμ. as *appropriating* dative (see Bernhardy, p. 88 f.) to χειρόγρ.: our *bond of obligation to the statutes.*[2] But if χειρόγρ. were *our* bond of obligation (subjectively), the expression τὸ καθ᾽ ἡμῶν χειρ. would be inappropriate, and Paul would have said merely τὸ ἡμῶν χειρ. τ. δόγμ. It is incorrect as to sense, though not linguistically erroneous, to connect τοῖς δόγμ. with ἐξαλείψας, in which case it is explained to mean (as by Harless on Eph. ii. 15) that the

---

[1] So also Wieseler in Rosenmüller's *Rep.* II. p. 135 ff. : τὸ χειρόγρ. τὸ τοῖς δόγμ. καθ᾽ ἡμῶν ὄν.

[2] Comp. Wieseler on *Gal.* p. 258 : "with reference to the statutes." He takes Paul's meaning to be, " our testimony with our own hand, that we have transgressed the statutes of the law of Moses."

abrogation of the law had taken place either *as regards its statutes* (Steiger) ; or *by the evangelical doctrines of faith* (the Greek expositors, Estius, Grotius, Hammond, Bengel, and others) ; or *nova praecepta stabiliendo* (Fritzsche, *Diss. in 2 Cor.* II. p. 168 f.). In opposition to these views, see Eph. ii. 15. Erasmus, Storr, Flatt, Olshausen, Schenkel, Bleek, and Hofmann have attached it to the following relative clause,[1] in opposition to the simple order of the words, without any certain precedent in the N. T. (with regard to Acts i. 2, Rom. xvi. 27, see on those passages), and thereby giving an emphasis to the τοῖς δόγμ. which is not warranted (for the law as such contains, in fact, nothing *else* than δόγματα). — ὃ ἦν ὑπεναντίον ἡμῖν] an emphatic repetition—bringing into more marked prominence the hostile relation—of the thought already expressed by καθ᾽ ἡμῶν, with the view of counteracting the legalistic efforts of the false teachers. Bengel's distinction, that there is here expressed *ipsa pugna*, and by καθ᾽ ἡμῶν, *status belli*, is arbitrary and artificial. It means simply : *which was against us*, not : *secretly* against us, as Beza and others, including Böhmer, interpret the word, which Paul uses only in this place, but which is generally employed in Greek writers, in the Apocrypha and LXX., and in the N. T. again in Heb. x. 27. The relative attaches itself to the entire τὸ καθ᾽ ἡμ. χειρόγρ. τοῖς δόγμ. — καὶ αὐτὸ ἦρκεν κ.τ.λ.] Observe not only the emphatic *change of structure* (see on i. 6) which passes from the *participle*, not from the *relative* (Hofmann), over to the further act connected with the *former* in the *finite tense*, but also (comp. on i. 16) the *perfect* (Thuc. viii. 100 ; Dem. 786. 4) : *and itself* (the bill of debt) *he has taken out of the way*, whereby the abrogation now stands *completed*. A *graphically illustrative* representation : the bill of debt was *blotted out*, and it has *itself been carried away and is no longer in its place ;* ἦρκεν αὐτὸ ἐκ τοῦ μέσου μὴ ἀφεὶς ἐπὶ χώρας, Oecumenius. αὐτό denotes the *handwriting itself, materialiter,*

---

[1] So also Thomasius, *Chr. Pcrs. u. Wcrk*, III. 1, p. 110. He considers as the χειρόγραφον not the Mosaic law itself, but the bill of debt which the *broken law* has *drawn up* against us. The very parallel in Eph. ii. 15 is decisive against this view.

in contrast to the just mentioned *blotting out* of its *contents*.
For He has *nailed* it, etc. ; see the sequel. Hofmann imports
the idea : *it in this* (hostile) *quality ;* as if, namely, it ran καὶ
τοιοῦτο ὄν (Xen. *Anab.* vi. 5. 13 ; Philem. 9). —— The ἐκ τοῦ
μέσου is our : " *out of the way,*" said of obstructions which are
removed. Comp. Plat. *Eryx.* p. 401 E ; Xen. *Anab.* i. 5. 14 ;
de praefect. 3. 10, and the passages in Kypke, II. p. 323.
The opposite : ἐν μέσῳ εἶναι, *to be in the way,* Dem. 682. 1 ;
Aesch. *Suppl.* 735 ; Dorv. *ad Charit.* vii. 3, p. 601. Thus
the law stood *in the way* of reconciliation to God, of the
χαρίζεσθαι κ.τ.λ. in ver. 13. — προσηλώσας κ.τ.λ.] προσηλοῦν
only found here in the N. T.; see, however, Plat. *Phaed.* p.
83 D (with πρός) ; Lucian, *Prom.* 2, *Dial. D. I.* (τῷ Καυκάσῳ
προσηλωμένος) ; Galen. IV. p. 45, 9 : τῷ σταυρῷ, 3 Macc.
iv. 9. Since the law which condemned man lost its punitive
force through the death of Christ on the cross, inasmuch as
Christ through this death suffered the curse of the law for
men (Gal. iii. 13), and became the end of the law (Rom. x.
4), at the same time that *Christ* was nailed as ἱλαστήριον to
the cross, the law was nailed to it also, and thus it ceased
to be ἐν μέσῳ. Observe, moreover, the logical relation of the
aorist participle to the *perfect* ἦρκεν. The latter is the state
of the matter, which has emerged and exists *after God has
nailed*, etc. The κ. αὐτὸ ἦρκεν ἐκ μέσου takes place *since* that
nailing. In the strong expression προσηλώσας, purposely
chosen and placed foremost, there is involved an *antinomistic
triumph*, which makes the disarming of the law very palpably
apparent. Chrysostom has aptly observed on the whole passage:
οὐδαμοῦ οὕτως μεγαλοφώνως ἐφθέγξατο. Ὁρᾷς σπουδὴν
τοῦ ἀφανισθῆναι τὸ χειρόγραφον ὅσην ἐποιήσατο ; οἷον πάντες
ἦμεν ὑφ᾽ ἁμαρτίαν κ. κόλασιν· αὐτὸς κολασθεὶς ἔλυσε καὶ τὴν
ἁμαρτίαν καὶ τὴν κόλασιν. Nevertheless, προσηλώσας neither
figuratively depicts the *tearing in pieces* of the χειρόγρ.
(Chrysostom, Oecumenius, Theophylact), nor is there any
allusion to an alleged custom of publicly placarding *antiquated*
laws (Grotius). According to Hofmann (comp. also his
Schriftbew. II. 1, p. 370 f.), a public placarding *with a view
to observance* is meant ; the requirement of Israelitish *legal*

obligation has become *changed* into the requirement of *faith* in the Crucified One which may be read on the *cross,* and this transformation is also the *pardon* of transgressions of the law. This is a fanciful pushing further of the apostolic figure, the point of which is merely the blotting out and taking away of the law, as the debt-document hostile to us, by the death of the cross. The entire representation which is presented in this sensuous concrete form, and which is not to be expanded into the fanciful figure of transformation which we have just referred to, is intended, in fact, to illustrate merely the *forgiveness of sins* introduced by χαρισάμενος κ.τ.λ. in ver. 13, and nothing more. Comp. 1 Pet. ii. 24. It is to be observed, at the same time, that the ἐξαλείφειν and the αἴρειν ἐκ τ. μέσου do not represent two acts substantially different, but the *same* thing, the perfect accomplishment of which is *explained* by way of climax with particularising vividness.

Ver. 15.[1] In this doing away of the law was involved the *victory and triumph of God over the devilish powers,* since the strength of the latter, antagonistic to God, is in sin, and the strength of sin is in the law (1 Cor. xv. 56); with the law, therefore, the power of the devil stands or falls. — If ἀπεκδυσ. ran parallel, as the majority suppose, with προσηλώσας, there must have been a καί inserted before ἐδειγμάτ., as in ver. 14 before the finite verb, because otherwise no connection would be established. Hence a full stop (Beza) must be placed before ἀπεκδυσ., or at least a colon (Elzevir, Bleek); and without any connecting particle the significant verb heads all the more forcibly the description of this final result expressed with triumphant fulness : *Having stripped the lordships and powers, he has made a show of them boldly, holding triumph over them in the same.* Observe the symmetrical emphatic prefixing of ἀπεκδυσ., ἐδειγμάτ., and θριαμβ. The subject is

---

[1] Holtzmann, p. 156 f., rejects this verse because it interrupts the transition of thought to ver. 16 (which is not the case); because διγματίζειν is un-Pauline (but in what sense is it un-Pauline ? it is in any sense a very rare word) ; because θριαμβεύειν is used here otherwise than in 2 Cor. ii. 14 (this is incorrect) ; but, especially, because ver. 15 can only be explained by the circle of ideas of Eph. iii. 10 and Col. i. 10 ; Eph. iv. 8, ii. 15 f. (passages which touch our present one either not at all, or at the most very indirectly).

still always *God*, not *Christ*,[1] as Baur and Ewald hold, following Augustine, Theodore of Mopsuestia, Erasmus, Grotius, Calovius, and many others; hence the reading ἀπεκδ. τὴν σάρκα in F G (which omit τ. ἀρχ. κ. τ. ἐξουσ.) Syr. Goth. Hil. Aug. was an *erroneous* gloss; and at the close, not αὐτῷ (Syr. Vulg. It. Theodoret, Luther, Melanchthon, Elzevir, Griesbach, and Scholz), instead of which G has ἑαυτῷ, but αὐτῷ should be written; see Wolf *in loc.* The figurative ἀπεκδυσ., which illustrates the *deprivation of power* that has taken place through the divine work of reconciliation, represents the ἀρχὰς καὶ ἐξουσ. as having been *clothed in armour* (comp. Rom. xiii. 12; Eph. vi. 11; 1 Thess. v. 8), which God as their conqueror stripped off and took from them; Vulg.: *exspolians.* Comp. on ἐκδύειν and ἀποδύειν, used from Homer's time in the sense of *spoliare*, Dem. 763. 28, 1259. 11; Hesiod, *Scut.* 447; Xen. *Anab.* v. 8. 23; 2 Macc. viii. 27; and on the subject-matter, Matt. xii. 19; Luke xi. 22. Moreover, we might expect, in accordance with the common usage of the middle, instead of ἀπεκδυσάμενος, which is elsewhere used *intransitively* (comp. iii. 9), the active ἀπεκδύσας (comp. Matt. xxvii. 28, 31; Luke x. 30); yet even in Plat. *Rep.* p. 612 A, the (right) reading ἀπεδυσάμεθα is to taken in the sense of *nudavimus;* and Xenophon uses the perfect ἀποδέδυκεν, which is likewise *intransitive* elsewhere (see Kühner, I. p. 803), *actively*, see *Anab. l.c.* : πολλοὺς ἤδη ἀποδέδυκεν, multos *veste spoliavit;* comp. Dio Cass. xlv. 47. Further, the middle, as indicating the victorious *self-interest* of the action (*sibi* exspoliavit), is here selected even with nicety, and by no means conveys (as Hofmann, in order to refute this explanation, erroneously lays to its charge) the idea: in order to *appropriate to Himself* this armour; see on the contrary generally, Krüger, § 52. 10. 1; Kühner, II. 1, p. 93 f. The disarming *in itself*, and not the *possession* of the enemy's weapons, is the interest of the victor. Lastly, the whole connection does not admit of any intransitive interpretation, such as Hofmann, in his *Schriftbew.* I. p. 350 f.

---

[1] Through this erroneous definition of the subject it was possible to discover in our passage the *descent into hell* (Anselm and others).

(and substantially also in his *Heil. Schr. in loc.*), has attempted, making the sense : God *has laid aside from Himself* the powers ruling in the Gentile world—which were round about Him like a *veil* concealing Him from the Gentiles—by manifesting Himself in unveiled clearness.   Something such as this, which is held to amount to the meaning that God has put an end to the ignorance of the Gentile world and revealed Himself to it, Paul must necessarily have *said ;* no reader could unravel it from so strange a mode of veiling the conception, the more especially seeing that there is no mention at all of the victorious *word* of Christ [1] converting the Gentiles, as Hofmann thinks, but on the contrary of what God has effected in reference to the ἀρχαὶ and ἐξουσίαι by the *fact of reconciliation* accomplished on the cross ; He has by it *rendered powerless* the powers which previously held sway among mankind ; comp. John xii. 30 f., xvi. 11.—That these ἀρχαί and ἐξουσίαι are two categories of *evil angels* (comp. Eph. vi. 12), corresponding to two classes of good angels similarly named (comp. ver. 10), is taught by the context, which has nothing to do with mediating beings intervening between God and the world (Sabatier), or even with human rulers.   Ritschl, in the *Jahrb. f. Deutsche Theol.* 1863, p. 522, understands the *angels of the law-giving* (comp. on i. 20), of whom God has *divested* Himself (middle), *i.e.* from whose *environment He has withdrawn Himself.*   Even apart from the singular expression ἀπεκδυσάμ. in *this* sense, this explanation is inappropriate, because the ἀρχαί and ἐξουσίαι appear here as *hostile* to God, as beings over whom He has *triumphed ;* secondly, because the angels who ministered at the law-giving (see on Gal. iii. 19) have no share in the *contents* of the law, which, as the νόμος Θεοῦ, is holy, righteous, good, and spiritual (Rom. vii.), and hence no deviation from God's plan of salvation can be attributed to the angels of the law ; and, finally, because the expression τὰς ἀρχὰς κ. τὰς

---

[1] In which sense also Grotius explained it, though he takes ἀπεκδυσάμ. rightly as *exarmatos.* See, in opposition to him, Calovius. Hofmann's explanation is also followed by Holtzmann, p. 222 ; it is an unfortunate attempt at rationalizing.

ἐξουσίας is so comprehensive that, in the absence of any more
precise indication in the text, it cannot be specially limited
to the powers that were active in the *law-giving*, but must
denote the *collective* angelic powers—hostile, however, and
therefore devilish. *Them* God has *disarmed, put to shame*,
and *triumphed* over, through the abrogation of men's legal
debt-bond that took place by means of the atoning death.
The emphatic and triumphant prominence given to this
statement was, doubtless, specially occasioned by those speculations regarding the power of demons, with which the false
teachers were encroaching on the work of Christ. — δειγματίζειν,
preserved only here and in Matt. i. 19 (comp. however,
παραδειγματίζειν, especially frequent in Polybius ; see Schweighäuser, *Lex.* p. 429), denotes, in virtue of its connection with
the conception of triumph, the making a show (Augustine, *ep.*
59 : " exemplavit ;" Hilary, *de trin.* 9 : " ostentui esse fecit ")
for the purpose of *humiliation and disgrace* (comp. Chrysostom), not in order to exhibit the *weakness* of the conquered
(Theodoret, Böhmer), but simply their accomplished *subju-
gation ;* comp. Nah. iii. 6 : θήσομαί σε εἰς παράδειγμα. —
ἐν παρρησία] is usually rendered *publicly, before the eyes of all*,
consequently as equivalent to φανερῶς in John vii. 10 (the
opposite : ἐν κρυπτῷ, John vii. 4 ; Matt. vi. 4 ; Rom. ii. 28) ;
but this the word does not mean (see on John vii. 4) ;
moreover, the verb already implies this idea ; [1] and the usage
of Paul elsewhere warrants only the rendering : *boldly, freely
and frankly.* Comp. Eph. vi. 19 ; Phil. i. 20. Hilary :
" cum *fiducia* ;" Vulgate : "*confidenter* palam." The objection
that this sense is not appropriate to the action *of God*
(Hofmann), overlooks the fact that God is here represented
just as a *human* triumpher, who freely and boldly, with re-
morseless disposal of the spoils acquired by victory, subjects

---

[1] Hence Hofmann joins it with θριαμβεύσας, in which, however, the idea of
publicity is obviously already contained. Hofmann, indeed, assumes a reference
of contrast to the *invisible* triumphs, which God has ever been celebrating over
those powers. But thus the idea of θριαμβεύειν is extended to an unwarranted
amplitude of *metaphorical* meaning, while, nevertheless, the entire anthropopathic
imagery of the passage requires the *strict* conception of the public θρίαμβος
Moreover, the pretended contrast is altogether foreign to the context.

the conquered to ignominious exhibition.[1] — θριαμβεύσας αὐτ. ἐν αὐτῷ] synchronous with ἐδείγμ.: *while He triumphed* over them.   Respecting θριαμβεύειν τινα, *to triumph over some one*, see on 2 Cor. ii. 14.   Comp. the passive θριαμβεύεσθαι, to be led in triumph, Plut. *Coriol.* 35.   αὐτούς refers κατὰ σύνεσιν to the devils *individually*, who are conceived as *masculine* (as δαίμονες, κοσμοκράτορες, Eph. vi. 12), see generally Winer, p. 138 [E. T. 183]; and ἐν αὐτῷ is referred either to the *cross* (hence, also, the readings ἐν τῷ ξύλῳ or σταυρῷ) or to *Christ*.   The former reference is maintained by the majority of the Fathers (Theophylact: ἐν τῷ σταυρῷ τοὺς δαίμονας ἡττημένους δείξας), Beza, Calvin, Grotius, and many others, including Böhmer, Steiger, Olshausen, Ewald, Weiss, *Bibl. Theol.* p. 432, ed. 2 ; and the latter, by Erasmus, Luther, Melanchthon, Wolf, Estius, Bengel, and many others, including Flatt, Bähr, Huther, de Wette, Baumgarten-Crusius, Bisping, Bleek, Hofmann, Rich. Schmidt.   The reference to Christ is erroneous, because Christ is not mentioned at all in ver. 14, and God pervades as subject the entire discourse from ver. 11 onwards. We must hold, therefore, by the reference to τῷ σταυρῷ, so that ἐν αὐτῷ once more places the cross significantly before our eyes, just as it stood emphatically at the close of the previous sentence.   *At the cross* God celebrated His triumph, inasmuch as through the death of Christ on the cross obliterating and removing out of the way the debt-bill of the law He completed the work of redemption, by which the devil and his powers were deprived of their strength, which rested on the law and its debt-bond.   The *ascension* is not to be here included.

Ver. 16. Οὖν] since ye, according to vv. 11–15, are raised to a far higher platform than that of such a legal system. — κρινέτω ἐν βρώσει] No one is to *form a judgment* (whether ye are acting allowably or unallowably, rightly or wrongly) con-

[1] It is an inconsiderate fancy of Hofmann to say, by way of controverting our explanation : Who would be surprised, that the triumpher should make a show of the conquered, "*without previously asking their permission*"?   As if such a thought, no doubt very silly for the victor, were necessarily the contrast to the frank daring action, with which a general, crowned with victory, is in a position to exhibit his captives without any scruple, without sparing or hesitation !   He has the ἰξουσία for the διγματίζειν, and uses it ἐν παῤῥησίᾳ.

cerning you in the point of eating (ἐν, comp. Rom. ii. 1, xiv. 22 ;
1 Pet. ii. 12). There is hereby asserted at the same time their
independence of such judgments, to which they have not to yield
(comp. Eph. v. 6). With Paul, βρῶσις is always *actio edendi*,
and is thus distinct from βρῶμα, *cibus* (Rom. xiv. 17 ; 1 Cor.
viii. 4 ; 2 Cor. ix. 10 ; also Heb. xii. 16), although it is also
current in the sense of βρῶμα with John (iv. 32, vi. 27, 55), and
with profane authors (Hom. *Il.* xix. 210, *Od.* i. 191, x. 176, *et
al.;* Plat. *Legg.* vi. p. 783 C ; Hesiod, *Scut.* 396). This we
remark in opposition to Fritzsche, *ad Rom.* III. p. 200. The
case is the same with πόσις (Rom. xiv. 17) and πόμα (1 Cor.
x. 4 ; Heb. ix. 10).— ἐν πόσει] Since the Mosaic law contained
prohibitions of *meats* (Lev. vii. 10 ff.), but not also general
prohibitions of *drinks*, it is to be assumed that the false teachers
in their ascetic strictness (ver. 23) had extended the prohibition
of the use of wine as given for the Nazarites (Num. vi. 3),
and for the period of priestly service (Lev. x. 9), to the Christians as such (as ἁγίους). Comp. also Rom. xiv. 17, 21. De
Wette arbitrarily asserts that it was added doubtless in consideration of this, as well as of the Pharisaic rules as to drinks,
Matt. xxiii. 24, and of the prohibition of wine offered to idols
(οὖν does not point to such things), but still mainly *on account
of the similarity of sound* (Rom. xiv. 17 ; Heb. ix. 10, and
Bleek *in loc.*).— ἐν μέρει ἑορτῆς κ.τ.λ.] ἐν μέρει, with the
genitive, designates the *category*, as very frequently also in
classical authors (Plat. *Theaet.* p. 155 E, *Rep.* p. 424 D ;
Dem. 638. 5, 668. 24) ; comp. on 2 Cor. iii. 10, and see
Wyttenbach, *ad Plut.* I. p. 65. The *three* elements : *festival,
new moon,* and *Sabbath,* are placed side by side as a further
classis rerum ; in the point (ἐν) of this category also no judgment is to be passed upon the readers (if, namely, they do
not join in observing such days). The elements are *arranged,*
according as the days occur, either at longer unequal intervals
in the year (ἑορτῆς), or monthly (νουμην.), or weekly (σαββάτ.).
But they are *three,* co-ordinated ; there would be only *one*
thing with three *connected* elements, if καί were used instead
of ἤ in the two latter places where it occurs. The three are
given in inverted order in 1 Chron. xxiii. 31 ; 2 Chron. ii. 4,

COL. 2 B

xxxi. 3. On the subject-matter, comp. Gal. iv. 10. Respecting the Jewish celebration of the *new moon*, see Keil, *Archäol.* I. § 78 ; Ewald, *Alterth.* p. 470 f. ; and on σάββατα as equivalent to σάββατον, comp. Matt. xii. 1, xxviii. 1 ; Luke iv. 16, *et al.* ἐν μέρει has been erroneously understood by others in the sense of a *partial* celebration (Chrysostom : ἐξευτελίζει λέγων· ἢ ἐν μέρει ἑορτῆς· οὐ γὰρ δὴ πάντα κατεῖχον τὰ πρότερα, Theodoret : they *could not* have kept *all* the feasts, on account of the long journey to Jerusalem ; comp. Dalmer), or : *vicibus* festorum (Melanchthon, Zanchius), or, that the *participation* in the festival, the *taking part* in it is expressed (Otto, *dekalog. Unters.* p. 9 ff.), or that it denotes the *segregatio,* " nam qui dierum faciunt discrimen, quasi unum ab alio dividunt" (Calvin). Many, moreover inaccurately, hold that ἐν μέρει means merely : *in respect to* (Beza, Wolf, and most expositors, including Bähr, Huther, and de Wette) ; in 2 Cor. iii. 10, ix. 3, it also denotes the *category.* Comp. Aelian. *V. H.* viii. 3 · κρίνοντες ἕκαστον ἐν τῷ μέρει φόνου.

Ver. 17.[1] An epexegetical relative sentence, assigning the ground for what has just been said.— ὅ, *which* (see the critical remarks), is not to be arbitrarily referred merely to the observance of feasts and days (Flatt and Hofmann), but to the things of the law mentioned in ver. 16 generally, all of which it embraces. — σκιά] not an *outline* (σκιαγραφία, σκιαγράφημα), as in the case of painters, who " non exprimunt primo ductu imaginem vivis coloribus et εἰκονικῶς, sed rudes et obscuras lineas primum ex carbone ducunt," Calvin (so also Clericus, Huther, Baumgarten-Crusius, and others), which σκιά does not mean even in Heb. viii. 5, x. 1, and which is forbidden by the contrast of τὸ σῶμα, since it would rather be the perfect picture that would be put in opposition to the outline.

---

[1] Holtzmann, without assigning his reasons, regards the entire verse as an "*extract from the Epistle to the Hebrews*" (Heb. ix. 6, 9 f., 25, x. 1, 11, viii. 5) ; he thinks that the whole polemic of vv. 16–23 was intended to introduce the more developed features of later heresy into the picture of the apostolic age. But the difficulty of ver. 18 (which Holtzmann considers utterly unintelligible) and ver. 22 f., as well as the alleged un-Pauline character of some expressions in ver. 19, does not furnish a sufficient basis for such an opinion. Comp. on vv. 18, 19, 22, 23.

It means nothing else than *shadow*. Paul is illustrating, namely, *the relation of the legal ordinances*, such as are adduced in ver. 16, *to that which is future*, i.e. *to those relations of the Messianic kingdom*, which are to be manifested in the αἰὼν μέλλων (neither ἀγαθῶν from Heb. x. 1, nor anything else, is to be supplied with τῶν μελλόντων), and in doing so he follows the figurative conception, that the μέλλοντα, which therefore, locally considered, are in *front*, have cast their *shadow* behind, which shadow is the Mosaic ritual constitution,—a conception which admirably accords with the *typical* character of the latter (Heb. viii. 5, x. 1), of which the constitution of the Messianic kingdom is the *antitype*. It is to be noted further: (1) The emphasis of confirmation lies not on τῶν μελλόντων (Beza), but on σκιά, in contrast to τὸ σῶμα. If, namely, the things in question are only the *shadow* of the Messianic, and do not belong to the reality thereof, they are —in accordance with this relatively non-essential, because merely typical nature of theirs—not of such a kind that salvation may be made dependent on their observance or non-observance, and adjudged or withheld accordingly. (2) The passage is not to be explained as if ἦν stood in the place of ἐστί, so that τὰ μέλλοντα would denote the *Christian* relations already *then* existing, the καινὴ διαθήκη, the Christian plan of salvation, the Christian life, etc. (so usually since Chrysostom); but, on the contrary, that which is spoken of *is* shadow, not, indeed, as divinely appointed in the law (Hofmann)—for of *this* aspect of the elements in question the text contains nothing—but in so far as Paul sees it in its *actual condition* still at that time *present*. The μέλλοντα have *not yet been manifested at all*, and belong *altogether* (not merely as regards their *completion*, as de Wette thinks, comp. also Hofmann) to the αἰὼν μέλλων, which will begin with the coming again of Christ to set up His kingdom—a coming, however, which was expected as very near at hand. The μέλλοντα could only be viewed as having already *set in* either in whole or in part, if ἦν and not ἐστί were used previously, and thereby the notion of futurity were to be taken *relatively*, in reference to a state of things then already *past* (comp. Gal.

iii. 23 ; 1 Tim. i. 16), or if ἐστί were meant to be said from
the standpoint of the *divine arrangement* of those things
(Hofmann), or if this present tense expressed the *logical*
present merely by way of enabling the mind to picture them
(Rom. v. 14), which, however, is inadmissible here, since the
elements indicated by σκιά still continued at this time, long
after Christ's earthly appearance, and were present really, and
not merely in legal precepts or in theory.   (3) The characteristic *quality*, in which the things concerned are meant to be
presented by the figurative σκιά, is determined solely by the
contrast of τὸ σῶμα, namely, as *unsubstantiality* in a Messianic
aspect : *shadow* of the future, standing in relation to it, therefore doubtless as typically presignificant, but destitute and
void of its reality.   The reference to *transitoriness* (Spencer, *de
legit. rit.* p. 214 f., Baumgarten-Crusius, and others) is purely
imported. — τὸ δὲ σῶμα] *scil.* τῶν μελλόντων, *but the body* of
the future.[1]   Inasmuch as the legal state of things in ver. 16
stands to the future Messianic state in no other relation than
that of the *shadow* to the living *body itself*, which casts the
shadow, Paul thus, remaining faithful to his figure, designates
as the *body* of the future *that* which is *real and essential* in
it, which, according to the context, can be nothing else than
just *the* μέλλοντα *themselves*, their concrete reality as contrasted with the shadowy form which preceded them. Accordingly, he might have conveyed the idea of the verse, but
without its figurative garb, in this way : ὅ ἐστι τύπος τῶν
μελλόντων, αὐτὰ δὲ τὰ μέλλοντα Χριστοῦ. — Χριστοῦ] *scil.*
ἐστί, *belongs to Christ.* The μέλλοντα, namely, viewed under
the figurative aspect of the σῶμα which casts the shadow
referred to, must stand in the same relation to Christ, as the
body stands in to the *Head* (ver. 19) ; as the body now
adumbrating itself, they must belong to Christ the *Head* of
the body, in so far, namely, as He is *Lord and ruler* of all the
relations of the future Messianic constitution, *i.e.* of the Mes-

---

[1] The explanation of Hilgenfeld, 1873, p. 199 : "the *mere* σῶμα Χριστοῦ, a
purely somatic Christianity," is at variance with the antithetical correlation
of σκιά and σῶμα, as well as with the apostle's cherished conception of the
σῶμα of Christ, which is contained immediately in ver. 19.

sianic kingdom, of the βασιλεία τοῦ Χριστοῦ (i. 13; Eph.
v. 5). Whosoever, therefore, holds to the *shadow* of the
future, to the things of the law (as the false teachers do and
require), and does not strive after the μέλλοντα themselves,
after the *body* which has cast that shadow, does not hold to
Christ, to whom as Head *the* σῶμα (τῆς σκιᾶς) *belongs as His
own.* This view, which is far removed from " distorting" the
thought (as Hofmann objects), is required by the natural
and obvious correlation of the conception of the *body* and its
head, as also by ver. 19. There is much inaccuracy and irrele-
vancy in the views of expositors, because they have not taken
τὰ μέλλοντα in the sense, or not purely in the sense, of the
relations of the αἰὼν μέλλων, but in that of the then existing
Christian relations, which in fact still belonged to the αἰὼν
οὗτος, and because, in connection therewith, they do not take
up with clearness and precision the contextually necessary
relation of the genitive Χριστοῦ as denoting Him, whose the
σῶμα is, but resolve it into what they please, as *e.g.* Grotius (so
also Bleek): " ad Christum pertinet, ab eo solo petenda est;"
Huther: " the substance itself, to which those shadowy figures
point, has *appeared in Christ;*" Ewald: " so far as there is
anything really solid, essential, and eternal in the O. T., it
belongs to Christ and to His Spirit;" Hofmann: " the body
of the future *is there, where Christ is,* present and given with
Him" (consequently as if ἐν Χριστῷ were used).—On τὸ σῶμα
in contrast to σκιά, comp. Josephus, *Bell.* ii. 2. 5: σκιὰν
αἰτησόμενος βασιλείας, ἧς ἥρπασεν ἑαυτῷ τὸ σῶμα. Philo, *de
conf. ling.* p. 434: τὰ μὲν ῥητὰ τῶν χρησμῶν σκιάς τινας ὡσανεὶ
σωμάτων εἶναι· τὰς δ᾽ ἐμφαινομένας δυνάμεις τὰ ὑφεστῶτα ἀληθείᾳ πράγματα. Lucian, *Hermot.* 29. Observe, however,
that σῶμα invariably retains its strict literal sense of *body,* as
a sensuous expression for the substantially real, in contrast
to the unsubstantial shadow of it.

Ver. 18.[1] Warning against a *further* danger, with which
they were threatened on the part of these false teachers. —
μηδείς] not different from μήτις in ver. 16, as if the latter
emphasized the verb and the former the subject (Hofmann).

---

[1] See upon ver. 18, Reiche, *Comm. Crit.* p. 277 ff.

This would be correct, if in ver. 16 it were μὴ οὖν κρινέτω τις ὑμᾶς. Comp. on μήτις, ver. 8, and on μηδείς, ver. 4. Moreover, the words cannot be regarded (with Holtzmann) as a duplicate proceeding from the interpolator, especially as they contain a *new* warning, and in such a peculiar form (καταβραβ.). — καταβραβευέτω] Let no one *deprive you of the prize.* καταβραβεύειν, which is not a Cilician word (Jerome; see, on the contrary, Eustath. *ad Il.* i. 93. 33 : καταβραβεύει αὐτὸν, ὥς φασιν οἱ παλαιοί), is only now preserved among ancient Greek authors in Dem. *c. Mid.* 544, *ult.* : ἐπιστάμεθα Στράτωνα ὑπὸ Μειδίου καταβραβευθέντα καὶ παρὰ πάντα τὰ δίκαια ἀτιμωθέντα, where it expresses the taking away of victory in a judicial suit, and the procuring of a sentence of condemnation, and that in the form of the conception : *to bring it about to the injury of some one, that not he, but another, shall receive the prize from the* βραβεύς. Midias had *bribed* the judges. The κατά intimates that the prize was *due* to the person concerned, although it has been in a *hostile* spirit (not merely *unrighteously*, which would be παραβραβεύειν,[1] Plut. *Mor.* p. 535 C; Polyb. xxiv. 1. 12) *withdrawn* from him and adjudged to *another.* The right view substantially, though not recognising the distinction from παραβραβ., is taken by Chrysostom (παραβραβευθῆναι γάρ ἐστιν, ὅταν παρ' ἑτέρων μὲν ἡ νίκη, παρ' ἑτέρων δὲ τὸ βραβεῖον) and Theophylact, also Suidas : τὸ ἄλλου ἀγωνιζομένου ἄλλον στεφανοῦσθαι λέγει ὁ ἀπόστολος καταβραβεύεσθαι. Comp. also Zonaras, *ad Concil. Laod.* can. 35, p. 351 : τὸ μὴ τὸν νικήσαντα ἀξιοῦν τοῦ βραβείου, ἀλλ' ἑτέρῳ διδόναι αὐτὸ ἀδικουμένου τοῦ νικήσαντος. The conception is : (1) To the readers as true believers *belongs* the Messianic prize of victory,—this is the assumption upon which the expression is based ; (2) The false teachers desire *to deprive them of the prize of victory* and to give it to others, namely, to themselves and their adherents, and that through their service of angels, etc. ; (3) Just as little, however, as in

---

[1] With which Theodoret confounds it (ἀδίκως βραβεύειν) ; he makes it the unrighteous awarding of the prize of victory : ἐπειδὴ τοίνυν καὶ οἱ τὰς νομικὰς παρατηρήσεις τῷ εὐαγγελίῳ παραμιγνῦντες ἀπὸ τῶν κρειττόνων αὐτοὺς ἐπὶ τὰ ἐλάττω μετέφερον, εἰκότως ἔφη· μηδεὶς ὑμᾶς καταβραβευέτω.

the case of the κρίνειν in ver. 16, ought the readers to *give heed*
to, or let themselves be *led astray* by, this hostile proceeding
of the καταβραβεύειν, which is based upon subjective vanity
and is (ver. 19) separation from Christ and His body,—
this is implied in the imperatives. Consequently, the view
of Jerome, *ad Aglas.* p. 10, is not in substance erroneous,
although only approximately corresponding to the expression:
" Nemo adversus vos praemium accipiat;" Erasmus is substantially correct: "*praemium,* quod sectari coepistis, *vobis inter-
vertat;*" comp. Calvin, Estius, Olshausen, Baumgarten-Crusius,
Ewald, and others; while the Vulgate (*seducat*), Luther ("*to
displace the goal*"), and others content themselves with a much
less accurate statement of the sense, and Bengel imports into
the passage the sense of *usurped false leading and instruction,*
as Beza similarly took it.[1] The βραβεῖον, to which καταβρ.
refers, is not *Christian liberty* (Grotius, who explains it praemium *exigere*), nor yet: "*the honour and prize of the true
worship of God*" (de Wette), but, in accordance with the standing apostolic conception (comp. Phil. iii. 14; 1 Cor. ix. 24):
the bliss of the Messianic kingdom, the incorruptible στέφανος
(1 Cor. ix. 25), the στεφ. τῆς δικαιοσύνης (2 Tim. iv. 8), τῆς
δόξης (1 Pet. v. 4), τῆς ζωῆς (Jas. i. 12); comp. 2 Tim. ii. 5.
With reference to the βραβεῖον, Elsner, Michaelis, Storr, Flatt,
Steiger, and others, including Bähr, Böhmer, Reiche, Huther,
and Bleek, following Photius in Oecumenius (μηδεὶς ὑμᾶς
κατακρινέτω), have taken καταβραβ. in the sense of *to condemn,*
parallel to the κρινέτω in ver. 16, or *to refuse salvation to*
(Hofmann). This rendering is not, indeed, to be rejected on
linguistic grounds, since Hesychius and Suidas both quote the
signification κατακρίνειν in the case of καταβραβεύειν; but
it cannot be justified by proofs adduced, and it is decidedly in
opposition to the context through the following θέλων κ.τ.λ.,
which presupposes not a *judgment* of the opponents, but an

---

[1] "Nemo adversum vos rectoris partes sibi ultro sumat." He starts from the
common use of βραβεύειν in the sense of *regere ac moderari* (see Dorvill. *ad
Charit.* p. 404). Comp. on iii. 15. But neither the passage of Dem. *l.c.,* nor
the testimony of the Greek Fathers, of Suidas, Eustathius, and Zonaras, nor the
analogy of παραβραβεύειν, would justify the adoption of this sense in the case of
the *compound* καταβραβ.

action, something *practical*, which, through their perverse religious attitude, they would fain *accomplish*. — θέλων] *sc.* καταβραβεύειν ὑμᾶς : *while he desires to do this*, would willingly accomplish it (comp. Dissen, *ad Pind. Ol.* ii. 97) by humility, etc. So rightly Theodoret (τοῦτο τοίνυν συνεβούλευον ἐκεῖνοι γίνεσθαι ταπεινοφροσύνῃ δῆθεν κεχρημένοι), Theophylact (θέλουσιν ὑμᾶς καταβραβεύειν διὰ ταπεινοφρ.), Photius in Oecumenius, Calvin, Casaubon, and others, including Huther and Buttmann, *Neut. Gr.* p. 322 [E. T. 376]. The "*languidum et frigidum*," which Reiche urges against this view, applies at the most only in the event of καταβραβ. being explained as *to condemn ;* and the accusation of *incorrectness of sense* (Hofmann) is only based upon an erroneous explanation of the subsequent ἐν ταπεινοφρ. κ.τ.λ. The interpretation adopted by others : *taking delight in* humility, etc. (Augustine, Castalio, Vatablus, Estius, Michaelis, Loesner, and others, including Storr, Flatt, Bähr, Olshausen, Baumgarten-Crusius, Bleek, Hofmann, and Hilgenfeld), is based upon the extremely unnecessary assumption of an un-Greek imitation of ב חפץ, such as occurs, indeed, in the LXX. (1 Sam. xviii. 22 ; 2 Sam. xv. 26 ; 1 Kings x. 9 ; 2 Chron. ix. 8 ; Ps. cxlvii. 10), but not in the N. T. ; for in Matt. xxvii. 43, θέλειν is used with the *accusative*, comp. on Rom. vii. 21. Moreover, in the O. T. passages the object of the delight is almost invariably (the only exception being Ps. cxlvii. 10) a person. Even in the Apocrypha that abnormal mode of expression does not occur. Others, again, hold that it is to be joined in an adverbial sense to καταβρ. It would then (see Erasmus, *Annot.*) have to be rendered *cupide* or *studiose* (Plat. *Theaet.* p. 143 D ; and see Reisig, *Conject.* p. 143 f.), or unconstrained, *voluntarily*, equivalent to ἐθελοντί, ἐθελοντήν, ἐθελοντής (Plat. *Symp.* p. 183 A, very frequent in Homer, Soph. *Phil.* 1327, Aesch. *Choeph.* 19. 790, and the passages from Xenophon quoted by Sturz, *Lex.* II. p. 21), which sense, here certainly quite unsuitable, has been transformed at variance with linguistic usage into the idea : "*hoc munus sibi a nullo tributum exercens*" (Beza), or : *unwarrantably* (Böhmer, comp. Steiger), or *of his own choice* (Luther, who, like Ewald, couples it with ἐμβατεύων), or :

arbitrarily (Ewald), or: *capriciously* (Reiche), etc. ; consequently giving it the sense of ἑκών, αὐτοθελής, αὐτοκέλευστος,
or αὐτογνώμων. Even Tittmann, *Synon.* p. 131, comes at length
to such an *ultro*, erroneously quoting Herod. ix. 14, where
θέλων must be taken as in Plat. *Theaet. l.c.* — ἐν ταπεινοφρ.
κ. θρησκ. τῶν ἀγγέλ.] ἐν is not *propter*, which is supposed to
have the meaning : because ταπεινοφρ. κ.τ.λ. is necessary to
salvation (Reiche) ; nor does it denote the *condition* in which
the καταβραβεύειν takes place (Steiger, Huther) ; but, in keeping with the θέλων, it is the *means* by which the purpose is
to be *attained : by virtue of humility and worshipping of angels.*
Thereby he wishes to effect that the βραβεῖον shall be withdrawn from you (and given to himself and his followers).
τ. ἀγγέλων is the genitive of the *object* (comp. Wisd. xiv. 27 ;
Herodian, iv. 8. 17 ; Clem. *Cor.* I. 45 ; see also Grimm on
4 Macc. v. 6, and the passages from Josephus in Krebs, p. 339),
and belongs only to θρησκ., not to ταπεινοφρ. That the latter,
however, is not humility in the *proper* sense, but is, viewed
from the perverse personal standpoint of the false teachers, a
humility in *their* sense only, is plain from the context (see below,
εἰκῆ φυσιούμ. κ.τ.λ.), although *irony* (Steiger, Huther) is not to
be found in the word. Paul, namely, designates the thing as
that, for which the false teachers held it themselves and
desired it to be held by others, and this, indeed, as respects
the disposition lying at the root of it, which they sought to
exhibit (ἐν ταπεινοφρ.), and as respects the abnormal religious
phenomenon manifested among them (κ. θρησκ. τ. ἀγγέλων) ;
and then proceeds to give a deterrent exposure of both of these
together according to their true character in a theoretical
(ἃ . . . ἐμβατ.) and in a moral (εἰκῆ φυσ. . . . τὴν κεφαλὴν)
respect. *How far* the false teachers bore themselves as
ταπεινόφρονες, is correctly defined by Theodoret : λέγοντες,
ὡς ἀόρατος ὁ τῶν ὅλων Θεὸς, ἀνέφικτός τε καὶ ἀκατάληπτος,
καὶ προσήκει διὰ τῶν ἀγγέλων τὴν θείαν εὐμένειαν πραγμα-
τεύεσθαι, so that they thus regarded man as too insignificant
in the presence of the divine majesty to be able to do without[1]

---

[1] Compare Augustine, *Conf.* x. 42 : " Quem invenirem, qui me reconciliaret
tibi ? Abeundum mihi fuit ad angelos ? Multi conantes ad te redire, neque per

the mediation of angels, which they sought to secure through
θρησκεία (comp. 4 Macc. iv. 11), thereby placing the merit of
Christ (Rom. v. 2) in the background. It is differently explained by Chrysostom and Theophylact (comp. also Photius
in Oecumenius): the false teachers had declared the *majesty of
the Only-Begotten* to be too exalted for lowly humanity to have
access through Him to the Father, and hence the need of the
mediation of angels for that purpose. In opposition to this
view it may be urged, that the very prominence so frequently
and intentionally given to the majesty of Christ in our Epistle,
and especially as above the angels, rather goes to show that
they had *depreciated* the dignity of Christ. Reiche and Ewald
(comp. Hofmann's interpretation below) find the ταπεινοφροσύνη in the ἀφειδία σώματος of ver. 23, where, however, the
two aberrations are adduced *separately* from one another, see
on ver. 23. Proofs of the existence of the *worship of angels*
in the post-apostolic *church* are found in Justin, *Ap.* I. 6,
p. 56,[1] Athenagoras, and others; among the *Gnostic heretics*
(Simonians, Cainites): Epiph. *Haer.* xx. 2; Tertullian, *praescr.*
33; Iren. *Haer.* i. 31. 2; and with respect to the worshipping
of angels in the *Colossian* region Theodoret testifies: ἔμεινε
δὲ τοῦτο τὸ πάθος ἐν τῇ Φρυγίᾳ καὶ Πισιδίᾳ μέχρι πολλοῦ· οὗ
δὴ χάριν καὶ συνελθοῦσα σύνοδος ἐν Λαοδικείᾳ τῆς Φρυγίας
(A.D. 364, can. 35) νόμῳ κεκώλυκε τὸ τοῖς ἀγγέλοις προσεύ-
χεσθαι, καὶ μέχρι δὲ τοῦ νῦν εὐκτήρια τοῦ ἁγίου Μιχαὴλ παρ'
ἐκείνοις καὶ τοῖς ὁμόροις ἐκείνων ἐστὶν ἰδεῖν. The *Catholic
expedients for evading* the prohibition of angel-worship in
our passage (as also in the *Concil. Laod.*, Mansi, II. p. 568)
may be seen especially in Cornelius a Lapide, who understands not all angel-worship, but only that which places
the angels above Christ (comp. also Bisping), and who refers
the Laodicean prohibition pointing to a "κεκρυμμένη εἰδω-
λολατρεία" ("ὅτι οὐ δεῖ Χριστιανοὺς ἐγκαταλείπειν τὴν ἐκκλη-

---

se ipsos valentes, sicut audio, tentaverunt haec, et inciderunt in desiderium
curiosarum visionum, et digni habiti sunt illusionibus." The (false) ταπεινοφροσύνη was the subjective *source* of their going astray to angel-worship.

[1] Hasselbach gives substantially the right interpretation of the passage in the
Stud. u. Krit. 1839, p. 329 ff.

σίαν τοῦ Θεοῦ καὶ ἀπιέναι καὶ ἀγγέλους ὀνομάζειν" κ.τ.λ.), in accordance with the second Nicene Council, only to the cultus *latriae*, not *duliae*, consequently to actual adoration, not τιμητικὴν προσκύνησιν. In opposition to the words as they stand (for θρησκεία with the genitive of the subject would necessarily be the cultus, which the angels present to God, 4 Macc. v. 6, 12; Joseph. *Antt.* xii. 5. 4; comp. Acts xxvi. 5), and also in opposition to the context (see ver. 19), several have taken τῶν ἀγγέλων as the genitive *of the subject*, and have explained it of a religious condition, which desired to be like that of the angels, *e.g.* Luther: "*spirituality of the angels*," comp. Melanchthon, Schoettgen (" habitus aliquis angelicus "), Wolf, Dalmer. Nevertheless, Hofmann, attempting a more subtle definition of the sense, has again taken τῶν ἀγγέλων as genitive of the *subject*, and joined with it not only θρησκεία, but also ταπεινοφροσύνῃ. The ταπεινοφροσύνη of the angels, namely, consists in *their willingly keeping within the bounds assigned to them as spirits*, and not coveting that which *man* in this respect *has beyond them*, namely, what belongs to the *corporeal* world. And the θρησκεία of the angels is *a self-devotion to God*, in which, between them and Him, *no other barrier* exists than *that between the Creator and His creatures*. That ταπεινοφροσύνη and this θρησκεία man makes into *virtue* on his part, when he, although but partially, *renounces that which belongs to Him in distinction from the angels* (ταπεινοφρ.), and, as one *who has divested himself as much as possible of his corporeality*, presents himself *adoringly* to God in such measure as he *refrains* from what was conferred upon him for *bodily* enjoyment. I do not comprehend how, on the one hand, the apostle could wrap up the combinations of ideas imputed to him in words so enigmatical, nor, on the other, how the readers could, without the guidance of Hofmann, extract them out of these words. The entire exposition is a labyrinth of imported subjective fancies. Paul might at least have written ἐν ἐγκρατείᾳ ἐπὶ τῷ ὁμοιώματι (or καθ' ὁμοίωσιν, or καθ' ὁμοιότητα) τῆς ταπεινοφροσύνης καὶ θρησκείας τῶν ἀγγέλων! Even this would still have been far enough from clear, but it would at

least have contained the point and a hint as to its interpretation. See, besides, in opposition to Hofmann, Rich.
Schmidt, *Paul. Christol.* p. 193 f. — ἃ ἑώρακεν ἐμβατεύων] Subordinate to the θέλων κ.τ.λ. as a warning *modal* definition to
it: *entering upon what he has beheld, i.e.* instead of concerning
himself with what has been objectively given (ver. 19), entering the subjective domain of *visions* with his mental activity,
—by which is indicated the *mystico-theosophic* occupation of
the mind with God and the angels,[1] so that ἑώρακεν (comp.
Tert. *c. Marc.* v. 19) denotes not a seeing with the eyes,
but a *mental* beholding,[2] which belonged to the domain of
the φαντάζεσθαι, in part, doubtless, also to that of visionary
ecstasy (comp. Acts ii. 17; Rev. ix. 17; ὅραμα in Acts ix.
10, 12, x. 3; 2 Chron. ix. 29, *et al.;* Luke i. 22). This reference must have been intelligible to the readers from the
assertions put forth by the false teachers,[3] but the failure to
observe it induced copyists, at a very early date, to add a
negative (sometimes μή and sometimes οὐ) before ἑώρακεν.
Ἐμβατεύειν (only used here in the N. T.; but see Wetstein,
also Reisig, *ad Oed. Col. praef.* p. xxxix.), with accusative of the
place conceived as object (Kühner, II. 1, p. 257), also with the
genitive, with the dative, and with εἰς, means *to step upon*, as
e.g. νῆσον, Aesch. *Pers.* 441; πόλιν, Eur. *El.* 595; γῆν, Josh.
xix. 49; also with reference to a *mental* domain, which is

---

[1] This fanciful habit could not but be fostered and promoted by the Jewish
view, according to which the appearances of angels were regarded as φαντάσματα
(Gieseler, *Kirchengesch.* I. 1, p. 153, ed. 4).

[2] Ewald regards ἑώρακεν as more precisely defined by ἐν ταπεινοφρ. κ.τ.λ., as if
it ran ἃ ἐν ταπεινοφρ. κ.τ.λ. ἑώρακεν : "*while he enters arbitrarily upon that, which
he has seen in humility and angel-worship* (consequently has not actually himself
experienced and known), and desires to teach it as something true." But such
a hyperbaton, in the case of the relative, besides obscuring the sense, is without
precedent in the N. T. Comp. on ver. 14. Besides, the thought itself is far
from clear ; and respecting θέλων, see above.

[3] For the sphere of vision of the ἑώρακεν lay not outside of the subjects, but in
the hollow mirror of their own fancy. This applies also in opposition to Hilgenfeld, who now (1873, p. 198 f.) properly rejects the μή, but takes ἃ ἑώρ. ἐμβατ.
incorrectly : "*abiding by the sensuous.*" Opposed to this is the very use of the
perfect ἑώρ. and the significant expression ἐμβατεύων. The apostle does *not* mean
the ὁρατά, but the ἀόρατα (i. 16), into which they ascend by visions which they
profess to have had.

trodden by investigation and other mental activity, as Philo, *de plant. Noë*, p. 225 C, *et al.;* see Loesner, p. 369 f. ; 2 Macc. ii. 30 ; comp. also Nemes. *de nat. hom.* p. 64, ed. Matth. : οὐρανὸν ἐμβατεύει τῇ θεωρίᾳ, but not Xen. *Conv.* iv. 27, where, with Zeunius, ἐμαστεύετε ought to be read. Phavorinus : ἐμβατεῦσαι· τὸ ἔνδον ἐξερευνῆσαι ἢ σκοπῆσαι. It is frequently used in the sense of *seizing possession* (Dem. 894. 7 ; Eur. *Heracl.* 876 ; Schleusner, *Thes.* II. 332 ; Bloomfield, *Gloss. in Aesch. Pers.* p. 146 f.). So Budaeus and Calvin (*se ingerens*), both with the reading μή, also Huther (*establishing himself firmly* in the creations of fancy); still the context does not suggest this, and, when used in this sense, ἐμβατ. is usually coupled with εἰς (Dem. 894. 7, 1085. 24, 1086. 19 ; Isa. ix. 3, *et al.;* 1 Macc. xii. 25). In the reading of the *Recepta*, ἃ μὴ ἑώρ., the sense amounts either to : *entering into the unseen transcendental sphere*,[1] wherein the assumption would be implied that the domain of *sense* was the only field legitimately open, which would be unsuitable (2 Cor. v. 7, xiii. 12) ; or to : entering into things, which (although he dreams that he has seen them, yet) *he has not seen*—a concealed antithetical reference, which Paul, in order to be intelligible, must have indicated. The thought, *in the absence of* the negative, is not *weak* (de Wette), but *true, in characteristic keeping* with the perverseness of theosophic fancies (in opposition to Hofmann's objection), and representing the *actual state of the case,* which Paul could not but know. According to Hofmann, the ἃ μὴ ἑώρακεν which he reads is to be taken, not with ἐμβατεύων, but with what goes before : *of which, nevertheless, he has seen nothing* (and, consequently, cannot imitate it). This is disposed of, apart even from the incorrect inference involved in it,[2] by the preposterousness of Hofmann's exposition of the ταπεινοφροσύνη κ. θρησκεία τῶν ἀγγ., with which the connection, hit upon by

[1] Comp. Chrysostom : they have not seen the angels, and yet bear themselves as if they had seen them.

[2] For even the *unseen*, which may in any other way have been brought to our knowledge, we may and under certain circumstances should imitate (comp. *e.g.* Eph. v. 1). And even the angels and their actions have been included among the objects of the divine revelation as to the history of salvation and its accomplishment.

him, of εἰκῇ with ἐμβατεύων (" *an investigation, which results in nothing* "), also falls to the ground.—εἰκῇ φυσιούμ. κ.τ.λ., and then καὶ οὐ κρατῶν κ.τ.λ., are both subordinate to the ἃ ἑώρακεν ἐμβατεύων, and contain two *modal definitions* of it fraught with the utmost danger. — εἰκῇ φυσιούμ.] for the entering upon what was seen did not rest upon a real divine revelation, but upon a conceited, fanciful self-exaggeration. Τὸ δέ γε φυσιού-μενος τῇ ταπεινοφροσύνῃ ἐναντίον οὐκ ἔστι· τὴν μὲν γὰρ ἐσκήπ-τοντο, τοῦ δὲ τύφου τὸ πάθος ἀκριβῶς περιέκειντο, Theodoret. On εἰκῇ, *temere*, i.e. *without ground*, comp. Matt. v. 22 ; Rom. xiii. 4 ; Plat. *Menex.* p. 234 C ; Xen. *Cyrop.* ii. 2. 22.   It places the *vanity*, that is, the objective groundlessness of the pride, in contradistinction to their presumptuous fancies, em-phatically in the foreground.   Even if ἐμβατ. is not taken absolutely with Hofmann, we may not join it with εἰκῇ (in opposition to Steiger, de Wette, Reiche ; Böhmer is doubtful), since it is not the *uselessness* (in *this* sense εἰκῇ would require to be taken, 1 Cor. xv. 2 ; Gal. iii. 4, iv. 11) of the ἐμβα-τεύειν ἃ ἑώρ. (or ἃ μὴ ἑώρ.), but this ἐμβατεύειν in and of itself, that forms the characteristic perversity in the conduct of those people—a perversity which is set forth by εἰκῇ φυσιούμ. κ.τ.λ., and in ver. 19 as immoral and antichristian. — ὑπὸ τοῦ νοὸς τῆς σαρκ. αὐτοῦ] becoming puffed up *by* (as operative principle) *the reason of his flesh.* This is the morally deter-mined intellectual faculty in its character and activity as not divinely regulated, in which unennobled condition (see on Eph. iv. 23) it is the servant, not of the divine πνεῦμα, whose organ it is designed to be, but of the materio-physical human nature, of the σάρξ as the seat of the sin-power, and is governed by its lusts instead of the divine truth.   Comp. Rom. i. 21, 28, iv. 1, vi. 19, vii. 14, xii. 2 ; Eph. iv. 17 f. ; see also Kluge in the *Jahrb. f. D. Theol.* 1871, p. 329 ff.   The νοῦς does not belong to the essence of the σάρξ (in opposition to Holsten) ; but, be it observed, the matter is so represented that the σάρξ of the false teacher, in accordance with its dominant superiority, appears *personified* (comp. Rom. viii. 6), as if the νοῦς, influenced by it, and therewith serviceable to it, were *its own.* In virtue of this non-free and, in its activity, sinfully-directed reason,

the man, who is guided by it, is *ἀνόητος* (Gal. iii. 1, 3 ; Tit.
iii. 3), loses his moral judgment (Rom. xii. 2), falls into *ἐπιθυμίας ἀνοήτους* (1 Tim. vi. 9), and withstands Christian truth
and purity as *κατεφθαρμένος τὸν νοῦν* (2 Tim. iii. 8 ; 2 Cor.
xi. 3), and *ἐσκοτισμένος τῇ διανοίᾳ* (Eph. iv. 18). — The
puffing up of the persons in question consisted in this, that
with all their professed and apparent humility they, as is
commonly the case with mystic tendencies, fancied that
they could not be content with the simple knowledge and
obedience of the gospel, but were capable of attaining a special
higher wisdom and sanctity. It is well said by Theophylact :
*πῶς γὰρ οὐ σαρκικοῦ νοὸς κ. παχέος τὸ ἀθετῆσαι τὰ ὑπὸ Χρισ-
τοῦ λεχθέντα,* John iii. 16, 17, 19, x. 26 f., *καὶ μυρία ὅσα* !

Ver. 19. *Καί*] annexing to *εἰκῆ φυσιούμενος κ.τ.λ.* a
further, and that a negative, modal form of the *ἃ ἑώρακεν
ἐμβατεύων.* This *ἐμβατεύειν* into what is seen takes place,
namely, in such a way, that one is puffed up by fleshly
reason, *and does not hold the Head,* etc. So much is it at
variance with the *nature and success, as respects unity, of the
church !* [1] — *οὐ κρατῶν κ.τ.λ.*] *not holding fast* (but letting it
go, comp. Song of Sol. iii. 4 : *ἐκράτησα αὐτὸν καὶ οὐκ ἀφῆκα
αὐτόν) the Head,* inasmuch, namely, as they seek *angelic* mediation. Bengel aptly observes : " Qui non unice Christum tenet,
plane non tenet." — *ἐξ οὗ κ.τ.λ.*] represents the whole objection-
ableness of this *οὐ κρατῶν τ. κεφ.,* and the absolute necessity
of the opposite. This *οὗ* is not to be referred to the verbal
idea (Bengel's suggestion : " ex quo sc. tenendo caput "),
but applies objectively (comp. Eph. iv. 15 f.) to that which
was designated by *τὴν κεφαλ.* In this view it may be *masculine,*
according to the construction *κατὰ σύνεσιν* (Kühner, II. 1, p.
49), as it is usually taken, but it may also—and this is prefer-
able, because here the personality is not, as in Eph. iv. 15 f.,
specially marked—be *neuter,* so that it takes up the Head, not

[1] The conduct of those men is the negation of this holy relation, a separation
from the organism of the body of Christ as an unity. The compressed characterizing of this articulated organism is therefore as suitable here as in Eph.
iv. 16, and by no means an *opus supererogationis* on the part of the author
(Holtzmann).

personally (though it *is* Christ), but in accordance *with the neuter idea : from which.* See Matthiae, p. 988 ; Kühner, II. 1, p. 55. Comp. Maetzner, *ad Antiph.* p. 201. The τ. κεφαλ. might also be taken attributively : not holding fast *as the Head* Him, from whom, etc. (Ewald), which would be, however, less simple and less forcibly descriptive. ἐξ denotes the *causal issuing forth* of the subsequently expressed relation, comp. Eph. iv. 16. — πᾶν τὸ σῶμα] consequently *no* member is excepted, so that *no* member can expect from any other quarter what is destined for, and conveyed to, the whole body from the head. The conception of the church as the body of Christ, the Head, is not in our Epistle and the Ephesian letter different from that of the other Epistles (in opposition to Holtzmann, p. 239 ff.). Comp. on 1 Cor. xii. 12 f., vi. 15 ; Rom. xii. 4 f. ; also 1 Cor. xi. 3. Any pressing contrary to the author's design of the thought of a σῶμα, which strictly taken is a *trunk,* is in this particular case excluded by the graphic delineation of the constantly living and active connection of the members with the Head. Every comparison, indeed, when pressed, becomes halting. — διὰ τῶν ἁφῶν κ. συνδεσμῶν ἐπιχορ. κ. συμβιβ.] The participial relation to the following verb is this : from the Head the whole body is furnished and bound together *and grows* in this way, so that ἐξ οὗ therefore is to be referred neither to the participles *only,* nor to the verb *only,* but to *both ;* and διὰ τ. ἁφ. κ. συνδεσμ. specifies by what means the ἐπιχορ. κ. συμβιβ., proceeding from the Head, is *brought about,* viz. *through the* (bodily) *nerve-impulses* (not *joints,* as it is usually explained ; see on Eph. iv. 16), which are conveyed from the Head to the body, and through *the bands,* which, proceeding from the Head, place the whole in organic connection. Observe that ἐπιχορ. refers to διὰ τ. ἁφῶν, and συμβιβ. to κ. συνδεσμ. Theophylact (comp. Theodoret) has aptly illustrated the former by the action of the nerves which is diffused from the head through the entire body, so that ἀπὸ τῆς κεφαλῆς ἐστι πᾶσα αἴσθησις κ. πᾶσα κίνησις. As, therefore, the body receives its efficiency from the head through the contact of *impulses* effected by means of the network of nerves, so would the church,

separated from Christ—from whom the feelings and impulses
in a spiritual sense, the motions and activities of the higher
ζωή, are conveyed to it—be without the supply in question.
Comp. the idea of the figure of the vine.   Further : as, starting
from the head, the whole body, by means of the *bands* which
bind member to member, is bound together into one organic
whole ; so also is the entire church, starting from Christ, by
means of the bands of Christian communion (κοινωνία), which
give to the union of individuals the coherence of articulate
unity.   *Faith* is the *inner ground* of the ἀφαί, not the latter
themselves (in opposition to Bengel) ; so also is *love* the inner
ground of the σύνδεσμοί of the mystical body, not these latter
themselves (in opposition to Tertullian, Zanchius, Estius,
Bengel, and others) ; and the *operative principle* on the part of
Christ the Head is the *Holy Spirit* (Eph. iv. 4 ; 1 Cor. xii. 3 f.,
7, *et al.*).   Theodoret erroneously (comp. Ewald) explains the
σύνδεσμοί as the ἀπόστολοι κ. προφῆται κ. διδάσκαλοι, and
Böhmer takes the ἀφαί and σύνδεσμ. as the *believers*.   The
latter, as also the teachers, are in fact the *members*, and *share
in experiencing* what is here asserted of the entire body.—
ἐπιχορηγούμ.] *receiving supply*, being furnished.   Comp. on
the *passive* expression, which is not un-Pauline (Holtzmann),
but in harmony with the general passive usage (Kühner, II.
1, p. 109), Polyb. iv. 77. 2 : πολλαῖς ἀφορμαῖς ἐκ φύσεως
κεχορηγημένος, iii. 75. 3, *et al.;* Diod. Sic. i. 73 ; Ecclus.
xliv. 6 ; 3 Macc. vi. 40.   The *compound*, not expressing " *in
addition besides* " (Bleek), denotes that the χορηγία *is coming
to, is being conveyed towards.*   Comp. 2 Cor. ix. 10 ; Gal. iii.
5 ; Dion. Hal. x. 54.   But it is not said *with what* the body
is provided, as χορηγεῖν (comp. also ἐπιχορ., Ecclus. xxv. 22)
is often used absolutely (see *e.g.* the passages from Polybius in
Schweighäuser, *Lex.* p. 663), and admits of its more precise
definition being supplied from the context, which, however,
here points not to *nourishment* (Grotius, de Wette), but to that
which is accomplished through the *feelings* (ἀφῶν), namely,
the *vital activity*, of which the body would be destitute in
the absence of the different impulses.   Comp. Chrysostom : τὸ
εἶναι καὶ τὸ καλῶς εἶναι, Theophylact : πᾶσα αἴσθησις κ.

COL.

2 C

πᾶσα κίνησις, and in the application : λαμβάνει τὸ ζῆν κ. αὔξειν πνευματικῶς. — τὴν αὔξησιν τοῦ Θεοῦ] denoted by the article as the divine growth absolutely ; τοῦ Θεοῦ is the genitive *auctoris : which God confers* (1 Cor. iii. 6, 7), with which ἐξ οὗ is not at variance (as Bähr thinks), since God is ranked above Christ (1 Cor. xi. 3), and is the supreme operating principle in the church (1 Cor. xii. 6 ; Eph. iv. 6). At once weak, and suggested by nothing in the text, is the view : " incrementum, quod Deus probat " (Calvin, Bähr[1]). What is *meant* is the gradual *growth* of Christians collectively toward *Christian perfection*. The circumstance that αὔξει as an intransitive only occurs again in Eph. ii. 21, comp. iv. 15, and αὔξησις only in Eph. iv. 16, cannot prove it to be an un-Pauline mode of expression (Holtzmann). Respecting the connection of the verb with the more precisely defined cognate noun, see Winer, p. 210 [E. T. 281]; Lobeck, *Paralip.* p. 507 f. ; Kühner, II. 2, p. 262 f.

Ver. 20 f. After these warnings, vv. 16–19, which were intended to secure his readers against the seduction threatening them, the apostle now returns for the same purpose once more to the two main foundations of the Christian life, to the fellowship with Christ in *death* (ver. 20), and fellowship with Him also in *resurrection* (iii. 1). His aim is to show, in connection with the former, the groundlessness and perversity of the heretical prohibitions of meats (vv. 20–23), and to attach to the latter—to the fellowship of resurrection—the essence of Christian morality in whole and in detail, and therewith the *paraenetic* portion of the Epistle (iii. 1–iv. 6), the tenor of which thereby receives the character of the *holiest moral necessity*. — εἰ ἀπεθάνετε κ.τ.λ.] the legal abstinence required by the false teachers (see below) stands in contradiction with the fact, that the readers at their conversion had entered into *the fellowship of the death of Christ*, and thereby had become loosed from the στοιχεῖα τοῦ κόσμου (see on ver. 8), *i.e.* from the ritual religious elements of non-Christian humanity, among which the legal prohibition of meats and the traditional regulations founded thereon are included. *How far* the man who

---

[1] Comp. Chrysostom and Oecumenius, who explain τοῦ Θεοῦ by κατὰ Θεόν.

has died with Christ has passed out of connection with these elementary things, is taught by ver. 14, according to which, through the death of Christ, the law as to its debt-obligation has been abolished. Consequently, in the case of those who have died with Christ, the law, and everything belonging to the same category with it, have no further claim to urge, since Christ has allowed the curse of the law to be accomplished on Himself, and this has also taken place in believers in virtue of their fellowship of death with Him, whereby the binding relation of debt which had hitherto subsisted for them has ceased. Comp. Gal. ii. 19, iv. 3, 9; Rom. vii. 4, *et al.* — ἀποθνήσκειν, with ἀπό, meaning *to die away from something, moriendo liberari a* (Porphyr. *de abstin. ab esu anim.* i. 41), is only met with here in the N. T.; elsewhere it is used with the dative, as in Gal. ii. 19, Rom. vi. 2, whereby the same *thing* is otherwise *conceived* in point of form. It is, moreover, to be observed, that *Christ Himself* also is by death released from the στοιχεῖα, since He was made under the law, and, although sinless, was destined to take upon Himself the curse of it; hence it was only by His death in obedience to the Father (Phil. ii. 8; Rom. v. 19), that He became released from this relation. Comp. on Gal. iv. 4. Huther erroneously denies that such an ἀποθανεῖν can be predicated of Christ, and therefore assumes (comp. Schenkel and Dalmer) the brachylogy: "if, by your dying with Christ, ye are dead from the στοιχεῖα τοῦ κόσμου." — τί ὡς ζῶντες κ.τ.λ.] *why are ye, as though ye were still alive in the world, commanded: Touch not,* etc. Such commands are adapted to those who are not, like you, dead, etc. As ἀποθανόντες σὺν Χ. ἀπὸ τ. στοιχ. τ. κόσμ., ye are no longer alive in the domain of the non-Christian κόσμος, but are removed from that sphere of life (belonging to the heavenly πολίτευμα, Phil. iii. 20). The word δογματίζειν, only found here in the N. T., but frequently in the LXX. and Apocrypha, and in the Fathers and decrees of Councils (see Suicer, *Thes.* I. p. 935), means nothing more than *to decree* (Diod. Sic. iv. 83; Diog. L. iii. 51; Anth. Pal. ix. 576. 4; Arrian. *Epict.* iii. 7; Esth. iii. 9; 3 Esdr. vi. 34; 2 Macc. x. 8, xv. 36; 3 Macc. iv. 11), and δογματίζεσθε is *passive: why are ye prescribed to, why do men make decrees for you (vobis)* ? so that it is not a *reproach* (the censure conveyed by the expression affects rather the *false teachers*), but a *warning* to those readers (comp. vv. 16, 18) who were not yet led away (i. 4, ii. 5), and who ought not to yield any compliance to so absurd a demand. That the readers are the *passive subject*, is quite according to rule, since the active has the dative along with it, δογματίζειν τινι (2 Macc. x. 8); comp. also Hofmann and Beza. The usual rendering takes δογματ. as *middle*, and that either as: why *do ye allow commands to be laid down for you* (Huther), *rules to be imposed upon you* (de Wette), *yourselves to be entangled with rules* (Luther) ? and such like;[1] or even: *why do ye make rules for yourselves* (Ewald) ? comp. Vulgate: *decernitis.* This, however, would involve a *censure of the readers*, and ὡς ζῶντες ἐν κόσμῳ would express the unsuitableness of their conduct with their Christian standing—a reproach, which would be altogether out of harmony with the other contents of the Epistle. On the contrary, ὡς ζῶντες ἐν κ. indicates the erroneous aspect in which the Christian standing of the readers was regarded by the *false teachers*, who took up such an attitude towards them, as if they were not yet dead from the world, which nevertheless (comp. ver. 11 f.) they *are* through their fellowship with Christ (iii. 3; Gal. ii. 19 f.; 2 Cor. v. 14 f.). The ὡς ζῶντες ἐν κόσμῳ, moreover, is entirely misunderstood by Bähr: "as if one could at all *attain to life and salvation through externals.*" Comp., on the contrary, the thought of the εἶναι ἐν τῇ σαρκί in Rom. vii. 5 and Gal. vi. 14. Observe, further, that this ζῆν ἐν κόσμῳ is not *one and the same thing* with εἶναι ὑπὸ τὰ στοιχεῖα τοῦ κόσμου (Hofmann, by way of establishing his explanation of στοιχεῖα in the sense of the *material things of the world*); but the ζῆν ἐν κ. is the *more general*, to which the special εἶναι ὑπὸ τ. στοιχεῖα τ. κ. is *subordinate.* If the former is the case, the latter also takes place by way of consequence. — μὴ ἅψῃ κ.τ.λ.] a vivid concrete representation of the δόγματα concerned, in a " compendiaria mimesis" (Flacius). The *triple*

---

[1] Comp. Chrysostom: πῶς τοῖς στοιχείοις ὑπόκεισθε ; similarly Theodoret, Beza; and recently, Bähr, Böhmer, Olshausen, Baumgarten-Crusius, Bleek, and others.

description brings out the *urgency* of the eager demand for abstinence, and the relation of the three prohibitions is such, that μηδέ both times means *nor even;* in the second instance, however, in the sense of *ne quidem,* so that the last point stands to the two former together in the relation of a climax : *thou shalt not lay hold of, nor even taste, nor once touch !* What was meant as *object* of this enjoined ἀπέχεσθαι (1 Tim. iv. 3) the reader *was aware,* and its omission only renders the description more vivid and terse. Steiger's view, that the object was suppressed by the false teachers themselves from fear and hypocrisy, is quite groundless. From the words themselves, however (γεύσῃ), and from the subsequent context (see ver. 23), it is plain that the prohibitions concerned certain *meats and drinks* (comp. ver. 16) ; and it is entirely arbitrary to mix up other things, as even de Wette does, making them refer also to *sexual intercourse* (θιγγάνειν γυναικός, Eur. *Hipp.* 1044, *et al.;* see Monck, *ad Eur. Hipp.* 14 ; Valckenaer, *ad Phoen.* 903), while others distinguish between ἅψῃ and θίγῃς in respect of their objects, *e.g.* Estius : the *former* refers to unclean objects, such as the garments of a menstruous woman, the *latter* to the buying and selling of unclean meats ; Erasmus, Zanchius : the *former* concerns dead bodies, the *latter* sacred vessels and the like ; Grotius : the *former* refers to meats, the *latter* to the "vitandas feminas," to which Flatt and Dalmer, following older writers, make ἅψῃ refer (1 Cor. vii. 1). Others give other expositions still ; Böhmer arbitrarily makes θίγῃς refer to the *oil,* which the Essenes and other theoso-phists regarded as a *labes.* That Paul in ἅψῃ and θίγ. had *no* definite object at all in view, is not even probable (in opposi-tion to Huther), because γεύσῃ stands between them, and ver. 23 points to abstinence from meats, and not at the same time to anything else.——Following the more forcible ἅψῃ, *lay hold of,* the more subtle θίγῃς, *touch,* is in admirable keeping with the climax : the object was to be even ἄθικτον (Soph. *O. C.* 39). Comp. on the difference between the two words, Xen. *Cyrop.* i. 3. 5 : ὅταν μὲν τοῦ ἄρτου ἅψῃ, εἰς οὐδὲν τὴν χεῖρα ἀποψώμενον (σὲ ὁρῶ), ὅταν δὲ τούτων (these dainty dishes) τινὸς θίγῃς, εὐθὺς ἀποκαθαίρῃ τὴν χεῖρα εἰς τὰ χειρό-

μακτρα, also v. 1. 16. In an inverted climax, Eur. *Bacch.* 617.
οὔτ᾽ ἔθιγεν οὔθ᾽ ἥψαθ᾽ ἡμῶν. See also Ex. xix. 12, where the
LXX. delicately and aptly render נְגֹעַ בְּקָצֵהוּ, *to touch the outer
border of the mountain,* by the free translation θίγειν τι αὐτοῦ,
but then express the general הַנֹּגֵעַ בָּהָר by the stronger ὁ ἁψά-
μενος τοῦ ὄρους. Hofmann erroneously holds that ἅπτομαι
expresses rather the *motion* of the *subject grasping* at something, θιγγάνω rather his *arriving* at the *object.* In opposition
to this fiction stands the testimony of all the passages in the
Gospels (Matt. viii. 3, ix. 20; John xx. 17, and many others),
in which ἅπτεσθαι signifies the actual *laying hold of,* and, in
Paul's writings, of 1 Cor. vii. 1, 2 Cor. vi. 17, as also the quite
common Grecian usage in the sense of *contrectare (attingere et
inhaerere),* and similarly the signification of the active *to fasten
to, to make to stick* (Lobeck, *ad Soph. Aj.* 698; Duncan, *Lex.
Hom.* ed. Rost, p. 150). The mere *stretching out the hand
towards something,* in order to seize it, is never ἅπτεσθαι.
Hofmann, moreover, in order to establish a climax of the
three points, arbitrarily makes the subtle gloss upon γεύσῃ,
that this might even happen more *unintentionally,* and upon
θίγῃς, that this might happen *involuntarily.*—Respecting the
aorist θιγεῖν (a present θίγειν instead of θιγγάνειν can nowhere
be accepted as certain), see Schaefer, *ad Greg. Cor.* p. 990,
Ellendt, *Lex. Soph.* I. p. 804; Kühner, I. p. 833.

Ver. 22. We are not to put in a parenthesis μὴ ἅψῃ ... ἀπο-
χρήσει (Erasmus Schmid, Heinrichs, and others), but merely
ἅ ἐστιν ... ἀποχρ. (Griesbach, Lachmann, Scholz, Ewald); for
the construction proceeds uninterruptedly to θίγῃς, is then only
broken by the judgment ἅ ἐστι π. εἰς φθ. τ. ἀποχρ., and thereafter runs on with κατὰ τὰ ἐντάλμ. κ.τ.λ. — ἅ ἐστι ... ἀποχρ.
is an inserted[1] *judgment of the apostle* anent that which the false
teachers interdicted by μὴ ἅψῃ κ.τ.λ.: *which all are destined
to destruction*[2] *through the using,*—from which it is to be rendered

---

[1] For it is only an *incidental* observation in opposition to the above δογματίζεσθαι; the main ground of opposition to the latter lies in εἰ ἀπέθαν. σὺν X.

[2] ἐστὶν εἰς φθοράν, it serves for destruction, *i.e.* it serves for the purpose *of being
destroyed.* See generally Winer, p. 173 [E. T. 229]; Buttmann, *Neut. Gr.*
p. 131 [E. T. 150 f.]. Comp. Wisd. iv. 18; Ecclus. xxxiv. 10; Judith v. 21, 24,
viii. 22.

palpably apparent, how *preposterous* it is to make such things a condition of eternal bliss by urging abstinence from them. We have here a similar line of argument to that in Matt. xv. 17. Comp. 1 Cor. vi. 13. Hence φθορά is meant to denote the perishing which takes place through the natural dissolution (digestion) of the meats and drinks ; and with this conception quite accords the purposely-chosen compound τῇ ἀποχρήσει, which, like *abusus*, indicates the *using up*, the *consuming* (Plut. *Mor.* p. 267 E ; Davis, *ad Cic. N. D.* iv. 60). So it is unanimously explained by Chrysostom, Theodoret (εἰς κόπρον γὰρ ἅπαντα μεταβάλλεται), Oecumenius (φθορᾷ γὰρ, φησιν, ὑπόκειται ἐν τῷ ἀφεδρῶνι), Theophylact, Erasmus, Luther, Beza, Calvin, Wolf, Grotius, Michaelis, and many others, including Bähr, Steiger, Olshausen, Ewald, Bleek, Hofmann. But, according to others, who likewise regard ἅ ... ἀποχρ. as a parenthetical judgment, the ἅ is to be referred to the prohibitions, ἀποχρ. to the *use, i.e.* the following of them, and φθορά (comp. Gal. vi. 8) to the destruction of the persons who follow them : *all which* δόγματα *by their use tend to* (eternal) *destruction.* So Ambrosiaster, Augustine, Cornelius a Lapide, Calixtus, Heumann, Junker. Erroneously ; because ἀπόχρησις never means merely *use,* and even the simple χρῆσις, in the sense of τήρησις, would be an unsuitable designation ; in fact, the entire addition, " by the use," would be utterly superfluous. On account of ἀποχρ., the expedient must also be rejected, on linguistic grounds, that ἅ ... ἀποχρ. are still *words of the false teachers,* which Paul repeats with irony : " *omnia haec* (vetita) *usu suo perniciem afferunt,*" Heinrichs, comp. Schenkel. By others, who, like Tischendorf, have deleted the marks of parenthesis, the whole down to ἀνθρώπων is taken together : all this, which the false teachers forbid, tends through the using to (" moral," de Wette) destruction, " si sc. *ex doctorum Judaicorum praeceptis et doctrinis* hac de re judicium feratur,"[1] Kypke ; so also

---

[1] Similarly Dalmer, who, however, takes τῇ ἀποχρ. in the sense of *abuse,* joining it immediately to κατὰ τὰς διδασκ. κ.τ.λ. But while ἀποχρῆσθαι (Dem. 215. 8 ; Herodian, v. 1. 13) is found in the sense of *abuse* (καταχρῆσις, παραχρῆσις), ἀπόχρησις is not, though it was so taken by Erasmus Schmid, Schoettgen, Zachariae, as also by Grimm in his *Lexicon.*

Vatablus, Storr, Flatt, Böhmer, de Wette, Baumgarten-Crusius (Huther is undecided between this explanation and ours). But in opposition to this it may be urged, that the compound ἀπο-χρήσει would be entirely *without a motive*, since not the *consumption*, but the *use* at all would be soul-destroying according to the maxims of those people. Our view alone supplies a *motive* for the use of ἀποχρήσει, and that through the *point* of its connection with εἰς φθοράν, in which case, however, the object affected by ἀποχρ. and εἰς φθορ. must be the *same* (the things forbidden). De Wette's objections are irrelevant, since the thought of the parenthesis ἅ . . . ἀποχρ. is expressed not strangely, but with Pauline ingenuity, the words κατὰ τὰ ἐντάλμ. κ.τ.λ. annexed to δογματίζεσθε are by no means superfluous (see below), nor does this annexation require us to begin the parenthesis with μὴ ἅψῃ and thereby to include heterogeneous elements together; for μὴ ἅψῃ κ.τ.λ. still belongs closely to δογματ., of which it is the contents, and κατὰ τὰ ἐντάλμ. κ.τ.λ. is then annexed, after the brief incidentally inserted remark, to δογματ. *and* its contents (μὴ ἅψῃ κ.τ.λ.). — κατὰ τὰ ἐντάλματα κ.τ.λ.] The article before ἐντάλμ., and extending also to διδασ-καλ., is *generic*. The μὴ ἅψῃ κ.τ.λ. was decreed by the false teachers *conformably to the commandments and doctrines of men*, not in consequence of what *God* had commanded and taught. This element, annexed to δογματίζ., is by no means superfluous (in opposition to de Wette), since, in fact, δόγμα in itself is a *command generally*, and may be one based upon *divine* authority; it rather serves to bring out with perfect clearness the conflicting relation, in which that δογματίζεσθαι stands to the ἀπεθάνετε σὺν Χριστῷ κ.τ.λ. For what the false teachers decreed was not the prohibitions of meats contained in the law of Moses as such, and these alone (although they too would have been incompatible with the ἀπεθάνετε σὺν X. κ.τ.λ.), but such as consisted in the human (Essene) definitions, expansions, and amplifications of the former (κατὰ τὴν παράδοσιν τῶν ἀνθρώπων, ver. 8). It was in this, and not in the mere setting up again of the Mosaic law abolished through Christ (Chrysostom and many others), that the δογματίζεσθαι was regulated by *human* standard, without the divine authority and warrant.

Moreover, διδασκ. is not *synonymous* with ἐντάλμ., but has a *wider* sense (in Matt. xv. 9 and Mark vi. 7, the narrower idea comes *after* as a more precise definition), so that the two together specify *the preceptive and generally* (καί) *the doctrinal standard.* Comp. Isa. xxix. 13.

Ver. 23. *And of what nature and quality* is that, which I have just termed τὰ ἐντάλματα κ. διδασκαλ. τῶν ἀνθρ.? — ἅτινα] *quippe quae,* i.e. *ita comparata, ut* (Kühner, *ad Xen. Mem.* ii. 1, 30). The conception was different in ἅ of ver. 22, where the thing in question was regarded purely objectively, as mere *object.* — ἐστί] belongs to ἔχοντα, without, however, being with this equivalent to ἔχει; it introduces what the ἅτινα *are* as regards their quality. If it belonged to οὐκ ἐν τιμῇ τινι (Bähr), or to πρὸς πλησμ. τ. σ. (Bengel), or to ἐν ἐθελοθρησκείᾳ κ.τ.λ. (that which *moves* and *has its being* in ἐθελοθρ. κ.τ.λ.), as Hofmann thinks, taking λόγον μ. ἔχοντα σοφ. parenthetically—why should it not have been actually *placed* beside that to which it would belong? Apart from this, Hofmann's connection of it with ἐν ἐθελοθρ. could alone deserve consideration, since from ἐν ἐθελοθρ. onwards all that follows is consecutive. But even this connection must be abandoned, because the sphere of subsistence indicated by ἐν ἐθελοθρ. κ.τ.λ. would be too *wide* for such special prohibitions, ver. 21, as are conveyed by ἅτινα, and because we have no right to put aside from the connection, as a mere *incisum,* the *important* thought (comp. ver. 8) expressed by λόγ. τ. ἔχ. σοφίας, which comes in with ἐστί so emphatically at the very *head* of the judgment, and appropriately, as regards meaning, attaches to itself all that follows. — λόγον ἔχειν, explained by many since Jerome approximately in the sense of *speciem* or *praetextum habere* (see Kypke, de Wette, Dalmer, and others; also Köster in the *Stud. u. Krit.* 1854, p. 318), may, according as we adopt for λόγος the signification *ratio* or *sermo,* mean either : *to have ground* (so in the passages from Demosth., Dionys. Hal., and Lesbonax in Kypke; from Plat. in Ast, *Lex.* II. p. 257; from Polyb. in Schweighäuser, *Lex.* p. 370[1]), in

---

[1] So Hilgenfeld, in his *Zeitschr.* 1870, p. 250, holding that what is rejected in the legal sense in ver. 22 is here "*permitted as voluntary asceticism.*" See,

which case the ground may certainly be only an apparent one, a pretext (comp. Ellendt, *Lex. Soph.* II. p. 36) ; further, *to have an insight* into something (often thus in Plato, *e.g. Rep.* p. 475 C), *to have regard to* (Herod. i. 62 ; Plat. *Tim.* p. 87 C) ; or : *to have a reputation*, so that one is in any relation the subject of *discourse*, of legend, of mention, of rumour, etc. ; see *e.g.* Plat. *Epin.* p. 987 B : Ἐωσφόρος . . . Ἀφροδίτης εἶναι σχεδὸν ἔχει λόγον (*dicitur*), Herod. v. 56 : λόγον ἔχει τὴν Πυθίην ἀναπεῖσαι, comp. ix. 78 ; Xen. *Oec.* 11. 4 (the same thing conceived under another form : λόγος ἔχει τινα, Herod. vii. 5, and frequently). The latter signification is here to be adhered to, because the subsequent οὐκ ἐν τιμῇ τινι, when correctly rendered, accords with it as bearing on the matter in hand, and is in sense appropriately correlative. Hence : *that which has a repute of wisdom*, popularly passes for wisdom. Comp. ὄνομα ἔχειν (Rev. iii. 1) and ὀνομάζεσθαι (1 Cor. v. 11). — μέν] without a subsequent δέ ; there was before the apostle's mind the contrast : *repute*, truly, *but not the reality*, οὐ δύναμιν, οὐκ ἀλήθειαν, Chrysostom. He omitted to express this, however, led aside by the progress of his discourse, so that instead of bringing in the antithesis of λόγον by δέ, he makes οὐκ ἐν τιμῇ τινι follow without δέ, and in contrast not to the λόγον, but to the ἐν ἐθελοθρ. κ.τ.λ.,—from which we are to gather in substance, what in starting with λόγον μέν it was intended to express. See Erasmus, *Annot.*, and generally Winer, p. 534 f. [E. T. 719] ; Buttmann, *Neut. Gr.* p. 313 [E. T. 365] ; Klotz, *ad Devar.* p. 656 ; Maetzner, *ad Antiph.* p. 153 ; Baeumlein, *Partik.* p. 163 f. The linguistic phenomenon of this μέν without an adversative word following is so common, that there is no ground for requiring before οὐκ ἐν τιμῇ τ. an ἀλλά (Hofmann), which *might* have been used (Baeumlein, p. 170), but not *necessarily*. Holtzmann also takes too much offence at the absence of a formal contrast, and finds in πρὸς πλησμ. τ. σαρκός an ill-inserted remnant of the original. — ἐν ἐθελοθρησκείᾳ] *instrumental*, specifying by what means it is brought about, on the part of those who lay down the com-

however, on the sequel, from which the impossibility of this interpretation is self-evident.

mandments and doctrines referred to, that the latter have a
repute of wisdom: *through self-chosen worship*, *i.e.* through a
cultus, which is not divinely commanded, but is the work of
their own self-determination. What was *meant* by this, the
reader was *aware;* and ver. 18 places it beyond doubt that the
worship of *angels* formed an essential and chief part of it,
though it need not, from the general character of the expression in our passage, have been meant exclusively; other forms
of capricious cultus may have been included with it. The
substantive ἐθελοθρ. does not occur elsewhere except in ecclesiastical writers; but the *verb* ἐθελοθρησκεῖν is explained by
Suidas: ἰδίῳ θελήματι σέβειν τὸ δοκοῦν, and Epiph. *Haer.* i. 16
explains the name Pharisees: διὰ τὸ ἀφωρισμένους εἶναι αὐτοὺς
ἀπὸ τῶν ἄλλων διὰ τὴν ἐθελοπερισσοθρησκείαν παρ᾽ αὐτοῖς
νενομισμένην. Comp. ἐθελοδουλεία (Plat. *Symp.* p. 184 C,
Rep. p. 562 D), ἐθελοκάκησις, ἐθελοκίνδυνος, ἐθελόπορος, ἐθελο-
πρόξενος (Thuc. iii. 70. 2, where the scholiast explains: ἀφ᾽
ἑαυτοῦ γενόμενος καὶ μὴ κελευσθεὶς κ.τ.λ.), and various others.
Hofmann erroneously takes away from the word in itself the
bad sense, and explains (after the analogy of ἐθελοπονία and
ἐθελουργία): worship, *which one interests himself in.* This
view is prohibited by the evident retrospective reference of
this word and the following one to ver. 18, where, according
to the right interpretation, the θρησκεία was certainly something bad. The unfavourable meaning, according to Hofmann's present explanation (he gave a different but also
erroneous view in his *Schriftbew.* II. 2, p. 72 ; see, in opposition to it, my third edition), is only got by the addition of
σώματος, which belongs to *all the three* points, so that ἐθελοθρησκεία σώματος must be understood as a worship gladly
and earnestly rendered, *but which is rendered only with bodily
demeanour.* But σώματος does not suit either with ἐθελοθρ.
or ταπεινοφρ.,[1] but only with ἀφειδίᾳ. For it is plain from

---

[1] According to Hofmann, namely, ταπεινοφροσύνη σώματος is a disposition of *self-
humiliation, which, however, only weakens the body by abstinences.* But it would
rather have the absurd sense : *humility of the body ;* for ταπεινοφροσύνη neither
means humiliation nor self-humiliation, but *humility, meekness*, ver. 18, iii. 12 ;
Phil. ii. 3.

ἀφειδίᾳ σώματος that σώματος is the genitive of the *object*,
from which it follows that θρησκεία σώματος would yield the
opposite sense: a θρησκεία *rendered to the body* (comp. θρησκ.
τῶν ἀγγέλων in ver. 18), which would come ultimately to the
idea of the λατρεύειν τῇ ἡδονῇ (Lucian, *Nigr.* 15), comp. Plut.
Mor. p. 107 C: λατρεία τοῦ σώματος, and on the matter conceived as θρησκεία, Phil. iii. 19. — ταπεινοφροσ.] from the
point of view of the false teachers (comp. ver. 18), what *they*
thus designated; although in fact it consisted in this, that, as
in all false humility, they with spiritual conceit (comp. ver. 18,
and subsequently πρὸς πλησμον. τ. σαρκός) took pleasure in
unduly undervaluing themselves — an ethical self-contempt,
which involved in relation to God the ἐθελοθρησκεία, and towards the body an *unsparingness* through mistaken abstinence
and mortifying asceticism, inconsistent with Christian liberty.
On ἀφειδίᾳ, comp. Plat. *Defin.* p. 412 D; Plut. *Mor.* p. 762 D;
further, ἀφειδεῖν βίου, Thuc. ii. 43. 3; ψυχῆς, Soph. *El.* 968:
σωμάτων, Lys. ii. 25, Diod. Sic. xiii. 60. — οὐκ ἐν τιμῇ τινι]
not through anything whatever that is an honour, not through
anything honourable, by which that repute would appear
founded in truth and just. The expression is *purposely chosen*,
in order to make the λόγος σοφίας appear as *repute without
honour*, *i.e.* without any morally estimable substratum on the
part of the persons concerned. The following πρὸς πλησμονὴν
τῆς σαρκός is also purposely chosen; in it πλησμον. significantly glances back to ἀφειδίᾳ, and τῆς σαρκός to σώματος,
and there is produced a thoughtful contrast, a striking ethical
oxymoron: *for the sake of fully satisfying the flesh*. Those commandments and doctrines have a repute of wisdom, etc., *in
order to afford thereby full satisfaction to the material-psychical
human nature*. Thus, while the repute of wisdom is procured
among other things by *mortifying* the body, the *flesh is satisfied;*
the fleshly sinful lust of these men gets *fully satisfying
nourishment* conveyed to it, when they see that their doctrines
and commandments pass for wise. *What* lust of the flesh it
is which Paul has in view, is placed beyond doubt by the case
itself and also by ver. 18, namely, that of religious *conceit and
pride*, which through the λόγον σοφίας ἔχειν feels itself flattered

and gratified in the fancy of peculiar perfection. This interpretation, which we have given of οὐκ ἐν τιμῇ τινι, πρὸς πλησμονὴν
τῆς σαρκός, is held in substance, following Hilary (" sagina
carnalis sensus traditio humana est"), by Bengel, Storr, Flatt,
Böhmer, Steiger, Bähr, Huther, Dalmer, Bleek, and others. Most,
however, refer ἐν τιμῇ τινι to the honour to be shown to the
body (or the σάρξ, see Luther), and πρὸς πλησμ. τ. σαρκ. to
bodily satisfaction, so that the sense results: *not in some esteeming of the body to the satisfying of bodily wants ;* [1] " sentit
apost., sapientiam illam aut praecepta talia esse, per quae
corpori debitus honor, pertinens ad expletionem, *i.e.* justam
refectionem carnis, subtrahatur," Estius. So, in substance,
Chrysostom, Theodore of Mopsuestia, Theodoret, Oceumenius,
Theophylact, Pelagius, Erasmus, Luther, Melanchthon, Calvin,
Musculus, Clarius, Zeger, Erasmus Schmid, Zanchius, Vatablus,
Calovius, Cornelius a Lapide, Wolf, Michaelis, Nösselt, Rosenmüller, and others, including de Wette and Baumgarten-
Crusius. It is fatal to this view:—(1) that ἐν τιμῇ τινι, as
is shown by the repetition of ἐν, is the contrast not merely to
ἐν ἀφειδίᾳ σώματος, but to the entire connected ἐν ἐθελοθρησκείᾳ ... σώματος, and hence the reference to the honour to
be shown to the *body* does not seem justified by the context ; [2]
(2) further, that for the designation of the mere *satisfaction*
at this particular place, where Paul could only have had a
πρόνοιαν τῆς σαρκός in view, as in Rom. xiii. 14, the term
πλησμονήν would be very inappropriate, especially in contradistinction to the mortifications of the false teachers, since it
denotes *filling up, satisfying fully,* even in Ex. xvi. 3 (see
generally the passages from the LXX. and Apocrypha quoted
by Schleusner, *Thes.* IV. p. 375 f.); comp. Plat. *Legg.* viii.
p. 837: Xen. *Mem.* iii. 11. 14, *rep. Lac.* 2. 5, *Cyrop.* iv. 2. 40,
Ages. 5. 1 ; Lucian. *Nigr.* 33, *Ep. Saturn.* 28 ; Polyb. ii. 19. 4 ;
(3) finally, that the interchange of σώματος and σαρκός, in

---

[1] " God will have the body honoured, *i.e.* it is to have its food, clothing, etc.,
for its necessities, and not to be destroyed with intolerable fasting, labour, or
impossible chastity, as the doctrine of men would do," Luther's gloss.

[2] This applies also in opposition to Olshausen, who in the case of ἐν τιμῇ τινι
follows the explanation of respect for the *body*, but with regard to πρὸς πλησμ.
τ. σαρκ. follows *our* view.

the event of the latter not being meant in an ethical character, would seem to be without a motive, while, according to our view, σαρκός stands in as ingenious correlation with σώματος, as πλησμονήν with ἀφειδίᾳ. These arguments apply also in opposition to Ewald's view; " what seems very wise, but is *in no value whatever*, is rather quite useless *for the satisfaction of the flesh*, which yet also demands its rights, if man would not wantonly disorganize his earthly life or even destroy it" (2 Cor. x. 3). Hofmann finally takes πλησμονὴ τ. σαρκός rightly, but explains οὐκ ἐν τιμῇ τινι in such a way as to make τινι *masculine*, and to attach it as appropriating dative to τιμῇ: " *not so that honour accrues to any one.*" This is to be rejected, because Paul, instead of simply and clearly writing τιμῇ τινος, would only have expressed himself in a way singularly liable to be misunderstood by τινί, which every reader was led to join as a feminine with τιμῇ ("in honore aliquo," Vulgate). Nor is it to be easily seen *what subjects*, beyond the teacher of the false wisdom himself, we should have to conceive to ourselves under τινί taken as *masculine*.

CHAPTER III.

Ver. 4. Instead of ὑμῶν, which Griesb. approves, and Lachm. puts in the margin, but Tisch. 8 in the text, ἡμῶν is read by Elz. Scholz, and Tisch. 7, in opposition to C D* E* F P G ℵ min. Arm. Slav. ed. Vulg. It. and many Fathers (not Origen). A is defective here. Considering this weighty evidence in favour of ὑμῶν, and seeing that the following καὶ ὑμεῖς suggested the change of person to the copyists, as indeed the beginning of a lesson with ver. 4 could not but have favoured the insertion of the general ἡμῶν, we have stronger grounds for regarding ὑμῶν as original than as a repetition from ver. 3. — Ver. 5. ὑμῶν] is wanting, indeed, in B C* ℵ* min. Clem. Or. (five times) Eus., but has all the vss. in its favour ; hence the evidence against it is not sufficient to warrant its rejection, with Tisch. 8, as an inserted supplement. —δι᾽ ἅ] C* D* E F G Clar. Germ. read δι᾽ ὅ or διό. Rightly ; the *Recepta*, though strongly attested, is an alteration to correspond with the plurality of the preceding objects under comparison of Eph. v. 6. — ἐπὶ τοὺς υἱοὺς τ. ἀπειθείας] is wanting in B D* (?) Sahid. Aeth. Clem. Cypr. Ambrosiast., bracketed by Lachm. and omitted by Tisch. The evidence against it is too weak to justify its rejection, especially in the face of the agreement of the passage otherwise with Eph. v. 6, and of the incompleteness of the thought which would remain, in case those words were omitted; Reiche properly defends them. — Ver. 7. Instead of τούτοις Elz. and Scholz have αὐτοῖς, in opposition to decisive Codd., although defended by Reiche. — Ver. 11. Before ἐλεύθ. Lachm. inserts καί; considerably attested, it is true (not by B C ℵ), but nevertheless an addition which crept in easily in consequence of the first two clauses of the verse; nearly all the same authorities (not A) have it also before Σκύθης. — Ver. 12. Instead of οἰκτιρμοῦ Elz. has οἰκτιρμῶν, in opposition to decisive testimony. — Ver. 13. ὁ Χριστός] Lachm. reads ὁ κύριος, following A B D* F G 213, Vulg. It. Aug. (once) Pel. Rightly ; the *Recepta* is an interpretation, instead of which ὁ Θεός (ℵ) and *Deus in Christo* (Arm. Aug. once) are also found. — Ver. 14. ὅς] A B C F G P Vulg. It. Clem. Chrys. read ὅ, which

is approved by Griesb. and adopted by Lachm. and Tisch. ὅς
(א*) and the *Recepta* ἥτις (א**) are emendations. — Ver. 15.
Instead of τοῦ Χριστοῦ Elz. has τοῦ Θεοῦ, in opposition to decisive
evidence, from Phil. iv. 7. — Ver. 16. The καί before ὑμν. and
ᾠδαῖς should in both cases be omitted (Scholz omits only the
first), in accordance with preponderating evidence. Borrowed
from Eph. v. 19. — ἐν χάρ.] Lachm. and Tisch. : ἐν τῇ χάρ., which,
on the authority of B D* E* F G א** Clem. Chrys. Theodoret,
is to be preferred. The article was passed over as superfluous.
— Following far preponderant testimony (also א), we must read
subsequently with Lachm. and Tisch. 8 : ἐν ταῖς καρδίαις ὑμ. τῷ
Θεῷ, not : ἐν τῇ καρδίᾳ ὑμ. τῷ κυρίῳ (Elz. Reiche), or : ἐν τῇ καρδίᾳ
ὑμ. τ. Θεῷ (Tisch. 7). Comp. Eph. v. 19. — Ver. 17. κυρίου Ἰησοῦ]
Lachm. : Ἰησοῦ Χριστοῦ, which is to be adopted on the authority
of A C D* F G min. vss. and Fathers; א has κυρ. Ἰησοῦ Χρ. —
καὶ πατρί] καί is to be omitted, with Lachm. and Tisch., following
A B C א min. vss. and Fathers ; from Eph. v. 20. — Ver. 18.
After τοῖς Elz. reads ἰδίοις, in opposition to decisive evidence ;
from Eph. v. 22. — Ver. 19. After γυναῖκας Lachm. has ὑμῶν,
which, with considerable evidence in its favour, is the more
especially to be adopted, as in Eph. v. 25 ἑαυτῶν is found. The
omission easily occurred, because τοῖς ἀνδράσιν previously was
also without genitival definition. — Ver. 20. Instead of ἐν κυρίῳ
Elz. has τῷ κυρίῳ, which is to be regarded on decisive evidence
as an omission of the apparently superfluous ἐν. — Ver. 21.
ἐρεθίζετε] Lachm. and Scholz, as also Griesb., recommend : παρ-
οργίζετε, following, it is true, A C D* E* F G K L א (παροργίζεται)
min. Vulg. It. Theodoret, ms. Theoph. ; but it comes from Eph.
vi. 4. — Ver. 22. Elz. and Tisch. have ὀφθαλμοδουλείαις, which
Reiche approves. But ὀφθαλμοδουλείᾳ (recommended by Griesb.
and adopted by Lachm. and Scholz) is the reading in A B D E
F G min. Damasc. Theoph.; and Chrysostom also by κατ᾽ ὀφθαλμο-
δουλείαν testifies in favour of the singular. The singular is to be
preferred as preponderantly attested, and because the final
syllable AI (ᾳ) might very easily bring about the conversion
into the plural. If the singular had come in from Eph. vi. 6,
Chrysostom's reading, κατ᾽ ὀφθ., would be more frequent. — Instead of κύριον Elz. has Θεόν, contrary to decisive witnesses. — Ver.
23. καὶ πᾶν ὅ, τι ἐάν] The reading ὅ ἐάν, which Griesb. approves,
and Lachm. Scholz and Tisch. have adopted, is decisively
attested ; the *Recepta* is from ver. 17. — Ver. 24. τῷ γάρ] γάρ
has so decisive witnesses against it (also א), that, with Lachm.
and Tisch. (Griesb. also condemns it), it is to be deleted
as a current connective addition. — Ver. 25. ὁ δέ] ὁ γάρ is

decisively attested (also by ℵ); it is approved by Griesb., and adopted by Lachm. and Tisch. The antithetical δέ crept in from misunderstanding. — κομιεῖται] The form κομίσεται (Lachm.) is found in B D*** E K L ℵ** min. Fathers. To these may be added F G, which have κομίζεται. The *Recepta* must give way to the more strongly attested κομίσεται. Comp. on Eph. vi. 8.

CONTENTS.—The *generally hortatory* second portion of the Epistle, preceded in ii. 6 merely by a *special* exhortation against the danger of heresy, does not begin with ii. 6 (Hofmann), but only now, and seeks to promote in the readers *the essential moral direction* of the Christian life (vv. 1–4); after which they are encouraged to lay aside and abandon everything which is contrary to that direction (vv. 5–11), and to adopt and follow all that is good and edifying in a Christian sense (vv. 12–17). Then follow exhortations in reference to the various relations of the household (ver. 18–iv. 1).

Ver. 1 f. *Εἰ*] does not make the relation problematical any more than in ii. 20, but sets it forth as an undoubted fact (ii. 12), from which the subsequent duty results, in syllogistic form, as is frequently the case in Paul's writings (see Fritzsche, *ad Rom.* I. p. 325), and also in the classics (Hartung, *Partikell.* I. p. 259 f.; Kühner and Herbst, *ad Xen. Mem.* i. 5. 1). The being risen with Christ, namely, is not meant in the sense of the regenerate *moral life* (see on ii. 12), but as the relation of *real participation* in the resurrection of Christ, which involves as its ethical correlate the obligation τὰ ἄνω ζητεῖν. To be risen with Christ and not τὰ ἄνω ζητεῖν, would be a contradiction. — *οὖν*] *therefore*, points back to ver. 20, and with logical propriety, since fellowship in the *resurrection* of Christ is the necessary consequence[1] of fellow-

---

[1] It is therefore with all the less reason that Hitzig, p. 23 ff., would have vv. 1, 2 regarded as "*a portion of the reviser's work,*" at the same time denying the integrity of the text in ii. 22, 23, declaring ii. 19 to be an interpolation, and very arbitrarily remodelling ii. 17, 18. He thinks that the interpolation of iii. 1 f. betrays times subsequent to the destruction of Jerusalem, when earthly grounds of hope had vanished, but not extending beyond the period of Trajan, —which is assumed to result from iv. 17. Combinations such as these are

ship in *His death*,—a fact which Paul had in view also in ver.
21, in writing ὡς ζῶντες ἐν κόσμῳ.   The οὖν is not intended
to be *resumptive*, namely, of what was said in ii. 12 (Hofmann) ; otherwise what comes after that verse down to the
present one must have had the nature of a parenthesis, or a
digression. — τὰ ἄνω] the opposite to τὰ ἐπὶ τῆς γῆς : that
which is in heaven (comp. John viii. 23 ; Gal. iv. 26 ; Phil.
iii. 14), by which is indicated the *Messianic salvation* which,
with its future blessings (ii. 17), is preserved in heaven to be
manifested and communicated at the Parousia (vv. 3, 4).
Comp. Matt. vi. 33, and the conceptions of the treasure in
heaven (Matt. vi. 20), of the heavenly βραβεῖον (ii. 18 ;
Phil. iii. 14), πολίτευμα (Phil. iii. 20), Jerusalem (Gal. iv. 26).
It is substantially the same as δόξαν κ. τιμὴν κ. ἀφθαρσίαν
ζητεῖν in Rom. ii. 7.   As a philosophical analogy, comp.
especially the ἄνω ὁδός in the beautiful close of Plato's *Re-
public*, and the farewell of Socrates in the *Phaedo*.   A *liturgical
colouring*, which such expressions as τὰ ἄνω (also τὰ ἐν τοῖς
οὐρανοῖς κ.τ.λ. in i. 16, 20) are alleged to have (Holtzmann),
is arbitrarily assumed as a criterion of a later age. — οὗ ὁ X.
ἐστιν κ.τ.λ.] furnishing a motive encouraging them to perfect
the fellowship.   " Par est enim illuc tendere studia curasque
membrorum, ubi jam versatur caput," Erasmus.   The event
of the bodily *ascension* (but not a definite form of the process)
is here, as in every case where the exalted Christ is the subject of discourse, *presupposed*.   Comp. especially Phil. iii. 21 ;
1 Cor. xv. 48.   Notwithstanding the local οὗ, Hofmann thinks
that Paul has conceived the supramundane existence of Christ
not at all locally.   Comp., however, on Eph. i. 20 and Mark
xvi. 19 ; and see the frequent and significant ὅπου ἐγὼ ὑπάγω
and ὅπου εἰμὶ ἐγώ from the lips of Jesus in John. — Ver. 2.
τὰ ἄνω] repeated with emphasis, and then still further
strengthened by the negative contrast.   The φρονεῖτε is *more*

beyond the reach of criticism.   According to Holtzmann, vv. 2, 3 presuppose
the destruction of all hopes connected with the continuance of the theocracy,
and directly allude to Heb. xii. 22 ; even the "sitting at the right hand"
(as in Eph. i. 20) is withal, notwithstanding Rom. viii. 34, assailed.   Of
the entire chapter, Holtzmann only leaves vv. 3, 12, 13, 17 to stand as
original.

comprehensive than ζητεῖτε, expressing not only the striving (comp. Rom. ii. 7), but *the whole practical bent of thought and disposition* (comp. Beck, *bibl. Seelenl.* p. 62), the moral *meditari*, Phil. ii. 5. — τὰ ἐπὶ τ. γῆς] *e.g.* money and estate, honours, comforts, etc. Comp. Phil. iii. 19 : οἱ τὰ ἐπίγεια φρονοῦντες, also 1 John ii. 15, *et al.* Neither the contrast nor the subsequent text warrants us in finding here a further reference to the requirements of the false teachers. So Theophylact : τὰ περὶ βρωμάτων κ. ἡμέρων ; Calvin : " adhuc persequitur suam disputationem de ceremoniis, quae similes tricis facit, quae nos humi repere cogant ; " comp. Beza, Michaelis, and others. The hortatory portion of the Epistle proceeds no longer at all in the form of statements opposed to the false teachers, but in that of general moral exhortations.—We have to observe, further, that the earthly is not *of itself* placed under the point of view of the sinful, which would be quite un-Pauline (1 Cor. vi. 12, x. 23), but is so as the contents of the striving which is *opposed* to the τὰ ἄνω φρονεῖν. Comp. the idea in Matt. vi. 21.

Ver. 3. Assigning a reason for the requirement of ver. 2. — *For ye are dead ;* how then could your mind be directed towards earthly things ! *and your life* does not belong to the realm of the visible world, but it *is hidden with Christ in God :* how should you not then τὰ ἄνω φρονεῖν ! It is a guide to a correct and certain interpretation of the passage, that this statement of a reason must affirm the *same* thing as was already contained, only without special development, in εἰ συνηγέρθ. τ. Χ. of ver. 1. This *special exposition* Paul now gives. Whosoever is risen, namely, has *died* and *lives,* and *these* are the two points to which ver. 3 refers. — ἀπεθάνετε] namely, by your having entered into the fellowship of the death of Christ. This being dead has dissolved in the consciousness of the Christian the ties that hitherto bound him to earthly things. He *finds himself* still in the realm of the earthly, but he no longer *lives* therein, ii. 21. Comp. Phil. iii. 20 ; Gal. ii. 20. — ἡ ζωὴ ὑμῶν] must necessarily be *the* life, which has followed the being dead ; consequently the *eternal life,* comp. ver. 4, which set in through the resurrection (of which Christians, in fact, have become partakers with Christ, ver. 1)—a life which the believer has, prior to the Parousia, as a possession that has not yet been manifested but is still in secret (οὔπω ἐφανερώθη, 1 John iii. 2), a treasure in heaven, possessed in hope and still unrevealed, destined to appear in glorious manifestation only at the Parousia. — σὺν τῷ Χριστῷ] For Christ Himself, apart from fellowship with whose life the ζωή of His believers cannot have its being and essence, is *hidden* till the Parousia; and only then sets in His φανέρωσις (ver. 4), ἀποκάλυψις (1 Cor. i. 7 ; 2 Thess. i. 7 ; 1 Pet. i. 7, 13, iv. 13), ἐπιφάνεια (1 Thess. ii. 8 ; 1 Tim. vi. 14), with which also the ἀποκάλυψις τῶν υἱῶν τ. Θεοῦ (Rom. viii. 19) will take place, ver. 4.   Comp. 2 Tim. ii. 10 f.; 1 John iii. 2. — ἐν τῷ Θεῷ] *in God*, in so far, namely, as *Christ*, who, according to John (i. 18), is εἰς τὸν κόλπον τοῦ πατρός, remains hidden in God till the Parousia, as σύνθρονος of God (ver. 1), living united with God in His glory hitherto unseen, in order thereafter to proceed from God and to manifest Himself with the full divine glory.   But, as with Christ, so also with our *life*, which is hidden σὺν τῷ Χριστῷ, and therefore can only issue forth at His second coming from God, and be received by us in real glorious communication and manifestation through our συνδοξασθῆναι (Rom. viii. 17, comp. v. 2, 10).   If the *coherence* of the relation expressed by κέκρυπται was asserted by σὺν τῷ Χ., so also is its *inherence* by ἐν τῷ Θεῷ.   The *essential* part of our explanation, viz. that ἡ ζωὴ ἡμ. is *eternal life*, is held also by Chrysostom, Theodoret (ἐκείνου γὰρ ἀναστάντος πάντες ἠγέρθημεν, ἀλλ᾽ οὐδέπω ὁρῶμεν τῶν πραγμάτων τὴν ἔκβασιν), Oecumenius (τῶν γὰρ ἀληθῶς Χριστιανῶν ζωὴ ἔστιν μένουσα, ἡ μέν τοι πάρουσα εἰκόνα μᾶλλον θανάτου ἢ ζωῆς ἔχει), Theophylact (Paul wished to show αὐτοὺς καθημένους ἄνω καὶ ἄλλην ζῶντας ζωήν, τὴν ἐν τῷ Θεῷ, τὴν μὴ φαινομένην), Calvin, Beza, Erasmus Schmid, Grotius, and others, including Baumgarten-Crusius.   The accurate contextual connection of this view with what precedes, and with ver. 4 (see above), excludes the explanation adopted by many, of ζωή in the *ethical*, *spiritual* sense.   So Erasmus, Vatablus, Calovius, Bengel, Flatt ("the inner, new, blissful life of true Christians"), Bähr,

Böhmer, Steiger, Olshausen,[1] and others, including Huther,[2] Bleek, and de Wette, who apprehends this life as being hidden in two respects : namely, as regards the *disposition* and striving, it is, because directed to the heavenly, *internal and ideal*, whereas the life of worldly men in the common sense is *real* or *manifest;* as regards the *imputation* or *recompense,* it lacks outward happiness, but enjoys internal peace, and is therefore in this respect also *hidden* or *ideal,* whereas the worldly life, in unison with the outer world, leads to external peace or to happiness, and is so far, therefore, *real* or *mἀnifest* also ; the σὺν τῷ X. denotes not merely the spiritual fellowship, but is "at the same time to a certain extent" to be understood in a local sense (comp. ver. 1), and ἐν τῷ Θεῷ denotes the sphere of the Christian life, or "its relation to the system of the universe, that it belongs to the invisible world, where God Himself, lives." Of all this there is *nothing* in the words, the *historical* sense of which neither requires nor bears such a spiritualistic idealisation with more senses than one, but, on the contrary, *excludes* it as caprice. The ἡ ζωὴ ὑμῶν does not refer to the *ethical* life of Christians at all, neither alone nor along *with* eternal life (Cornelius a Lapide, Estius ; comp. Bleek and Ewald). On the contrary, it is aptly said by Kaeuffer, *de ζωῆς αἰων. not.* p. 93 : "vitam enim piam et honestam, quam homo Christianus in hac terra vivere possit ac debeat, P. dicere non poterat nunc cum Christo in Deo (in coelis putc. in quibus Christus nunc est) reconditam esse, atque olim in splendido Jesu reditu de coelo revelatum iri ; haec non nisi vitae *coelesti* conveniunt." Hofmann's distinction is less clear and definite : the ζωή is meant as the blessing, in which Christians have an advantage over the world, by their

---

[1] "The life of believers is said to be hidden, inasmuch as it is internal, and what is external does not harmonize with it ;" and in ἐν τῷ Θεῷ God is conceived as the element, "into whose essence believers, like Christ Himself, are assumed and enwrapped."

[2] In whose view the Christian leads a life in God, and this is a hidden life, because the world knows nothing about it (comp. Erasmus : "juxta judicium mundi"); in fact, to the Christian himself its full glory is not manifest (comp. Bengel) ; and by σὺν τῷ X. it is shown that the Christian leads such a life not of himself, but only in his fellowship with Christ. Dalmer gives an obscure and heterogeneous explanation.

having participated in the death and resurrection of Christ,—
a life, which is indeed life in the full sense of the word, but
which does not appear before the world as what it is, so long
as Christ is hidden from the world and in God. Notwithstanding, Hofmann properly rejects the explanations referring
it to the *holy* life of the Christian, and to the holy *and* blissful
life *together*. —— Observe, further, the difference in the *tenses*,
the *aorist* ἀπεθάνετε denoting the accomplished act of dying at
conversion, by which they entered into the fellowship of the
death of Christ ; and the *perfect* κέκρ., the continuous subsisting
relation in reference to the present up to the (near) Parousia.

Ver. 4. And what a blissful *future* is connected with the
ἡ ζωὴ ὑμῶν κεκρ. κ.τ.λ. ! This bright, favourable side of the
previous thought is the continuation of the proof of ver. 2
begun in ver. 3, detaching them thoroughly from earthly
pursuits and elevating them to the courage of victory ; vividly
introduced without connecting particle (καί) : " repentina luce
percellit," Bengel, which Hofmann fails to perceive, when he
objects to the absence of δέ. The relation is not antithetical at all. —— φανερωθῇ] *shall have become manifest*, have come
forth from His present concealment, namely, by His Parousia.
See on ver. 3.—— ἡ ζωὴ ὑμῶν] *your life.* Christ Himself is
thus designated (comp. ἡ ἐλπίς in i. 27), because He is the
personal author, possessor, and bearer of the eternal life of
His believers (comp. John xiv. 6, xi. 25), and this, according
to the context, inasmuch as they have entered into the fellowship of His resurrection : they are alive[1] *with Him* (σὺν τ.
Χ., ver. 3) ; *His* life is *their* life. The definite object of this
apposition, moreover, is *argumentative,* for the following τότε
κ.τ.λ. —— καὶ ὑμεῖς] as *Christ*, so *also ye* with Him. The two
subjects have the emphasis. —— φανερωθ. ἐν δόξῃ] Comp. συν-
δοξασθῶμεν in Rom. viii. 17. It means nothing else than the
glory of the Messianic kingdom, in which believers (also glorified
bodily, 1 Cor. xv. 43 ; 2 Cor. v. 1 ff. ; Phil. iii. 21) shall be
manifested visibly. The offence which Holtzmann takes at
the use of φανεροῦσθαι (instead of ἀποκαλύπτεσθαι, Rom. viii.

[1] Comp. Ignatius, *Eph.* 3, where Christ is designated τὸ ἀδιάκριτον ἡμῶν ζῆν,
also *Magnes.* 1, *Smyrn.* 4.

17 ff.) and ζωή, presupposes a too limited range for Paul's manipulation of language. Our passage has nothing to do with 2 Cor. iv. 10 f. Nor does it even "almost look" (Holtzmann) as if the author were conceiving the readers as already dead at the Parousia. The φανερωθῆναι ἐν δόξη takes place in the case of those still *alive* through their *being changed*, as the reader was aware.

Ver. 5.[1] Οὖν] draws the inference from vv. 3, 4, in order now to lead to that which must be done with a view to the carrying out of the μὴ τὰ ἐπὶ τ. γῆς. The inference itself is: "Since, according to vv. 3, 4, ye are dead, but have your life hidden with Christ in God and are destined to be glorified with Christ, it would be in contradiction of all this, according to which ye belong no longer to the earth but to the heavenly state of life, to permit your earthly members still to *live;* no, ye are to *put them to death*, to make them die" (Rom. iv. 19 ; Heb. xi. 12 ; Plut. *Mor.* p. 954 D) ! — νεκρώσατε] prefixed with emphasis as the point of the inference ; the term is *selected* in significant reference to ἀπεθάνετε and ἡ ζωὴ ὑμῶν, vv. 3, 4. — τὰ μέλη ὑμῶν] means nothing else, and is not to be explained otherwise than : *your members* (hand, foot, eye, etc.). That these were not to be put to death in the *physical* sense, but in an ethical respect (comp. ii. 11)—seeing, namely, that they, as the seat and organs of sinful lusts (Rom. vii. 23), which they still are even in the case of the regenerate (Gal. v. 17, 24), are to lose their vigour of life and activity through the Christian moral will governed by the Holy Spirit, and in so far to experience ethical deadening (comp. Rom. vii. 5, 23, viii. 13, and the analogous representation by Jesus as to plucking out the eye, etc., Matt. v. 29 f., xviii. 8 f. ; comp. also xix. 12)— was self-evident to the reader, as it was, moreover, placed beyond doubt by the following appositions πορνείαν κ.τ.λ. Hence there was neither ground nor warrant in the context to assume already here (see ver. 9) the conception of the *old man*, whose *desires* are regarded as members (Beza, Flacius,

---

[1] In the section vv. 5-17, in which Hönig, in relation to Eph. iv. 1-5, 20, finds the stamp of *originality*, Holtzmann discovers the concentrating labour of the *interpolator*, whose second (and better) effort is the passage in Colossians.

Calvin, Estius, Cornelius a Lapide, Calovius, and others, including Böhmer, Olshausen, and Bleek), although the required putting to death presupposes that the old man is still partially alive. Nor is *sin itself*, according to its totality, to be thought of as *body* and its individual parts as *members* (Hilary, Grotius, Bengel, Bähr, and others; comp. also Julius Müller, *v. d. Sünde*, I. p. 461, ed. 5, and Flatt),—a conception which does not obtain even in ii. 11 and Rom. vi. 6, and which is inadmissible here on account of ὑμῶν. The view of Steiger, finally, is erroneous (comp. Baumgarten-Crusius), that the entire *human existence* is conceived as σῶμα. We may add that the νέκρωσις of the members, etc., is not inconsistent with the death (ἀπεθάνετε, ver. 3) already accomplished through conversion to Christ, but is *required* by the latter as the necessary, ever new act of the corresponding morality, with which faith lives and works.[1] And in view of the ideal character of this obligation the command νεκρώσατε κ.τ.λ.—this requirement, which is ever repeating itself, of the *ethical mortificatio*—is never superfluous. — τὰ ἐπὶ τῆς γῆς] *which are upon the earth*, corresponds to the τὰ ἐπὶ τ. γ. in ver. 2 ; in contrast, not to the glorified human nature of Christ (Hofmann, *Schriftbeweis*, I. p. 560), but to *the life hidden with Christ in God*. In this antithetical addition is involved an element which *justifies* the requirement νεκρώσατε τ. μ. ὑμ., not expressing the *activity* of the μέλη for what is *sinful* (de Wette, comp. Flatt and others, in connection with which Grotius would even supply τὰ φρονοῦντα from ver. 2), which the simple words do not affirm, but : that the μέλη, as existing upon earth, have nothing in common with the life which exists in heaven, that their life is of another kind and must not be spared to the prejudice of that heavenly ζωή ! Comp. also Hofmann's present view. The context does not even yield a *contrast of heavenly members* (Huther), *i.e.* of a life of activity for what is heavenly pervading the members, or of the members of the new man (Julius Müller), since the ζωή is not to be understood in the sense of the *spiritual*,

---

[1] Chrysostom illustrates the relation by comparing the converted person to a cleansed and brightened statue, which, however, needs to be afterwards cleansed afresh from new accretions of rust and dirt.

ethical life. — πορνείαν κ.τ.λ.] Since Paul would not have the members slain as such absolutely and unreservedly, but only as regards their ethical side, namely, the sinful nature which dwells and works in them (Rom. vii. 23), he now s bjoins detailed instances of this sinful nature, and that with a bold but not readily misunderstood directness of expression *appositionally*, so that they appear as the *forms of immorality* cleaving to the members, *with respect* to which the very members are to be put to death. In these forms of immorality, which constitute no such heterogeneous apposition to τὰ μέλη ὑμ. as Holtzmann thinks, the life of the μέλη, which is to be put to death, is represented *by its parts*. Paul might have said: λέγω δὲ πορνείαν; but by annexing it directly, he gave to his expression the form of a distributive apposition (see Kühner, II. 1, p. 247), more terse and more compact after the σχῆμα καθ᾽ ὅλον καὶ μέρος. It is neither a sudden leap of thought nor a metonymy. — ἀκαθαρσ.] in reference to *lustful* uncleanness; comp. on Rom. i. 24; Gal. v. 19; 2 Cor. xii. 21; Eph. iv. 19, v. 3. Paul gives, namely, from πορν. to κακήν, *four* forms of the *first* Gentile fundamental vice, *unchastity*, beginning with the special (πορνείαν), and becoming more and more general as he proceeds. Hence follows: πάθος, *pas ion* (the ἡττᾶσθαι ὑπὸ τῆς ἡδονῆς, Plat. *Prot.* p. 352 A; D m. 805. 14; Arist. *Eth.* ii. 4), *heat;* Rom. i. 26; 1 Thess. iv. 5; and Lünemann *in loc.* Comp. also Plat. *Phaed.* p. 265 B: τὸ ἐρωτικὸν πάθος, *Phaedr.* p. 252 C. And finally: ἐπιθυμ. κακήν (Plat. *Legg.* ix. p. 854 A), *evil desire*, referring to unchaste longing. Comp. Matt. v. 28; Breitenbach, *ad Xen. Hier.* 6. 2. *Unnatural* unchastity (Rom. i. 26. f.; 1 Cor. vi. 9) is included in ἀκαθ., παθ., and ἐπιθ. κακ., but is not expressly denoted (Erasmus, Calovius, Heinrichs, Flatt, Böhmer) by πάθος (comp. *pathici*, Catullus, xvi. 2; παθικεύεσθαι, Nicarch. in *Anth.* xi. 73), a meaning which neither admits of linguistic proof, nor is, considering the general character of the adjoining terms (ἀκαθαρσ. ἐπιθ. κακ.), in keeping with the context. ἐπιθ. κακ. is to be *distinguished* from πάθος as the more general conception; the πάθος is always also ἐπιθυμία and relatively ἐπιθ. κακή, but not the converse, since a ἡγεῖσθαι or κρατεῖν τῆς ἐπιθυμίας may also take place. — κ. τὴν πλεονεξίαν] After the vice of uncleanness comes now the *second* chief vice of the Gentiles (comp. on Eph. iv. 19): *covetousness.* Hence the connection here by means of καί, which is not *even,* but (in opposition to Hofmann) the simple *and,* and the *article,* which introduces the *new* category with the description of its disgraceful character,[1] associating this descriptive character as a special stigma with the vice of πλεονεξία. In opposition to the erroneous interpretations : *insatiable lust* (Estius, Michaelis), or : *the gains of prostitution* (Storr, Flatt, Bähr), see on Eph. *l.c.,* and Huther. The πλεονεξία is not *separated* by the *article* from the appositional definitions of the μέλη, and *co-ordinated* with τὰ μέλη, so that the latter would only be "the members which minister to unchaste lust" (Huther) ; for τὰ μέλη ὑμ. can only denote the members generally, the collective members ; and ἐν τοῖς μέλεσιν (Rom. vii. 5, 23) understood generically, and not as referring to particular individual members, sin is operating with *all* its lusts, as, in accordance with this ethical mode of viewing the matter, the collective members form the σῶμα τῆς σαρκός of ii. 11. Bengel remarks aptly that the article indicates *totum genus vitii a genere commemoratarum modo specierum diversum.* — ἥτις ἐστὶν εἰδωλολατρ.] *quippe quae est,* etc., further supports the νεκρώσατε specially in reference to *this* vice, which, as the idolatry of money and possessions, is κατ᾽ ἐξοχήν of a *heathen* nature. It has been well said by Theodoret : ἐπειδὴ τὸ μαμωνᾶ κύριον ὁ σωτὴρ προσηγόρευσε, διδάσκων, ὡς ὁ τῷ πάθει τῆς πλεονεξίας δουλεύων ὡς Θεὸν τὸν πλοῦτον τιμᾶ. In 1 Cor. v. 11, the εἰδωλολατρ. is to be taken differently (in opposition to Holtzmann). Moreover, see on Eph. v. 5. Observe, further,

---

[1] Looking to the so closely marked *twofold division* of the vices adduced, it is inconsistent with the text to take, with Hofmann, the three elements, ἀκαθαρσ., πάθος, and ἐπιθυμ. κακ., in such a *general* sense as to make ἀκαθαρσία mean every "*action which mars the creaturely honour* (?) *of* man," πάθος, the passion *which enslaves through excitement of the blood,* and ἐπιθυμία κακή, *all evil desire, which is, as such, a morbid excitement of the blood.* The *excitement of the blood,* thus sanguinely enough invented without any hint whatever from the text, is then held to convert the second and third elements into cases in which one sins *against his own body,*—a characteristic point, which Paul has not in view at all in connection with the apposition to τὰ μέλη κ.τ.λ., as is plain from the appended κ. τ. πλεονεξ.αν belonging *to the same apposition.*

that the addition of the πλεονεξία to unchastity (comp. 1 Cor. v. 11) can afford no ground for supposing that the author of the Ephesians borrowed this combination from 1 Thess. ii. 3, and that it was taken into our present Epistle from that to the Ephesians (Holtzmann). Comp. also 1 Cor. vi. 9 f.

Ver. 6. This relative affirmation stands in a confirmatory reference to the νεκρώσατε κ.τ.λ. above, the omission of which would draw down upon the readers, instead of the φανερω-θῆναι ἐν δόξῃ of ver. 4, a fate such as is here described. — δι' ὅ (see the critical remarks) has the significant stress of the relative clause: *on account of this immorality mentioned in ver. 5.* The *Recepta* δι' ἅ is to be taken just in the same way, and not to be referred to the μέλη (Bähr), since it is not the latter themselves, but their life activities specified by πορνείαν κ.τ.λ., which call forth the wrath of God. — ἔρχεται] namely, at the judgment. Comp. Eph. v. 6; 1 Thess. i. 10: ἡ ὀργὴ ἡ ἐρχομένη; Matt. iii. 7: ἡ μέλλουσα ὀργή. Hence: ἡμέρα ὀργῆς in Rom. ii. 5; Rev. vi. 17. Chrysostom well says: Paul warns διὰ τῶν μελλόντων ἐξ ὧν ἀπηλλάγημεν κακῶν. See also on Eph. v. 6. The frequent reference to the manifestation of the divine wrath (comp. Rom. i. 18 ff.) *in the course of this temporal life* (Huther and many others) overlooks the correlation with ver. 4, and the apostle's conception of the *nearness* of the Parousia. Hence, also, the combination of the *two* references (Theophylact and others, also Flatt) is to be rejected. — Respecting the υἱοὺς τῆς ἀπειθ. (the Jews and Gentiles, who reject the gospel and thereby disobey God), comp. on Eph. v. 6, and as to this mode of expression generally, Steiger on 1 Pet. i. 14.

Ver. 7. Transition to the following exhortation; and how touching through the effect of the contrast! — ἐν οἷς] is, with the reading δι' ὅ in ver. 6, necessarily to be referred to the υἱοὺς τ. ἀπειθ.: *among whom ye also walked once,* by which is meant, not external association (which in fact was not cancelled by conversion, 1 Cor. v. 10), but the *fellowship of moral conduct.* But, even with the reading δι' ἅ in ver. 6, ἐν οἷς is to be taken (comp. Eph. ii. 2 f.) as *inter quos* (Vatablus, Rosen-müller, de Wette, Schenkel, Bleek), and not to be referred, as it commonly is (Chrysostom, however, seems to understand it

as masculine) to the vices named in ver. 5, because the relative most naturally attaches itself to what immediately precedes, in order to continue the discourse, and because, if ἐν οἷς
refer to the sins, then ἐζῆτε ἐν τούτοις once more asserts substantially the same thing, so that the discourse gains nothing
in thoughtfulness through the two verbs, as in Gal. v. 25,
but is unduly amplified.   The distinctions which in this
case have been attempted between περιπατεῖν and ζῆν still
make the one or the other appear as self - evident.   See
e.g. Calvin : vivere and ambulare are distinguished from each
other like *potentia* (comp. Grotius : " moveri ") and *actus*, the
former preceding and the latter following ; Beza (and Estius) :
vivere denotes *naturae habitum*, ambulare, ἐνέργειαν *ipsam* ;
Bähr (comp. Olshausen and Reiche) : the former refers more
to the disposition, the latter to the outward conduct ; Hofmann : the *state of life* (ἐζῆτε), with which *the conduct in
detail* (περιεπατ.) harmonized. — ὅτε ἐζῆτε ἐν τούτοις] ἐζῆτε
stands emphatically and pregnantly first : when ye *lived* in
these, *i.e.* when ye *were alive* therein, inasmuch as the ἀπεθάνετε
of ver. 3 had not yet set in in your case, the requirement of
the νεκροῦν in ver. 5 was still strange to you, and these disgraceful things formed the element and sphere of activity of
your *life*.   On ζῆν, *to be alive*, in contrast to the being dead,
comp. Rom. vii. 9 ; 2 Cor. xiii. 4 ; also Col. ii. 20 ; ἐν τούτοις[1]
is *neuter*, grouping together demonstratively, and setting forth
contemptuously, the states of vice spoken of.   According to
Flatt, Böhmer, and Huther, it is *masculine :* " then, *when ye
belonged to the children of disobedience*," so that ζῆν ἐν κόσμῳ
(ii. 20) and ἀναστρέφειν ἐν τῷ κόσμῳ (2 Cor. i. 11) would
have to be compared.   In opposition to this view it may be
urged that ὅτε ἐζῆτε ἐν τούτοις, in *this* sense, would be a very
meaningless and superfluous more precise designation of the
ποτέ, whereas, according to the view above adopted, it is
thoughtful and characteristic.[2] — On the change from the

---

[1] With the *Recepta* αὐτοῖς any other reference than that, which οἷς has, is
excluded ; hence the *origin* of αὐτοῖς.

[2] Hence not to be attributed, with Holtzmann, to the tautological style of the
author, in remembrance of 1 Cor. vi. 11.

merely historical *aorist* to the descriptive *imperf.ct*, lending a lively colour to the representation, and claiming the closer attention of the reader who had passed more rapidly over the περιεπατ., comp. Kühner, II. 1, p. 133, and Reisig, *ad Soph. O. C.* p. 254 f.

Ver. 8. Νυνὶ δέ] In contrast to the past, which has just been described : *but now*, when ye are no longer alive in those things. — καὶ ὑμεῖς] does not refer to the fact that the *Ephesians* also are thus exhorted (Eph. iv. 22, 25, 31), as Holtzmann here contrives critically to suggest; but as ϗαὶ ὑμ. in ver. 7 reminded the readers of the immoral pre-Christian society, which *they also* had formerly resembled, so *this* καὶ ὑμεῖς reminds them of the moral *Christian* society, which *they also* ought to resemble now. — τὰ πάντα] *the whole* of these, *i.e.* the things indicated by ἐν τούτοις without any exception ; ye shall retain *nothing* of them, " ne quid veneni resideat" (Grotius). To this τὰ πάντα the apostle then annexes directly and in rapid asyndetic *continuation* yet *other* sins, which are likewise to be left off. Bleek erroneously takes ὁ ϗγὴν κ.τ.λ. as in *apposition* to τὰ πάντα ; for the latter can only be retrospective (comp. Hofmann), and cannot, consistently with the text, be taken as meaning, " everything *that belongs to the old man.*" — ἀπόθεσθε] like garments (see on Eph. iv. 22); a lively change of figures ; the conception of members is laid aside. — θυμόν] distinguished from ὀργήν as the ebullition, the effervescing of the latter (Eustath. *ad Il.* i. p. 7. 17). See on Rom. ii. 8 ; comp. Eph. iv. 31 ; Rev. xvi. 19 ; Ecclus. xlviii. 10 ; 1 Macc. ii. 49 ; Hom. *Il.* ix. 629 ; Plat. *Phil.* p. 47 E : τοῖς θυμοῖς κ. ταῖς ὀργαῖς. — κακίαν] *wickedness, malicious nature.* Comp. on Rom. i. 29 ; Eph. iv. 31. — βλασφημίαν] *slander,* not against God, but against others, as oral outbreak of the evil dispositions mentioned. Comp. Eph. *l.c.* ; 1 Cor. iv. 13 ; Rom. iii. 8 ; Tit. iii. 2 ; frequently in classic writers ; in Dem. 312. 19 joined with συκοφαντία. — αἰσχρολογίαν] only used here in the N. T.: *shameful discourse,* which, in accordance with the category of all the sins here named, is not to be understood of *unchaste* discourse, as, following the Fathers (see Suicer, *Thes.* I. p. 136), it has commonly been taken (Hof-

mann: "obscene" discourse); comp. Epictet. *Enchir.* 33.
16; Xen. *de Lac. rep.* 5. 6; αἰσχρολογοῦντας in Plat. *Rep.*
p. 395 E; *Pollux,* iv. 105; and the passages in Wetstein;
also αἰσχροεπέω in Athen. xiii. p. 571 A; and respecting the
αἰσχρολογία ἐφ' ἱεροῖς, see Lobeck, *Aglaoph.* p. 689. Rather:
railing speech (Polyb. viii. 13. 8, xxxi. 10. 4), forming one
genus with βλασφημίαν, but a wider idea. Comp. αἰσχρὰ
ἔπεα, Hom. *Il.* iii. 38, xxiv. 238. *All* the elements in
ver. 8 specify the *malevolent and hostile disposition;* and the
two last, especially the *oral manifestation* thereof; hence the
addition of ἐκ τοῦ στόματος ὑμ., which, without arbitrariness,
cannot but be referred to *both* words (so also Bleek), not to
αἰσχρολ. alone, and is, with Grotius, to be conceived as depending on the still operative idea of ἀπόθεσθε, so that it
may not be characterized as a "secondary malformation"
(Holtzmann). The readers are *to lay aside,* generally, ὀργὴν,
θυμὸν, κακίαν; and to lay aside *from their mouth* βλασφημίαν, αἰσχρολογίαν. We are not to suppose any special
purpose in connection with the addition; it serves merely
for the concrete representation; but, if we should regard it as
the more precise definition of αἰσχρολ. (Hofmann), or should
even, as is often done, by supplying an ἐκπορευομένην, join
it with αἰσχρολογ., or with βλασφ. and αἰσχρολογ., it would
be utterly void of meaning. The special idea of *that which
defiles* (Chrysostom), or of the opposite of Christian *praise
to God* (Hofmann), does not form the basis of the ἐκ τ. στόμ.
ὑμ.; on the contrary, it is the conception in general of *what
is unsuited and foreign* (comp. on νυνὶ δέ) to Christian fellowship and intercourse, which serves as the presupposition for
the entire exhortation. Comp. Eph. iv. 29.

Ver. 9. Μὴ ψεύδεσθε εἰς ἀλλ.] *i.e. lie not one to another,* so
that εἰς expresses the *direction* of the ψεύδεσθαι (comp. ψ.
κατά τινος in the sense of the *hostile* direction, Plat. *Euthyd.*
p. 284 A, *al.;* Jas. iii. 14), like πρός in Xen. *Anab.* i. 3. 5;
Plat. *Legg.* xi. p. 917 A; Lev. vi. 2. It is different in
Susann. 55. 59. It connects itself with what precedes, and
hence it is to be separated only by a comma from ver. 8
(with Lachmann and Tischendorf); the following ἀπεκδυσά-

μενοι κ.τ.λ. adds a determining motive for the whole ἀπόθεσθε
. . . ἀλλήλους : *since ye have put off the old man . . . and put
on the new*, etc., with which the retaining of wrath, etc., and
the further lying (observe the *present* ψεύδ.) would not be
consistent ; on the contrary, this transformation which, in
principle, has taken place in and with the conversion to Christ,
must manifest itself practically by the laying aside of those
vices.   Accordingly, the *aorist* participles are not *synchronous*
with the foregoing (*exuentes*, etc., so Vulgate, Luther, Calovius,
and others, including Flatt, Olshausen, Huther, de Wette, Ewald,
and Bleek), but *precede* it ; they are not included in the
exhortation, for which reason 1 Pet. v. 6 f. is inappropriately
appealed to, but *assign a ground* for it.   This is clear, even in
a linguistic point of view, from the fact that ψεύδεσθε is the
present ; and also, as regards the sense, from the circumstance
that if the words be regarded as part of the exhortation itself,
as a definition of the mode of what is required, the *exuentes*
only, and not the *induentes*, would correspond with the requirement to lay aside and to abstain from lying.   Besides, ver. 11
is inappropriate as a constituent part of an exhortation, but
suits well as an argumentative enlargement.   Finally, the
assumed figurative exhortation only comes in expressly at
ver. 12, and that by way of inference (οὖν) from what had
been said previously from ἀπεκδυσάμ. onwards in the same
figure, though not yet in paraenetic form.   Without any
sufficient reason, and out of harmony with the simple paraenetic form of the entire context, Hofmann begins with ἀπεκδυσάμ. a new period, whose protasis ends in ver. 11, and
whose apodosis begins with οὖν in ver. 12 (comp. on Rom.
ii. 17 ff.) ; by this we gain only a more clumsy complica-
tion of the discourse, especially as the supposed apodosis
has again participial definitions.   The entire practical part
of the Epistle proceeds in plain sentences, not dialectically
joined together.   Comp., moreover, on ver. 12. — Respecting the *double compound* ἀπεκδυσ., comp. on ii. 11. — The
terminus ante quem for παλαιός is the adoption of Christianity, so that, by the whole expression ὁ παλαιὸς ἄνθρωπος
generically the collective *pre-Christian condition* in a moral

respect[1] is presented as personified.[2]   Comp. on Rom. vi. 6 ;
Eph. iv. 22. — σὺν ταῖς πράξεσιν αὐτοῦ] not generally : with
his *doing* (Hofmann), but in the bad sense : *along with his*
evil practices, with his bad tricks.   Comp. on Luke xxiii. 51
and Rom. viii. 13.

Ver. 10. The positive aspect of the transformation (regeneration) wrought by God through conversion to Christ ; *and since*
ye have put on, etc. — τὸν νέον] The collective new Christian-
ethical condition, conceived as personified and set forth *objec-*
tively, so that it appears as *becoming individually appropriated*
by the putting on.   It might, with equal propriety, be designated from the point of view of *time* as the *homo recens* in
contrast to the decayed and worn - out nature of the pre-
Christian moral condition (comp. the νέον φύραμα in 1 Cor.
v. 7), as from the point of view of the new, altogether different,
and previously non-existent *quality* as the homo *novus*.   It is
the former here,[3] the latter in Eph. iv. 23 (comp. also ii. 15),
where καινὸς ἄνθρ. is used.   See regarding the difference
between the two words, Tittmann, *Synon.* p. 59 ff.   The specification *of quality* is then further added by τὸν ἀνακαινούμ.
κ.τ.λ.   The notion of *not growing old* (Chrysostom, Oecumenius,
Theophylact, Erasmus) is not implied in νέον. — τὸν ἀνακαι-
νούμενον] The homo *recens, so far, namely, as the converted*
person has appropriated it as his moral individuality, is not
something ready-made and finished, but (comp. 2 Cor. iv. 16)
in a state of *development* (through the Holy Spirit, Rom. vii. 6,
viii. 2 ; Tit. iii. 5), by means of which there is produced in
him *a new character and quality specifically different from that*

---

[1] *Original sin* is not *denoted* by the expression and the conception to which it
is subservient (in opposition to Calvin : "veteris hominis nomine intelligi pra-
vitatem nobis ingenitam ;" comp. Calovius : "concupiscentiam pravam con-
genitam ") ; it is, however, according to the biblical view (Rom. vii. 14 ff.), its
presupposition and the regulative *agent* in the moral character of the old man.

[2] With the entrance of Christianity into the life of humanity, the old has
passed away, and all things have become new (2 Cor. v. 17).   But the old man
was *individually* put off *by the several subjects* through their own historical
conversion to Christ.   The Χριστὸν ἐνεδύσασθε of Gal. iii. 27 is not *in substance*
different from the having put on the new man.

[3] In the ethical sense Christians are, as it were, the νεολαία (Blomfield, *Gloss.*
Pers. 674) of humanity.

of the old man. Comp. Rom. xii. 2. Hence the *present* participle, which is neither to be taken as *imperfect* (B.-Crusius), nor as *renewing itself* (Bleek); and ἀνα does not refer to the relation of *re*-establishment,[1] namely, of the justitia originalis (since τοῦ κτίσαντος does not directly mean the *first* creation), but only to the *old* constitution, the transformation and new-moulding (*renewal*) of which forms the process of development of the νέος ἄνθρωπος. Comp. Winer, *de verb. c. praepos. compos.* p. 10 f. The καινότης of the νέος ἄνθρ. is *relative*. In Greek authors ἀνακαινόω is not found, but ἀνακαινίζω is (Isocr. *Areop.* 3, *App.* 2, p. 13; Plut. *Marcell.* 6), Heb. vi. 6; also in the LXX. — εἰς ἐπίγνωσιν] is to be taken along with the following κατ᾽ εἰκ. τ. κτίσ. αὐτόν, and with this expresses the *end* aimed at by the ἀνακαινοῦσθαι. Through the latter there is to be produced a *knowledge, which accords with the image of God.* Comp. Beza. God, as respects His *absolute* knowledge, *i.e.* a knowledge absolutely adequate to its objects, is the model, with which the *relative* knowledge of the regenerate to be attained in the course of their being renewed, *i.e.* their increasing penetration into divine truth, is to be accordant. And the more it is so—the more fully it has developed itself in accordance with the divine ideal—the more is it also the determining power and the living practical agent of the whole conduct, so that all those vices enumerated in ver. 8 are excluded by it, and even become morally impossible. Hofmann rightly takes κατ᾽ εἰκ. τοῦ κτίσ. αὐτόν as the more precise description of ἐπίγνωσιν, though defining the sense to this effect, that the new man "*everywhere looks to, and estimates everything by the consideration, whether he finds the stamp of this image.*" But, in that case, an object (πάντων) would

---

[1] "*Renovatus* autem dicitur novus ille homo, *quia novus quondam fuit in prima creatione,*" Calovius. Comp. Steiger, Huther, de Wette, Philippi, *Dogm.* II. p. 375 ff., ed. 2, and many others. Thus we should have for the νέος ἄνθρωπος, not the conception of a *nova* creatura (καινὴ κτίσις, 2 Cor. v. 17; Gal. vi. 15), but that of a *redintegrata* creatura. But it is to a *new* life that the believer is regenerated, raised up, etc. by God. This new creation is not the *redintegratio* of the first, though it is its *antitype*, as Christ Himself, so far as in Him the new creation is founded and begun (*how*, see Rom. v. 15, 17–19, vi. 1 ff.), is the antitype of Adam (Rom. v. 14; 1 Cor. xv. 45). Consequently this passage is only *indirectly* probative for the doctrine of the image of God as innate.

COL. 2 E

necessarily stand with ἐπίγνωσιν, and the idea of ἀνακρίνειν or δοκιμάζειν would be substituted for that of ἐπίγνωσις. The κατ᾽ εἰκόνα κ.τ.λ. is usually connected with ἀνακαινούμ. and εἰς ἐπίγν. taken by itself, in connection with which Steiger, Huther, de Wette, and Bleek (comp. also Ewald) arbitrarily adopt the view, that the prominent mention of the knowledge was occasioned by a polemic opposition to the false teachers and their tendencies to false *gnosis*. But how abrupt, isolated, and indefinite would the εἰς ἐπίγν. thus stand! No; the subsequent κατ᾽ εἰκόνα κ.τ.λ. just serves as a more precise characteristic definition for the—in theory and practice so extremely important—point of Christian knowledge. The expression of this definition *in this particular way* comes very naturally to Paul, because he is speaking of the homo *recens creatus*, in connection with which, after the analogy of the creation of Adam, the idea of the image of God naturally floated before his mind, —the image which that first-created man *had*, and which the *recens creatus* is *to attain and present* by way of copy in that towards which he is being developed, in the ἐπίγνωσις. This development is only completed in the αἰὼν μέλλων, 1 Cor. xiii. 12; for its aim *before* the Parousia, see Eph. iv. 13 f. — τοῦ κτίσαντος αὐτόν] A description of *God*, harmonizing with the conception of the νέος ἄνθρωπος, who is God's *creature*. Comp. on Eph. iv. 24. It is erroneous, with Chrysostom, Theophylact, Ewald, and others, to understand *Christ*[1] as referred to; for *creating* is invariably represented in Scripture as the work *of God* (even in i. 16), and especially here where a parallel is instituted with the creation of Adam after God's image. Comp. Eph. ii. 10, iv. 24. Olshausen, indeed, understands τοῦ κτίσ. αὐτ. to mean God, but would have the *image* of God, in accordance with i. 15, taken of *Christ*, who is the archetype of man. There is no ground for this view in the context, which, on the contrary, reminds us simply of Gen. i. 27; comp. κατὰ Θεόν, in Eph. iv. 24, a simpler expression, which has found here a significant more precise definition out of the riches of the apostle's store of ideas (not a fanciful

[1] So also Julius Müller, *v. d. Sünde*, II. p. 496, ed. 5; see, on the other hand, Ernesti, *Urspr. der Sünde*, II. p. 133 ff.

variation, as Holtzmann thinks) in vivid reproduction. —
αὐτόν] must refer to the νέος ἄνθρωπος, whom God has created
by regeneration, not to τ. ἄνθρωπον alone (" which is the
substance, on which the *old* and *new* qualities appear as acci-
dents," de Wette), as the orthodox explanation is forced to
assume contrary to the text; see *e.g.* Calovius : " Per imaginem
ejus, qui creavit ipsum, imago Dei, quae in *prima creatione*
nobis concessa vel concreata est, intelligitur, ad quam nos
renovamur, quaeque in nobis *reparatur* per Spiritum sanctum,
quae ratione intellectus consistebat in cognitione Dei, ut
ratione voluntatis in justitia et sanctitate, Eph. iv. 24. Per
verbum itaque τοῦ κτίσαντος non nova creatio, sed *vetus illa
et primaeva* intelligitur, quia in Adamo conditi omnes sumus ad
imaginem Dei in cognitione Dei." Rather, the divine creation
of the *new* man had that *primaevam creationem* for its sacred-
historical type, and is the work of salvation antitypically corresponding with it, which the Creator has done in Christ ;
hence also Paul has not written κτίζοντος (as Philippi, *l.c.*
p. 376, thinks might have been expected), but κτίσαντος,
comp. iv. 24, ii. 10 ; 2 Cor. v. 17 ; also Jas. i. 18.

Ver. 11. *Where all the separating diversities have ceased,* by
which those phenomena of malevolence and passion mentioned
in ver. 8 were occasioned and nourished. Comp. Gal. iii. 28,
of which passage Baur indeed sees here only an extended and
climactic *imitation.* — ὅπου] *where* there is not, etc. ; namely
there, where the old man has been put off, and the νέος κ.τ.λ.
put on, ver. 10. It represents the existing *relation* according
to *local* conception, like the Latin *ubi*, i.e. *qua in re*, or *in quo
rerum statu*, like the local ἵνα ; comp. Kühner, *ad Xen. Mem.*
iii. 5. 1 ; Ellendt, *Lex. Soph.* II. p. 331 f. The relation is
one *objectively real, historically* occurring (comp. Gal. iii. 28 ;
Rom. x. 12 ; 1 Cor. xii. 13), present in renewed humanity.
Consequently ὅπου is not to be referred to the ἐπίγνωσις, and
to be interpreted *within which, i.e.* in the *Christian consciousness* (Schenkel) ; but just as little is the relative clause to be
joined immediately with εἰς ἐπίγνωσιν κατ᾽ εἰκόνα κ.τ.λ. so
that it affirms that *there, where this image is found,* all
contrasts. etc., have vanished ; so Hofmann in connection with

his erroneous explanation of εἰς ἐπίγνωσιν κατ᾽ εἰκόνα κ.τ.λ.,
see on ver. 10. — Respecting ἔνι, equivalent to ἔνεστι, see on
Gal. iii. 28. — ῞Ελλην κ. ᾽Ιουδ.] *national* diversity, without
taking ῞Ελλην, however, with Chrysostom, Theophylact, and
others, in the sense of *proselyte*. — περιτ. κ. ἀκροβ.] *theocratic*
diversity.[1] — βάρβαρος κ.τ.λ.] In the increasing vividness of
conception the arrangement by *pairs* is dropped, and the
nouns are placed beside each other asyndetically.   Paul does
not couple with βάρβαρος, as he does again in the case of
δοῦλος, *its opposite*, which was already adduced (῞Ελλην, comp.
on Rom. i. 14), but proceeds by way of a *climax*: Σκύθης.
Bengel (comp. Grotius) well says : "Scythae . . . barbaris
barbariores ; " they were *included*, however, among the bar-
barians (in opposition to Bengel, who thinks that the latter
term indicates the *Numidians*).   For instances in which the
Scythians are termed βαρβαρώτατοι (comp. also 2 Macc. iv.
47 ; 3 Macc. vii. 5), see Wetstein.   We may infer, moreover,
from the passage, that among the *Christians* there were even
some *Scythians*, possibly immigrants into Greek and Roman
countries. — ἀλλὰ τὰ πάντα . . . Χριστός] the dividing circumstances named, which, previous to the putting on of the νέος
ἄνθρωπος, were so influential and regulative of social interests
and conduct, have now—a fact, which was beyond doubt not
recognised by the Jewish prejudice of the false teachers —
since the Christian renovation (comp. 2 Cor. v. 17) ceased
to exist in the fellowship established by the latter (ideal
expression of the thought: their morally separating influence
is abolished) ; *whereas Christ is the sum total of all desires
and strivings, and that in all individuals*, without distinction
of nations, etc. ; He "solus proram et puppim, ut aiunt,
principium et finem tenet " (Calvin).   All are one in Christ,

---

[1] For even a ῞Ελλην might be circumcised and thereby received into the
theocracy. — The fact that ῞Ελλην stands *before* ᾽Ιουδ. (it is otherwise in Gal.
iii. 28 ; 1 Cor. xii. 13 ; Rom. x. 12, *et al.*) ought not to be urged, with
Holtzmann, following Baur and Hökstra, against the originality of the passage.
Paul does not arrange the designations mechanically, as is evident from the
second clause.   Holtzmann, however, justly denies, in opposition to Mayerhoff
and Hökstra, that the arrangement is so inserted in antagonism to the Jewish
people.

Gal. iii. 28, v. 15; Rom. x. 12; 1 Cor. xii. 13; Eph. ii. 14. Comp. on this use of the τὰ πάντα in the sense of *persons*, who *pass for everything*, 1 Cor. xv. 28; Herod. iii. 157, vii. 156; Thuc. viii. 95. 1; Dem. 660. 7; Hermann, *ad Viger.* p. 727. — Χριστός] the subject put at the end with great emphasis. *He*, in all His believers (ἐν πᾶσι) the all-determining principle of the new life and activity, is also the constituent of the new sublime unity, in which those old distinctions and contrasts have become meaningless and as it were no longer exist. The Hellene is no longer other than the Jew, etc., but in all it is only Christ, who gives the same specific character to their being and life.

Ver. 12. Οὖν] for these virtues are in keeping with the νέος ἄνθρωπος, according to what has been said in ver. 11; it would be a contradiction to have put on the new man, and *not* to have put on these virtues. The *new moral condition*, into which ye have entered by your conversion, passing thereby into the *fellowship of equality and unity* in Christ described in ver. 11, *binds* you to this by the necessity of *moral consistency*. The οὖν therefore serves for the introduction of the direct summons *by way of inference* from its foregoing premises, just like the οὖν in ver. 5, but not for the introduction of the apodosis (Hofmann; see on ver. 9), as if it were *resumptive*. — ἐνδύσασθε] for, although the putting on of the νέος ἄνθρ. *has taken place* as a fact historically through the conversion to Christ, nevertheless it has also, in accordance with the ethical nature of the νέος ἄνθρ. (comp. τὸν ἀνακαινούμενον κ.τ.λ. in ver. 10), its *continued* acts, which *are to* take place, namely, by appropriation of the virtues which the new man as such must have. — ὡς ἐκλεκτοὶ κ.τ.λ.] as it becomes such; ἐκλ. τ. Θεοῦ is the *subject*, and ἅγ. κ. ἀγαπ. its *predicates*. The consciousness of this distinguished bliss, of being the *elect of God*—chosen by God from profane humanity for eternal Messianic salvation (Eph. i. 4; Rom. viii. 33; Tit. i. 2, *al.*), who as such[1] are *holy* (through the ἁγιασμὸς πνεύματος, 2 Thess. ii. 13), and *beloved* of God (Rom. v. 5; Eph. i. 6),—

---

[1] For the act of the divine ἐκλογή, which in itself is before time, has come into temporal realization and manifestation through the calling (comp. ver. 15).

how could it fail to touch the consciences of the readers, and incite them to the very virtues, corresponding to so high a position, — virtues of that fellowship described in ver. 11, which are required from them as renewed men! Observe, moreover, that the ἐκλογὴ τ. Θεοῦ is the presupposition of what is said by ἀπεκδυσάμενοι κ.τ.λ. in vv. 10, 11, and that therefore ὡς ἐκλεκτοὶ κ.τ.λ. is not inserted without significant connection with what goes before. It is likewise admissible to take the words ἅγιοι κ. ἠγαπ. *substantively*, either as *co-ordinate* with the ἐκλεκτοὶ τ. Θ. and *explanatory* of this idea ("as the elect of God, holy and beloved," Luther, Calvin, Grotius, and the majority, including Bähr, Böhmer, Huther, de Wette, Hofmann), or so that ἐκλεκτ. τ. Θεοῦ stands in adjectival relation to them (Bleek: "elect holy and beloved ones of God"); but it is more in keeping with the purposely chosen order of the words to concentrate the whole stress on ἐκλεκτοὶ Θεοῦ. Bengel, connecting as we do, aptly observes: "Ordo verborum exquisite respondet ordini rerum: electio aeterna praecedit sanctificationem in tempore; sanctificati sentiunt amorem et deinceps imitantur." Theophylact (comp. also Steiger) took ἅγιοι as the chief word, which is more precisely defined by ἐκλ. τ. Θεοῦ and ἠγαπ. (ἐγένοντο μὲν γὰρ ἅγιοι, ἀλλ' οὐκ ἐκλεκτοὶ οὐδὲ ἠγαπημένοι· ὑμεῖς δὲ ταῦτα πάντα). Neither supported by the position of the words nor by the context, which does not suggest any contrast. — σπλάγχνα οἰκτιρμοῦ] οἰκτ. is the genitive of *quality*, and the expression is quite similar to that in Luke i. 78, σπλάγχνα ἐλέους; see *in loc.* Hence σπλάγχνα is not to be taken here in the abstract sense (*love*, so usually), but in its proper sense: *viscera*, as the *seat* of sympathy; consequently: a heart, the moving feeling of which is sympathy. Comp. Ewald and Hofmann. The two are separated in Phil. ii. 1. As to the conception of οἰκτιρμ., comp. on Rom. ix. 15 — χρηστότητα] *kindliness*, the opposite is ἀποτομία, Rom. xi. 22. Comp. Eph. iv. 32. See generally, Tittmann, *Synon.* p. 140 ff. — ταπεινοφρ., *humbleness*, which is meant here, however, according

Comp. generally, Weiss in the *Jahrb. f. Deutsche Theol.* 1857, p. 78 ff., and *Bibl. Theol.* § 88, ed. 2.

to the entire context, not towards *God* (Böhmer), but (see ver. 11) in relation to *others*, as the opposite of haughtiness (ὑψηλοφρονεῖν); Eph. iv. 2; Phil. ii. 3. — On πραοτ., *gentleness* (opposite: Eph. iv. 31, and ἀγριότης, Plat. *Conv.* p. 197 D), and μακροθ., *long-suffering*, bearing with immoral opposition (comp. Eph. iv. 2, and on Gal. v. 22), ver. 13 throws fuller light.

Ver. 13. Neither the second part of the verse, καθὼς ... ὑμεῖς, nor ἀνεχόμενοι ... μομφήν, is to be parenthesized; for the whole is an uninterrupted continuation of the construction. — ἀνεχόμ. ἀλλ.] modal definition of the ἐνδύσασθαι *of the last two* virtues, informing us how the required appropriation of them is *to manifest itself in active conduct: so that ye*, etc. This conduct is conceived as developing itself in and with the completion of the required ἐνδύσασθε; hence ἀνεχόμενοι ἀλλήλ. is not to be regarded as only " *loosely appended* " (Hofmann) to μακροθ. — καὶ χαριζόμενοι κ.τ.λ.] for the endurance (comp. Eph. iv. 2) is to advance to positive *forgiveness*, and not to remain a mere passive attitude. Observe here the alternation of ἀλλήλων (*one the other*) and ἑαυτοῖς (*yourselves each other*); the latter is used, because to the χαρίζεσθαι of the *Christians*, which they are to show *to themselves* mutually, there is proposed as pattern *the* χαρίζεσθαι which they have experienced from above, from *Christ*. Comp. Kühner, *ad Xen. Mem.* ii. 6. 20. — μομφήν] *blame, reproach*, only here in the N. T., not found at all in the Apocrypha and LXX., but very common in the classics, especially the poets, also with ἔχειν, to find fault with something, Eur. *Phoen.* 780, *Alc.* 1012, *Or.* 1069 ; Soph. *Aj.* 179, and Schneidewin *in loc.* ; Pind. *Isthm.* iv. 61. — καθὼς καὶ κ.τ.λ.] The duty of the χαρίζεσθαι ἑαυτ. is so essentially Christian and important, that Paul goes on further to hold up before the readers the great motive and incitement for its fulfilment, namely, the forgiveness which they themselves have experienced, which *Christ* (ὁ κύριος, see the critical remarks) has bestowed upon them. Comp. Eph. iv. 32, where, however, the *principal* subject of the χαρίζεσθαι is indicated, namely, *God* (comp. ii. 13), who has pardoned *in Christ*. To the expression in our passage—and a consideration of the

circumstances of the Colossian church naturally prompted the
emphasizing of the merit *of Christ*—corresponds the frequent
ἡ χάρις τοῦ κυρίου ἡμῶν, Rom. xvi. 20, 24 ; 1 Cor. xvi. 23 ;
2 Cor. viii. 9, xii. 9, xiii. 13 ; Gal. i. 6, vi. 18 ; Phil. iv. 23.
There is no trace here of " an advanced Christology " (Holtzmann).   The *divine* pardon obtained *for* us by Christ in His
work of atonement (Rom. v. 6 f., 15), and continuously procured through His intercession (Rom. viii. 34), is in so far *His*
(in the sense that *He* is the pardoning subject) as He is the
procurer, bearer, and accomplisher of the divine grace (Eph. ii.
16 ; Col. i. 19 f.), and *God's* love is *His* love (Rom. viii. 35,
39 ; Eph. iii. 19 ; Rom. v. 7 f.).   The pardon received from
Christ, however, binds us by moral necessity (Matt. xviii. 33 ;
and generally, Rom. viii. 9) to forgive also upon our side ;
—anything beyond this, namely, what is contained in Matt.
vi. 12, as de Wette thinks, is not conveyed in the words, but
results as a consequence. — καὶ ὑμεῖς] *sc.* χαριζόμενοι.   The
context suggests this, and not the imperative ; hence the
orderly connection is not broken, and the whole verse contains
accompanying participial definitions, after which, in ver. 14,
the discourse continues uninterrupted. — Respecting the
double καί of the comparison, see on Rom. i. 13. — It is to be
observed, moreover, that καθώς refers only to the *pardon itself*,
and does not concern the service *by which* Christ has procured the pardon, the death, namely, which the Christian
ought to be ready to undergo for the brethren, John xiii. 34,
as Chrysostom, Theophylact, and others think, but which would
be *here* an irrelevant *importation*.

Ver. 14. *In addition to all this, however,* put on *love, by
which Christian perfection is knit.*   In making τ. ἀγάπην
dependent on ἐνδύσασθε, Paul abides by his figure : becoming
added (Kühner, II. 1, p. 433) to all those virtues (regarded
as garments), love is to be put on like an upper garment
embracing all, because love brings it about, that the moral
perfection is established in its organic unity as an integral
whole.   Thus love is the *bond* of Christian perfection, its
συνδετικὸν ὄργανον ; without love, all the individual virtues,
which belong in themselves to that perfection, would not unite

together into that necessary harmonious entirety, in which
perfection consists.   Not as if the latter were already *existent
without* love (as Schenkel objects to this view), but love is the
σύνδεσμος *constituting* its perfection ; *apart from* love *there is* no
τελειότης, which has its conditio *sine qua non* only in the in-
clusion of its other factors in love ; *how* love accomplishes this,
no one has better shown than Paul himself in 1 Cor. xiii.[1]   Nor
is it as if the genitive would necessarily be a *plurality* (as Hofmann objects) ; on the contrary, the τελειότης according to its
nature and to the context is a *collective* idea, with which the
conception of a σύνδεσμος well corresponds.   It might, moreover, occasion surprise, that *love*, which is withal the principle
and presupposition of the virtues enumerated, is mentioned *last*,
and described as *being added* ; but this was rendered necessary
by the *figurative* representation, because love, from its nature,
in so far as it *includes in principle* the collective virtues and
comprehends them in itself, necessarily had assigned to it in the
figure of putting on garments the place of the *upper garment*,
so that Paul rightly proceeds in his description from the under
garments to the upper one which holds all the others together,
and with whose function love corresponds.   Accordingly the
absolute ἡ ἀγάπη is not to be taken in any other sense than
the general and habitual one of *Christian brotherly love* (i. 8, ii.
2 ; 1 Cor. xiii. ; Phil. i. 9) ; nor yet in any sort of reference
limiting it to special qualities, *e.g.* as by de Wette : " as active,
beneficent, perfecting love." — ὅ (see the critical remarks),
which, namely love, conceived of as *neuter*, as in our "*that is.*"
Comp. on ἐξ οὗ, ii. 19. — σύνδεσμος τῆς τελειότ.] *bond of perfection, i.e.* what binds together the Christian moral perfection
into the totality of its nature, συνδεσμεύει, Polyb. iii. 42. 8 ;
ξυνδεῖ καὶ ξυμπλέκει, Plat. *Polit.* p. 309 B.   Chrysostom
(though mingling with it the foreign figure of the *root*) aptly
says : συγκράτησις τῶν τὴν τελειότητα ποιούντων.   Comp.
Theophylact : πάντα ἐκεῖνά, φησιν, αὕτη συσφίγγει παροῦσα·
ἀπούσης δὲ διαλύονται καὶ ἐλέγχονται ὑπόκρισις ὄντα καὶ οὐδέν.
The genitive, which is that of the *object*, denotes (it is otherwise
in Eph. iv. 3 ; comp. Acts viii. 23 ; LXX. Isa. lviii. 6) that

---

[1] Comp. Clem. *Cor.* I. 49 f.

which is held together by the bond.   Comp. Plat. *Rep.*
p. 616 C : εἶναι γὰρ τοῦτο τὸ φῶς ξύνδεσμον τοῦ οὐρανοῦ ...
πᾶσαν ξυνέχον τὴν περιφοράν, also p. 520 A : τὸν ξύνδεσμον
τῆς πόλεως, *Polit.* p. 310 A : τὸν ξύνδεσμον ἀρετῆς μερῶν
φύσεως ἀνομοίων.   Taken as the genitive of *quality*, it would
yield the *adjective* sense : *the perfect bond,* "animos sc. con-
jungens," Grotius.   So also Erasmus, Vatablus, Calovius,
Estius, Wolf, Michaelis, Rosenmüller, Flatt, and others.   But
how arbitrary this would be in itself, and especially in view of
the fact that, in the event of τ. τελειότ. being disposed of as an
adjective, the more precise definition of σύνδεσμος would have
to be *gratuitously introduced !*   Taken as the genitivus *causae*
(Schenkel), it would not correspond with the *figure,* though it
is *in substance* correct that that, which as a bond envelopes perfection, only thereby brings about its existence (comp. above).
According to Huther, the sense is : " by man's putting on love
he is girt with perfection ; whosoever lives in love is perfect."
Thus the genitive would have to be conceived as genitive of
apposition, which would yield an incongruous analysis of the
figure, induced by the opinion that ὅ does not refer to the ἀγάπη
itself, but to the ἐνδύσασθαι τὴν ἀγάπην.[1]   According to
Hofmann (comp. Ellicott), the genitive is meant to be that of
the *subject,* and the τελειότης is to indicate the completeness
of the *Christian state,* of which love is the bond, *inasmuch as*
it binds *Christians together among themselves, wherever that
completeness exists* (John xiii. 35).   This is erroneous ; for if in
some curious fashion the abstract ἡ τελειότης (consequently an
aggregate of attributes) were to be the acting subject, which
makes use of love as a bond (consequently for the purpose of
binding), yet *the Christians among themselves* could not be
conceived as the object of that binding, but only the πάντα
ταῦτα in accordance with the immediate context (ἐπὶ πᾶσι δὲ

---

[1] σύνδεσμος, namely, would apply to the *girdle,* as Clericus, Ewald, and
Schenkel make it do.   But to that view the ἐνδύσασθε to be supplied would be
contextually less suitable (comp. Eph. vi. 14) ; while after what has gone before
the reader would most naturally think of love simply as a *garment,* and not as
the *girdle,* "which holds together all individual efforts towards perfection"
(Ewald).   Besides, it would not at all be easy to see why Paul should not have
used the definite word ζώνη instead of σύνδεσμος.

τούτοις). The apostle would have been able to express the tenor of thought forced upon him by Hofmann simply and clearly by some such phrase as ὅ (or ὅς, or ἥτις) ἐστι σύνδεσμος τῶν ἐν Χριστῷ τελείων (comp. i. 28). Others take it as the *sum* of perfection. So Bengel, Zachariae, Usteri, Böhmer, Steiger, de Wette, Olshausen (" inasmuch as it comprehends in itself —bears, as it were, bound up in itself—all the individual aspects of the perfect life, all virtues"). Comp. on the subject-matter, Rom. xiii. 10. This explanation cannot be justified linguistically (not even by Simplic. *Epictet.* p. 208, according to which the Pythagoreans termed friendship : σύνδεσμον πασῶν τῶν ἀρετῶν, *i.e.* the bond which knits all the virtues together), unless we take σύνδεσμος in the sense of a *bundle*, as Herodian uses it, iv. 12. 11 (πάντα τὸν σύνδεσμον τῶν ἐπιστολῶν), which, however, even apart from the singular form of the conception in itself, would be unsuitable to the context, since love is to be *added* to all the previously enumerated elements of perfection, and may therefore well be termed the *bond* that holds them together, but not their *bundle*, not the *sum* of them. The word σύνδεσμος itself, which except in our two parallel epistles does not occur in Paul's writings, is too hastily assigned by Holtzmann "*to the range of language of the Auctor ad Ephesios.*" As if we had the whole linguistic range of the copious apostle in the few epistles which bear his name ! Indeed, even ἐπὶ πᾶσι δὲ τούτοις (comp. Eph. vi. 16) is alleged to betray the *auctor* in question. — In opposition to the Catholic use of our passage to support the *justificatio operum*, it is enough to observe that the entire exhortation has justification as its *presupposition* (ver. 12), and concerns the moral life *of those who are already justified.* Irrelevantly, however, it is urged in the *Apol. Conf. Aug.* 3, p. 104 f. (comp. Calovius and others), in opposition to the Catholics, that τελειότης is the *integritas ecclesiae,* and that through love the church *is kept in harmony,* as Erasmus, Melanchthon, and others also explained it.

Ver. 15. All these virtues, however, along with the love which binds them together, must have their deep living foundation in the *peace of Christ,* which reigns in the heart, and their abiding incitement in *gratitude* towards God for the salvation received in Christ. Hence now the further summons —appended by the simple καί—to the readers, to let that *peace* reign in their hearts and to be *thankful.* The εἰρήνη τοῦ Χριστοῦ is the holy *satisfaction of mind wrought by Christ* through the Spirit, the blessed inner rest, of which the atonement and justification appropriated in faith (Rom. v. 1) are the presupposition and condition. See on Phil. iv. 7. Comp. Luther, Bengel, and others, including Flatt, Bähr, Olshausen, Huther, de Wette, Baumgarten-Crusius, Ewald, Bleek, Hofmann. To understand the peace of mutual *concord* (the Greek Fathers, Erasmus, Calvin, Grotius, Calovius, and many others, also Reiche, *Comm. Crit.* p. 297), is less in accordance with the universality of the connection, which here descends to the deepest ground of the Christian life in the heart ; and besides, the concord in question already *follows of itself* on the virtues recommended. Moreover, there is implied in βραβ. the determining and regulating power, the *supreme authority,* which the peace of Christ is to have in the Christian heart, which suits most fully the above interpretation alone. — βραβενέτω] βραβεύειν only found here in the N. T., but as little un-Pauline as καταβραβ. in ii. 18 (in opposition to Holtzmann); it means primarily : *to arrange and conduct the contest* (Wisd. x. 12, and Grimm *in loc.*) ; then : *to confer the prize of victory,* to be βραβεύς, *i.e.* umpire (Plut. *Mor.* p. 960 A ; Diod. Sic. xiii. 53) ; finally : to *govern*[1] generally. See for the last signification especially Dem. 36. 7, 1231. 19 ; Eur. *Hel.* 1079 ; Isocr. *Areop.* p. 144 B ; Polyb. vi. 4. 3, xiii. 1. 5, xxvii. 14. 4, *et al. ;* passages from Josephus in Krebs, and from Philo in Loesner. Considering its very frequent occurrence in the latter sense, and its appropriateness in that sense to ἐν τ. καρδ. ὑμ., and seeing that any reference to the Messianic βραβεῖον (comp. ii. 18) is foreign to the context, the majority of modern expositors have rightly interpreted it : the peace of Christ must *rule, govern* in your hearts. So Luther ("let it be master and keep you in all tribulation"), Castalio, Beza, Bengel, and many others, including Flatt, Bähr, Olshausen,

---

[1] The Vulgate incorrectly renders : *exultet.* So also the Gothic.

Steiger, Huther, de Wette, Baumgarten-Crusius, Dalmer, and
Bleek. The conception involves the *superintending*, arranging,
and administering activity, and that in *supreme deciding* com-
petence (comp. Ewald and Hofmann), as it ought to be exercised by the εἰρήνη τ. Χ. in the heart, quite like the German
verfügen [*to dispose of*]. Bremi says aptly, *ad Dem. Ol.* p.
179, Goth. : it is not simply equivalent to διοικεῖν, " sed pleno
jure et ex arbitrio διοικεῖν." Chrysostom and his followers
have retained the meaning : *to confer the prize of victory*, but
with ideas introduced to which nothing in the text points.
Theophylact : ὑβρίσθημεν πολλάκις ὑπό τινος· ἀγωνίζονται παρ'
ἡμῖν λογισμοὶ δύο, ὁ μὲν εἰς ἄμυναν κινῶν, ὁ δὲ εἰς μακροθυμίαν.
Ἐὰν ἡ εἰρήνη τ. Θεοῦ στῇ ἐν ἡμῖν, ὥσπερ τις βραβευτὴς
δίκαιος, τουτέστι κριτὴς καὶ ἀγωνοθέτης, καὶ δῷ τὸ βραβεῖον
τῆς νίκης τῷ κελεύοντι μακροθυμεῖν, παύσεται ὁ ἀνταγωνιστής.
Comp. also Erasmus, Vatablus, and Calvin, who, however, explain it erroneously : palmam *ferat*. Grotius : " *dijudicet*,
nempe si quid est *inter vos controversum*." So also, substantially, Hammond, Kypke, and others ; similarly, Melanchthon :
" gubernet omnia *certamina*." Comp. βραβεύειν ἔριν (Plut.
Rom. 9) and the like. See Dorville, *ad Charit.* p. 445. But
the context points to deeper matters than disputes, upon which
the peace of Christ in the heart is to decide. — εἰς ἣν κ. ἐκλ.
κ.τ.λ.] argumentative, supporting the exhortation just uttered ;
for which ye also (καί expressing the *corresponding* relation)
were called, etc. ; εἰς ἥν, *in behalf of which*, i.e. *to possess which
peace*, is not the *final aim* of the calling, which is rather participation in the Messianic kingdom, but a *mediate aim*. Comp.
1 Pet. ii. 21. — ἐν ἑνὶ σώματι] not instead of εἰς ἓν σῶμα
(Grotius, Flatt, and many others) ; nor yet : " as *growing to be*
members of a single body" (Hofmann, gratuitously importing),
but (comp. Ellicott and Bleek) as the *result* of ἐκλήθητε,
announcing the relation of fellowship, into which the individuals are translated through their calling, and *in which* they
now *find themselves* continuously. This abiding condition was
the *predominant* conception ; hence the *pregnancy* of the expression (Kühner, II. 1, p. 469) ; *so that ye are in one body*,
namely, as its members. The element of unity, added with

emphasis, and that quite in Pauline form (Rom. xii. 5 ; 1
Cor. x. 17 ; in opposition to Holtzmann), stands in appropriate
reference to the entire requirement.   To have become by the
calling one body with those who share in that calling, and yet
not to let the holy moral disposition, for the sake of which we
are called, be the common ruling power of life—what a contradiction !   In that case there would be wanting to the ἐν
σῶμα the ἐν πνεῦμα accordant with the calling (Eph. iv. 4 ;
1 Cor. xii. 13).— The mention of this *calling*—the great blessing which makes everything, that is at variance with what has
hitherto been demanded (ver. 12 ff.), appear as *ingratitude
towards God*—induces the apostle to add still further the
highest motive of all for every Christian virtue (comp. ii. 7,
i. 12): κ. εὐχάριστοι γίνεσθε: *and become ye thankful* (comp.
on Eph. iv. 32) ; in which the γίνεσθε (not equivalent to ἐστέ)
requires the constant striving after this exalted aim as something not yet attained ; comp. *e.g.* John xv. 8.   It was nothing
but a misconception of that inner connection and of this significance of γίνεσθε, which led to the taking εὐχάρ. as *amabiles,
friendly*, and the like (comp. Eph. iv. 32 ; Prov. xi. 15).   So
Jerome, Erasmus (not in the *Paraphr.*), Calvin, Vatablus, Beza,
(*benefici*), Cornelius a Lapide, Wolf, Krebs, and many others,
including Bähr, Steiger, Olshausen, and Reiche.   The linguistic use of εὐχάριστος in this sense in the classical writers
is well known (Xen. *Cyr.* ii. 2. 1, *Oec.* v. 10), but equally so is
also its use in the sense of *thankful* (Xen. *Cyr.* viii. 3. 49 ;
Herodian, ii. 3. 14 ; Diod. Sic. xviii. 28) ; and the N. T., in
which, moreover, the adjective is nowhere else found, has, like
the Apocrypha, εὐχαριστεῖν and εὐχαριστία only in the latter
signification (comp. ver. 17), the reference of which in our
passage to *God* after εἰς ἣν κ. ἐκλήθ. (it is *God* who calls) is
self-evident, but not (in opposition to Grotius and Calovius)
the *mutua* gratitudo.   The ascription of the words κ. εὐχάρ. γίν.
to the *interpolator*, who is also supposed to have inserted ἐν
εὐχαριστίᾳ in iv. 2 (Holtzmann), is destitute of ground either
in the language or in the matter of the passage.   It is not at
all easy to see why εὐχάριστος should be " as un-Pauline as
εὔσπλαγχνος in Eph. iv. 32."

Ver. 16 f. The series of exhortations begun in ver. 12 is now closed,[1] and Paul proceeds to give, before going on in ver. 18 to the duties of particular callings, an encouraging allusion to the *Christian means of grace* for furthering the common life of piety, namely, the *word of Christ.* This ought to dwell richly among them, so that they might by means of its operation (1) *instruct and admonish each other* in all wisdom with psalms, etc.; (2) by the divine grace sing to God *in their hearts;* and (3) *let all that they do,* in word or deed, be done *in the name of Jesus* with thanksgiving to God. Accordingly, the previous paraenesis by no means ends in a *"loose aggregation"* (as Hofmann objects), but in a well-weighed, steadily-progressive, and connected conclusion on the basis of the λόγος of Christ[2] placed at the very beginning. According to Hofmann, ver. 16 f. is only meant to be an amplification of the εὐχάριστοι γίνεσθε in ver. 15. This would be a *disproportionate* amplification—especially as εὐχ. γίν. is not the leading thought in the foregoing—and could only be plausibly upheld by misinterpretations in the details; see below. — ὁ λόγος τ. Χριστοῦ] *i.e.* the *gospel.* The genitive is that of the *subject;* Christ causes it to be proclaimed, He Himself speaks in the proclaimers (2 Cor. xiii. 3), and has revealed it specially to Paul (Gal. iv. 11 f.); it is *His* word. Comp. 1 Thess. i. 8, iv. 15; 2 Thess. iii. 1; Heb. vi. 1. The designation of it, according to its *principal* author: ὁ λ. τοῦ Θεοῦ, is more current. — ἐνοικείτω ἐν ὑμῖν] not: *among you* (Luther and many others), which would not be in keeping with the conception of *in*dwelling; nor yet: *in animis vestris* (Theodoret, Melanchthon, Beza, Zanchius, and others, including Flatt, Böhmer, and Olshausen), so that the indwelling which

---

[1] Lachmann and Steiger have put ὁ λόγος . . . πλουσίως in a parenthesis, which just as arbitrarily sets aside the new and regulative idea introduced by ὁ λόγος, as it very unnecessarily comes to the help of the construction.

[2] This applies also in opposition to Holtzmann, p. 54 f., who finds in ver. 16 an echo of Eph. v. 19, which at the same time interrupts the entire connection, and presents something un-Pauline almost in every word (p. 164). Un-Pauline, in his view, is ὁ λόγος τ. Χριστοῦ (but see 1 Thess. i. 8, iv. 15); un-Pauline the juxtaposition of ψαλμοῖς, ὕμνοις, ᾠδαῖς (the reason why it is so, is not plain); un-Pauline the ᾄδειν itself, and even the adverb πλουσίως. How strangely has the apostle, so rich in diction, become impoverished!

depends on *knowledge* and *faith* would be meant, since the subsequent modal definition is of an *oral* nature : but *in you*, *i.e.* in your *church*, the ὑμεῖς, as a *whole*, being compared to a house, in which the word has the seat of its abiding operation and rule (comp. Rom. viii. 11 ; 2 Tim. i. 5). — πλουσίως] *in ample measure.* In proportion as the gospel is recognised much or little in a church as the common living source and contents of mutual instruction, quickening, discipline, and edification, its dwelling there is quantitatively various. De Wette explains it, not comprehensively enough, in accordance with what follows : " so that many come forward as teachers, and often." In another way Hofmann limits it arbitrarily : the letting the word of Christ dwell richly in them is conceived *as an act of gratitude.* How easy it would have been for Paul to have indicated this intelligibly ! But the *new* point which he wishes to urge upon his readers, namely, to let the divinely-powerful *means of Christian life* dwell richly in them, is placed by him without any link of connection, and independently, at the head of his closing exhortation. — The following ἐν πάσῃ . . . τῷ Θεῷ is the modal definition of the foregoing : *so that ye*, etc. ; construction according to the logical subject, as in ii. 2.—ἐν πάσῃ σοφίᾳ] Since what precedes has its defining epithet in πλουσίως, and that with all the emphasis of the adverb put at the end, and since, moreover, the symmetry of the following participial clauses, each of which begins with ἐν (ἐν πάσῃ σοφίᾳ . . . ἐν τ. χάριτι), ought not to be abandoned without some special reason, the ἐν τ. σοφ. is to be referred *to what follows* (so Bos, Bengel, Storr, Flatt, Bähr, Steiger, Olshausen, Huther, de Wette, Baumgarten-Crusius, Ewald, Dalmer, Reiche, Bleek, Hofmann, and others ; Böhmer hesitates, and Beza *permits* this reference), and not to what *precedes* (so Syriac, Chrysostom, Luther, and many others). Comp. i. 28. Every sort of (Christian) wisdom is to be active in the mutual instruction and admonition. Regarding the details, see on i. 28. — ἑαυτούς] mutually, *among yourselves*, comp. ver. 13. — ψαλμοῖς κ.τ.λ.] *modal* definition of the mutual διδάσκειν and νουθετεῖν, which are to take place *by means of* (see below, ἐν χάρ. ᾄδοντες κ.τ.λ.) psalms, etc. It is all the more arbitrary to refer it merely to νουθετ. (de Wette), seeing that the position of ἑαυτούς binds the two participles together, and seeing that inspired songs by no means exclude a *doctrinal* purport. The conceivableness of a didactic activity in mutual *singing* (in opposition to Schenkel and Hofmann), and that without confounding things radically different, is still clearly enough recognisable in many of our best church songs, especially in those born of the fresh spirit of the Reformation. Storr and Flatt, Schenkel and Hofmann join the words with ᾄδοντες, although the latter has already a definition both before and after it, and although one does not say ψαλμοῖς κ.τ.λ., ᾄδειν (*dative*), but ψαλμοὺς κ.τ.λ. (*accusative*), as in Ex. xiv. 32; Plat. *Symp.* 197 E, *Rep.* p. 388 D, and in all Greek authors. The *dative of the instrument* with ᾄδειν would be appropriate, if it had along with it an accusative of the object praised (as *e.g.* Eur. *Ion.* 1091). See, moreover, on Eph. v. 19. Concerning the distinction between ψαλμοί (religious songs after the manner of the Psalms of the O. T., to be regarded partly as Christian songs already in use, partly as improvised effusions, 1 Cor. xiv. 15, 26) and ὕμνοι (songs of praise), to both of which ᾠδαὶ πνευματικαί (*i.e.* songs inspired by the Holy Spirit) are then added as the general category,[1] see on Eph. v. 19. Observe, moreover, that Paul is here also (comp. Eph. *l.c.*) speaking not of *divine worship*[2] in the proper sense of the term, since the teaching and admonition in question are required from the readers *generally* and *mutually*, and that as a proof of their *abundant* possession of the word of Christ, but rather of the *communication one with another in religious intercourse* (*e.g.* at meals, in the agapae and other meetings, in family circles, etc.)—in which enthusiasm makes the fulness of the heart pass from mouth to mouth, and brotherly instruction and admonition thus find expression in the higher form of psalms, etc., whether these may have been

---

[1] Many arbitrary more special distinctions are to be found in expositors. See Bähr. Even Steiger distinguishes them very precariously into (1) songs accompanied by stringed instruments; (2) solemn church songs; (3) songs sung in the house and at work.

[2] This applies also in opposition to Holtzmann, who discovers here and in Eph. v. 19 an already *far advanced stage* of worship.

songs already well known, or extemporized according to the
peculiar character and productive capacity of the individual
enthusiasm, whether they may have been sung by individuals
alone (especially if they were improvised), or chorally, or in
the form of alternating chants (Plin. *Ep.* x. 97). How common religious singing was in the ancient church, even apart
from divine service proper, may be seen in Suicer, *Thes.*
II. p. 1568 f. The existence of a multitude of rhythmic
songs, composed ἀπ᾽ ἀρχῆς by Christians, is attested by Eus.
H. E. ii. 17, v. 28. Regarding singing in the agapae, see
Tertullian, *Apol.* 39 : "post aquam manualem et lumina, ut
quisque de scripturis sanctis vel proprio ingenio potest, provo-
catur in medium Deo canere." See generally, Augusti, *Denkw.*
II. p. 110 ff. — The *asyndetic* (see the critical remarks) juxtaposition of ψαλμ., ὕμν., and ᾠδαῖς πν. renders the discourse
more urgent and animated. — ἐν τῇ χάριτι ᾅδοντες κ.τ.λ.] is
commonly regarded as *subordinate* to what goes before ; as if
Paul would say : *the heart also is to take part in their singing,*
οὐχ ἁπλῶς τῷ στόματι, ἀλλ᾽ ἐν τῇ καρδίᾳ, ὅ ἐστι μετὰ προσ-
οχῆς, Theophylact. But Paul himself has not in the least
expressed any such *contrasting* reference ; and how superfluous,
nay, even inappropriate, would such an injunction be, seeing
that the διδάσκειν and νουθετεῖν takes place in fact by the
ψαλμοὶ κ.τ.λ., and this is to be the outcome of the abundant
indwelling of the gospel ; and seeing, further, that there is no
mention at all of a stated common worship (where, possibly,
lip-service might intrude), but, on the contrary, of mutual
edifying intercourse ! The entire view is based upon the
unfounded supposition of a degeneracy of worship in the
apostolic age, which, even though it were true in itself, would
be totally inapplicable here. Moreover, we should expect the
idea, that the singing is to be the expression of the emotion of
the heart, to be represented not by ἐν τ. καρδ., but by ἐκ τῶν
καρδ. (comp. 2 Tim. ii. 22 ; Matt. xii. 34) or ἀπὸ τ. κ. Comp.
Wisd. viii. 21, also classical expressions like ἐκ φρενός and
the like. No, the participial clause is *co-ordinate* with the
preceding one (as also at Eph. v. 19, see *in loc.*), and conveys
—after the audible singing for the purpose of teaching and

admonition, to be done *mutually*—as a *further* element of
the pious life in virtue of the rich indwelling of the word
of Christ, the *still singing of the heart*, which each one must
offer to God *for himself inwardly ;* *i.e.* the silent praising
of God, which belongs to self-edification in the inner man.
Chrysostom already indicates this view, but mixes it up, notwithstanding, with the usual one ; Theophylact quotes it as
another (ἄλλως), giving to it, moreover, the inappropriate antithesis : μὴ πρὸς ἐπίδειξιν, but adding with Chrysostom the
correct illustration : κἂν γὰρ ἐν ἀγορᾷ ᾖς, δύνασαι κατὰ σεαυ-
τὸν ᾄδειν μηδενὸς ἀκούοντος. Bengel well describes the two
parallel definitions ἐν πάσῃ σοφίᾳ κ.τ.λ. and ἐν χάριτι κ.τ.λ.
as *distributio* of the πλουσίως, and that *mutuo* et *seorsim.* — ἐν
τῇ χάριτι] does not belong to ᾠδαῖς πνευμ. (Luther: "with
spiritual *pleasant* songs," also Calvin), but to ᾄδοντες as the
parallel element to ἐν πάσῃ σοφίᾳ. In the same way, namely,
as the teaching and admonition above mentioned are to take
place *by means of every wisdom*, which communicates and
operates outwardly through them, so the still singing of the
heart now spoken of is to take place *by means of the divine
grace*, which stirs and moves and impels men's minds,—a
more precise definition, which is so far from being useless and
idle (as Hofmann objects), that it, on the contrary, excludes
everything that is selfish, vain, fanatical, and the like.
Chrysostom says rightly : ἀπὸ τῆς χάριτος τοῦ πνεύματος,
φησὶν, ᾄδοντες κ.τ.λ. ; comp. Oecumenius : διὰ τῆς παρὰ τοῦ
ἁγίου πνεύματος δοθείσης χάριτος, also Estius and Steiger.
Hofmann's view is erroneous : that ᾄδειν ἔν τινι means to sing
of something, thus making the grace experienced the *subject-
matter* of the songs. This it does not mean even in the LXX.
Ps. cxxxviii. 5, where בְּ is taken in a *local* sense.[1] The
subject-matter of the singing would have been expressed by
an *accusative* (as μῆνιν ἄειδε), or with εἰς.[2] Inappropriate as

---

[1] As in the Vulgate, and by Luther.
[2] Nevertheless, Holtzmann, p. 164, adopts the linguistically quite incorrect
explanation of Hofmann : he thinks that it alone yields a tolerable sense,
but that it is foreign to the linguistic usage of *Paul* (no, it is foreign to *all*
linguistic usage).

to sense (since the discourse concerns singing *in the heart*) is the view of others : *with gracefulness.* So Theophylact (who, however, permits a choice between this and the true explanation), Erasmus, Luther, Melanchthon (" sine confusione, εὐσχημόνως"), Castalio, Calvin, Beza, Grotius, Calovius, Cornelius a Lapide, Wetstein, Bengel, and others, including Bähr, Baumgarten-Crusius, Schenkel, Reiche. Even though the singing in *public worship* were spoken of, the injunction to sing *gracefully*, and especially with the emphasis of being placed first, would touch on too singular an element. Anselm, and in more modern times Böhmer, Huther, de Wette, and Bleek take it : with *thankfulness*, in which case the article, which Bleek rejects (see the critical remarks), would denote not the gratitude *already required in ver.* 15 (so Huther), but that which is *due*. But the summons to general thanksgiving towards God (in ver. 15, grateful *conduct* was meant by εὐχάρ. γίν.) only follows in ver. 17 ; and inasmuch as the interpretation which takes it of the *divine grace* is highly suitable both to the connection and to the use of the article (which sets forth the χάρις as a conception *formally set apart*), and places an admirably characteristic element in the foreground, there is no reason for assuming here a call to thanksgiving.—— As ἐν ταῖς καρδ. ὑμ. was contrasted with the preceding *oral* singing, so is τῷ Θεῷ contrasted with the destination for *others; the* still heart-singer sings *to God*. It is just *for this reason* that the otherwise superfluous τῷ Θεῷ is added. Comp. 1 Cor. xiv. 28.

Ver. 17. The apostle having announced in ver. 16 the *first* way in which the abundant indwelling of the word of Christ must manifest itself by ἐν πάσῃ σοφίᾳ διδάσκοντες . . . πνευματικοῖς, and having set forth as the *second* the ἐν τῇ χάριτι ᾅδοντες κ.τ.λ., now adds the *third*, and that, indeed, as one embracing the entire conduct of life ; the καί, *and*, attaches it to the two participial clauses in ver. 16, not, however, introducing another participial mode of expression conformed to the foregoing, but leading over, through the verb to be supplied, into the *direct* form of discourse : *And whatsoever ye do by word or by work, do all in the name of Jesus.* The πᾶν ὅ,

τι ἂν ποιῆτε . . ; ἔργῳ is the *absolute nominative,* placed at the
beginning with rhetorical emphasis, and syntactically independent. See Kühner, II. 1, p. 42 ; Winer, p. 534 [E. T.
718]. — *ἐν λόγῳ ἢ ἐν ἔργῳ*] Comp. Aesch. *Prom.* 659 : τί χρὴ
δρῶντ᾽ ἢ λέγοντα δαίμοσιν πράσσειν φίλα. See Pflugk, *ad Eur.
Hec.* 373 : " Dictis factisque omnis continetur actio." For
instances of *λόγος* and *ἔργον* associated in that order and
conversely, see Bornemann, *ad Xen. Mem.* ii. 3. 6 ; Lobeck,
Paral. p. 64 f. — *πάντα*] again emphatically prefixed, not,
however, taking up again the previous *πᾶν,* but rather : in the
case of *everything* which is done by word or deed, *all* is to take
place in the name of Jesus ;[1] no element of the doing is to
be out of this sphere ! The imperative *ποιεῖτε* is to be *supplied* from the context. Comp. on Eph. v. 21. — *ἐν ὀνόμ.*]
Not : *with invocation of* (Chrysostom, Oecumenius, Theophylact, Melanchthon, and others), but : so that the name is the
holy moral *element, in which* the action *proceeds,* inasmuch,
namely, as this name, as the sum of the faith which moulds
the new life, fills the consciousness, and gives to the action its
specific Christian quality and consecration. *Ἐν Χριστῷ
Ἰησοῦ* would not be substantially different. Comp. on Eph.
v. 20 ; Phil. ii. 10 ; John xiv. 13. " Illum sapiat, illum
sonet, illum spiret omnis vestra vita," Erasmus. The *ideal*
character of the requirement is misapprehended, when, with
Cornelius a Lapide, it is lowered to a mere *consilium.* See,
on the contrary, Calovius.—*εὐχαρ. τῷ Θεῷ κ.τ.λ.*] accompanying definition : *whilst ye at the same time give thanks,* etc.
Comp. *ἐν εὐχαριστίᾳ* in ii. 7, iv. 2, i. 12 ; Phil. iv. 6. In the
apostle's view, there belongs essentially to the devoutness of
Christian *life* the self-expressing piety of thankfulness for all
Christian bliss, in the consciousness, assurance, and experience
of which one does everything in the name of Jesus. Since
εὐχαρ. denotes *thanksgiving,* Grotius ought not to have taken
the participle in a declaratory sense ("*quid sit* in nomine
Christi omnia facere et loqui ") ; a misinterpretation, which

---

[1] Paul, as is well known, is fond of placing close beside each other different
forms of *πᾶς* with different references. See Wilke, *Rhetor.* p. 381; comp. also
on Phil. iv. 12.

Hofmann rightly rejects, but substitutes another explanation which neglects the verbal import of εὐχαριστεῖν : namely, that Paul *declares* the *doing* here required *to be a thanksgiving*, etc., doing, which is *practical* thanks. Εὐχαριστεῖν is never in the N. T. equivalent to χάριν ἀποδοῦναι, *gratias referre*. — πατρί] Father of Jesus. — δι' αὐτοῦ] For Jesus, as the personal historical mediator of Messianic bliss through the work of atonement, is therewith for the Christian consciousness the *mediator of thanksgiving;* He it is, *through whose benefit* the Christian *can* and *does give* thanks. Comp. Rom. i. 8, vii. 25, *al.* Hence in Eph. v. 20 : ἐν ὀνόματι κ.τ.λ. Both the thought and expression were so habitually in use and belonged so essentially to the circumstances of the case, that the hypothesis of a contrast to the mediation of *angels* (Theodoret, Bengel, and many others, including Bähr) is unfounded, more especially seeing that the entire context has no polemical reference.

Ver. 18 to iv. 1.[1] Instructions for the different portions of the *household.* Why Paul should have given to the churches such a table of household rules only in this Epistle and in that to the Ephesians (comp. also 1 Tim. and Tit.), must be left wholly undecided (Chrysostom exhausts himself in conjectures). They are not polemical; but possibly, in the presence of a theosophico-ascetic atmosphere, the practical rules of healthy domestic life seemed to him the more seasonable. They do not contain traces of a *later* development of church-life (Holtzmann). The circumstance that the precepts for the several forms of domestic society uniformly (vv. 18, 20, 22 ff.) begin with the *subordinate* party, as also at Eph. v. 21 ff., is to be

---

[1] This domestic code is held by Holtzmann to be an insertion of the interpolator from Eph. v. 21–vi. 9. He groundlessly questions the genuineness of the expressions εὐάρεστος, ἀδικεῖν, ἐρεθίζειν, ἰσότης, τὸ δίκαιον, ἁπλότης τῆς καρδίας, and even appeals to the use of ἀνθρωπάρεσκος, ἀνταπόδοσις, and the formula τῷ κυρίῳ Χριστῷ δουλεύειν as direct evidence against its Pauline origin. Might not, however, the word ἀνθρωπάρεσκος have been sufficiently familiar to Paul from the LXX. (Ps. liii. 5) and otherwise (Lobeck, *ad Phryn.* p. 621), and have been used by him in the two parallel epistles? Is not ἀνταπόδοσις a term in general use since Thucydides? Is not "*to serve the Lord Christ*" a Pauline idea, and even (comp. Rom. xvi. 18) literal expression? The danger of a *petitio principii* only too easily steals upon even the cautious and sober critic in such points of detail. He finds what he *seeks.*

regarded as having occurred without any set purpose ; the idea
of *obedience* was primarily present to the writer's mind. If
Paul's aim had been to counteract *the abuse of Christian freedom
and equality*, or in other words, perverse desires for emancipation,
he would not have considered so weighty a purpose sufficiently
met by the mere mode of arrangement, but would have
entered upon the matter itself (in opposition to Huther and de
Wette) ; and this we should have to assume that he would
have done also *in the event* of his having had in view an
attitude of resistance on the part of those bound to obedience
as the thing most to be feared (in opposition to Hofmann).
Just as much might such an attitude be a thing to be feared
from the stronger party. Respecting the *nominatives* in the
address, see especially Stallbaum, *ad Plat. Symp.* p. 172 A. —
ὡς ἀνῆκεν] not the *perfect* (with present signification), as
Huther thinks and Bleek does not disapprove, but the *imperfect*, which has its logical reference in the ἐν κυρίῳ to be
connected with it : *as was fitting in the Lord, i.e.* as was becoming in the relation of the ἐν Χριστῷ εἶναι (Philem. 8), as
was appropriate to the Christian state, but had not yet been
in this way realized. The imperfect (comp. Acts xxii. 22)
denotes, therefore, as also in χρῆν and ἔδει, the incomplete
condition, which extends even into the present. See Kühner,
II. 1, p. 176 f. ; Bernhardy, p. 373. Similarly, Winer, p. 254
[E. T. 338]. Comp. also Buttmann, p. 187 [E. T. 216].
We are not to think of an omission of ἄν ; see Kühner, *l.c.*
The connection of ἐν κυρίῳ with ὑποτάσσεσθε (Chrysostom,
Theophylact, Estius, Rosenmüller, Hofmann, and others)—in
which case Hofmann imparts into ὡς ἀνῆκεν the abstract idea :
as was *already in itself* fitting—is opposed by the position of
the words themselves, as well as by the parallel in ver. 20 :
εὐάρεστόν ἐστιν ἐν κυρίῳ.

Ver. 19. Comp. Eph. v. 25 ff., where this love is admirably
characterized according to its specifically Christian nature. —
πικραίνεσθε] *become* not *embittered*, description of a spitefully
cross tone and treatment. Plat. *Legg.* v. p. 731 D ; Dem. 1464.
18 : μήτε πικραίνεσθαι μήτε μνησικακεῖν. Philo, *Vit. Mos.* II.
p. 135. Comp. πικρῶς διακεῖσθαι πρός τινα, Polyb. iv. 14. 1 ;

LXX. Ex. xvi. 20; Ruth i. 20; 3 Esdr. iv. 31; ἐμπικραί-
νεσθαί τινι, Herod. v. 62.

Ver. 20 f. Comp. Eph. vi. 1–4, where likewise is given a
characteristic development in fuller detail of what is here
only succinctly stated. — κατὰ πάντα] not to be restricted;
for Paul is quoting the *rule*, that which holds good *principaliter*
in the relation of children, while possible *exceptional cases*
obviously come under the principle of obeying God rather
than man (Oecumenius: δίχα τῶν εἰς ἀσέβειαν φερόντων).
Comp. Eph. v. 24. — εὐάρεστόν ἐστιν ἐν κυρίῳ] In connection
with this reading (see the critical remarks), to supply τῷ Θεῷ
to εὐάρ. is arbitrary (in opposition to de Wette and Baumgarten-Crusius), since this is not suggested by the context as
in Rom. xii. 1, 2 ; nor is ἐν κυρίῳ to be taken as instead of
the dative (Flatt, Bähr, Bleek), or in the sense : *coram* Domino
(Böhmer), but rather as in ver. 18. We have to leave εὐάρ.
without any other more precise definition than what is contained in ἐν κυρ., so that it is affirmed of childlike obedience,
that it is *well - pleasing*, and that indeed not in a worldly
fashion apart from Christ, οὐκ ἀπὸ τῆς φύσεως μόνης (Chrysostom), but in a definite *Christian* character ; consequently
the *Christian ethical beauty*, in which the δίκαιον (Eph. vi. 1)
of that virtue manifests itself. Comp. προσφιλῆ in Phil. iv. 8.
It would be a perfectly groundless violence to couple, with
Hofmann, ἐν κυρίῳ with ὑπακούετε τ. γ. κ. π., notwithstanding
the clause which is introduced by γάρ.——Ver. 21. οἱ πατέρες]
they, and not the mothers, are addressed as holding the
government of the household, also in reference to education.
Comp. on Eph. vi. 4. — ἐρεθίζετε] *irritate*, very frequent in
the classics and LXX., especially in connection with *anger*,
as here (comp. Eph. vi. 4). This irritation takes place through
unjust or over-severe (ἐστὶν ὅπου καὶ συγχωρεῖν ὀφείλετε,
Chrysostom) treatment, which the child, provoked thereby to
anger, must *bear* without being able to get satisfaction for its
injured sense of justice ; whereby it becomes liable to a spirit-
less and sullen, and therefore immoral, resignation, a despair
paralysing all moral power of will ; hence ἵνα μὴ ἀθυμῶσιν.
This verb is only found here in the N. T., but frequently in

LXX., also Judith vii. 22; 1 Macc. iv. 27; and in classic writers from the time of Thucydides (v. 91. 1, vii. 21, *al.*). Its opposite is θαῤῥεῖν. Bengel aptly says: "fractus animus pestis juventutis."

Ver. 22. Comp. Eph. vi. 5 ff. The minuteness with which Paul enters into this point in comparison with the others, may naturally have been caused by the flight and conversion of Onesimus, who was a Colossian slave. — τοῖς κατὰ σάρκα κυρίοις] the masters, who are so after a *fleshly* manner, *i.e.* in respect to material-human nature; a description, which pre-supposes another relation belonging to the higher pneumatic sphere, in which, namely, *Christ* is (ver. 24) the master. Comp. Rom. ix. 3. — μὴ ἐν ὀφθαλμ. ὡς ἀνθρωπάρ.] See on Eph. vi. 6. The obedience of Christian slaves becomes *men-pleasing,* and, to appearance, *eye-service,* when it is not subordinated to, and normally conditioned by, the fear of Christ (2 Cor. v. 11) as the higher Master. See below, where ἐν ἁπλότ. καρδίας (see on Eph. vi. 5) corresponds to the ἐν ὀφθαλμοδουλ., and φοβούμ. τ. κύριον to the ὡς ἀνθρωπάρ. Eye-service presupposes insincerity of *heart,* and *men*-pleasing takes for granted a want of the fear *of Christ.* Comp. on the latter, Gal. i. 10.

Ver. 23 f. More precise explanation of the ἐν ἁπλότ. καρδ., φοβούμ. τ. κύρ. just required. — ποιῆτε] in your service. — ἐκ ψυχῆς] μετὰ εὐνοίας, μὴ μετὰ δουλικῆς ἀνάγκης, ἀλλὰ μετὰ ἐλευθερίας καὶ προαιρέσεως, Chrysostom. Comp. on Eph. vi. 6. — ἐργάζεσθε] *execute, carry out,* not equivalent to ποιεῖτε, but correlative with it, hence also not in the narrower sense: *labour* (as *e.g.* in Xen. *Oec.* iii. 4 with reference to slaves). — ὡς τῷ κυρ.] Point of view of the ἐργάζ.; this is to be regarded as taking place for Christ, rendered as a service to Him. Comp. Eph. vi. 6 f. And the relation to the *human* masters, to whom the slaves belong, is in this higher aspect of the service thrown so much into the background as not to be taken into account at all, in accordance with the principle that no man can serve two masters; hence οὐκ is not relatively, but *absolutely* negative. Respecting the *contrast* of ἀνθρ. and Χριστός, see on Gal. i. 1. — εἰδότες κ.τ.λ.] Ground of the

obligation in one's own consciousness for the ὡς τῷ κυρίῳ κ.
οὐκ ἀνθρ.: *since ye know that ye shall receive from the Lord,*
etc. On εἰδότες, comp. iv. 1. — ἀπὸ κυρίου, excluding the
human recompense, stands first with emphasis, and ἀπό (*on
the part of*) denotes, not expressly the *direct* giving (παρά),
through which the recompense is received, but generally the
issuing, proceeding from the Lord, who is the possessor and
bestower, although the receiving of the recompense at the
judgment *will be* in reality direct (Eph. vi. 8 ; 2 Tim. i. 18).
Comp. on 1 Cor. xi. 23 ; Winer, p. 347 [E. T. 463]. — τῆς
κλήρον.] In the Messianic κληρονομία, *i.e.* in the future
possession of eternal bliss (see on Gal. iii. 18 ; Eph. i. 11 ;
Col. i. 12 ; Rom. iv. 13), the reward *consists.* The motive for
its purposely-chosen designation by *this* particular term lies in
the fact, that in human relations slaves are not usually *heirs,*
comp. Gen. xxi. 10.   Hence also this closing word, next to
the ἀπὸ κυρ., has special emphasis : from the *Lord* ye shall
receive the recompense of the *inheritance.*   Comp. as to substance, Ignat. *ad Polyc.* 4 : ἵνα κρείττονος ἐλευθερίας ἀπὸ Θεοῦ
τύχωσιν. — On ἀνταπόδοσις (only found here in the N. T.),
comp. Thuc. iv. 81. 1 (where, however, the sense is different) ;
Plut. *Mor.* p. 72 F ; Polyb. vi. 5. 3, xx. 7. 2, xxxii. 13. 6 ;
passages from Diod. Sic. in Munthe's *Obss.* p. 390 ; and from
the LXX. in Schleusner, I. p. 296 ; also ἀνταπόδομα in
Rom. xi. 9. — τῷ κυρίῳ Χ. δουλεύετε] without γάρ (see the
critical remarks) embraces succinctly the *whole summary of
the Christian duty of slaves* in accordance with the principle
already laid down in the ὡς τῷ κυρίῳ κ. οὐκ ἀνθρώποις ;
Χριστῷ is not to be taken as appositionally equivalent to ὅς
ἐστι Χριστός (Hofmann), but in accordance with the quite
common usage ; hence : *to the Lord Christ be serviceable !* It
is properly rendered thus *imperatively* in the Vulgate ; also by
Ewald, Dalmer, Schenkel, and Bleek. The whole significant
emphasis lies upon τῷ κυρ. Χριστῷ ; *His* slaves they are
to be in the relation of human service. Where the γάρ is
regarded as not genuine,[1] the *indicative* interpretation (the

---

[1] The decisive preponderance of the witnesses omitting this γάρ renders it
quite impossible to uphold it by subjective criticism (in opposition to Hofmann),

usual one) makes the utterance—which, moreover, would be
superfluous after ver. 23 — vapid, especially without the
addition of an οὕτως.

Ver. 25. Ground of *encouragement* (γάρ, see the critical
remarks) to fulfil the precept τῷ κυρ. Χ. δουλεύετε : *for he
who does wrong shall carry off* (the penal recompense of) *what
wrong he has done,* — a *locus communis*, of which the slaves
were to make the *application*, that the unjust treatment which
they experienced from their *masters* would not go unpunished ;
hence they could not but feel themselves the more encouraged to
be in their relation of servitude slaves of no other than *Christ*,
and to permit no unjust treatment to make them deviate
from that principle.   Paul therefore adds for their further
encouragement : [1] καὶ οὐκ ἔστι προσωποληψία, *and there is no
partiality*, of which likewise general proposition the intended
application is, that in that requital the impartial Judge
(Christ, comp. ver. 24) will not favour the masters, and will
not injure the slaves, comp. Eph. vi. 9.   The correct view
is held substantially by Theodoret, Beza, Calvin, Estius,
Zachariae, Ewald, and others.   Others have understood ὁ ἀδικῶν
as referring to the *slave* who violates his duty, in which case
ἀδικεῖν is taken either in the strict sense of the *trespass of
him* who *intentionally injures* his master (Hofmann, comp.
Philem. 18), or loosely and generally in the sense of *doing
wrong*, comp. Rev. xxii. 11 (Chrysostom, Theophylact, Bengel,
Heinrichs, Storr, Flatt, Steiger, and others).   But against this
view the κ. οὐκ ἔστι προσωπολ. may be decisively urged,

proceeding on the supposition that its omission may be traced to an artificial
combination of ideas, which is imputed to the copyists.   Just as little is the
Recepta δέ (instead of γάρ) in ver. 25 to be defended.

[1] Hofmann finds it incredible that Paul should have closed the section
referring to the slaves with a proposition couched in such general terms as
ver. 25, which applies *not to the slaves*, but to the *masters*.   This, however, is
an erroneous view.   For in vv. 22–24 the apostle has instructed the slaves
regarding their *active* bearing in service, and he is now, in the general proposition of ver. 25, suggesting for their reflection and deliberate consideration
the proper soothing and elevating point of view regarding their *passive* bearing
in service also.   Thus ver. 25 also applies to the *slaves*, and forms merely the
transition to the precept for the masters in iv. 1.   This applies also in opposition
to the doubts expressed by Holtzmann, p. 44 f.

which assumes that the subject to be punished is *higher*, of superior rank ; for the idea which has been imported into the passage is purely fanciful : " Tenues saepe putant, sibi propter tenuitatem ipsorum esse parcendum ; id negatur," Bengel, in connection with which Theophylact appeals to Lev. xix. 15. And if on account of οὐκ ἔστι προσωπολ. the unjust *masters* must be taken as meant by ὁ ἀδικῶν in the application of the sentence, the reference to *both* parties, to the masters *and the slaves* (Erasmus, Grotius, and others, including Bähr, Huther, Baumgarten-Crusius, and Bleek, following Jerome and Pelagius), is thereby excluded, since προσωπολ. is appropriate *only* to the masters. — κομίσεται] *shall carry off for himself* (sibi), refers to the Messianic judgment, and ἠδίκησε to that which he, who is now ἀδικῶν (*present*), has (shall have) then done.   On the expression κομίζεσθαι κ.τ.λ., used to express the idea of a recompense equivalent to the deed in respect of its guilt, comp. Eph. vi. 8, and on 2 Cor. v. 10. — Respecting προσωποληψία, see on Gal. ii. 6.

CHAPTER IV.

Ver. 1. οὐρανοῖς] Lachm. and Tisch. read οὐρανῷ, follo wing
A B C ℵ* min. vss. Clem. Or. Damasc. The plural is from Eph.
vi. 9. — Ver. 3. δι' ὅ] Lachm. reads δι' ὅν, following B F G.
Not attested strongly enough, especially as after τ. Χριστοῦ the
masculine involuntarily suggested itself. — Ver. 8. γνῷ τὰ περὶ
ὑμῶν] A B D* F G min. Aeth. It., and some Fathers have γνῶτε
τὰ περὶ ἡμῶν.[1] Recommended by Griesb., received by Scholz,
Lachm. and Tisch. 8, approved also by Rinck and Reiche ; and
rightly, because it has preponderant attestation, and is so
necessary as regards the context that it must not be regarded
as an alteration from Eph. vi. 22 (comp. *in loc.*). The *Recepta*
is to be regarded as having arisen through the omission of the
syllable τε before τα. — Ver. 12. Instead of στῆτε Tisch. 8 has
σταθῆτε, only on the authority of A* B and some min. —
πεπληρωμένοι] A B C D* F G ℵ min. have πεπληροφορημένοι. Recommended by Griesb., received by Lachm. and Tisch., and justly ;
the familiar πεπληρωμ. crept in involuntarily, or by way of gloss.
— Ver. 13. ζῆλον πολύν] Griesb. Scholz, Lachm. Tisch. Reiche
read πολὺν πόνον, following A B C D** ℵ 80, Copt., while D* F G
have πολὺν κόπον, and Vulg. It.: multum *laborem.* Accordingly
the *Recepta* is at any rate to be rejected, and πολὺν πόνον to be
preferred as having decisive attestation ; πόνον was glossed partly
by κόπον, partly by ζῆλον (πόθον and ἀγῶνα are also found in codd.).
Neither ζῆλον nor κόπον would have given occasion for a gloss ;
and in the N. T. πόνος only further occurs in the Apocalypse.
— Ver. 15. αὐτοῦ] A C P ℵ min. have αὐτῶν ; B : αὐτῆς. The
latter is the reading of Lachm., who with B** instead of Νυμφᾶν
accents Νύμφαν. The αὐτῶν, which is received by Tisch. 8, is
to be held as original ; the plural not being understood was
corrected, according as the name Νυμφ. was reckoned masculine
or feminine, into αὐτοῦ or αὐτῆς.

Ver. 1. Τὴν ἰσότητα] not: *equity,* for the word signifies
aequalitas, not *aequitas, i.e.* ἐπιείκεια (in opposition to Steiger,

[1] ℵ* has γνω τε τα περι υμων ; ℵ** deletes the τε, and is thus a witness for the
Recepta.

Huther, de Wette, Ewald, Bleek, and most expositors), but: *equality* (2 Cor. viii. 13 f.; very often in Plato, Polyb. ii. 38. 8, vi. 8. 4; Lucian, *Herm.* 22, *Zeux.* 5, also the passages from Philo in Wetstein, and the LXX. Job xxxvi. 29; Zech. iv. 7), so that ye, namely, *regard and treat* the slaves *as your equals.*   What is herein required, therefore, is not a *quality of the master*, and in particular not the *freedom from moral unevenness*,[1] which is equivalent to δικαιοσύνη (Hofmann), but a *quality of the relation*, which is to be conceded; it is not at all, however, the equalization of the *outward* relation, which would be a *de facto* abolition of slavery, but rather *the* equality, which, amidst a continued subsistence of all the outward diversity, is brought about in the Christian κοινωνία by kindly treatment.   While τὸ δίκαιον (*what is right*) expresses that which, according to the Christian consciousness of right, belongs *as matter of right* to the slave, τὴν ἰσότητα requires the concession of the *parity* (*égalité*) implied in the *Christian* ἀδελφότης.   Paul has in view (in opposition to Hofmann) merely *Christian* slaves (whom he has exhorted in iii. 22 f.); otherwise, in fact, the conception of ἰσότης would be not at all appropriate.   It is just by the Christian status of *both* parties that he desires to see their inequality in other respects ethically *counterbalanced.*   A commentary on τὴν ἰσότητα is supplied by Philem. 16.   At variance with the context, Erasmus, Melanchthon, Vatablus, Cornelius a Lapide, Böhmer, and others understand the *equality of impartial treatment,* according to which the master does not *prefer one slave to another.*   This would not in fact yield any definite moral character of the treatment in itself, nor would it suit all *the*

---

[1] This conception, *coincident with* δικαιοσύνη, does not pertain to ἰσότης at all; and just as little to ἴσος in Soph. *Phil.* 685, where ἴσος ἐν γ' ἴσοις ἀνήρ is nothing else than *par inter pares*, namely, to his friends a friend, to his foes a foe. Comp. Schneidewin *in loc.*   At many other passages ἴσος denotes *the equality of right,* that which is *impartial*, and is hence often combined with δίκαιος (*righteous* in the *narrower* sense).   But ἰσότης is always (even in Polyb. ii. 38. 8) *equality ;* see *e.g.* Plato, *Rep.* 658 C, where it is said of the democracy : ἰσότητά τινα ὁμοίως ἴσοις τε καὶ ἀνίσοις διανέμουσα, that is, it distributes uniformly to *equal* and *unequal* a certain *equality.*   In such passages the conception of *égalité* comes into view with special clearness.   Hofmann has explained our passage as if ἰσότης and ὁμαλότης, or λειότης (*levelness*), were identical conceptions.

cases where there is only *one* slave. As to the *middle* παρέχεσθε (Tit. ii. 7 ; Acts xix. 24), observe that it is based simply on the conception of the self-activity of the subject; Kühner, II. 1, p. 97. — εἰδότες] consciousness, that serves as a motive, as in iii. 24. — καὶ ὑμεῖς κ.τ.λ.] Theophylact says correctly : ὥσπερ ἐκεῖνοι ὑμᾶς, οὕτω καὶ ὑμεῖς ἔχετε κύριον, and that *in heaven,* namely *Christ.*

Vv. 2–6. After having already concluded the *general* exhortations at iii. 17, Paul now subjoins some *by way of supplement,* and that in aphoristic epistolary fashion, concerning *prayer* along with *intercession* for himself (vv. 2–4), and *demeanour towards non-Christians* (vv. 5, 6). How special was the importance of both under the circumstances then existing !

Ver. 2. *To prayer apply yourselves perseveringly ;* comp. Rom. xii. 12 ; Eph. vi. 18 ; Acts i. 14 ; also 1 Thess. v. 17 : ἀδιαλείπτως προσεύχεσθε, which is substantially the same thing. Comp. Luke xviii. 1. — γρηγορ. ἐν αὐτῇ] modal definition of the προσκαρτερεῖν : *so that ye are watchful* (that is, *alacres,* mentally attentive and alert, not weary and distracted, comp. 1 Thess. v. 6 ; Eph. vi. 18 ; 1 Pet. iv. 7, v. 7 f. ; Matt. xxvi. 41) *in the same.* ἐν, not to be taken as instrumental, is meant of the business, *in the execution of which* they are to be vigilant, since it is *prayer in itself,* as an expression of the spiritual life, and not as *an aid to moral activity,* that is spoken of. Hence we must not interpret it, with Hofmann, as indicating *how Christian watchfulness ought to be* (namely, a watching *in prayer*), but rather how one ought to be *in praying* (namely, *watchful* therein). The point of the precept is the *praying ;* and hence it is continued by προσευχόμενοι. — ἐν εὐχαρ.] accompanying attitude, belonging to γρηγ. ἐν αὐτῇ ; *with thanksgiving, amidst thanksgiving,* namely, for the benefits already received. Comp. i. 12, ii. 7, iii. 17 ; Phil. iv. 6 ; 1 Thess. v. 17. This is the essential element of the *piety* of prayer :[1] αὕτη γὰρ ἡ ἀληθινὴ εὐχὴ

---

[1] But Olshausen incorrectly says : "the prayer of the Christian at all times, in the consciousness of the grace which he has experienced, can *only* be a prayer of thanksgiving." He holds the more general προσευχή to be *more precisely*

ἡ εὐχαριστίαν ἔχουσα ὑπὲρ πάντων ὧν ἴσμεν καὶ ὧν οὐκ
ἴσμεν, ὧν εὖ ἐπάθομεν ἢ ἐθλίβομεν, ὑπὲρ τῶν κοινῶν εὐερ-
γεσίων, Theophylact. The combination with τῇ προσευχῇ
προσκαρτ. (Böhmer, Hofmann) is without ground in the context, although likewise suitable as to sense.

Ver. 3. Comp. Eph. vi. 19 f.— ἅμα καὶ περὶ ἡμ.] *while
your prayer takes place at the same time also* (not merely for
yourselves, for others, and about whatever other affairs, but at
the same time also) *for us,* includes us also. This ἡμῶν, not
to be referred to Paul *alone,* like the singular δέδεμαι subsequently and ver. 4, applies *to him and Timothy,* i. 1. — ἵνα]
contents of the prayer expressed as its *purpose,* as in i. 9 and
frequently.—θύραν τ. λόγου] is not equivalent to στόμα (Beza,
Calvin, Zanchius, Estius, Cornelius a Lapide, Bengel, and
others, comp. Storr and Böhmer)—a singular appellation which
Eph. vi. 7 does not warrant us to assume—but is rather a
figurative way of indicating the thought : *unhindered operation in the preaching of the gospel.* So long as this does not
exist, there is not opened to the preachers a *door for the word,*
through which they may *let* it *go forth.* Comp. 1 Cor. xvi. 9 ;
2 Cor. ii. 12 ; Dion. Hal. *de vi Dem.* p. 1026. 14 : οὐδὲ
θύρας ἰδὼν λόγος, also Pind. *Ol.* vi. 44 ; πύλας ὕμνων
ἀναπιτνάμεν, Bacchyl. *fr.* xiv. 2. The παρρησία of the preaching (Chrysostom, Oecumenius, Theophylact), however, lies not
in the θύρα and its opening, but in what follows. Hofmann
incorrectly holds that the closed door is conceived as being on
the side *of those, to whom* the preachers wished to preach the
word, so that it could not *enter in.* This conception is
decidedly at variance with the immediately following λαλῆσαι
κ.τ.λ., according to which the hindrance portrayed (the door
to be opened) exists on *the side of the preachers.* Moreover,
in this ἵνα ὁ Θεὸς κ.τ.λ. the wish of the apostle, as regards his
own person, is certainly directed to *liberation from his captivity*
(comp. Philem. 22), not, however, to this *in itself,* but to the
free working which depended on it. It was not the *preaching
in the prison* which Paul meant, for that he *had;* but he
defined by ἐν εὐχαρ. Against this view the very ver. 3 is decisive, where, in
fact, Paul does *not* mean a prayer of thanks.

longed after the opening of a θύρα τοῦ λόγου; God was to *give*
it to him. Perhaps the thought of liberation suggested to
himself the choice of the *expression*. Nor is the plural
ἡμῶν and ἡμῖν, embracing others with himself, at variance
with this view (as Hofmann holds); for by the captivity of
the apostle his faithful friend and fellow-labourer Timothy,
who was with him, was, as a matter of course, also hindered
in the freedom of working, to which he might otherwise have
devoted himself. This was involved in the nature of their
personal and official *fellowship*. Observe how it is only with
δέδεμαι that Paul makes, and must make, a transition to the
singular. This transition by no means betrays (in opposition
to Hitzig and Holtzmann) the words δι᾽ ὃ καὶ δέδεμαι, ἵνα φαν.
αὐτό to be an interpolation from Eph. vi. 20. The fact, that
Paul elsewhere (Rom. vii. 2; 1 Cor. vii. 27, 39) has δέειν in
the figurative sense, cannot matter; comp., on the contrary,
the δεσμός and δέσμιος which he so often uses. — λαλῆσαι
κ.τ.λ.] infinitive of the aim: *in order to speak the mystery of
Christ*. The emphasis is on λαλῆσαι: *not to suppress it*,
but *to let it be proclaimed*. Comp. 1 Cor. ii. 6; 2 Cor. iv. 13;
1 Thess. ii. 2. — τοῦ Χριστοῦ] genitive *of the subject*, the
divine mystery contained in the appearance and redemptive
act of Christ (comp. Eph. iii. 4), in so far, namely, as the
divine counsel of redemption, concealed previously to its being
made known by the gospel, was accomplished in Christ's
mission and work (i. 26, ii. 2; Eph. i. 9; Rom. xvi. 25).
Thus the μυστήριον *of God* in ii. 2 is, because *Christ* was the
bearer and accomplisher of it, the μυστήριον τοῦ Χριστοῦ.—
δι᾽ ὃ καὶ δέδεμαι] δι᾽ ὅ applies to the μυστήρ.; and the whole
clause serves to *justify the intercession desired*. When, namely,
Paul wishes λαλῆσαι τὸ μυστήρ. τ. Χ., he therewith desires
that, which is in such sense his entire destination, that on
account of this mystery—because, namely, he has made it
known—he *also bears* his *fetters*. This καί is consequently
the *also of the corresponding relation*, quite common with re-
latives (Baeumlein, *Partik.* p. 152).

Ver. 4. Ἵνα κ.τ.λ.] cannot, seeing that the preceding ἵνα ὁ
Θεὸς ἀνοίξῃ κ.τ.λ. means the *free* preaching *outside of* the

prison, be dependent either on δέδεμαι (Bengel, Hofmann, comp. Theodoret) or on προσευχόμενοι, so that it would run parallel with ἵνα in ver 3 (Beza, Bähr, de Wette, Baumgarten-Crusius, Dalmer, and others) ; it is *the aim of the* λαλῆσαι τὸ μυστ. τ. Χ. : *in order that I may make it manifest* (by preaching) *as I must speak it.* Comp. also Bleek, who, however, less simply attaches it already to ἵνα ὁ Θεὸς ἀνοίξῃ κ.τ.λ. The significant weight of this clause expressing the aim lies in the specification of mode ὡς δεῖ με λαλῆσαι, in which δεῖ has the emphasis. To give forth his preaching *in such measure, as it was the necessity of his apostolic destiny to do* (δεῖ)—so frankly and without reserve, so free from hindrance, so far and wide from land to land, with such liberty to form churches and to combat erroneous teachings, and so forth—Paul was unable, so long as he was in captivity, even when others were allowed access to him. There is a *tragic* trait in this ὡς δεῖ με λαλῆσαι, the feeling of *the hindered present.* The *traditional* explanation is that of Chrysostom : μετὰ πολλῆς τῆς παῤῥησίας καὶ μηδὲν ὑποστειλάμενον, namely, *in captivity,* where Paul longed to speak *in the right way* (de Wette; so usually), or *conformably to higher necessity* (Bähr, Huther, comp. Beza, 1 Cor. ix. 16), or *without allowing himself to be disturbed in his preaching as apostle to the Gentiles* by his imprisonment occasioned by *Jewish-Christian* hostility (Hofmann). But in opposition to the reference of the whole intercession to the ministry *in prison,* see on ver. 3. The wish and the hope of working once more *in freedom* were so necessarily bound up in Paul with the consciousness of his comprehensive apostolic task, that we can least of all suppose him to have given it up already in Caesarea, where he appealed to the emperor. Even in the Epistle to the Philippians (i. 25, ii. 24), his expectation is still in fact directed to renewed freedom of working.

Ver. 5 f. Another exhortation, for which Paul must still have had occasion, although we need not seek its link of connection with the preceding one. Comp. Eph. v. 15 f., where the injunction here given in reference to the non-Christians is couched in a general form. — ἐν σοφίᾳ] Practical

Christian *wisdom* (not mere prudence ; Chrysostom aptly quotes
Matt. x. 16) is to be the *element,* in which their walk amidst
their intercourse with the non-Christians moves. πρός of the
social direction, Bernhardy, p. 205. As to οἱ ἔξω, see on
1 Cor. v. 12. Comp. 1 Thess. iv. 12. — τὸν καιρὸν ἐξαγορ.]
definition of the mode in which that injunction is to be carried
out : *so that ye make the right point of time your own* (see on
Eph. v. 16), allow it not to pass unemployed. *For what ?* is to
be inferred solely from the context ; namely, *for all the activities in which that same wise demeanour in intercourse with the
non-Christians finds expression*—which, consequently, may be
according to the circumstances very diversified. Individual
limitations of the reference are gratuitously introduced, such
as " ad ejusmodi homines meliora docendos," Heinrichs, comp.
Erasmus, Beza, Calovius, and others, including Flatt and
Böhmer ; or : " in reference to the furtherance of the kingdom
of God," Huther, Hofmann. There is likewise gratuitously
imported the idea of the *shortness* of time, on account of which
it is to be well applied (Chrysostom, Oecumenius, Castalio,
and others, including Bähr), as also the view that the καιρός,
which signifies the αἰὼν οὗτος, is not the property of the
Christian, but belongs τοῖς ἔξω, and is to be made by Christians their own through good deeds (Theodoret, comp. Oecumenius), or by peaceful demeanour towards the non-Christians
(Theophylact). Lastly, there is also imported the idea of an
evil time from Eph. v. 16, in connection with which expositors have in turn lighted on very different definitions of the
meaning ; *e.g.* Calvin : " in tanta saeculi corruptela eripiendam
esse benefaciendi occasionem et cum obstaculis luctandum ;"
Grotius : " effugientes pericula." — Ver. 6. ὁ λόγ. ὑμ.] *what ye
speak,* namely, πρὸς τοὺς ἔξω ; the more groundless, therefore,
is the position of Holtzmann, that ver. 6 is a supplement
inserted at a later place, when it should have properly come in
at chap. iii. between vv. 8 and 9. ἔστω is to be supplied,
as is evident from the preceding imperative περιπατεῖτε. — ἐν
χάριτι] denotes *that with which* their speech is to be *furnished,
with grace, pleasantness.* Comp. on Luke iv. 22 ; Ecclus.
xxvi. 16, xxxvii. 21 ; Hom. *Od.* viii. 175 ; Dem. 51. 9. This

χαριέντως εἶναι of speaking (comp. Plato, *Prot.* p. 344 B, *Rcp.*
p. 331 A) is very different from the χαριτογλωσσεῖν of Aesch.
Prom. 294. — ἅλατι ἠρτυμ.] *seasoned with salt,* a figurative
representation of speech as *an article of food,* which is
communicated. The *salt* is emblem of *wisdom,* as is placed
beyond doubt by the context in ver. 5, and is in keeping with
the sense of the following εἰδέναι κ.τ.λ. (comp. Matt. v. 13 ;
Mark ix. 49, 50). As an article of food seasoned with salt [1]
is thereby rendered *palatable,* so what is spoken receives
through wisdom (in contents and form) its morally *attracting,*
exciting, and stimulating quality. Its opposite is the *stale,*
ethically insipid (not the morally *rotten* and *corrupt,* as Beza,
Böhmer, and others hold) quality of speech, the μῶρον, μωρο-
λογεῖν, in which the moral stimulus is wanting. The designation of *wit* by ἅλς (ἅλες) among the later Greeks (Plut. *Moral.*
p. 685 A ; Athen. ix. p. 366 C) is derived from the *pungent*
power of salt, and is not relevant here. Moreover, the relation
between the two requirements, ἐν χάριτι and ἅλατι ἠρτυμένος,
is not to be distinguished in such a way that the former shall
mean the *good* and the latter the *correct* impression (so, arbitrarily, Hofmann) ; but the former depicts the character of the
speech *more generally,* and the latter *more specially.* The good
and correct impression is yielded by *both.* — εἰδέναι κ.τ.λ.]
taken groundlessly by Hofmann *in an imperative sense* (see on
Rom. xii. 15 ; Phil. iii. 16), is, as if ὥστε stood alongside of it,
the *epexegetical* infinitive for more precise definition : *so that*
ye know ; see Matthiae, § 532 f., p. 1235 f. ; Winer, p. 296
[E. T. 398]. This εἰδέναι (*to understand how,* see on Phil.
iv. 12) is, in fact, just an ability, which would not be found in
the absence of the previously-described quality of speech, but
is actually existent through the same. — πῶς] which may be
in very different ways, according to the varieties of individuality in the questioners. Hence : ἑνὶ ἑκάστῳ, "nam haec
pars est non ultima prudentiae, *singulorum* habere respectum,"
Calvin. — ἀποκρίνεσθαι] We may conceive reference to be

---

[1] The poets use ἀρτύειν often of articles of food or wines, which are *prepared*
in such a way as to provoke the palate. Soph. *Fragm.* 601, Dind. ; Athen. ii.
p. 68 A ; Theoph. *de odor.* 51 ; Symm. *Cant.* viii. 2. Hence ἄρτυμα, *spice.*

made to questions as to points of faith and doctrine, as to
moral principles, topics of constitution and organization, historical matters, and so forth, which, in the intercourse of Christians with non-Christians, might be put, sometimes innocently,
sometimes maliciously (comp. 1 Pet. iii. 1), to the former, and
required *answer*. Paul does not use the word elsewhere.
Comp. as to the thing itself, his own example at Athens, Acts
xvii.; before Felix and Festus; before the Jews in Rome, Acts
xxviii. 20, and so forth; and also his testimony to his own
procedure, 1 Cor. ix. 20–22. Chrysostom, Theodoret, Calovius, and others, inappropriately mix up *believers* as included
in ἑνὶ ἑκάστῳ, in opposition to ver. 5.

Vv. 7–9. Sending of Tychicus, and also of Onesimus.
Comp. on Eph. vi. 21 f. — By ἀδελφ. Paul expresses the *relation of* Tychicus as a *Christian brother generally ;* by διάκονος,
his *special* relation as the apostle's official *servant*, in which
very capacity he employs him for such missions; and by σύνδουλος (i. 7) he delicately, as a mark of honour, places him as
to official category *on a footing of equality with himself;* while
ἐν κυρίῳ, belonging to the *two latter* predicates,[1] marks *the
specific definite character*, according to which nothing else than
simply Christ—His person, word, and work—is the sphere in
which these relations of service are active. Comp. Eph.
vi. 21. — εἰς αὐτὸ τοῦτο] *for this very object*, having a
retrospective reference as in Rom. xiii. 6, 2 Cor. v. 5 (in
opposition to Hofmann), *in order, namely, that ye may learn
from him all that concerns me*. The following ἵνα γνῶτε τὰ
π. ὑμῶν (see the critical remarks) is explicative; πάντα ὑμ.
γνωρ. τὰ ὧδε in ver. 9 then corresponds to both. Comp. on
Eph. vi. 22. — παρακαλ.] *may comfort*, in your anxiety concerning me, respecting my position. With the reading γνῷ
τὰ περὶ ὑμῶν, the reference would be to the sufferings of the
readers; δείκνυσι καὶ αὐτοὺς ἐν πειρασμοῖς ὄντας καὶ παρακλή-
σεως χρήζοντας, Theophylact, comp. Chrysostom. — σὺν Ὀνη-
σίμῳ] belonging to ἔπεμψα. As to this slave of Philemon, see

---

[1] διάκονος and σύνδουλος are also connected by the common attribute πιστός,
and separated from ἀδελφός, which has its special adjective. Chrysostom, moreover, aptly remarks on the different predicates : τὸ ἀξιόπιστον συνήγαγεν.

Introd. to the Epistle to Philemon. Paul commends him[1] as his *faithful* (πιστός, as in ver. 7, not : *having become a believer*, as Bähr would render it) *and beloved brother*, and designates him then as *Colossian*, not in order to do honour to their city (Chrysostom, Theophylact), but in order to bespeak their special *sympathy* for Onesimus, the particulars as to whom, especially as regards his conversion, he leaves to be communicated orally. — ἐξ ὑμῶν] As a Colossian he was *from among them*, that is, one belonging to their church. Comp. ver. 12. — τὰ ὧδε] *the state of matters here*, to which τὰ κατ᾽ ἐμέ, ver. 7, especially belonged.

Ver. 10. Sending of salutations down to ver. 14. — ᾽Αρίσταρχος] a Thessalonian, known from Acts xix. 29, xx. 4, xxvii. 2, Philem. 24, was with Paul *at Caesarea*, when the latter had appealed to the emperor, and travelled with him to Rome, Acts xxvii. 2. — ὁ συναιχμάλωτός μου] Οὐδὲν τούτου τοῦ ἐγκωμίου μεῖζον, Chrysostom. In the contemporary letter to Philemon at ver. 24, the same Aristarchus is enumerated among the συνεργοί; and, on the other hand, at ver. 23 *Epaphras*, of whose sharing the captivity *our* Epistle makes no mention (see i. 7), is designated as συναιχμάλωτος, so that in Philem. *l.c.* the συναιχμάλωτος is expressly distinguished from the mere συνεργοί, and the former is *not* affirmed of Aristarchus. Hence various interpreters have taken it to refer not to a *proper, enforced* sharing of the captivity, but to a *voluntary* one, it being assumed, namely, that friends of the apostle allowed themselves to be temporarily shut up with him in prison, in order to be with him and to minister to him not merely as visitors, but continuously day and night. Comp. Huther, de Wette, and Fritzsche, *ad Rom.* I. p. xxi. According to this view, such friends *changed places* from time to time, so that, when the apostle wrote *our* letter, *Aristarchus*, and when he wrote that to Philemon, *Epaphras*, shared his captivity. But such a relation could the less be gathered by the readers from the mere συναιχμάλωτος (comp. Lucian,

---

[1] And how wisely and kindly, after what had happened with Onesimus ! Yet Holtzmann holds that of the whole verse only the name Onesimus is characteristic, and reckons the verse to owe its existence to that name.

As. 27), seeing that Paul himself was a prisoner, and consequently they could not but find in συναιχμάλ. simply the
entirely similar position of Aristarchus as a συνδεσμώτης (Plat.
Rep. p. 516 C; Thuc. vi. 60. 2), and that as being so at the
same time, not, as in Rom. xvi. 7, at some earlier period. Hence
we must assume that *now* Aristarchus, but when the Epistle to
Philemon was written, Epaphras, lay in prison at the same
time with the apostle,—an imprisonment which is to be regarded as detention for trial, and the change of persons in the
case must have had its explanation in circumstances to us
unknown but yet, notwithstanding the proximity of the two
letters in point of time, sufficiently conceivable. It is to be
observed, moreover, that as αἰχμάλ. always denotes captivity
in war (see on Eph. iv. 8; also Luke iv. 18), Paul by συναιχμ.
sets himself forth as a captive *warrior* (in the service of
Christ). Comp. συστρατιώτης, Phil. ii. 25; Philem. 2.
Hofmann (comp. also on Rom. xvi. 7) is of opinion that we
should think "of the *war-captive state of one won by Christ
from the kingdom of darkness,*" so that συναιχμάλωτος would be
an appellation for *fellow-Christian;* but this is an aberration,
which ought least of all to have been put forth in the presence of a letter, which Paul wrote in the very character of *a
prisoner.* — Upon ἀνεψιός, *consobrinus, cousin:* Herod. vii. 5.
82, ix. 10; Plat. *Legg.* xi. p. 925 A; Xen. *Anab.* vii. 8. 9,
Tob. vii. 22, Num. xxxvi. 11; see Andoc. i. 47; Pollux,
iii. 28. Not to be confounded either with *nephew* (ἀδελφι-
δοῦς) or with ἀνεψιάδης, cousin's son, in the classical writers,
ἀνεψιοῦ παῖς. See generally, Lobeck, *ad Phryn.* p. 506. To
take it in a wider sense, like our "kinsman, relative" (so in
Hom. *Il.* ix. 464, who, however, also uses it in the strict
sense as in x. 519), there is the less reason, seeing that Paul
does not use the word elsewhere. Moreover, as no other Mark
at all occurs in the N. T., there is no sufficient ground for the
supposition of Hofmann, that Paul had by ὁ ἀνεψ. Βαρν.
merely wished to signify *which* Mark he meant. Chrysostom
and Theophylact already rightly perceived that the relation-
ship with the highly-esteemed Barnabas was designed to
redound *to the commendation* of Mark. — περὶ οὗ ἐλαβ. ἐντολ.]

in respect of whom (Mark) *ye have received injunctions*[1]—a remark which seems to be made not without a design of *reminding* them as to their execution. *What* injunctions are meant, *by whom* and *through whom* they were given, and whether *orally* or *in writing*, Paul does not say; but the recalling of them makes it probable that they proceeded *from himself*, and were given ἀγράφως διά τινων (Oecumenius). Ewald conjectures that they were given in the letter to the Laodiceans, and related to love-offerings for Jerusalem, which Mark was finally to fetch and attend to. But the work of collection was probably closed with the last journey of the apostle to Jerusalem. Others hold, contrary to the notion of ἐντολή, that *letters of recommendation* are meant from *Barnabas* (Grotius), or from *the Roman church* (Estius); while others think that the following ἐὰν ἔλθῃ κ.τ.λ. forms the contents of ἐντολάς (Calvin—who, with Syriac, Ambrosiaster, and some codd., reads subsequently δέξασθαι,—comp. Beza, Castalio, Bengel, Bähr, and Baumgarten-Crusius),—a view against which may be urged the plural ἐντολάς and the absence of the article. Hofmann incorrectly maintains that περὶ οὗ ἐλάβ. ἐντολάς is to be taken along with ἐὰν ἔλθῃ π. ὑμ.: *respecting whom ye have obtained instructions for the case of his coming to you.* This the words could not mean; for ἐὰν ἔλθῃ π. ὑμ. signifies nothing else than: *if he shall have come to you*, and this accords not with ἐλάβ. ἐντολ., but only with δέξασθε αὐτόν,[2] which Hofmann makes an exclamation annexed with-

---

[1] περὶ οὗ is not to be referred to Barnabas, as, following Theophylact and Cajetanus (the former of whom, however, explains as if παρ' οὗ were read), Otto, *Pastoralbr.* p. 259 ff., has again done. The latter understands under the ἐντολάς instructions formerly issued to the Pauline churches *not to receive Barnabas*, which were now no longer to be applied. As if the παροξυσμός of Acts xv. 39 could have induced the apostle to issue such an *anathema* to his churches against the highly-esteemed Barnabas, who was accounted of apostolic dignity! Paul did not act so unjustly and imprudently.—Comp., on the contrary, Gal. ii. 9 and (notwithstanding what is narrated at Gal. ii. 11) 1 Cor. ix. 6.

[2] In 1 Tim. iii. 14 f., a passage to which Hofmann, with very little ground, appeals, the verb of the chief clause is, in fact, a *present* (γράφω), not, as would be the case here, a *praeterite*, which expresses an act of *the past* (ἐλάβετε). There the meaning is: *In the case of my departure being delayed, however, this my letter has the object*, etc. But *here*, if the conditional clause were to be annexed to the past act ἐλάβετε, the circumstance conditioning the latter would logically

out connecting link (that is, with singular abruptness).—ἐὰν
ἔλθῃ κ.τ.λ.] Parenthesis ; Mark must therefore have had in
view a journey, which was to bring him to Colossae. δέχεσθαι
of *hospitable* reception, as often in the N. T. (Matt. x. 14 ;
John iv. 45) and in classical authors (Xen. *Anab.* iv. 8. 23).
From the circumstance, however, that δέξασθε stands without
special modal definition, it is not to be inferred that Paul was
apprehensive lest the readers should not, without this summons, have recognised Mark (on account of Acts xv. 38 f.) as
an apostolic associate (Wieseler, *Chronol. des apost. Zeitalt.*
p. 567).   Not the simple δέξασθε, but a more precise definition, would have been called for in the event of such an
apprehension.

Ver. 11. Of this *Jesus* nothing further is known. — οἱ ὄντες
ἐκ περιτ. is to be attached, with Lachmann (comp. also Steiger,
Huther, Bleek), to what follows, so that a full stop is not to
be inserted (as is usually done) after περιτ.   Otherwise οἱ
ὄντες ἐκ περιτ. would be purposeless, and the following οὗτοι
μόνοι κ.τ.λ. too general to be true, and in fact at variance with
the subsequent mention of Epaphras and Luke (vv. 12–14).
It is accordingly to be explained : *Of those, who are from the
circumcision, these alone* (simply these three, and no others)
*are such fellow-labourers for the kingdom of the Messiah, as have
become a comfort to me.*   The *Jewish-Christian* teachers, consequently, worked even at Caesarea to a great extent in an
anti-Pauline sense.   Comp. the complaint from Rome, Phil. i.
15, 17.   The nominative οἱ ὄντες ἐκ περιτ. puts the *generic*
subject at the head ; but as something is to be affirmed not
of the *genus*, but of a *special part* of it, that general subject
remains without being followed out, and by means of the
μετάβασις εἰς μέρος the special subject is introduced with
οὗτοι, so that the verb (here the εἰσί to be supplied) now
attaches itself to the latter.   A phenomenon of partitive
apposition, which is current also in classical authors.   See
Kühner, II. 1, p. 246 ; Nägelsbach and Faesi on Hom. *Il.* iii.

have to be conceived and expressed in *oblique* form (*from the point of view of
the person giving the injunction*), in some such form, therefore, as : εἰ ἔλθοι πρὸς
ὑμᾶς (comp. Acts xxiv. 19, xxvii. 39 ; Klotz, *ad Devar.* p. 491 f.).

211.   Comp. Matthiae, p. 1307.   Hence there is the less reason for breaking up the passage, which runs on simply, after the fashion adopted by Hofmann, who treats ἐκ περιτο- μῆς οὗτοι μόνοι as inserted parenthetically between οἱ ὄντες and συνεργοί.   The complimentary affirmation is to be referred to all the three previously named, without arbitrary exclusion of Aristarchus (in opposition to Hofmann).   At any rate, *Caesarea* was a city so important for the Christian mission, that many teachers, Jewish-Christian and Gentile-Christian, must have frequented it, especially while Paul was a prisoner there ; and consequently the notice in the passage before us need not point us to *Rome* as the place of writing. — παρη- γορία] *consolation, comfort,* only here in the N. T. ; more frequently in Plutarch ; see Kypke.   Μέγιστον ἐγκώμιον τὸ τῷ ἀποστόλῳ γενέσθαι θυμηδίας πρόξενον, Theodoret.   Bengel imposes an arbitrary limitation : " in *forensi* periculo."

Ver. 12. Ἐπαφρᾶς] See i. 7 and Introd. — It is to be observed that, according to ver. 11, Epaphras, Luke, and Demas (ver. 14) were *no Jewish*-Christians, whereas Tiele in the *Stud. u. Krit.* 1858, p. 765, holding Luke to be by birth a Jew, has recourse to forced expedients, and wishes arbitrarily to read between the lines.   Hofmann, refining groundlessly (see on ver. 14), but with a view to favour his presupposition that all the N. T. writings were of Israelite origin,[1] thinks that our passage contributes nothing towards the solution of the question as to Luke's descent; comp. on Luke, Introd. § 1. — ὁ ἐξ ὑμῶν] as in ver. 9, exciting the affectionate special *interest* of the readers ; ὑπὲρ ὑμῶν afterwards thoughtfully corresponds. — δοῦλος X. is to be taken together with πάντοτε ἀγωνιζ., but ὁ ἐξ ὑμῶν is not to be connected with δοῦλος (Hofmann) ; on the contrary, it is to be taken by itself as a special element of recommendation (as in ver. 9) : Epaphras, your own, a servant of Christ who is always striving, etc.—ἀγωνιζ.] Comp. Rom. xv. 30.   The more *fervent* the prayer for any one is, the more is it a *striving for him,* namely, in opposition to the dangers which threaten him, and which are present to the vivid conception

---

[1] This postulate, wholly without proof, is also assumed by Grau, *Entwick- elungsgesch. d. neutest. Schrifth.* I. p. 54.

of him who wrestles in prayer. Comp. also ii. 1. The striving of Epaphras in prayer certainly had reference not merely to the *heretical* temptations to which the Colossians, of whose church he was a member, were exposed, but—as is evident from ἵνα στῆτε κ.τ.λ. (purpose of the ἀγωνιζ. κ.τ.λ.)— to *everything* generally, which endangered the right Christian frame in them. — στῆτε] designation of *stedfast perseverance ;* in which there is neither wavering, nor falling, nor giving way. To this belongs ἐν παντὶ θελήμ. τ. Θ., expressing *wherein* (comp. 1 Pet. v. 12) they are to maintain stedfastness; *in every will of God,* that is, *in all that God wills.* Comp. on στῆναι ἐν in this sense, John viii. 44; Rom. v. 2; 1 Cor. xv. 1, xvi. 13. This connection (comp. Bengel and Bleek) recommends itself on account of its frequent occurrence, and because it completes and rounds off the whole expression ; for στῆτε now has not merely a *modal* definition, τέλ. κ. πεπληρ., but also a *local* definition, which admirably corresponds to the figurative conception of *standing.* This applies, at the same time, in opposition to the usual mode of construction with τέλ. κ. πεπληρ., followed also by Hofmann, according to which ἐν π. θελ. τ. Θ. would be the moral sphere, "*within which* the perfection and firm conviction are to take place," Huther.[1] — τέλειοι καὶ πεπληροφορημένοι] *perfect and with full conviction* (comp. ii. 2; Rom. iv. 21, xiv. 5; and see on Luke i. 1) obtain through the context (στῆτε ἐν π. θελ. τ. Θ.) their more definite meaning; the former as *moral* perfection, such as the true Christian ought to have (i. 28); and the latter, as stedfastness *of conscience,* which excludes all scruples as to what God's will requires, and is of decisive importance for the τελειότης of the Christian life; comp. Rom. xiv. 5, 22 f.

[1] If we follow the *Recepta* πεπληρωμένοι (see the critical remarks), on the other hand, we must join, as is usually done, following Chrysostom and Luther, ἐν π. θελ. τ. Θεοῦ to πεπληρωμ. : *filled with every will of God,* which, instead of being transformed into "voluntatis divinae verae et integrae *cognitio*" (Reiche, comp. Beza), is rather to be understood as denoting that the heart is to be full of all that God wills, and that in no matter, consequently, is any other will than the divine to rule in the believer. Respecting ἐν, comp. on Eph. v. 18. Bähr incorrectly renders : "*by virtue of* the whole counsel of God," which is not possible on account of the very absence of the article in the case of παντί. Grotius, Heinrichs, Flatt, and others, erroneously hold that ἐν is equivalent to εἰς.

Ver. 13. *General* testimony in *confirmation* of the *particular* statement made regarding Epaphras in πάντοτε κ.τ.λ. ; on which account there is the less reason to ascribe to the interpolator the more precise definition of ἀγωνιζ. ὑπ. ὑμ., which is given by ἐν ταῖς προσευχ. (Holtzmann). The γάρ is sufficiently clear and logical. — πολὺν πόνον (see the critical remarks) ; *much toil*, which is to be understood of the exertion of *mental* activity—of earnest working with its cares, hopes, wishes, fears, temptations, dangers, and so forth. The word is *purposely chosen*, in keeping with the conception of the conflict (ver. 12) ; for πόνος is formally used of the toil and trouble *of conflict*. See Herod. vi. 114, viii. 89 ; Plat. *Phaedr.* p. 247 B ; Dem. 637. 18 ; Eur. *Suppl.* 317 ; Soph. *Trach.* 21. 169 ; often so in Homer as *Il.* i. 467, and Nägelsbach *in loc.* ; comp. Rev. xxi. 4. — καὶ τῶν ἐν Λαοδ. κ. τ. ἐν Ἱεραπ.] Epaphras had certainly laboured in these adjoining towns, as in Colossae, which was probably his headquarters, as founder, or, at least, as an eminent teacher of the churches.

Ver. 14. *Luke the physician, the* (by me) *beloved*, is the *Evangelist*—a point which, in presence of the tradition current from Iren. iii. 14. 1 onward, is as little to be doubted as that the Mark of ver. 10 is the Evangelist. Luke was with Paul at Caesarea (Philem. 24), and travelled with him to Rome (Acts xxvii. 1), accompanying him, however, not *as* physician (as if μου or ἡμῶν had been appended), but as an associate in teaching, as συνεργός, Philem. 24. Hofmann calls this in question, in order to avoid the inference from ver. 11, that Luke was a non-Israelite. The addition, moreover, of ὁ ἰατρός is simply to be explained after the analogy of all the previous salutations sent, by assuming that Paul has appended to *each* of the persons named a special characteristic description by way of recommendation.[1] The case of Δημᾶς is the only exception ; on which account it is the more probable that the latter had

---

[1] In the case of Luke, the attachment of the honourable *professional* designation ὁ ἰατρός to the name suggested itself so naturally and spontaneously—considering the peculiarity of his professional position, to which there was probably nothing similar in the case of any other συνεργός—that there is no reason to assume any special purpose in the selection (Chrysostom, Erasmus, and many, suggest that the object was to distinguish Luke from others of the same name).

even at this time (at the date of 2 Tim. iv. 10 he has *aban-doned* him) seemed to the apostle not quite surely entitled to a *commendatory* description, although he still, at Philem. 24, adduces him among his συνεργοί, to whose number he still *belonged*. Hence the assumption of such a probability is not strange, but is to be preferred to the altogether precarious opinion of Hofmann, that Demas was the *amanuensis* of the letter, and had, with the permission of the apostle, inserted his name (comp. Bengel's suggestion). Whence was the reader to know that? How very different is it at Rom. xvi. 22! The name itself is not Hebrew (in opposition to Schoettgen), but Greek; see Boeckh, *Corp. inscrip.* 1085; Becker, *Anecd.* 714.

Ver. 15. Messages down to ver. 17. — The *first* καί is: *and especially, and in particular,* so that of the Christians at Laodicea (τοὺς ἐν Λαοδ. ἀδελφ.). *Nymphas* is specially[1] singled out for salutation by name. In the following καὶ τὴν κατ' οἶκον αὐτῶν ἐκκλ., *the church which is in their house,* the plural αὐτῶν (see the critical remarks) cannot without violence receive any other reference than to τοὺς ἐν Λαοδ. ἀδελφοὺς κ. Νυμφᾶν. Paul must therefore (and his readers were more precisely aware how this matter stood) indicate a church *different* from the Laodicean church, a *foreign* one, which, however, was in *filial* association with that church, and held its meetings in the same house wherein the Laodiceans assembled. If we adopt the reading αὐτοῦ, we should have to think, not of the *family* of Nymphas (Chrysostom, Theodoret, Calvin, and others), but, in accordance with Rom. xvi. 5, 1 Cor. xvi. 19, Philem. 2, of *a portion of the Laodicean church,* which held its separate meetings *in the house* of Nymphas. In that case, however, the persons here saluted would have been already included among τοὺς ἐν Λαοδικείᾳ ἀδελφούς. The plural αὐτῶν by no means warrants the ascribing the origin of ver. 15 to an unseasonable reminiscence of 1 Cor. xvi. 19 and Rom. xvi. 5, perhaps also of Philem. 2 (Holtzmann). What a mechanical procedure

---

[1] Nymphas appears to have been specially well known to the apostle, and on friendly terms with him; perhaps a συνεργός, who was now for a season labouring in the church at Laodicea.

would that be!—The *personal name* Nymphas itself, which
some with extreme arbitrariness would take as a symbolic
name (Hitzig, comp. Holtzmann), is not elsewhere preserved,
but we find *Nymphaeus, Nymphodorus, Nymphodotus,* and *Nymphius,* also *Nymphis.*

Ver. 16.[1] This message presupposes essentially similar
circumstances in the two churches. — ἡ ἐπιστολή] is, as a
matter of course, the present Epistle now before us; Winer,
p. 102 [E. T. 133]. Comp. Rom. xvi. 22; 1 Thess. v. 27.—
ποιήσατε, ἵνα] *procure, that.* The expression rests on the conception : *to be active, in order that* something may happen,
John xi. 37. Comp. Herod. i. 8 : ποίει, ὅκως κ.τ.λ., i. 209;
Xen. *Cyrop.* vi. 3. 18. The following καὶ τὴν ἐκ Λαοδ. κ.τ.λ.
is, with emphatic prefixing of the object, likewise dependent
on ποιήσατε, not co-ordinated with the latter as an independent
imperative sentence like Eph. v. 33—a forced invention of
Hofmann, which, besides, is quite inappropriate on account of
the stern command which it would yield.[2] — τὴν ἐκ Λαοδικείας]
not : *that written to me from Laodicea.* So τινές in Chrysostom,
who himself gives no decisive voice, as also Syriac, Theodoret,
Photius in Oecumenius, Erasmus, Beza, Vatablus, Calvin,
Calovius, Wolf, Estius, Cornelius a Lapide, Storr, and others,
as also again Baumgarten-Crusius. This is at variance with
the context, according to which καὶ ὑμεῖς, pursuant to the
parallel of the first clause of the verse, presupposes the Laodiceans, not as the *senders* of the letter, but as the *receivers* of the

---

[1] See Anger, *Beitr. zur histor. krit. Einl. in d. A. u. N. T.* I. ; *über den
Laodicenerbrief,* Leip. 1843 ; Wieseler, *de epistola Laodicena,* Gott. 1844 ; and
Chronol. d. apost. Zeit. p. 450 ff. ; Sartori, *Ueber d. Laodicenserbrief,* Lüb.
1853.

[2] Hofmann needed, certainly, some such artificial expedient, wholly without
warrant in the words of the text, to favour his presupposition that the *Epistle to
the Ephesians* was meant, and that it was a *circular* letter. For a *circular* letter
goes through the circuit destined for it *of itself,* and there is no occasion to ask
or to send for it in order to *procure, that* (ποιήσατε, ἵνα) people may get it to read.
But the effect of the forced separation of the second ἵνα from ποιήσατε is, that the
words τὴν ἐκ Λαοδικείας are supposed only to affirm that the letter "*will come*"
from Laodicea to Colossae, that it "*will reach*" them, and they ought to *read*
it. In this way the text must be strained to suit what is *à priori* put into
it. This applies also in opposition to Sabatier, *l'ap. Paul,* p. 201, who entirely
ignores the connection with ποιήσατε ("la lettre *qui vous viendra* de Laod.").

letter, by whom it was *read*. How unsuitable also would be
the form of the message by ποιήσατε! Paul must, in fact,
have *sent* to them the letter. Lastly, neither the object aimed at
(Theophylact already aptly remarks : ἀλλ' οὐκ οἶδα, τί ἂν ἐκείνης
—namely, that alleged letter of the Laodiceans—ἔδει αὐτοῖς
πρὸς βελτίωσιν), nor even the *propriety* of the matter would be
manifest. Purely fanciful is the opinion of Jablonsky, that
Paul means a letter of the *Laodiceans to the Colossian overseers,*
as well as that of Theophylact : ἡ πρὸς Τιμόθεον πρώτη· αὔτη
γὰρ ἐκ Λαοδικείας ἐγράφη. So also a scholion in Matthaei.
In accordance with the context—although Lange, *Apost.*
Zeitalt. I. p. 211 ff., denounces the idea as a " fiction," and
Hofmann declares it as excluded by the very salutations with
which the Colossians are charged to the Laodiceans—we can
only understand it to refer to *a letter of Paul to the Laodiceans,*
which not merely these, to whom it was written, but *also the*
Colossians (καὶ ὑμεῖς) were to read, just as the letter to the
Colossians was to be read not merely by the latter, but also in
the Laodicean church. The *mode of expression,* τὴν ἐκ Λαοδικείας, is the very usual form of attraction in the case of pre-
positions with the article (comp. Matt. xxiv. 17 ; Luke xi. 13),
so that the two elements are therein comprehended : the letter
to be found in Laodicea, and to be *claimed or fetched from*
Laodicea to Colossae. See generally, Kühner, II. 1, p. 473 f.,
and *ad Xen. Mem.* iii. 6. 11, *ad Anab.* i. 1. 5 ; Stallbaum, *ad*
Plat. Apol. p. 32 B ; Winer, p. 584 [E. T. 784]. This letter
written to the Laodiceans has, like various other letters of the
apostle, *been lost.*[1] In opposition to the old opinion held by
Marcion, and in modern times still favoured especially by such
as hold the Epistle to the Ephesians to be a circular letter

---

[1] The apocryphal letter to the Laodiceans, the Greek text of which, we may
mention, originated with Elias Hutter (1599), who translated it from the Latin,
may be seen in Fabricius, *Codex apocr.* p. 873 ff., Anger, p. 142 ff. The whole
letter,—highly esteemed, on the suggestion of Gregory I., during the Middle Ages
in the West, although prohibited in the second Council of Nice, 787 (to be found
also in pre-Lutheran German Bibles),—which is doubtless a still later fabrication
than that already rejected in the Canon Muratorianus, consists only of twenty
verses, the author of which does not even play the part of a definite situation.
Erasmus rightly characterizes it : " quae nihil habeat Pauli praeter voculas
aliquot ex ceteris ejus epistolis mendicatas."

(Böhmer, Böttger, Bähr, Steiger, Anger, Reuss, Lange, Bleek, Dalmer, Sabatier, Hofmann, Hitzig, and others), that the *Epistle to the Ephesians* is to be understood as that referred to, see Introd. to Eph. § 1 ; Wieseler, *Chronol. d. apost. Zeitalt.* p. 435 ff. ; Sartori, *l.c.* ; Reiche, *Comm. crit. ad Eph.* i. 1 ; Laurent in the *Jahrb. f. D. Theol.* 1866, p. 131 ff. The hypothesis that the *Epistle to Philemon* is meant (so Wieseler, also Thiersch, *Hist. Standp.* p. 424 ; and some older expositors, see in Calovius and in Anger, p. 35) finds no confirmation either in the nature and contents of this *private* letter,[1] or in the expressions of our passage, which, according to the analogy of the context, presuppose a letter to the whole church and for it. Even the *Epistle to the Hebrews* (Schulthess, Stein, in his *Comm. z. Luk.*, appendix) has been fallen upon in the vain search after the lost ! According to Holtzmann, the words are intended to refer to the Epistle to the Ephesians, but καὶ τὴν ἐκ Λαοδικ. ἵνα κ. ὑμ. ἀναγν. is an insertion of the interpolator ;[2] comp. Hitzig.

REMARK.—It is to be assumed that the Epistle to the Laodiceans was composed *at the same time* with that to the Colossians, inasmuch as the injunction that they should be *mutually* read in the churches can only have been founded on the similarity of the circumstances of the two churches as they stood at the time. Comp. ii. 1, where the καὶ τῶν ἐν Λαοδικείᾳ, specially added to περὶ ὑμῶν, expresses the similar and simultaneous character of the need, and, when compared with our passage, is to be referred to the consciousness that the apostle was writing

---

[1] For, although it is in *form* addressed to several persons, and even to the church *in the house* (see on Philem. 1, 2), it is at any rate in *substance* clear, as Jerome already remarks : "Paulum tantummodo ad Philemonem scribere, *et unum cum suo sermocinari.*" Besides, it is to be inferred from the contents of the Colossian letter, that the Laodicean letter meant was also *doctrinal* in contents, and that the reciprocal use of the two letters had reference to this, in accordance with the essentially similar needs of the two neighbouring churches.

[2] Because, if we annex ἵνα to ποιήσατε, an awkward sense arises, "seeing that the Colossians can only cause that they *get* the letter *to read*, but not that they *read* it." That is a subtlety, which does injustice to the popular style of the letter. But if we take ἵνα independently (as Hofmann does), then Holtzmann is further of opinion that the author of Eph. iv. 29, v. 27, 33, is immediately betrayed—an unfounded inference (comp. Winer, p. 295 [E. T. 396]), in which, besides, only the comparison of Eph. v. 33 would be relevant, and that would be balanced by 2 Cor. viii. 7.

to *both* churches.   And the expression τὴν ἐκ Λαοδικείας produces the impression that, when the Colossians *received* their
letter, the Laodiceans *would already have* theirs. At the same
time the expression is such, that Paul does not expressly *inform*
the Colossians that he had written also to the Laodiceans, but
speaks of this letter as of something *known to the readers*,
evidently reckoning upon the oral communication of Tychicus.
The result, accordingly, seems as follows : Tychicus was the
bearer of *both* letters, and travelled *by way of Laodicea* to
Colossae, so that the letter for that church *was* already in
Laodicea when the Colossians *got* theirs from the hands of
Tychicus, and they were now in a position, according to the
directions given in our passage, to have the Laodicean letter
forwarded to them, and to send their own (after it was publicly
read in their own church) to Laodicea.

Ver. 17. The particular circumstances which lay at the
root of this emphatic admonitory utterance[1] cannot be ascer-
tained, nor do we even know whether the διακονία is to be
understood in the narrower sense of the office of *deacon*
(Primasius), or of any other office relating to the church
(possibly the *office of presbyter*), or of the calling of an *evangelist,* or of some individual *business* relating to the service of
the church. We cannot gather from ἐν κυρίῳ any more precise definition of the Christian διακονία. Ewald conjectures
that Archippus was a still younger man (Bengel holds him to
have been sick or weak through age), an overseer of the
church, who had been during the absence of Epaphras too
indulgent towards the false teachers. Even Fathers like
Jerome and the older expositors regard him as bishop (so
also Döllinger, *Christenthum u. Kirche,* ed. 2, p. 308), or as
substitute for the bishop during the absence of Epaphras
(similarly Bleek), whose successor he had also become (Cornelius a Lapide and Estius). Comp. further as to this
Colossian,[2] on Philem. 2. — The special motive for *this precise*

[1] Bengel : "vos meis verbis dicite tanquam testes. Hoc magis movebat, quam
si ipsum Archippum appellaret."

[2] Theodoret already with reason declares himself against the opinion that
Archippus had been a *Laodicean* teacher (so Theodore of Mopsuestia, Michaelis,
and Storr), just as the *Constitt. apost.* vii. 46. 2 make him appointed by Paul as
bishop of Laodicea. Recently it has been defended by Wieseler, *Chronol. des*

form of reminding him of his duty is not clear.[1] But what
merits attention is the relation of *disciplinary admonitive
authority*, in which, according to these words, the *church* stood
to the office-bearers, and which should here be the less called
in question with Hofmann, since Paul in the letter to
Philemon addressed jointly to Archippus would doubtless
himself have given the admonition, if he had not conceded
and recognised in the church that authority of which he in-
vokes the exercise—and that even in the case, which cannot
be proved, of the διακονία having been the service of an
evangelist. The expedient to which Oecumenius and others
have recourse can only be looked upon as flowing from the
later hierarchical feeling : ἵνα ὅταν ἐπιτιμᾷ Ἄρχιππος αὐτοῖς,
μὴ ἔχωσιν ἐγκαλεῖν ἐκείνῳ ὡς πικρῷ . . . ἐπεὶ ἄλλως ἄτοπον
τοῖς μαθηταῖς περὶ τοῦ διδασκάλου διαλέγεσθαι (Theophylact).
— βλέπε κ.τ.λ.] Grotius, Wolf, Flatt, Bähr, and many, take
the construction to be : βλέπε, ἵνα τὴν διακ. ἣν παρέλ. ἐν κυρ.,
πληροῖς, from which arbitrary view the very αὐτήν should
have precluded them. The words are not to be taken otherwise than as they stand : *Look to the service* (have it in thy

apost. Zeitalt. p. 452, and Laurent in the *Jahrb. f. D. Th.* 1866, p. 130, arguing that, if Archippus had been a Colossian, it is not easy to see why Paul,
in ver. 17, makes him be admonished *by others ;* and also that ver. 17 is joined
by καί to ver. 15 f., where the *Laodiceans* are spoken of. But the form of
exhortation in ver. 17 has a motive *not known* to us at all ; and the reason based
on καί in ver. 17 would only be relevant in the event of ver. 17 following immediately after ver. 15. Lastly, we should expect, after the analogy of ver. 15,
that if Archippus had not dwelt in Colossae, Paul would have caused a *salutation*
to be sent to him as to Nymphas. Besides, it would be altogether very surprising that Paul should have conveyed the warning admonition to Archippus
through a *strange* church, the more especially when he had written at the same
time to himself jointly addressed with Philemon (Philem. 2).

[1] Hitzig, p. 31 (who holds also vv. 9, 15, 16 to be not genuine), gives it as
his opinion that Archippus is indebted for this exhortation, not to the apostle,
but to the *manipulator*, who knew the man indeed from Philem. 2, but
probably had in his mind the *Flavius Archippus*, well known from Plin. *Ep.*
x. 66–68, and the *proconsul* Paulus, when he adjusted for himself the relation
between the *Apostle* Paul and his *fellow-warrior Archippus* (Philem. 2). I do
not understand how any one could ascribe even to an interpolator so singular an
anachronistic *confusion of persons.* Yet Holtzmann finds the grounds of Hitzig
so cogent, that he ultimately regards vv. 15–17 as the *rivet*, "by means of which
the *Auctor ad Ephesios* has made a connected triad out of his own work, the
interpolated Colossian epistle, and the letter to Philemon."

view), *which thou hast undertaken in the Lord, in order that thou mayest fulfil it*, mayest meet its obligations; ἵνα αὐτ. πληρ. is the *purpose*, which is to be present in the βλέπειν τ. διακ. κ.τ.λ. Comp. 2 John 8. On πληροῖς, comp. Acts xii. 25; 1 Macc. ii. 55; Liban. *Ep.* 359; Philo, *in Flacc.* p. 988: τὴν διακονίαν ἐκπλήσαντες. — ἐν κυρίῳ] not: *from the Lord* (Bähr); not: for *the sake of the Lord* (Flatt); not: *secundum Domini praecepta* (Grotius). Christ, who is served by the διακονία (1 Cor. xii. 5), is conceived as the *sphere, in which* the act of the παραλαμβάνειν τὴν διακονίαν is accomplished objectively, as well as in the consciousness of the person concerned; he is in that act not out of Christ, but *living and acting in Him.* The ἐν κυρ. conveys the element of holy *obligation.* The less reason is there for joining it, with Grotius, Steiger, and Dalmer, to the following ἵνα αὐτ. πληρ.

Ver. 18. Conclusion written with his own hand; comp. 2 Thess. iii. 17. See on 1 Cor. xvi. 21. — *Be mindful for me of my bonds,* a closing exhortation, deeply touching in its simplicity, in which there is not a mere request for intercession (ver. 3), or a hint even at the giving of aid, but the whole pious affection of grateful love is claimed, the whole strength of his example for imparting consolation and stedfastness is asserted, and the whole authority of the martyr is thrown into the words. Every limitation is unwarranted. Τοῦτο γὰρ ἱκανὸν εἰς πάντα αὐτοὺς προτρέψασθαι, καὶ γενναιοτέρους ποιῆσαι πρὸς τοὺς ἀγῶνας· ἅρα καὶ οἰκειοτέρους αὐτοὺς ἐποίησε καὶ τὸν φόβον ἔλυσεν, Oecumenius, comp. Chrysostom. — ἡ χάρις] κατ᾽ ἐξοχήν: *the grace of God bestowed in Christ.* Comp. 1 Tim. vi. 21; 2 Tim. iv. 22; Tit. iii. 5. Comp. on Eph. vi. 24.

Adam (J., D.D.)—AN EXPOSITION OF THE EPISTLE OF JAMES. 8vo, 9s.

Ahlfeld (Dr.), etc.—THE VOICE FROM THE CROSS: Sermons on our Lord's Passion by Eminent Living Preachers of Germany. Cr. 8vo, price 5s.

Alexander (Prof. W. Lindsay)—SYSTEM OF BIBLICAL THEOLOGY. Two vols. 8vo, 21s.

Alexander (Dr. J. A.)—COMMENTARY ON ISAIAH. Two vols. 8vo, 17s.

Ante-Nicene Christian Library—A COLLECTION OF ALL THE WORKS OF THE FATHERS OF THE CHRISTIAN CHURCH PRIOR TO THE COUNCIL OF NICÆA. Twenty-four vols. 8vo, Subscription price, £6, 6s.

Augustine's Works—Edited by MARCUS DODS, D.D. Fifteen vols. 8vo, Subscription price, £3, 19s.

Bannerman (Prof.)—THE CHURCH OF CHRIST. Two vols. 8vo, 21s.

Bannerman (Rev. D. D.)—THE DOCTRINE OF THE CHURCH. 8vo, 12s.

Baumgarten (Professor)—APOSTOLIC HISTORY. Three vols. 8vo, 27s.

Beck (Dr.)—OUTLINES OF BIBLICAL PSYCHOLOGY. Crown 8vo, 4s.

———— PASTORAL THEOLOGY IN THE NEW TESTAMENT. Crown 8vo, 6s.

Bengel—GNOMON OF THE NEW TESTAMENT. With Original Notes, Explanatory and Illustrative. Five vols. 8vo, Subscription price, 31s. 6d. *Cheaper Edition, the five volumes bound in three*, 24s.

Besser's CHRIST THE LIFE OF THE WORLD. Price 6s.

Bible-Class Handbooks. Crown 8vo.

  BINNIE (Prof.)—The Church, 1s. 6d.

  BROWN (Principal)—The Epistle to the Romans, 2s.

  CANDLISH (Prof.)—The Christian Sacraments, 1s. 6d.

  ———— The Work of the Holy Spirit, 1s. 6d.

  ———— Christian Doctrine of God. 1s. 6d.

  DAVIDSON (Prof.)—The Epistle to the Hebrews, 2s. 6d.

  DODS (MARCUS, D.D.)—Post-Exilian Prophets, 2s. Book of Genesis, 2s.

  DOUGLAS (Principal)—Book of Joshua, 1s. 6d. Book of Judges, 1s. 3d.

  HAMILTON (T., D.D.)—Irish Presbyterian Church History, 2s.

  HENDERSON (ARCHIBALD, M.A.)—Palestine, with Maps. *The maps are by Captain Conder, R.E., of the Palestine Exploration Fund.* Price 2s. 6d.

  KILPATRICK (T. B., B.D.)—Butler's Three Sermons on Human Nature. 1s. 6d.

  LINDSAY (Prof.)—St. Mark's Gospel, 2s. 6d.

  ———— St. Luke's Gospel, Part I., 2s. ; Part II., 1s. 3d.

  ———— The Reformation, 2s.

  ———— The Acts of the Apostles, Two vols., 1s. 6d. each.

  MACGREGOR (Prof.)—The Epistle to the Galatians, 1s. 6d.

  ———— Book of Exodus, Two vols., 2s. each.

  MACPHERSON (JOHN, M.A.)—Presbyterianism, 1s. 6d.

  ———— The Westminster Confession of Faith, 2s.

  ———— The Sum of Saving Knowledge, 1s. 6d.

  MURPHY (Prof.)—The Books of Chronicles, 1s. 6d.

  SCRYMGEOUR (WM.)—Lessons on the Life of Christ, 2s. 6d.

  STALKER (JAMES, M.A.)—Life of Christ, 1s. 6d. Life of St. Paul, 1s. 6d.

  SMITH (GEORGE, LL.D.)—A Short History of Missions, 2s. 6d.

  THOMSON (W. D., M.A.)—Christian Miracles and Conclusions of Science. 2s.

  WALKER (NORMAN L., M.A.)—Scottish Church History, 1s. 6d.

  WHYTE (ALEXANDER, D.D.)—The Shorter Catechism, 2s. 6d.

Bible-Class Primers. Paper covers, 6d. each ; free by post, 7d, In cloth, 8d. each ; free by post, 9d.

  CROSKERY (Prof.)—Joshua and the Conquest. GIVEN (Prof.)—The Kings of Judah. GLOAG (PATON J., D.D.)—Life of Paul. IVERACH (JAMES, M.A.)—Life of Moses. PATERSON (Prof. J. A.)—Period of the Judges.

Bible-Class Primers—*continued.*

 ROBSON (JOHN, D.D.)—Outlines of Protestant Missions.
 SALMOND (Prof.)—Life of Peter. The Shorter Catechism, 3 Parts. Life of Christ.
 SKINNER (J., M.A.)—Historical Connection between Old and New Testaments.
 SMITH (H. W., D.D.)—Outlines of Early Church History.
 THOMSON (P., M.A.)—Life of David.   WALKER (W., M.A.)—The Kings of Israel.
 WINTERBOTHAM (RAYNER, M.A.)—Life and Reign of Solomon.
 WITHEROW (Prof.)—The History of the Reformation.

Blaikie (Prof. W. G.)—THE PREACHERS OF SCOTLAND FROM THE 6TH TO THE 19TH CENTURY. Post 8vo, 7s. 6d.

Bleek's INTRODUCTION TO THE NEW TESTAMENT. Two vols. 8vo, 21s.

Bowman (T., M.A.)—EASY AND COMPLETE HEBREW COURSE. 8vo. Part I., 7s. 6d.; Part II., 10s. 6d.

Briggs (Prof.)—BIBLICAL STUDY: Its Principles, Methods, and History. Second Edition, post 8vo, 7s. 6d.

—— AMERICAN PRESBYTERIANISM. Post 8vo, 7s. 6d.

—— MESSIANIC PROPHECY. Post 8vo, 7s. 6d.

Brown (David, D.D.)—CHRIST'S SECOND COMING: Will it be Pre-Millennial? Seventh Edition, crown 8vo, 7s. 6d.

Bruce (A. B., D.D.)—THE TRAINING OF THE TWELVE; exhibiting the Twelve Disciples under Discipline for the Apostleship. 3rd Ed., 8vo, 10s. 6d.

—— THE HUMILIATION OF CHRIST, in its Physical, Ethical, and Official Aspects. Second Edition, 8vo, 10s. 6d.

Buchanan (Professor)—THE DOCTRINE OF JUSTIFICATION. 8vo, 10s. 6d.

—— ON COMFORT IN AFFLICTION. Crown 8vo, 2s. 6d.

—— ON IMPROVEMENT OF AFFLICTION. Crown 8vo, 2s. 6d.

Bungener (Felix)—ROME AND THE COUNCIL IN 19TH CENTURY. Cr. 8vo, 5s.

Calvin's INSTITUTES OF CHRISTIAN RELIGION. (Translation.) 2 vols. 8vo, 14s.

Calvini Institutio Christianæ Religionis. Curavit A. THOLUCK. Two vols. 8vo, Subscription price, 14s.

Candlish (Prof. J. S., D.D.)—THE KINGDOM OF GOD, BIBLICALLY AND HISTORICALLY CONSIDERED. 8vo, 10s. 6d.

Caspari (C. E.)—A CHRONOLOGICAL AND GEOGRAPHICAL INTRODUCTION TO THE LIFE OF CHRIST. 8vo, 7s. 6d.

Caspers (A.)—THE FOOTSTEPS OF CHRIST. Crown 8vo, 7s. 6d.

Cassel (Prof.)—COMMENTARY ON ESTHER. 8vo, 10s. 6d.

Cave (Prof.)—THE SCRIPTURAL DOCTRINE OF SACRIFICE. 8vo, 12s.

—— AN INTRODUCTION TO THEOLOGY: Its Principles, its Branches, its Results, and its Literature. 8vo, 12s.

Christlieb (Dr.)—MODERN DOUBT AND CHRISTIAN BELIEF. Apologetic Lectures addressed to Earnest Seekers after Truth. 8vo, 10s. 6d.

Cotterill—PEREGRINUS PROTEUS: Clement to the Corinthians, etc. 8vo, 12s.

—— MODERN CRITICISM: Clement's Epistles to Virgins, etc. 8vo, 5s.

Cremer (Professor)—BIBLICO-THEOLOGICAL LEXICON OF NEW TESTAMENT GREEK. Third Edition, with Supplement, demy 4to, 38s. SUPPLEMENT, separately, 14s.

Crippen (Rev. T. G.)—A POPULAR INTRODUCTION TO THE HISTORY OF CHRISTIAN DOCTRINE. 8vo, 9s.

Cunningham (Principal)—HISTORICAL THEOLOGY. Review of the Principal Doctrinal Discussions since the Apostolic Age. Two vols. 8vo, 21s.

—— DISCUSSIONS ON CHURCH PRINCIPLES. 8vo, 10s. 6d.

Curtiss (Dr. S. I.)—THE LEVITICAL PRIESTS. Crown 8vo, 5s.

Dabney (R. L., D.D.)—THE SENSUALISTIC PHILOSOPHY OF THE NINETEENTH CENTURY CONSIDERED. Crown 8vo, 6s.

Davidson (Professor)—AN INTRODUCTORY HEBREW GRAMMAR. With Progressive Exercises in Reading and Writing. Ninth Edition, 8vo, 7s. 6d.

Delitzsch (Prof.)—A SYSTEM OF BIBLICAL PSYCHOLOGY. 8vo, 12s.
———— NEW COMMENTARY ON GENESIS. Two Vols., 8vo, 21s.
———— COMMENTARY ON JOB. Two vols. 8vo, 21s.
———— COMMENTARY ON PSALMS. Three vols. 8vo, 31s. 6d.
———— ON THE PROVERBS OF SOLOMON. Two vols. 8vo, 21s.
———— ON THE SONG OF SOLOMON AND ECCLESIASTES. 8vo, 10s. 6d.
———— OLD TESTAMENT HISTORY OF REDEMPTION. Cr. 8vo, 4s. 6d.
———— COMMENTARY ON ISAIAH. Two vols. 8vo, 21s.
———— ON THE EPISTLE TO THE HEBREWS. Two vols. 8vo, 21s.
Doedes—MANUAL OF NEW TESTAMENT HERMENEUTICS. Cr. 8vo, 3s.
Döllinger (Dr.)—HIPPOLYTUS AND CALLISTUS ; or, The Roman Church in the First Half of the Third Century. 8vo, 7s. 6d.
Dorner (Professor)—HISTORY OF THE DEVELOPMENT OF THE DOCTRINE OF THE PERSON OF CHRIST. Five vols. 8vo, £2, 12s. 6d.
———— SYSTEM OF CHRISTIAN DOCTRINE. Four vols. 8vo, £2, 2s.
———— SYSTEM OF CHRISTIAN ETHICS. 8vo, 14s.
Eadie (Professor)—COMMENTARIES ON ST. PAUL'S EPISTLES TO THE EPHESIANS, PHILIPPIANS, COLOSSIANS. New and Revised Editions, Edited by Rev. WM. YOUNG, M.A. Three vols. 8vo, 10s. 6d. each ; *or set*, 18*s. nett.*
Ebrard (Dr. J. H. A.)—THE GOSPEL HISTORY. 8vo, 10s. 6d.
———— COMMENTARY ON THE EPISTLES OF ST. JOHN. 8vo, 10s. 6d.
———— APOLOGETICS. Three vols. 8vo, 31s. 6d.
Elliott—ON THE INSPIRATION OF THE HOLY SCRIPTURES. 8vo, 6s.
Ernesti—BIBLICAL INTERPRETATION OF NEW TESTAMENT. Two vols., 8s.
Ewald (Heinrich)—SYNTAX OF THE HEBREW LANGUAGE OF THE OLD TESTAMENT. 8vo, 8s. 6d.
———— REVELATION : ITS NATURE AND RECORD. 8vo, 10s. 6d.
———— OLD AND NEW TESTAMENT THEOLOGY. 8vo, 10s. 6d.
Fairbairn (Principal)—TYPOLOGY OF SCRIPTURE, viewed in connection with the series of Divine Dispensations. Sixth Edition, Two vols. 8vo, 21s.
———— THE REVELATION OF LAW IN SCRIPTURE, 8vo, 10s. 6d.
———— EZEKIEL AND THE BOOK OF HIS PROPHECY. 4th Ed., 8vo, 10s. 6d.
———— PROPHECY VIEWED IN ITS DISTINCTIVE NATURE, ITS SPECIAL FUNCTIONS, AND PROPER INTERPRETATIONS. Second Edition, 8vo, 10s. 6d.
———— NEW TESTAMENT HERMENEUTICAL MANUAL. 8vo, 10s. 6d.
———— THE PASTORAL EPISTLES. The Greek Text and Translation. With Introduction, Expository Notes, and Dissertations. 8vo, 7s. 6d.
Forbes (Prof.)—SYMMETRICAL STRUCTURE OF SCRIPTURE. 8vo, 8s. 6d.
———— ANALYTICAL COMMENTARY ON THE ROMANS. 8vo, 10s. 6d.
———— STUDIES IN THE BOOK OF PSALMS. 8vo, 7s. 6d.
Frank (Prof. F. H.)—SYSTEM OF CHRISTIAN EVIDENCE. 8vo, 10s. 6d.
Gebhardt (H.)—THE DOCTRINE OF THE APOCALYPSE, AND ITS RELATION TO THE DOCTRINE OF THE GOSPEL AND EPISTLES OF JOHN. 8vo, 10s. 6d.
Gerlach—COMMENTARY ON THE PENTATEUCH. 8vo, 10s. 6d.
Gieseler (Dr. J. C. L.)—ECCLESIASTICAL HISTORY. Four vols. 8vo, £2, 2s.
Gifford (Canon)—VOICES OF THE PROPHETS. Crown 8vo, 3s. 6d.
Given (Rev. Prof. J. J.)—THE TRUTHS OF SCRIPTURE IN CONNECTION WITH REVELATION, INSPIRATION, AND THE CANON. 8vo, 6s.
Glasgow (Prof.)—APOCALYPSE TRANSLATED AND EXPOUNDED. 8vo, 10s. 6d.
Gloag (Paton J., D.D.)—A CRITICAL AND EXEGETICAL COMMENTARY ON THE ACTS OF THE APOSTLES. Two vols. 8vo, 21s.
———— THE MESSIANIC PROPHECIES. Crown 8vo, price 7s. 6d.
———— INTRODUCTION TO THE PAULINE EPISTLES. 8vo, 12s.

Gloag (P. J., D.D.)—Introduction to the Catholic Epistles. 8vo, 10s. 6d.
—— Exegetical Studies. Crown 8vo, 5s.

Godet (Prof.)—Commentary on St. Luke's Gospel. Two vols. 8vo, 21s.
—— Commentary on St. John's Gospel. Three vols. 8vo, 31s. 6d.
—— Commentary on Epistle to the Romans. Two vols. 8vo, 21s.
—— Commentary on 1st Epistle to Corinthians. 2 vols. 8vo, 21s.
—— Lectures in Defence of the Christian Faith. Cr. 8vo, 6s.

Goebel (Siegfried)—The Parables of Jesus. 8vo, 10s. 6d.

Gotthold's Emblems; or, Invisible Things Understood by Things that are Made. Crown 8vo, 5s.

Grimm's Greek-English Lexicon of the New Testament. Translated, Revised, and Enlarged by Joseph H. Thayer, D.D. Demy 4to, 36s.

Guyot (Arnold, LL.D.)—Creation; or, The Biblical Cosmogony in the Light of Modern Science. With Illustrations. Crown 8vo, 5s. 6d.

Hagenbach (Dr. K. R.)—History of Doctrines. Three vols. 8vo, 31s. 6d.
—— History of the Reformation. Two vols. 8vo, 21s.

Hall (Rev. Newman, LL.B.)—The Lord's Prayer. 8vo, 10s. 6d.

Hamilton (T., D.D.)—Beyond the Stars; or, Heaven, its Inhabitants, Occupations, and Life. Crown 8vo. (*New Edition in Preparation.*)

Harless (Dr. C. A.)—System of Christian Ethics. 8vo, 10s. 6d.

Harris (Rev. S., D.D.)—The Philosophical Basis of Theism. 8vo, 12s.
—— The Self-Revelation of God. 8vo, 12s.

Haupt (Erich)—The First Epistle of St. John. 8vo, 10s. 6d.

Hävernick (H. A. Ch.)—Introduction to Old Testament. 10s. 6d.

Heard (Rev. J. B., M.A.)—The Tripartite Nature of Man—Spirit, Soul, and Body. Fifth Edition, crown 8vo, 6s.
—— Old and New Theology. A Constructive Critique. Cr. 8vo, 6s.

Hefele (Bishop)—A History of the Councils of the Church. Vol. I., to A.D. 325; Vol. II., A.D. 326 to 429. Vol. III., A.D. 431 to the close of the Council of Chalcedon, 451. 8vo, 12s. each.

Hengstenberg (Professor)—Commentary on Psalms. 3 vols. 8vo, 33s.
—— Commentary on the Book of Ecclesiastes. Treatises on the Song of Solomon, Job, and on Isaiah, etc. 8vo, 9s.
—— The Prophecies of Ezekiel Elucidated. 8vo, 10s. 6d.
—— The Genuineness of Daniel, etc. 8vo, 12s.
—— History of the Kingdom of God. Two vols. 8vo, 21s.
—— Christology of the Old Testament. Four vols. 8vo, £2, 2s.
—— On the Gospel of St. John. Two vols. 8vo, 21s.

Herzog—Encyclopædia of Biblical, Historical, Doctrinal, and Practical Theology. *Based on the Real-Encyklopädie of Herzog, Plitt, and Hauck.* Edited by Prof. Schaff, D.D. In Three vols., price 24s. each.
—— Encyclopædia of Living Divines, etc., of all Denominations in Europe and America. (*Supplement to Herzog's Encyclopædia.*) Imp. 8vo, 8s.

Hutchison (John, D.D.)—Commentary on Thessalonians. 8vo, 9s.
—— Commentary on Philippians. 8vo, 7s. 6d.

Janet (Paul)—Final Causes. By Paul Janet, Member of the Institute. Translated from the French. Second Edition, demy 8vo, 12s.
—— The Theory of Morals. Demy 8vo, 10s. 6d.

Johnstone (Prof. R., D.D.)—Commentary on First Peter. 8vo, 10s. 6d.

Jouffroy—Philosophical Essays. Fcap. 8vo, 5s.

Kant—The Metaphysic of Ethics. Crown 8vo, 6s.
—— Philosophy of Law. Trans. by W. Hastie, B.D. Cr. 8vo, 5s.

Keil (Prof.)—Commentary on the Pentateuch. 3 vols. 8vo, 31s. 6d.

Keil (Prof.)—COMMENTARY ON JOSHUA, JUDGES, AND RUTH. 8vo, 10s. 6d.

—— COMMENTARY ON THE BOOKS OF SAMUEL. 8vo, 10s. 6d.

—— COMMENTARY ON THE BOOKS OF KINGS. 8vo, 10s. 6d.

—— COMMENTARY ON CHRONICLES. 8vo, 10s. 6d.

—— COMMENTARY ON EZRA, NEHEMIAH, ESTHER. 8vo, 10s. 6d.

—— COMMENTARY ON JEREMIAH. Two vols. 8vo, 21s.

—— COMMENTARY ON EZEKIEL. Two vols. 8vo, 21s.

—— COMMENTARY ON DANIEL. 8vo, 10s. 6d.

—— ON THE BOOKS OF THE MINOR PROPHETS. Two vols. 8vo, 21s.

—— MANUAL OF HISTORICO-CRITICAL INTRODUCTION TO THE CANONICAL SCRIPTURES OF THE OLD TESTAMENT. Two vols. 8vo, 21s.

—— HANDBOOK OF BIBLICAL ARCHÆOLOGY. Two vols. 8vo, 21s.

Keymer (Rev. N., M.A.)—NOTES ON GENESIS. Crown 8vo, 1s. 6d.

Killen (Prof.)—THE OLD CATHOLIC CHURCH; or, The History, Doctrine, Worship, and Polity of the Christians, traced to A.D. 755. 8vo, 9s.

—— THE IGNATIAN EPISTLES ENTIRELY SPURIOUS. Cr. 8vo, 2s. 6d.

König (Dr. F. E.)—THE RELIGIOUS HISTORY OF ISRAEL. A Discussion of the Chief Problems in Old Testament History as opposed to the Development Theorists. Crown 8vo, 3s. 6d.

Krummacher (Dr. F. W.)—THE SUFFERING SAVIOUR; or, Meditations on the Last Days of the Sufferings of Christ. Eighth Edition, crown 8vo, 6s.

—— DAVID, THE KING OF ISRAEL: A Portrait drawn from Bible History and the Book of Psalms. Second Edition, crown 8vo, 6s.

—— AUTOBIOGRAPHY. Crown 8vo, 6s.

Kurtz (Prof.)—HANDBOOK OF CHURCH HISTORY. Two vols. 8vo, 15s.

—— HISTORY OF THE OLD COVENANT. Three vols. 8vo, 31s. 6d.

Ladd (Prof. G. T.)—THE DOCTRINE OF SACRED SCRIPTURE: A Critical, Historical, and Dogmatic Inquiry into the Origin and Nature of the Old and New Testaments. Two vols. 8vo, 1600 pp., 24s.

Laidlaw (Prof.)—THE BIBLE DOCTRINE OF MAN. 8vo, 10s. 6d.

Lange (J. P., D.D.)—THE LIFE OF OUR LORD JESUS CHRIST. Edited, with additional Notes, by MARCUS DODS, D.D. Second Edition, in Four vols. 8vo, Subscription price 28s.

—— COMMENTARIES ON THE OLD AND NEW TESTAMENTS. Edited by PHILIP SCHAFF, D.D. OLD TESTAMENT, 14 vols.; NEW TESTAMENT, 10 vols.; APOCRYPHA, 1 vol. Subscription price, nett, 15s. each.

—— ON ST. MATTHEW AND ST. MARK. Three vols. 8vo, 31s. 6d.

—— ON THE GOSPEL OF ST. LUKE. Two vols. 8vo, 18s.

—— ON THE GOSPEL OF ST. JOHN. Two vols. 8vo, 21s.

Lechler (Prof. G. V., D.D.)—THE APOSTOLIC AND POST-APOSTOLIC TIMES. Their Diversity and Unity in Life and Doctrine. 2 vols. cr. 8vo, 16s.

Lehmann (Pastor)—SCENES FROM THE LIFE OF JESUS. Cr. 8vo, 3s. 6d.

Lewis (Tayler, LL.D.)—THE SIX DAYS OF CREATION. Cr. 8vo, 7s. 6d.

Lichtenberger (F., D.D.)—HISTORY OF GERMAN THEOLOGY IN THE 19TH CENTURY. 8vo, 14s.

Lisco (F. G.)—PARABLES OF JESUS EXPLAINED. Fcap. 8vo, 5s.

Lotze (Hermann)—MICROCOSMUS: An Essay concerning Man and his relation to the World. Second Edition, two vols. 8vo (1450 pages), 36s.

Luthardt, Kahnis, and Brückner—THE CHURCH. Crown 8vo, 5s.

Luthardt (Prof.)—ST. JOHN THE AUTHOR OF THE FOURTH GOSPEL. 7s. 6d.

—— ST. JOHN'S GOSPEL DESCRIBED AND EXPLAINED ACCORDING TO ITS PECULIAR CHARACTER. Three vols. 8vo, 31s. 6d.

—— APOLOGETIC LECTURES ON THE FUNDAMENTAL (*Sixth Edition*), SAVING (*Fifth Edition*), MORAL TRUTHS OF CHRISTIANITY (*Third Edition*). Three vols. crown 8vo, 6s. each.

T. and T. Clark's Publications.

Macdonald—INTRODUCTION TO PENTATEUCH. Two vols. 8vo, 21s.
———— THE CREATION AND FALL. 8vo, 12s.

M'Lauchlan (T., D.D., LL.D.)—THE EARLY SCOTTISH CHURCH. To the Middle of the Twelfth Century. 8vo, 10s. 6d.

Mair (A., D.D.)—STUDIES IN THE CHRISTIAN EVIDENCES. Cr. 8vo, 6s.

Martensen (Bishop)—CHRISTIAN DOGMATICS: A Compendium of the Doctrines of Christianity. 8vo, 10s. 6d.
———— CHRISTIAN ETHICS. (GENERAL ETHICS.) 8vo, 10s. 6d.
———— CHRISTIAN ETHICS. (INDIVIDUAL ETHICS.) 8vo, 10s. 6d.
———— CHRISTIAN ETHICS. (SOCIAL ETHICS.) 8vo, 10s. 6d.

Matheson (Geo., D.D.)—GROWTH OF THE SPIRIT OF CHRISTIANITY, from the First Century to the Dawn of the Lutheran Era. Two vols. 8vo, 21s.
———— AIDS TO THE STUDY OF GERMAN THEOLOGY. 3rd Edition, 4s. 6d.

Meyer (Dr.)—CRITICAL AND EXEGETICAL COMMENTARY ON ST. MATTHEW'S GOSPEL. Two vols. 8vo, 21s.
———— ON MARK AND LUKE. Two vols. 8vo, 21s.
———— ON ST. JOHN'S GOSPEL. Two vols. 8vo, 21s.
———— ON ACTS OF THE APOSTLES. Two vols. 8vo, 21s.
———— ON THE EPISTLE TO THE ROMANS. Two vols. 8vo, 21s.
———— ON CORINTHIANS. Two vols. 8vo, 21s.
———— ON GALATIANS. 8vo, 10s. 6d.
———— ON EPHESIANS AND PHILEMON. One vol. 8vo, 10s. 6d.
———— ON PHILIPPIANS AND COLOSSIANS. One vol. 8vo, 10s. 6d.
———— ON THESSALONIANS. (Dr. Lünemann.) One vol. 8vo, 10s. 6d.
———— THE PASTORAL EPISTLES. (Dr. Huther.) 8vo, 10s. 6d.
———— THE EPISTLE TO THE HEBREWS. (Dr. Lünemann.) 8vo, 10s. 6d.
———— ST. JAMES' AND ST. JOHN'S EPISTLES. (Huther.) 8vo, 10s. 6d.
———— PETER AND JUDE. (Dr. Huther.) One vol. 8vo, 10s. 6d.

Michie (Charles, M.A.)—BIBLE WORDS AND PHRASES. 18mo, 1s.

Monrad (Dr. D. G.)—THE WORLD OF PRAYER. Crown 8vo, 4s. 6d.

Morgan (J., D.D.)—SCRIPTURE TESTIMONY TO THE HOLY SPIRIT. 7s. 6d.
———— EXPOSITION OF THE FIRST EPISTLE OF JOHN. 8vo, 7s. 6d.

Müller (Dr. Julius)—THE CHRISTIAN DOCTRINE OF SIN. An entirely New Translation from the Fifth German Edition. Two vols. 8vo, 21s.

Murphy (Professor)—COMMENTARY ON THE PSALMS. 8vo, 12s.
———— A CRITICAL AND EXEGETICAL COMMENTARY ON EXODUS. 9s.

Naville (Ernest)—THE PROBLEM OF EVIL. Crown 8vo, 4s. 6d.
———— THE CHRIST. Translated by Rev. T. J. DESPRÉS. Cr. 8vo, 4s. 6d.
———— MODERN PHYSICS: Studies Historical and Philosophical. Translated by Rev. HENRY DOWNTON, M.A. Crown 8vo, 5s.

Nicoll (W. R., M.A.)—THE INCARNATE SAVIOUR: A Life of Jesus Christ. Crown 8vo, 6s.

Neander (Dr.)—GENERAL HISTORY OF THE CHRISTIAN RELIGION AND CHURCH. Nine vols. 8vo, £3, 7s. 6d.

Novalis—HYMNS AND THOUGHTS ON RELIGION. Crown 8vo, 4s.

Oehler (Prof.)—THEOLOGY OF THE OLD TESTAMENT. 2 vols. 8vo, 21s.

Oosterzee (Dr. Van)—THE YEAR OF SALVATION. Words of Life for Every Day. A Book of Household Devotion. Two vols. 8vo, 6s. each.
———— MOSES: A Biblical Study. Crown 8vo, 6s.

Olshausen (Dr. H.)—BIBLICAL COMMENTARY ON THE GOSPELS AND ACTS. Four vols. 8vo, £2, 2s. Cheaper Edition, four vols. crown 8vo, 24s.
———— ROMANS. One vol. 8vo, 10s. 6d.

Olshausen (Dr. H.)—CORINTHIANS. One vol. 8vo, 9s.

—— PHILIPPIANS, TITUS, AND FIRST TIMOTHY. One vol. 8vo, 10s. 6d.

Orelli—OLD TESTAMENT PROPHECY OF THE CONSUMMATION OF GOD'S KINGDOM. 8vo, 10s. 6d.

—— COMMENTARY ON ISAIAH. 8vo, 10s. 6d.

Owen (Dr. John)—WORKS. *Best and only Complete Edition.* Edited by Rev. Dr. GOOLD. Twenty-four vols. 8vo, Subscription price, £4, 4s.
The 'Hebrews' may be had separately, in Seven vols., £2, 2s. nett.

Philippi (F. A.)—COMMENTARY ON THE EPISTLE TO THE ROMANS. From the Third Improved Edition, by Rev. Professor BANKS. Two vols. 8vo, 21s.

Piper—LIVES OF LEADERS OF CHURCH UNIVERSAL. Two vols. 8vo, 21s.

Popular Commentary on the New Testament. Edited by PHILIP SCHAFF, D.D. With Illustrations and Maps. Vol. I.—THE SYNOPTICAL GOSPELS. Vol. II.—ST. JOHN'S GOSPEL, AND THE ACTS OF THE APOSTLES. Vol. III.—ROMANS TO PHILEMON. Vol. IV.—HEBREWS TO REVELATION. In Four vols. imperial 8vo, 12s. 6d. each.

Pressensé (Edward de)—THE REDEEMER : Discourses. Crown 8vo, 6s.

Pünjer (Bernhard)—HISTORY OF THE CHRISTIAN PHILOSOPHY OF RELIGION FROM THE REFORMATION TO KANT. 8vo, 16s.

Räbiger (Prof.)—ENCYCLOPÆDIA OF THEOLOGY. Two vols. 8vo, 21s.

Rainy (Principal)—DELIVERY AND DEVELOPMENT OF CHRISTIAN DOCTRINE. (*The Fifth Series of the Cunningham Lectures.*) 8vo, 10s. 6d.

Reusch (Prof.)—NATURE AND THE BIBLE : Lectures on the Mosaic History of Creation in Relation to Natural Science. Two vols. 8vo, 21s.

Reuss (Professor)—HISTORY OF THE SACRED SCRIPTURES OF THE NEW TESTAMENT. 640 pp. 8vo, 15s.

Ritter (Carl)—THE COMPARATIVE GEOGRAPHY OF PALESTINE AND THE SINAITIC PENINSULA. Four vols. 8vo, 26s.

Robinson (Rev. S., D.D.)—DISCOURSES ON REDEMPTION. 8vo, 7s. 6d.

Robinson (Edward, D.D.)—GREEK AND ENGLISH LEXICON OF THE NEW TESTAMENT. 8vo, 9s.

Rothe (Prof.)—SERMONS FOR THE CHRISTIAN YEAR. Cr. 8vo, 4s. 6d.

Saisset—MANUAL OF MODERN PANTHEISM. Two vols. 8vo, 10s. 6d.

Sartorius (Dr. E.)—DOCTRINE OF DIVINE LOVE. 8vo, 10s. 6d.

Schaff (Professor)—HISTORY OF THE CHRISTIAN CHURCH. (New Edition, thoroughly Revised and Enlarged.)

—— APOSTOLIC CHRISTIANITY, A.D. 1–100. 2 vols. Ex. 8vo, 21s.

—— ANTE-NICENE CHRISTIANITY, A.D. 100–325. 2 vols. Ex. 8vo, 21s.

—— POST-NICENE CHRISTIANITY, A.D. 325–600. 2 vols. Ex. 8vo, 21s.

—— MEDIÆVAL CHRISTIANITY, A.D. 590–1073. 2 vols. Ex. 8vo, 21s.
(*Completion of this Period, 1073–1517, in preparation.*)

—— MODERN CHRISTIANITY, A.D. 1517–1530. 2 vols. Ex. 8vo, 21s.

—— THE TEACHING OF THE TWELVE APOSTLES. The Didachè and Kindred Documents in the Original. Second Edition, ex. 8vo, 9s.

Schmid's BIBLICAL THEOLOGY OF THE NEW TESTAMENT. 8vo, 10s. 6d.

Schürer (Prof.)—HISTORY OF THE NEW TESTAMENT TIMES. Div. II. Three vols. 8vo, 31s. 6d.

Scott (Jas., M.A., D.D.)—PRINCIPLES OF NEW TESTAMENT QUOTATION ESTABLISHED AND APPLIED TO BIBLICAL CRITICISM. Cr. 8vo, 2nd Edit., 4s.

Shedd—HISTORY OF CHRISTIAN DOCTRINE. Two vols. 8vo, 21s.

—— SERMONS TO THE NATURAL MAN. 8vo, 7s. 6d.

—— SERMONS TO THE SPIRITUAL MAN. 8vo, 7s. 6d.

—— DOGMATIC THEOLOGY. Two vols. Ex. 8vo, 25s.

Simon (Rev. Prof. D. W.)—THE BIBLE ; An Outgrowth of Theocratic Life. Crown 8vo, 4s. 6d.

Simon (Rev. Prof. D. W.)—THE REDEMPTION OF MAN. 8vo, 10s. 6d.

Smeaton (Professor)—THE DOCTRINE OF THE ATONEMENT AS TAUGHT BY CHRIST HIMSELF. Second Edition, 8vo, 10s. 6d.

———— ON THE DOCTRINE OF THE HOLY SPIRIT. 2nd Ed., 8vo, 9s.

Smith (Professor Thos., D.D.)—MEDIÆVAL MISSIONS. Cr. 8vo, 4s. 6d.

Stalker (Rev. Jas., M.A.)—THE LIFE OF JESUS CHRIST. New Edition, in larger Type. Crown 8vo, 3s. 6d.

———— LIFE OF ST. PAUL. Large Type Edition. Crown 8vo, 3s. 6d.

Stanton (V. H., M.A.)—THE JEWISH AND THE CHRISTIAN MESSIAH. A Study in the Earliest History of Christianity. 8vo, 10s. 6d.

Steinmeyer (Dr. F. L.)—THE MIRACLES OF OUR LORD : Examined in their relation to Modern Criticism. 8vo, 7s. 6d.

———— THE HISTORY OF THE PASSION AND RESURRECTION OF OUR LORD, considered in the Light of Modern Criticism. 8vo, 10s. 6d.

Stevenson (Mrs.)—THE SYMBOLIC PARABLES : The Predictions of the Apocalypse in relation to the General Truths of Scripture. Cr. 8vo, 3s. 6d.

Steward (Rev. G.)—MEDIATORIAL SOVEREIGNTY : The Mystery of Christ and the Revelation of the Old and New Testaments. Two vols. 8vo, 21s.

———— THE ARGUMENT OF THE EPISTLE TO THE HEBREWS. 8vo, 10s.6d.

Stier (Dr. Rudolph)—ON THE WORDS OF THE LORD JESUS. Eight vols. 8vo, Subscription price of £2, 2s. Separate volumes, price 10s. 6d.

———— THE WORDS OF THE RISEN SAVIOUR, AND COMMENTARY ON THE EPISTLE OF ST. JAMES. 8vo, 10s. 6d.

———— THE WORDS OF THE APOSTLES EXPOUNDED. 8vo, 10s. 6d.

Tholuck (Prof.)—THE EPISTLE TO THE ROMANS. Two vols. fcap. 8vo, 8s.

———— LIGHT FROM THE CROSS. Third Edition, crown 8vo, 5s.

Tophel (Pastor G.)—THE WORK OF THE HOLY SPIRIT. Cr. 8vo, 2s. 6d.

Uhlhorn (G.)—CHRISTIAN CHARITY IN THE ANCIENT CHURCH. Cr. 8vo, 6s.

Ullmann (Dr. Carl)—REFORMERS BEFORE THE REFORMATION, principally in Germany and the Netherlands. Two vols. 8vo, 21s.

———— THE SINLESSNESS OF JESUS : An Evidence for Christianity. Fourth Edition, crown 8vo, 6s.

Urwick (W., M.A.)—THE SERVANT OF JEHOVAH : A Commentary upon Isaiah lii. 13–liii. 12; with Dissertations upon Isaiah xl.–lxvi. 8vo, 6s.

Vinet (Professor)—STUDIES ON BLAISE PASCAL. Crown 8vo, 5s.

Walker (J., D.D.)—THEOLOGY AND THEOLOGIANS OF SCOTLAND. New Edition, crown 8vo, 3s. 6d.

Watts (Professor)—THE NEWER CRITICISM AND THE ANALOGY OF THE FAITH. Third Edition, crown 8vo, 5s.

———— THE REIGN OF CAUSALITY : A Vindication of the Scientific Principle of Telic Causal Efficiency. Crown 8vo. 6s.

Weiss (Prof.)—BIBLICAL THEOLOGY OF NEW TESTAMENT. 2 vols. 8vo, 21s.

———— LIFE OF CHRIST. Three vols. 8vo, 31s. 6d.

White (Rev. M.)—SYMBOLICAL NUMBERS OF SCRIPTURE. Cr. 8vo, 4s.

Williams—SELECT VOCABULARY OF LATIN ETYMOLOGY. Fcap. 8vo, 1s. 6d.

Winer (Dr. G. B.)—A TREATISE ON THE GRAMMAR OF NEW TESTAMENT GREEK, regarded as the Basis of New Testament Exegesis. Third Edition, edited by W. F. MOULTON, D.D. Ninth English Edition, 8vo, 15s.

———— THE DOCTRINES AND CONFESSIONS OF CHRISTENDOM. 8vo, 10s. 6d.

Witherow (Prof. T., D.D.)—THE FORM OF THE CHRISTIAN TEMPLE. 8vo, 10/6.

Workman (Prof. G. C.)—THE TEXT OF JEREMIAH; or, A Critical Investigation of the Greek and Hebrew, with the Variations in the LXX Retranslated into the Original, and Explained. Post 8vo, 9s.

Wright (C. H., D.D.)—BIBLICAL ESSAYS. Crown 8vo, 5s.

Wuttke (Professor)—CHRISTIAN ETHICS. Two vols. 8vo, 12s. 6d.